TAPE OP

TAPE OP

A Book About Creative Recording

Edited by Larry Crane
Introduction by Tony Visconti

Table Of Contents

Chapter 1: Home Recordists

Chapter 2: Artists and Bands

Tape Op: The Book About Creative Music Recording
copyright 2000 by Larry Crane

All rights reserved.

ISBN: 0-922915-60-1

Feral House
2554 Lincoln Blvd. #1059
Venice, CA 90291

www.FeralHouse.com

Design by Brian Shevlin
Cover by Sean Tejaratchi
Art Direction by John Baccigaluppi

10 9 8 7 6 5 4 3 2 1

Chapter 3: Engineers, Producers and Studios

Chapter 4: Knowledge and Techniques

Chapter 5: Recording Equipment

Introduction:

I thought I subscribed to all the audio magazines until I had two copies of a *Tape Op* shoved into my hands by Larry Crane one fine autumn afternoon in Portland, Oregon. I was a speaker on a panel, along with Mark Hudson and Phil Ramone, sponsored by the North West Chapter of the Recording Academy. Not until my return flight to New York did I finally stick my nose inside *Tape Op*. I couldn't believe what I was reading: Real articles about recording by the seat-of-your-pants. Articles written by heart thumping, out-in-the-real-world engineers and producers, who make records passionately, the same way as I do. There were no stories about state-of-the-art studios in Nashville, Los Angeles or New York, where the monitors are resting on the bedrock of the state, costing half a million alone. No "...hard disk recording has changed the way I edit..." articles that are a dime a dozen in glossier mags. Nothing about MIDI software or virtual anything (okay, some articles about computer recording did creep in)! But these articles were written by sonic pioneers – in far away places – making recordings with not so conventional gear!

All too often I work with younger engineers who are shy of reaching for the EQ strip on the console or plugging a compressor in line to record an instrument. Recording "flat" seems to be the preference of today because it is believed that all the fancy stuff takes place in the mix, and usually by another engineer more qualified to EQ and compress. What utter nonsense. If one reduces engineering to just placing a microphone in front of an instrument or singer and recording flat with no sonic embellishments, then a bright child could be taught to do that in a few minutes.

by Tony Visconti

Recording is an art. Steadily we have been given more brushes and colors for our palette over the years. I have often been asked how we got our records to sound the way they did in the '60s, '70s and early '80s. Before I could answer, I would be told it was all down to analog tape and vintage consoles, just fill in the blanks. *Nothing was further from the truth.*

Analog tape in the '60s was appalling. The best manufacturers couldn't stop it from shedding. One particular brand left a small hill of oxide under the tape heads at the end of the day. Our "vintage" consoles were brand new then and were built to last maybe ten years or so. They weren't very versatile either – parametric EQ was yet to come. So analog tape and the limitations of primitive recording consoles were our enemies which we constantly battled.

We knew that we had to make the music louder than the hiss. We had to record everything at the highest level possible but avoid saturation and distortion. It was always walking a fine line between hi-fi and grunge in those days. Usually, after we got a great sound balance of the group, the energy level of the musicians would inevitably go up with subsequent takes and that fine line was crossed more often than not. Mixing was both a creative exercise and a salvage exercise in one. A saturated kick drum needed a few tricks to make it sound like a punchy kick drum again. That's a different approach than today. It's very difficult to saturate modern analog tape as easily and impossible to saturate digital recordings. Now a punchy kick drum usually stays punchy – it doesn't need fixing.

But the fixing was part of the art. In 4 and 8-track days the entire drum kit was recorded on one or two tracks. An engineer had no option but to equalize, compress and sometimes even add reverb or slapback, which were impossible to remove after they were printed to tape. This wasn't a bad thing. This created a vibe, a sonic reference which would guide the overdubs that followed. Musicians loved what they heard and were inspired by it. As the tape shedded its oxide, high frequencies would noticeably decline. Mixing then became an exercise of adding EQ and compression to something already submixed, EQ'd and compressed, to restore its luster. It's my theory that this constant battle against the diminishing returns of the wear and tear of analog tape and the twice and thrice time processing of the original sound is what younger musicians and engineers mean when they say "analog."

I see lots of engineers of this generation using analog tape and vintage gear all the time, but I don't hear many new records sound like (or as good as) the great recordings of Led Zep, Fleetwood Mac, Beach Boys, The Who and (of course) The Beatles. The difference is that we committed sonic ideas to tape and this generation hardly ever does.

That's where *Tape Op* comes in. There are members of this generation who have rediscovered the blissful art of making bold, vivid strokes on oxide. Within its pages, there are guerrilla recording tactics, advice like using microphones bought from toy stores, using a guitar pickup as a microphone, getting the most bang for the buck from Radio Shack gear and making "real" loops from tape spliced in a loop! The truth is that any piece of equipment has a personality. Although the Neumann U87 is one of my favorite microphones, it is as predictable as hell. So the other day I had my singer do a vocal in a kick drum mic (I'm not telling you which one). The vocal was a happily kept keeper.

I'm not saying that excellent high-end gear is an anathema to the writers and readers of *Tape Op*, they've just learned how to make great sounds without them – as well as with them. I have seen articles in there by great modern icons such as Joe Chiccarelli, who's list of personally owned gear had me drooling. But racks of gear don't get out of the box by themselves, walk into the studio and make records on their own.

Tape Op is an adventure magazine. You'll be gripping your seat in anticipation of the next paragraph.

(Tony Visconti has produced records by David Bowie, T Rex, The Boomtown Rats, Badfinger, Iggy Pop, Thin Lizzy and many, many others.)

Tape Op:
The Book About Creative Music Recording

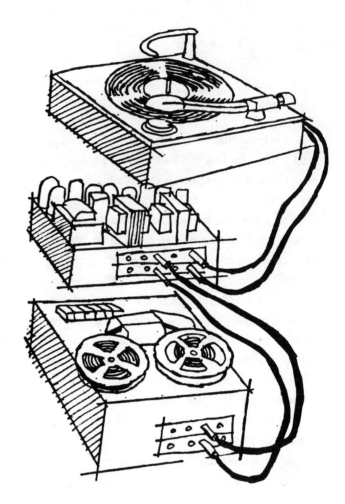

It is the intent of *Tape Op* to make people aware that there are many ways to make a great recording. The main constrictions that affect the recording of music are time and money. If there isn't enough time, because of money, to get the performances and sounds needed for a project, then the issue becomes getting more time. By using small studios, home recording gear, creative engineers or judicious pre-production, better recordings can be achieved. In other cases money is no object, but the best use of available time becomes important. It all comes down to trying to capture the finest performances of the material one is working with, and sometimes the relaxed atmosphere of a home recording setup is key. Other times the abundance of gear in a studio makes capturing takes easier. There are many different approaches.

Some recording enthusiasts assume that there is a "right" and "wrong" to the art of capturing sound. This is false and anathema to the creative recording process. By worrying about the correctness of mic placement one might miss a golden opportunity to record an amazing take. There are no rules to this game. Many creative recording advancements have nothing to do with what is technically "better" and were discovered by engineers or artists through curiosity and experimentation. Don't feel that you have to know "everything" in order to press record. Knowledge is great, but people play electric guitars that have no idea of how their instruments work.

Audio recording gear is only a tool. It is a way to record sounds in order to play them back later. A person who picks up a hammer to frame a house may use a different hammer than another but, given the drive to get it done, they will still build a house. The gear used is not important. The end result can be.

Use what you have. Learn everything that can be done with it. Try things you think you shouldn't do. Record in different places. Put the "wrong" mics on things. Try to capture the loose first takes. Experiment. Only when you have outgrown your gear (and you *will* know) might you need to search for more. Never blame your lack of time spent recording on not having the "right" equipment. There is no excuse to not record. There is every reason to record.

XXXXXXXXXXXXXXXXXXXXXXXXXXXXXXXXXXXXXXXXXXXXX

I remember hooking two home cassette decks together in 1980 in order to overdub the weird electronic drones I was creating. I soon built a little mixer, analog echo box, and other gizmos to work with. Later I borrowed the "new" cassette 4-tracks from friends to make more annoying "solo" cassette releases. Eventually I found myself in a band (Vomit Launch), playing bass, and we made four records. They were all done at "smaller" studios and I had a large hand in the way they sounded. I enjoyed learning from the engineers (Greg Freeman and John Baccigaluppi) and would record demos on my 4-track while we worked on pre-production for our albums.

In 1993 I moved to Portland, Oregon, and started furiously 4-tracking in my basement room. These songs formed the basis of what became Flaming Box of Ants (with Marila Alvares and Dewey Mahood – it later mutated into Elephant Factory). When Marila and I found a house with a cool basement what started out as a practice room became a studio when Dewey dropped off a pair of Teac 1/4" reel-to-reel decks.

I recorded my first "outside" project in 1994, in our basement studio (known as Laundry Rules). It was a 7" single for my friends, the Maroons. We used a borrowed (from Quasi) Fostex 1/4" 8-track analog machine and horrible Fostex board along with my Mackie 1202 mixer, mics, headphones and such. The Maroons single was the first time someone had enough faith in me to trust me with an actual release. Soon after I bought a Tascam 1/2" 8-track deck and Soundcraft Spirit board and started charging $10 an hour for my services. A Maroons CD followed as did sessions with Versus, Catpower, 2 Foot Flame, Jr. High and others.

Around the time I went "semi-pro" I started to get the idea for what became *Tape Op*. I'd written for music magazines, like: *BravEar*, *Sound Choice*, *You Could do Worse*, *File 13* and others (all long gone), for years and had even done my own Xeroxed 'zine in 1986. I still wanted to do something with music journalism, but something different. At the same time I was trying to learn about music recording. There were some great books that I found at the library that helped me with basic concepts of how microphones and tape decks worked. There were also magazines like: *Mix*, *EQ*, *Electronic Musician*, and *Recording*, but none of these resources talked about making the kind of music that I recorded or listened to.

The music that let me know that I could do my own recordings was varied. East River Pipe had some amazing albums out that were recorded in an apartment yet sounded huge and spacious. Bruce Springsteen's *Nebraska* had an intimate quality that was so far from his other bombastic releases. The Young Marble Giants were an English trio who had recorded some minimalist pop masterpieces on minimal gear. Guided By Voices had released some of the best and rawest rock-and-roll 4-track records ever. The Clean were a New Zealand band who recorded masterpieces on 4-track. Pete Townshend's *Scoop* albums consisted of fascinating demos and home recordings. The Soft Boys' *Underwater Moonlight* had mostly been tracked in 4 and 8-track studios and had been a favorite record for years. I had worked with Greg Freeman who had started a studio (Lowdown) with an 8-track and minimal gear in the mid '80s and did some great records with Barbara Manning, Thinking Fellers Union Local 282, X-Tal

and others. Pavement's *Slanted and Enchanted* was a straight-up, simple recording with great songs. Elliott Smith had recorded a couple of 4 and 8-track records that were getting a lot of attention. All of this told me that it was okay to record at home or in a small studio. We didn't need huge budgets and fancy studios to make great records. But how were these records made? I certainly didn't read about this in *Mix*.

The debut issue of *Tape Op* featured interviews with F. M. Cornog of East River Pipe, Greg Freeman and a few studio stories from pals of mine and came out in April, 1996. It was Xeroxed at a friend's workplace, in the off-hours, and then I spray-painted the cover with a reel flange as a stencil. 600 copies went pretty fast; soon we had subscribers, mail coming in, and free CDs in the mail! I stuck to a quarterly schedule and started getting articles from contributors, a few record company ads, and a lot of support.

Soon after interviewing Elliott Smith, we ended up joining forces to open a studio. Jackpot! Recording Studio began in February 1997, with the Maroons as our guinea pigs in the MCI 2" 16 track experience. Elliott tracked a bunch of "demos" for his next album (some of which found there way onto *XO*) and we even recorded an Oscar-nominated song ("Miss Misery") for *Good Will Hunting* before he moved to New York. I carried on doing lots of projects, many with bands I had interviewed (Quasi, Poolside, Varnaline, Reservoir). I learned more and more about recording, many times from interviews done for *Tape Op*.

In Fall, 1998, John Baccigaluppi and his partner Sonny Mayugba plied me with Cajun food and Schlitz in an attempt to work with me in bringing *Tape Op* into the world of "real" publishing

via their Substance Media Works. I fell for it, and in January 1999, the magazine appeared as a much thicker read with a color cover and, finally, ads for pro-audio gear. They started offering free subscriptions and kicked the circulation up to 25,000. The year 2000 saw the magazine move into a bi-monthly release schedule and get even "glossier." Now there's even a book. Welcome to *TAPE OP: The Book About Creative Music Recording*.

– Larry Crane

CHAPTER 1
Home Recordists

East River Pipe

Dump

The Barn

Quasi

Sea Saw

The Apples in Stereo

Sue Garner

Alastair Galbraith

Linda Smith

Chad Crouch

Robert Poss

Track Star

Papas Fritas and the Columnated Ruins

A Trip to Athens

East River Pipe

ONE MAN

by Larry Crane

Steve Satterwhite

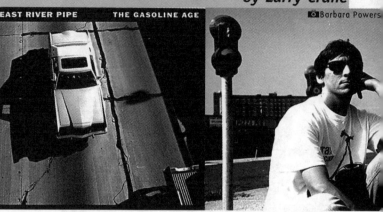
EAST RIVER PIPE   THE GASOLINE AGE
Barbara Powers

East River Pipe is one man, Fred M. Cornog. He makes beautiful and dreamy pop records. The early ones were recorded in a small apartment in New York, which he shared with Barbara Powers [who's played a large part in getting his music released], but they now have a house in New Jersey. His music is so well-crafted and recorded that many listeners never realize that what they are hearing is not a "full" band or even that there's no drummer, only an older model drum machine. Check out his CDs: *Shining Hours in a Can*, a collection of singles (on Ajax records), *Poor Fricky*, *Mel*, and *The Gasoline Age* (all on Merge records).

I remember reading that you were into Tom Verlaine and Television.

When I finally moved to the city [NY], I was looking at this Television bin... One was *Marquee Moon* and one was *Adventure*. I was looking at *Marquee Moon* and it was too scary to pick that up, because that's a Mapplethorpe photo on the cover and it looks like their veins are sticking out, every hideous blemish on their face is amplified. I only picked up *Adventure* because it looked less scary to me, more accessible. I started out listening to "Glory," "Days," "Foxhole" and stuff like that, rather than "Marquee Moon" and "See No Evil."

I think I actually heard Tom Verlaine's solo stuff before I heard Television.

There's kind of this drug element to everything Tom Verlaine does that I really like, although I don't take any drugs anymore! There's still this residual, leftover thing of acid in my head that will never go away. Television and Tom Verlaine stuff always seemed like really good drug music to me.

How did you start recording your own music?

When I was a kid, 15 years old or so, I had two little cassette players and I'd record a piano part and then I'd rewind it and play that back and play another piano part over that [previous] piano part with the other one on record. I'd

essentially be bouncing off these cheap things. As soon as those mini-studios came on the market, I knew I wanted one of those things. The first one I got was a Tascam Porta-One 4-track. I guess how I got into it was by a fascination with songwriting and tape machines at the same time. I put in a lot of time listening to records, and I still do. If you listen to late-period Beatles records, put the headphones on and listen to "Strawberry Fields Forever," and one thing will be coming out of the left earphone, one thing will be coming out of the right, and one thing will be going down the center. I didn't know how they did that, and I still don't, but that it could be done seemed really interesting to me – that it wasn't all just coming down the center of your head. It seemed like another world, an inner world. Listening to late-period Beatles records and also wanting to write songs on my own, that's what's led to this disaster known as East River Pipe.

So when you realized there were these 4-track things you automatically understood what they were capable of?

Oh yeah! I was like, "Boy, I'm gonna get one of those!"

How old were you when you got your first 4-track?

About 23 or something. I've been messing around with it for about ten years.

What are you using now? Is it an 8-track?

I have a Tascam 388. It's an 8-track reel-to-reel but it lays flat and it's on 1/4" tape. It's not compatible with anything. You can't bring that tape into a real recording studio.

It won't play on a Fostex 8-track?

It won't play on anything. It doesn't sync [align] up with it. What you'd have to do, if you were gonna bring that into a *real* studio, would be to bring the whole machine in. One person *could* carry it but it's pretty huge. I love this machine. For me, it's miles ahead of the cassette decks. You get a better fidelity. I'm not trying to get a bad fidelity recording. Why not try to make it as good as it can be? At the same time, I'm not a tech-head. I don't know anything about recording, I've never read the manual for this Tascam 388 because, quite frankly, I don't like to use things the way everybody else uses things. I never read the manuals for anything I get. I just turn the thing on and pluck the guitar and that's it. I just learned over time how to use it more efficiently, or in a way that suited my music the best.

It seems like you've experimented with a lot of the sounds over time, and have all this you can draw from to put things together.

Barbara and I got it [the 8-track] used in 1989. I'd say the first two years of stuff that I did sounded very shrill, kinda harsh and claustrophobic, but over time, it's just like everything else... You do it enough, you get better at it. I just kept doing it, day in and day out, and here we are six years later, with the same machine and it's still working, and I use it a lot. It's a really good, durable machine that sounds good.

I thought it was an 8-track cassette recorder.

I know that some people like to use these ADAT machines, those digital things. I don't like digital and I couldn't afford one to begin with. There's this kind of war going on between people that believe in digital or analog, and I'm not at war with anybody, but I really believe in the analog sound. I don't care if the fidelity isn't as crisp or something. It just sounds natural, the way it comes over the speakers. Digital kinda reminds me of a cheap Formica table and analog reminds me of a nice, wood-grained table. There's something about digital things that I don't like.

What do you mix down to?

Well, I have a whole bunch of things. I have a cassette player. "Happytown" and "Times Square Go-Go Boy"... that's where the masters for those came from. I have a reel-to-reel, which is a 2-track thing, and I have a DAT machine. I've been using the DAT machine more, recently, just because it's fast. It works fast... it's like a fancy cassette machine... it's growing on me – but not the sound of it.

Have you gotten a chance to do any digital editing for your albums?

I'm not up to that level of sophistication.

You just rent some studio time and you patch it all together on a computer.

There's a guy, his name's Danny Caccavo, and he works at a place called This Way Productions in Manhattan and he masters my stuff. What we do, Barbara and I, is we give Danny a whole bunch of DATs, or cassettes, or reels and just go, "Okay, it's mix number three on this tape" and he'll sequence it, trim the ends, slightly EQ it and slightly compress it.

So that's being done, you're just not there.

I don't have a clue about that stuff. I'm so naive about the whole expertise of that. I just plug in the guitar and go. People wonder, "How'd you do that?" or, "That's amazing." It's really not amazing at all. All it is, is plugging in a guitar and then playing a part over that and then maybe adding a keyboard or playing bass. I think the hard part about this whole thing is writing a good song and getting a decent performance of that song. Writing a good song, that's the important part. It's the most simplest thing but it's sometimes lost. Once you have a good song, how can you fuck up a good song production wise? I was playing "Chicken Blows" by Guided By Voices and Barbara was going, "Oh my God, listen to that!" But it's such a great song, it doesn't even matter if all of the sudden this background vocal comes flying out at you. It works. It's very simple to me why that works, because it's a very good song.

It probably facilitates what you want to do, having the little home setup and doing it all at your own speed as opposed to trying to take it into a pay-by-the-hour studio.

Yeah, I couldn't even imagine, aside from the money part. Even if it was 25 dollars an hour, I think it would cost a fortune to record an East River Pipe album in the studio because I like to use the recording process as the creative process. In order to do that in a *real* recording studio, I guess you have to either have a friend that owns the studio that's gonna give you a real cut rate, or no rate, or you're gonna have to have a lot of money to blow.

Like the Rolling Stones, or something.

Yeah, look at the Beatles! They could fuck around with "A Day in the Life" or "Strawberry Fields" because by that time they were millionaires. I think they owned Abbey Road! You can just sit there and camp out. Christ! Elton John used to rent out a studio in France for three months and just sit there. I never liked the clock ticking over my head when I'm trying to do something creative. It's the antithesis of the creative mindset. "I'm paying $50 an hour for this..." I can't imagine the spontaneity level either, because of what I try to do... Usually I'm just kinda diddling around on the guitar in front of the TV and I'll go, "This sounds like a half-decent song." So I'll just go over to the mini-studio and flip it on, play something, and it captures the moment. It captures the moment when you're actually really excited about the thing. With most bands, I guess the guy who writes the songs will do a little demo for his friends and then they'll practice it. By the time you get around to booking time or deciding you're gonna go over to the studio and record the song, I don't know if the idea's there any more. Or, you have to manufacture a spontaneity. Like, "Okay, let's try to play this like the first time we played it." Now, don't you wish you had a decent studio that you could capture that first time you play that song with your band? That's what I try to do. "Wow, I feel excited about this now, I'm gonna go in and I'm just gonna do it, right now."

Are a lot of songs written that way? Do you find that sometimes you sketch something out and never finish it?

Yeah, that happens a lot. I would say that about ten percent of my stuff gets out. Ninety percent gets trashed or recycled. Most of it gets trashed. I would think that those numbers would be pretty representative of just about everybody.

Let's get technical. When you're using a drum machine do you print the effects?

Yeah. Whatever effects you hear on my records... I never add effects later, assuming that's what print means.

Yeah, sorry.

Okay, I learned a new term tonight! So I always print with effects, I add nothing afterwards.

A lot of times people don't have the balls to do that.

I'm just having a little fun here. If you like the way your guitar sounds, or your bass, your vocal. I like to sing with effects on 'cause I think it makes you more adventurous. If you just want to fuck around and experiment then fuck around and experiment. The thing I hate about all these tech people, that are into the technical side of recording, is they always tell you, "Naw, you can't do that, nobody does that." Or, "I really don't want you to sing with the reverb on 'cause that'll be down on tape and we can't get rid of it." I'm like, "Why not?" I don't care. I'm just having fun here. That's one of the reasons I record by myself. Then I don't have some technical engineer guy telling me I can't do that. Not that anything I do is all that strange or weird, but for me, the technical process of this thing is just not that important, really. You should control the technology instead of the technology controlling you. Some of these engineers, they're kinda in this rut of the way they do things and they can only see it that way. "Why would you want to record two guitars doing the same thing when I can run your one guitar through this stereo flanger thing and we can get the same effect?" That's a different thing. That's an artificial way of getting what I want and it's not the same thing. Don't tell me that it's the same thing – it's not. I'm very hard headed about that stuff. I just really enjoy dicking around by myself. All I'm doing is just dicking around. I'm not trying to make some great technological recording or something. I'm just trying to have fun. I don't have any rack mounted gear or anything. If I got a bunch of rack mounted stuff, I would spend so much time fucking around with dials I wouldn't get a song done. Or the songs would go in a different direction, and I think it would be an unhealthy direction. You would focus more on the technology of the thing, like, "Oh, maybe if I used this gated, reverse reverb instead of the room #2 reverb it would sound that much better." My philosophy is, "Fuck man! Just get it done." I'm just doing a home recording here. It's not like I'm the Beatles or Pink Floyd or something. I've always kept this set up really simple. I have about four guitar stomp boxes, and that's it. I've got a reverb – a stupid, little guitar reverb thing. I also bought a compressor thing, which I'm very impressed with. And a distortion pedal – just a cheap little $40 distortion pedal.

That's the extent of your effects?
That's the whole thing.

What kind of reverb is that?
Let's see. It says, Boss RV-2 digital reverb. It's just a guitar stomp pedal and it's got six different reverbs on it and I don't even use half of them.

Do you run your guitar direct into your mini-studio and listen to it through your stereo while recording?
I play everything back and I mix through the stereo.

Do the neighbors like you?
Well, when I do a mix I might do ten mixes. One guy upstairs was going, "Boy, you were listening to the same song today for six hours!" He doesn't even know I'm a musician, he thinks I'm some obsessive/compulsive person. The neighbors have never complained about anything, and I always play and sing and carry on pretty loud.

Does Barbara mind it?
She always likes it, because when I'm messing around with a song I'm not bothering her.

What kind of mics do you use?
One's a Shure PE15H. I've had this thing since I had my little Tascam Porta-One. This engineer guy said, "You gotta get a Shure SM 58." So I bought one but I don't like it; it's too sensitive. This PE15H thing, I'm so used to it vocal-technique-wise. I have another mic I use when I do acoustic guitar. It's a Beyer Dynamic M69N.

Is that a ribbon mic?
I don't know anything about that! The only ribbon I know is for wrapping presents. I used to be really militant about having cheap stuff but I'll tell you, I got a cheap compressor 2 years ago, it was an Arion compressor, and the thing would pop. You'd hit a louder note and, "crack!"

You could hear the compressor grab onto it. Recently I got this Boss compressor/sustainer and what a difference, it's amazing. I'm kind of getting rid of my bullshit bias for really cheap gear.

There are certain limits.
I got a little impatient with *really* cheap, low-end stuff.

Is there any inspiration for your recording style?
Two years ago I was sitting around listening to all this *hip alternative bullshit* and after two hours, I put on Lou Reed's *Magic and Loss*. I put that on and it's just guitars – electric guitars, just really thickly done, no heavy-duty effects; recorded nicely. Clean guitars. And a voice, bass and drums. It was just so simple that it reduced those other albums to a pile of shit. It was just so obvious that that was the way to go. Wow, a simple song with simple chords, recorded simply [don't get too fancy] and trying to communicate with people. Try to do something beautiful, but don't get complicated; keep it simple. That's been my mantra for a long time. When I picked up Lou Reed's *The Blue Mask* in 1983, that showed me how little it takes to really create a great album. That album just blew my mind. Listening to Lou Reed albums, I think the way those albums are recorded, that's what spoke to me, the directness of *The Blue Mask* or *Magic and Loss* seemed to speak to me in a way that was very direct and I said, "That's the ticket. The rest of this stuff is bullshit." Now, I love albums like Marvin Gaye's *What's Going On*, the Beach Boys' *Pet Sounds*. Those are also beautiful albums, but they're more ornate, perhaps. Late-period Beatles records. I love *Sister*, by Sonic Youth. These are all different records that are all great records that create their own space. Production wise, what spoke to me were Lou Reed solo records. That's in your face, no bullshit.

It's funny, 'cause I'm trying to get you to get technical about how you record and we keep discussing songs.
A friend of mine, who's much more technical than I am, was recording an album in a studio that cost about $40 an hour. He invited me down, just to sit there. I'd never been in a real recording studio. His singer in the band is singing this thing and it sounds really good to me. He's singing it through some Shure mic, like a 57. Afterwards, we're driving home and he's playing the tape for me and he goes, "You know, this is gonna be really good when he sings this with the Neumann mic." And I'm thinking to myself, "This guy's fuckin' insane." The performance was there, a great performance, and now they're gonna go back, it's not gonna be spontaneous, they're gonna have this mic, it's not gonna be the same. He just doesn't understand what it's about. The recording using the 57 mic was great. Leave it. It has an intensity to it. Why go back and spoil a perfectly good recording just to get a slightly better sound?

That points out problems in the whole recording process.
And it also points out priorities that don't necessarily revolve around the performance, which is the important thing. Christ, let the music live. Let the band be the band. Keep that spontaneity there at all costs. A vast majority of these engineer types have always seemed rigid to me. Technical. They impede the creative process.

Contact Mr. Cornog c/o: PO Box 701, Summit, NJ 07902, MoonRideNJ@aol.com, www.bilner.com/erp.html

Dumb

📷 Rafael Fuchs

JAMES McNEW AND HIS 4-TRACK BAND

by Larry Crane

Yeah. So I had heard of Dump, the bass player from Yo La Tengo, who did these great songs he recorded at home on 4-track. But I had never stumbled across any of his CDs until a bunch showed up in the mail a while back. Well damn, they're good. So, I set up an interview to see where this guy was coming from and boy, was he a nice fellow.

Is *A Plea for Tenderness* the same kind of album where you recorded it all on your 4-track?

Yeah, and mostly at home.

What kind of machine is it?

A Tascam Porta 5 I got in '86. It's still the same one. I've had a couple of bands replaced inside it. There must be something wrong with it 'cause it still works. I saw one exactly like mine in a pawn shop in Florida a couple of weeks ago and I almost bought it. A friend for my old one! There've been times when I've thought about upgrading, but I just can't. Until this one catches fire and melts into a ball of goo – I don't think I can replace it.

Upgrading to what?

A better 4-track. This guy, Peter Walsh, who really helped me mix the last couple of things I've done, knows all about *real*, *actual* recording equipment and he was trying to talk me into the MiniDisc thing. "You should do it." Maybe eventually – one day.

But it's not analog. You wouldn't get those tape dropouts and things.

I know. I've become quite an expert at those. I am sort of scared of that "cold-crisp" sound.

You should be. So your first record, was that stuff you'd been putting together over the years?

A little bit of it was. I put out a single before the first CD that came out on the 18 Wheeler label in 1992. I'd sorta been using the 4-track for a long time and my friend Tom, who runs the label, suggested putting out a single. I was pretty happy with that. It was stuff I'd done over

the last year or two prior to that. I recorded almost all of it in Providence actually. Brinkman Records got a hold of that single and called me and asked if I wanted to make a record. I said I'd rather make a single and then I got a scathing letter from Brinkman saying, "No! Make an album. What are you, chicken?" So that's what I did. *Superpowerless* was recorded almost all in New York, mostly in the apartment.

That's what I was gonna ask you. You do a lot of real drums...

Yeah, that stuff I do at the Yo La Tengo practice place.

So you'd track that down there and then go home and add guitars and vocals?

Yeah, pretty much.

Ever the other way around?

No. I can do the drums at practice and piece it together. Mostly, I like to do as much of it as I can at home. I'm always kinda happy with the sounds I can get. It seems to work out okay. It's much easier to bounce stuff down, being at home and able to concentrate. The playback is the stereo in my bedroom. I've really gotten used to the sound of it and how to interpret it.

Do you do a lot of bouncing down?

Oh yeah. The new record, I took it a lot further than I usually do. I tried to make more of a production out of it. There's lots more tracks and tricks and stuff like that. On a lot of the stuff, I just tried to go as far as I could. I think it came out really great. It took me a really long time, (two years) to make.

Well, you've been busy with Yo La Tengo.

Yeah, but... I really have been working on it. I finally got it together, sequenced it, and got it the hell out. I just got my copies of the record and it's a nice feeling to know that it's done. I gotta get on with my life.

You don't have any roommates I assume...

Uhhh, my girlfriend and I live together.

Does she get tired of hearing the stuff?

She almost never hears it.

You try to do it when she's away?

There is some stuff that I've recorded while she's asleep. Any keyboard and really quiet guitar stuff. There's at least one whole song on the new record that was recorded in the middle of the night, not to her knowledge.

That's kind of a common occurrence. People recording stuff real quiet...

I've done that a couple of times, recording an electric guitar being played without an amp and then just crank up the volume so it has this really crazy windy-day quality to it. When I do stuff like that, on occasion you can actually hear the television on or something else going on in the house. There was one thing I recorded where I was watching a basketball game and some of the commentary made it onto the end of the track.

Do you ever have trouble with the other people living around you?

We just moved, and at our old place there was never any problem with volume and I just had everything turned up really loud all the time. For a while, I was used to the other people's schedules in the building but then, after a while, I didn't care. Just let it fly! They never said anything. So we moved, and I'm in that kind of paranoid, good neighbor thing. I don't know how noisy I can be yet.

What kind of microphones do you use at home?

I only own one. A lot of stuff that I use, including the only "proper" microphone, a Shure SM 58, is borrowed. A lot of it's borrowed from my friend Dave who used to be in the group Hypnolovewheel and was my neighbor for a long time. I just keep borrowing his stuff and I'm sure he'll want it back, someday. He's busy with a real job and two daughters and he doesn't have time for his equipment anymore. I like to keep his equipment happy. The only microphone that I have, Rick Brown [Run On] gave to me. He found it in Chinatown. It's sort of an old reel-to-reel type microphone, really bizarre looking little thing. A Unichord or something. It's the greatest sounding thing. It gives you that Headcoats sound! The Billy Childish-a-phone! I use that almost exclusively and I just love the way it sounds.

What about effects?

I did one upgrade recently. Peter talked me into getting a little one-channel tube preamp.

Is it one of those Art TubeMP's?

Yeah. It makes all the difference and sounds terrific. You can really screw around with them and overload them. That's been just about the biggest addition to the family. I found a Realistic reverb unit for $15 at a flea market in Denver. It's a screwy analog, Lee Perry-in-a-box kind of thing. I've been having fun with that. I've gotten a really good collection of effects and things I use for all of the wrong reasons. There's a Dunlop RotoVibe that I use a lot. I bought a tremolo pedal made by Voodoo Labs and it sounds really good. It's really crazy. It has that Mission of Burma non-Fender tremolo. It sounds exactly like that.

I've always thought that stuff sounded so great. It has a sharp attack and decay.

Yeah. Plus the rate can go tons slower or faster. I use that a lot. I bought an E Bow. Those are fun. I love the E Bow. I've come up with a couple more keyboards that I've found on the road. I've had a Moog for a really long time. There's a single that came out last year that I recorded right after

I bought it and it sounds exactly like that. I try to use it so that it doesn't sound like a Moog synthesizer.

There's a lot of people using them that don't know how to.

Yeah, I agree. I found a keyboard bass made by the Rheem company. I think they make air conditioners. It's really great. My friend Mark from this group called Medicine Ball (in Providence) plays one. In the "Whip It" video, one of the Devo guys is playing one. I found one for really cheap, but it's out of tune and I opened it up to fix it, but I have no idea. I've never seen anything like it. It's powered by fireflies or something. It's kind of useless right now. If I write to the Rheem company they're just gonna say, "We have no idea what you're talking about." Maybe if I can get an air conditioner guy out to the house, he can service it!

Do all the notes play out of tune from each other?

Yeah. Every note is out of tune in a different way. It looks beautiful. I just bought a Roland organ and string ensemble synthesizer for $100 and it's very "Goth" sounding like the *Pornography* era Cure sound. I was playing it and I started laughing. It sounds really great.

I always feel like instead of buying a $5000 synthesizer you could buy 20 funny little keyboards that all have a unique sound for a lot less.

I'm beginning to understand the logic behind all of the modern stuff, in that, when you want to play, you don't have to bring all 40 of them and hope that they all work. But they're so cool.

Do you mix your recordings with someone else?

This was the first time a new record was mixed almost all by someone else [Peter].

What did you mix to before?

I would just borrow somebody else's DAT. Fred Brockman, who did some demos with Yo La Tengo and ran an 8-track studio in Hoboken for a while, had a board and a DAT and some outboard gear. That's how I mixed the first two records and a bunch of singles. I'd hook up the 4-track to the board, just 2 channels out, and ran it to the DAT and that's it! I set levels through the board and mixed everything on the 4-track. The mixing for the new record was a much fancier approach but I wasn't there for a lot of it. I thought he did a really terrific job. It was a whole new approach, but it sounded almost exactly like I wanted it to sound.

He didn't add tons of reverb?

Nah! He was very true to the project.

Do you think you'll ever record a Dump record not on a 4-track?

Probably not. It's not a group, so I don't think so. I think the equipment is a large part of the group. The most important part of the group! Someday I'm gonna get a letter from the 4-track's lawyer! That's the fun of it… Having it at home for me to do it whenever I want it.

DUMP, PO Box 6028, Hoboken, NJ 07030

The Barn

A VISIT TO THIS STUDIO IN RURAL NEW MEXICO
"YOU SHOULD RECORD. ANYONE CAN THINK OF AN EXCUSE NOT TO."

by Larry Crane

📷's Larry Crane

The common image of a studio is a warehouse or basement setup in a decent sized city. Or maybe it's a fancy resort styled place in the woods where millionaire rockers can relax and make hit records. One doesn't usually conjure up images of an adobe building 7 miles from the smallest of towns in the high desert of New Mexico. Yet, that's where we found the MudHive. Dave and Anne Costanza moved out here 10 years ago from San Francisco, where they had been in The Whitefronts, one of that city's most overlooked treasures. All along, they had planned to build a recording studio and a home. Somehow they ended up living in the recording studio, where they've done albums for Granfaloon Bus, Hieronymus Firebrain, Dent, and ten cassettes for their own band, The Lords of Howling (since mutated into Art of Flying). I interviewed Dave while Marila Alvares and I were visiting during a "vacation." We had all played music together, and recorded some the night before (and it was quite fun).

So how did you end up with this recording gear?

We saw an ad in the paper that said, "Wanted: wood floors refinished in exchange for recording equipment."

It really said that?

We were like, "This is not for real." We didn't really have any gear. We used to just record direct to cassette; that was cool for live. So we went to this guy's house and he had cases of wine. He had just done recording in exchange for wine. We had this idea that we wanted a Sennheiser mic, that's all we knew, and he was, "What kind of gear do you have?" We had an AKG microphone. We had never heard of old gear. Finally he decided, "You know floors and you don't know shit about recording so I'll just give you stuff." It was like magic beans. We did floors in three different houses and we got two Neumann KM53 mics. Someone might know about them. If you get the stuff that's harder to sell that's not name brand...

Neumann's a name brand...

Right, but people know KM84s and U47s. These are tube omnis and they're just amazing. Then he gave us two C12As, which we had never heard of. They're little babies of the big C12s, with the exact same diaphragm.

Those little AKG ones?

Yeah, like the grandfather of the 414. The guy who I was working with, Bill, was just like, "Dude, what is going on here?" Then I got the two Big Red monitors that used to belong to Blue Oyster Cult. They're great speakers, but people aren't really using big speakers to monitor anymore. They're cool for the room and we can use them as a PA.

What brand are they?

They're Altec, I think. I took them in [to be worked on] and the guy was all, "They're cast magnets!" To be honest, for what the floor would have cost and what I could sell this for now, I could get 20 times [more back]. The money would've been spent. His theory was get a good mic, a good preamp and it didn't matter what the deck was. We had an Otari at the time, which disappeared. We used a Teac 1/4" 4-track. All our tapes, from one to ten, are all 1/4" 4-track, and now we're gonna start doing the 8-track, which definitely sounds better. The difference between the Teac with worn heads and the Otari [5050] is a lot more than I thought it was gonna be. Anyway, he gave us those [mics] and the API preamps that he built into a box for us – I have four of them. I went back and did more work and I got those 2254E Neve compressors. So we got all this amazing shit that we probably shouldn't have and we can't afford to fix. No one in town would even know how to do it. I had to send a cord back because someone twisted it and the wires came out and there was no way to figure it out. I guess I could've gotten a schematic but it's hard to find a schematic for a 50 year old microphone. So that's how the gear showed up. That was ten years ago and it probably took 8 years for me to get any clue on how to use it. We thought, "It's a great microphone, just shove it in a room and record and it'll sound great." But the way they work, they hear so much, as opposed to most mics, which are kinda deaf, and they can cancel so much worse.

They're omnidirectional.

We record 6 tracks at once. We kind of know how to work this room, like where to put the vocalists, and we always do that basic setup. That kind of showed us. The deck [Otari 5050] I just bought. That's recent. I got it for $800.

No way.

It didn't work when I got it. It had a bad transformer and a bad spindle. It's in a rack and came with a remote, which was a real intrigue. The plate reverb came later.

What kind is that?

It's an EMT 140 S. They made a small one with a 12" plate. This one is 3' x 5'. It weighs 435 pounds. It had to be brought out here in a U-Haul.

Its outside dimensions…

It's 8' x 4' x 1'. Then we got this board, that 1604 Mackie.

It only has six mic inputs.

We don't use them except for a PA. They have one now with 16 inputs. Why put 16 cheap ones when you could put 6 high quality, professional mic preamps in there?

Well you know… selling points once again. What other projects, besides the Lords, have you done here?

The first Granfaloon Bus CD, *A Love Restrained,* was done here. We did *There* by Hieronymus Firebrain. They did *Here* and *There*. One's here and one's in Oakland, CA. Mostly Lords. In the last three years we've done 33 reels of 1/4".

What kind of deck was that on?

Teac 2340 SX. Someone gave it to me, and we got a lot of use out of it. When we used the 4-track, we printed left and right of the room. We had the bass, electric guitar - we ran the acoustic through an amp – and the drums…all sharing two mics. Then we sang on track 3 and we used track 4 for overdubs. One advice we got was never to use the board and print straight through, which actually people are doing in studios. The signal path is the Neumann [mic] to the API [preamp] to the [Neve] compressor to tape. No EQ, just 'cause we don't have any to run it through.

Well, you're lucky to have a good sounding room.

I guess so. We didn't know. We have a 21-foot ceiling, in the middle. The wood floors might be somewhat of a problem but the room sounds good. You can play in here.

It's got some reverberation. It's not tiny.

Actually it is a good sounding room.

See. Told you so.

The walls are mud [adobe]. Maybe that's the secret. They're softer than brick.

They don't seem to reflect much. How do you get around working without a control room?

We built one up there, which is now my little girl's room. When she got old enough to turn knobs we decided to move out. Now, she knows how to fade this down and she knows how to press play and record. They think that by 8 she'll be running the tape deck. She'll press play and record but at 6, she starts to lose interest. She falls asleep with the headphones on. She's heard a lot and she's on a lot of the tapes. We just let a lot of the noise in. It just seems ridiculous to have this recording scene and be all, "Hush everyone!" As soon as you shut the world out then everything seems all over-important and it's really stupid. "We just spanked all the kids to be quiet and now we're doing this dumb little song." So now we just do it and let them run around. One time we wanted them to be on tape and they shut up. Then it seemed kinda stupid to ask them to talk while we were recording. There was a period, when we started, that someone came through

and he isolated every track. Every track had to be done separately even though it drove the musicians crazy. You'd be trying to do a song, "How many verses?" He used to fade up a track and go, "Look at all that bleed. I can hear a little bit of guitar on it." We'd go a whole day with bleed and the way we did it. A friend of mine that worked in LA at a real studio was, "Go with what's more for playing." So we started at square one and it didn't sound too bad. We thought if we could hear the vocals it was okay. The stuff sounds great, like grainy old films. What I found, from having a lot of the similar gear to big studios, is until you have tons of it and tons of time, you're never gonna sound like that. Not in your wildest dreams. They've set up this weird thing… I was thinking the other day, the hippies don't like to eat white bread but they sure like to make it. The studios like, just torture yourself and do this really clean, processed stuff. So I was playing, going up and down the stairs, in and out of the booth, so we just put it [the deck and mixer] in where it is. That isn't a problem unless your tape deck makes a lot of noise. My reel-to-reel was scraping and you could hear it on the quiet songs. It's actually pretty cool on one song, but after a while we were getting tired of it.

It's always there. So basically, when you're recording you'll be playing at the same time.

I used to walk over, which kept me out of the first verse. Chris doesn't like to waste tape so he would start. Now we always start, as soon as we press play we start and then we come together and play. Now I have my volume pedal and distortion box back at the board. I feel a little isolated but not too much 'cause we all wear headphones. Everyone's used to that.

I couldn't hear the banjo last night so I took them off.

With a room mic going last night and a wild free-for-all it's kind of fun. I went without them too. When we play, we play real quiet, and our drummer, Peter, plays to the mics. Now we are dealing with 5 years of experience with just this exact setup. Now we're kinda spoiled – we couldn't go anywhere else! We have enough decent gear to do it. It almost isn't flexible for other bands. It isn't really a studio for hire. It doesn't work really well. It's built around our scene. None of the gear's paid for itself, just spiritually.

The projects that you've done here, like Granfaloon Bus, that's your brother's band.

They like the vibe. They come here for the space. It works pretty good for them - they get a completely different thing. I realized that some things don't work. The drummer plays louder so a lot of this stuff had to be regrouped. We ended up redoing vocals after, which they like doing anyway. A lot of our songs, you'd never find it. We do vocals live. As long as anything else isn't louder than the thing you're trying to record on the track. You don't have to try to make the drums sound like they're in a room. Sometimes the vocal bleed on the main mics can be kinda bad. Kinda cavernous. So I try to keep that to a minimum.

How?

Like if Chris is singing, and he gets picked up by the Neumanns [overheads] on the drums. It's almost a slapback. Our room is the size that's really the minimum to really record live in. We're 20' x 30'. That's kind of a luxury. We just kind of do it. We had somebody basically choose the equipment for us. Used the tape deck that somebody gave me. That's the thing that I think for people… really to use what you have, not to think about what you don't have. Go to a studio and find out what you will never have and by the time you have it, it will be either broken or out of date! I'm kind of a slack engineer, and that's why the compressors help. These are real accurate and you don't notice it sounding squashed. They do a good job.

They're not tube, are they?

Someone else would know more; I'd hate to say the wrong thing. They're from the '70s.

They're probably transistor.

They're discrete. You pay more for that these days. This is early '70s Neve stuff.

Your tapes seem to present a good feel of the band playing.

That's underrated in the studio world.

You find more of that in jazz. Especially early recordings which were done with a few mics.

But those are amazing sounding. What I consider a great sounding album is [Coltrane's] *A Love Supreme*. Wasn't that as part of a soundcheck for some other project? That's what I consider a great sounding album. I don't consider ELO a great sounding album even though there's 5001 tracks.

But the way you're approaching it is like that. The drummer would learn to play so the parts he wants to get heard cut through.

Right. Those Neumanns, we hang them from a beam [above the drummer]. When we first started we used the omnis in an X/Y pattern on a coffee table, and I guess you can't do that with omnis. They cancel like crazy. Chris put the lyrics on the table and sang into the X/Y, the drums were right behind him, the bass was behind the drums, the acoustic guitar was printing straight into a mic, and the electric lead was going – no compression, straight in. Then we'd do 2 tracks of overdubs. That was our tapes: 2, 3, and 4 were all done that way. When I go back, it's really strange sounding. The slightest movement changes all these cancellations. I was in Nashville, a friend of mine works in a fancy studio and he's the mastering engineer. In Nashville, you can't be upfront about smoking pot ('cause it's all red, white and blue) so they have to hide it. They hide in the mastering room with a friend of mine and smoke pot. So this big engineer's in there smoking pot and I'm like, I've got a captive audience, let's listen to the Lords. So I find the cassette deck and I'm blasting it through this million dollar system and they guy's like, "Y'all getting a lot of signal cancellation. You got two omni-directionals too close together." He heard it! He told me you've got to be at least three feet apart. The other advice he taught me was how to print reverse reverb. Just to flip your tape, run whatever tracks through the reverb, and then print that to another track. I think that's a great sound. We get kinda hooked on it, actually. The plate's a great sound.

You said you were using a spring reverb before?

I got a Master Room and I gave it away. It was noisy and took a lot of volume and then it would crash. I actually never used reverb on anything. I used the chorus a lot, I think it sounds a lot better, that Roland Tape Chorus.

Does it have a built in spring reverb too?

It has a spring.

I used a Master Room reverb and we gated it, so it would cut out the noise when it wasn't being used.

I always wanted to buy one of those gates 'cause when you compress stuff, it boosts the noise level when people aren't doing stuff. I don't know what that'll do to my sound – another thing in the chain.

They're tricky.

We kind of slam the tape. We don't care much if it distorts.

Do you ever hear any distortion?

I don't. I haven't heard much. I think it can take a lot more than those meters. I know how to bias it and stuff now. You have the advantage, at least, that you know where you stand. This is biased at minus 3/250. If you bias it at something else, it's all relevant. I've had the meters all slamming. Some people look at those, and if it's not zero they get all weird.

My meters stick all the time. Especially channel 8. It'll fly over and stick. You have to tap it.

That's a good machine [the Otari]. The difference between that and the bigger ones is not as much as it was jumping from the 4-track to that.

But you've got the same track width as the 4-track.

But it's twice the speed. It's got better heads. It was a lot better sounding than I thought it would be. We record 6 tracks live and then do overdubs. Then we mix down to DAT and then we make the cassettes from the DAT. That was why we got the DAT. Instead of having to print 100 of each, we just print them to order. I'm wondering when that will wear out my DAT. I'll worry about that later. It's funny, I don't know what sounds good. Things are so different. People are reading about it – you go from one tip to the next, and you should record. Anyone can think of an excuse not to.

Write The Barn at HC 81, Box 629, Questa, NM 87556

Quasi

UNEARTHING THE PARANORMAL.
SECRETS OF RECORDING WITH
PORTLAND'S SONIC ADVENTURERS

by Larry Crane

QUASI R&B TRANSMOGRIFICATION

John Clark

G.W.T

Quasi is a unique band. Sam Coomes and Janet Weiss play all the instruments and both sing; though Sam's forte is manic guitar and keyboard work and Janet is a drummer extraordinaire. They used to be in Motorgoat, a more conventional "rock" trio and Sam was in the fine Donner Party combo from San Francisco. They've been playing out as Quasi since mid 1993, sometimes employing extra musicians, but lately not.

Their first CD, *Early Recordings*, is an amazing release. There's pop songs, there's noises and there's always a keen sense of musical and sonic adventure going on. They're nearly done with a new album [*R&B Transmogrification*], which is set to be even stronger in the pop song department and will have a different sound, due to the use of rock band Pond's nifty little recording setup.

I met up with Quasi after band practice at Sam's late one Friday night....

How did you guys come about recording at home and having the 8-track?

S: Before my first band, Donner Party, I had this friend who was the original guitar player in that band. He got a settlement from a malpractice suit and got all this money. We were playing music and this was when home 8-tracks first came out.

J: Way back in the old days!

S: 1982 or 83. We went to the music store and bought this equipment and he paid cash for it. We used that to record Donner Party stuff, later on. A couple of years later we moved up to San Francisco and he dropped out of the band and eventually dropped out of music. I never saw the stuff 'til years later. He moved up to Portland and I was, "What are you doing with that 8-track stuff?" He said it was in boxes at his parent's house. I said, "I'd love to buy it off you if you were gonna sell it cheap." So, I got it from him.

Pretty cheap?

S: I think we paid a thousand bucks for a board, an 8-track, a 2-track, some cables, a delay unit, a couple of mics...

J: We got a lot of other stuff at Portland Music's half price sale. Have you been to that? Invitation only. We got tons of stuff. Mics and cords and mic stands. It was great and I've never been invited again.

Freeloader. What type of decks and mixing board did you end up with?

S: It's a Fostex A8.

J: Bottom of the line.

S: You can only record 4 [channels] at a time. The next year they came out with a deck that you could record all 8 at the same time.

What was the mixing board?

S: A Fostex model 350 mixer.

J: It doesn't have much EQ on it.

When you do stuff what do you mix to? Do you borrow a DAT?

J: For Motorgoat stuff we went right to DAT.

S: We used the 2-track [Fostex 1/4"] for Quasi.

And then dump that to DAT?

S: Yeah, and then use the DAT to master [the CD].

So the Motorgoat stuff you did straight to DAT. Did you notice a difference?

J: I did. The Motorgoat stuff actually sounds pretty good. We labored over it a lot more. But the music isn't as good! The recording is surprisingly good. The Quasi stuff, we just try to get the songs out. More performance orientated instead of worrying about if the rack tom is mic'd right.

Aren't you doing 3 mics on the drums?

S: We used a lot of different ways.

J: I'd read about triangle mic'ing in some stupid drum book and we'd try it and it'd be horrible. We wouldn't redo it, we'd just leave it.

S: We tried a pretty wide variety. I think that four mics is good for what we do. You can mic the snare and the bass drum and then two just stereo in the air.

The simplest way.

J: You can lose a lot of toms.

S: It's the principle of diminishing returns. If you set up those four mics you get pretty good to totally fine, and then you could spend hours and hours getting just slightly better than that.

J: Sam's the impatient one and I'm the perfectionist.

You like to get it sorta rough, "It'll work," and run with it?

J: It depends.

S: I don't like to spend a lot of time dillydallying over little increments of sonic quality. As long as it sounds pretty good...roll tape!

Do you ever get mad at him for working too fast that way?

J: No, because if I do feel like we gotta work on it more, we'll work on it more. He always lets *me* work on it more. *He* just doesn't want to work on it more.

S: It's not so much recording, it's also mixing.

J: He kinda shuts off.

S: I'll get it to a point where I'm happy and then if it needs to go further I'll just leave it.

J: It was nice mixing with Charlie [from Pond] around, because he's like me. He could work on one thing... small changes. Once I zone in on something, it's gonna bug me if I don't fix it. If I don't notice it, I don't notice it. If I notice it then I gotta work on it. By listening to our records you would never think that it was like that. It's all really loose.

S: People are surprised that we did it on a 1/4" home studio. I was talking to Mike from Poolside, and he said, "We just recorded and we used 2" tape."

J: 2" tape? Where'd they get that?

S: I was, "Why are you doing that? What's the deal?" I told him we recorded on 1/4" 8-track and he was, "Really?" 2" tape? Just leave that for big budget studio people who have 2 inches worth of tape to waste.

J: But to be inexperienced...

A band can be wasting their time on some of their first ventures into the studio, spending a lot of money, and still getting something that doesn't sound good to them when they could just buy a 4-track cassette deck.

S: An inch and 3/4's of tape is not gonna magically make you sound better!

J: Not to rag on Poolside, though.

S: They haven't had that much experience.

J: It's hard to experiment on 2" tape. There's something about paying $12 for a reel of tape. You can goof around. You can spend the whole reel playing one note.

S: A lot of stuff on our record, we'd just roll tape 'til the tape ran out. We went back and we'd overdub over parts that sounded cool.

I'd find it hard to imagine Quasi going into a studio and being able to work. Playing at home you can take your time.

S: It's been pointed out, by prominent thinkers in the past, that it's very important for the workers to own the means of production. You will always have abuses and oppression if a third party is in control...

J: The record business, right there!

S: People are surprised that you can make an album.

J: You don't need a lawyer to make an album!

S: You can make an album in a cheap studio and nobody will even know the difference. The average person can't tell the difference and doesn't care.

A lot of times they'll spend a lot of time trying to get something to sound as gritty as an inexpensive studio. When you go to record, where do you do it? Do you do it here?

S: We recorded the first record at Janet's house. The basement and living room.

J: Drums sound much better in the kitchen. The cymbals sound better. We had everything set up in the basement. It's out of the way and we had all the cords running through the floor. You could turn the tape on and run downstairs. At any time it was set up. Here, we actually did some stuff in the kitchen too. On the new record.

S: We finished another record. We did it on Pond's deck, an Otari 8-track 1/2". We're moving up. We've doubled our tape volume!

J: I think it makes a difference.

Catches more.

J: Yeah. We have better room mics now, too.

What kind of mics do you guys like to use?

S: We used only [Shure SM] 57s on our whole first record.

J: Think we could get an endorsement?

S: We used Pond's gear. Still a lot of 57s, but they have some other stuff.

J: A kick drum mic. Some condenser mics. I think the 57's sound exactly the same. Maybe even better. But I'm totally sold on the condenser mics. You could just have those and something on the bass drum and it would be good. Your snare might not be quite as loud as you want it to.

S: They're pretty specialized for drums or a room mic for some ambient thing.

Sometimes they're too sibilant, like for vocals.

S: A 57's fine for vocals as far as I'm concerned. I'm used to the sound of my voice in a 57.

J: We had another one, it looked Las Vegas-y, with a silver round top.

S: That was a 58, I guess.

J: It never really worked.

S: It's fine.

J: It doesn't work. You have to give it so much power to get a signal out of it.

S: It's not distorted, it just doesn't seem to have the output.

Are there any "odd" pieces of gear you use?

J: The secret weapon.

S: We have a [BBE] Sonic Maximizer.

J: And the delay.

S: The delay's busted. It doesn't work anymore.

J: We would use it instead of using reverb on the snare. We would use really heavy delay. Like slapback.

S: The drums were fucked on that record [*Early Recordings*], 'cause we recorded on the fly and didn't pay much attention to the sound. I used distortion boxes on the drums. I just did all kinds of fucked up things to make it sound interesting.

While you were mixing it?

S: While mixing and while recording. I would put the mics up and listen to it and it would not sound too great. It would be better to make it sound deliberately fucked up.

J: There are drums on that record where the cymbals are so loud. It's hard to listen to sometimes. I like it in a way. But the Sonic Maximizer really helped.

Do you use that for tracking?

S: Mixing.

J: It brightens it up a little. You have to make sure you don't put too much on.

S: We got really excessive with it. Just put a tiny bit on there and it's pretty noticeable. You think, "If it sounds good with a little bit, it'll sound great with a lot." You have to hardly use it at all. It adds a little more vibrancy to the mix.

Do you have any idea what it's doing?

S: I had it explained to me once. There's an [Aphex] Aural Exciter and the Sonic Maximizer and they work with two different principles and I can't remember which is which. I think The Sonic Maximizer takes the high end of the spectrum and the low end and separates them out and it puts a teeny bit of delay on the rest of the spectrum so that the high end is hitting your ear first and it jumps out at you. The Aural Exciter works with harmonics.

It takes high harmonics and distorts those and blends them back in.

S: Yeah. That's what the Aural Exciter does.

I thought the Sonic Maximizer gave you the low end first. In a straight mix the lows are arriving to the listener after the high end, because of physics.

S: It has only a couple of knobs. Low and high. It's really simple, but it definitely makes a difference. It's pretty subtle, but it's a nice thing.

Did you use that on *Early Recordings*?

S: That album's pretty weird. It was mixed at different times. It was all these tapes lying around. We just piled them up and dumped them onto a DAT. There was no method applied to that project at all. That's just the nature of how that was. The second record – that we've finished mixing, it hasn't been mastered – was more traditional.

How do you approach a recording session?

J: We've done it every different way. There's some stuff where Sam plays everything and there's some stuff where I play everything. It could just have started by putting a guitar line down and making it into a song. There was a song where I played the drums, in some weird format, and then made a song on top of it. Sam, certain times he'd put the guitar down and I'd have to overdub the drums. It was really hard. Sometimes we play guitar or bass and drums together. We've done it a lot of different ways.

S: The approach that we used on the record that we're working on now was more standard. We recorded basics together, then overdubbing.

Do you think that came from playing live more?

S: Yeah. We had the songs already worked out. The stuff we have now is just like our live set and then we put little treats on top of it.

Do you guys ever bounce tracks?

S: I don't do full bounce. Like taking all the tracks down to 2 and then freeing up 6. Sometimes I'll take 2 tracks and I'll mix them onto one track. Like two vocals and bounce them into one harmony track to free up another track. I do limited bouncing.

Is there noise reduction on that deck?

S: Yeah, I think there's Dolby on it but I don't use it.

J: No Dolby. Noise. That's what it's all about.

S: We'll reduce the tape hiss and we'll also lose the top end. Tape hiss is really only noticeable when the music is quiet which doesn't happen all that often with Quasi.

Is there anything either of you have been listening to lately that you like the sound of?

J: I've been listening to *Alien Lanes* by Guided By Voices. That's the greatest. That's such a perfect example. They obviously didn't get caught up in making it sound perfect, but it comes across as better. The songs are good and it sounds better. It's not all fancy. It's more the spirit of the recording. The buzz of the amp adds some texture. I've been really pleased with listening to that. You put it on and you don't think, "Well, they should've gone into a big studio."

S: The only name that comes to mind that's been doing something consistently interesting is Jim O'Rourke of Brise-Glace, Faust, and Gastr Del Sol. Pretty much anything he does is interesting. He's such an advocate of tape splicing and loops and I've been thinking I really want to start messing around with that.

You could record 8-track loops on your deck.

S: This friend of mine made a whole tape for me of different loops that he had done on a 2-track deck that he found in a garbage can. It's great. Just think what you could do with 8-track loops.

contact Quasi c/o Up Records PO Box 21328 Seattle, WA 98111-3328.

Sea Saw

SHORTS

by Larry Crane

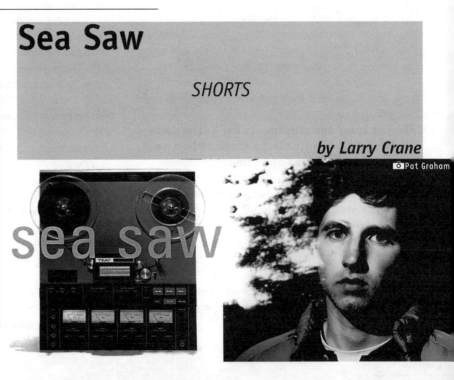

This was originally going to be just a short review of a record I liked very much, but as time went by I listened to it way too much and wanted to know more about how it was recorded and put together. The album is by a band called Sea Saw and is called *Magnetophone*. Sea Saw is really only Trevor Kampmann, a one-man-band home recordist who used a 4-track reel-to-reel deck to it's fullest potential in creating *Magnetophone*. His work is nothing short of meticulous, finding the right sounds for the instruments, layering a thick buzzing pop drone, and when it's time to write a catchy hook (and there's a good handful here) he delivers the goods. Plus, a lot of the tunes use lyrics about recording technology as analogies for personal trouble, like: "microphone has died, lose the tone" or "erase my tapes, my batteries are low." It totally hit home here at recording-geek central.

How did you get started doing recordings?

In college I took an engineering class. I was a politics major, but I just decided to take one thing that I thought might be interesting. It turned out to be really interesting. I wasn't really super into recording but it was a fun class. It was an 8-track analog recorder but I wound up gravitating toward the 4-track.

Do you have any idea why?

It was easier to manipulate. Initially, the 4-track was it. When I was in my bedroom I had to keep things really, really quiet. With 4-track you can make things sound loud even though they're really quiet. It's like the opposite of big, multitrack recording. Things sound puny, but collectively they become a big, huge thing.

You were just concentrating on individual sounds and making them big?

Yeah.

Are you still using the TEAC 3440 [1/4" 4-track], that's on the album cover?

I got this Scully flatbed. It's a 1/2" 4-track industrial thing. It's the type *Pet Sounds* was recorded on.

Do you like the sound of it better?

It's amazing. It soaks in lots of low end, but I want to sell it 'cause I just got an ADAT. It's not what people think it is. I'm going through a [Roland] Space Echo so it goes onto tape and the output sounds like analog tape, because it is. I also did that with the Scully, have that rolling and do some drum things. You can only do that with the initial tracks 'cause there's a [tape] delay, but I actually could delay it on my ADAT after I record it. The ADAT is a great medium.

You have 8 tracks to play with.

It's a huge plus. I like it 'cause I can do all these experimental things with degrading sound, but it's there. It'll be there forever. I like using crummy mics that have really colored sounds.

Are there any mics you really like?

I work in the audiovisual department for this corporation that's really old and they have this "museum" of audio equipment. That's where I got the Scully. I use this Electro-Voice, one of those real industrial-type mics. They're thin and they've been around since the '60s. It's a great, really bright sound. I always use that on vocals. I have this Shure Pro Log, the crummiest Shure you can find. I use that for warmer stuff. And just a host of Radio Shack mics. I just bought a *real* AKG, a *real* microphone! But the new stuff is still totally lo-fi. That's the funniest thing – I must just be drawn towards those sounds.

The Apples in Stereo

WITH GARY LUCY

by Larry Crane

We caught the Apples at a strange Portland gig opening up for some shitty local bands. Many people who came to see them play ended up seeing us interview the band instead. They're a wonderful, pop-psychedelic combo based in Denver, Colorado and they love to record their own music... as well as play live. Their first album, *Fun Trick* *Noisemaker*, was out and they had a unique deal going with their record label, SpinArt, who not only encouraged them to record on their own... well, you'll see! Robert Schneider, who's the main songwriter, singer and plays melodic leads on his guitar, did most of the talking. Hilarie Sidney, the drummer with the minimal kit, had a lot to say too, but John Hill (rhythm guitar) and Eric Allen (bass) were either running around or rather quiet.

How did you get into recording yourselves?

I guess that's the way that we've always done it. We've all been recording for a long time on 4-track and stuff. I started when I was 15. We recorded two EPs and some 7" records on a 4-track and we couldn't afford, or didn't want to go, to a recording studio. Plus, it was a really distasteful sound to our ears.

Have any of you been in bands that used a "real" recording studio?

We'd never been in other bands. We didn't really know, when we first started recording on the 4-track [cassette], that you couldn't make something sound as good as a recording studio. We knew the Beatles recorded on a 4-track; therefore, why couldn't we? Then we found out you can't, so we got a reel-to-reel 4-track. Now we have an 8-track.

What kind of 8-track?

An Otari 5050 1/2". It sounds great. We've got good mics. I recorded a few albums, last year, after our own. I recorded the Neutral Milk Hotel album [on Merge]. We did that on our 4-track, reel-to-reel. Then I recorded the Olivia Tremor Control and the Felt Pilotes on 8-track. I've gotten a lot better engineering since then. We're almost hi-fi!

That's cool, you graduated from 4-track...

We told SpinArt that we'd been in recording studios and we knew how to record. They told us they'd buy us an 8-track if we got an engineer to help us with it. We didn't have either experience or an engineer!

How many reels of tape sound really bad?

None. With those good mics, you just set them up anywhere, never change the settings, and it sounds great. Even a SM 57 on the bass drum sounds really good. So, we just figured it out. It was good enough on the 4-track, we just wanted 8 tracks and with these better mics it's gonna be better anyway. We didn't end up having an engineer. We went to a friend's house in California and recorded. We've become expert, technical engineers!

What kind of mics have worked really good for you guys?

The Audio-Technica 4033. It rules. It's so great. They took the analog EQ curve from a bunch of great '60s mics and then they averaged it out and copied it on that mic. It sounds real old fashioned and real warm. The 4050, the next model up, is too pristine. It's a bit too fat and bassy sounding too.

Does everyone get into recording?

We all do.

How did you get SpinArt to offer the cash to set up the studio?

They offered. That was why we decided to do a record with them. They liked our stuff and they wanted to put one of our songs on a compilation. I told them how I really wanted to get an 8-track and they said, "Hey, we'll buy you an 8-track." They knew about the equipment and they suggested some stuff and my friend Kyle had a studio, and he suggested some more stuff. We ended up getting some high-end equipment.

A lot better than a regular advance!

Yeah! We can keep it forever. Not like we'll piddle it away. I've recorded three other albums; I'm getting to be a pretty good engineer. We got the money back and I got to live off that all year.

But these guys [the other Apples] are the ones who helped you get the equipment and you get the money [from outside productions]? [Laughs] I'm sorry. What are some of your favorite records that sound cool to you?

I love the new Lilys album. It's not out yet. It's called *Better Can't Make Your Life Better*. It's amazing. It sounds like the Kinks in 1966. It's totally mod and it's beautiful and it's great songwriting. I'm really jealous that he recorded such a great album. I love Pavement records.

What about the Beach Boys influence? On the album there's that one song with that total fuzz bass.

"Lucky Charm". Like "Good Vibrations". That little piece is exactly a rip. SpinArt were thinking about putting that song out as a single and we went and remixed it and it's really strange, they insisted that we take out the bridge. It's my favorite part of the whole song. They thought it was too weird for radio. That seems bizarre, 'cause it's a rip of "Good Vibrations" and that's what they told Brian [Wilson] in the old days – that it was too weird for radio – and it was a big hit.

So you guys will borrow a friend's house, you'll take your 8-track, record your basic tracks, and do some overdubs. When it comes to mixing do you take it somewhere else?

We might do that more in the future. Maybe the record after next. It's good to have all those compressors and stuff. It'd be good to have another set of ears for mixing, too. It'd be good to have somebody else so you could bounce ideas around. I'd still have to mix everything myself because I have a really strong idea of what it has to sound like. Everything is all connected musically. There's not a whole lot of room for this or that to be different. That's all sub-mixed, so it's all pre ordained.

So you do a lot of bouncing?

Yeah. We bounce everything. We recorded that album [*Fun Trick Noisemaker*] on 8 tracks and then dumped it to a DAT machine, put it back on 2 tracks of the 8-track and then kept going. It works really well, a stereo mix and everything.

And you save your old tracks just in case..

Exactly. That works great. That's how we did most of the stuff. The new stuff, some of it will be submixed to stereo and some of it will be ping-ponged on the 8-track. It's better to ping-pong than sub mix 'cause you have more control in the end. If you submix, all the overdubs are real crisp and the submix is on 2 tracks. Those 2 tracks can sound awfully puny once you start overdubbing other tracks. I've gotten better at EQ and stuff, so I think I can make them sound less puny.

Do you record guitar, bass and drums initially?

Track the drums first with a scratch guitar, overdub rhythm guitars and acoustic guitars, and maybe overdub some keyboards and piano. Submix all that down to stereo. Go back to the tape, add all the harmonies, keyboards, slide guitars, everything. Submix all that stuff to a couple more tracks. Bass and the lead vocals are the last things to go down. So the bass can have it's own track - it always gets drowned out in the submix. The vocals have 2 tracks, one for each lead vocal.

[To Hilarie] You seem to sing a lot less live than on the record.

Yeah. Well, I'm kinda shy. I don't want to sing flat. It's hard with the PAs; we're all real soft singers. If I can't hear myself, I'm real self-conscious that I'm singing totally off. I can't hear myself over my cymbals. I wish I was really confident and knew I was gonna sing it right. Sometimes we'll record the parts, but we never practice them, so I'll forget what the part is.

It seems like you guys, as a band, enjoy recording and operating in this way.

It's fun to learn. It's a thrill on it's own. Plus we're never, "Oh shit, time's ticking away! It's $20 an hour!" We're just sitting there, smoking pot and having a really good time. Taking all night to do a guitar track if you have to. Like the guitars on "High Tide." All the lead guitars on that - I just stayed up all night with a pillow, on my back, with the remote for the 8-track next to me and just recorded all the lead guitars, there's 3 or 4 of them on there. It took all night. I was just baked, smoking pot, lying down on the floor. It was really fun.

Cool. So you're pretty adamant about doing the next few records yourselves?

We're gonna do them all. We're always gonna do our records on our own. We'll just get higher budgets and more great equipment. Someday we'll have a 16-track, maybe. Right now we're happy with the 8-track; there's a long way to go with it, with the new mics and new board.

What kind of board is it?

A Mackie 8 buss, 24 channel. It's a really great board. It's got a lot of EQ options. The one we used to have was the Mackie 1604. That's what we did our album with, mixed it and everything. So our next album's gonna be a lot better. Even in the submixing, you can make it sound a lot better. It's really amazing.

How do you mic the drums?

We use a snare drum mic, a bass drum mic and an overhead. Even with other bands, when they have tom toms and stuff. Put it on 3 tracks and submix it to one track.

You don't do stereo drums?

We did on our album but not anymore. I realized after that album that every single album I love has mono drums. Our album was different 'cause we really wanted it to sound like a band in a room; a roomy, real, right-there kinda sound. But you just get a better sound with mono drums, I think. The Beatles, The Zombies, The Beach Boys, Phil Spector. The best drum sounds are all mono.

Have you heard the Beatles *Anthology 2*? The drums sound so fat on that.

That's the drum sound we want. That perfect, flat, just slightly overdriven drum sound.

So do you use much reverb?

Just on the harmonies, some slide guitar, maybe. We have two [Roland] Space Echoes. That's all we use. We use tape delay and spring reverb. That's all we need. We used to have a digital delay and I traded it for my tube 4-track.

Any last words on recording?

We love it. It's part of the writing of songs for us. We're gonna keep doing it and get better and better. We're in control, like, "Let's make it sound better on the next record." Not, "I hope it sounds better." We're not just a rock band. We're producers and we want to be engineers. Someday we might not be a rock band, but we may still want to write songs and record them.

The Apples in Stereo can be reached at their record label: Elephant 6 Records, PO Box 9935, Denver, CO 80209 or at elep6recco@aol.com

MARBLES
Pyramid Landing (SpinArt)

Marbles is a CD of 4-track goodies from Robert Schneider [of the Apples in Stereo] featuring songs he recorded 1992-93 before they got the band together. It's exuberant pop experimentation where you can hear him exploring the recording process, figuring out how to layer all the parts to mimic his favorite psychedelic records and learning how to compose some catchy tunes. It's a good listen, and maybe, even more than the Apple's work, showcases Robert's mastery of recording as a great songwriting tool. –Larry Crane

THE APPLES in Stereo
Tone Soul Evolution (SpinArt)

I've only had time to listen to the first few songs on this record but one thing's for sure - you need this album. The Apples continue on their bright pop path, this time recording at home on the 8-track and also at Studio .45 in Hartford, CT. If you remember correctly, you'll place that studio at the heart of the last Lily's CD, another fine psychedelic pop record. Once again, lead Apple Robert produced, but Studio .45 main man Mike Deming co-engineered and mixed with him. It's great, trust me. –Larry Crane

NEUTRAL MILK HOTEL
In the Aeroplane Over the Sea (Merge)

Solidly recorded, exquisitely lyrical folk music from Jeff Mangum, produced in Denver by Robert Schneider [of The Apples in Stereo]. Although Jeff still writes all the songs, the arrangements here have more of a band feel than his previous full-length, *On Avery Island*. The central guitar/vocal axis is hung at various points with organ, singing saw, flugelhorn, bowed banjo, and a whole stable of other instrumental esoteria. Jeff does a good job mixing pretty melodies with his own distinctive vocabulary. It's not every songwriter who will get you singing "semen stains the mountaintops" as you walk down the street. –Leigh Marble

MARBLES
"I the Summer" b/w " Our Song" 7" (Elephant 6)

Once again, Robert from the Apples in Stereo proves his pop worth with a couple of super-well crafted gems that he recorded and performed on his own. I swear these sound like Beach Boys or Association outtakes. I think he's the master of the pop 8-track recording session... –Larry Crane

Sue Garner

WITH A RECORD THAT WAS NEARLY TITLED *TWO ADATS AND A MICROPHONE*, YOU CAN REST ASSURED THAT THERE'S A *TAPE OP* STORY INVOLVED

by Larry Crane

© Chris Toliver

Sue Garner has been a member of many New York based bands over the years: Fish and Roses, The Shams, Run On and others. Generally she can be found playing bass and singing. After all those years in bands Sue's first solo record, *To Run More Smoothly*, has finally appeared on the fine Thrill Jockey imprint. Recordings for the album were done in her apartment [which she shares with husband Rick Brown, drummer for Run On and Les Batteries], her band's rehearsal space and at Chris Stamey's Modern Recording in Chapel Hill, NC. Chris used to be a member of the legendary DBs and was the one responsible for nearly naming Sue's album, *Two ADATs and a Microphone*. I met up with Sue during her soundcheck in Portland for a swank gig opening for Mark Eitzel and we had a fun chat. By the way, the show was great too.

Had you been working on solo recordings before or did Thrill Jockey approach you with the idea of doing one?

No, I had been working on some stuff and over the last couple of years I had made a 4-track tape that sat around the house for a year and then I made some copies and they sat around the house for about 6 months. Finally I got them out to a couple of places and Bettina [Thrill Jockey owner] said, "Yeah."

I thought Matador would jump on it first...

They didn't. It does help any sort of conflict of interest that might arise.

So did some of the stuff from that 4-track tape appear on the album?

No.

Were these songs that Run On didn't use?

Just songs that didn't really seem to fit the band. Or I'd even brought them in but no one was interested. You don't want to push it.

The album was all done on ADAT, right?

Yeah.

A single ADAT?

I have one but I would get copies made so I could add more tracks. Not that everything has that many tracks to it but that way I could try something else. I made three copies: A, B and C. I would try different things. Sometimes it wasn't until we mixed that I realized if it worked or not because I'd never heard them all together!

Were you tracking everything at home?

I tried. There were 4 or 5 songs that the vocals and basic guitars were done at Chris Stamey's house. Then I did all the other stuff at home. Then, when I was mixing, there were a couple of tracks where I was like, "It'd sound good with this here."

So you did a lot of the work on this record with Chris Stamey?

He has a lot of really good tube compressors, Pro Tools for editing... He's got the business going down there. It was great working with him.

So he does a lot of commercial work? What's his studio called?

Modern Recording. I highly recommend it. It was a really nice experience working with him. He's a great musician, really tireless and has good ears. That's important. I would be,"That's fine, let's stop." He would say, "Let's get it perfect."

Oh yeah. I know how that goes. So I assume you live in an apartment, especially from that song, "Box and You". Do you record in a corner of the place or something?

We have a room, a recording room, and we have a rehearsal room...

In your apartment?

No! Not in our apartment! For loud guitar and drums I'd go down there. Take my ADAT to the rehearsal room.

What kind of stuff do you use for preamps or a mixer?

I have that one, actually I'm using it as a preamp for my guitar tonight. It's an Art [tube] MP. I use that and we have a little Mackie board.

The 1202? Does it have faders or little round knobs instead?

Little round knobs. I use those preamps too. When I just need one preamp I use the Art, but if I need more than one I just use the mixer.

What do you listen back to the ADAT on?

The Mackie. I'm always having to re-patch stuff. We're gonna try and get a little bit clearer setup. You know how the ADATs have the Elco cables? Well, I didn't buy them 'cause they were an extra $150. I think I will get those.

I've hardly ever worked with ADATs.

I like my little ADAT. It's like a really souped-up 4-track. It's portable.

Do you ever do that stuff where you can set up punch in points?

Yeah, but I don't do a lot of that. I'll just track the whole thing. I have a hard time with punch-ins anyway. One thing I had was time, so I would tend to do it over.

I used to do that when I was 4-tracking. If you messed up a vocal you just do it all over.

I never did one vocal. One of the tapes was just for vocals and I just sang it seven times. We'd listen to the seven takes, make a chart, and if you liked a line you'd X it. If you really liked it you'd double XX it. If you *really* liked it you'd star it. I like to try to get it as much from one as possible, but I love studios and I love the fact that you can do that!

Some times people are afraid of working that way... What kind of mics did you use for recording your album?

We used what we had! A couple of [Shure] SM 57s... I bought one good mic, A Rode NT-2. We had an SM 58 Beta, but I didn't like the way it recorded. I like it live, for vocals, 'cause I tend to be quiet and it helps.

What places has Run On recorded at?

Idful, Greenstreet...

Where's that?

In New York. Nice place and a really great engineer, Rod Hui. Also at Rare Book Room in Brooklyn. We did stuff with John McEntire in Chicago.

How was that?

It was great. John's really great. Unfortunately, the DAT that we were mixing down to messed up so we couldn't mix down. That was a long time ago! I think he's got his DATs working now!

That happened to me before... Which studios did you enjoy working at?

I really liked working at Greenstreet. It's a 24-track analog machine with 2" tape. They've made their living doing hip-hop records.

Just like Run On...

Exactly! At the same time, with Casey [Rice, at Idful], there were certain things that would never sound that good with anyone else. One of my favorite songs on that record is "Days Away," and I don't think anyone else would have made it sound as good as Casey. We were really too pressed for time with that record.

How long did you have?

We did it in two and a half weeks. 16 days. Without a day off. Really long days.

You can lose perspective at the end of that.

It's not a good way to work. We thought it would be; to go and immerse yourself in this thing. It's not a good way to make a record.

What do you think would be ideal?

Having a really great studio in your house!

Or the practice place/studio like Sonic Youth.

Exactly. I think they have found the perfect solution. That is what I want to try and get going, somehow.

Get another ADAT, a small mixer and a couple of mics... you're on your way!

And then go mix it at places that have all the analog stuff and tubes. I think it is a good idea to mix with other people 'cause it gets it out of yourself so much.

It seems like your band might do really well with that sort of thing. Are other people in the band tech-heads when it comes to recording?

Rick's the biggest tech-head.

Did he help you get some of your stuff together?

Yeah, he helps me a lot.

Doesn't he play a little synthesizer and drums on the album too?

He plays a snare drum and a cold cream thing with beans in it.

You don't have to chase him off when you're trying to record stuff?

There are times where, "No, I don't want help. Okay?" I don't go to him when he's working, "Don't you want my help?"

What other stuff does he have going on besides Run On and Les Batteries?

He's got tapes and tapes of these great loops and stuff that he's made. Our next records gonna have a lot of loops. We actually sat down for a few hours one day and went through some DATs and made notes on what was on them and what sounded good.

Are they things you could build songs around?

Yeah. What I would love to get would be another ADAT, Pro Tools and a mixer. In this world, the amount of money I need is so small. So anyone reading...!!

Alastair Galbraith

THE MANY RECORDING ADVENTURES OF ALASTAIR GALBRAITH

by Larry Crane

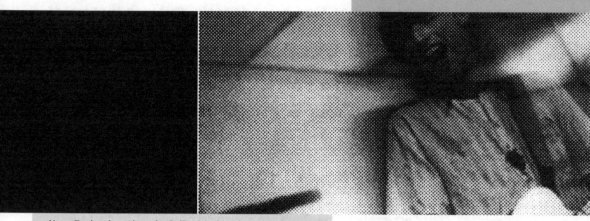

New Zealander Alastair Galbraith has been recording his music on 4-track decks in a non-studio environment since he did *Stormed Port* by his "group" The Rip in 1987. Turned on to the possibilities of "home-recording" by Peter and Graeme Jefferies during those sessions, he went on to record with Peter as Plagal Grind and finally branched out on his own in the recording realm. Since then, he's recorded most of his music at home on an old Tascam 3440 late at night, out in the country, and at his own pace. He's also done various collaborations with Graeme Jefferies and John D's Mountain Goats by sending reels of tape through the mail and adding parts as needed. We got to chat over the phone after his first coffee and cigarette of the day.

So your first recording experience was with The Rip in a "real" studio.

That's right. We were about 16 or 17 years old and pretty easily led. At that time there seemed to be a few less people making their own recordings and there was no other label than Flying Nun that [we] could release stuff on. We just went the direction we were led, which was towards a large studio in Christchurch. An engineer did the engineering and I sat back and laughed. When we brought it home it sounded nothing like what it sounded like on the beautiful ten thousand-dollar speakers. It was a real disappointment.

Did those recordings get released?

The Rip, an EP called *A Timeless Piece,* Flying Nun 23 or something.

Did you immediately start thinking about recording on your own?

Peter and his brother Graeme Jefferies came down from the north island of New Zealand. Graeme owned a Teac 4-track and Peter suggested that we record with him and he would produce and engineer it. They lived in an old store in Dunedin and I went around there in the evenings when my band had just split up. Basically the next Rip record for

Flying Nun was a solo thing. Graeme played guitar on a song and Robbie Muir played bass on one song. Peter engineered and explained what he was doing as he did so and Graeme engineered a couple of the songs as well. I got the picture of what it was like to record yourself through that experience.

That's cool of Peter to teach you like that.

And Graeme, both equally.

So, that was an eye opening experience in seeing that you could record on your own?

Yes and no, because they did it and I was in another room. They explained what they were doing, and what they thought would be good to do next, but I still wasn't there with my hands on the machine. I didn't really know how to do it. Shortly after, somebody got me to look after their warehouse and there was a cassette PortaStudio there. That's when I really got the hands-on experience. I recorded the song "Midnight Blue" by playing some guitar and then turning the cassette backwards and finding out it was really easy to slow down and speed up and make it go backwards and so on.

Did you move up to a reel-to-reel?

Yeah, I got the same kind of machine that Graeme Jefferies had [Teac 3440].

So most of your recordings have been done in this format since then. I heard you dumped some stuff to 8-track at one point.

We did that for the Plagal Grind EP. That was a beautiful 8-track that was 1" tape with lots of headroom on each track. There were one or two tracks that were a bit dodgy and two that sounded beautiful. You had to watch where you put stuff. It was fun doing that as well, but definitely everything else has been done on the Teac and I haven't really felt the need for more than 4 tracks.

Do you have it set up at home?

Yeah, the 4-track goes straight into the stereo. I don't use a mixing desk. I plug directly into it because it has such a nice sound anyway. As a result with no mixing desk and nothing to pan things, tracks 1 and 3 of the 4-track go left and tracks 2 and 4 go right and there's extreme separation. When it comes time to actually "mix" something down I just turn the output knobs on the 4-track and do it hard left and hard right. A lot of the records have that extreme separation or else I just press the mono button on my stereo if I don't really think it should be separated.

So you do all your recording that way?

Yeah. Once or twice I've borrowed a small little panning device that a friend made for about $2 with a little knob off a guitar. He just soldered it onto a bar of metal. You plug 2 things in and then you turn the little knob left or right.

That's crazy. What do you mix down to?

Well, generally what they want is a DAT. In the past I've hired one, but now I bought this really cheap DAT thing that's really a still video recorder. It takes a normal DAT tape, but it's a very odd machine. Most of the time it's good enough.

When you're going straight into your deck... are there preamps built into that?

There must be. I know so little about it. The level thing, with all those machines, you're pretty safe. There is no need to increase anything or do anything to it. Even if you record it all at a real extreme +3 all the time the natural distortion that machine has is beautiful. I do record like that, in the red all the time, and it's got a really warm distortion.

Any thoughts on microphones?

If anyone that's into home recording is reading this, and they want to know about a really good cheap microphone, get a PZM microphone.

We did an article on them.

You can get them for $60. I find them to be just the best vocal mic. I love to hold that big plate in my hand at a distance of 2 or 3 centimeters. It has about the same treble response as the very best valve [tube] microphone.

Do you use any effects to run things through before it goes to the tape deck?

Generally I haven't bothered for myself. The effects I use are not really effects like that. I've got a big, old fan and I broke a blade off it so that it really has an odd, eccentric motion and I stuck it on my chest and sang. That is a really great effect, if you can adjust the speed of the fan.

Were you singing through the fan?

No, no. Just hold it on my chest. I've done things like sing down a pipe or, in one case, get a big polystyrene picnic hamper thing, stick that over my head and make a hole in it and stick a microphone in and you get an extreme deepness that can't be beaten. That kind of thing interests me a lot more than buying a box that has little wires in it.

Do you make a bit of racket there at your house? Do you have a room set aside?

I do have a room that's mainly used for that. Because I'm plugging the guitar straight in, I'm not using an amp, except for what comes back through the stereo; it's like the music has never existed except for in the 4-track itself. Except for singing.

How have you felt working with the Bats? [in bigger studios adding violin to their songs]

You're just a session musician. I don't do that anymore. It's always been really fun to play with them, especially live because it's pure improvisation. In the studio, when there has been a producer, it's been difficult because they want to know what you're going to do. You don't know what you're going to play when you're improvising. That's kind of the point of being in that band and being a member who didn't have any idea what was going to happen; that was important.

So you'd come in and be like, "Well, let's see what happens."

Yeah.

And the producers and engineers...

Producers. They had a couple of well-known American producers where that was definitely not allowed. So I stopped at that point.

I assume you're still friends with the Bats?

Yeah, they're great.

Do you find that having this recording setup at home is conducive to your way of working?

Yes, because otherwise you'd be worrying about how much money or time you had. I find that I generally record in the evenings, at night really, and I live in the country and there's nobody to annoy if I ever make too much noise. It's a good thing to be able to start it when you like and stop it when you like. To have no set agenda of what must be done. That's the other thing about working alone, that you really are totally free when you are writing and recording. You work on what you want to work on. I want to keep doing that for as long as I live. It doesn't mean you can't work with other people. I worked with John from the Mountain Goats and also Graeme Jefferies in this way as well: They would send me 4-track tapes with 2 tracks filled up with the songs they wanted me to work on. I still work on it alone, at my own pace, without them even knowing what I'm gonna do to it. It's exciting for them to get the tape back and not know what's gonna be there.

Have your collaborators been pretty happy with the results?

Yeah. It's my favorite way to work 'cause there's no one looking over your shoulder. I'm sure if you see the process of improvising on somebody else's material there will always be a point where it will not sound good. It's important to go through that part of the process. Otherwise it's not real experimentation. I make wine at home and there's a point where it tastes out-n-out awful.

When it's just starting to ferment?

Yeah.

Some musician from New Zealand had mentioned the lack of decent places to record being an impetus for doing recording on their own.

That probably holds true for people who have the money to consider the option of going into a studio. If I had several hundred dollars at my disposal to record the next thing instead of fifty dollars for tape and splicing patches. Even if I had the option I wouldn't take it anyway. I do know people, like Fish St. studios who I would trust if I were in that type of position, but I still wouldn't pursue it. I want to be the engineer and producer myself anyway. I've got the freedom to take a year to do something. If you're going to work in a studio you're doing it mainly 'cause your record company has told you to go to this studio and you want this kind of album. I think that's really the main reason, in most cases, that people have worked in a particular studio instead of at home. If most people were given the option of owning their own gear or going into a studio they'd rather get their own gear.

Write to: Alastair Galbraith, PO Box 1376, Dunedin, New Zealand

Linda Smith

HOME TAPER

by Diana Froley

Linda Smith is a home recordist from Baltimore. She has released several tapes on her own label, Preference, and she has released the 1996 CD *Nothing Else Matters* (on Feel Good All Over) and 1998's *Preference* plus *Selected Songs 1987-1991* (on Harriet), as well as several singles. Her suitcase-full of ethereal pop tunes and her singular approach to recording make her one of Baltimore's brightest secret stars.

Tell me how you started playing and recording music.

Well, I started playing music a long time before I started recording it. I didn't start playing music until I was about 25, in the early '80s. I got a little guitar, and a little amp. I had been wanting to do it for a couple of years, since I had started re-listening to pop music. I hadn't listened to pop music since I was a kid, but I got into it again because I heard Patti Smith, the English groups like The Raincoats and people like that. What they did seemed very simple but it had a lot of energy. It was kind of like people playing who didn't really know how to play, in the accepted sense. That's why I was drawn to it, although I've always liked more slick pop music, I also liked the idea that people don't have to know a lot of chords, and have chops, and all that. So I was into music at that time (late '70s). I learned a few chords, I wrote a few songs, and I thought it was time to find some people to play in a group with, because that was what you did. It was a little while before the personal 4-tracks came out, so I didn't think of recording initially because the technology wasn't there for people to go to a music store and buy a 4-track. There were the professional machines, the big clunky things, but I didn't even think of recording. I hadn't even written any songs but one or two. I put an ad in the *Baltimore City Paper*, because I didn't know anybody who was a musician, and I was particularly looking to play with other women because I liked the idea of The Raincoats, which was all

women at the time. I ended up meeting just about all the people in the Baltimore area who I still know, from that ad.

So what did the ad say?

Something about looking for people who don't know how to play and who are into The Raincoats or into the Young Marble Giants, or Patti Smith. Basically I was looking for beginning musicians, like myself. Of course I got a lot of responses from people who had been playing for years and years and years – they don't read! It didn't sink in. A couple of people I did go out of my way to meet, and find out what they were about, and I did end up playing with a couple of them, but not for about a year after that ad. I got together with this one guy who played bass, and he liked all the same groups I did, but he didn't play bass very well. In fact he played less well than I did, and I didn't play well at all, but mainly I'd go to his basement and we'd play records. We didn't really play any music. I think he was a lot younger than I was, but he was fun. He was cute, he was fun. Then a year later I went to this party, I don't know how I got invited to this party in a big old house and I thought, "Well I'll go." At this party were a couple of the people I had met in the previous year. One person, I re-met at the party, was a woman who played drums in a band called the 45's. They were still together when I originally met them, but they had since broken up. They were like an early Slits girl group, and they had played at the Marble Bar occasionally. So the drummer and I decided to get together and start playing music. That was Peggy [Bitzer]. Peggy and I and the guy from the basement decided to make a little trio, and we went to his apartment downtown, where Peggy set up her drums. It was above a bar and we could just be as loud as we wanted. What happened was he would never play, but we would play.

Did he do anything?

Well, he'd smoke cigarettes. He had a bass and he wasn't any worse than we were, but he didn't have any motivation. He liked the idea of saying he was in a band. We were thinking we were musicians at that point. Even though we hadn't made any songs. I didn't sing at that point. I played some chords I liked and Peggy would beat on the drums. I didn't have a microphone. After a while Kenny, the bassist, was out of the picture, but we met up with Peggy's friend Nancy [Sexton] and started a trio, and she played the bass, and I played guitar. Then we started to figure words into it, actually writing songs with words. That was called the Symptoms, and we played a few times down at the Marble Bar, art happenings, places like that. Nancy played saxophone also. She gradually drifted away and

Peggy and I joined up with a couple of other people who we rented a house with who were just starting to play music – Nancy Andrews and Liz Downing, who now have other pursuits. That group was called Ceramic Madonnahead. That was probably the first group for them, and that was the first time Liz had ever sung. The first show we played as a foursome was at the Congress Hotel, at this kind of art festival, and Liz was so frightened by being onstage that she ran off the stage. She got through one song, she looked at us, and she just disappeared. Which is kind of hard to imagine now, but she was petrified. So I had to say, "Would Miss Downing please return to the stage" and I think she did come back up. We even made a recording in a studio, and at that time an apartment in NY opened up and Peggy and I decided to go try that out, to do music in New York. They weren't interested in that, so in New York, Peggy and I met up with a couple of guys who wanted to play, and one of them played cello and one of them played drums. Peggy switched over to bass, and we switched vocals with the guys too. They had written songs also, so we had more of a songwriting collaboration with different people writing songs. We did some recordings and made a single for a friend's label, another Baltimorean, who put out a couple of singles. The name of the band, and it wasn't my idea and I didn't like it, was The Woods. We played a few shows. None of us had the whatever it takes to go out and get shows, but we did practice a lot, at our little practice space in Manhattan, and we'd go there every week and practice. The last time we played, we did a show at CBGBs and I just remember it was the low point of the morale of the group. The guy who played drums in the band kind of didn't feel like things were going the way he wanted them to.

With the sound or with the way you were being received?

It almost seemed like an inferiority complex, like he wanted to be more creative and have more input. I was writing a lot more songs; I had more than we had time to really practice. And we didn't play out a lot. We'd started doing some recordings at a studio in Manhattan, and that was fun. I liked that. I think he wanted a different kind of sound, he was more into ambient kind of stuff though he did like songs. Anyway, we were playing (at CBGB's) and [during] the whole set, he kept putting us down in between songs.

Was that considered a big deal then? You always hear about it.

Not then, it was past the time. Although a lot of bands played there and a lot of bands still do, it wasn't the kind of prestigious thing it was in the late '70s when all the good groups played there. But it was nice to get to play there; and I enjoyed it except when he was making apologies for how bad he thought we sounded. Just asides, to the microphone.

That's terrible! You should never apologize.

Yes, even if you sound like total shit, you should never apologize, but people do it. It was the deciding moment for me to get out of bands. Yeah, he was apologizing for out of tune guitars, for off-key singing, whatever, the things that people don't really hear when they're sitting there listening to music. I just thought, "This is it, I can't do this." I guess that was about 1985, and around that time I noticed in the paper these ads for 4-tracks just starting to come out, and I thought, "Why don't I just buy one of these and to hell with this." At that show I decided I didn't want to play in a group anymore, and I told them that, and that was that. I put a 4-track on layaway, and finally I got it, and I started doing 4-track recordings of my songs. To me this was just the greatest thing to happen, it was just one of those revelations, like, "Oh, this is fun. This music sounds like what I want it to sound, and I don't have to argue with people who think that what they have to offer is better than my suggestion." Sometimes they did come up with nice things, but then nobody wanted to listen to my suggestions. Everybody had this idea, or there was this idea I had which they couldn't execute, for whatever reason. At that point I was a little more advanced than they were, and also I had definite ideas about what I wanted to do, and they didn't know yet what they wanted, and they weren't really capable of carrying out what I wanted them to do on my songs. Not that what I was doing was so virtuosic.

But the sound that you end up with is really unique.

I felt like I had a unique idea. All the elements themselves are very basic, but when I put them all together, they add up to something that's kind of quirky. It just didn't work with a group of people.

Is that when you wrote these songs (on *Preference*)?

Some of these are the first songs I recorded on 4-track. Like "Wishing Well" and "Girl on the Train."

Are those the actual first recordings?

All these I recorded up in NY in my apartment in Brooklyn.

That's so great. They sound a little bit rougher then you do now, but it's like you got that 4-track and you were fully realized.

I thought the technology hadn't been available to most people, and you know there are so many electronic stores in New York, whereas here I might not have noticed it, because we had so few outlets. I just got the most basic one you could get. It was smaller than this little mixing board. It was a Fostex X15, which actually was my favorite 4-track. I've had two over the years. I got another one because I thought, "I want more stuff, more things, more whatever." The one I got was a Tascam. It was bigger, but it didn't really sound as good to me – it didn't really sound any better. It was the same amount of tracks, just bigger. There were more inputs for the effects, but I didn't have any effects. It was twice the price of the first one. I never really did understand why I bought that. I guess I needed a step up, but it really wasn't. It had inputs to record four things at once, where the other one didn't. You could only record two things at once.

But since it was just you playing, did that really apply?

No, it didn't.

How soon after you started recording with your 4-track did you start making tapes?

After I had a collection of songs together: I had eight. Also what attracted me was that there were all these magazines that did reviews of cassettes. The most widely read at that time was *Option*. I think that it had just started; the early issues contained a whole section of reviews of home tapes. I put an ad in one of their issues, to sell this first tape. The ads weren't very expensive then, so I thought, "This is a good way to start out, I'll get one of these out there." The review was in the same issue that the ad was in, and that kind of got things rolling. I got all kinds of letters and stuff from people who wanted to trade tapes, or wanted to just buy a tape. I was getting a lot of mail and I felt that it was a lot more rewarding than playing in a band. I remember some of the letters I got were like, do they want a tape or do they want a date?

You want some response to your music. Just not too much. You want it kept on a certain level. In a way it's perfect because you've got everything you need right here.

I have a mixing board, I have a reel to reel 8-track, I have a set of monitors, I have an amplifier, and I have kind of a cheap tape deck that I mix down to sometimes. But I don't have mixing equipment. I have one effects processor, but I don't have real mixing capabilities. No compressor, and all that junk that people use to alter and make a particular sound. To take the original and make it something bigger, or fuller.

Would you take your 8-track and go to a studio?

That's what I've done, except for the *Preference* CD. Those were mixed down at a friend's studio, actually the guy who used to play drums in The Woods. He had a little studio in a closet in his apartment. He had more capabilities for mixing. But *Nothing Else Matters* was mixed in a bigger studio in Hampden. He had all kinds of stuff; it's called Track in the Box. It's not ultra big, like Oz downtown, but it has computer capabilities and lots of processors. The main problem I have doing recording here in the apartment is the ambulances, because of the hospital. And the last place I lived was near a fire station. So buried in the mix of a lot of these songs are these ambulance sounds, because they're there all day. It's constant and I can hear some of them at the beginning of a song.

Does that bug you?

It bugs me if it's too loud. If it's just a little bit I don't mind. If it is too loud I'll just chop it off.

Do you play quietly so you don't bug your neighbors?

Most of the time I just record direct. I don't usually use these monitors to record with. I use them to listen to CDs on. I like mixing through headphones. Originally I felt like if I was working late at night, people in apartments would hear that. You have to turn it up to a certain level to hear it. I've had to get so many pairs of headphones because one side always goes out. I'm not one of those people who wants to solder stuff.

Do people still write you for CDs?

I never bothered to get a PO Box. I've been lazy about it. I've never gone that route because I thought the label would get that. A lot of people aren't as inclined to write to a label, as they would be if they saw it was your own PO Box, so I don't sell my tapes anymore. It's just the CDs and a few old singles, but they have old addresses on them. Everybody suggested I get an e-mail address, but I don't have a computer. I'm not up with the times. If you don't have a computer or an e-mail address, you might as well forget it. They don't review tapes in magazines anymore, which is one of the reasons I stopped making cassettes. There used to be a lot of magazines that would do it. I always regret that I

wasn't able to get a vinyl album out. By the time I got to wanting to put things out on a bigger format, there was no reason. I didn't get a CD player 'til a year ago. Last time I read *Magnet* I got the CD they sent, and as I paged through the magazine I noticed that most of the bands on the CD had purchased large ads in the magazine. And I thought, how much did these labels pay for an ad, and to get on the compilations CD? Which is unlistenable, mainly. I just throw all those compilation CDs in the trash. Sometimes now I don't even listen to them at all.

The whole thing is terrible? Or maybe one good song?

Maybe there was half a good song. So it comes down to those listening stations in record stores, and those are paid for by the record companies. So if you don't have money to pay for that you're going to have much less exposure. You do have to put up a certain amount of money to sell it. Even if you make 1,000 copies of something. That seems like a lot of copies. If bigger labels put out a small edition of something they'll press 30,000.

But to you and me 1,000 is a lot.

You might sell them in 10 years. Unless you get some big interest in your stuff. But it's slower. I've thought that I want to release my own stuff. Because I'm tired of labels who give me 100 copies and I get a couple reviews and that's it. I'd rather have control over it. I can send out copies of CDs just as well as they can. At this point I feel that I can go after a distributor because my stuff has been distributed already. They may know it. I don't know if it sells now, but I'd be better able to follow that if I do it myself in the future.

You probably could get a distributor.

At least one. That experience with those little labels laid a little groundwork. If I had started putting out my stuff alone, I'd probably have a lot more problems getting it out there now. At this point I feel like I should do it myself. Even if I make 500 copies, and then go on to the next thing. They always say, "If you get more made, it's less per copy."

If you buy the 50-pound tub of butter it's cheaper, but you might not need that much butter.

I thought, maybe I don't want 500 more copies at this point. I could always have them re-pressed, if there's more demand it's not that much different, except it clutters up your life. I know there are a lot of women who do music, though.

But usually there's some guy standing there recording them.

Right, they usually go into a studio and have somebody else record them. Even if it's some guy with a 4-track. They'd usually rather have somebody else turning it on, off, turning the knobs, and hooking up the microphones. It hasn't really changed that much. Although now when I read some of the fanzines I see there are a few female artists who are recording some of their own stuff at home. Like Lisa Germano's first 2 albums, and maybe her new one. It sounds very, not low fi, but not a big studio sound. I would think that women would be more interested in that because it allows them the freedom to record at home without the inhibiting ears or eyes of men in a recording studio, who they might feel more intimidated working with. I mean I know a lot of men probably feel intimidated going into a recording studio, setting up the first time and playing. One of my main interests in recording at home was doing it without having anybody tell me it sounded like shit, or sounded great, or whatever. I could put it all together myself and put it out myself without anybody saying one word. Now perhaps a lot of women don't feel the confidence to be able to sit down and trust their own instincts. Certainly I've gotten a lot of tapes from guys who don't feel that inhibition. They just say, "It's me, and the world should hear it," and they don't have that lack of confidence. The basic 4-track is no harder to use than a typical cassette deck. So I don't get it. I think it's the confidence thing and the lack of encouragement perhaps in younger years, to use equipment. I know it's all seen as a guy thing. Equipment – guitars, like if you go to a music store it's all guys.

And the way they talk to you!

You do feel like an outsider. You feel odd because you're in there looking at equipment.

When I went to buy my 4-track, a (female) friend came with me and the guy in the store kept assuming I was buying it for someone else. My friend said, "This guy doesn't understand that you're going to use it yourself, I don't think you should buy anything here." Just try to buy a microphone, it's intimidating.

Maybe that's why there aren't more women doing home recording. Like: "I'd like to record at home, but I can't stand the thought of going to this music store and trying to buy it." Or, "I don't know which is the best one, and I'm afraid to ask."

I hate when they act like, "Oh, typical dumb girl."

You do see more women buying guitars. So maybe the recording will come at some point. The desire to put their own music down. The thing about that is it can bring more self-confidence to do that. You put down 4 tracks and you want to do more. I wish more women musicians would do that to start with, instead of thinking, "Oh I gotta get a band, I gotta find a producer, I gotta show people I'm serious, or I gotta show off my looks." The thing about playing at home is you can make a whole tape and not put your picture on the CD. Not go that route. Which is the way that most major labels, to be sure, market women. Always have to have your picture on the front, and maybe 10 of them inside. All in different poses with hair blowing, or whatever. The male-oriented albums have more pictures of guitars. They all look the same. T-shirts. Some of them may be cute and some of them may be fat but it does not matter. They can look like big old slobs, and if their music is big old slob music that's fine. But a woman can't really get away with that. The major labels would not accept that.

Both those covers (*Nothing Else Matters* and *Preference*) are beautiful, but you might lose some people who want to know, "What do her tits look like?"

Yes, those are both thrift store paintings. Because Fiona Apple looks like a cute little girl, they don't really care what she's singing. If they couldn't make videos of her half-dressed, it wouldn't be so easy to market her. There may be more women in music, but the image they project is not more advanced than years ago. The more independent types don't rely as much on looks. They don't sell as many records, but those are the people I would listen to. Liz Phair started out as an indie, and she recorded herself, but when she went to make her bigger move she took on the "tough chick" role. She posed for pictures that displayed that image. They had to have a picture that went with the image. I would like to hear more women who don't depend on that at all, where that is not part of their packaging.

Linda Smith, <www.homemademusic.com>, Diana Froley/Serious Records, P.O. Box 24564, Baltimore MD 21214, or <dfroley@erols.com>

Linda Smith's recording equipment:
Fostex R8 reel to reel 8-track
Mackie 1202 12 channel mixer
Alesis RA 100 reference amplifier
Yamaha NS 10M studio monitors
Alesis Midiverb III multi effects processor
AKG D 120 ES microphone

DIANA FROLEY
Pet My Kitty Mr. NYC CD

Several adjectives come to mind when listening to *Pet My Kitty Mr. NYC*. Minimal. Unique. Innocent. Intimate. While Froley possesses a flirtatious lyrical style, some of the songs feature virtually nothing more than her voice backed by banjo, accordian, bass, or trumpet while other songs have more of a straight-forward, guitar-bass-drums approach.

Five of the disc's sixteen songs were recorded in "Ken Herblin's air-conditioned studio one Saturday in June" on an analog 8-track setup. The rest was recorded on ADAT at the Dead Chicken Ranch in Baltimore by drummer Jim Doran [also credited as a co-producer], mostly in one day. I personally can't hear any difference between the analog and ADAT songs. They all fit together nicely and form a really good album. –*Rob Christensen*

LINDA SMITH
Preference CD

Baltimore's Linda Smith uses a home recording format to make intimate and unique songs. The songs on *Preference* span four years of songwriting and living fraught with a strong narrative element. However, Smith manages to leave room for the listener to maintain a degree of mystery. Working on her own terms and her own equipment enables Smith to capture a generous amount of clarity and warmth that might have been lost had her ideas been run through the filters of other musicians or music industry demands. Her songs are efficiently arranged - strummed guitars, percussive sounds and cool keyboards - everything that happens, counts. This efficiency can be attributed to her smart songwriting as much as the constraints of small-scale recording. Her unaffected voice is as important as any other component of the recordings - drifting from spooky and droll on "Looking at the Scenery Alone" and "Because You Asked Me", to lush and poppy on "But is She Happy?" and the gorgeous "Confidence".

Smith's music is hard to pin down at times, due in part to her rarity: how many albums have you heard of women recording themselves during the 1980s? Jangley guitars and obtuse pop structures dominate, but overt references to other bands are lacking here. Smith's influences show up more in small sections of songs. The instrumentation and chord progressions of "An Ideal View of the Ideal City" hint at the Beatles' "Fool on The Hill", while (oddly enough) the circular lyrics and subject matter of the song suggest an introverted postscript to Petula Clark's "Downtown".

Linda Smith's creations conflict. Small and big, personal and aloof, sing-songey and wise. The way she makes music has allowed her to maintain an untainted perspective, but it also guarantees her relative obscurity. What's clear is that making the effort to hear *Preference* means there will be one more Linda Smith fan. –*Amy Annelle*

Chad Crouch

PORTLAND'S ONE-MAN SHOW

by Matt Mair Lowery

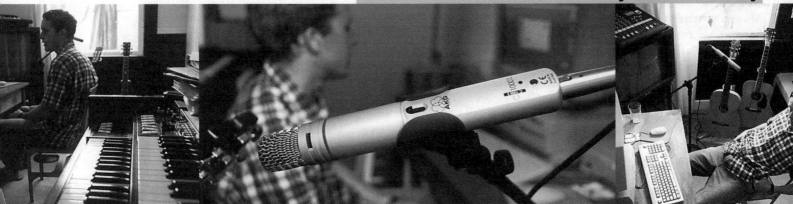

In addition to being a prolific singer/songwriter (as well as multimedia artist), Chad Crouch runs Hush Records, a singer/songwriter-oriented label he started in 1996. Chad has recorded many of Hush's highly praised releases on an Apple Macintosh G3 in either the lofts he has previously inhabited or in the basement studio he recently completed in his newly acquired Portland home. The warm sound he has achieved on these CDs reflects the casual, homey environments they were recorded in and his direct style of production shows a great regard for capturing the essence of the songs. I sat down with Chad to see how he has utilized the advantages of digital technology to capture and fine-tune the performances of some of the Northwest's up-and-coming singer/songwriters.

Since you started recording in earnest back in college, you've worked on a wide variety of machines and in a wide variety of environments, and I was wondering if you could recall the progression: from 4-track to now.

Well, I did about a dozen tapes on 4-track [Laughs]. No, I did about four or so on 4-track, then I bought my first Apple Quadra audio/video computer about a year after it was released. When the Quadra was affordable, and that was the first A/V computer that was all ready to go. It had the sound card and the video card. So I thought, "Well, I'm going to do video, audio and everything," and I bought a little program called DigiTrax. That was a 6-track multitrack and it was like $150; so compared to a 4-track it made a lot of sense. I didn't even sink any money into preamps and microphones until later, I was just using that little Apple plastic microphone [laughs]. Anyway, the thing that came to me as the most immediate advantage was sampling. Suddenly you could sample stuff and loop it, and it was just easy to rip-off drum loops. I made some tapes with that. Then, right after that, I went to a world class studio [to record *Portland, OR*].

That was Clark Stiles' studio?

Mm-hmm. And recorded on a 32-track system with both digital and analog capabilities and $5000 microphones. That wasn't something I could have really handled myself, it was kind of another world, but it showed me a lot about where to put money. You know, what was and wasn't important, per se. And really, any technical stuff isn't that important as long as you've got a decent microphone, and it just takes one. Then I kept going and got more adept at using the software, which is like anything. You use PhotoShop and you start learning the key commands and then you're hardly using your mouse and stuff. Then I got a better computer and a better multitrack recording program called Deck, and that's what I do everything on now. Deck II, and I get as many tracks as you want on that.

Do you bounce tracks on that?

You can bounce. I can probably get, on my configuration, 30 tracks real time with faders and EQs and stuff. The thing about digital is that you can use any software you can get your hands on. All you need is the hardware.

So have you done most of the Hush stuff on that then?

Yeah, everything. Except Kim Norlen's *And*, [recorded at Jackpot!] and one of Ben Barnett's [from Kind of Like Spitting] releases was recorded on an 8-track.

So what kind of computer do you have now?

A G3.

Is that billed as a multimedia, too?

Yeah, they all are now.

You still have that same board you used to have?

Yeah, it's just a powered mixer. So you can use it as a PA or a mixer.

Do you know what it is?

Yamaha. EM1600.

What microphones are you using now?

Whatever I can get my hands on. Usually low impedance, but nothing special. Generally vocal mics. I don't know what directional quality they are. I just put them close to the thing, whether it's a snare or whatever. I usually do the drums with just two mics.

What on?

One closer to the kick and one kind of near and above the snare and the hi-hat.

Were the drums on Paul Hixon Pittman's album room mic'd or...

They were close, maybe two feet away.

So you haven't sunk any money into real expensive mics or anything like that?

I haven't spent anything. That's where the money should go, but no, I haven't. [*Note:* Chad recently purchased a couple AKGs, including a C-1000S, which he uses for vocals and overheads.]

So probably the big difference between Clark's and your studio was that he had a bunch of stuff and you basically had the computer, the mixing board and the mic. That's about it.

Yeah, but if you put a decent $120 mic next to anything it's going to give you a good signal.

So you didn't feel limited at all coming back to your studio after doing *Portland, OR*?

No, you just don't have maybe quite as much of the depth or the shimmering quality, but you can get pretty damn close. With digital you don't have any tape hiss, so it's still very clear.

Aside from clarity and the loops, what other advantages to digital do you see?

Yeah, the loops and the built-in EQs. You can EQ a thing like crazy and you don't have to buy any boxes or get any special things. I think it sounds pretty genuine and doesn't sound too tweaked or weird. There are so many plug-ins that you can get in Deck, you can do all the effects after, like phaser, pitch or shifting.

Can you apply those when you're recording?

Just afterwards. So that's an advantage. Another advantage is just [saving on] time spent rewinding. You just push the return key. Or finding a cue point in a song is real easy that way, if you just want to do accents on the choruses or extra vocals. Cut and paste editing. It's a whole different way of making music. You can kind of session track by track and then cut out the bad stuff and suddenly it takes on a different quality and sounds pretty cohesive. So it's a different way of getting at making music. You can be pretty sloppy and clean up afterwards. We always would take out notes. If they hit a bad note or something we could take out a bad snare hit, a bad note, anything, if it's not too obvious. Whereas with tape that would be really, really difficult.

Do you see any disadvantages to the digital stuff?

Yeah. I mean, if you listen to Portishead or something you can tell that it's digital. I think it's true that you can tell, especially some stuff, the difference between digital and analog, but I think that has more to do with the fragmentation, the way it's edited. It has to do with samples. You can play a straight song and record a straight band and I would doubt you'd be able to tell the difference, personally. But aficionados say that analog has a warmer sound to it, and for the most part I trust that, but I don't really notice.

Well, I think with your stuff you get a really warm sound anyway. Most of the music

that's recorded digital that you know is recorded digital is all the cut and paste stuff, and most of the stuff you do is pretty straight and song oriented. And it's different from the stuff where they're really exploiting the digital technology in creating the music rather than just utilizing it to record the songs, like you are often doing.

Yeah. Most of what I record are singer/songwriters. It's hard not to sound analog.

Overall, on your albums the sound is really rounded out, it's not like anything is cold and heartless. Besides running the mic through the board to preamp it, do you add any effects going in?

I sometimes apply the built-in reverb on the board.

On Paul's album and on any of the more full-on band stuff, do you record it live for the most part?

No, there are a lot of overdubs. I'm dealing with a paucity of microphones, and given that I'm not set up as yet to record multitrack through different mics to mix those tracks afterwards, I mean most people would think that you couldn't make shit with that because it's not even as good as a 4-track. I mean, in terms of recording a band you have to get creative then and isolate sounds and so it takes longer. For example [in the loft] we would record drums and maybe a bass line at the same time and put the drums downstairs and the bass upstairs and make sure I got a good mix on them, and then also Paul would play acoustic a little bit just to give the song its natural flow, for the drummer, and that would bleed onto the take, but it would make the guitar sound fuller in the end. You get a fuller sound that way, but it's piecemeal and I wouldn't really want to do it for a long time; and the hardware nowadays isn't that expensive. Four inputs isn't very expensive.

Change the sound card?

PCI, yeah.

That's cool that it wasn't all done absolutely live and yet it has a really live feel.

It was live in its essence.

Do you see a big difference in how you started out on the 4-track and where you are now in terms of the mixing process? With all the stuff that you can do; does it become more time consuming than just mixing down four simple tracks, or does the efficiency of the computer make up for all that?

I don't know about most 4-track users, but after the first tape I realized it was fun to do more. To put more tracks on than just a vocal and guitar. And you continually push that by bouncing tracks analog. You can really get into the new method. If it's a drum track, it's a lot faster. You can just take one bar out and loop it. So, yes and no. It depends on which way you are going. For straight recording it's faster, and you get a much better result, because you can tweak stuff.

How did you record the violin on "Opening Theme" on the *Less* compilation?

I don't know much about engineering at all, but someone suggested that we put the mic well above the violin, so we had it on a boom stand and it was probably a good three feet above the violin. They're loud, for one thing. And so it was just a vocal mic above the violin.

It sounds really good. The guitars on that song, and on other songs where they're super tight and each note is essential, did they ever play through a pick-up and then straight into the board at all or were they just mic'd?

Just mic'd. I personally have done that [played straight through on an electric] 'cause I didn't own an amplifier, but generally you want to play through the amp.

It's a better sound. It has more body, it has more tone, it's more authentic.

On the acoustic guitars, have you done anything with acoustic pickups?

That sounds awful [laughs]. I mean it gives you that real Ani DiFranco live sound, which doesn't sound like an acoustic guitar, it sounds like an acoustic guitar as captured through a Piezo pickup, which isn't an acoustic guitar. It's making the signals electric. The only thing I would really record straight through would be a bass and even then sometimes I go through a guitar amp, cause I don't have a bass amp. But that gives it a really bassy sound, if you go straight through. Otherwise, if it's an acoustic instrument or if it depends a lot on how it sounds outside it. Like you can't plug in an organ. Generally, mic everything.

When you have people over to record do you try and do anything like a producer might do to create a comfortable environment for everything to happen in?

Yeah, [when Paul came down] I did. We had the basketball courts and I was big on having fruit salads at the time and so, I mean, you need to keep fed when you're recording and you need to get outside every now and then. You can't just hole yourself up forever. Apart from that, just being sincere and other stuff. I didn't go out of my way to create an environment.

So did you use getting out and eating to break up recording and mixing or just everything?

Whenever I felt like we needed it. We were getting tired or it was getting old or things didn't seem to be gelling, you know. Just get out. And another thing is you have to keep the people who aren't playing and doing takes kind of occupied, so it's good to have lots of magazines or be located in an area where they can just walk around and they'll be something to look at or do. It was good that I lived downtown.

So are you still doing everything from recording to pressing the discs?

Yeah. That's the great thing about digital recording. You've got it, you mix it on the hard drive, it never leaves one place. It's always stays in that little box and then you write it onto the disc and then it comes out. So you might as well just write a bunch and then sell it. And then you have a record label. It's a good way to get started, especially if you're fast at it or you have the time to do it. And then if you sell enough, which we have, you can start financing pressings of your recordings (rather than CD-Rs) and so that's kind of my "pull myself up by my bootstraps" kind-of ethic to having a record label.

So is there mastering? What's the process once you've got all your tracks recorded and you've got your mix saved? Where do you go from there to get it on the CD-R?

You just drag it into a little square that says "Soundfiles." You just drag the thing in and then sequence it. On the flashy CD-R programs you can decide how much time you want between each song. That's about it.

So there's no equivalent to mastering?

Oh no, I master, I'm sorry. There is an equivalent and I use a different program. I master because you have to or else... The biggest part of mastering is making things as loud as possible and making sure they all sound like they're at the same volume. And that's basically what it is for me. Then fine tuning the EQs. I master in a program called Peak and I think the pros use it. You just highlight the whole thing and apply different filters and stuff and add gain. Mostly, all I use is gain and the EQing features. Unfortunately, it's not real time. You can preview the song with the EQ, but it takes, even on a super fast computer, it takes like maybe 20 seconds to change it. Especially the EQ. Gain takes about ten seconds.

So do you compress it at all on there?

You can compress it, but it doesn't work the same way as if you had analog compression. It doesn't sound right, at least to me. Sometimes I go through and if there's a loud bit in the song I take some gain off of it, take some volume out, and it's rarely discernible, so it's like a manual compression. And if there's an odd hi-hat hit or a boom, usually it's a bass sound that will start to clip, then you just have to shrink it. You just take the gain out of that boom as it's highlighted. You see the song in a wave form and then you just highlight the bit that looks like it's clipping and shrink it. So yeah, the compression feature doesn't work that well in Peak, in my own experience.

For your own material, what do you want to do next?

There's two facets of my own stuff. The one is the real stripped down aesthetic and the other is the kind of cut and paste sound. I think it's comparable to Beck, even though most people wouldn't compare me to Beck. Just the throw everything in for a kind of sound and getting kind of cheeky with it, like a lot of tempo shifts, which is my new bag. Right now I'm just working on beats as an art form, almost. Taking a snare hit and a bass kick and using those as elements in and of themselves, like a hip-hop producer would, and not using whole phrases like I used to, but out of sampling little bits and putting them together in weird ways. And doing a lot of sampling so it makes this really thick, strange beat. But I've been doing it more with brush sounds that I've been recording, so you have more the singer songwriter aesthetic with these weird loopy sounding backwards and forwards and shuffling beats and it just doesn't sound like a drummer could do all those things. That's what I'm working on.

Have you been pulling those samples off records?

No, I recorded my drummer [Greg Lind, of the Portland band Brigantine] at a good studio. It's new bits, and we just do that to DAT and then I cut it up. So I've got excellent source material to work with. I don't know what'll come out of it, but I want to try and merge the two, the singer songwriter and the alchemist music, hip-hop kind of thing. I mean, it's hard when you're doing that stuff to write as poignant lyrics as if you're strumming a sad loping kind of thing rather than just a jammin' beat. I don't think that a hip-hop person would say jammin'. I don't know, tight, or... anyway.

So you just grab one beat at a time and paste it together?

It's easiest to take a bar of what he's doing and get a full phrase, something that resolves itself that you can loop easily and then just add a bunch of stuff on top of that. Other drum sounds, like hi-hat or something that's not already substantially coming through. Then you're suddenly becoming this electronic drummer. It's hard, because when you're doing it in a hip-hop realm you've got a sequencer and a click track and your sample is set to a trigger, whereas I've just got to put them together like Legos. It's really visual, so I'm looking at little mountains and peaks and valleys and thinking "Well, if this mountain comes off of this mountain it will happen for me and it will sound right." It's really trial and error and sometimes not as intuitive as a sequencer or something would be. So I don't really recommend doing beats this way, but it's a different take and so you're going to get different kinds of stuff out of it this way.

I remember on DigiTrax that if you copied something you could condense it or crop it to the portion you wanted. Can you do that on Deck?

Yeah, it has a memory so whatever you initially captured will stay there and you can back it up or crop it or expand it or whatever. Basically, apart from how you sequence it on the track display, you can get everything back to the original, unless you lose the whole thing somehow.

How many times has that happened?

It hasn't happened at all with Deck, apart from me just accidentally trashing stuff. That's the one really bad thing about recording digital, is you do stand a chance of losing it all. But it diminishes year by year as software and hardware gets better.

You said you had the beats going backwards, can you do then the equivalent of flipping the tape over and recording a backwards guitar solo or something on Deck?

I don't know. I suspect there's a way you could work it out. You could record the song straight and then turn it around and play with it backwards and then flip everything again. So, no, you couldn't do it in the same way that you flip a tape over, but there's a solution to everything.

Hush Records, PO Box 12713, Portland, OR 97212, chad@hushrecords.com, www.hushrecords.com

Robert Poss

by Heather Mount

I briefly met Robert Poss back in the fall of 1993, when Band Of Susans performed in Bratislava at the U Club, an amazing underground bunker that had once been used as a bomb shelter by the local Slovak powers. I next caught up with him in the Fall of 1996, at a Lincoln Center performance of works by Nicolas Collins and Alvin Lucier. My first impression was that this was a guy both whip smart and off the wall. He skated saucily through life's mires, taking jovial punches at politics (sexual and otherwise), the state of music appreciation and depreciation, and the pitfalls of what he likes to call showbiz. At that time, Robert was threatening to leave music for a career with the U.S. Postal Service. It became clear that underneath the unpretentious, playful chat, that this was a guy who really knew music. Getting to know Robert could not happen without also getting to know his music. Robert began playing electric bass,

as a young lad of 12, and soon drifted over to blues/rock guitar, continuing through college (at Wesleyan). He was in some blues bands early on, and later embraced the punk and post-punk aesthetic in bands like Tot Rocket and Western Eyes. He then co-founded Band of Susans, an influential art-rock/guitar wall band that cut its teeth in the mid '80s. Although outnumbered by splendiferous Susans in the band, Robert was the driving force of the guitar-writing; with other co-founder Susan Stenger sharing the singing, songwriting, and the all-over sound and fury of the band. Band of Susans developed quite a name for themselves, and put records out on such labels as Blast First, Rough Trade Germany and Restless. Disbanding, due to basic life stuff, Susan and Robert continue to collaborate on projects both here in NYC and in England. Robert Poss' interest in recording goes way back into his teens growing up, and through the days with BOS. Gleaning techniques from various engineers with whom BOS worked during the '80s, Robert learned what he liked and what he didn't like. He produced all of Band Of Susans releases except for their Peel Sessions. In 1995, he started acquiring gear for serious home recording. Since then the obsession and fascination with recording has grown, as has his studio and its potential. Robert has begun recording various indie bands (Nickel Hex, Combine, the Croutons, Skulpey, Tone), and recently teamed with ex-BOS member Page Hamilton [Helmet] to do a major label remix for the infamous Skeleton Key. Poss has been impressing audiences with his live solo shows. He is also working on a variety of new material, embracing his own brand of electronica, fractured rock and densely textured guitar minimalism.

During the years you've been in bands you have been constantly busy playing, touring and recording. Recently, you had a solo-guitar performance at the Cooler, which blasted my socks off. What else have you been up to over the past 2+ years?

In 1996 I spent quite a bit of time in The Netherlands, working on solo guitar and electronics material in Amsterdam at the STEIM music think-tank; performing a few solo shows, working with Nicolas Collins, and also working in an ensemble with composer David Dramm. David, myself and two wonderful Dutch percussionists had a residency in Utrecht, working on David's song cycle, "All Lit Up." I did the live electronic processing – with distortion, resonant filters, various kinds of delays. I did things like put heavily gated contact mics on the vibes and hi-hats, and run them through heavy distortion, or have them key-trigger gates on other instruments. I got a great deal of use out of my Peavey Spectrum Analog Filter. In the fall of 1996 I went to London and performed at the South Bank Centre as part of The Brood - a group comprised of Susan Stenger [from Band Of Susans], Justine Frischmann from Elastica, Sonic Boom from Spaceman Three, Robert Grey [Gotobed] from Wire, and me. We performed pieces by LaMonte Young, Phill Niblock and Rhys Chatham. Panasonic also performed - they're really fine. BOS did a cool show with them at the Knitting Factory in '95. The Aphex Twin, Bruce Gilbert [also from Wire] and Caspar Brontzmann/F.M. Enheit were also on the bill. In 1996, Susan Stenger, Bruce Gilbert and I also performed in London and Manchester as a trio, so-called GilbertPossStenger. I had a solo show at Roulette in 1997, and did some record engineering/producing: Tone [for Dischord/Independent Project], Seth Josel [for O.O. Disk], local bands The Negatones, and Nickel Hex, another called Mold, and Skulpey. Several months ago I did a remix in my home studio of a Skeleton Key song with Page Hamilton. That was cool, because we ended up working with only 8 tracks out of a 48 [two slaved 2-inches], and I did things like run the percussion track through a Rat and a Dunlop tremolo pedal, and looping one measure of the bass guitar track on the hard drive and running it through two cascading digital delays – a Korg SDD-2000 and the ultra wacky Ursa Major MSP-126 – to make a rhythmic overlay. We did that remix on my Akai DR4ds. I guess I also worked a bit with composer Phill Niblock – recording Jim O'Rourke and David First for him – and performed his guitar piece a number of times. The rest of the time I've been getting my home studio together and doing day job work (I do location video sound for television, mostly for the BBC). The thing I'm just finally getting to now is recording some new material on my own. I've been in foreplay mode on that for almost three years, it seems. I just hope I won't hate myself in the morning.

You really seek the cutting edge in the equipment aspect of studio recording, obviously committed to constantly improving your studio's production capacity. As you have tried out tons of different models, what are some pieces of outboard effectry that you have found less satisfying than their reputation would have them seem?

Some of the real low budget stuff that is cheap, you expect it to be halfway decent, but it is absolute crap. I put the Alesis 3630 compressor in this category, as well as some of the current cheaper DBX stuff. Yuck! For under $200, you can go out and buy an RNC1773 [the Really Nice Compressor] from a guy in Texas [FMR 800-343-9976]. I have two of them, and you get an astonishing good piece of gear. There are times when the RNC sounds better on a given instrument or pair of tracks than my Joe Meek optical compressor, a unit that costs ten times as much. The AKG C3000 microphone has been a disappointment to me. I used it one night on my guitar amp in Germany in '95, and was very impressed. I bought one when they became available in the U.S. and haven't ended up using it very much at all. I guess I should have known better, since I've never really liked the AKG 414, which is the mic that the C3000 is ostensibly patterned after. Now that they've cut its list price in half, the C3000 isn't such a bad deal, though.

At what point did you really dig in to furnishing your own equipped home studio?

I never really wanted to have a home studio, because I felt that I had been "spoiled" by working with all of the great gear at places like Baby Monster. I always wrote and demoed songs on 4-track cassette, and loved the sound of it. In fact, I still think some of the 4-track demos have better guitar sounds in places than some of the BOS records we released. Maybe it has something to do with the in-line impedance transformers I used, and the input stages of the Tascam or Fostex. I loved to pack the level on. Meters be damned! It had long occurred to me that it would be wonderful to do stuff in my apartment that was spontaneous, but a bit higher fidelity than the 4-track cassette stuff. In 1995, I started getting more interested in getting a home studio together. I bought two Akai DR4ds [stand alone hard drive machine] because I had heard such horror stories about ADAT transports. The first things that were done at the studio, that were released, were the last BOS tracks we ever recorded, two cuts for two Wire tribute CDs. Part of what made the studio possible was that I was given some fine equipment from my brother-in-law, who had decided to dismantle his own home multimedia studio. So I ended up with wonderful stuff I never could have afforded: a Bryston 4B power amp, two Westlake BBSM-6 monitors, a Lexicon PCM-70... It snowballed from there, and I realized that my pathological equipment lust had a purpose. I could learn a lot by actually owning the gear because I would have time to experiment and really learn the engineering stuff that I had never had a chance to learn while we were paying by the hour.

What are some of the main things that you have learned in general about the recording process? What advice would you give to recordees, as they approach the notion of recording music in a studio?

A studio makes most musicians self-conscious. The easiest parts and riffs suddenly seem difficult, the grooves that were so effortlessly attained in rehearsal seem stiff and stilted. The problem is that in the studio, most people think too much and concentrate too hard. And there's time pressure, money pressure and a sense that the work is going to be permanent – a statement of sorts. Ideally, one should book enough time so that there's time to get acclimated, to make mistakes, to fool around a little without losing focus. In my best recording situations, that nervousness and sense of expectation was channeled into an intensity, an urgency that meant that the performances were one of a kind. I seem to recall vodka and whiskey also playing a role here. I guess a certain amount of preparation is important, if you do music that requires such things. With BOS, basic parts had to be learned and perfected beforehand, because our sound relied on a great deal of precision. I would also spend a great deal of time in the session auditioning and choosing guitars, and various permutations of amps, speakers and mics. I was very hands-on when it came to mixing those BOS records; the engineer would usually leave the room for awhile and just let me do my thing, and then return and be horrified by how upfront the guitars were. Don't always settle for the speaker close-mic'd with a Shure SM57. Experiment, but always have a sonic goal in mind. Otherwise it can become aimless, self-indulgent and costly. I've always thought that live performances and studio recordings were completely different types of events. A gig is like a play. Making a record is like shooting a film. There's a level or artifice and manipulation permissible in a session that is analogous to the way a film narrative is structured through direction and editing. A play or a concert on the other hand, exists in real time and has a whole different sort of aura. So, I've never been obsessed with things being "live" in the studio.

What has become of BOS recordings? Any thoughts on remixes?

I still have all of the 2" masters. We've always owned our own publishing, and I think the rights to our recording have reverted or are in the process of reverting back to us. It's a little complicated, since we were on Restless in the U.S., Rough Trade Germany World Service in Europe, and Blast First in the U.K. I sometimes think about dumping some 2" masters down to 16 tracks of ADAT [sacrificing some of the tracks, in other words] and doing some remixes in my apartment. It would be great fun, and I know so much more about engineering than I did when I did those records. On the other hand, the mixes on those records are very extreme, and when I go back and listen to them I find flaws, but I also marvel at how gutsy we were to have the guitars so loud. At the time, everyone seemed to be in "a guitar band", but most of those bands had very loud vocals and drums. We were truly guitar heavy, and we were involved with approaches to overtones and textures and drones that only became popular in the last few years. In the late '80s we used to talk to writers from *Melody Maker* and *Spin* about LaMonte Young, Alvin Lucier, Phill Niblock and Tony Conrad and they didn't know who the hell we were talking about.

You now play and record your own solo works, which generally involve multiple guitars, and amplifiers ranging in power from 1 to 200 watts - your sound is a rich, loud, swirl... How do you plan to record this stuff?

The core of my live sound is a signal chain that I devised early on, I guess in 1986 and 1987. I take a G&L SC-1 – the world's finest guitar with the world's finest guitar pickup – and run it through a Tube Screamer, a Rat, a DBX 463x noise gate, an original Yamaha SPX-90 [used primarily for its gain stages] and then into a clean, high-powered Park or Marshall tube amp. With BOS live I would run a 100-watt non-master volume tube Park head and a 100-watt Marshall Dual Reverb head through the four twelves in my Marshall (or later Laney) speaker cab. Of course, the Park had to be green and the Marshall had to be purple. Since the cab was stereo, I could use one bottom with two heads. The Park took the processed signal, and the Marshall took the straight guitar signal. I would also usually run a another small combo amp across the other side of the stage for stereo dispersion. The gain out of my system was so high that, even playing outside at the Roskilde festival in Denmark, I never ran the Park head volume more than about 2 out of 10. It all has to do with cascading gain stages, and being able to control feedback so that a shift in position will cause precise overtones to sound. I generally used MesaBoogie tubes in my amps, even though I hate the sound of their guitar amps generally. Of course now with my solo stuff, and playing in small clubs, I use multiple small amps – Fender, Laney, Ampeg, Crate, Traynor – and split the signal in various ways. I also make use of: a Gibson ES-135 hollow body, a Yamaha hollowbody with Gretsch Filtertron pickups, a Fender Stratocaster 12-string that I have in a bizarre tuning with metal koto-like bridges placed under the strings along the neck, and my other old standbys, two aluminum-bodied semi-hollow Tokai Talbo Blazing Fire guitars in various odd tunings I've devised. I use two Lexicon JamMans and a Boomerang for live looping. Of course, BOS started back in 1986 with me using three old digital delays to do looping, so I'm pretty familiar with all that stuff. Playing in a band is great, but it has all the blessings and curses of being in a cult. But after all the intensity of collaboration, I'm finding it liberating to be on my own just now. No band meetings, no arguments, no explanations. Just me and my big fat ego. I've also been getting back into pure electronic music which is something I've been involved with since the mid-1970's, using oscillators and filters and those sorts of things. I'd like to release a solo record or two, maybe something a little like BOS with a beat and something else purely electronic/noise.

We could do a whole interview based on the wonders of different kinds of mics, and mic techniques. Which of the mics that you use these days do you find to be high both in performance and versatility? What are your picks for vocals and snare?

Even though most engineers obsess over the snare, I generally just stick a 57 on it and vary the timbre by mic positioning and adjusting/tuning the snare itself. Then a whole range of stuff can be done with it in mixdown. For kick, the important thing is distance and placement, determined as always by educated guesses and refined by trial and error. Electro-Voice RE-20s and the standard Beyer or AKG kick mics tend to work well. For guitars, I use a wide variety of mics. I very much like the Audix D3. I like the SM-58 rather than the 57. I'm fond of the Sennheiser 441 (one of my favorite dynamic mics) and of course the Coles 4038, a mic that I fell in love with when I first used one in London in 1988. I like using the Langevin CR3A, sometimes placing it behind and above the speaker cabinet to get resonance and bass. I think omnidirectional dynamic mics are great, like the EV-635. And I've used Beyer ribbon mics (the M260) since 1989. I have a pair on semipermanent loan from Nicolas Collins and recently had them re-ribboned at Beyer. I have a few other old ribbon and dynamic mics kicking around as well... And a few oddball condensers, though I can't afford the old classic ones. For vocals, almost anything will work. It depends on the situation, and what sort of timbre and response you're looking for. I'm partial to the Shure SM-7, the RE-20, the CR3A, the AudioTechnica C-87 MKII, and the 441.

The issue of tubes came up the other day, and you led me to checkout a cool book on the history of tubes and tube amplifiers called *The Tube Amp Book*, written by Aspen Pittman of Groove Tubes fame. What tubes do you use in your mics and amps?

I grew up in the era of monophonic sound and of tubes. When we would go to the record store, the records came in two flavors, stereo and mono. My earliest musical memories are of listening to music through a mono tube hi-fi set played through a 15" JBL D-130 speaker that my father had rigged for the living room using the basement staircase as an infinite reflex speaker cabinet. He cut a hole in the wall, in other words. A well-designed tube circuit with the proper transformers and plate voltages sounds fabulous. A well designed discrete Class A solid state circuit (like API) can sound just as good. Luckily the fad [which became a movement] for vintage and tube recording gear has meant that more companies are making tubes, and tube-based equipment. Some of the circuits sound terrible, but some sound just great. There also some great solid state stuff out there. I love the EL-8 Distressor.

We [Skulpey] were getting some buzz the other day, which occurred on the bass track of the recording that we were working on. You were quiet for a couple of minutes, then you jumped up, started to wire up your Stro-Lion to sample the buzz, and to create a phase shift great enough to cancel out most of the buzz. We were very impressed. What other noise reducing tricks have you found to work?

The Roland SN-550 and SN-770 do an amazing job on hum and hiss reduction in real time. They're very sophisticated, and somewhat expensive. The Stro-Lion N'Hummer can sometimes work wonders by nulling the hum through adjustable phase cancellation in the sidechain. Downward expansion gates, like the 463x, can also work wonders. I never understand why so many guitarists settle for loud hum in the spaces between their playing. Gating is so simple, and something like the Behringer Intelligate, which can be made frequency selective, is quite fast, cheap, and simple to use. If it's done right, gating can be totally invisible and unobtrusive.

Tell us about that beautiful purple-knobbed Avalon monotrack processor...

I like the Avalon, Joe Meek, and API stuff that is currently being made quite a bit, and some of the TL Audio stuff (even if it's not purist tube stuff) can be useful. The Avalon VT-737 (which is a bit extravagant, I know) will probably hold its value for a long time. It is very well made, and very highly thought of. So, when I need to sell it, I'll get a fair amount of money. A lot of midrange equipment has virtually no resale value, so it often pays to buy very cheap or reasonably expensive stuff, and avoid the midrange stuff for the long haul. By the same token, I'm always on the lookout for old, cheap stuff made by companies like Altec. Of course, room mics can still be squashed effectively with a $70 Alesis MicroLimiter, and I love doing perverse things like using an old multiband passive architectural EQ made by Altec to process bass guitar, or using dirty White 4001 room EQ's – highly resonant – on kick and snare. I love the response and ballistics of old VU meters, and classic old equipment just looks so fine. It instills confidence even when it's broken. Of course, as we all know, the most important thing in audio is how the equipment looks. The rest is easy.

SKULPEY
The Chopper CD (Pedigree)

This fine record was recorded by the esteemed Robert Poss, who used to be in the sublime Band of Susans and has also produced Tone and Skeleton Key. Here, he aids this quirky trio in capturing some riveting performances in startling clarity. The music is rock, yet somewhat arty, with odd time signatures and busy sections, but the honest, upfront female and male vocals keep it all down to earth. Apparently the basics were tracked in a barn and then all the overdubs and mixing was done at Robert's apartment. It's one of those records where, in lesser hands, the production could be so wrong and ruin it, yet *The Chopper* sounds so fresh and inviting that I can't help but keep listening to it. –*Larry Crane*

TONE-The Guitar Ensemble
Sustain (Dischord/Independent Project)

With no vocals, (at least) 5 guitars, 2 basses and a drum set they certainly are a guitar ensemble. This is their second release and it was recorded at WGNS and Inner Ear in the DC area (two fine studios) and produced by Robert Poss, of the late Band of Susans. I listen to this one a lot, as it reminds me of Stereolab or Pell Mell, and the big droning sound is enjoyable. Plus, among other notable musicians involved is drummer Phil Krauth, who used to be in Unrest and knows just how to power these workouts. –*Larry Crane*

Track Star

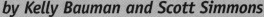

by Kelly Bauman and Scott Simmons

track star

San Francisco. Wyatt, Todd and Mark. They record their own releases. They rock.

On the No Big Deal 7", your first release, which was recorded in 1994, you recorded in your practice space. Is this the same narrow, kind of boxy space you shared with a bunch of bands?

Yeah.

So you recorded that there on what?

4-track [cassette]. Tascam 421.

421. I believe that's the model you can only record two tracks at a time. Is that right?

Yeah.

It just has a high and a low EQ doesn't it? So did you take the 421 and submix down from a small mixing board and record a lot of things onto, two tracks live or...

I don't really remember. I think we did the drums through a little Mackie...

A mini-Mackie, like an 8 channel Mackie?

Yeah.

So, 421 for this recording.

I lent it to somebody who put the wrong power supply in it and ever since then it runs the same as a regular tape player.

I didn't think the 421 even had a variable tape speed.

You can adjust the pitch. I think it used to be like 3 3/4 now it's 1 7/8 .

I'm amazed you recorded the *Sometimes, What's the Difference?* EP on the 4-track. I love that. I listened to that today. I like the tone and the sound of that record from beginning to end.

We recorded that in '95, that's when we recorded in the theater, over three or four late nights. I think around that time, as a band we had that kind of 4-track recording energy. It was a good time.

Did the size of the theater make a difference?

I don't think it really made that big of a difference 'cause everything we did was close-mic'd.

That's what I was going to ask you next. It seems like on the Communication Breaks album I hear a little reverb somewhere.

We didn't have anything like that until that last record.

Mostly I noticed that a lot of the drums are close mic'd and I actually like the snare sound a lot on pretty much everything. Do you guys record all the guitars live?

I think the drums most always came first and there's only a couple things that have both guitars live and drums too. For the last record I was able to borrow a couple Shure SM81s. So we had drum overheads and the guitars would bleed when we tried to do it live so we tried to do one guitar playing with the drums just to get the drums down.

That's a good thing to talk about. One thing that distinguishes yours as quality recordings is that there's not a lot of bleed. The drums sound clean. So it's all one instrument at a time?

Pretty much. There are a couple exceptions, like maybe some of the louder songs. When we did that in the theater it was a piece of cake because we had the drums close mic'd in front of the stage and then we had the guitar amps on the far sides of the stage and behind the curtains.

Interesting. I think your music is the kind of music that can be recorded that way, I think that's a great coincidence. I think your recordings sound good. When you're recording on 4 tracks, if you get a lot of bleed and you're not paying really close attention to that, it's going to sound like dog shit, ultimately.

I mean, like recording live... I don't really concern myself with getting the live feel or the sound of the band live. I really don't agree with the idea of trying to achieve that in recordings. It's like what's the use of having all this crazy, sophisticated stuff if you're not going to do something different than what you do live? We're totally limited when we play live. So I think it's two pretty different things, the record and then seeing us play, because we're extremely limited in what we can do when we play shows. We can always do a lot more when we record. I'd like to see that variation between the record and the live show get even greater and try even more stuff with recording.

Do you guys spend a lot of time with takes?
We have.

Do you believe in the perfect take?
I don't. I can't do anything perfect but I like it at least to sound pretty good. So, as long as we have everything set up and we have the time, I'd rather take the time to make it sound as good as I can. Probably everything we've done, whatever's ended up on the record it's been like, "Well, that's good enough." I don't think we've ever done anything like "Fucking Perfect!" It's the kind of thing where the 12th take and the 30th take are probably as good as the first take.

Sure. From the EP to the album, live, it sounded like you guys had perfected your soft/loud thing. So, as long as you could record that well, you didn't have to worry about mixing it so it sounds louder when you go into the heavy part.
I think we try to record like we play a live show. Like I don't want the soundperson messing with the dynamics [in that situation].

On some of the earlier recordings, it's strange, I think the nature of the machines you were using, they tend to automatically compress, like when all of the sudden the guitars crunch, the machines would almost automatically compress it. Which I thought was cool. It sounded different at the time, different than a soft guitar, loud guitar, soft guitar, loud guitar. It didn't sound mastered, it just sounded compressed. I thought that was a neat thing. Which also leads me to something else that I think is a really distinguishing sound of you guys that I like a lot: the way you don't have a bass player. But when you get both guitars overdriven and rolling pretty good, it sounds like the low end is crapping out on the tape.
I don't know if that's good.

I think it's great. I hear it on one of my favorite songs on the new record "This Is Number 42." When it's going crazy, and in the guitar part you hear the waver in the pitch catching up with the other part. Did you do 2 tracks of vocals for that screaming part, a distorted track at the end, or did you just scream and overdrive it?
It's the screaming, but if you listen to it you can tell...

That it's crapping out, and sounding good crapping out. That's the mystery of recording, that something like that will happen...

Five years from now it will be charming. [Laughter]

Recording, guitar wise, when you mix, do you EQ the guitars a lot? Do you know frequency? Are you that scientific in your approach?
I'm learning that better as we go along, but I only can realize what's missing or what needs to be cut, but I can't... I can say where it probably is, but I can't pinpoint it.

You can narrow it down to like high mids, mids, lows...
For the loud guitars we used to set the mids out and give the distorted guitars a real metal low-mid sound, but that doesn't sound good recorded unless you throw a mess of guitars on. If you have the mids boosted more I think it preserves the effect. It's weird the way the mids on the guitar amps are when you're recording, the level decreases almost, it doesn't actually decrease but it sounds like it does.

You're saying when you take away the mids?
Yeah.

I agree. You get white noise if you don't have a lot mids in there. I think especially on "This Is Number 42," that guitar that comes in at the end sounds super mid-range and crankin'.
That's just maxing out the EQ pedal.

Right. When you mix down do you use any outboard effects, like EQ pedals?
The last record, the LP, was the only time I've had a reverb thing.

What kind was it?
It was like the cheap Midiverb.

Alesis Midiverb?
Just that, and barely on anything. I don't even want a compressor so there's none of that. And you can tell how dry the drums are. The only thing that really has reverb is the vocals and really not that much.

I noticed on your vocal sounds, you do this real wispy thing. It has a real airy quality and I'm wondering if you tweek your vocals, or do you keep the EQ pretty much straight up and down.
When I record them I almost always put my mic through a Rat pedal, and not like distort it...

But use it as a preamp.
Just kind of make it a little warmer. Barely turn up the gain.

Yeah, I did that a few of months ago. Just put it through a distortion pedal. You hear so much more of the voice, you hear all the sounds, all the air moving around.
Sometimes I'll use that and then put a mic in the room too and put them on separate tracks and then mix them together, usually with the room mic lower. I bring up the close mic to where I want the level to go, then bring up the room mic maybe pan it over to the opposite side of the close mic and bring it up until you can just hear it; so that you're not really aware that there are two tracks but it has a different quality. Then recently my roommate gave me, we haven't recorded with this yet, one of those Roland Chorus Echoes and I've been using that, going out of that onto a different track, putting just the echo to a different track.

Yeah, those have a cool infinite decay setting that I like a lot. Did you master this record?
No, some high priced mercenary did.

But it was mastered?
Yeah.

You know, what I noticed is that the record is pretty dynamic, and if it was mastered that's pretty cool. Most mastering to me seems like they really like to compress.

It was done by John Golden. I think he's expensive, but people like him cause he's actually into this kind of music. We wrote out a bunch of instructions, like "Don't make us look stupid."The mastering guy can do that. That's the danger.

What kind of mics did you start out using?

[Shure SM] 57s. That's all we had.

How many?

A couple. My friend worked at a rental place so he'd give me some. But we just got some used ones. My friend had an AKG, and he'd give us a bunch of 57s and then later they got some of those SM81s and then I picked up a couple of mics, like the AKG C1000.

You can put a battery in it and you don't need phantom power to run it.

Right, and then [our friend] Amy has this big, CAD mic that looks like an old tube mic and I borrow that sometimes, but not on anything we've done yet.

Do you prefer the sound of condensers over the sound of dynamic microphones or do you like them with different things or do you still like to record guitars with 57s?

Yeah. Oh, I also have this totally cheap Audio Technica, it's like a kick drum mic, just a large diaphragm dynamic mic, it's like $90. It's pretty good. I use it for everything. I put it on guitars, maybe that with a 57 and stick them right next to each other. I use it on vocals too, I use it on anything. You can scream into it and stuff and it won't hurt it. I like lately, though, getting more of a room sound on the drums, so starting out with a condenser in the room with the drum mix and then a kick and snare mic until it fills it out a little bit.

So that's how you start out, you don't start with a close mic and bring in the rim, you start with the rim and bring in the close mic?

Lately that's what I've been doing.

What kind of machine are you using now?

An Otari 5050 1/2" 8-track and then I have an Otari same model 1/4" that we mix down to.

And then you recorded the _Slower Than_ stuff on the same setup?

Yeah. That suffered a bit I think. I haven't heard it since we did it, and it sounds pretty good but it suffered a little bit 'cause we did it so fucking fast. They did like 5 or 6 songs in two days, and we just did it in mostly one or two takes and rushed it through. It sounds all right. We recorded the Poundsign record on that stuff too, with my girlfriend Alicia, that's her band and she owns this stuff. We own it together. That record sounds really good. It sounds better than our record. The last thing recorded was Aislers Set. That was Amy, our friend who has the same machine we have (5050). She recorded most of it at her house and then we mixed it at my house to the 1/4".

What kind of board did you use?

It's a Soundcraft. I don't know what the number is but it's a 16 channel with 4 buss.

How do you like the EQ on it?

It's good, it's got two mids. The person who owned it before upgraded it and put two in for effects returns.

Interesting. How do you conceptualize recording? How do your attitudes develop?

I think one thing that wasn't covered yet was how we record. A lot of times it was very mobile. We had to record often times in different places and that puts a whole new spin on recording, like spending four hours to set up, you know, and a couple car loads full of stuff. A bunch of times with the record we would set up and record all day. You know, set it up, try and get the drum sound and stuff and then fucking scrap the tape. Maybe we'll get one song out of it, and then a month later we all get some time and try and do it again. The whole album gets changed. We were into that too, but also I'm just talking about the prep work, like right now the studio's set up, but we've always recorded like commandos. You're fucking tired. We're all participating in setting up the studio, Wyatt's doing the technical, we're all doing the physical. Then it's "Let's be creative and record." You've got to try and get there, to that point. When we recorded at the theater we had to wait until the movies got out so we'd go in at midnight and record 'til nine in the morning.

Did you all have to work the next morning?

I'm sure we all did.We'd be hallucinating if not just tired. So that's why our records end up a little trippy. Like I said before, I'm not totally into recording. I think it'd be a good thing for me to learn. I know Todd and I talked about texture, and that sounds kind of cheesy, but I think that's why I like playing live, cause you can choose what you're gonna do. You have the structure of the song, but you can hit it this way or hit it that way, whereas when you record you have to pick, do you want to upstroke this or downstroke this? So, for me I like the live aspect, `cause maybe you have two or three ideas for an area and you can mix it up when you play live.

You guys have always turned a song that was once slow into like a one minute fast song or else a fast song would be drawn out, you would change every measure. It seems like if a band is going to be interesting it has to go back and reinterpret.

I think about recording too, once you record something you're hearing it totally different. When you record you can hear what works and what doesn't work. Some things work very well from just a songwriting aspect, and some things don't and once it's recorded you can tell that a part's weak and try and make it better.

There's a strange physics to the placement of something onto tape and then hearing it back. I think people operate from the perspective that mics pick up sound and that's all there is to it, but mics don't hear the way your ears do. They can't. There's no way, and that's really tricky. But as far as producing your own records, do you guys all get involved in that process, do you take rough mixes home?

We have, but so far it's always more rushed than that. It's more last minute.

Just trying to get it on tape?

We get it on tape and then it's like, "We have to mail this out." We always have good intentions of doing that [closer production], and we've done it on occasion, but we've scrapped stuff too. People give us a hard time like, "Are you going to take two years to record your next album?" and it's just frustrating. It's not like we spend two years or a year or a year and a half or six months everyday straight, so that's just hard. I think by having Wyatt have all his stuff set up, in the future, things will be a lot more workable. It's an evolution from the 4-track to the 8-track. That's encouraging. The other thing that's nice about recording ourselves is that there's nobody I would rather have do it. Having a band member record your own music, I know we're going to do the right thing. We have a shared view of what we want. I'm never worried. It's always going to be good.

So you guys aren't excited to get into a studio and work with a producer anytime soon.

I don't think we'd turn it over to somebody and be like, "Yeah, just do whatever." Every engineer has their own way of doing things and they're going to do stuff to your sound, like add effects, that you're not aware of. Somewhere in that mass of equipment, something's going to be there. So it really takes the guesswork out, doing it yourself. `Cause you just never know. Some

engineers will think, "Well, these guys don't know what the fuck they're doing," and after you leave they'll just go back...

I think a lot of people start with the idea that a studio is just them taking what they do in and this guy just puts it on tape. But at that point you're taking out that person's role as an artist as well.

But see, I look at that person as a technical person. If I want them to be an artist, if I'm hiring a producer someone who has a sound [that's different]. But if I'm just going to the corner recording studio to put some songs down, I don't know who this guy is or what his thing is so I have him there for the technical skills, getting the levels there and stuff. And it's always those guys who are so bored that they do what they want anyway, because that's the only fun they get to have, you know, schmoes coming in there paying them to do it.

Papas Fritas and the Columnated Ruins

AN INTERVIEW WITH TONY GODDESS OF PAPAS FRITAS

by Leigh Marble

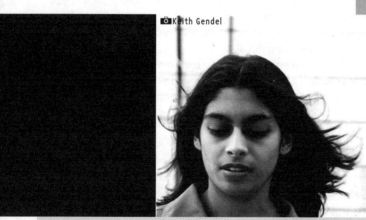

Keith Gendel

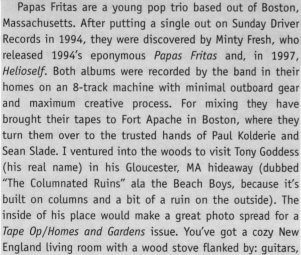

Papas Fritas are a young pop trio based out of Boston, Massachusetts. After putting a single out on Sunday Driver Records in 1994, they were discovered by Minty Fresh, who released 1994's eponymous *Papas Fritas* and, in 1997, *Helioself*. Both albums were recorded by the band in their homes on an 8-track machine with minimal outboard gear and maximum creative process. For mixing they have brought their tapes to Fort Apache in Boston, where they turn them over to the trusted hands of Paul Kolderie and Sean Slade. I ventured into the woods to visit Tony Goddess (his real name) in his Gloucester, MA hideaway (dubbed "The Columnated Ruins" ala the Beach Boys, because it's built on columns and a bit of a ruin on the outside). The inside of his place would make a great photo spread for a *Tape Op/Homes and Gardens* issue. You've got a cozy New England living room with a wood stove flanked by: guitars,

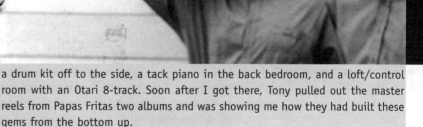

a drum kit off to the side, a tack piano in the back bedroom, and a loft/control room with an Otari 8-track. Soon after I got there, Tony pulled out the master reels from Papas Fritas two albums and was showing me how they had built these gems from the bottom up.

In what order do you generally lay down tracks when you're recording?

Usually it's the drums first, with a scratch guitar and vocal track. On our first album [*Papas Fritas*], the drums were mostly done with a single PZM mic.

Really?

Yeah, we'd put it under the snare. On a few tracks we also used a [SM] 57 on top, and on "TV Movies" we used a 414 to pick up the brushes better. But mostly a PZM. On our second album [*Helioself*] we used four mics for the drums. We'd track them all to separate tracks, but we always bounce the drums down to mono as soon as we need the space. Vocals come next to make sure there's enough space to get them together. You know, enough room to bounce stuff around, submix harmonies and doubled harmonies. The most important thing is to get the drums, get the track together, but then get the vocals and build around the vocals. I don't know enough about mixing; maybe guys can make room for the vocals at that stage no matter what. But that way, everything else gets built around the drums and vocals, so that the other parts are reacting to what are really the most important parts.

Yeah, there are guys who can mix and make space for vocals, but it might take a lot of EQ.

With vocals, getting the performance is the most important thing. I don't mess around that much with mic'ing techniques but more with which mic I'm using. You're singing the melody, and you just want to get that strong and in front. You're not going to create space with vocals, you're going to create it with other instruments. So after we do the vocals, usually bouncing them down to 2 or 3 tracks, we build around them. Guitar, piano, organ, other percussion come next. Sometimes these get bounced, if there's two parts in different frequency ranges and I need the space I will combine them on one track. Sometimes I'll mix two parts on a bounce, but one really quiet if it's a part that I don't really care if it gets lost. If it pops up in a couple spots, that's cool, it adds to the layering without really taking up room. Bass goes down last, on it's own track, to keep it punchy.

Let's talk about history a little. Were you doing 4-track stuff before you got together with Keith and Shivika?

No, that's really how the band started. I had gotten a 4-track and was just starting to mess around with that stuff a bit. I was in the big band at school and in a smaller jazz ensemble and then a free improvisation ensemble. I got a 4-track to start recording that stuff. And then I was getting into the idea of, instead of just recording spontaneous improvisation, getting into layering. I was listening to bands like Sebadoh, Tall Dwarves, and stuff like that. Stuff where you knew they were 4-tracking. Shivika inherited a drum kit from her cousin, I knew her because we're both from Delaware, we went to high school together, and she wanted a place to keep it, and I wanted to start writing songs to record; and it just kind of grew out of that. Keith was around too. We kind of formed to play at a friend's party but it started on 4-track, just messing around with that, but we got pretty into it. We didn't have much for gear, had a standard grey Tascam 424. I had a 57. I used a headphone for the bass drum microphone... Have you ever done that, plug the headphone out into the input jack?

Did you think that one out, like, "Oh, that'll be like a large diaphragm mic, good for bass?"

Oh, no [laughs]. It was just there. And I have a silver Electrovoice mic from the '50s that I inherited from my grandfather. The kind you might see on old Byrds records.

A condenser?

No, dynamic, kind of what was a 57 back then. A live mic for bashing. And we were recording and playing some parties. We had done some songs and a friend of mine said, "Do you want to put that out as a single?" We were just mixing down to cassette at that point. So we went into a 16-track studio in Boston, a place called Birdog Studios, and started recording some stuff there. We tried "Lame to Be," which is on our first album. They had a 16-track 1", and a pretty big room. I was starting to have some idea of how I wanted it to sound, but I really didn't have a very clear idea. I was like, "Make the guitars sound like tin foil." And the guy was like, "What are you talking about?" He just wanted to set up the mics, record what we do live, and make it sound professional. He didn't really want to produce... His idea of producing was setting up mics and recording. But we had no idea what we wanted to do either. So that just didn't work out. My big trip with it is that, when you're playing live, people can see you, there's more than one sense being engaged. And when you're recording, you can't just record what you do and put some reverb on it, unless you're such an amazing performer. You've got to make a listening experience. They've already looked at your CD booklet a couple times, there's not more visuals than that, so you've got to make the listening experience more visual. You've got to create a sound environment that the listener can enter into, or hear textures develop and shift, you know what I mean? You're creating a picture. With the latest album we took that even further. With that song, "Say Goodbye," that's about turning into an angel. So we wanted to have lots of soft and airy sounds, like the organ with the high bells. And there's that song, "Live By the Water," which is about moving out into the country. You're going to use acoustic instruments; you're not going to use electric guitars to write a song about living in the country. And there's "Rolling In the Sand," which is about when we played at a bar where a fight broke out, so we used an old saloon-style piano with thumbtacks. Just trying to create a picture with sound. The downside of that is that sometimes people thought the music was too theatrical, too much like a show tune. Minty Fresh contacted us, and we hadn't had a good experience in the studio, so we decided to get our own stuff. I got the 8-track [a 1/2" Otari] and a Mackie 1604, we bought a [AKG] 414, and a couple PZMs. Minty Fresh is in Chicago, so they got me in touch with Brad Wood, who said, "Oh, Radio Shack has these PZMs, you should check them out." I think he had only done the first Liz Phair album by then, he wasn't quite so well known. So I got that stuff, and I just concentrated on drums a lot. I knew I didn't want big, loud drums. Just figuring out, "Oh, I'll mic it from there, or put towels over them," which is anathema to most drummers. "How dare you duct tape tissues to my drums?" But it's just a question of what works. We just started recording the album in our basement. We realized we had all these songs from when we started playing, but how were we going to make a band out of this? We had recorded them as we went along, and it sounded like too many different styles. How to unify it, through different arranging techniques? Like the muted guitars and drum sounds, that was trying to make it more unified. Reading interviews with Lindsey Buckingham, he said, "My greatest contribution to Fleetwood Mac wasn't as a guitar player or a singer or a songwriter, but being able to take these three songwriters and create an identity for the band." Realizing that it's not just recording a drum kit, or getting a cool guitar sound, it's creating a whole sound for the band. There's a quote from Brian Wilson, talking about Phil Spector, where he says, "I wasn't really into production until I realized it's not just the song, it's like you're creating a two-minute experience for the listener, not just a two-minute song. A great record should be like an experience they've had, that they can go back to whenever they put on that record." I have pretty grandiose role models [laughs].

Did you kind of bash around in the dark awhile when you first got the 8-track? While you were trying to get this vision together?

Yeah, for a really long time. Our first single was "Passion Play," with a string section. I thought that would be cool, but I didn't really know what I was going for, I just thought it sounded kind of retro. And "Lame To Be," our first version was what we did live, distorted guitars, but on the album, I knew I wanted it to sound different but I didn't know what it was. When we play it live, it's like this, [plays descending bar chords]. But I realized I wanted it to be like this [plays descending bass line with suspended harmony]. It's not just sound that makes a recording, it's how you decide to harmonize.

There's that piano part on there too, that ascends at the end of each line.

Yeah, to break all the parts up, [plays parts on piano]. That's when I started to learn to play piano a bit too. And realizing what a lame instrument the guitar is because you're just playing chords [laughs]. In that song "For No One" by the Beatles, he just plays a C chord the entire time. Same with "Penny Lane", he just plays a C chord the whole time and moves the bass down with his left hand. But with guitar, you see the natural relationships...

The three and the five always following the root.

Yeah, exactly. So I was just getting into that - there was a lot of bashing around.

Did you reach a point where you said, "Okay, I've got it now, we're going to start with the first song and do it right"?

Kind of. I started getting some things together. It was kind of like when you're bashing around on a paper for school and it takes you forever to figure out how you want the paper to be but once you do you're like, "Fuck, now I gotta write the thing." So, yeah, I got the drum sound in place, and the whole muted guitar thing came from thinking of how to make the rhythm more harmonic. Putting polyrhythms in there that aren't just percussion, that are harmonic or melodic too. Like guitar parts that hit the chords on the two and the four with the snare. It was kind of a drag because I'd play it for my friends and they'd be like, what is this? This doesn't sound like you guys. We sound like one thing live, but this is what we sound like in the studio. I always like that, when you see a band live and it's different from the record and you've learned something more about them, as opposed to just hearing them play the record. So yeah, we were bashing around, the record company was like, "Just record it!"

Had they seen you live at that point?

They hadn't seen us live before. Anyhow, from playing jazz in the big band, the guitar players in those bands are never just strumming chords, you know, they're filling in holes and hitting spots. So I've never been the kind of guitar player that just strums chords, I've always wanted the parts to be smaller.

So once you have the drums and vocals down, do the other parts develop out of improvisation, or do you know what everything is going to be before you roll tape at all?

I think generally, in songs like "Explain," or "TV Movies," the ballads, you've got the rhythm but the rhythm has so much space in it. There's so much space between every beat. A song like "My Revolution", the rhythm is quick enough that you don't want too much stuff messing around between the beats. But a ballad that is slower, you gotta think, "How am I going to float chords in there without having these sharp edges. How are you going to get harmony in there?" We didn't have an organ for the first album, but organ is so unobtrusive, you just kind of float it. But for other things, how am I going to float the harmony in there without getting attacks. And that's using the volume swells or some slight lead guitar playing. But like in jazz, even when you're playing "My Funny Valentine" for the hundredth time, you're expected to come up with a new piece of music. When we're playing around with arrangements, I'm playing Rhodes or piano or guitar and Shiv is playing drums or just maracas and tambourine, it's not improvising, but it's creating new pieces of music with the same harmonic material. So that's what I mean, when you're casting around for a direction for a production. It's the satisfaction of trying out different ways to play a song. You feel like you're using your musical vocabulary, almost improvisational, and you keep pushing it around until you hit on something and then you fine-tune it. And on the last album too, we spent a lot of time around the piano working on vocal harmonies. And also saying, who should sing this song, or on "Hey Hey You Say," getting into trading off the vocals.

It's clear a lot of work and refining went into that song.

Sometimes I put so much time and effort into a song, I think it's going to translate into a really heavy listening experience. But to most listeners it's just notes coming out of a speaker. They don't hear the hours of work. Sometimes I think I need to focus on it being a more immediate experience.

Oh, it's quite immediate. But for people who think about how it was recorded, it's also clear that it was a lot of work.

People think our music is so light. But it's hard to make music that feels good. I think of it as, not sober music, but serious and emotional music to me, but many people think it's just "la dee da," that it just comes out all peppy. But I worked my ass off on that! [laughs] Great music, great creation in general, doesn't say, "Hey look at me, I'm a great creation." It just, you never question it, it just sounds right. But the reason a tambourine is there is because I put it there, it didn't happen on accident. That handclap or that harmony, it doesn't just come out when you open your mouth. Nothing exists naturally in music, you are making conscious decisions about each sound, more or less. That is my biggest problem with music made electronically. All music is made of the ability to make a sound and the ability to organize it. I think electronic music is only organization. To play guitar, it's a combination of your body's ability to play the guitar and your brain wanting to play the notes in that sequence and with that tone. And with a lot of electronic music, at least what I've heard, I'm not aware of any physical component. You know, I might want to sing like Aretha Franklin, but my physical body can't. And when you eliminate the physicality of the human body making the sounds I think it leaves something to be desired. Maybe I just like working with limitations. When you EQ and sample drum kits, you have all these variables, you can make it sound however you want. But you need to say, that's wood there that's making the sound of the drum, or I may want to play guitar like Jimi Hendrix, and I may have all the fuzz pedals, but it's not going to come out like Jimi Hendrix, it's going to come out like a different human being. So sometimes with electronic music, I get scared that it's all made by the brain, it's not made by the body.

So is struggle part of what you want to hear?

Yeah, and I think it comes from jazz too, hearing a guy improvise, hearing him push himself. That's what I like about the guitarist in Pavement, or J Mascis, they're improvising, you can hear them learning about their instrument. I do like some electronic music. But I look at music as having four components: rhythm, melody, harmony, and tone. And to me, the rhythm is the engine. Rhythm is time, and music doesn't exist if time doesn't exist; and melody and harmony are like the steering wheel on the engine. It's what gives it direction. I think that more and more people now, they don't want to agree on, they don't want to be a part of larger things. I don't think rhythm inherently has emotion. I think it's melody and harmony that gives music human resonance, outside of the physical resonance. People more and more right now don't want the emotion, they want engines and they want energy and they want physicality. When I listen to electronic music, rhythmically and tonally it's pretty advanced, but harmonically and melodically it doesn't satisfy a lot of my needs. I like the Chemical Brothers, it's fun to improvise to, it gives you a beat and you're just jamming. But it never changes key. A friend of mine has this theory that people's belief systems go through cycles every couple hundred or thousand years, that people's belief systems are based outside their bodies, like in Christianity, and then Pagan beliefs are of course all concerned with the body and earth. And he thinks that electronic music, it has no melody or harmony to give it this "larger than the body" feeling, it's all rhythm, it's Pagan music, rhythm-body music. That's generally what I listen to it for, I don't sit down and listen, but it helps me do the chores.

Do you want to talk about your songwriting process?

Yeah, we just had a band meeting, and I think what I've realized is the different roles you play when you're in a band producing yourself. There are three roles you have: moment capturer, sound designer, and public relations specialist. One, you capture moments; that's the songwriting process. You sit at the piano and you get some chords and a rhythm together until all of a sudden, this is kind of cheesy, but a crack in time opens up, so you can go back and play that and all of a sudden you're back in that moment. And after the first album I got so much into the sound design that I forgot where the raw material came from. I'd start playing and automatically I'd start thinking, "Oh I'm going to have the bass guitar hitting on this beat and the piano doing this," and I just got real hung up on that stuff. I was writing songs with

just the production instead of the moment. Sometimes that's cool if you just want to do a groove song, but usually you want to capture a moment. So that's the first role; and then sound design, that's where you further define this moment that you've created. You flesh it out with whatever instruments you use. All the production decisions about how you choose to make that moment sound. You want to make it as true to the moment as possible and also as creatively rewarding as possible, but you also want to make it, if you're concerned about this, and we definitely are, commercial. You can make a moment pretty esoteric, but we want to make it stick. That's where public relations comes in. Public relations and sound design are pretty intermingled. You know, say, that people react to a certain rhythm, or you refine the lyrics, to make them a little more accessible to people. So that's pretty much our songwriting process. I write whatever I want and then we'll play it and put it through those filters, as opposed to always worrying while I'm writing, "Is this going to work? Will this fit with our image?"

It's a way to make space.

Yeah. A lot of times I'll just have a chorus, or some chords that'll work for a verse, and I bring it to the band, and we just kind of play it. We bounce it around, figure out the bigger picture like the intensity level of the song, who's going to sing it... All these different puzzle pieces that we work with until we say, "Oh, of course it's going to be that way."

You were saying that for the first album you wrote most of the material on your own. Was the second album written more as a group?

Yeah, a lot more group. I just didn't realize that we were going to have to tour for ten months and have an album coming off of it. I've never written on tour. It's hard to get a song together in the back of a van. You're never alone for ten minutes. For, like, "Say Goodbye" I had all the chords and the chorus but I didn't have how we were going to play it. When we played it live I was just doing the chords as an arpeggio thing. So then we decided Shiv was going to sing it. I had the chorus already, "Say goodbye to all your friends," whatever that might be, and she decided it was about becoming an angel. And that's when we decided, oh we'll use airy sounds. Or on "Hey Hey You Say", we just had that riff and we played it over and over, and I had the "man on the telephone" part. We just kind of scatted lyrics until we said, "Okay, everyone go home and write a verse and bring it in," and we just kept doing that. It was also we were kind of pressed for time. We had all these fragments, but then you've got to say, "Okay, these twelve are going to make an album." You can't just try to write twelve hit singles, but maybe you'll make an album that by the end is taking you someplace. One thing I want to say about recording it ourselves is that music is a very organic thing. When you wake up in the morning you put on some music to wash the dishes to, or when you're going out on a Friday night you put on different music. It's part of life; and the recording of it should relate to that. Some records are almost like a study of a place; you get such a sense of where it was recorded. My favorite groups, it's all part of the production, songwriting, image of the band. Like Cheap Trick. I like the production on their early records, I like the performance, the sound, the image. The Band's *Songs From Big Pink* is like that, there's a strong sense of the room that they wrote and performed the songs in. And on our first album, we recorded it in this completely dead 10 x 10-ft. room, the sound has that quality and if you listen to it enough you pick up on that.

Are there any technical things you'd like to add, about gear or mic choice mic or placement?

The gear thing, it's all so subjective. Our drum kit is a piece of crap that we inherited, we've had it for years. But sometimes you might want the snare to sound like a cardboard box. It's all context. I guess you can make a thousand-dollar drum kit sound like a cardboard box, but you can't make a fifty-dollar drum kit sound like a thousand-dollar kit. You know, I paid $75 for that organ, and $150 for that piano. But it's not about that, it's about being aware of frequency ranges, stuff like that, and you'll get it okay. So many bands, I think, say, "Oh we'll go to a studio with a Neve and a bunch of really great mics." They think that's all of a sudden going to arrange their music, that because they recorded it on a Neve all of a sudden the bass guitar and the bass drum are going to lock up right. You've got to arrange that yourself, you know? You want a good mic for your vocal, that's what I'm learning more about. The first time all we had was a 414 and I don't like what that does to my voice. It's good for Shivika's voice, it gives her a nice light high end – it's airy, which is good for her. But I want my voice to be more of a tight, punchy sound. The [Sennheiser] 421 is better for my voice. I have a really rough voice and I don't usually sing out of my range. My voice is not a pure tone, so I want a mic that doesn't capture all the little resonances. I want a mic that makes all the edges and crooks of my voice sound like more of a pure tone. Whereas Shivika's voice is more of a pure tone, so we use a mic that captures as many edges as she can. On the first album I did more stuff like wrapping stuff in T-shirts, or putting the mic across the room. Then on the second album when Bryan [Hanna] came out to help us engineer he'd just do whatever, put a 57 on top of the snare drum. And he tuned drums, that's something I'm learning about. For electric guitars I mostly use the SansAmp, because I'm doing them myself up in the control room and I don't want to be running downstairs messing with a mic. When I started 4-tracking I'd try to get a cool guitar sound or just a crazy part [plays me some early stuff, one of which features the sound of a shower running in the background throughout] I didn't really hear the sounds as working towards the song.

It was like, "Yeah, showers!"

Yeah, "That would be cool if I record it in the shower. Next song I'll record it on the bottom of my swimming pool." But, yeah, as far as the technical stuff, it's just thinking about frequency ranges. In terms of thinking about parts, it's about leaving space, especially if you're a rock band. Technically, on the bass, we always compress the hell out of it, and use a lot of muting with our palms, to try and be consistent. I like a bass sound that has a lot of punch to it, a lot of attack and edge. Keith uses flatwound strings. Not on everything, but on a lot of stuff. On the guitars I use a lot of muting too, with the direct in with the SansAmp. I wish I could concentrate on getting different guitar sounds a little more. We don't have any delays or reverbs here, so that's not something we play with. We do play with compression a lot, not just as something to use to make sure it sits okay, but as an effect.

You were saying with the handclaps, you use a lot of compression on that to bring out the room sound?

On the drums too. Those Zeppelin records, recording in castles, they'd just stick a mic on the kick, mic on the snare, and then they had a couple of ambient mics just compressed to hell. Same with, you know the Flaming Lips, they were saying on the last song on, I think, the "She Don't Use Jelly" album, they got a huge Zeppelin drum sound. Compress the hell out of the overheads. And using compression on guitars alters the sounds, whether it's really clicky or punchy. On the handclaps, you affect the attack and release and get some cool effects out of that. You can get some cool effects out of just about any instrument that way.

When I was listening to your first album, I thought it was compression on the snare that gave it that sound.

It was recorded really tightly. You can have the most rickety snare drum in the world, when you put a towel over it it's gonna go "tink." We do a lot of speeding up and slowing down sometimes with vocals, if it's not a word part. You record it slower, so it's lower and easier to sing, then when you speed it up it brightens them. You want your background vocals to be bright. But also you're speeding up time so if you're singing out of tune it's, less time you're singing out of tune. It can brighten them and bring the background vocals together. Or if you want a loose draggy drum sound, record it faster then slow it down so the drums have a deeper tone. The whole sonic identity thing, that's why I like older records I think. So many of them have more sonic identity than records these days. I'm not talking about the way they play their instruments, but what comes out of the speakers. Right now, I feel I could put on a Nirvana record, a Pearl Jam record, and maybe even a rap record; they all use the same frequencies, and they have the same presence of sound. Before recording gear was mass-marketed, people had to customize gear more, so a record made in Detroit sounded different than a record made in Philadelphia. I don't think vintage rules, I don't have any vintage gear, but it's that attitude.

A Trip To Athens

by Brian McTear

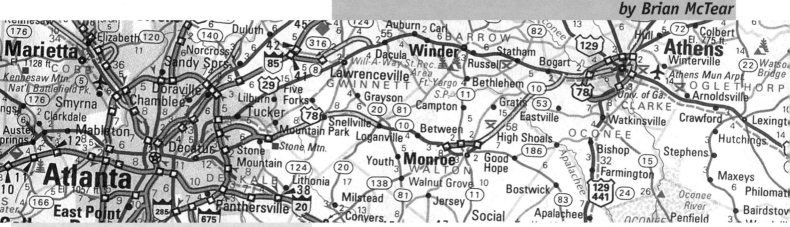

I am a musician. At least that is what I tell my parents when they ask. In early March of last year, my band, The Marinernine; played at a house in Athens, GA, appropriately called The Landfill. The show was sparsely attended, but everybody in that room – everybody in Athens, it seemed – was in a band. Talking to people that night, it was apparent that although there was a resurging network of musicians, there were few resources for them besides the University radio station and a few fledgling record labels in that town. There was only one recording studio that was within affordable price range, a digital studio called Rock Central, but from the sounds of it, they were booked pretty far in advance, and prices were kind of high.

I had told a few people about our studio in Pennsylvania [Miner Street, then located in our living room in West Chester], and their reaction to our $10/hour rate was very enthusiastic. But let's face it, Athens is fourteen hours away from West Chester. It was pretty obvious that no one in their right mind would make a trip like that for a studio, and two "producers" they'd never heard of. It wasn't until a few days later that I came up with the idea that would occupy my thoughts for the next several months. If they needed a studio, and I wanted to be a "producer," then maybe my partner Jason ["J"] Knight and I could just bring our studio to them.

June 15:

Lots of phone calls and three months later, on Saturday, we packed up the Marinernine van and headed off once again for the deep South. I had contacted eight bands, and booked five: Kincaid, The Possibilities, Ceiling Fan, Stunt Double, and The Lost Man; all committed to two days each. After we arrived I filled the remaining days with three others: Rug Boy, Gritty Kitty, and Joe Christmas.

We arrived at around 10 PM. Long trip? Yes. We carried our things inside with Ryan and Dan from Kincaid. They were very quick to inform us that Michael Stipe lived across the street in what appeared to be, impressively, a regular, "old shack" of a

house with lots of bamboo, and a red porch light (I wasn't sure if it was a "bug-zapper" or not). We would be recording there for the next two days, then the remainder of the recordings would take place at the Landfill where we played in March. Needless to say, as we drifted off to sleep on the floor of their practice space, flashbacks to those tenth grade dreams of someday meeting my high school hero danced in my head.

June 16:

We began setting up at around 11 AM. The practice room was a bedroom adjacent to the living room, so we set the recording gear in front of the TV, and ran cables between the rooms, under the door.

One major shortcoming within our system at the time was that our board had no tape sends, and no pre-tape EQs (it was a live soundboard). This meant that we had to use the inserts as tape sends and rely exclusively on the quality of the source signal and mic placement in lieu of EQs. This actually forced us to learn a lot about mic placement, a valuable asset for sure. And it's never bad to know how to get a good sound from your amplifiers, drums, etc. I'll say it now: Much of the equipment in our system is actually pretty shitty, but we have made the most of it. And instead of getting angry with it, it has always felt better to cherish it for all the valuable lessons it has imparted on us. (I have this dream of having all of the stuff we replace with higher quality equipment dipped in chrome and hung in the studio where they can be preserved and appreciated for eternity.)

Anyway, the drummer used a very small kit, luckily for us since our board had no sub mix channels. We set up an SM 57 on the snare, D112 on the kick, both to their own tracks with the 3630 for compression. On a third track we decided to use the E100 for an overall drum mix, but with little luck. The room was ultra-carpeted and padded, with everything from extra curtains to styrofoam insulation board and the cymbals, therefore, were instantly soaked up, making an even balance between the floor tom and overhead impossible. In the spirit of "rigging it" we used a Y chord to patch the E100 on the floor tom [with the -20 dB pad on], and my brand new Realistic Electret as an overhead into the third track. (In case you never heard of the Electret, that's probably because it's such a piece of shit – made by Shure for Realistic I had heard, but shit nonetheless.) Later we discovered our D112 was making a "pop" noise, so we had to replace it with the EV 257. The guitar amps, one Fender Twin Reverb and another solid-state Fender amp, were outside the room around the corner, making it impossible for us to hear much out of the monitors. The bass amp (Fender Bassman) stayed in with the drums, and was recorded with the Revox and the DBX for compression.

"Yikes!" you say. Well, rightly so. The overall set up may have been pretty laughable, but at least we were smart enough to act like it was all okay. It was our first day there, for God's sake. So we pretended everything was just fine and in the end it pretty much was. The Twin Reverb came out great; the other solid-state Fender was okay. (I have a really hard time getting any warmth out of solid-state amps. Jason was much more patient and it ended up paying off.) The bass sounded nice and full. The drums ended up all right, with some (lots of) EQing. By 7 PM or so we recorded eight songs! All were well performed and tight, and everybody seemed very happy.

Then something strange happened. At about 7:15 all of their girlfriends called and they all had to rush home. So we called it a night and drove to The Manhattan. Now, if you are planning a trip through Athens, this is a must see. It's dark, has lots of red velvet and brass, and they sell cans of Schlitz for $1. We made a night of it.

June 17:

The next day we began vocals at 1 PM. We used the E100 (pad off) through the DBX compressors. That went by smoothly as well, so by about 5:30 we started the mix. Unfortunately we were not very aware of mixing room acoustics back then. The sound of your mix depends greatly upon the room in which your system is located. The size of the room, the height of the ceiling, the hardness or softness of the walls and floor, and even how it is furnished – these all have a large effect on what your ears "think" the speakers are "saying." I don't pretend to be an expert in this area, but I can say in retrospect that this was no "dream" setting for a control room. It was about 15' x 20', but it opened into another similarly sized dining room. This made it too large for our "bookshelf"-sized monitors and 50-watt receiver. Because of this we ended up switching between our monitors and Ryan's stronger stereo system for different perspectives on the mix. After a while we began to rely on his stereo speakers. It was only after five songs or so that I realized that he preferred his stereo to sound really bass heavy. When we mixed, these things resulted in us "undermixing" the low end on those songs. We did some back tracking, but in the end it was only a satisfactory mix.

Later that night, J and I started brainstorming how we could correct this for the coming sessions at the Landfill. Our final resolution was to set up an equalizer that would correct for the qualities of our next control room with respect to the sound that was going to tape. That sounded easy, but in essence it was still a very "shady" move loaded with all sorts of variables. It was an improvement, nonetheless.

There were some other mistakes in retrospect: (This is the embarrassing part) using the Y cord in the recording process was probably the worst mistake. It's a bad idea to try to mix two different signals to one track via a $4.95 piece of cable. For one thing, the shielding is likely to be cheap. This is the metal covering which keeps the frequencies intact (i.e. especially with longer cables, high-end frequencies can be lost) and protects the wire from picking up outside interference such as radio waves, etc. Also, even if your Y cord has not seen extensive use,

the thin bundles of wire on the inside can become frayed causing everything from crackles and distortion when the cable is moved. Cables, connectors and wiring work in a lot of ways by the same principles as your tape format. The larger the tape format, the stronger the signal it can take, and the more your recording has room to "breathe". By the same token, the thicker the cable and the better the solder joints, the stronger the signal it can convey. Also, just as your better quality tape uses better glues and plastics to preserve your recordings over time, a good cable will have heavier, better quality shielding and solder joints to preserve the signal from source all the way to tape. We still occasionally use Y cords today, but only in mixing scenarios.

June 18:

The next morning involved breaking down at the Kincaid House, and setting up at the Landfill. Until now the temperature had been pleasant. Today would be different, humidity, storms – the works. By early afternoon, we had set up the studio equipment in another "bedroom-adjacent-to-the-living room" situation. This time it seemed like it would work better. We were used to our living room in West Chester, which had about a ten-foot ceiling, hard walls and hardwood floor. This was similar. There was also a fireplace (good to put an amplifier in) and a sloped section of the ceiling under the stairs going to the second floor.

When Matt and Bob from The Possibilities arrived (Kevin, the guitarist, was at a doctor's appointment) we began by setting up the drums under the sloped ceiling. He played a four-piece, big rock TAMA set. This time we set the same snare setup, plus the E100 about 1 ft. above the rack tom, picking up the overhead and the tom itself very nicely (I think the room had a lot to do with it), and our PZM on the floor about 1.5 feet from the kick and the floor tom. It ended up boosting the ride as well. This setup worked really well, and served as the model for the rest of our time in Athens. Their guitars were beautiful. They were a three-piece, with bassist and guitarist switching throughout, but when they played their Telecaster (late '60s vintage), they used an old Fender Bassman, and when playing their SG (early '70s), they used an old Marshall amp. (They did this live also.) Whatever the case, both lineups sounded brilliant. As usual, an SM 57 through the DBX, and that was that.

There was one problem, however – the bass guitar. Their equipment was fine enough, nothing fancy, just a Fender P Bass and a big Peavey combo amp. The problem was the sound they insisted on recording. This has been a recurring problem: how do you tell a bassist that he or she does NOT have to turn up the low end all the way on the amplifier? Everyone wants a super-warm, full low end, but if it's not 100% there on the tape, it's not too hard to boost the EQ in the mix. If there is too much, on the other hand, the result is an uncontrollable ball of mush. Well, we recorded it like he had it, anyway, through the Revox and DBX compression.

Kevin's appointment went late. In the meanwhile, a motherfucker of a storm rolled through. I understand it was something of a typical midday summer storm in the South: clouds, heavy rain, thunder, lightening, AND sunshine all at once. By the time it was thoroughly gone (didn't want to trust the surge protectors on our $20 power strips anyway), Kevin showed up. We started at around 4 PM, and kicked out five songs by 8:00 or so, vocals included. These Athens people were proving to be quite proficient. What a great band, too! They were Southern through and through, hard rock at times reminiscent of Skynyrd, but strong country tendencies the likes of Uncle Tupelo and family. What set them apart from those, however, were Bob's and Kevin's accents kicking through - the South's equivalent to Morrissey. Actually, they were originally from Bainbridge, GA, which is true "deep South", but decided to move to Athens for the music. As you can tell, I really liked this band.

June 19:

The next day's mix had to be postponed because the DAT player we were using (a Sony DTC 690) was discovered to have bad head alignment when Kincaid brought their DAT to Rock Central to have a copy made for a compilation. To their horror it was laden with glitches and squeals. When it was played on the machine we recorded it on, however, it was fine. When a DAT player's heads are out of alignment, tapes recorded on that machine will display moments of high pitched "squeals" and "chirps" when played on other machines. When it's really bad, the player won't even play DATs recorded on other machines without similar results. All of this is usually the result of the machine being moved around a lot, which was the case with this machine. Every band in town had borrowed it at one time or another. Nonetheless, Kincaid needed the player for the day, so we couldn't mix. For the rest of the sessions we could mix to this player, but I'd have to find another DAT player that I could copy our mixes to before we left GA.

June 20th and 21st:

Ceiling Fan had an interesting setup of guitar and bass. The guitar was split between a Silvertone 212 amp, and one of those tiny plastic Marshall amplifiers that looks like a half stack but is actually about 6 inches tall. We put the Marshall in the fireplace, although we could have used a shoebox for isolation. The levels were sent really hot to tape to add some "fire" to the otherwise cold solid state sound. The bassist used an upright for a few songs, through a Fender Bassman. In their remake of "God Made the Flowers" (by the late Athens band The Roosevelts), Jesse, the bassist steps on a distortion pedal with the upright causing everything in the room to come through his bass, which had become a giant overdriven microphone.

June 22nd & 23rd:

We recorded and mixed Stunt Double; a rock-a-billy Jon Spencer inspired threesome. The session went incredibly well, and when we mixed one of their songs, "Amazing Daredevils", we set up a microphone pointed directly into a fan through a Rat pedal and into the board. At the climax of "Amazing Daredevils" we activated the channel as everyone in the room began screaming and clapping. The combination sounded like fucking Armageddon on the mixdown.

Week Two

June 24:

The Lost Man. Going down to Athens, this was the only band we had heard before our arrival. We played with them when our band was at the Landfill in March. They were a lot to be excited about: a threesome, playing super intense, sometimes rock-a-billy, other times Louisville KY, stopping and starting rock songs. On top of that they had one of the most unconventional drummers I have ever seen. Not solid not necessarily good, but who's to say? Rob was somehow smooth, and undoubtedly awesome. He actually plays in Stunt Double as well, but at the time he really shined with The Lost Man.

We set up the drums and guitar as usual. Matt, the bassist had the same insistence on adding ass-loads of low end to his amp; we just went with it. Rob wanted some grit to his drums, so we ran levels high. We began recording right away, but unfortunately about five songs into their set, we noticed that the DBX was turned off on the machine. Boy, what a fuck up. People criticize the DBX built into the TSR 8, but we have become so accustomed to it that we just weren't prepared to deal with that at the moment. It turned out that of the ten or so songs they had planned to record, the second half were instrumental. So we

turned it on at the break between the vocal set and the instrumental set. That way, when we mixed the following Saturday, we'd have consistent levels and EQs for the two blocks of songs. In addition, we added some extra room mics for the second block of songs that we knew wouldn't be requiring vocals.

June 25:

Rugboy. This band had no drums. Thank God. They had a cellist who was wired through a solid-state Silvertone 212. We thought he would be playing with effects, or we would rather have put the E100 on it. As it turned out he didn't use any effects. For guitars, they switched between acoustic and electric. For all else they had this guy who just did weird shit on everything from percussion to keyboard to bass. They were the first to record and mix in the same day. When they initially said they planned on six songs, we were doubtful. They ended up finishing eight!

June 26:

Gritty Kitty. I booked this group after we were in Georgia. J and I figured we should record on the days we had originally set aside to fuck around. This ended up being the best quality recording of the trip. The drums had a full tone with a pleasant ambient ring about them. I think they were vintage Ludwigs, or at least cheap "look-a-likes". The guitarist had a brand new Peavey tube amp. I had never seen the model before. I guess I, like many others, am guilty of harboring ill feelings toward Peavey equipment, probably because it was the only brand my high school would consider purchasing. This amp, however, did change my mind. Lastly, the one thing that set this recording above the others – Polly had a big phat bass, and cabinet.

Unfortunately they were only able to do three songs, of which they were only happy with one. They eventually didn't even use that.

The story behind it is actually somewhat humorous. Gritty Kitty was a somewhat loose cutie-pop outfit that wrote songs with hints of Small Factory and the like. They especially wanted to record their song "Dumpy" for a split with Rug Boy (a highly unusual combination), but it was, as with the others, a bit of struggle involving many takes. We were able to get two takes of "Dumpy" to tape, but when it came time to add vocals I mistakenly rewound to the first take which was to be the throw away cut. J and I couldn't tell the one take from the other, but they both seemed to be on equal ground, loose in some parts, right on in others. Then when J went to mix (sometimes we switched on and off to preserve our ears) he went to the second cut, which was the correct one (even though through the whole vocal overdub the band themselves couldn't tell the difference). They were somewhat disappointed, but mixed the song anyway. About a week after we left they added a new band member, so they decided to start over and record again. We have a copy of the mix and I still think it was our finest quality job of the trip.

June 27:

This would be the day of our rescheduled mix session for the Possibilities. We had drawn a model of the board and its settings from the previous week, along with the settings of compressors, effects, etc. People say this never works, that something always changes. But I think it can work, especially if you understand that those levels are only going to be starting points for the mix. Let's face it, we had been listening to that band all day – really loud at times when we wrote out the levels. Our ears were in no condition to make final decisions anyway. But when we put up the reel, and repositioned the settings, we were about 90% there.

The Possibilities mix went really smoothly. We even did some extra mixes of one song, "New Tradition." All sounded great. Like I said before, I'm still trying to figure out how to get this band up to Philadelphia. That afternoon I took a few hours to go to Red House Studio to copy all of our DATs from the machine with the bad head alignment to a good machine. This place was a trip. It was located outside of town on the same property as a tent-city commune. The front door was open when I got there. I peeked my head inside and was greeted by a large man with hair and beard down to the middle of his chest. He set me up in the control room space, a big heap of a mess, with an old 16 X 8 board which he claimed REM's *Chronic Town* EP was recorded on. Throughout the four hours I was there, probably twenty different people of all ages, shapes, sizes passed through in tie-dyes, loin cloths, bikinis, beaded hair, dreads – I felt like I was tripping. When I was finished he only charged me $20. (Every other place wanted at least that per hour.) Nice people. Another place to stop when in Athens, to see the sights.

June 28:

This was another "add-on" since our arrival. Joe Christmas was a group of young fella's (some of whom lived in the Landfill) who had just recently returned from recording with Bob Weston in Chicago, and a full US tour. They also had recently filmed a real music video with all the locals in an Athens roller-skating rink. Rumors were also about that Michael Stipe had shown up to their recent homecoming performance at the 40-Watt Club. They were, in short, the current "home town heroes" in Athens.

They were only going to record one song for a split 7 inch" with Kincaid. I split for a few hours to run some errands, thinking that by the time I returned, J would have been setting up the mix. When I did return, however, I learned that they apparently hadn't even written the song yet. Worse yet, the process was floundering about rather awkwardly while my poor partner tried to move things along. They began at noon, and by 5 PM they decided to call it quits for a few hours, at which time they all went to sleep.

At around 8:00 they resumed. J went out to get drunk. He had earned it. I would later meet him at the 40 Watt to see Servotron. The Joe Christmas session ended up coming together at about 11 PM and we finished up for the night at 11:30. We hadn't done vocals or mixed though, and the next day, our last day in GA, was already scheduled for the mix of The Lost Man. In the end, Zach, the singer, and I got up at 8:30 AM. We finished it all just as The Lost Man was coming in at around noon.

June 29:

Our Last Day! The mix for The Lost Man came together pretty well. I have to say the whole thing suffered greatly because we forgot the DBX on the first five songs. There were some highlights, though. Rob's drumming – that smooth, jostled, almost arrhythmic style – was accentuated well by overdriving the drums through the board (they were already "hot" to tape). We also managed to salvage some of the overblown bass tones. Ryan, Matt and Rob were very excited in the end, as well they should have been. Their music was incredible, and their lyrics were intense and outrageous at the same time. One thing I wouldn't have known from seeing them play earlier that week at The Atomic was that much of their lyrical content was pointed very strongly towards lampooning industry people and musicians of the day. "Infectious" is about a local writer for *The Flagpole* who worships "All things Archers of Loaf", and another song is aimed at Kim Gordon called "There's No Such Thing as a Free Kitten."

By 4:30 we had finished and loaded the van. It was late afternoon. We knew we'd have to contend with traffic, but we were homesick. So we said our good-byes and hit the road. This had certainly been one of the most draining, yet rewarding "vacations" both of us had ever had on. In the end we had recorded over forty songs by eight bands in fourteen days and nearly one hundred hours of studio time. We had driven roughly 1300 miles, spent $160 on gas, and less than $150 each on food, beer, and other "recreation".

This brings me to the "Special Thanks" part. J and I became great friends with Landfill Proprietor Phil Waldorf. He not only allowed us to set up all our shit in his living room, bring five to ten other strangers into his house each day and make lots of noise – but he also fed us daily via his management position at The Taco Stand, brought Jason in for his radio show at WUOG (he was the station manager of Univ. of GA's radio), and (in all other respects) showed us a great time. It was Phil also who introduced us to the music of The Olivia Tremor Control. As their success grows I wonder why we didn't try harder to get them in on our project. (Probably because Phil said we didn't have a chance.) I did call once, but I guess I just didn't have the steam pursue it.

Additional Shouts go out to Jon Milavec for additional good times, Ryan Lewis and Megan Wargula for allowing me to stay in their air conditioned house while Jason slept with the roaches at the Landfill, and lots of other people - too many to mention.

One last thing: On the first day we were there, J and I met my high school hero Michael Stipe. Fortunately for you all, I have told the story so many times that I can't bear to tell it again. I will say, though, that I found out a few weeks later that only shortly before our meeting in the street in front of his house, REM had resigned with Warner for $80 million. For someone that rich, he was way down to earth. Thank god. If he were a dick, I'd have to reassess my whole high school experience.

Songs recorded during that trip have appeared on the following releases:
The Treble Revolution vol. 2, "Eleanor Roosevelt" by **Kincaid**, Kindercore Record's kc003
Rug Boy/Gritty Kitty **Split 7"**, *"Place Holder"* 18" kc004
Joe Christmas/Kincaid **Split 7"** *"Two Ways a Thousand Times,"* "Eleanor Roosevelt" kc005
The Lost Man **3 Song 7"** EP *"Natural Disaster," "Infectious"* kc006
Stunt Double EP *"Swingin' Daredevils,"* King Tone Records KTR001

Studio Equipment:

1. Tascam TSR 8, 1/2" analog recorder
2. Peavey 12X2 PA mixing Board
3. 4 SM 57s
4. 1 SM 58
5. 1 CAD "Equitech" E100 condenser mic
6. 1 Revox mic (model unknown)
7. 1 (Borrowed) Realistic PZM
8. 1 AKG D112 mic (borrowed)
9. 1 Realistic Electret Condenser mic
10. 1 EV ND257 mic
11. 1 EV PL 78 condenser mic
12. Alesis 3630 Stereo Compressor
13. DBX 166 Stereo Compressor
14. Tascam RS 20 Spring Reverb
15. DOD R-870 Flanger and Doubler (Borrowed)
16. Lexicon LXP1 effects unit (Borrowed)
17. Digitech DSP 16
18. Korg SR-120 "Beat Box" Drum Machine
19. Eight Reels of Ampex 456 1/2" tape
20. One Case of DATs
21. Other [Assorted mics, noisemakers, and knick knacks, too many to list]

Note: You may notice the absence of a mix down deck of any sort. We made arrangements to use someone's DAT player down there. It was a Sony DTC 690, consumer model unit. This turned out to be a BIG MISTAKE since it was in bad need of head alignment, and there was no place within fifty miles of the town that could do it in the two week period that we were there.

CHAPTER 2
Artists and Bands

Guided By Voices
Varnaline, Reservoir and
Space Needle
Elliott Smith
Poolside
Paul Marotta
A Quick One With the Revelers
Martin Phillips of the Chills
Grandaddy
Pavement: Steve Malkmus
Gary Young
I have a question for you

Guided By Voices

by Larry Crane

Taylor Crothers

If there's one person *Tape Op* readers have been dying to see interviewed in these pages it would have to be Robert Pollard, the dynamic, engaging leader and frontman of the popular combo known as Guided By Voices. I know a lot of kids out there see Bob as some sort of messiah of lo-fi, the guru of 4-track or the inventor of the practice-tape-as-LP concept, and while I do find his music entertaining, I see him more as a great pop songwriter and less as a recording guru. Nevertheless, I tracked him down after soundcheck when the supercharged GBV (Cobra Verde + Bob) blew through town in support of their new CD, *Mag Earwhig* (Matador Recs). The secret origins of lo-fi appear here courtesy of John Petkovic, guitarist for GBV and Cobra Verde. And apologies are extended to Kim Pollard.

People are always writing in and they're saying that you're the candidate they want me to interview. I heard a story that the first time you recorded somewhere you hated it so much you actually burned the master tapes.

That was Blue Oyster Cult.

You were in that band too?

They were called Soft White Underbelly then. I have never actually burned a tape, but I have shit-canned a project. I taped over it. We've had completely finished records in the can, packaging and everything, ready to go to mastering, and at the last second said, "No." Shit-canned the whole thing.

Because of the sound?

Yeah, the recording sound and other factors involved like I didn't like the way it was sequenced, but mainly the recording part. I've never actually burned tape. I may have erased it.

A lot of times people thought you were holding up a banner of lo-fi.

John Petkovic: I'll tell you why. I'll relate a secret about lo-fi. This is true. You know why he's lo-fi? His wife Kim would not allow him to spend money in a big studio. She won't even let me buy pot. She's the reason for lo-fi. Really. She wouldn't let me buy a 4-track.

John: That's why there was lo-fi.

Musically, all I have to my name is a Harmony guitar that my brother gave me and a really cheap little solid-state tape recorder that my brother-in-law gave me.

Is that what you demo stuff on?

Yeah. The whole lo-fi thing... We ran out of ideas for that as far as how far we could go with that. You can only go so far with lo-fi. You can only move the amplifiers around the room so many different ways and use so many devices and play on the side of the washer and dryer. You can only do that for so long.

It was kind of a dead end for you after a certain number of albums?

I like the immediacy and I like the warmth of a lo-fi recording. When I started a band I wanted to make big, good-sounding rock music. It was never a conscious effort to say, "Let's be lo-fi." We just retreated to the basement because of negative feedback. "So we'll just do it ourselves, for ourselves, and fuck it all. We're having fun and no one else likes it, but we like it so we'll just keep it to ourselves."

John: And your wife wouldn't let you spend money on it. I'm blowing your cover. I'm sorry.

That's okay.

The last album you did at Easley Studios and I remember reading these stupid reviews which said that your sound had changed drastically. I didn't think that it had changed that much.

It's not that drastic. It's not that slick. If you want to hear hi-fi, listen to the new Foo Fighters album. Not to say it's bad, 'cause it sounds fuckin' good. To get a sound like that, you have to pay dearly. You gotta get a producer that costs $100,000.

[Someone mentions Steve Albini]

You pay Steve Albini what you can afford. He records bands for free if they can't afford it and if a band's on a major label he makes them pay more. He worked with Bush didn't he? I don't know if I should say this, but I think we were $1000 a day.

John: I think he was working with Bush only so he could get some major label cred.

John's opinions do not necessarily reflect mine 'cause I don't know if John's a big fan of Steve Albini. I like him.

You did some stuff with John Croslin [Spoon, Reivers] too.

I like John.

Was he just coming through town?

He came in specifically for that. I think it sounds good, but the guitar sound's not very good. That's not his fault, it's the place we recorded. They put the amps in these really thick-walled little rooms. Maybe he should have said, "Bring those out of there." I don't know. He's good. I heard that stuff he did with Spoon and it sounds really, really good. Britt's a good songwriter.

So what about the aesthetics of studios?

I still want it to sound raw. I don't want it to sound studio-slick. It's a carryover from the basement. We finally got the sound we wanted in the basement and there was only so much we could do with it; and now the challenge is to get the vocal sound we like and the noise sounds we like. To try to use that, somehow, in the big studio. You've got to have a studio you're comfortable with. You've got to be as comfortable in a big studio as you are in a basement and that's a tough thing. I never did like studios.

Too sterile?

Too sterile; too removed. Working with engineers that really don't give a fuck about you. They're doing their best just to tolerate you.

I would think that at this point there would be a logical progression where there are comfortable studios and there are people who give a fuck about you.

There might be some people who are like, "I'd like them to be lo-fi forever". When would that dwindle? People would start dropping off. "Oh, I've had enough of that."

I can't see that an outsider has a place to tell a band what to do in the first place.

I don't regret the days of lo-fi, but now if I make a compilation tape of GBV for somebody, I wish that some of these songs were recorded better so the compilation tape would all be big rock songs. When we were making lo-fi in the basement we only used a 4-track. You know how some bands want to be lo-fi. We were more experimental. We wouldn't care if the drums were in sync with the guitars. To me, that's not lo-fi. That's just being silly and experimental like the Beatles *White Album* type stuff.

Goofing around and having the freedom to feel like you could do that.

But the whole "lo-fi" thing... at least it opened the doors for us. There was something for us to jump on. Something people could associate our music with. It was a genre that came about because there was nowhere left to go.

And then lump a bunch of people together that don't necessarily have the same aesthetics. So what's Cro-Magnon studios [in Dayton, OH]?

That's a 24-track setup. They've got ADAT's. The guy's working there are really cool. They let you do what you want and it sounds good, but I don't know. I haven't heard anything come out of there with a big, booming guitar sound. Maybe it's ADAT. I don't know. Maybe they don't know how. I've heard that when you turn the amp volume down real low, where you can get it real dirty without feeding back, and then you turn it up in the mix.

Little tiny practice amps can sound real good.

On a song on the new album, "The Old Grunt," we had some of those little bitty Marshalls [MS-2 mini amp] and the guitar part in the middle was through one of those.

They cut through.

Then you turn it up in the mix.

Are there any plans for the future. Are you recording after the tour?

We're gonna do some more touring and work this album a little bit longer. We may start recording in November. I have the next album written; as a matter of fact it was almost all written in one day. I like them that way. I haven't done that in a long time, where I was inspired to write 20 or 30 songs in one day.

How do you like working with Don Depew [at 609 in Cleveland]?

Don's good. We were real uncomfortable with each other on this last album but that's gotten better. I wasn't as experimental with the vocal sound as I'd have liked to have been. I'm real happy with the drum and guitar sounds. I think it sounds good.

Was he making you sing through his Peavey mics?

Umm, yeah.

I heard you were really into some Radio Shack mic.

On our 4-track stuff we did through some Radio Shack... a wide head, wide mouth mic.

Do you remember what it was called, what number it had or anything?

I don't know. Realistic or something. It was so wide that it captured more, like the whole room or something. That's what we called the "Hot Freaks" sound. When we first got a good vocal sound was the "Hot Freaks" song. That's the sound I want to get. I think on the next album I'm gonna try to get that in a big studio. We tried to get that on *Under the Bushes, Under the Stars* and we had to actually use a fuckin' 4-track to do it. And we had to use that mic. I want to try to get that where it sounds like that, but it's bigger.

Do you play around with effects and stuff?

We play around with pedals and sing through amps. Toby [Sprout, former guitarist] had a thing called a Memory Man [analog delay]. We used that for the "Hot Freaks" sound. You should check out a Memory Man sometime.

What other technical stuff can you think of?

Did you say testicle stuff? I got a vasectomy and my nuts got this big [indicates a large area in his lap]. Dude, it was purple, it fucked me up and I thought I was gonna die. I had to go back and they cut it open and they squeezed all that puss out.

That sounds painful. No, technical questions.

You can ask me technical questions, but I don't know how much I can answer. You just want to capture the song the way you hear it in your head. That's the art and the difficult part. And you don't want to spend too much time on it 'cause it loses something if you do.

With all these different tracks recorded at different studios... Do you record multiple versions of the same songs at different places?

Occasionally, but not usually. That's been the case for the last couple of albums 'cause I've been kind of in the dark trying to figure out how to bridge this gap between lo-fi and hi-fi studios. I've been just kinda feeling around trying to work with people. The next album's gonna be really solid because I know where I'm at and what I want now.

Do it all at the same studio?

Maybe, but even if I don't I know what I want and where, on the last couple of albums, I wasn't quite sure whether I wanted to be half lo-fi and half hi-fi... I didn't want to jump too abruptly into the next level. Now I'm ready and I'm ready to push. But then again, I always change my mind. I'm gonna quit telling people what I'm gonna do 'cause I always change my mind.

I don't expect a careful outline of a plan...

It's gonna rock. Another White Album.

GUIDED BY VOICES

Under the Bushes Under the Stars (Matador)

Do I really need to tell you this is great? If you're reading Tape Op and you've never heard GBV then get to it, okay? They embody every screw-the-studio, let's just do it concept that I'm trying to get across. Rumor has it that the tapes from their first studio session were burned by the band in disappointment. Yay! [But unfortunately not true!] –*Larry Crane*

ROBERT POLLARD

Not In My Airforce (Matador)

First off, I must confess that this record rocks in the most positive sense of the word. In an era of polished, overproduced rock music and sleepy "underground" bands, Not In My Airforce comes bursting out of the speakers to proclaim that rock-n-roll can still be exciting and meaningful. While the easiest point of reference would be Paul McCartney and Thurston Moore in a jam session, Pollard most brings to mind the sad, yet playful world of Robert Wyatt. Even Pollard's liveliest songs are infused with a deep melancholy that both recognizes the burden of existence and laughs at it. These raw sketches of drunken 4-track recordings just might cause you to jump up and do the air-guitar dance. –*Dewey Mahood*

GUIDED BY VOICES

Sunfish Holy Breakfast (Matador)

Since an album of GBV stuff seems like a rag-tag collection of stuff it makes sense that weird EPs and shit they toss out are just as good. One song is from the Kim Deal/Easley sessions, the rest being either some small studio or home recorded. Who cares? It's all great, and ends up sounding the same when you sing through Radio Shack mics and drink a lot of Bud. –*Larry Crane*

Varnaline, Reservoir and Space Needle

by Larry Crane

So, this story all starts with the New York combo Space Needle, formerly just a duo of Jud Ehrbar and Jeff Gatland who recorded some spacey yet catchy stuff on a 4-track and managed to get it (*Voyager*) released on the aggressive Zero Hour records. When it came time to tour, Jud recruited old friend Anders Parker, who was living in Portland, Oregon, at the time, to come play guitar, drums, etc. for the band. Anders brought with him a just-finished cassette of his solo work, under the moniker Varnaline. Zero Hour decided to put out Varnaline's *Man of Sin* as a CD and so Anders, to tour, needed a band. He grabbed his brother John Parker to play bass and Jud to drum. In the meantime, Jud recorded some really wacky stuff at home under the name Reservoir that sounds like Eno's *On Land* meets gritty synth-pop. It came out on Zero Hour as well. Out of all this activity, some really interesting homemade recordings have seen the light of day. I caught them before a show at Portland's Satyricon in the middle of Varnaline's 1996 U.S. tour, and we chatted about recording, of course. Obviously, Jeff from Space Needle wasn't present, so Anders and Jud did the yakking.

So let's talk about Varnaline first. Did you record that on an 8-track cassette or a 4-track cassette?

A: Actually, it's the first 4-track that went on the street. An old Tascam 144. An ancient machine. I bought it for $50 off of someone, 'cause one of the channels was busted. I would use it once a year. I recorded some of my older bands occasionally. It sort of gained inertia as I went along, and the last few years I really started to understand what was going on with it.

Any noise reduction on it?

A: You know, I don't think there is. It's really funny, 'cause when the tape is moving you can hear creaking, so on certain songs, at the very end of the fadeout, you can hear *eerreek, eerreek* from the machine just because the mechanism is so loud.

How did you get all that stuff onto 4 tracks?

A: For the stuff that sounds pretty layered, I would do 4 tracks and fly it down to my cassette deck and tape that back to 2 tracks stereo on the 4-track. Some of the songs were 6 tracks, basically.

I thought it was an 8-track, given the layers.

A: Yeah. I experimented a lot with stuff, but that was the best thing that came out.

Did you mix that anywhere else, or did you mix it at home?

A: All the mixes are basically first mixes. It was always the first mix that was "there." You're in that space where it just happens. All I did was, when I went to make the tape, I took the original mixes that I'd done off the cassette and mixed those down to a portable DAT player that somebody let me borrow. Then I did some EQ. When it went to CD, I went to the mastering studio at Zero Hour and did a final EQ and mastering compression.

On the single ["Party Now" & "Iron Horse"], was that recorded on the same kind of setup?

A: Yeah, basically. I got a new 4-track about a year ago. On "Party Now", if you listen to the sound, there's this ominous death rattle to it. I taped the PZM mic to the door of my room and John's bass was making the whole room and the door vibrate. So, if you listen to it you can hear the mic vibrate.

So that was recorded with a full band?

A: It was recorded at my folks' house in New York.

Could you make a bit of racket up there?

A: Yeah, we could turn it up. All the stuff on the Varnaline album was done, mostly, at conversation level. I couldn't turn it up. I had this friend who lived across from me, it was this U shaped apartment building, and she told me she could hear everything! In the summertime she said, "Oh, I listened to you all day, it was great."

Have you got a whole new album ready to go?

A: We're gonna record a new album in May after we get off tour. We're going to record at a 16-track studio this time.

Big jump!

A: Exactly.

Are you gonna record with Adam Lasus [at Studio Red]?

A: Yeah. We did the Space Needle album there on 8-track and it's kinda the same attitude... whatever goes. Any idea is open to use. He had one thing where he would use a [recording] Walkman, run a line out of it, and just put it by the drums, and it sounded amazing. It totally overdrives the Walkman. He's just got that anything goes attitude, which is great.

He's probably not really expensive.

A: It's pretty reasonable. He works with this guy, Jason [Cox], they're like a demented co-producing team. They're pretty crazy.

Back to the home stuff; you were talking about PZM mics. What were they picking up?

A: Just for the room. We did the basics tracks live: bass, drums, and guitar. One mic on the guitar, direct out of the bass, one mic on the drums, and then the PZM to get the sound of the room.

Mix those all together and run them to one track of the 4-track?

A: Pretty much

On the stuff you did earlier, the Varnaline album, how did you do the drums?

A: It was all brushes, actually. The one mic that I got was this pretty cool Tascam condenser mic that has a screw-on head for omni and unidirectional. I used that for the drums and some of the vocals. I'd have a snare drum, a bass drum, a high hat and a ride cymbal; I'd stick it right over the snare drum, kind of between the snare drum and the high hat. Sometimes, I'd put something in the bass drum, like this shitty kind of Audio Technica mic that I use for all the guitar mic'ing.

You'd throw that in the kick drum?

A: Yeah, but sometimes I didn't even need it. I had a wood floor so it would come through the mic stand. Other times I'd put the stand on a pillow, so you wouldn't hear the vibration through it.

You don't see that in pro studios! A lot of the sounds, like the drum sounds, are about to crack up on that. Are you pushing the inputs on that?

A: Totally. I would drive it really hard. I knew on some of the songs I would do more than 4 tracks. I knew if it weren't really hot I'd get all sorts of tape hiss. I wanted to make it really hot, especially between the 4-track and cassette and then back to the 4-track and then mixing down again. There was so much possibility of losing the signal. For me, the one rule of 4-track is to drive everything really hard.

When you did that, where you mixed 4 tracks down to stereo and than added 2 more, what was on those tracks? Vocals?

A: Usually on all those songs I would use one mic, that condenser mic, and do acoustic guitar and vocals at the same time. Instead of doing the vocals last I would do them first. Except for "The Hammer Goes Down," the vocals came later on that, but usually on the 5th or 6th track would come a backing vocal or another guitar or something like that.

So, on a lot of the songs you would record yourself just playing the song and would build around it with other instruments?

A: Yeah, exactly. Half the songs, maybe over half the songs, were originally done with acoustic [guitar] and voice over the first track. I would do it to one track, I didn't separate the two. I have a hard time singing after-the-fact, to kind of get a vibe or whatever.

Reservoir

Did you do the Reservoir album at home?

J: Yeah, at my apartment on 4-track. All direct [into the tape deck] except for the first song, which was a PZM [mic] on my guitar amp. Other than that everything was direct.

You were able to be pretty quiet, then!

J: Yeah! In fact, a lot of those I did at night when my girlfriend was sleeping.

Headphones?

J: Yeah! I had to be pretty quiet. A lot of that stuff... I'd just gotten my new drum machine. The first time I ever put it to tape was one of those songs. It was also, pretty much, the first time I used that keyboard at my apartment. They're just really early, messing around things, and they happen to be the best. With that kind of stuff, I find that if you really think about it too much and plan it out, it just sucks.

It's funny, 'cause what you're playing with there could make a really shitty new age record, but instead it's all overdriven and avoids all that.

J: Yeah, hopefully! I went with all first takes and I'd like to think there's something that isn't really boring about it.

I think Eno had a quote, something about new age music lacking any undercurrent of danger or edge to it.

J: Or it's all too planned out.

A: I like on that first song, where you hear the amp click on!

J: The horrible thing is that when we mastered it, the guy who mastered it cut that part out. I was there for the whole thing, and we were, "Alright, excellent." And then he went back later and thought, "Oh, that must be a mistake" and cut that out. We printed it, I got it and I was just, "AAARRRGGHH." I called him up but, whatever. He didn't know. They had to redo it.

A: We've heard so many stories of getting stuff back and channels being switched, left being the right and right being left. People cutting things out or cutting things off 'cause they thought it was wrong, which you can understand. With special stuff like Space Needle and Reservoir, how are they supposed to know what's supposed to be there and what's not? To me, it's like, "Jeez, it's a big part of the song and it's cut off."

J: I don't think you can really expect someone who's mastering a lot of albums to care or catch it. On weirder sounding stuff, they're not gonna know.

Space Needle

Are there more guitars and stuff on it than the previous one?

A: Yeah... it's kinda weird. It's all over the place. There's some stuff that's more representative of us as a three-piece and there's stuff that's kinda like... not at all! We had this violin player come and play on a couple of tracks. There's a couple of pop songs that Jud did on 4-track.

With Space Needle, do you create in the studio?

A: We try to keep it as live and as off-the-cuff as possible. We kind of had an idea of what we wanted. We'd been playing all these new songs after I joined the band. By the second day it just kinda gained its own momentum and went its own way.

J: I think it was good that we went in with that.

A: Yeah, exactly. Start out live and let's get all the effects and everyone layer their part. We got pretty much everything that we wanted to get done as far as what we'd been performing live and this other stuff kinda sprung out of it. It turned out really cool.

Were you editing a lot of stuff together?

J: We really tried to stay away from studio trickery. It would be the logical thing to do, considering the sounds, we really tried to avoid it and it ended up that weird things happened on their own. There are a couple of tracks where the keyboard's just total white noise and we didn't know it was doing that. We were playing live and it was kinda loud and then we go in to listen to it and it was ridiculous. It takes over the track! It sounds like we meant to do it.

A: It also comes down to the mix. It's one of those things you can alter.

J: I didn't realize it was like **that!**

The concept changes when you listen to the song.

A: It's great. It's a lot of fun.

You did the new album on 8-track?

J: Yeah.

You did some of Voyager on 8-track too, didn't you?

J: Umm. Not really. We did the whole thing on 4-track and then we went to mix it through a board to make it sound real good and it didn't come out that good. We ended up recording two live to DAT things there. But it was really all 4-track. I think one mix that we used had more.

I tried to figure out if it might have been taped at a different session.

J: The middle of the last song, "Scientific Mapp," that we ended up remixing.

A: But that was on the 4-track.

J: Yeah. We didn't change anything at all, just added some panning to it.

How did you get into recording your stuff?

J: The thing that got me into recording... the first things I did was on a rap mixer. You'd do a tape and then run the tape back to one channel and go back to another tape deck. Primitive 4-track. When we put the stuff in the phono inputs it made this great sound. Really great distortion. We used it live and I played bass through that. The whole last song on Voyager I remixed through that. It's a great distortion. I still don't own a 4-track. Jeff [Gatland – the other Space Needle] bought one and I borrowed it for the last year and a half. I just gave it back to him, so right now I'm basically without stuff.

Are you thinking of buying anything?

J: I'm talking of possibly getting an ADAT. I've got to learn a little more about it. It seems to be the direction I want to head. I definitely want to make better sounds than the Reservoir stuff.

Do you have a DAT player?

J: I got one. I'm definitely still learning all these things. There's a lot to learn.

But each of you has taken good advantage of what you had in front of you.

A: I bought a compressor! One of those DBX stereo compressors. I still don't feel like I really understand what it does.

I've had one for a year and I always wonder if it's really doing any good.

A: That's one thing about recording really hot to the tape, it naturally compresses everything.

SPACE NEEDLE

The Moray Eels Eat the Space Needle (Zero Hour)
This is probably one of my favorite records of the moment. Produced by Adam Lasus on 8 track, it's a sonically dense album compared to their first, *Voyager*, which was done mostly on 4 track cassette.

There's more references to Eno ("Hyapatia Lee"), unashamed digital drum machine ("Never Lonely Alone"), retro Rhodes piano ("Love Left Us Strangers"), prog rock ala King Crimson ("Hot For Krishna"), and some crazy buildup/freakout stuff ("Where the Fucks My Wallet?"). It's all over the map, and together, makes a nice sonic journey. It definitely shows a creative use of the studio environment. –*Larry Crane*

Elliott Smith

FROM HOME 4-TRACKING TO HEATMISER ROCK BAND TO SEVERAL SOLO RECORDS...

by Larry Crane

Larry Salcedo

Joanna Bolme

It was, strangely, a sunny day in the middle of a Portland winter when I came by to pry Elliott out of a studio/office space [actually, it's a room off the side of the Undercover Inc. office] where he was working on "leftovers" from his album-in-progress. We went to a bar next door that had seating out back and sat in the sun. It was a pleasant, yet odd setting to be discussing the creation and recording of his soul-wrenching music. In earlier work with Heatmiser, angst and loud guitars careened around. On his solo albums, minimal yet precisely double tracked guitars and vocals ache with guilt and longing. During the recording of the 3rd Heatmiser album, *Mic City Sons*, he was witness to the disintegration of the band in the studio. Yet we sit and talk of the craft of songwriting and recording, how they've intermeshed for him in the past, and how they're leading to *Either/Or*, his third solo album.

Had you done 4-tracking before your first solo album was even a thought?

I've done it since I was 14 or so. Hours and hours of unmarked blank tapes. I've been doing that for a long time, I just didn't play them for anybody.

As a way to write songs?

Just to record. I could borrow a 4-track. It was something I could understand. Mixing boards, 8-tracks, 24-tracks and all that seemed like a really complicated nightmare. It seems like there's some point where the guy who works at the studio doesn't know what in the world is going on and is running around, checking all the connections – can't figure out why he's not getting tape delay on the snare or whatever.

Seeing that from the perspective of a band that's recording...

Pretty intimidating.

So you borrowed a 4-track back then?

I borrowed one for a really long time. A year at a time. It was a friend of mines' brother-in-law's, and he didn't really need it. One of those old Tascam ones with the big knobs.

Were you using that before you were ever playing music in a band?

Yeah. Sometimes I would sync up two of them by cueing them up and hitting play at the same time and constantly adjusting the speed on one of them to catch up with the other.

No way.

That's not that hard to do. It seems like it'd be a nightmare. A lot of them [4-tracks] don't have speed controls now. The old ones had sweepable mids for EQ and speed control.

Did you record with drums and stuff or did you just do guitar?

Mostly just guitar. A lot of piano. I didn't have any drums.

Were you playing around with sounds or were you working more on songs?

I didn't really look at it as separate aspects back then. I was really taken with the prospect of being able to record one thing and then another thing at a different time that would play at the same time. It was all about parts and I didn't think much about sounds. I EQ'd things, but I just did it instinctively.

Did you have one mic you used on everything?

Basically. I think it was a [Shure SM] 57.

It's probably the best choice.

It's a good mic. People overlook it as soon as they can afford a more expensive one sometimes. It's the one. Somebody told me that the [Shure SM] 58 is really the same mic with a different grill.

It's got a boost in the high end so there's more treble to it. The screen can help dampen the popped p's but not completely.

The 57s are great. You can't really break them.

So you were 4-tracking. Did you find yourself playing music with others eventually?

I was in a band in high school. We didn't really play out - we just made tapes. We'd be recording an "album," so to speak, except it'd be an album we'd record to cassette 4-track and then make some tapes.

Was everybody in the band into the recording process?

Yeah, everybody was pretty into it. It was pretty exciting. It was something to do. It was a good way to spend time. I can't say much for the music though.

How would you record those kind of things? Would you record the drums first or would you play live?

The first thing that we did, we had this drum machine called Dr. Rhythm, which was not slick in any way at all. It didn't sound even remotely like real drums.

Analog sounds.

The cymbal went, "Chhhhhhhh."

White noise with a gate on it.

So we'd program that and play that and something else at the same time onto a track. We did a lot of bouncing or ping ponging, whatever you want to call it. We'd try not to put more than a couple of things on the same track. Everything was totally dead. We didn't have any effects at all. The next year after that, we had a real drummer and two 4-tracks and we were syncing them up like I was talking about. We'd do the drums to two tracks in stereo because that was of the *utmost importance* to have the drums in stereo 'cause they could be now. We'd have that [the drums], the bass and one other thing on one 4-track, and the other one would be mostly for vocals. We'd just chase the drum…

Start the 4-track with the drums and try to follow it?

Right. Follow that one with the vocal.

I can't believe you were doing that.

It's not that hard. It just sounds like it would be a nightmare. You have to have some patience.

Keep trying it over and over until you get it right. You'd just mix down to a cassette deck?

I had a friend who had a Nakamichi. One time we mixed down to Beta videotape 'cause supposedly that sounded better than cassettes. I couldn't really tell.

Did you use SM 57s for that stuff?

We'd get kind of extensive with mic'ing the drums. We'd round up as many mics as we could. Sometimes I'd even use some headphones for a mic.

Did you have a little mixer to run them into?

Eventually. All we had were normal mics. We didn't have any fancy stuff.

Did you ever do any 4-track recording with Heatmiser?

That went straight to a real studio.

Obviously Tony Lash [Heatmiser's drummer and producer/engineer] was involved.

He was the guy who was in control of that and he was good at it. I was used to hearing things a certain way so it sort of threw me off the first time we went into a studio. It sounded extremely clean and I was really excited because it was a new way to do things. Over time I reverted back to things I initially liked, soundwise.

When did you think of doing a solo album? Did anyone approach you at first?

The first one [*Roman Candle*] was just the most recent 4-track stuff. I played the tapes for a couple of people. They encouraged me to play it for a couple of other people and send it to Denny and Christopher at Cavity Search Records to see if they wanted to do a single. They just wanted to put the whole thing out.

How did you record that stuff?

It was two 4-tracks. One was Neil's [Gust – other songwriter/guitarist in Heatmiser] and also this guy Jaime's. There was an SM 57 and a Radio Shack mic.

What kind?

I don't even know. It's one of those kind that you can't even take the cord off of and has an off/on switch. I didn't have many options 'cause the songs were really quiet. All I could do was plug in the mic and turn everything all the way up. The fader and the preamp and all that.

You put as much as you could to tape?

Yeah, but even at that there wasn't a whole lot getting to tape. It was really noisy. I kind of liked it. That was the way it had to be. There's something to be said for things having to be a certain way. Then you stop worrying whether you should have made this decision or that about how things sounded and just get down to the business of making songs.

I assume it was all mixed down to DAT.

It was, and Tony helped me do that.

Was there any way to clean tape hiss up, like EQ it out or anything?

There was a minimum of stuff done, but it sounded a lot better coming through the [direct] tape outs and into the Mackie [board]. It sounded a lot better. He had a compressor that he put on a couple of things, but everything seems to sound compressed on a cassette 4-track.

Did you bounce tracks much? It's pretty minimal music.

Most of it was straight double tracking. Two guitars, two vocals. Towards the end, there's a song, "Last Call," which has more stuff going on. That was 4 tracks of guitars bounced down to two on another cassette and I put that cassette into the recorder [and added two more tracks]. The last song, that's an instrumental, was a really old recording from several years before.

A song that fit in with the new stuff?

Yeah.

During all this time there were Heatmiser records being made, with Tony producing. Were you happy with that stuff too?

Tony has a great ear. He's totally gifted. I wasn't happy with those records, but it wasn't just because of how they sounded. Sometimes I tried to make the way they sounded be the scapegoat, in my mind, but the problem was that I was really having a hard time thinking of anything that I wanted to be singing about at the top of my lungs all the time. I was trying to do that but my head was in a different space. I wasn't even happy with the songs that I had written so everything else further down the line was not gonna be right 'cause it wasn't starting out intact.

Were you happy with the process of working in a bigger studio as opposed to 4-tracking?

At the time it was pretty exciting to be in a real studio. Looking back, I prefer to be left alone, without a timeline, to not have to go and record an entire record in four days and have a cold and still have to sing all the songs.

After that, you started working on your second solo album on the 8-track. Was that done on your Tascam 38?

That was done on a Tascam, but it wasn't mine, it was Leslie Uppinghouse's. So I was going over to her house every day for a couple of weeks and recording in a big, pretty much empty, wooden room. She had a 57 and a 58 and this tube preamp that someone had built for her that just had one big knob on the front. I was running everything through that, mostly 'cause I couldn't hear it, not because I could. That was cool because there were four extra tracks now.

You seem to love doubling your voice.

Sometimes it's better not to. It's a really old studio trick. That, and cutting the tape - which I don't really do.

I saw that splicing block on your deck.

Yeah, but I don't have any splicing tape and it makes me nervous. I've seen people do it and it's like, if you're confident, you have a better chance of not fucking it all up.

Where did you end up mixing the second solo album?

I mixed it with Tony in his basement. He had a 12 channel rack-mount Mackie board. You couldn't do anything complicated on it. No sweepable mids. This stuff was all the reverse of Heatmiser, where the mix would be up on the board for 2 to 3 hours. I would take my solo stuff over to Tony's and mix the whole thing in a day or two. He was doing it as a favor.

You don't want to waste his time. For Heatmiser's third album [recorded for Virgin, out on Caroline] you bought your own recording gear.

We got the big check from Virgin, and then we were on a big do-it-yourself kick. We didn't know that Virgin wasn't gonna really fuck with us. People are always saying, "Oh major labels, they'll tell you what to do and make you do this and that." So we were totally paranoid going in to that

deal and held out for a year, for total control, and then went so far as to buy our own stuff. They never bothered us at all. We got two of those Tascam DA-88s, which I don't recommend.

Why don't you recommend them?

The technology's not worked out yet. We had lots of problems with digital spikes that would have ruined our songs if we didn't know someone who had a computer and could take them out. It happened on almost every song. Say you have one machine on "slave," following another deck, and you're punching in on track two of the slave machine. If you do it too many times it'll create spikes in tracks three and one, the adjacent tracks. Someone said that every time you punch in on one of those machines it picks up all the data that was on the tape and adds the new number in and puts it all back on the tape. Every time it does that, it makes a few little errors and after time they build up and the error light starts coming on. Then you see a digital spike. It was totally infuriating. We had an Otari [analog] 8-track that was also synced up. When we were using that, which we didn't need most of the time, the digital machines were chasing that. We got a bunch of stuff that was pretty good - it's all been sold now. Some of it was really clean and didn't have much of a sound, but some things really did have a sound. We got some API preamps, solid state, and they totally have a sound to them. If I was gonna get a good piece of equipment, I would recommend them. They've been making them the same way for a long time.

I think they're all discrete components. There's no integrated circuits in there. Most every processor thing you buy now has a couple of integrated circuit chips inside like a little computer. There's a difference, and it costs a lot more to make stuff like the API. What kind of mixing board did you buy?

It was a Soundcraft, Spirit. It was really big but it wasn't heavy.

Was that nice, soundwise?

It was okay. To my ears, it didn't have any color. It was the link in the chain that I never noticed. We had a couple of tube preamps and stuff like that. A lot of the tube preamps that you can get now, maybe they have one little tube at some stage but they're mostly solid state. They will not sound noticeably different from solid state stuff. You buy it thinking it's gonna sound like George Martin or something, and it's so disappointing.

Like those ads, "Sgt. Pepper's was recorded on a 4-track, buy a PortaStudio." Sure. You got some mics too, like that one you brought over.

That was a mic I bought. A Langevin. There's this company called Manley that makes obscenely expensive mics. They're really amazing sounding but they're also really bright. Langevin is in the same factory, supposedly. Manley is all the tube stuff and Langevin is all the solid state. It's nowhere near as expensive. If it's worth $2000 and it doesn't have wheels and an engine it's hard to justify it.

You guys picked up all this stuff and rented that house over in Northeast Portland. Did you make isolation rooms in the house?

We got a lot of foam, the kind that looks like egg cartons, and we made a dead room and had the kitchen for a live room. We'd take off the foam on the ceiling of the dead room sometimes and rearrange it depending on how we wanted it to sound. We got these big blocks of foam that were about a foot wide and you could stack them up on each other. We'd make the main room into two rooms by building a wall with those because the control room was not separated from the place where the drums were being recorded. We tracked everything there and we mixed in California, at the Bong Load studio. Then Tony mixed a couple of things back at our studio that used to be.

How long did you have that up?

Maybe half a year.

It seems like such a cool idea to record this way.

Yeah, it was good and bad. Instead of one person being at the helm there were a lot more people putting their two cents in. It was too many cooks in the kitchen.

Sam (Coomes, bassist for Heatmiser and Quasi co-leader) kept out the way, right?

For the most part, yeah. Everybody was extremely dissatisfied in one way or another. Some aspect of it rubbed somebody the wrong way.

What was bugging you?

Mainly, what was bugging me was everybody else's problem, whatever it was. I was trying to keep it together and trying to keep it going. Then again, it may have been my perception of their problem, which may not have been a problem. It was highly stressful. Our days were numbered and everybody knew it. We weren't unified. Nobody could speak for anybody else. The producers were supposed to direct traffic. They did that. It's a little weird, because previously it had been strictly within our band. It was unusual, to begin with, to have had a member that was a really good producer. The first two albums sound great. He always does a great job. He's really good. He makes things make sense, soundwise. Part of my deal was that I didn't want things to make too much sense and that can throw people off. They don't know where it stops and starts. On the other hand, at certain times I'd be really picky about what someone was playing on my songs and at another time I'd be like, "Just do whatever you want."

Do you think you're difficult to work with?

No I don't, but I don't think that was the right mix of people. I don't think that Tony's difficult to work with or Sam or Neil, but for me it was often difficult to work in that situation. It was also hard for them.

What if you had just gone to a studio? Would that have made things easier?

Maybe. It would have been the same problem anywhere. It would have been better if everyone had put their trust in one person to take the reins. No one could put their trust in anybody else. It was kind of a nightmare.

When I heard that you guys were gonna record that way I thought that it was so cool.

It could've been.

It sounded good, like you'd have a lot of control over it, and it seemed really smart, financially.

It probably worked out about the same. We didn't, personally, make very much money. You sign, and you're gonna get a couple of hundred thousand dollars, and then you end up getting a check for eight thousand bucks. It's still a lot more than I'd ever had before but everybody else made more money – the lawyer and all that stuff.

I think a lot of bands will let the label tell them where to record.

You have to pick your battles. Some bands, they're not gonna

be upset if their label strongly encourages them to put this song on instead of that song because what they want is for the song to be successful and if the label says, "That's the one," then they'll go, "Yay!" If that's not your battle, then why spend the time holding out for artistic control so you can tell your friends you have it. Some people are really better with somebody organizing for them. We didn't want that to be happening. There was nobody checking up on us. They were interested, and it was cool, but they knew that Tony was good and he wasn't gonna let anything by that was gonna be totally insane. They knew who the producers were. They had done Beck's first record. Rob [Schnapf] and Tom [Rothrock] had some kinda cool mics that I hadn't heard of. They're called Coles. [4038]

I've heard of them.

They used those a lot for room mics on drums. They put them down by the floor. They look sort of like a frying pan, it's not a normal shape, they're black, and they don't look like microphones. I think they're ribbon mics, actually. They were really dark sounding; they weren't dropping frequencies, but they weren't really "glassy" like the Manleys. We had a Manley [not a gold plated one] but it was so incredibly expensive.

The Coles you'd use for stereo drum mics?

They'd set them several feet off the floor and point them at whatever they wanted to pickup. They'd use them, sometimes, to pick up the kick drum from ten feet away. They were doing lots of stuff with the drums that I thought was really cool and I hadn't seen before. Tony had a toy drum set that he played on at least one song. We made some drum loops on a computer for one song. I learned a lot of things from Rob and Tom.

They seem to have a real creative approach to recording. Their records sound fun.

They have a feel for the event of a song. They would always be zooming in and out. In to the details of how the compressor was set but then they'd zoom out and see how that fit into the song. I have a pretty high tolerance for fussing with things, but I've never found it fruitful to fuss with things for very long. I'm totally capable of obsessing over a ridiculous detail. A week or month later, if I hadn't spent that extra hour trying to accomplish some small little task, I wouldn't remember. Nowadays I try to, mixing-wise, get it to sound like the song is happening and you can hear the things that you want to be heard. If it has good feeling to it just put it down like that. Why drive yourself insane?

Did you all go down to California for the mixing?

Yeah. They have a studio built in a barn out behind Tom's mom's house. There's a big panel with an X like a barn has and it just slid aside and there's a door. It didn't look like a dentist's office. They had a really cool mixing board that was built by this guy from Cuba and it used to be at some studio in L.A. and the first couple of Tom Waits records were done on it. It was all API parts and was all metal with big knobs. The mutes were switches.

Not buttons?

You had to flick them all on with your forearms. It was a really nice mixing board.

Did you spend a lot of time mixing this album?

Yeah, it was less than a week. We were mixing three songs a day. A lot of attention was paid to that. It didn't go to the point where everyone was totally fatigued.

I like it a lot. It's such a different record compared to your first two.

I like it a lot better than those other ones. It was a really stressful time.

So you're working on your third solo album.

Most of that was done at my house, some stuff was done at Joanna's [Bolme, Elliott's pal and bassist for local combo, Jr. High] house on a 4-track, a couple of songs at Mary Lou Lord's house on her 4-track, some on 16-track in California... all over the place.

Now you've got to pull it all together and finish it up.

Which was kind of hard. Everything sounded different. I kept recording more songs with no regard whether or not they were gonna be on anything. That's what I'm used to doing; recording all the time and not going, "What should I record for this record?" Usually it's put out whatever happened in the last 6 months. With this, I had way too many songs and no mechanism for picking between them.

Now you have to sit down and figure out which songs are gonna be on the album.

I think I did that last night. I've done that several times now and I hadn't been happy with it. There seemed to be no path through any 10 or 12 of them that made any sense. I think I happened on it last night. I'm kind of pleased to not have another decision to make. The records we were talking about before, at Leslie's house and on 4-track, were totally limited and there was no choice about what to use. Then I got my own stuff, and an 8-track, and I have a choice between a couple of different mics, I got a compressor and one of those boxes that will make any effect that you have the patience to try to program. I fooled with it for two hours to make something that sounded like a plate reverb. That's pretty much all I ever use it for. I got lost in a sea of decisions that didn't really matter.

How do you balance the technical and songwriting ends?

It's hard to wear all the hats, but it just makes it harder if you get bogged down in sweating the small stuff, which I did for months. I like it, as long as I don't get really frustrated. I follow a few simple, provisional rules: Don't, while mixing, keep the mix up for more than 20 minutes or half an hour. Don't drive yourself crazy with mic placement when all you're doing is an acoustic guitar track that's gonna be overlooked for the main melody of the song. When you're doing drums by yourself and you've got three mics on them, you have to be extremely patient to play and then playing it back and see how it sounds. I just watch the lights. If there are too many red lights coming on the compressor I make it so only three come on. I make sure some signal is getting to tape. If I had more patience, I'd be very concerned about tape levels.

That's what we're talking about. You might lose the feel of the song.

I got extremely interested in the technical stuff in the last year. I read all this stuff about the Beatles' sessions, even though there's no way to recreate those kind of sounds now. When I was recording Pete [Krebs, of Hazel/Golden Delicious for his second solo LP on Cavity Search] I was being very careful to get the level that I wanted to get.

It's easier when you're not having to perform.

I could hit the tape really hard with this guitar solo he's doing so it could imperceptibly compress and distort without sounding distorted. I don't have the patience to do that when I've just made up a song and want to record it.

Are you finished with Pete's record?

It's all tracked except for one song. I'm mixing it next week. I really like this record and hopefully I can do justice to it.

Poolside

WHAT? A BAND THAT DOESN'T ENJOY THE RECORDING PROCESS?

by Larry Crane

There was a brief mention of Poolside in the interview we did with Quasi, wherein Quasi questioned Poolside's choice of studios and the use of 2" tape. Curious about Poolside's perspective on the matter, I chatted with them and discovered their phobia of studios and an amazing history full of all sorts of different experiences in the recording realm. No, you won't find any mic'ing tips here, but I would hope that in reading these tales, other bands might take heed and avoid some of the worst situations. By the way, Poolside is a great band. Look for their album *Indyglow* on Bong Load Records.

The very first Poolside recording session?

Mike Wu (guitar, vox): The very first one was in California, what was that town called?

Eric Diaz (analog synths): Did you go to the same place that we went to? It's a suburb of San Francisco.

Daly City?

M: No. I don't know. We did it with this guy named Jim Day.

E: 8-track.

M: It was all one room, a garage. We didn't know what we were doing. We went in with the drummer from Samiam [Dave Ayer], who did another recording with us later on. It was just Claire [bass/vox], him and me. We just did four songs.

Joe Fitzgibbon (drums): Was that the tape you guys gave me?

M: Yeah. He [Jim Day] had no idea...

E: He didn't know much.

M: He played weddings. He liked real slick production. He was really happy to have us in there, but he didn't know anything...

How much was it per hour?

E: It was like $8, $10, $14?

M: Something like that.

What kind of deck were you recording on?

E: 8-track?

M: We're not gonna have any specifics about recording!

This is good. Was it on a cassette? Reels?

E: It was on a reel-to-reel and it was mixed down to a DAT.

And you'd record in this guy's garage?

M: It looked okay, but there was no separation.

Between the control area and the band?

M: Right, and we didn't put the guitar in another room or anything.

J: It sounded okay. I was happily surprised.

M: The circumstances were funny.

What did you find difficult about it?

M: I think that we just didn't know what we were doing and Claire came down, from Seattle, just to do that and she was real freaked out. It was the first time she'd ever recorded. It was just kinda weird. I hate recording.

What's wrong with recording? 'Cause it's different from live?

M: Everything about it.

J: With recording in general, you realize just how much practicing you need to do.

M: And how much you let slide when you're playing live. It's like you're paying for every minute and you've got to get it right and someone does it wrong and you've got to do it over.

E: You never have enough time either.

How did you feel about the sound of what you ended up with?

M: It was very flat, unflattering and hard to listen to. We didn't know what we were doing and he didn't know anything about our [kind of] music.

What was your next recording session? Was it in Portland?

M: It was here. That was pretty easy; it was no stress.

[To Joe] Are you on that one?

J: Yeah.

M: Joe was drumming with us.

J: It was probably the same setup. The 8-track was right there in the same room. It was pretty low budget.

M: Extremely! It was a friend of ours [Ben].

J: The first time we did it, we just bought him a six-pack of beer.

M: We were the first thing he did. It sounded better than our first tape.

E: That was recorded on Quarterflash's old 8-track!

M: The quality is already there! We just had fun with it, as much fun as we possibly could. We didn't waste that much time. We just did it. Some songs came out okay, but some weren't that good. It was probably the least stressful [session] ever.

Was that in his house?

M: In his basement. He carpeted every section of the room. We helped him put it up. I guess that was part of the payment. It turned out as fine as it could be, I guess. We did six songs.

Was that the tape that you had for sale?

M: It sold real well 'til we stopped making copies. I don't even know where the master is. I hear that it's being played in Alaska.

What more can you ask?

J: For some Eskimos up there.

M: Some guy said, "I have a friend who's a DJ in Alaska and he has your tape and he plays it all the time."

So what happened after that?

J: There was one more at Ben's. That was right when I was still in, right before I quit.

E: You were thrown out.

J: Oh, that's right. There were just three songs.

M: We didn't do anything with them; we didn't put vocals on them. So then, a little while later we changed drummers. At the time our friend in San Francisco, who did our first tape, Dave Ayer [who drummed for Samiam and Porch] called up and said I'm gonna come visit you guys and you should record. He suggested that it should be something worth putting out and it should be this, this, this and this. So we're, "Uhh, okay." We ended up giving him the list of all the studios in town and he called them all. He found one of the only places in Oregon with a 2" [16-track] deck. So we set up a time there, it was $25 an hour, and we planned it out for three days, so many songs, in and out. I went and checked it out before we actually went in there. It's really a cool studio, a whole basement. The control room is in one room and all the recording is done in a converted garage and it's all carpeted. There's a shower-type thing that's all cemented and that's where they put the bass. He had great equipment, great mics. So Dave flew up, with all his drums, and we practiced the songs the night before we went in (another big mistake). Eight songs he had never heard before. We went in there and it was immediately tense. This guy [the engineer] had never done anything remotely close to rock. He did ballad-type country music. He played us a little of it and it was all pristine sounding. At one point, after we had been recording, he so much as admitted that, "It's all alien to me. I don't know what you guys want" and backed away from the board. That was after lots of other stuff. So we went in there the first day and that was all tense and weird 'cause it always is. Laying down the tracks for eight songs, trying to get them right, everyone's getting on each other's nerves. We spent the next day doing vocals and mixing and the third day we were mixing. It sounded okay, but we couldn't quite get what we wanted.

It sounds like the engineer didn't help much in that department.

M: He's this nervous guy and he was always scratching his hair, coming in and fixing something and something would be going wrong with his board and he'd be behind it, switching stuff. I guess that's kind of normal but...

Not always...

M: He was stumped a lot of times. He didn't know what was wrong with his equipment and he'd get really mad. Dave was like, "I've never seen anyone that unprofessional before." He freaked us out. We mixed the last two songs while he just stood there. We moved the knobs and stuff. We got out of there and paid $750 for the whole thing, not including the tape. In the end we got a CD made off the DAT and couldn't stand any of the songs on it. Finally I picked four that I sort of liked and when I transferred from the CD to cassette tape I boosted the levels.

It livened it up a little?

M: Yeah. There were only four songs I could stand of the eight songs that we did. Everyone said it sounded fine. Joe thought it sounded great.

E: I didn't think it was that good.

M: I thought it was okay.

[To Claire] What do you think of it?

C: I was not happy with it at all and I think a lot of it was our fault. Just feeling a little rushed. We didn't have a chance to relax, which I think is really important.

E: I wish somebody else would pay for it!

That didn't sound like fun. What was the next recording session?

M: After that I hated recording so much that I wouldn't do it. We did "Union City Blues" with Tony Lash [producer/musician with Heatmiser] for the *Undercover* record. We did that in a night.

C: That was good.

M: He knew what the hell he was doing!

He knows what a guitar-heavy rock band sounds like.

M: And I completely trust him.

Where was that done? The Heatmiser house?

M: I guess they rented a house.

Where they recorded their album [*Mic City Sons*].

M: We were one of the last things done there and then they tore the studio down. It [the recording] turned out fine.

E: The vocals took the longest.

Are those double-tracked?

C: Yeah.

M: He [Tony] was great.

E: He's not very talkative!

M: We just did whatever he said. And we weren't paying for it.

C: You have to pay to talk to him!

M: We didn't have anything to do with the mixing either.

C: He did the whole thing. We just got a tape. They just said, "This is pretty much it."

J: But the [finished] record sounds better.

C: I was really scared.

M: It was scary because the tape sounds different than the record. I think they worked on it more.

Plus when they master the record they can EQ it and stuff. So the next session would be your most recent one.

M: Yeah we just did a demo tape.

C: That was fun wasn't it?

M: Yeah

E: It was rushed again.

C: It wasn't that rushed.

E: If we had the opportunity, I would do it all over again. I wouldn't have saved any of it. It could all be better.

C: You can say that about anything.

M: I just remember it being very hot.

C: Yeah, well, it was hot.

M: It was in the basement and it should've been cooler, but it felt hotter.

You're probably trapped in a room with the door shut.

M: Yeah.

J: We did it with Mark [Edwards].

M: At Fresh Tracks. It's an okay studio.

E: He's a very nice guy.

J: We appreciate everything he did for us.

E: We don't have very much money.

M: That wasn't free. It was $10 or $12 an hour and then we paid Mark.

For a 16-track? That's a really good deal. $12 will usually only get you an 8-track studio.

E: He kind of "donated" his time so there was only so much you could expect from him. I think we tortured him.

Does he talk to you guys still?

M: Oh yeah. We'd been friends with him long before we planned to do this recording. He was always offering. It turned out pretty good.

Is this something you're gonna use to shop around to labels?

M: We sent it off to Mercury Records.

C: They called us.

M: I don't know why they called us.

E: Is that all we did was two songs? See we didn't have much time.

M: Yeah we did.

E: We could've done more.

M: I think it was good that we just focused on two songs.

What sorts of things about recording have bothered you the most?

M: I think we really need to work with someone who knows what they're doing. That takes away all the pressure.

It sounds like when you worked with Tony Lash you came in and did your thing and, boom, you were done.

M: And I just knew it was gonna be okay. It's fine if you want to do it yourself, you just need time.

E: It was nice to have Tony do it all, but experimenting more would also be fun. That wasn't an option. Partly because of the song we were doing, but also because he was doing a favor for us.

Any other comments on recording? You guys ever thought of buying a 4-track?

M: We have one.

Do you play around with that much?

C: No. Basically we don't know how to record. Those guys set it up so we just have a room mic for taping practices.

M: I could see how if you put it in the right place...

That place doesn't really exist.

J: I think we don't take the time to learn how to use the 4-track.

M: I think we want to concentrate more on writing songs than learning how to record them.

Paul Marotta

by Larry Crane

's John Morton

Where were you in 1973? Maybe you were a 10-year-old kid like me, or maybe a bit older and checking out your older siblings' record collections. Hell, maybe you weren't even born yet. I bet you weren't running around Cleveland in a VW bus full of recording gear and instruments. I'll also bet you weren't ever credited with being in a "punk" band before punk even existed.

Paul Marotta was there. He's a man of many talents and contradictions. Maybe he helped usher in the early art-punk scene in Cleveland, but now he manages the not-for-profit New World Records: a classical, jazz, folk, and world-beat label. He created some of the most whacked out music ever heard, but he'll suggest that musicianship is a very important quality. He's also considerably gracious and a blast to talk to! Consider this quote from Paul (from the recently released *Those Were Different Times* CD booklet on Scat Records):

"Our personalities, musical and otherwise, forced us to work in a vacuum. There were no record labels that would pay for recordings, no "producers" to help us get a sound, no engineers to teach us about recording. Low-cost home recording equipment wasn't invented yet. None of the bands even had a guy hanging out to do sound for us at our gigs. Consequently, the master tapes I used were either live cassettes (the mid '70s was still relatively early in the development of cassette recording technology), basement tapes, and some studio recordings; all of widely varying quality."

So what was the gig you just had? Was that a Styrenes gig?

Umm, no. I also play bass in a swinging bachelor-type band. It's a nice, easy gig and I just like to play. We did a CD that just came out and that's nice too. Then, last night, we did a Styrenes session at a 24-track studio here.

No way.

We did four new songs.

Who all's in the band at this point?

Well, Mike Hudson [of the Pagans] is still singing with us. The bass player 's Al Margolis and the guitar player's a friend of mine. I'd played with his band in Germany and he came in for the week so he played guitar with us. That was piano, guitar, bass, drums and vocals.

Did you have a good time with it?

We had a great time. It was a good, hard session. One of the problems that I have leading Styrenes is that I play the piano and that means that most small studios don't have pianos. If I want to play a piano that's got any kind of tone to it I have to go to an expensive studio. That's okay. There's a 24-track here, it's a big studio, and the rate's $65 an hour including engineer. You know, we cut four songs last night and we're gonna have to redo the vocals, but essentially we're almost done. The session and tape, together, cost me about $900. It's not bad.

It should sound like a piano, not like some strange, muffled, over EQ'd thing.

Right.

Well, this conversation's mostly gonna be about the ... *Different Times* CD. It mentioned in the liner notes that you pulled up in the microbus with all this recording gear. Was that in '74?

Actually in '73.

What kind of stuff did you have back then? I think a lot of our readers can't understand that you couldn't even get 4-track cassette decks back then.

Right! At that time, I would have brought a tube reel-to-reel deck, 1/4" 7 1/2 ips. A cassette deck. Four small mixers. Cables. Mostly lots of microphones and cables; with all that crud, you've got to patch it all. That's where it starts to get weird. We used to use Shure Vocalmasters as recording mixers and one of the advantages to that particular unit was you didn't need to have speakers plugged into it. Most PA amplifiers, if you don't have a load on it, it blows out. The Vocalmaster was always cool because you didn't need to have speakers plugged into it.

So you could just use it as a mixer.

Like you said, people forget that those things didn't exist. A board that had line outs was unusual.

Would you record a lot of stuff as a practice session and a home recording session?

What I liked to do a lot was to double-tape microphones [together] so that the band would play as if they were regularly practicing and not really pay attention to the recording and not try to worry about the sound. Then there'd be a second microphone that was essentially taped right to it. That feed would go into the recording. That way, if the singer needed to get on top of the microphone for rehearsal, he could do so without blowing up the recording.

So you would have that running to a separate mixer and have that going to your reel-to-reel?

Right.

You see that in older films of bands playing where they used to do that before they figured out mic splitting.

All the stuff that's been out by the Electric Eels was recorded that way.

Totally homemade. Did you know any other people doing stuff like that back then?

Around that time there was another group... they were more a bunch of jazz-bo's. They called themselves Moonbeams or Moondream or something like that. They actually had a 4-track Ampex and I thought that was pretty cool. We bought our first 4-track Teac 3440 in 1975 and I think it ran us about $1700. In 1975 dollars, man that was expensive!

When you got a hold of that thing did that open up a world for you there?

Oh yeah. We did all the things that any goofy person does when they get their first 4-track. The way we ping-ponged was; I would take the four tracks and mix it down to two. We had a pretty good Tascam mixdown machine. It was a half-track with a split preamp section and came in a large, rolling, console. So we'd mix down to the 2-track and then I would take that exact same reel and put it back onto the 4-track and it would open up two more tracks. The pitch was a little funky, but you could essentially get six tracks with only one reduction.

That's pretty amazing.

A lot of the stuff on the Styrenes CD was recorded like that. Some of the overdubbed stuff that's coming out on the *Different Times* record was done on two reel-to-reels or two cassettes bounced back and forth for each overdub.

You're playing it back and playing to it and mixing them together.

Mixing them together. Of course, you don't get remix capabilities!

I know later on you guys had some sessions on 1" 8-track. Was that Earthman Studios?

No. Earthman was our 4-track! The 1" 8-track was at Owl in Columbus. That was a 1" Scully... actually it was the 1" machine from Woodstock. That's a really cool way to record. Even in the '80s there was a studio here that ran 1" 8-track at 30 ips. It was really quiet, really nice. I've got some of those masters and I have no place to play them back any more. You can put the 1" tape on a 1" 16-track and they'll play back pretty good.

You gang up the channels.

I think one of the tracks on the *Different Times* collection says it was recorded at Owl and remixed at Noise New York. That's exactly what we did. That was a 1" 16-track.

I've heard you can play a 16-track 2" on a 24-track machine. You can gang up certain tracks and actually mix it.

I don't know if I would do it with the bass guitar tracks but most of the overdub tracks you can usually squeeze a little space out. The 1" 8-track... they had a homemade board and it was a little noisy. They were somewhere in between wanting to do a recording studio and wanting to do live sound. Jack of all trades, master of none sort of thing. Their mic technique was not particularly great and the studio vibe... it was hard to work there. The isolation booths didn't have glass in between them. The piano was 75 feet away from the band in a room where you can't hear or see anything.

It's not set up to be comfortable.

My overriding philosophy of recording has been that the recording process should never diminish the musicians' enjoyment. It's almost a cliché, but it really happens. The musicians should just play and not pay attention to the wires and everything. That's the engineer's job to do that. Which is why so much of the stuff we recorded didn't come out good. The main reason we were there was to play and make music. It wasn't necessary to make recordings. We were playing way too loud. It's ridiculous to have a band rehearsing in a basement using the size amplifiers we did. That was part of the '70s. The idea of playing through a Fender Princeton amp would have been offensive. That's probably what we should have been doing. Instead of having Vox Super Beatles we should have had Vox Pacemakers, with one 10" speaker and 18 watts. It would have been plenty!

But no one wants to do that.

I'm playing in a band (Amoeba Raft Boy) with John Morton from the Eels. We've got small Marshalls; 25 watts. They're great. Any place you play that's big enough is gonna mic you any way and we've got the stage sound down, together, finally. It took us 25 fuckin' years. We finally don't overpower each other. We did a cut on the *Cle* sampler that we recorded in our rehearsal studio. The studio has a Mackie board and it's got enough sends that we recorded right to DAT and it came out okay.

That's an economical way to go. With all the gear you used to use, what kind of mics and headphones did you have?

The mics were AKG D1000s or Shure SM 57s and 58s. Around '76 or '77 Audio Technica brought in this line of battery-powered condenser mics. I forget the model numbers, but they were great! You couldn't phantom power them but that was okay because the boards that we had didn't have phantom power. They used to eat batteries like crazy. Boy, what a difference that made for recording the vocal track.

Just for the clarity...

Uh huh. They were cheap; just 60 or 70 bucks. If they still made them here now, I'd buy some. People ask me all the time what kind of mic you can use for cheap vocal recording and there isn't such a thing, really.

Everything's got its fault.

But the Shure SM 57 is still such a standard. We didn't bother with headphones. In the basement where we recorded the Mirrors and early Styrenes stuff - I walled off a small area where I put the mixers and keyboards and sometimes I would play, walled off from the band so I could monitor a little bit. I had some Koss headphones that were so tight on your ears that it was painful. It was good for playing with the band 'cause you didn't hear the band. I used these really cheap Radio Shack mixers with no preamps.

Those little black ones with the four faders?

Yeah. I used to hook a speaker send through them so I could run the monitor back out through the PA so they could hear what's going on.

We're delving into some very primitive techniques that all worked. So later you got the 4-track.

We bought some Tascam equipment. We went from the model 2 to the model 3 to model 5 and had a couple of model 5's ganged together.

The mixers?

Yeah. That worked pretty good. We used those for a live PA as well. At one point, where we started to work with the acoustic piano a little more, in a live setting, we bought tri-amped stereo hookup for the PA. That was, again, carrying ridiculous amounts of equipment with us. We were able to bring acoustic piano in a punk rock setting and actually make it work. We had bass bins, mid range horns and tweeters. Everything powered by separate amplifiers of course.

You'd haul all this stuff around to every gig?

We used to haul the piano around. It was very different. Clubs didn't have PAs then. You were expected to come in to a show and do four of five sets.

There's probably a lot of bands that wouldn't bother if that was the case these days.

That's for sure. Here in New York, without any transportation it'd be impossible.

Did you ever look into getting some 8-track gear?

No. We moved to New York in 1979. When we had our studio in Cleveland we were renting it out and we were able to get $25 an hour for a 4-track. That was in '78. By 1979 and '80 we came to New York and 16-track time you could get for $10 an hour. Nobody was gonna book our studio. We came here with these big plans and after four months we realized, "This is bullshit!" The truth is that I sold all the recording gear. The technology was changing so fast it was the last business on earth I wanted to be in. Although, in one of the most harebrained things I've ever done, we bought a 1" 8-track, model number 3. Literally, this was the third one that Ampex built in 1969 and they built it for the Motown studios. They built two of them for Atlantic and then this one for Motown. When Motown moved to LA they sold it at an auction. We had this idea that we were gonna open up an all-tube studio. This was in the late '80s. All the electronics were custom made by Ampex. The thing generated enough heat that you could heat your living room with it. The signal to noise ratio was 55 dB. I think cassettes are better than that. It was pretty cool but it never happened. I couldn't find anybody to work on it. Jaime [Klimek] still has it. We bought a tube board. In the '80s there was so much tube equipment that the professional places were just filled with this stuff. Anyway, the last stuff that we did a few years ago was done at this place in New Jersey that had the Abbey Road board. Lenny Kravitz owns the studio. He's a tube recording freak and he bought all the Abbey Road stuff. That was kinda cool.

How did it sound?

It sounds okay. Essentially that was his toy. He didn't like to let people use it. They had other stuff. Let's see... Tape configurations were a little bit different in the '70s. We had a lot of flaking going on. I work at a label now, and they started in 1976. The tapes that we did in '76 we're having a big problem with now when we reissue them on CD. They almost all have to be baked. Stuff I have from the early '70s I have no problem playing.

I heard that had to do with whale oil.

I heard that too. It could be 'cause they were experimenting with different tape configurations.

At some point in the '70s they stopped using whale oil as an adhesive. When they started using synthetics to hold the tape to the backing it was actually not working as well. It's a strange story. So you're able to bake a lot of those for the label?

Actually, they just plain bake them.

Kinda low for a few hours...

Yeah! And you don't really know if it works until you make a pass. We haven't lost anything yet though. What else can I tell you? Mic'ing technique?

Sure.

Well, we didn't use a lot of microphones 'cause it would just make more and more bleed. The idea was to use as few as possible. We had a lot of success mic'ing drums with just two microphones... usually placed fairly close to the bass drum rather than overhead. Usually, with younger, more energetic type drummers, they're bashing the fuck out of the cymbals anyway. They're cutting through. We even bothered to do it in stereo.

So you put them down low?

And the vocal mics end up picking up a lot of the bleed of the drums. There was always so much going on. The hardest thing to get was any good low end. It was really easy to get a good distorted guitar sound, but to get some kind of clarity on a bass drum...

Did you try taking a line out on the bass?

Just mics. It really was hit or miss. Hell, there were no compressors around! We never found anything that really worked that we could keep coming back to over and over again. If you listen to the Electric Eels stuff, in particular, we'd started to get some sense of what we were doing recording wise, but there's a distinct difference in the groups of tracks. Five songs sound one way and four songs sound the other way and they were recorded a few days apart. They didn't do anything different – they had the same amplifiers!

As far as outboard gear, you guys were lucky if you could patch in a guitar effect.

There was no patching. I had an early DBX unit that was sold for stereos. It was made to be patched into home stereos and was designed to be a DBX noise reduction unit, but it worked great as a compressor.

Just to squeeze it a little?

What we used it for was to eliminate background noise, like a noise gate, on the vocal tracks. I just got rid of it no more than six months ago. A strange-looking little device with controls that made no sense whatsoever. No LED's or anything. I'm trying to remember why we bought that. Somebody must have seen us coming and said, "Try this guys." There were no reverb units. Echoplex. The MXR phase shifters had just come out! Fuzztone. That's what you had for effects was a Fuzztone.

Do you have a cassette 4-track at home these days?

No. It's funny, 'cause I've been looking and thinking about doing it. For home recording now, I'm not sure what I would buy. I was ready to buy a 4-track cassette, but I thought maybe I should buy an 8-track cassette. There's these MiniDisc recorders... apparently you can do all the real digital editing and the cross-fading on them. They're about $1000. Should I wait a year and see how technology changes? Then I'm looking at the Yamaha 4-track cassette and it looks pretty good. $600 and you can record on all four channels. Also, I've got the concept down so I really think things through in my head without needing the 4-track.

You've written and played music for a number of years. You also seem to be the one who had the most training in music. You knew about recording but also played a few different instruments.

Well. The musical training is somewhat accidental. This is probably a theoretical thing, and a discussion that could go on forever, but, personally, I do not believe it is ever wrong to have knowledge. I think that one of the biggest fallacies is when I hear rock players say, "Oh, I don't want to learn to play good because that'll make me think stupid thoughts." I think that's just so bogus. I think that culture has bought into that. Because you can play good doesn't mean you have to. I have no problem throwing out every bit of knowledge I have to play a one-note guitar solo, but I want to be able to do a run, from the bottom of the guitar to the top, if I choose to. If you don't have the skill you can't do that. I think that if your physical technique limits your mental vision then that's a problem. I still play hard-edged, simple, two-chord stuff and I also still take piano lessons.

But I think you find a lot of players that can't step back and play a Lou Reed song or something. They think it's dumb and smirk at the simplicity of it.

One of the guys who plays in the bachelor pad band I play in is always making rude comments about rock players. He drives me crazy. I can't stand that attitude. The guy can't play a fucking major chord. He's gotta throw a 9th into it. I really believe that the bass guitar should just play the root. I think finger popping on the bass is the worst thing that could ever have happened. It's a sound I don't ever want to hear in my entire life. Walking bass lines, I think, are bullshit. Keep it simple and get out of the way.

Switch to guitar, buddy. Back to your current job... What is your job there anyway?

I'm the managing director of the company. I still do some producing. I tend to do the things that are really weird. The label I work for is a classical/jazz label and a not-for-profit foundation. The PBS of the record business. We do a lot of classical and jazz but we also do folk, bluegrass, Native American and Americana. I produced a session of "shape note" singers. It's a kind of rural, religious music that's open harmonies, a capella style and it's done in a community setting where a different person is called up to lead every single song. They sit in a square, divided up by their vocal parts. I produced that. I'm producing a 19th century brass band that uses 19th century instruments. They have a 24" snare drum and a 32" bass drum. I'm doing that in about two months in Michigan. I'm not sure

how the hell I'm gonna record them because they make so much sound. It was made to be played outside. Every city in America, in the 19th century, had a brass band that used to come out and play on Sunday morning. They kind of wanted to go into a studio and I'm thinking, "Maybe we should just go right outside, dammit!" I'm not sure what we're gonna do. They did music in the baseball show that Ken Burns did and that was done in the studio. These are academic fans and they got a taste of studio life and the "big time" and they thought that was pretty cool. I have booked a classical engineering company called Soundbite to record them 2-track digital. I'm not sure yet what we're gonna do. It might be just two microphones. It depends how much they want to walk around, 'cause they like to walk when they play.

This sounds like a nightmare!

I enjoy this kind of stuff. The regular classical recording bores me.

It's very structured...

It's structured and it's just, God, you make so many takes and you edit it together in so many small pieces. Uggh... It's too tedious for me.

With the shape note singers... did you do it live on location?

Yeah. It was a church in rural Alabama down by the Florida border. I contracted a heavy metal PA company to come out and give me an electrical feed off the power line 'cause there was no good electricity in the church. They didn't even have a telephone. We built a small metal scaffold around the edges of the church up over the top for microphone poles. It was essentially three microphones. We had a stereo cross-pair and then there was one for the leader of each song. Being a bunch of New Yorkers coming down to a rural town, I really wanted to be inconspicuous.

That's great that you still get to play with recording. It's a big part of your life.

I can't say I've got any complaints about that. I suppose if I got to drive a Mercedes and made a lot of money that'd be the icing on the cake. That's okay... I get to learn interesting things.

So yeah, check out Those were Different Times, *a compilation of tracks by the Electric Eels, The Mirrors, and the Styrenes, all bands Paul was involved in. Paul Marotta can be contacted through Scat Records, 6226 Southwood, St Louis, MO 63105.*

A Quick One With the Revelers

by Mike McDonald

The Revelers are a rare treat: A band in the true sense of the word. An "us against the world" attitude pervades everything: their beer selection, their songwriting, their dress, their live shows, their equipment, their van, and their ideas about recording. Andrej and Joel both sing and play guitar, Tommy drums, and George plays bass. Whenever we spoke about recording over the past few months, it always reminded me of a *Tape Op* article. Hence, the interview:

Let's see... You guys have recorded on 24-track, 16-track, 8-track analoge, 8-track ADAT, and cassette 4-track, unless you've done something else I'm not aware of. Which do you prefer? Do you have a preference at all?

Joel: I don't know... There's certain things that I like about all the different recording experiences.

Andrej: [laughing] You're the perfect guy to answer that question! "There's certain things I like about everything".

Joel: Ummm... Ahhhh...

Well, you seem to like your 4-track recordings more, from what I understand.

Joel: Yeah!

Why so?

Tommy: I think that we're more relaxed recording in our own space, and I think that's what comes across when we are recording like that. We're more confident with doing 4-track.

Andrej: Well that could just be not being on the clock... A money thing, you know? It's just in the back of your mind. Maybe that's what it is. I don't know, it's weird. It is a different atmosphere for sure.

Joel: The 4-track recordings seem to sound more like what I, personally anyway, imagine us sounding like, whereas once you get into a 24-track studio like Kramer's, it's just so... Ahhhh...

Tommy: They're intimidating! So much you can do!

Joel: Plus, you're standing out there in the studio, playing your guitar through this amplifier, and it sounds, you know, great! Then you hear it back on the tape, and it doesn't sound good at all. Whereas on 4-track...

Andrej: I don't know if that's true, though. I mean, that stuff sounds pretty much the way it sounds; you just don't get it all muddied up and distorted. Maybe that's the thing.

You think 4-track is more forgiving?

Andrej: I think it blends everything together.

Tommy: Plus, I think what happens is that a lot of times, if you really have the time to work with the final mix, then 24-track is the way to go. I think we've had bad experiences where we've had all these options, but not enough time to spend to really get the sounds we were looking for.

Bad experiences just because you didn't have the cash?

Tommy: Sure, sure.

Andrej: It, also, could be that the style of music that we play just doesn't sound good like some other stuff sounds great, like done really separated and clean. I keep thinking, I don't know what to compare it to... You know how you see a realistic painting of a cheesy landscape? No matter how good it is, it's cheesy. I think that if you screw it up a little, maybe you take the cheese out of it. If you polished us up, we'd just look like any other band.

Do you think that having no producer or anyone to tell you what to do has helped you?

Tommy: I think that's helped us quite a bit.

Joel: Yeah.

Tommy: Situations that we've been in, working with you included, when we've been able to say exactly what we want have been good. You came and saw us live a lot of times, other people have very seldom seen us live.

They don't know what you're going for?

Andrej: I don't know if that makes much difference. I think you're just like us. Other people we've worked with, they didn't like this kind of music particularly. They might have seen the quality in what we do, but it's not their kind of music.

What do you think the role of the producer should be? I mean, if you don't like someone getting on your shit, do you think a producer should just sit back and let you twist any knob you want?

Andrej: What the producer should do is to get people to buy the record because his name's on it! [Laughs] That's the role of the producer!

Tommy: You know, I think that the producer is there to make sure things don't get messed up, but...

Andrej: Keep the beer fresh, make sure you never run out of cigarettes...

George: The tour guide!

Tommy: I don't know when things are getting to the point when things are getting messed up in the mix, or when they sound just crazy. I know what I want to hear and if I'm not getting that, then it's the producer's job to remedy that.

Andrej: But the thing is that some of the things you try to do aren't possible. You can't make a band's sound live, sound that way on record.

No, no. I think you can. I personally haven't accomplished it yet.

Andrej: With almost any band that you would say is a good rock band, their records and their live shows are almost completely different things. They make great records and they play great live, but they're not the same thing.

See... That's interesting. The goal where I try to go, and I don't know if one can achieve it, but you guys are such a good live band that I want to capture that on tape.

Andrej: Can't be done, can't be done, can't be done!

So you don't even want to try it?

Andrej: We have been trying it for the last six years! It can't be done. We're approaching the problem all wrong, that's what I think. When we rocked super hard on some of our records, and you listen to it... It's like we're taping!

So you don't think live intensity shows up on tape in the slightest bit?

Andrej: I think they're two different things. Look at Elvis and Chuck Berry and stuff. They were just able to make records that sound exciting. There's some talent to that. But, you can't compete with the sheer volume of air that you move when it's a real drum set and a real amplifier that you're listening to.

So what other records do you like?

Andrej: I like the way that the Studio One stuff sounds.

Tommy: Yeah. They did all the hot bands back in the '60s. A lot of the ska, the rock steady.

Andrej: Those records sound like those guys didn't have a clue about the technical stuff, they just made it sound cool. They don't sound like any records today's pros make.

Tommy: They're more like Stax or Motown.

Andrej: They have uniqueness to them. Today, everybody makes records that sound like everybody else's records. Then, there was a clear difference between Phil Spector and Atlantic.

There's a formula now.

George: When you go into a studio now and you say, "I want to do this." They say, "No, this is the way we do this." Like, "This is the way we do drums."

Joel: Unfortunately, if you don't have that much experience in the studio yourself, you can't tell somebody what to do. You don't know what to do to make it sound different.

Andrej: One thing gets popular, and then everything sounds like that. Nobody seems to put their own stamp on stuff.

What current bands do you guys like?

Tommy: Guided by Voices.

Andrej: I like *Crooked Rain* by Pavement.

Joel: I like the Flaming Lips' records. They're a lot more creative than a lot of the bands out there.

It sounds like, as in a live situation, you'd rather hear someone go out on limb on a record as far as production quality. It may fall on its face in some aspects of quality, but if it works overall, at least it's exciting to listen to.

Andrej: Exactly. I read someplace where Thelonious Monk was talking about playing. He said that a lot of the time, it's just accidents, and you kind of build on them. I think recording has got to be the same thing. You've got to be that open to accidentally come upon something. It doesn't seem like people do that anymore.

George: Some stuff can only happen with the time spent in the studio. With all the records I've been involved with, it's been like, "We've got this much money, we've got this much time."

Andrej: There's such a huge difference between major label budgets and the budgets that independent, regular people trying to make records have. To major labels, spending $10,000 on a band is cheap!

Then how come the major stuff sounds so generic compared to the stuff that has no money?

Andrej: The bands that do have the power to do something crazy, don't.

THE REVELERS
The Afterbirth of Cool 7"
On Top CD, Better Get Hit in Your Soul CD (Inbred)

It's rare that I get sent some stuff out of the blue and it's any good. Sorry, but true. The Revelers are a Cleveland band I've never heard of but they're a great '60s style mod/pop/garage band. The 7" was recorded on a Fostex 4 track and sounds surprisingly good. The *On Top* CD was recorded on a single ADAT machine and sounds rough and good and the more recent CD was done in four days at Noise New Jersey with Kramer. They're currently working with Mike McDonald so I'm sure it'll be cool. Fun. –Larry Crane

Martin Phillipps of the Chills

by Larry Crane with Richard Baluyut

Karl Buckley

First off, let me state that The Chills are one of my favorite pop bands ever. When I heard there was a new album (*Sunburnt*) coming out, and a tour to follow, I was overjoyed. Then I thought, "Hey, why not interview Martin for *Tape Op*?" Eventually, there I was, a wee bit tipsy after a few too many pints of Pabst, doing an interview after the Martin Phillipps and The Chills show here in Portland. The intensity with which he delved into the subjects at hand startled me at first, but then I realized that this band, off and on and in its many permutations, has been a big part of his life for the last 16 years. On with the interview!

I'd like to start talking about the new stuff, but I think we'll just skip to the chase. There's one question that's been bugging me. It popped up with the Barbara Manning snippet that we did in the first issue. She brought up the *Brave Words* incident. She said it had taken her a long time to connect Mayo Thompson to Red Krayola and the production on your record. I remembered that you had mentioned in interviews that you had wanted-ed to remix it and call it *Braver Words*.

The problem with *Brave Words* is that it was done really, really fast. It was recorded and mixed in about two weeks. Obviously, that's the first album after 7 years, plus that band was about 2 1/2 months old at that stage. In all aspects, that record was really done fast. We basically just recorded things as they had been live. Then we went back and sort of went overboard trying to redo some stuff to make it sound as big as we'd been hearing it.

Was that you guys or Mayo?

Everybody. We probably did some technical things, but I'm not sure how we could've made it better. The main problem we had was that the pressing was absolutely atrocious. The mastering...

Of the vinyl?

Yes, and also the CD. They're mastered terrible – it's mushy. A difference needed to be made at the studio. I didn't know as much then as I know now. When we did the *Heavenly Pop Hits* compilation last year, two tracks from *Brave Words* were remixed, "Look for the Good in Others" and "Wet Blanket." That was a sort of test run for the others .

I didn't get to hear that yet. [Later I did - the songs sound much better]

There's also a new vocal on "Wet Blanket" as well. I sung it really badly at the time. I sang them [originally] with reverb in the headphones – "Everything sounds great!" The band played really strongly on the recording, but there are things of much higher priority to be done before [remixing *Brave Words*].

I always liked the songs on that album but thought the sound was a bit off. Richard said he thought it sounded fine.

Richard: I think it has incredible sound, that record. It's so... different.

Martin: It was that. People who knew the band live were the most disappointed.

R: I just come from hearing that and not being familiar with your other records. It seems like, through the murk, you can find these things. It may be a little more difficult, but it's more rewarding.

M: There's quite a unique quality, like listening to AM radio, but that's not really how...

R: It's not like a bad demo. It's a more interesting sound than that.

It definitely worked and captivated a lot of people. With *Sunburnt*, you worked with Craig Leon, who has a famous pedigree, although a lot of people don't know who he is. It was done in England. Had you played the songs with a full band before going over to record?

Some of it. I'd been writing ever since the band broke up in '92, so there was 2 or 3 years of material to choose from. All the darker stuff got put to one side [*Shadow Ballads* is the working title] that may hopefully end up as an extra CD with the next album. It's a plan of mine, anyway. We just realized – myself, Craig and the record company – that it'd be crazy to come out with a dark album after four years, especially following *Soft Bomb*. I wanted something that was much more positive and optimistic. Once we decided that was what it was going to be, it was pretty easy [to see] which songs fit together well. Probably about a third of them I worked on with Jonathan [Armstrong/drums], 'cause he's been with me now for a couple of years and Steven Shaw [the bass player] and the keyboardist, Dominic Blaazer. We realized it wasn't worth taking Dominic over 'cause I was going to be playing the keyboard parts myself and sequencing them. The rhythm section came over about two weeks after I got there only to be stuck at Heathrow airport immigration and promptly flown on the next flight back to New Zealand. We had to come up with ideas, that's how we ended up with the two Daves. Dave Mattacks, drummer for Fairport Convention and Dave Gregory from XTC, who's actually a keyboardist, but claimed to me that he played rudimentary bass.

He played a lot of guitar on XTC stuff.
He's a real guitar maniac and he's got a huge knowledge. He's the one that put me on to the Charvel guitar.

Did you and Craig Leon do a lot of pre-production? Picking through the songs and arranging stuff?
I was there about two weeks. I had my own rhythm section tuned up; we spent at least a week and a half trying different approaches to different songs. We had to refer closely to my home demos.

For arrangement?
A lot of it is actually close to what I had. Which, with hindsight, I think forced my hand to make a really solid record.

Like having too many options?
I'm sure if the band had come up, it would once again have a diluting effect. The two Daves couldn't come in at the same time, even though they had worked as a rhythm section previously. So they came in for two days each.

Did you track with the drummer first?
Yes! They're both great rhythmic people. They really enjoyed it and it worked out well.

The album previous to that, *Soft Bomb*, was done with Gavin MacKillop producing. Where was that done?
That was done in Los Angeles at Master Control Studios.

To me, I think it's one of your best sounding records.
I really like it. A lot of people never really gave it a chance 'cause they were looking for another *Submarine Bells*. That's a reasonably dark album. Actually, that's one point why the records have been done overseas (especially the last one, where right up until two weeks before we started was supposed to be recorded in New Zealand). It actually ended up being cheaper to fly the entire band to England than to fly the producer and his partner to New Zealand.

How come?
Because the cost of studios in England is just so much cheaper with all the competition. New Zealand has some good ones, but they're overpriced for what they are.

Supply and demand.
Basically. The top line studios there charge top line fees even though they're actually B or C studios. So, we just couldn't afford it. There was also free accommodations thrown in with the studio we did it in. We've been trying really hard to record in New Zealand for ages 'cause we've never done an album there. Probably the next one will be, because there's such a tiny budget.

Were you happy to make an album and not be in a US studio?
I think it's a real "indie" myth that somehow you go to an American studio and make an American sounding record. It totally comes down to who you're working with. In the studio, once you close the door, you could be anywhere. *Soft Bomb* sounds like it does because of other factors and it sort of got out of control in the production sense.

Do you think things got out of hand?
In a way it's not... actually it sounds quite amazing, especially when you crank it up on a good stereo... but it's not what I've been trying to catch with The Chills. It's somebody else's angle on it. I made decisions with that album where I felt I didn't know enough about the recording process to justify throwing away tons of extra things. Better to let the people who've got expertise. Through that record I realized that I did have a reasonably good ear and a surprising amount of knowledge built up from the years. So come *Sunburnt*, I was a lot more active and it's really paid off.

It doesn't sound like someone took it and ran off in the wrong direction.
Craig Leon, and his partner Cassell Webb, she's got the title of Production Coordinator. She basically makes sure we're free to concentrate. Between the two of them, they made it the most enjoyable recording process I've ever been in. That was really good and Craig really encouraged me to stick with the original arrangements that I had done. A lot of the keyboard sounds were a cheap little Casio organ I picked up once during a writing sabbatical. There's a certain sort of glee using this reasonably big budget recording and this little Casio organ. It really works. There's this really beautiful drum sound and this cheesy organ. I love contrast.

Your earliest stuff was done with Doug Hood and Chris Knox.
Mainly Doug. Chris kinda hovered around and threw in the odd suggestion. He was a really good balancing influence 'cause Doug would always have the tendency to make things sound more professional. Chris was a really good one to say, "Stop, you don't need this overdub." Sometimes he's wrong, too. I was always satisfied to prove Chris Knox wrong on a point.

There's a certain feeling on that old stuff... a kind of innocence.
The interesting thing is, even at the time, especially in the early '80s, I was listening to a lot of '60s garage rock and we were by no means trying to do a sort of retro recording. We turned out the best possible recordings we could. People think we were trying to make it sound like that. If we'd had access to a full studio we would've gone straight in and it probably would've sounded pretty much the same, I imagine. The point was, we could be talked into a better studio to try and catch the band. It's this ongoing battle about whether it works or not. I don't feel it's a mistake to go to the most expensive studio in the world and capture your raw sound, if that's what you're trying to do. I've been lead astray, or lead myself astray on some of the records, but I still believe, and I think *Sunburnt* proves more than the others, that you can catch that raw sound, but in a really well recorded way. As opposed to having a "try-hard" indie recording. It really irritates me when people are still doing indie recordings after 10 years. It's not honest anymore. It's as phoney as somebody going to a big studio and losing sight of it. I always try to encourage people not to be scared of big studios; just trust their ears and demand what they know they can do.

And you've proven it a few times. How was it working with Gary Smith [on *Submarine Bells*]?
I've learned an awful lot from all the producers I've worked with. It's probably Gary and Gavin MacKillop where I was challenged to explain things or justify why I wanted things a certain way, because they had their own ideas about recording

things and what worked. A lot of people were disappointed with *Submarine Bells* for the fact that the guitars were so cleaned up and mixed back. The nature of The Chills live, maybe more so then than now, was the real clash of guitar and keyboards creating a third instrument. As it's played on record, it's like half a picture. They kind of proved it to us every time we'd start doing a mix, 'cause my guitar playing was so rough if we turned it up it would sound worse. When we'd bring it back, the overall sound was much better. It was too late to change it 'cause it was how the whole project had gone. I guess we didn't realize until it was mixed just how clean the whole thing was. It's still got a gorgeous sound on that record. Again, it wasn't what we were trying to do. Gary felt under a lot of pressure, with the size of the budget we had from Warner Brothers, he felt that he must be expected to produce this little friendly record. It was actually Warner Brothers that first said, "Where are the guitars?" It was quite ironic that it was Warner Brothers that wanted what they'd seen live. I suspect that it contributed to Gary giving up production. In another 2 or 3 years he would stop producing. I never had the chance to sit down with him. We were all really happy with the record - it's a fine record.

It's a beautiful record.

There's a song, "Dark Magician", a b-side of "Part Past Part Fiction" that was an example of what didn't work. That song had an extra minute, and it went back to a slower chorus for the second time and at that stage was still meant to be on the album. Gary said, "Look, structurally it will work much better if you just drop that section all together and go straight to the tail section." Eventually he kinda talked us around and we less wanted to hear it. "Okay, that sounds alright." It didn't end up being on the album anyway, and that really pissed us off, 'cause we could've just left it as it was. Especially, with hindsight, it was much better with that extra section. The scope of The Chills material has proven to be too much for most producers. They always like elements of it, but there's always things they don't like. Gary wasn't fond of the long-winded dark stuff. Gavin MacKillop, on the other hand, loved the dark stuff and couldn't stand the fluffy pop stuff. On the *Soft Bomb* album it was a real haggle to get songs like "Double Summer" and "Ocean Ocean" even on, and they'd come out so much more lightweight than they needed to be. He couldn't understand this thing I was trying to achieve; this real sonic but beautiful pop music. So, it sort of came out kind of reasonably twee, which is a major factor why that album bombed. Either "Ocean Ocean" or "Double Summer" were meant to be the successor of "Heavenly Pop Hit". With both of them being handicapped and having to go with "The Male Monster From The Id" as the single... it's sort of a dead topic now...

What a way to go out.

The good thing is now people tell us it's quite a good album.

Where have you done your demos for the albums?

Submarine Bells and the first album I started writing was on a Tascam Porta 5, 4-track cassette, so I've been using one of those ever since. That's just completely bitten the dust now, so I have to make a jump into the computer world and start doing it that way. I've always had really shoddy rough takes too. It was a mistake, but I was just doing it so I could be reminded of things. Never realizing that these recordings have a real special feel, and that if I just put a bit more care into them, could be up for releasing one of these days. As it was, I was taking the Porta Studio down to Volt where Brendan was working and we tidied them up as much as possible. I think I'll probably do it again at some stage. Those will be made available someday. We're setting up the ICE Club – International Chills Enthusiasts – an internet home page and mail order thing. Possibly even a magazine. I'll make available those demos and outtakes and stuff. Hopefully things like Peel Sessions and so forth.

You have quite the cult following.

Well the nature of The Chills' true fans is they want to hear all the little variations. I'm quite eager to get stuff out.

Write to Martin and The Chills at PO Box 705, Dunedin Central, New Zealand

Chills Album Discography
Kaleidoscope World, early comp tracks, singles, and EP that led up to the first album. Mostly produced by Doug Hood and a lot on 4-track!
Brave Words, the 1st proper LP, produced by Mayo Thompson of Red Krayola fame. Great songs – washy production.
Submarine Bells, 2nd album, produced by Gary Smith who's done The Walkabouts, Pixies, The Connells, Scrawl. Kinda glossy sound but it works well with the mood.
Soft Bomb, 3rd album, produced by Gavin MacKillop who also did the Straightjacket Fits' *Melt* [which is great but sounds weird]. *Soft Bomb* sounds fine and has moody tunes.
Sunburnt, 4th and most recent "comeback" album, was produced by Craig Leon who did early Blondie, Ramones, Suicide and recently *Rock Animals* by Shonen Knife [a way overdone record]. Craig catches Martin at his best here, and the two Daves don't hurt any.
Heavenly Pop Hits, a compilation of "hits" over the years. Probably a good place to start, although I'm biased towards the *Kaleidoscope World* stuff.

Grandaddy

"REAL STUDIOS ARE LIKE HOSPITALS"
A CHAT WITH JASON LYTLE

by Larry Crane

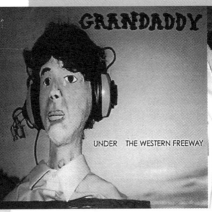

GRANDADDY

UNDER THE WESTERN FREEWAY

Grandaddy is a band I knew very little about until recently. I had heard rumors of a band locked away in their own studio in Modesto, a farming town in California's Central Valley, making some mind-blowing records, but I had never seen or heard any records until recently. When I did hear one (*A Pretty Mess By This One Band*), I sent a copy of *Tape Op* to them and got a response right away. Jason and I chatted a little bit and he sent more stuff to listen to, including their fresh new album *Under the Western Freeway* and a cassette of an EP called *Machines Are Not She*. It's all amazing listening and the recording quality is brilliant. Then we had this long talk. Thanks are due to Adam Selzer and Jed Brewer for turning me on to this stuff.

How did you end up with this recording gear working on your songs? Had you been recording on 4-tracks for years?

Yeah. I'm sure my story's pretty similar to a lot of people. I just ended up buying a microphone and a Yamaha MT 100 cassette 4-track. I had this job where I used to make a reasonable amount of money, but it didn't leave me with a lot of spare time. I would just work and buy stuff... fill up this bedroom at my parent's house... hoping that one day I could just quit and use it all. I ended up quitting and I got this house with a basement. I think that's when I really started to write songs. The songwriting and the learning of the recording process all bloomed together.

So you weren't even writing or recording much, but you accumulated this gear and it all came together?

Yeah, it's kind of weird. The whole recording and songwriting thing... it's almost like they've been siblings. I wasn't like some huge, aspiring songwriter who needed to get their ideas out.

Had you played in bands or wrote songs before?

Uhh... I started out playing drums. I didn't really like the whole "band" thing. I would hear stories about people having to answer ads at music stores... the whole dating service thing. That never appealed to me. The people that are in my band right now are people that were my good friends. People that didn't even know that I played music. I'd rather have a band full of mediocre musicians and be really good friends than so-and-so commutes from this town... there's all this pressure. Varying degrees of potential career-minded people there.

What led you to start acquiring all the recording gear?

The simplest ideas are what led me to it. I got the 4-track. I would record things and I would go, "Wow. That doesn't sound anything near to what these things I like, sound like. What can I do to try and get them to sound a little more like that." That leads to having to read about the different types of gear and what different things do. It's kind of been this ongoing quest to make records that I would want to listen to. I pretty much don't like 80% of the recordings that I've made to date.

Just 'cause you know what you'd change?

Maybe that whole *unsatisfied artist-y* thing too. You're never gonna be pleased and you're always gonna just try to better your craft. It usually turned out that the stuff that I spend the most time on and really labor over ends up not being anywhere as neat or magical as the stuff that you just kind of plopped out and is riddled with accidents.

You had told me before how trying to work out of a different ["real"] studio didn't work out for you. It seems like a lot of what you're working for is avoiding a "pressure" situation.

I think the main thing, which can be said for many facets of life, is the fact that you just need to find out what works. The studio thing was a real good example too, because the two people I was working with there were super nice - it was such a pleasant atmosphere and it was just us three the whole day. If anything should have worked, it should have been in that sort of atmosphere but... I think I've always tried to be really accommodating. I don't want to bore the shit out of people and I want everything to chug along at a nice pace. I guess it would be my problem, 'cause I should just not give a shit. They're all big boys and they can take care of themselves. The fact that somebody is there and something is taking a long time... you just feel that pressure. You just want to say, "Go away for 3 hours and come back." All of a sudden you're saying go away for another hour and come back. Shit, you might as well say, "Go away all together." I found this really good way to work. If it ain't broke, don't fix it.

It seems like you want to be left on your own to work everything out. A "studio" obviously isn't the best environment for that.

It seems like the place that I try to get to is kind of this "other-world" that doesn't really exist. When I feel like I've really succeeded is when I feel like I've tapped into this whole transcendence thing. It doesn't have a whole lot to do with people. It's a place that you have to get to. I don't want to start sounding all mystical.

It seems to me, that in a recording session everything becomes organized around the process and not the art.

Salvador Dali would sit there with a spoon in his hand and fall asleep in front of a canvas and as soon as he would drop it and awake he would immediately start painting. If you can have everything all set up and ready to go and hopefully get inspired and then get there as fast as you can – that's the thing I'm trying to shoot for. I'm really good about having notes. I'll have cassette tapes and pieces of paper taped to those cassette tapes… songs: what I was thinking and what I was trying to get across. Do everything you can to document everything that was going on when the song hit and then you can actually put it away and let it sit. If you're really lucky, you can look back into those notes and you can get right back to that place where you were.

Do you find yourself coming up with stuff when you lay down right before you fall asleep? Do you run down and start recording?

Yeah. I've heard people say that you can't sit around and wait to be inspired. The whole elbow grease thing is so important.

You mean, like when something isn't terribly inspired, but to keep working it out?

You don't even know what'll happen from there, though. I read somewhere that Tom Petty said he didn't worry about not being able to remember songs because there'll always be another one. I don't really agree with that too much. One of the best things I did was that I bought this little teeny guitar that I can put behind the seat of my truck and one of those notepads that attaches to the front window and a mini-cassette player. Sometimes what should have taken me an hour will take 4 1/2 hours, 'cause I'm constantly pulling over to the side of the road. I told myself that I had to take the responsibility to do what it took to document this stuff. I don't always feel like it will be there forever. I see it dissolving and being gone one day.

I doubt that will happen, but it's probably a good attitude to take. So where's your studio stuff set up?

Right now it's in an industrial warehouse space next to cabinet and sign shops. There were two rooms within it already and I just kind of threw a bunch of mattresses up against the walls and a bunch of couch cushions to make the control room not as ridiculous as it was. The bass response was just wacko all over the place.

So that's a temporary setup?

I'm in the process, right now, of relocating, but I'm not sure where.

As far as a living and recording space?

Yeah. As a matter of fact, I'm living in a tent right now. Our manager has a house and I'm living in this tent for the time being.

Until your tour starts?

Yeah.

So what kind of gear are you using these days?

A Fostex 16-track [1/2"]. The board is a Soundcraft Series 600 with a TT patchbay inside of it. I spent a shitload of money having to get all these converter cables.

What kind of mics and stuff do you use there?

I'm actually doing alright on mics, I guess. This one that I just bought used recently ended up being pretty darn good. I have a few of those Rode mics and they were kind of accentuated on the wispy end. My friend brought this Equitek CAD 200. It ended up being a halfway decent mic and it wasn't really overbearing in the high end. I've got a [Shure] Beta 57 and a regular 57, a couple of 58s. There's two Shure SM 81s.

For drum overheads?

Yeah. I have a couple of AKG C1000S. An [Electrovoice] RE 20.

Do you use that on kick and bass amps?

I have a D112 that I was pretty sold on, but I was having to crank the high end and had a really noisy kick channel. I started using an RE 20 and that doesn't require any high-end boost. It's good for rockin' songs that require a clicky kick drum, but I don't think it's all that fitting for slower stuff. I think it's a really good guitar cabinet mic and for rocking kick drum, but I think the D112 would be more suited for a mellower sounding kick. Oh god, I forgot to mention what is probably my favorite mic that I have right now… That Coles 4038. I was reading some Steve Albini article and he said that if he was to only have one ribbon mic it would be the Coles 4038. I looked into that and found out that they weren't terribly expensive. It's so *non-electric* sounding. It's good for a lot of stuff. It probably is good for vocals, but I still haven't found one really good vocal technique with any mic. I've had shitty luck so far.

It's probably hard 'cause you're recording yourself.

What I'll do is I'll record little projects for other bands and it really helps me to get technique down. I'll end up charging them for supplies and stuff 'cause we're both getting something out of it.

Do you like doing that sort of work?

Occasionally. The band I'm doing right now… I forgot how taxing it really was. I recorded them a year and a half ago. That whole, "put on your game face" thing. It's a challenge, but it's kinda weird. I manage to document, as thoroughly as possible, all the signal routing so when it comes time to do our stuff it'll be like, bam-bam-bam. It's just so not sitting in a meadow under a shady tree with a pen and paper writing poetry.

You're telling me… I was gonna ask you what was the Circuit City/Good Guys scam you mentioned the other day?

Well, they basically have that 30-day, money back - no questions asked guarantee. That pretty much says it all. If you were really inclined and determined enough you could go in there and buy a washer and dryer and do all your laundry and take them back. We have benefited with speakers and amps and VHS machines. You just keep it for about 28 days. They end up selling the stuff as opened box deals. It's just kind of one of those things that's there for the offering.

Don't they have a couple of consumer grade DAT machines? We'll mention that for people that need to mix something down.

Or tape duplication.

Get 4 or 5 decks and knock out all your tapes for your band's demo. But we're not suggesting that.

Oh no! This is kind of a risky venture, but say you're going on a road trip for 2 or 3 weeks and you wanna videotape it... [*much laughter ensues*]

But you've never done that, right?

I've known people that have.

What kind of keyboards do you use on your recordings? It sounded like Casios.

We have two keyboards. One, which has been a total mainstay [I've had this thing for about 10 years] and every time I can find one I buy it so I always have backups, is a Kawai PH 50. It's just like a pop keyboard that came out around when Miami Vice was really popular so its got all these Jan Hammer sounds on there. For some reason, when I bought the thing I took a liking to it. The one I have right now is falling apart 'cause we've been touring with it. I like the idea of nailing your equipment down to the floor and getting used to what you have instead of it turning into this big, revolving quest for whatever's bigger and better. The other one is a Yamaha PSS 270. There's this art to shitty little keyboards because some of them do have a bunch of really crappy sounds. This one has 100 sounds on it and I, seriously, really like 85 of them. That's pretty darn good. It's got a portamento setting on it too, which is pretty good. I have two keyboards on stage and the dedicated keyboard player has two of them. I can write all these parts and figure out how we're gonna play them later.

So you have a touring band...

I started the band 6 years ago and we started off as a 3 piece and we're still together. I added two other guys and we've been playing as a 5 piece for the last two years. On top of all the recording and everything, I stress the fact that we're a halfway decent live band.

With the recording process is the whole band involved?

It's pretty much been primarily me, although for the recent recordings, another guy in the band was an extra set of hands as far as engineering and all that. It's just this thing that I have no trouble spending exhausting, ridiculous amounts of time doing.

There's no resentment or anything?

No, no. It works out kinda neat like that 'cause I'm making these songs and the rest of the band really likes the songs so we practice in order to get the songs to sound like they do and we all kind of benefit. We all have a pretty good time. When we play live it's just kind of frustrating because we know how good rehearsals sound and there's all the kind of shit you have to deal with bad rooms and incapable sound people. That's when it gets kinda frustrating.

Have you recorded with the full line up?

The drummer plays on 80% of the recordings. The fact that I started off as a drummer means that I have the option if something needs to be done, but my drummer's a lot steadier than I am. I just recorded a live show of ours the other day with two stereo mics about ten feet out from where we were playing at this place in downtown Modesto. It turned out really good. We made about 15 cassette copies of it and sold some at this show that we played the other night. I've recorded rehearsals that we've done. I have these DAT copies of all this stuff that I'm hoping to do something with eventually.

www.grandaddylandscape.com

GRANDADDY
Under the Western Freeway CD (Will)

This is one of those records that *Tape Op* readers will love to listen to. Its full of creative production ideas with each song employing a different recording approach. Chief songwriter Jason Lytle recorded this magnum opus on his 16-track at Floater and Headcorders in Modesto, California. The opening track, "Nonphenomenal Lineage," starts with a murky keyboard and electric guitar intro and proceeds into a desolate acoustic guitar and vocal part which is soon accompanied by a perfectly placed mono recording of a drum kit reminiscent of garbage cans. There are a lot of unique keyboard sounds throughout the record, some tracks are more pop oriented and some are more stripped down entering into folk territory. Regardless of lineage, the entire record is well thought out and like all creatively recorded records, it gets better and more interesting with each listen. –Adam Selzer

Pavement: Steve Malkmus

by Larry Crane

's Joanna Bolme

Pavement slowly emerged out of California's Central Valley in the late '80s with a handful of cryptic releases. When the time came, they emerged as a band, built around Steve Malkmus and Scott Kannberg with engineer-turned-drummer Gary Young (see his story next), bassist Mark Ibold and gambler/utility player Bob Nastanovich in tow (who were later joined by Steve West when Gary got out-of-hand). The recordings that they created always seemed like studio creations, especially their first album, *Slanted and Enchanted*, which literally bubbled with catchy little overdubs. I cornered Steve Malkmus in order to cover the history of Pavement recording sessions and dispel the myth of lo-fi and 4-tracks.

It seemed that Pavement started as a studio band. My impression is that you and Scott [Kannberg] would come home from college and go make some recordings. Is that what the case was?

Essentially. We were in a band before that, an instrumental band with another guy from Stockton, CA. It was sort of like Echo and the Bunnymen, The Ventures, and Sonic Youth put together. They were like punk songs. That passed when I went to school and Scott was living in Sacramento. I was finished with college by the time it started. Scott never finished. I didn't want to be in a college rock band during the time I was in college – I just skipped the band thing. I thought I would try to get laid the hard way or whatever. It seemed that most of the guys at my school were in Grateful Dead cover bands.

Where were you going to school?

Virginia. That's where I met Bobby [Nastanovich]. So the band started after that.

So you finished, came home for the summer, and Pavement sort of started.

Yeah we would have jam sessions at my house.

Just the two of you?

Yeah, doing covers – Dinosaur, Talking Heads, probably some New Zealand bands and Chrome. We liked Chrome a lot.

How long was it until you went in to record the first single?

Um, not very long. From being at my college's radio station, I think it was sort of decided that people would be into obscure things. I knew we really didn't have to be a band because that's how I knew all bands anyway - just second-hand, through records - and we thought that's all a band really was. Bands came through the college to play, but to me they only really existed on vinyl. I was also listening to English groups too. You never got to see them. Or Chrome - we knew that Chrome couldn't play live due to the way their albums sounded. So we thought, "That's cool. We'll just make up fake bands." So that's what we did, but we didn't get started until we went to Gary [Young]'s studio. We made the single and we didn't rehearse or anything really. Maybe once in my garage, just me and him. I might have said, "Well these five will be kind of like this. We'll just do it later." I had more experience recording, anyway, than Scott. At the time I knew about overdubbing and I'm sure he did too, but I knew you could just sort of throw things together.

How did you find out about Gary's studio then?

I think Scott probably did or maybe I did, I can't remember. It was probably somebody from the earlier punk band. He was in this band called Death's Ugly Head, which would play at the punk shows that I would play when I was in a punk band. They were this joke band – they did metal songs and covers and glammed it up. So, he was around and I heard he had a studio – I think he also recorded the Authorities, this really good punk band from Stockton. We kind of knew about him, it sounded fine to me. I didn't expect him to play drums – I just went to use the place and it turned out that he could play. There were a couple of things on our first single where we couldn't play, or it wasn't a straight song like "Box Elder," and he just went in and did it. We said, "Well that was good why don't you play on this other one." He played on two songs. On the next single he didn't play because it was going to be me and Scott with other people. Scott had some other friends that played drums on the first single. "Forklift," the third single, Gary played a little bit on and so I decided to let him play – to have a more collaborative thing - let him play and actually rehearse, because up to that point we never rehearsed.

Just show up and have him put something on it?

Yeah, like lay out a track and have him drum. We did that on the last single.

As far as sessions, did you go into the studio and do the first single and then put it out?

Yeah, the single had five songs and then we did two extras that weren't good enough. I went on this trip to Europe for ten months and I came back and we did the second single. I moved to New York and when I came back for Christmas, we did the third single. Then we did the album [*Slanted and Enchanted*] in the summer.

It seems interesting that you and Scott apparently had a concept of not making a demo tape, not trying to record a whole album, but making little documents each time you went in. You guys were coming through as cryptic as a band from New Zealand, or Germany or something. Just little packages of singles and certain things on small labels. There was this mysterious element it had to it.

It was easy to do knowing Chrome and working at an art museum and stuff. Just trying to make it have more of an aura. English bands were like that – the Jesus and Mary Chain. Ten times more hype. There was some of that, but it was tongue in cheek in some ways -people didn't realize. We kept that going after *Slanted and Enchanted,* but then it just got to be too much. If you keep on doing that it gets to be frustrating. A lot of those people that do the cryptic thing don't have much to say or they're not that interesting. It just turned out we probably had more to say, or at least I did – and Bob. It was kind of an interesting story, you just can't keep on doing that for years and years. You could if you wanted to be the Residents.

But that's a really special case. Somebody who nobody knows who they are and they hide behind the music.

We just kind of got rid of that and started acting like a normal indie rock band or whatever.

Then you started working on an album?

All of it [*Slanted and Enchanted*] was done at Gary's studio.

And that was an 8-track studio at his house?

No, it was 16-track 1" Tascam and he had that board that was pretty cool, he'll tell you about it. Other than that, he really didn't have any good effects or anything. It was all just cheap reverb and compressors so we decided not to use them in any way. We thought it was like what Steve Albini said you were supposed to do or whatever. Just to be like the Pixies or something, with no reverb, that was cool. Also, that just simplified things because we were mixing it ourselves and we didn't really know what we were doing. We weren't listening for hi, low or mids. We didn't have any low, except for the kick drum, that also made it easier.

In the very early stuff there's layers of distorted guitars and different things. Did both you and Scott kind of jump at that idea of putting different things on there and filling it up?

Yeah, I did most of it, but he was up for it. He was an enthusiastic backer, and he liked the noise stuff. He wasn't afraid of it sounding weird or anything. He might seem conservative sometimes, but he's not always. He was a good foil I guess. He was the steady one, but he also taped some weird stuff on his own and he would put little noises he thought were cool and random on the songs.

It seems like no one in the States were doing what you were doing. Pop songs underneath, but a really chaotic approach on top sometimes.

I'm trying to remember what was going on, it wasn't much. There would be people who would say we were trying to sound like Some Velvet Sidewalk or Sebadoh - sort of lo-fi. They were also groups that just released one single, like Royal Trux. It was definitely different from the other stuff that was coming out.

When you guys started working on *Slanted and Enchanted*, it did seem like it took a different step. Your songwriting got a little poppier and it seemed that every little nook and cranny was filled with a hook. If the vocals stopped...

The guitar would come in.

It sounded like some of those things were created in the studio to fill it up.

Almost all of it was. Again, it was more of a concerted effort because we thought we had some attention from people. It would have been too outrageous to do that on your first album. You want to sort of build it up. You could have done that back then, *Slanted and Enchanted*, those kind of songs, but I didn't know it was going to turn out that good, or anything like how it turned out. It was just slightly more songs and more Fall influence on the songs that aren't pop songs. Basically, songs influenced by the Fall and then pop songs. It's very simple. I was into repetition, into My Bloody Valentine's *Isn't Anything* – I thought that it was really good for some reason. It is pretty good, but it's weirdly recorded.

Strange detuning and strange recording.

Yeah, it's still kinda cool. I thought that was a good fidelity to have. So that was like the production style, just raw like that.

I always thought when I first heard your record... "These guys like the third Velvet Underground album."

Yeah, I really like them, but I was trying to hide the Velvet Underground influence, I had already been through them in college. When I was singing in deadpan, it was kinda like Lou Reed on helium or something.

All the stuff on that record you've been saying was done in the studio, and you hadn't even gone out and played a gig or had you?

Before *Slanted and Enchanted* we had been playing the East coast. We played the Philly Record Exchange, Maxwell's...

Who was playing with you, just you three or...

No we had another guy. Gary came out, his parents lived in New York. We had Bob and we had this other guy, who won't be named. He was in this band called Sugartime. He was kind of this depressed guy who might assassinate me one day.

That's nice.

He's very competitive.

How did Bob get hooked into things?

I lived with him in New York. When we were sort of starting I said, "You could be the drummer if we ever played." I figured we just wanted a Mo Tucker type drummer. I thought he could do it because he's a good athlete. I would like to do a test to see what drummers are actually athletic, and which ones are dorks. Find out who's good and who's not. Cause Steve, our drummer, is really uncoordinated, but he can keep a good beat. I don't remember Gary being able to shoot baskets. We decided that Bob could be in our group - he ended up getting us our Suburban to travel to Charlottsville. He was our driver and he sort of became... we didn't know that Gary was such a freak. We knew that he was like a hippie and kinda flaky, but we didn't know he had such a bad drinking problem at the time. We found that out on tour, because he really got sick from being nervous. I think that was one of the reasons for drinking – to compensate for his lack of confidence. He was extra strong on that tour. That's why I let Bob be in the band... "Keep the beat going if Gary passes out." That sort of lightened the grooves, the band became less cryptic and people who cared about it found out about the wild, drunken drummer. Back then, celebrating alcoholism was still in with bands like Mudhoney. So, that's how Bob got in the band and then later came Mark. After *Slanted and Enchanted* was recorded we decided to get a bass, just for a change, so we got him and that was the line-up.

Did you record any bass on *Slanted and Enchanted* or was it just...

There's one song "In the Mouth A Desert." It's the third or fourth song. I did the bass just at the last minute, the song was already recorded. It was one of the last songs we did, we added the bass and he put reverb on it and we remixed that song at the last moment. It turns out it's good that big because it's one of the better mixed songs. I remember going into Gary's by myself and doing that the day before I left.

Did you and Scott have that kind of control in the studio with Gary? Did you have Gary mix things or would you all get in there?

We pretty much all would. I would say that there was some drum equalization that Gary would have to do. Like the band before we even came in, we used their settings for the drums, I remember that. It was one of those Stockton metal bands with this pseudo producer guy. I think they just used Gary's drums, they were already set up. It was primarily tracked with just me in the control room and Gary trying to get his drums. Scott would play the guitar through a bass amp and I would sing, and tell him what to do – "Go to the ride" and "Rock out man."

Instead of lyrics you were guiding the performance.

Yeah, just go "La la la la la la la. Now we're really going to rock." You can say to Gary, "Rock out now" and he does a good job. You can't say that to some drummers – they'll stop, or they're not creative.

You still do that though. I remember watching you guys working up songs for the new album and you would go to Steve and talk to him.

Gary worked a lot quicker. Steve's really great, but we were able to do the whole record in ten days, even though they were easier songs. Gary came up with some beats, some beats we told him to do... it was just kind of a mix. If he came up with something good, that was fine. If it wasn't

good I would just say, "Do something else." He also had some advice about certain things, certain ways we should play things. His brother is a recording engineer in New York, so he knows about recording and where to put the mics. Gary engineered it more than we did, that's for sure. He kept everything sort of under control. He winds the tape machine, he knows how to use a razor blade and he's pretty responsible in that way. It was pretty surprising; it was just a garage studio. Still, you know, it's a lot to keep track of just the patch bay.

After that you did *Watery, Domestic*?

Yeah, that was the last thing we did at Gary's. Everyone was there for the end of it. Mark held down some keyboard note and he whispers and Bob does some talking. That was when, "Oh, we're becoming like a real group." I was trying to sort of use everybody, sort of how Scott got to be in it a certain amount... Gary was going to be in it more, everyone was going to be in it more. I didn't know that then... I didn't know I was being a control freak.

After that you guys started to work on a new album with Gary didn't you?

Yeah, we did try to record with Gary again. We'd been touring across the US and Europe a lot and we weren't getting along too well. We kind of wanted to not record with him anymore, but we were too nice to fire people or even really talk about it. We started to rehearse songs – we didn't even know what. I flew out from New York and ended up staying at Gary's house and it just wasn't going that well. We recorded some basic tracks – Gary had moved the studio, he had a new place and a new board, one of those digital Tascams. It was this really big, silver, ugly thing. I think he admits now that it was a mistake. He basically took his Pavement money and put it into this studio, to make it nicer. We tried to record there, but it wasn't sounding good and he didn't have his studio ready and he was also in a drinking funk. He was supposed to be getting the studio ready months before and it wasn't ready. That didn't work out, he ended up retiring and quitting too. At that point we loved the way he drummed, but it just wasn't worth the psycho. Then we got Steve, it was just peaceful because he's such a nice guy.

Didn't Bob know him?

Yeah, they went to high school together and Steve was in this REM-ish band in high school and he tried to make it big with them. They were pretty good, just American sounding. They weren't capturing people's imagination enough at the time. They were an '80s band that didn't make it.

There were a lot of those. After that you guys went to New York and started recording *Crooked Rain, Crooked Rain*.

We started rehearsing. I rehearsed more with Steve because we lived in the same town. It turns out that he's best when he has a lot of time to rehearse. His performances were best on that record because he had a lot of time to learn the stuff. We recorded that in this little studio [Random Falls]. It's not even a studio, it's really just a room in the Fur district of New York. This guy [Mark Venezia] worked at this used music gear store - he was a really interesting character, very enthusiastic. He had a Studer 24-track and some kind of board that was from that shop.

Did you record at the music store?

Well, it was all down below and he lived there too. Kurt Ralske [UV Scene, producer, etc.] has a studio in this place. There were a lot of other studios and rehearsal rooms. Tape machine and speakers, and that's it. We were going directly into it through some cool mic preamps that he had gotten from upstairs that were really nice. You had to do one thing at a time. It was basically me and Steve who did that album anyway, just the basics of it. Scott came in, but he was just coming in from out of town and he contributed some interesting parts, like an interesting organ part on the last song and he did "Hit the Plane Down" there. He did a couple of other songs that didn't get used. It wasn't like going back to Stockton, it was more like a New York band for that album. Mark was around – Bob really wasn't there.

Did Mark play bass on most of the album?

Hmmm, I think he plays on the second song. "Unfair" and "Gold Soundz" don't have bass they just have guitar. He didn't play on "Range Life", he might've played on "5 - 4..." He probably didn't play on the last song, but he might've. He was still kind of new to it and we weren't really rehearsing too much together since a lot of the songs didn't have bass, that's the way it works. "Stop Breathing" was such a weird song and it was detuned so I played it.

So did you record the same way you did with Gary? Put a scratch down and have Steve play along and build up from there?

Yeah, except I was the guy playing with him more because I didn't have a chance to run through the songs with Scott and they were a little more complicated. They weren't just the same things over and over like *Slanted and Enchanted*. Almost every song, except for "Jackals...," "Fame Throwa" and "Zurich is Stained," are kind of these patterns that just repeat over and over. They all have patterns, but half of them are just exactly the same thing like "Summer Babe," "In the Mouth a Desert" and "Conduit For Sale!." It just seemed hard. I could probably do it if I had three days, but it didn't seem that we had time for that. We were just recording ourselves there. There was no punching in, all the guitar parts I would do all the way through. Sometimes Mark, the engineer, would say, "Okay, you can punch in." He might help me just fix one little thing. I would just do three vocal takes and leave them for later.

Do it in the mix?

Yeah, when we got to the studio where we mixed.

Mark was doing all the engineering for you?

Yeah, he was great. I said co-engineer on the album, which was kind of unfair because he was the main engineer, but we were recording ourselves a lot. We thought we also engineered it, but really he deserved to be... he was engineer 'cause he did set the mics in phase...

Things you might've not known about?

Yeah, where to put the kick drum mic - we didn't know that. We just did a lot of the recording of ourselves.

Seemed like you learned how to run the machine and to put tape on.

Yeah we did that.

How did you pick up that stuff? Just from working with Gary before?

Yeah, or Mark told us. We'd never used one of those big machines. It was manually recorded, half of it without the time thing [counter]. It wasn't working always, it was totally primitive, but it was good in some ways.

Did you spend a lot of time on the tracking?

There was at least a month of going in there for a few hours and fiddling on different amps. There's a lot more variety of guitar sounds. There were more amps and guitars than other things we had done. When we mixed it, we ended up

going to Baby Monster, this really nice studio in New York [now closed]. It's small, but it was my first run-in with expensive equipment like the Neve board. It was just fifty-dollars an hour, because they didn't know who we were and we were lucky. We also didn't plan this out... "Well, we're just going to mix it now and we'll do it ourselves, like our other albums and it will work out fine." We ended up going to this place where Bryce [Goggin], the house engineer, was there and he sort of took control when we got in there. It was fine with me, cause when we listened to it, the guitars were recorded awesomely, the vocals were fine, but the drums were fucked up. We weren't listening to it carefully during tracking and we thought we could fix it when we mixed it. Bryce fixed it. He made it sound like it was sort of professional when we recorded, compared to *Slanted and Enchanted*, which is so raw. Bryce was really into bass, and he made the bass really loud, which we had never done before.

There's a totally different feeling. That record feels warm and fuzzy while the other record seemed kind of sharp.

Exactly, scratchy and more angular. That was good, we were proud of ourselves, that we sounded different on a second record more than most bands do. We were really happy with the job we did; we were amazed that he made it sound so good.

And he shows up later in the story.

In the interim we were recording songs at Mark Venezia's that turned up on *Wowee Zowee*. "Best Friends Arm" and "Extradition".

Where did you do "Picket Fences"?

That was done at the place where Jon Spencer recorded in New York... that guy who lives in Tuscon now – Jim Waters... Waterworks. So was "Heaven is a Truck" and then on *Wowee Zowee* there's this "We Got the Money" song, which was recorded during *Crooked Rain* and also "Grounded", but we redid "Grounded". But that was directly taken from that session. Four songs and B-sides that eventually came out were done at Mark's, but they were all mixed at the same time as the stuff from Memphis. We tried to re-record all those songs but we just couldn't do it. It was just really slow sounding and sloppy. We just kept my roughs, like "AT & T," of those songs. We tried to get Steve to play, but it's not his style, the real energetic style so we kept the spastic take. We went down to Memphis – it was really fun. I'd made a Silver Jews album [*Starlight Walker*] there. Easley Recording is great, it's a nice building, it's big. I don't really remember - it was all really quick at that point. I got some basics done there and the rest of that was done with me and Bryce at a variety of studios. Whichever one's the cheapest, like Big House or Baby Monster. We were just sort of moving quick and mixing things really fast.

That's a pretty long record too.

Just at the end there was no real coherence to it, so I decided instead of trying to fake it to just put all the different songs on there.

It just feels like a collection of all kind of ideas and things that were flying around.

That's what I ended up wanting to do. I didn't feel like making a big statement, or something. We were getting too much like, "Oh, this was like what their next album was." This way and that way. I just felt like falling out of that and making this spastic...

Which left a lot of people scratching their heads, or loving it.

Yeah some people really liked it and continue to. A lot of my friends, people's opinions that I respect, they still listen to it. They don't listen to the other ones, but they probably got tired of the other ones because they liked them so much.

You never know.

It never happened really. Yeah, it came out and it didn't get very good critical respect. It sold like half as much as the one before that. Maybe not half, but it was okay... I didn't care.

There's an attitude of looking at the long term instead of the immediate gratification of the band. It's more, "Let's create a body of work." I always took the band like this and it always amazed me when people took it all on the short term like, "The new album sucks. I like the old one."

It's true. If you're trying to be like an artist, that's how you want it to be anyway.

You don't sit there and say, "When Rene Magritte did 'This is Not a Pipe.' I was really into his work, but when he did that one painting of his wife I thought he was terrible."

For better or worse, no matter what people say like that, you find out that there's just a few people who do really get things, like music. Maybe they don't always hit it right, but you kind of trust that they're going somewhere with it.

Your early recordings were referred to as lo-fi, but you started on 16-track and moved up to a 24 on your second full album. I don't see it as a style, yet here are things being done in an actual studio and being called lo-fi. What are you're feelings on that?

I don't know. I guess at the time it was a way to say, "You could buy this and not feel ripped off." They had to say the production was part of the style. It's not just that somebody was too lazy or cheap to do it right. We were just trying our best to make it sound cool to our ears. Your ears probably get used to a certain kind of sound. Just like Guided By Voices fans are supposedly up in arms about their new album.

Fuck 'em.

It's sad.

It seems weird.

It's never been a political thing... fidelity.

I just thought it was strange that you were even called lo-fi. Even when things like "You're Killing Me", the really early stuff, it's noisy, but it's clear.

It's not 4-track-y. It sounds fine to me.

It doesn't sound like a Loverboy album.

Well, there were some noises and stuff on it. They were probably trying to see a trend in it. Do-it-yourself style, when it was coming up, and there were other different things like Liz Phair. Yeah, that is sort of small sounding compared to Alanis Morrisette. Even she is supposed to be small sounding compared to Madonna, leaving Alanis Morrisette being lo-fi... things change.

I always wonder why that sort of thing happens in the first place. But that deals more with journalism and the boxes that people put things in.

It is pretty raw sounding, compared to a lot of music, so, I can understand – just relative to other things, not to itself. It kind of sounded the way it sounded. That was the idea - whatever came out you sort of lived with that.

The next album was *Brighten the Corners*?

We did the "Give it a Day" single and we did that at Easley too. Then we did *Brighten the Corners* at Mitch Easter's.

Was that the first time you demoed stuff on your own? Playing drums and other things and bringing it in to show people, or to sketch your ideas on?

I started to think that might be the best way. I did a couple of songs that way, but I don't know how many they actually listened to, or what happened. There were only three or four songs that we demoed that appeared on the album, and those are different. I think three or four of the songs we were already playing live, or we just knew the riffs. Like "Stereo" and "Starlings on the Slipstream." That funky one, I can't remember what's it called... there's like three anyway and Scott had his two numbers that we didn't know yet. So that left the other demoed ones. That album, to me, was getting all the stuff finished with it all around. Anything that anyone kind of knew. There's a couple of new things on that album, like "Type Slowly," that was a new thing. I guess "We Are Under Used", the really classic rocky one, was sort of new. People really didn't like that song. Those were different ones that were new; the rest was just sort of sweeping out this old stuff. The new ideas – just sort of wrapping up that side of the band.

Things that were half finished, stuff you kind of knocked around live?

Yeah.

That's one of the things I noticed too. I have a bootleg of the Peel Session with "Kentucky Cocktail" and that stuff. Those aren't on any records and they're really interesting. They seem like sketches for different ideas that are going places. But you were out playing live and even on the Peel Session.

We were just making up things. We didn't have a chance to rehearse. It was our chance to try something new and see if it would work. A lot of the good bands take those Peel Sessions and do interesting things with them, like Mercury Rev or something. One thing you could say about them is that they would actually try to do something original in their Peel Sessions instead of just playing their four hits, in a live setting. So that, again, we were sort of taking that stride. Even though they are pretty simple songs compared to what something like Mercury Rev would probably do, 20 overdubs and piano with the mic far away or something. There's still a chance to experiment and learn.

The Peel Sessions, I don't know if people understand it sometimes. It really is a studio session, it's just very fast.

You get a half-day to do it. They have cool engineers. We got a good guy named Midi. We've had him five times and he now requests us. He likes American bands more than English bands. He has a pint at midday. I'm not sure if I'm totally into his sound actually, but he knows. It's mixed for radio and stuff, so you kind of have to let him do it. How over compressed it is or something, he's trying to imagine what it's going to be like on the radio.

It's not going be a surprise. It's not going to pump and grind.

The way the drums are always on those things. They sound like...

Mid-rangey.

Just squashed. Like when they say things sound squashed, they really do sound that way.

Well the bootleg I have is probably off the radio. So it's even worse. Over the radio, then into someone's crappy tape recorder receiver. Hey, it was eight dollars.

That's not bad.

So that's cool to understand that the record [Brighten The Corners] was actually a lot of ideas coming together too. That was done at Mitch Easter's right?

Yeah, that was all done at the same place. Then we mixed it in New York at this place with Bryce. Bryce recorded and mixed most of it. Mitch recorded half of it when Bryce had to leave. It was done in his house; it was a nice place, but a little too cramped for us really to play in. Mitch's house has fantastic gear and it's really nice. You could do something really cool there if you wanted.

Is that the newer studio [Fidelitorium]?

Yeah, I heard he might be doing something different. I mean the mixing room is in his living room – that kind of thing. So, guitars in the next room... It's a strange way of doing it. There are so many nice people in the recording business that it's sort of unfair. I'm sure he has work, Doug has work and Bryce too. But they're all really nice people. It's amazing all across the board. I haven't ever met any really nasty engineer types. There are guys who'll say, "More emotion." No one has ever asked me to do that... more like, "Sing in tune." They can say that, that's fine with me if someone's like, "You were flat there, or you were wavering." That's where we're getting to with Nigel now. I can understand that.

The first time you used a producer was just recently. You never had anyone officially produce. Bryce is probably the closest.

He had a lot to do with how our last album [Brighten the Corners] sounded. He did a great job – he's definitely creative. He gets credit, but he could've been called the producer of the last album if he had really pressed for it, but we were sort of against that title anyway. We still are, we don't think we ever get produced, but by this point it's sort of old. It was... "Nigel wants to be producer? Well that's fine with us." We've done this for five albums now, and we wanted to work with him too.

He's creative.

He's really creative, and he works with Radiohead, which I think is a really cool band. We found out that Nigel wanted to record with us. We didn't request him, he just said he would do it and we were excited 'cause we knew that they were a cool band, even though I hadn't listened to Ok Computer all that much before we got a hold of him. We decided we wanted a producer and he decided he wanted to do it and we didn't want to ask anybody. We didn't want to look and he'd asked. So I called him up and he was a really nice, friendly guy. He had just done the Beck album [Mutations] and I like Beck.

That's a good sounding record.

Those are two really good records and the two coolest popular bands, just about. We were originally going to do it in Sonic Youth's studio [Echo Cañon], because we were just supposed to record on the cheap, like we always do. "They'll have a bunch of different little toys," 'cause they're

Sonic Youth. Their studio had a good tape machine, like the 2" 16 [Studer]. We went there with Nigel and started to record there (this is after rehearsing at your place and Steve's for a while). Nigel couldn't get his head around it. All he brought were some speakers and one microphone. He just wanted to use everything else there. It was really weird, the faders are backwards.

You pull them down for the sound to go up?

You'd be surprised how that can freak you out, things like that. There were weird things you had to do with playback and listen back, and there were no headphone mixes per se. We left and were going around to other studios in New York, 'cause there are inexpensive ones in Brooklyn that are still cool. He didn't care about working in the nicest studio. But he knew, cause he mixed REM at RPM, that he liked it fine. He said, "We should go check it out." We were all sitting there like, "We can record anywhere." It's just a professional, impersonal studio. That's where we did a lion's share of the recording. It's very comfortable but, I mean, I wouldn't go back there really.

You got an advance from Matador for the first time ever too, didn't you?

Yeah, this was more expensive then any of our other records. The last one wasn't cheap either, just because of flying and paying Bryce and then mixing. It wasn't as much as this one, it just kind of started getting expensive. Again, for me, I just wanted to get it done. Done well – I didn't really care at this point. I just figured we could be irrational for once in our lives. Just do that big thing and see if it's fine, but still, that being said, we were still kind of grasping. We only did twelve days there or something. Basically, we wanted to have all the drums and everything but the vocals done – we didn't quite do that. We went to London to do the vocals and mix it – get a break. We went to this place where Nigel was a tea boy and started his stuff. He met Radiohead when they were doing The Bends at RAK. That's when he agreed to become their mate. When John Leckie was passed out or something, he was there helping.

Being a tape op?

Totally. So, we were in the third room. Bernard Butler was there, from Suede, in the big room. Stephen Street was mixing Crissie Hynde's album. We were the underdogs in the cheap room. That's where we did the remainder of the recording. In this room, it was really cool, an API board with a big upstairs with a big glass partition. That's where the producer stayed, kind of in a control room or a disco booth, but up top. The studio was down below. We did three songs there with another drummer [Dominic Mercott, of the High Llamas] because we didn't get good performances on a couple of songs. We finished it up and we were going to mix there, but Nigel got paranoid about it and didn't like it. We went to this other place that's even nicer. That was a pretty cheap place, it was like 200-300 pounds a day, which is like $450, but we could stay there too. It had all this nice stuff. It had more of a vibe than RPM but it was also an impersonal studio, but that stuff never really bothered me that much. It doesn't matter if it's impersonal or not, I just want to do the record. I don't need to have all this vibe necessarily.

You're comfortable with the recording process. You started out with the recording process.

I mean, if you saw where we did Crooked Rain... it wasn't like that guy was going to get all these jobs when they came to see that place. It was just a room, like a black room, with drums and a couple of keyboards in the back. There wasn't a poster on the wall. Just cereal bowls and....

No lava lamps?

No. You just want stuff to work and I guess you want it to sound like what it really sounds like outside the studio – that's really important. The place we went to was called Mayfair and that's where we mixed it. Nigel got a deal, because he works there a lot. That was nice, it was more of a place where they have cable TV and big menus to order from. That sort of place is fun, but they do make you pay for it. Everything's marked up 200%, not just the tape. Nigel did most of the mixing himself; he wouldn't let us touch the board. It was the first time we didn't touch the board when we were mixing.

You were there though.

Yeah, we were there, except when he remixed a couple of them. "Carrot Rope" and "Billie" he did again one more time. He was a multiple pass guy. He had a different style than Bryce or me. We just sort of go through and mix it and that's it. It was this existential battle where we conquered the song right then in the spirit of the moment and it was done. But that means we did go back and do a couple of them again. Nigel was sort of the same way, but he had more of a hit or miss style. It seemed like he would just do it, take a pass and mix it in two hours. Then he would take it to his house and decide there. Some songs he did over and over. Like "The Hexx" he might have done that one too much actually. It's hard to say, but just about everything he did more than once. He ended up automating, it was pretty easy automation. He did it really quickly, it didn't take long, like SSL style. He ended up doing that and he did a really good job, I think.

I always thought he had a style. *OK Computer* is a very stylized record. A lot of distorted compression on drums, and all these things that he does. When I heard [Beck's] *Mutations* I was like, "Maybe he doesn't do that." It's a very low-key record, I always feel like the band is in a nice wood living room. Your record doesn't sound like that or Radiohead, it's an entirely different thing. What kind of things did you feel he brought to it?

Beyond the bare bones of recording, and whatever he did like limiting to tape and EQing to tape, he did more of that than we have before.

With drums?

Yeah, drums and guitars. Everything was a little more effective when it went to tape. We normally just did everything raw, onto tape, then fix it in the mix or change it later. His way was actually smarter, because you knew exactly what you were getting. Like when you mentioned mixing, all you had to do was balance the levels and maybe do some echoplexing or plate reverbs – things like that. Besides doing that, he was occasionally more active in trying to get things done with cutting tape and we had some slave stuff. We've never done that before.

Two tape decks?

Yeah, he would just copy a drum thing and put it back where there was a mistake. He was just more into noticing rhythm and with singing, given the time he had, he tried to make me sing better.

How did he go about doing that?

He just would say, "That was a little flat, do it again." He was also into my rough takes. He listened to the tape so much he got used to those. He wanted me to sing sort of like that, but in tune. Once or twice, like on "Ann Don't Cry" I had something else in mind, but didn't feel like fighting. He was like, "You do it like that or like this." I mean the lyrics don't mean anything, they are really sort of demo-y.

Were they one's where you were sketching it out?

Yeah, I was just doing that, and sometimes he would want that. Other than that it was, "Would you do that again? It was wobble-y. That's out of tune."

Would he do multiple passes and comp things out and try to put that together?

We tried that at first, but then he sort of... as we got tired we hoped it would be the right one. Originally, we did three passes and I'm getting into it and he would listen back and try to comp it. Then he'd try to fix things. I mean if I was a better singer, or if I was singing better, which I wasn't really, for some reason, it could've gone faster. I never really had problems like that before. Then again, if you listen to the last record, there are some bad vocals on *Brighten The Corners*. But with *Slanted and Enchanted* and stuff it just seemed like I did it normally. I think these are harder songs, and sort of dependent more on the singing and a little slower. It easier to sing and you can express more when a song is slower. You can express more, but also there's more pressure on your singing. We did some doubling, very subtle, not obvious doubling. Occasionally he would come up with little ideas, like the thing on "Hexx", with noises. Just his choice of Echoplex or reverb – sounds and phases. That was more his ideas, and we were happy to let him contribute. I was already contributing and I wanted someone else to contribute, to make it different.

I keep reading things about you being the leader of the band and you finally admitting it.

I don't mind that. I always thought that, but I just figured people would find out eventually. Nobody wants to hear that Billy Corgan made the whole Smashing Pumpkin's album. It's not that interesting, when you're in a band. I think everyone was like, "Whatever it takes to get it done." That was enough for people. If Mark thought I thought I could do it better, he would be happy. If I really thought I wanted to do the bass on one song, and it was a good idea, I would just do it. Even like "Spit on a Stranger," I play bass on that song just because I thought I had a bass line that was better. If Mark's is better, then we use that. We listened to them both and mine just turned out to be better, so it was like, "Let's just keep that." It's just a matter of time in the end as well. The control freak aspect has a lot to do with time. You know when someone teaches you to play a song, how long it takes for you to get into it.

It's rare when it's really fast.

There were some straight songs where you could do it. You're trying to make a new sound for a band - if Mark only has two weeks to learn twelve songs, that's a lot. He had more time this last album so it was better. Or Scott, they don't know what to add, so they just play it straight and that's fair. I've lived with the stuff more, and we don't have forever to make an album and we don't live in the same place. So, everyone knows why it happens. With Bob, he's like, "I'll just be touring, I don't care if I play." That's his attitude, maybe a defense mechanism, not contribute as much as he could. Again, if you live in different places or even if you didn't. I'm glad that our guys are however musical they are. They aren't playing all the time. If you say, "Play a C", Mark has to think for a second... "Okay C is here." It doesn't mean he's bad, but he just doesn't think that way. Those guys that "play" C are going, "Doo Doo dwiddle Doo." They know where every C is located.

It seems like having a producer is good for you. Having someone else in there going, "I've got sonic ideas, things to take to the band." Maybe push you a little, whereas Scott and everyone else is saying, "Do what you want!" The band could succeed or fail on one of your performances. I'm not saying Bryce wouldn't pay attention. He would, I'm sure.

If he's in the role.

Bryce would have told you if he thought something was really not working.

He did that, probably... I mean I would ask, "What do you think of that."

It seems like a good point to start working with producers.

It's fun, it's like an extravagance, really. They take a big percentage of your record. A lot of them take up front money. I wouldn't recommend it to bands that couldn't afford it, no matter how great it is. For me, it was an extravagance. I wasn't thinking, "Oh this is costing that much." Originally I was thinking that. "Oh they are sort of scam artists, producers. When you're in a real band you don't need anyone's help." As I got older I realized that I was wrong. I just wanted to work with this cool person who is talented. Like you were saying, it didn't have anything really to do with that producer mold. It was more like somebody else in here just to see if it was good. I didn't know what it was like, I had never done it before. At a time when you're not so precious of what you're sound is like, is another good time to do it. Maybe when you're first starting you're like, "Oh I need to be this way." You're also worried that you're going to sound like some other band... "We sound too much like Radiohead." It's more of a risk. At our point, we didn't feel that it was that much of a risk. We don't have to worry if it sounds too much like this or that

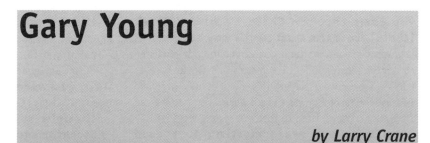

Gary Young

by Larry Crane

Gary Young was the flamboyant original drummer for Pavement. He was also the engineer for all their recordings up through the *Watery, Domestic* CD. He still resides in Stockton, California, and runs his Louder Than You Think [16-track 1" analog/ Pro Tools system] studio out in the walnut orchards. He's recently completed a self-released album [Gary Young's Hospital, *Things We Do For You*] and did some recordings with Scott Kannberg [of Pavement] that are to be released as Pavement B-sides.

How did you meet up with the guys in Pavement?

They just came here.

Do you know how they found out about your studio?

In the newspaper, or the fact that I was just local. You know, I was cheap.

How much were you charging back then?

I charged twenty dollars [per hour] then, I charge thirty dollars now.

That's pretty affordable.

Yeah, and I have a lot of stuff. What I had then was an MCI console and a 16-track. I have a Tascam MS-16.

A one inch?

Yeah, which I really like. I'd like to have 24-track if at all possible. People complain about the DBX and that it only goes 15 ips, but I know how it works. I can make drums sound really good because I drum. I recently got a pretty nice Pro Tools thing here, but I put it all on the tape machine first. I like the way the tape machine makes the vocals sound.

There's something different there isn't there?

Yes, when I put it on straight, it sounds kind of funny. Anyway, they [Pavement] came here and they had never been to a recording studio before. What I remember was that they had wanted to do this guitar noise kind of thing. They came and recorded that and I said to them, "This really doesn't sound like much, my drums are here, should I drum?" They agreed, so I just drummed that day and that's the first record. We did it all in one day. The second record was pretty much the same; they came and played guitar and I drummed that day. The third record had a slight amount of preparation, the 10" one. The other one [*Slanted and Enchanted*], we went over it for a few days before we recorded it. Again, there wasn't a great amount of preparation or anything that you would call practice. I don't really think that Kannberg [Scott] played much at the onset. More of what happened was that Steve would play the chords and say, "Change" or "Fast part" through the dummy mic we had set up. I would make up drum parts or flounder around a bit. Did you ever see us play?

Yeah, I helped do sound for you guys when you came through Chico. I'd known Mark [Ibold] from the Dust Devils way back.

Well, it was much better after it was so organized. If you listen to any of those bootleg live records you would have to know what we were playing to know if it was any good because the recording was so bad. When I listen to it I can sit and say, "Wow, listen to that". We were good.

By the time you were starting to record *Slanted and Enchanted*, were you in the band at that point?

We had played before then. We went to New York and played, not with Mark though. We had done about seventeen shows with a third guitar player and Bob [Nastanovich]. Mark came on before the *Slanted and Enchanted* tour, he wasn't on the record at all. There is only bass on one song on either "Here" or "Home."

There is low end on the record though, what's going on there?

I had an amplifier, now it doesn't work anymore, but it was an amplifier called a Lounge Casino. Basically, it was this bass amplifier for this cheesy nightclub thing. Scott [Kannberg] played all the guitar through that, so that's what sounds like bass.

Just kind of deeper and muddier sounding...

But there's no single-note kind of bass.

When you were in the band it was always 16-track recordings and from there they went on to 24-track 2". Besides some weird demos, nothing's ever been done on less than 16 tracks for the proper albums. Yet, you would read reviews of *Slanted and Enchanted* or other records and they would mention "8-track recording" or "lo-fi." Were you personally offended by that?

No. It's really not that lo-fi.

Right, I don't think it is either.

Whatever is on the album was intended. I didn't really understand this music then, my favorite band was Yes. I'm 46 years old now, the reason I liked that music [Yes] was because we started listening to the Beatles. I lived in New York so we had New York radio at home. In the late '60s, there was all this slop music, then all of the sudden here were all these guys that could really play. Yes was complicated and hard, so me and my brother really zoned in on this. We said, "Wow, this is really hard to do." So that's how we got involved in that. I can't make records like that, those are really hard to make. Short of that, I can make any kind of record you want. Anyway, I had just gotten my mixing console and I didn't know how it worked very well, it was made for broadcast. It had a switch that switches the EQ from a playback mode to a record mode. Well, we did one whole part of the album with the drums having no EQ. When the drums went onto tape it was really flat but I did EQ it after the fact. One of the reels of the tape didn't have any of the EQ on the drums incoming. The guitars sounded the way they wanted them to sound. I thought that for the other stuff besides *Slanted and Enchanted*, it was just pretty much noisy stuff.

Yes there is definitely some noisy stuff going on like on the songs they compiled on the *Westing by Musket and Sextant* CD. It's just got some crazy noise stuff, but then there are these beautiful little pop songs too.

Right, which is sort of what bugged me. I said, "There's some good songs here, but if you can't hear them then what's the point? Obviously my foresight wasn't any good.

Well, you were listening to Yes. [Laughter] I was living down in Chico, California, when that early stuff came out. I thought, "This is strange that there's people down in Stockton making records like that." It definitely has something to do with Stephen's vision of what they could do.

I don't know how much credit Stephen gives me, but those guys were completely clueless about recording.

Stephen said they really didn't know much of anything or what they were doing, and they would try to help mix...

Well, they would say to me, "We want this to sound like this, how do you that?" And I would do it. I had a lot of junk lying around that they would use.

To get the sounds?

Yes.

I heard some story that the drumset was set up from a heavy metal session that you had done right before, and they came in to record and you just used the same exact sounds. It was your drums that you had used for both sessions, right?

I don't know about that.

That's the rumor that goes around about *Slanted and Enchanted*.

Well, what does set up mean?

Exactly, that's what I always wonder. Was it mic'd up?

They're always mic'd up, the mics are just there. Again I'm not sure if it was the first or second album that has no EQ, so what does that mean? I have standard mic set up for the drums. My standard drum kit would have a D12 for kick drum, a SM57 for snare drum, 421s for tom-toms, Neumanns on the overheads and the 414s if you wanted a mic on the hi-hat or the ride cymbal. I generally use six mics on the drums, one for each tom-tom, kick, snare and two overheads. If the hi-hat isn't loud enough I just move the overhead near it.

I've never wanted to hear more hi-hat very often.

I also like to use a 414 for guitar amplifiers, SM57s are okay, but it's kind of middie for me. The thing about a 414, to me, is wherever you put your ear and you like what the amp sounds like, you put a 414 there and you're pretty well assured that it's going to sound like what you heard. I'm pretty sure that was the microphone we used for the amplifiers.

Yeah, real lo-fi there Gary! [Laughter]

It's funny. I have a Tascam mixing console now, which is okay. If I were going to start my recording studio business again right now, I'd buy an 8-track mixing board and spend every penny I had on microphones.

It's well worth it, don't you think?

The other thing is, you buy a decent one and it's worth as much as you pay for it or more. A good microphone never goes down in price.

Is your studio still in your house?

It was in my garage, but my neighbors gave us a hard time. We got really lucky; we bought a house that's seven miles outside of town on an acre in the corner of a walnut orchard – it's got two whole houses. The day before we signed the papers to buy the house someone came and bombed one house. The guy who lived there before us was a junkie. Of course, the bank wouldn't sell me the house because it was burnt down and the insurance company wouldn't pay me because it wasn't mine. I haggled these people for a year and finally they all agreed to fix it and sell it to us at the agreed upon price. The frame of the house remained, but most of the inside was fixed. In that budget was enough to add on a 20 X 30 room extended from the other house. The other house had a garage about 30 X 30 turned into a living room, which became the band room and the 20 X 30 room became the control room; the closets became isolation booths. My brother swiped a computer program that costs $50,000 for the design of the room. We built the control room five-sided with canted walls and no right angles – a really fancy control room design. You can walk around and there is very little change as to what anything sounds like, no matter where you sit in the entire room. I was lucky to have somebody tell me how to do it.

So you have no neighbors...

Well, they're three quarters of a mile away. I could put the drums on the roof and they wouldn't know or care anyway. It turns out that my soundproofing is more to keep noise out than in.

You get to the point where that's the reason, obviously.

Have you heard my new record yet?

No, I haven't heard that.

I made a thousand of these things, because after I had the "Plant Man" thing...

Yeah, did that do alright?

No, because that's when Big Cat records quit with everybody. What happened was that we had the record, the video came out and then the record company quit. Pavement – I understand them quitting with me because I was drunk and stuff, which I'm not anymore.

You don't drink anymore?

It's been thirteen months.

That seemed to be the biggest grievance that everyone in the band had.

Yeah, but we certainly attracted a lot of attention. They complain about it, but if it wasn't for me, with all that antics, I don't think it would have gone quite as far as it did. There's no question that it was out of hand but that's part of life... in a way.

Hey, it was fun. So you got dropped right after the first record came out?

Yeah and I made this other one. I had a thousand pressed and I still have 950 of the damn things.

Did you do all the recording and writing? Did you play all the instruments yourself?

I don't do all that on purpose – I just can't get anybody to help me! I can strum a guitar and I can play chords on a piano and I drum okay. Drumming I don't really have a problem with. I don't think I sing worth a shit. I have two guys who play in the band who are good singers, but they refuse to sing. They say my voice has character so I sing. I'm getting better at it; the new one is more in key than the old one. Do you have a Pro Tools thing?

No, I've used one for mastering, but I don't have anything here.

Well, I just got that auto-tune thing, I put it on my vocals because I just wanted to see and it's not that far off.

Those auto-tuners scare me.

What I would use it for is if someone played a really great solo but there was one wrong note, you could change the note.

And fly it over to another track?

Yeah, I would consider it for that. I think the Pro Tools thing is good for mixes. What I really like about it is that it remembers everything. The problem with me is if you do one band and then another band comes in, the guy from the first band will call you next week and say, "I love the whole thing but the vocals aren't loud enough." You're fucked. I don't know if you can, but I can write all the settings down and come back the next week and put them back the way they were and for the life of me it never sounds the same.

I totally agree, I don't even try anymore – it doesn't work that way.

Pro Tools remembers all that junk and you can do that kind of stuff.

So you'll do most of the main tracking on your 16-track and then put it in Pro Tools and maybe add a few things if you need to?

Yeah and the other thing that's cool about it is that you can physically go in and do a fade. You don't have to worry about twisting the knobs at the end of the song to get rid of that guitar noise. Another cool thing about it is you can erase stuff in between... like at the beginning of a guitar solo when the guitar player starts up and click, click... I'm always scared of doing that on my regular tape machine, with Pro Tools you can do that.

Do you feel like it makes work a lot faster?

I don't think it makes it any faster because I think you have to dick with it. I think that it makes it more repeatable and if you're really stuck on using analog, the SMPTE slave driver thing syncs up to my multi-track dead on, two samples off. What you can do is fly a vocal track onto the Pro Tools, fix it and put it back. I snagged one of these things used with a computer for $3,000.

That's not bad.

If you're interested, Digi-Design has a website where they have them used.

I'd have to save money up for awhile. So what kind of work have you been doing for the last few years?

I do ska bands. I've done 4 ska CDs, in the past year, of 4 different bands. It's a big thing here now.

Real young kids?

Well, college or high school, yeah. I also did something with [Scott] Kannberg.

I heard about that, can you elaborate on that?

It was sort of like Pavement. He came and we did two songs. One of them is really good – I played it for somebody and they said, "This sounds more like Pavement." I'm bummed about this because, in a lot of ways, I wish that they would come here and let me make another good one. I think that it would happen. To me, the drums on all the new albums...

I love this [Steve West] guy, he's a great guy and everything, but he sucks. He's got no inventiveness; all the drums sound the same on all the songs. When I found out that Nigel Godrich was going to do this I said, "Wow, this is going to be really great." They sent it to me a few months ago and there's nothing really interesting to me at all. Have you heard the new one?

Yeah, I actually helped do some demos. They were mostly just practicing here. I did demos for the previous record [Brighten the Corners] too, with just Stephen [Malkmus] on an 8-track and I like the demo stuff better! I just like the looseness and stuff.

To me, I'm prejudiced against it – I'm not a good judge of it. I just wish that they would make something more interesting. They did, and I know they can.

contact Gary Young at garytheplantman@email.msn.com
or at P.O. Box 1059, Linden CA. 95236

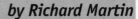

I Have a Question for You

by Richard Martin

Timmy Taylor of Brainiac

Brainiac's Touch and Go release, Hissing Prigs in Static Couture, has some of the weirdest sounds on any recent rock record. Girls Against Boys' Eli Janney produced most of the songs, which were recorded at Water Music in lovely Hoboken, New Jersey. Steve Albini had to get a piece of the action, so he put "Nothing Ever Changes" to tape in his basement. The creepiest and catchiest song, however, is "This Little Piggy," which features an electric voice that sounds like the computer in that old Matthew Broderick movie, War Games.

That's a Texas Instruments' home computer, the TI-994. I got that when I was 11 years old. We had it up in the attic for years, and I remembered that it had this speech pack, a

metal box that you snap into one of the ports on the side. Then you type in simple sentences. I didn't have any of the books any more, so I just started going around to thrift stores in Dayton and by luck one of them had a complete TI setup with this book that explained how to program it. I didn't want to pay the 25 bucks, so I stuffed the book down my pants and went home and learned how to program in basic again. I was able to write a simple program where you could feed sentences into it. It was really laborious – we had to feed it, then find the point in the song and punch it in. It took like three hours to get it all on tape.

Doug Scharin of Rex and Him

Doug Scharin, formerly with Codeine, now drums in Rex and spends his spare time in his Williamsburg, Brooklyn apartment fiddling with his 4-track while creating the electro-dub sounds for his project Him. Both Rex and Him have albums on Southern Records.

Do you find that Rex's trance-y waltz music is a response to the bustling New York environment?

I do on a personal level. Musically, I feel like it directly relates to it as well – I guess we all feel it. I've been living in Williamsburg for four years. I'm definitely influenced by the industrial vibe here and the sound structure you are forced to deal with every day living in this kind of situation. I don't know if it comes across so much on Rex music as it does on some of the other stuff I've been working on. We have this other side project here that I've been working on called Him. It's an ambient sound scapey dub sort of project. I go record outside and incorporate those kinds of environmental sounds into it. I have a 4-track and I've learned how to use it in such a way as to get the optimum sound that you could possibly get from cassette 4-track. Also, I've found ways to jam a lot of information on the tape to make it sound okay.

Kelley Deal of the Kelley Deal 6000

The Kelley Deal 6000's debut, Go To the Sugar Altar, *was produced by Ms. Deal herself, with some help from Dave Shouse of the Grifters. She started her own label, Nice, and released the record herself. It was recorded at Pachyderm and Terrarium in Minnesota, with Brent Sigmeth mixing.*

I thought Dave Shouse was supposed to produce your record?

I had been listening to the Grifters' *Eureka* EP all last summer, and of all the new music I'd heard, if something

moved me, that did. I had met Dave one time. I called him and said, "Hey, Dave, I'm gonna go in the studio. Do you wanna produce my record for me?" He says, "Well, I'm getting married on Saturday. I can be there on Tuesday."

Did he bring his wife?

No, Jenny stayed home. They delayed their honeymoon. They'd been living together for years. It was so funny. So, he comes up here and only has a week and a half that he can give. He's just Mr. Music. He and Jimmy Flemion both [Flemion played guitar and sang backup]. I would work with them at the drop of a hat. They walk around and notes spring from their step. I envision these little black quarter notes. Anyway, I told Dave I wanted a music box on the song "Nice" and he says, "Let me see what I can do." Then he goes on the Wurlitzer and he gets a sound that's exactly like a music box. After he had to go, we went to Pachyderm and re-recorded five of the songs. We didn't credit Dave as producer because all the songs he worked on were remixed and re-recorded. He hadn't even heard the record, so I couldn't put him down as producer: What if he hates it? Anyway, you can tell I feel bad about it.

Matt Kadane of Bedhead

Bedhead's latest Trance Syndicate effort, Beheaded, *was recorded in Austin, Texas, with Adam Wiltzie behind the boards. Wiltzie is in Stars of the Lid Symphony Orchestra, which has their own album out on Kranky.*

What was the story with the recording?

We recorded last summer. In fact, we started recording the summer before. It takes a while for us to mix. It doesn't take so long for us to record, but mixing takes a long time when you're dealing with three different guitars that sometimes have the same tones and sometimes have different tones. When you're doing a lot of ambient mic'ing, and trying to keep the cymbal out of the guitar mics at one point and have them in at another point and when you're dealing with all the contingencies of recording live, mixing is a real time-consuming thing.

CHAPTER 3
Engineers, Producers and Studios

Steve Albini

DOES THIS MAN NEED AN INTRODUCTION?

by John Chandler

© Cynthia Connolly

Steve Albini has become a somewhat legendary figure in the recording world these days. Enjoy this introduction into the mind of an engineer who will not be labeled a "producer". –Larry Crane

Going back in history a little bit, I remember reading that in your college days you would incite people to try and attack you by insulting them from behind a Plexiglass barrier.

That was one specific art project that I did. It was a piece of process sculpture. The remains of that Plexiglas screen and all the objects that were thrown at me were meant to be displayed, were meant to be shown as the result of the process, the process being taunting.

In terms of the music you create, from Big Black to the present with Shellac, would you say that confrontation and provoking people to react by raising their ire or frustrating them is a concept you've maintained.

No, not at all. I actually feel quite the opposite – that what the bands that I've been in have been about has been specific and within the band, and the outside world only enters into it really as sort of the proving grounds of the experiment. The reactions of other people are not the product of what we do. Other people's reactions, are in a lot of ways, immaterial. It's always satisfying if you feel like you're communicating with somebody and they're participating in what you're doing, almost on equal footing, with what the people in the band are doing. But that sort of camaraderie doesn't happen every time, and when it does happen it's an unusual, surprising and exciting event. So most of the time what we are doing is for ourselves.

With the Shellac album, *Terraform*, one gets the idea of a barren landscape that is reborn, or repopulated or re-foliated to resemble Earth, or the familiar. Yet at the

same time it's distinctly alien. In the same way there are elements of familiar or mainstream rock that occur on the album and yet are mutated to an extent to create new sound. Is that more or less the idea or am I just shooting blanks?

Well, we chose the name for the album on purpose. Being in a band is a construction process. You're putting together your aesthetic, you're putting together the songs, and you're putting together the relationships of the people within the band and the relationship that you're going to have with the people you're playing in front of. And if you direct those decisions after a specific effect, and say, "Well, we wanted to end up like this." You're going to be disappointed. So all you can really do is start processes underway, like start a methodology underway, and wait and see what happens. And that's sort of the modus operandi of the band on all fronts. We've got an idea of how we want to conduct ourselves and we've got an idea of what things we want to try, but the end result of that is what actual habitat we end up in, and what actual songs and sounds. What net effect do we have on the people that are in the band and the people that we play with? All of that's unknown.

I was intrigued, because when I brought the album home one of my roommates said, "Oh, the artwork reminds me of Shusei Nagaoka," who did a lot of those Electric Light Orchestra and Earth, Wind & Fire albums during the '70s, and so he was wondering if it was kind of a deliberate throwback thing or...

The choice of Chesley Bonestell is actually very specific. When I was a kid, there was a children's book called *From The Earth To The Moon*, which was illustrated by Chesley Bonestell. It was actually illustrated using a number of paintings he had done for *Collier's* magazine in the '40s and '50s about what space travel would be like. The illustrations were done during a period when there hadn't even been any exploration of the upper atmosphere. It was an entirely theoretical proposition, space travel. And the thing that amazed me over time was how many insights Chesley Bonestell had just from a purely academic knowledge and from an Earth-based knowledge of what the other planets were like and what space travel would be like. It was amazing how often he was right about how things would go. And about how things would look. It's not amazing that he got some of the things wrong that he got wrong. But that blend of just this uncanny prescient quality of being able to discern how things would go, long before anyone had even postulated the ideas, paired with just a naive perception of what technology would be around, and an unavoidably naive perception of what technology would really be here, I think gives his paintings a real charm, and I don't know of anyone who's working in an equally futuristic vein at the moment. There are a lot of buzz words and catch phrases that get kicked around in popular culture and fine art, you know, the information age and technology and all that kind of nonsense. But here's a guy who imagined that space travel was possible, found out everything he could about the methodology that would probably be employed and did these incredible, meticulous illustrations of what it would be like. And he was right far more often than he was wrong. He's a really remarkable character.

What was it about the music you were creating with Shellac at the time that made you return to those images?

Really, it's sort of been a long standing affection of mine, and there were some reprints of his stuff done in a couple of magazines, so I got a chance to show them to Bob [Weston] and Todd [Trainer] and they all thought that it was apropos. You know, there's a parallel between his artwork and everybody in the band. How you can imagine how something would be and present your take on it and then you're either proven right or proven wrong, and the degree of rightness or wrongness isn't as important as that it's possible to be right or wrong. In a complex subject there may be 150 specific elements that you could analyze as being right or wrong. 149 of them you can get totally wrong. But the one that you get right, if that's something that wasn't blatant and obvious, then you've had a unique insight.

You seem to be most comfortable musically playing in trio settings. Have you had any desire to work in any wildly different configurations at some point?

Well, as it happens, I'm only really comfortable playing as part of a band, that is, a band that is a permanent embodiment of a set of ideas that everyone is committed to. I've done occasional things where I've played as a side musician for somebody else, and that's almost always as a personal favor to someone.

Have you ever considered film scoring or things like that?

Again, only to help someone out. It's not an interest of mine. People that do that sort of stuff as a profession do that very well and understand the complexities of it, understand what's required of it. And me, from a naive perspective doing it, I would make countless callous blunders, you know.

Shifting gears, how did your working relationship with Jimmy Page and Robert Plant [on... *Clarksdale* album] come about and what sort of experience was it for you?

It was an enormously rewarding experience, just being in the company of people of that sort of significance, people with that kind of history behind them, you know. Definitely we got along really well and I consider them great friends and I had a fantastic time working on their record.

Was it a case of them approaching you, or was it a project you were interested in from day one and said, "I'd like to do this."

I got a call, I actually got a fax, from their management company that said they were interested in having me work on a record, would I be free to come to England to meet them? And I replied that I was a little bit humbled by them approaching me at all, and of course something like this is an opportunity that doesn't come along very often. But my time is generally committed pretty far in advance and I wasn't able to just drop everything and fly over, but if they wanted to schedule a session where we could get to know each other and possibly even get some work done toward a record, that would be the best way to evaluate whether or not we would get along and whether or not we could do a record together. 'Cause I didn't feel comfortable strapping into an extended project of that magnitude without them being completely sold on me and without me being completely comfortable with the way they wanted to make the record. So we did a short test session in June of '97 and that went well and at that point everybody committed to doing the record in September. We started in September, and then we just carried on.

It's interesting because I seem to recall an interview in the late '80s with Robert Plant in which he professed his admiration for bands like Hüsker Dü and the Violent Femmes. Is he a person who keeps up with less mainstream music?

Well, both he and Jimmy Page are pretty much the same rabid music fans that they've always been. Robert Plant still buys, I would guess he buys ten records a week. He's not operating in a vacuum. A lot of moribund rock stars sort of hole up in their castles and never venture out into the outside world. And Robert is so full of life and so full of the experience of day to day life that that sort of lifestyle just isn't possible for him. And Jimmy Page sort of came out of his shell a few years ago and since then he's made a lot of friends and he's developed a real affection for a lot of contemporary music. Which wouldn't be expected from somebody who had such a strong legacy to stand on his own, but they're constantly talking about this or that new record that they love or this or that band that they're crazy about. And there is also an inexhaustible archive of old material for them, which they keep discovering, like old blues stuff and old juke joint music and old ragtime. There really isn't a single genre of music that they don't have some affection for.

So, the most cynical scenario is where the cigar-chomping money guys say, "Let's get some hot young producer to update their sound," or something like that.

Well, for what it's worth, absolutely no one at the record company was involved in making the record. I remember once the album was finished and mastered, Robert was even skeptical of sending them a cassette for fear that somebody in the office would bootleg it. No, the people involved in the commercial side of the record were not involved at all in the making of the record. By and large they didn't even hear it until it was ready to be put on the shelves.

And from your point of view, you probably had the usual indie cynics going "What the hell? It must just be for a big money gig," or something like that.

Well, you know, I remain blissfully ignorant of what all the nose pickers say about me on the internet. It really doesn't matter to me. I mean, my rationale for the way I conduct myself is, in my mind, bulletproof and people can say whatever they like about me. I honestly don't care. I know that my motives are pure and that my sympathies lie with the bands and my sympathies will always lie with the bands. You know, there are people in my position who make records for a living who want to be part of the music establishment. They want to be part of the network of people who manipulate, and make profit off manipulation of careers, and I have no interest in that. I want to make good records and I want to be in cahoots with bands that want to make the record of their dreams. That's my role in all of this.

Have you ever felt the temptation to do a full-on Phil Spector approach with a band and try to shape their sound on an album from the ground up?

It doesn't have any interest for me. None whatsoever. I feel like the few times when I have been in a position where I've had to exert sort of creative energy for a band that just, for one reason or another, couldn't get their record made otherwise, I feel like I haven't done as good of a job as when a band takes the initiative on their own and comes up with their own agenda and executes it. It hasn't happened in a long time. By and large people who approach me about making records don't do it because they want me to create the record for them and put their name on it. They want to make a record themselves and they want someone who can avoid ruining it in the process.

Have you ever taken or absorbed something from one of the bands you are recording to the extent that it follows you into the music you are creating yourself?

Well, it's part of the life experience that's embodied in everything, all the music that my band does.

I partly think it would be hard to watch somebody like Jimmy Page and just be oblivious...

Well, I'm not much on imitation, but I can be inspired by an attitude quite comfortably without wanting to ape the moves that somebody else makes. And if I can be as full of life in my 50s as Jimmy Page and Robert Plant are, then I'll feel like I've really accomplished something.

There must have been some good exchanges, because the history of Led Zeppelin is always produced by Jimmy Page...

To his credit, Jimmy Page has grown a lot as a person. I think that when he was young and headstrong he wanted to be the auteur of everything that he was involved in. And you can't fault the results. You know, you can't criticize just the impeccable, consistent quality of the stuff that Led Zeppelin did. And that's stuff that was recorded under the most ridiculous variety of circumstances in the most extreme conditions. Everything from recording in a barn or in a castle to recording in state-of-the-art studios. Everything from the highest to the lowest technical standards and it all comes out sounding consistently good. You really can't fault the results. And so his working method for the time validated itself in the results. And his working method now is much more of a collaborative process with Robert because they've got a complete spectrum of things going on in their lives. You know,

they've both got intensive family obligations and they've both got quite rich personal lives. So to expect them to drop all of that and start behaving like they were adrenaline-charged and chemically-charged teenagers I think is unrealistic. And I also don't necessarily think it would make for a stable working relationship, because Robert's been on his own for eight or ten years and doing quite well. He's quite comfortable as a solo artist, and I think it took a lot of personal strength... personal growth, on both their parts, to be collaborative again.

Have you done any recording and engineering work in the electronica or dance music field?

Well, I work with a lot of experimental artists who incorporate that sort of stuff, but the genre that's referred to as electronica, which is basically just another variation of dance music that makes no pretenses about having an organic origination, I really haven't participated in that just because I don't have any feel for dance music. I don't understand it, I don't know why people make music like that, and it has no intrinsic appeal to me. And if I tried to work on it I would probably do a bad job. I think there are people who understand that music and who love it and for whom it is a part of their soul, you know, and those people will do a much better job of it than I would, so there's no reason for me to dabble in it and make a bunch of lousy records in that genre.

How concerned or dedicated to state-of-the-art technology are you? Do you work with vintage gear?

I like to work with good equipment, and the construction standards and the sound quality standards have not improved in the last 20 years, with a very few exceptions. So I tend to use a lot of older equipment. Not because I'm going after any sort of a retro vibe or a vintage sound, but just because that's the best equipment that's ever been made for a lot of purposes. Like a lot of microphones that were made 30 or 40 years ago are the ideal transducers. They're perfect for their chosen applications. So there's no reason to fiddle around with a bunch of new, cutting-edge nonsense if it doesn't do the job as well. The other side of the same coin, though, is that there are some things that are better pieces of equipment now than were available 20 years ago. And using them means using the best and that appeals to me. Specifically, the last generation of analog tape machines that were designed incorporated utility functions, utility features and are of a general sound quality which hasn't been duplicated and hasn't been surpassed by anything since. So, given my choice, I would work on technically sophisticated analog recording equipment.

On the evolutionary time line of music can you see anything big coming next, or will music for the foreseeable future continue to fragment into smaller niches?

Well, one thing that's happened on a cultural and on a musical level in the last couple years is that the mainstream record companies and the mainstream music industry has pretty much given up on rock music. And that, to me, is a great development from a cultural and aesthetic standpoint because it removed the patina of business from what should be a purely creative enterprise. And now people that are devoted to making, for lack of a better term, personal or experimental rock music, there is now no hint of commercial enterprise to it and I think that's a very freeing development. On the other hand, financially it's been very, very hard, because anyone whose livelihood depends on making records is going to be affected by the trend in the industry away from just the sort of blind infusion of money that took place in the '90s.

So you pretty much see the whole indie integrity vs. corp. contamination debate as a moot point.

Well, at the moment the mainstream record labels and the mainstream music business are not interested in anything of substance. They're not interested in quality music anymore. It's back to the state of affairs that it was in the late '70s and early '80s where the records that are on the radio are of a totally different stripe from the records I would listen to at home. Whereas, in the '90s, there was some crossover in that, between the two. And at the moment there's a much broader variety of sound, there's a much wider palate being explored in the underground than there was for a few years in the mid to late '90s. You know, almost every band fit into one of a few specific categories, even within the underground, and that's not the case anymore. Now the eggshell's busted pretty much wide-open and people are working on a much smaller scale, but are making much more personal music, making music that appeals to a smaller audience. And the people that are doing it are doing it because it means something to them, and as a consequence of that they have to make themselves content with the scale that they're working on. And I think that culturally that's a great development.

So in a sense it's as if we removed big money contracts from pro sports and said, "Well, anybody who still likes to play basketball can, you just won't make 12 million dollars a year."

It's a totally different perspective, I think. I mean there's no question that basketball is played at a higher level of expertise now than it was 20 years ago, but with the exception of the Chicago Bulls, there really aren't any dynasties anymore, you know. There aren't any teams that can hold their roster, there aren't any teams that stay intact for five or ten years where players can really develop a relationship with a coach and a group of teammates over a long-term period. Baseball has been most affected by that trend. Since the onset of free agency the greatness of the sport has probably been attenuated, although the players themselves are doubtlessly doing better.

In general how do your recording jobs materialize? Do they break down along a sliding scale from major label bands to more of pro bono thing for indie bands?

I would say 99 percent of the work that I do is for bands in the underground. That is, bands that have no financial backing and have no business interest involved in their records. On average over the last 10 years it's been about one or two records a year that I'll work on, out of 50 to 100 that have any affiliation with a larger corporate entity. There are people in my position who work almost exclusively with big label bands because it allows them to make one or two records a year and make a comfortable living. I'm really not interested in making a living. I'm interested in making myself available to a broader spectrum of people and making myself available as part of a community of people who make music and make records as a creative output and as sort of one of the bones in the backbone of their existence. People that I work with, in general, are making music because it means a lot to them. It is their life's work and that's what they do as their creative expression, and I feel better about being a participant in that, in both a cultural sense and on a personal level. I feel better about doing that than I would about making commodity music which would make me rich or, you know, would make me a player in the music business. I have no interest in being part of the music business. My interests are exclusively to be part of a community of people who are creative and intelligent and expressing themselves uniquely. Those people and that way of doing things is what I hold dear. Being a part of the business is of no interest to me.

Mitchell Froom

by John Baccigalupi

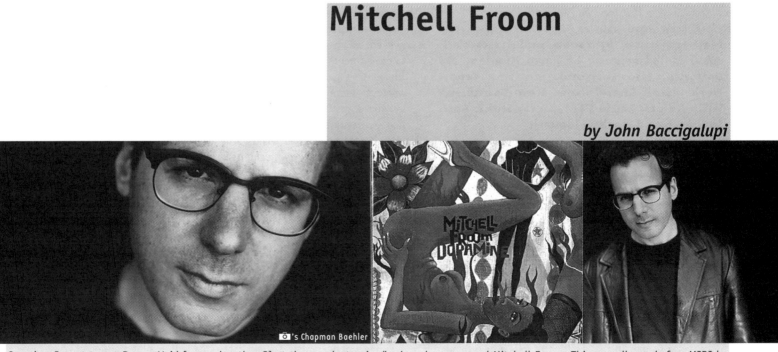

One time I went to see Romeo Void [remember them?] at the California State Fair here in Sacramento. It turned out that they were opening for a band called Gamma, which was Ronnie Montrose's new project and was only him and some electronics/keyboards guy named Mitchell Froom. This was all way before MIDI by the way. Well, Sacramento is a cool town in a lot of ways, but we've got an overly high share of white-trash trailer park meth lab types here, and I'm pretty sure they were all in attendance at this show. I really felt sorry for Romeo Void because the crowd kept yelling, "Moooontrooooose," really loudly and "You guys suuuuck," in between songs. Then they started throwing things and the band finally left the stage in the middle of a song. My hometown. So finally Gamma comes out and they start playing this prog-rock techno stuff and the crowd quits yelling for Montrose and starts yelling, "Bad Motor Scooterrrrrr," instead. Finally Ronnie Montrose sits down to play some kind of screaming 64th note acoustic guitar piece, but before he does he says, "You guys are serious assholes. Romeo Void's our good friends and we're not gonna' play 'Bad Motor Scooter' so why don't you all leave?" I thought that was pretty cool of Ronnie, and you gotta' admit the first Montrose record rocks pretty hard still. [Way back when Sammy Hagar just went by Sam.] What does this have to do with Mitchell Froom? Not much really, except that he was there and it's a funny story. A few years later, I heard the first Del Fuegos record that he produced and I thought it was really well produced with a light, but sure touch, especially for an era when most production was very heavy handed and obvious. The record sounded great, but was really raw and had a great feel to it. He went on to work with Crowded House next and has since worked with Los Lobos, Elvis Costello, Richard Thompson, Ron Sexsmith, American Music Club, Cibo Matto, Maria McKee and Suzanne Vega whom he married after they made the excellent *99.9 F* album. He's still making great records today and I was stoked for the opportunity to interview him for *Tape Op*.

You were in Gamma with Ronnie Montrose right?

Wow! Yeah I was in that band for two seconds.

On his new solo album 'Dopamine' [which features music by Froom and lyrics and vocal melodies sung by David Hidalgo, M. Doughty, Lisa Germano, Suzanne Vega, Mark Eitzel, Sheryl Crow, Steve Donnelly, Miho Hatori, Louie Perez, Jerry Stahl, Ron Sexsmith and Mark Feldman]:

Tony Berg at Geffen gave me the go ahead to do it. But it took three years to do it because our budget was really small and I had a lot of people's schedules to work around. By the time it was finished, the hierarchy at Geffen had changed and they had gone in a different direction, so it ended up on Atlantic. Initially it was really fun to make. Towards the end I scheduled a couple of weeks to finish everything off and it got kind of scary then. I had to come to terms with it, which I'd never had to do before. When I produce records the individual or the band, the highlight's there. With this record that wasn't really there. When it's yourself it's quite different. So I started to think in terms of it being an arranger's record and then it started to make more sense to me. In the tradition of people like Henry Mancini, I hoped to make something in that vein.

On Not Losing an Artist's Identity with Production:

You look at each artist and see what their strengths are and you push them right to the forefront. The trick is to make everything around it strong and not too overly respectful because if what you add is very, very subtle you tend to soften down the result. So, each album comes with it's own set of problems.

Working With Tchad Blake:

Our relationship began to be more successful when we gave each other more space. When we first started working together I was more concerned about the sounds and it got a little bit strained for a while but all of the sudden we started finding our way around the [*Los Lobos*]*Kiko* record. It's a real delicate thing and it's continually evolving. Tchad will continually evolve new techniques and I try to bring new things to the table. We work at the relationship a lot. I would say in general I'm a more conceptual guy. I work with the artist, improvise and get arrangements together. Tchad doesn't spend time with the music beforehand, he just reacts and I think that's a good combination. The kind of thing I'm interested in is musical hybrids. I'm not interested in making records that are retro records. I like a lot of kinds of music and if you can somehow manage to make the music a bit of a hybrid of different things it seems to be more lively

The early days:

I was a struggling musician for a long time. There weren't a lot of opportunities for me in San Francisco. In 1983 or '84 I scored a film that started to take off in the midnight movie slots called *Cafe Flesh* and the soundtrack was on Slash records. At that time they had signed the Del Fuegos and nobody wanted to produce them and the people at Warner Bros. were saying, "How could you sign a band this bad." Now the soundtrack I did was done on an 8-track so the president of Slash said, "Well you're good with 8-track tape decks, why don't you take these guys and make an 8-track tape and if it works out, we'll let you make the record." So that's what we did. And then we did their second record and Warner Bros. really liked it and they seemed to think I was good at my job if I could take a band that nobody liked and make them sound good. The next band I did was Crowded House and things kind of got rolling from there.

Choosing Projects:

It would feel presumptuous for me to pursue a project. If there was an artist I really liked, why would they need me? I already like them the way they are. It has to come from the band or the artist. If the project engages my imagination and I have some good ideas then it's something I would want to do. Sometimes, for whatever reason, I simply can't hear anything except what's there and then I'll say you're wasting your time and money. That would be more like a job, I can't find my way into it. It's really good, but it's not the right thing for me.

On Not Getting Burnt out:

Not letting it become a job. Keeping a sense of adventure to things. Sticking to a true collaboration where you feel you're going after things. I don't like the music business, but I really love music.

Balancing Studio Work with a Personal Life:

It's a struggle.

Session length:

Eight or nine hours, after that it's diminishing returns. You need to be able to concentrate and have fresh ears. It's better to come back to something later with fresh ears.

Other Interests:

Besides Suzanne and our child, my personal life, and my job I don't really have any hobbies or other artistic outlets. Music is plenty for me, I'm always working on it in one way or another. I'm very interested in it in a lot of different ways. I like to drink wine and read at night. Right now I'm reading *Underworld* by Don Delillo.

The importance of recording technology versus musical performance:

Wherever I go in the world, when people talk to me about records of mine they've liked, nine times out of ten they talk about the Latin Playboys record. That record was recorded on a 4-track cassette recorder and then bounced over to 24-track tape. It's all feel and performance. Not only that, but people say that's one of the best sounding records I've worked on, which made me feel kind of peculiar. It's so beautiful and the 4-track cassette tape is the sound of that.

You get these peculiar things that are part of the sound of the record that people say is the best sounding record I've ever made. What that tells me is that it has a lot to with performance, and it has a lot to do with musical ideas. Those are the main things. Whoever feels that you can't make a great record with a 4-track recorder because of the quality of the 4-track sound? Don't think that. Don't try and make it sound like a 24-track recording, sometimes you'll get something that's much better than what you would have gotten. It's like trying to over reach on an instrument and make it do things that it really can't do.

The Wavelab

TUCSON, ARIZONA ISN'T KNOWN AS A RECORDING MECCA, BUT THE WAVELAB, WITH RECORDS BY CALEXICO, OP8, BARBARA MANNING AND RICHARD BUCKNER, IS MAKING ONE HELL A NAME FOR ITSELF

by Adam Selzer

's Bill Carter

Once upon a time, a record under the guise of OP8 was released which was a collaboration between Howe Gelb, Joey Burns, John Convertino [all of Giant Sand] and Lisa Germano. It's one of those records that creates such a strong vibe, which has a great deal to do with the way it was recorded. Around the same time, Richard Buckner released *Devotion and Doubt*, which is one of the purest and most beautiful recordings I had heard in a long time. Both were recorded at Wavelab Studios in Tucson, Arizona, by Craig Shumacher who has also recorded Barbara Manning, Friends of Dean Martinez, Bill Janovitz [of Buffalo Tom] and Calexico. I called him at his studio one day to talk to him about his methods and ideas.

It seems like whenever I see your name credited on records, it's along with Nick Luca, Joey Burns, and John Convertino. What is your working relationship with those guys?

Well Nick, he's the other engineer here. He has a master's degree in music. He came here with a four-piece jazz combo and started recording with me a number of years

ago and then he had graduated from school and had nothing going on at the time. He wanted a job so I said, "I can't pay you, but you can hang around the studio" and he said, "Sure."

So would you say you're more of the expert at the studio?

No, not really, I mean, I'm the owner more or less. The studio is a sole proprietorship in my name, but Nick had a lot of experience in music and engineering doing things at school and he really took to it. Around that same time, we were sort of getting inundated with requests to make records with Joey and Johnny because they were the rhythm section du jour for a number of projects. I originally met those guys through Howe Gelb with Giant Sand and that splintered into the Friends of Dean Martinez record, which I believe brought in other artists who wanted that sound. That sound is really made up of those two guys, John's drum and vibe playing and Joey's cello, guitar, accordion, and general madness... and this place here being a big warehouse has a rather ambient sound...

I wanted to ask you about that. That sound is so unique; with the playing of those two guys and the way you capture the sound. I refer to it as 'desert core.'

That's a nice title, I like that. Desert core.

It has that real 'Arizona-it's-hot-out' feel.

That's probably because it's real hot in the studio when we're doing it.

Is there any instruments that those guys don't play?

As far as I know harmonica. That's my gig. And horns. If there's ever any bad trumpet or trombone that's usually me. Joey plays cello, mandolin, guitar, bass, accordion and then anything else he can get his hands on pretty much. I just finished a record with this duo from France, which was kind of like a Calexico thing but a little more edgy, a little more eclectic with just drums and guitar, but more rock than Calexico.

How did you get that job – a band from France?

Well, the same thing really – this one guy's wife has lived in the States, in Tucson, and she was a big Giant Sand fan. They moved here and got to know Joey and Johnny and all those guys and they came to me and said we want to make a record at Wavelab – we're almost done with that one – so they were looking for sort of the same thing.

What kind of setup do you have out there?

The actual studio itself is in a big warehouse by the railroad tracks hence the trains in all of our recordings.

That's great! You've got to take advantage of your surroundings.

The building is an older building for Tucson. This is a pretty young city so some parts of this building go back to 1910.

That sounds like up here in Portland.

Yeah, there's that industrial area... I'm sure it's pretty similar. The West has that sort of tendency, so these are all turn of the century buildings that then grew through the various times of America's development. You can definitely trace the areas – here's the pre World War II section and then here's the post war section. This whole building is over 80,000 square feet of which I occupy a little over 3,000.

That's big – is it basically just one big open room?

I have one really big open room, which is the main cutting room, and then there's two other rooms. I have a vocal booth and the control room, which is also fairly large, but most of the tracking is done in the big room.

I assume you record all of your drums in there.

Yeah, pretty much. Most drummers will come in and set up their drums and the first time they hit their drums they'll say something like, "Oh my god! They sound so great!"

I wanted to ask you some more about that. I was listening to the OP8 record and was really impressed with the drum sounds.

Yeah, that's Johnny's whole schtick there.

How do you go about mic'ing drums in that room?

With John, I have a tendency to use only about four mics. Generally an AKG D112 on the kick, a SM 57 on the snare, and two overheads of some kind. Now if it's my deal, and nobody has any money [which most people don't], I'm using (AKG) C1000s. But if someone's paying, we go and rent a couple of (Neumann) U87s from another studio in town.

So you don't have a large mic collection?

No, I have not made the big leap. My top mics in the arsenal are an (AKG) 414 and an (Audio Technica) 4050. Those are my two large diaphragms. The C1000s I've been leaning heavily on for a number of years. They're really nice overhead mics.

I have one of those, but I've never used a pair.

Well they're nice and they've come way down in price.

Yeah, they're under $200. AKG for some reason has reduced the price of a lot of their mics. Their C3000s are under $300 now.

Yeah. And then the other mic I use a lot – I have a lot of AKGs for some reason, I think it's because Rainbow Guitars here in town is the most pro-audio music store – he's the guy I always go to for advice – he says, "You've got to try this one" and I do and then I keep them. I have a small condenser of theirs, I think the number is a 460 – and I use that a lot. I use it on acoustic guitars. For cello and stand-up bass I use the 414. I use the 4050 for vocals, but on the OP8 record all of Lisa Germano's vocals were done with a 57.

Really!

Yeah, she held a 57 in her hand. She wouldn't have anything to do with that standing up thing. She sat on a bench.

It's really encouraging to know you're getting such great recordings with minimal techniques, especially your drum sounds.

Well, a lot of it has to do with the player's kit. You get a good drummer with a good kit and you can get a great sound with one mic. I don't mic the inside of a kick drum, I always, like with John, mic the kick with a D112 about six to eight inches, sometimes even a foot away. Sometimes I use five mics. I'll use the C1000s sort of as lower overheads to pick up the toms and cymbals and then place a large diaphragm mic as the higher overhead behind his head.

You'll use your 4050?

The 4050 or the 414 or, if I've rented, the U87. On some of the records we played around with some figure eight patterns – one in front of the kit and one behind. I stumbled across this "behind the head" technique which I'm sure other people have done. The first time I did that I remember John coming into the control room and hearing that mic and saying, "That's how my drums sound!" I thought, "Well, that makes sense... I sort of mic'd his head."

I've heard about people putting mics right by the drummer's ears because they're so used to hearing it that way.

Yeah, it really makes them happy. In fact, I acquired a Beta 56, the right angle housed Shure, and I was all hot-to-trot to use it because it was a Beta Shure and it was built like a tank. I put that on his snare and he wouldn't have anything to do with it. He was upset. He said, "That doesn't sound good!" If I don't put a 57 on his snare he's pretty upset.

That's the way everyone's always heard a snare.

Yeah. I don't really have any expensive mics to use anyway. If I need them I rent them. When we did the Friends of Dean Martinez record Sub Pop was paying so we rented the U87s for a couple of weeks

How much does that cost you?

Well, I get a good break from a studio in town. This is a small town so there's a pretty good working relationship between everybody. I don't consider myself in competition with any of the other studios because I'm my own animal. I didn't go the ADAT route; I use a 2" 16-track...

What kind is it?

It's an MCI built in 1977. I only run it at 15 ips with (Ampex) 456 mainly because the machine doesn't like to run at 30 ips. When we did the Richard Buckner record we pushed it at 30 ips because MCA was paying and we had to pretend we were a big studio, and it was a nightmare because you get all those motors rolling twice as fast and all the control logic changes so there were some dicey moments, but the whole time that was going on it was supposed to be demo work so my attitude was "Hey, its a demo, what do you want me to do? I'm not getting paid like its some whoop-dee-dink record."

That's really interesting because I think that record sounds amazing.

Most all the drums and guitars and vocals were recorded here. My friend JD Foster, who produced it, wanted Rick to come out here to get into the desert vibe and work with Joey and Johnny. We had a lot of fun. The song "On Traveling"... there's some cello stuff, and John is doing some ambient drumming, and Rick is playing a chord organ and singing, and we have a cricket going on. That was the first night they were here. Rick went to a thrift store and found this Magnus chord organ...

I see those at every thrift store I go to.

Yeah, he found one here and he plugged it in and started playing and singing and JD said, "We gotta get this" so we mic'd him up and the next thing you know Johnny jumps out there rumbling on his thunder drum and toms and Joey starts doing his squeaky cello thing and then there was this cricket that was kind of bugging us so JD said, "The hell with it! Mic the cricket!" So then the cricket had the nerve to stop playing so we had to loop the cricket.

Was the cricket particular as to what mic you were using?

Well, the cricket, just like everyone else, had red light fever. When we started recording he just stopped. There was a lot of wackiness going on during that time. JD Foster is a brilliant producer. It was a big deal for me to be involved in the record, it being on MCA and all. I had all these aspirations...

But at the time you thought it was a demo?

Well, yeah, but I also thought that if I did a good job I would get more work down the road and at that time I could get a much better rate than I normally charge. So anyway, we were having some problems with running the machine at 30 ips, it was warbling, and I thought, maybe it's a sign that I'm getting ahead of myself, maybe I should just stick to what I do best. So then I decided the hell with it, if they don't come back, at least we had a good time doing it, we cut some good tracks. There's not much anyone else can ask for. But they did come back, that was in July which is monsoon season so that really put some interesting vibe on the record. We had one day that went from dry and hot to humid and hot and we couldn't tune a guitar to save our lives. So this storm came in and started rattling the vents on the roof as well as the roll up door. We had the U87s sitting in the middle of the room both in figure eight, and JD said "This sounds pretty cool, why don't you get some of it on tape." Then Rick jumps up and say's, "I want to sing" so he starts singing "Fader" and he sang it for so long that the storm ended, but while he was singing there was so much noise from all the rattling and dust and dirt blowing up against the door, I mean, this place is so "not studio" it's not even funny. I can't afford to put in big thick doors with perfect insulation... I don't even have air conditioning; I use a swamp cooler for god's

sakes! Listen, there's a train going by right now [clearly audible over the phone], I have many people say, "How can you be a recording studio with that environment?" So, back to the story, we have multiple takes of him singing on DAT. I flew his vocal, the stereo Neumanns, onto the computer; I use an Audiomedia card with a Macintosh and Sound Designer. I used the takes without the storm, after it was over. I edited together the best version of the verses. Then we flew that back to the 2" tape in stereo. Then I randomly edited together the storm, and just by sheer luck it was magic to the point where when he would pause there would be percussive sounds or rocks and dust hitting the building like it was a drum. We were floored by it. But, we were using used tape that had been spliced together and we experienced drop out. We had to go back and recreate our perfect accident! I actually had to do it again recently for some sort of interview/out-take collection – I only had it saved on the computer in backup. MCA called and said they wanted it for this project so I figured it was a way to make some more money...

You gotta milk the majors for all you can...

Yeah, but they never pay you like they say they will, but that's another story. And if they do you're going to wait a long time. Oh, another good story about that session is the take of "Lil' Wallet Picture." The guitar and vocal on that was cut live at four in the morning the last day they were here, before they were about to go to Austin to start over dubbing. We had several renditions of the song including versions with bass and drums and other instruments, but it never quite came together to Rick's satisfaction. JD was really pushing for the song because it was a little more poppy, more radio friendly than most of his other songs, but Rick wanted a more heartfelt version and he was really bucking the idea of a produced version. Syd Straw and the Skeletons were playing at Congress and Howe Gelb had just gotten back into town from Europe and they all came over and Syd got us all stoned and started telling us all these horror stories about being on the road with Bob Weir and all. Then they left, and Rick stood up and said, "I want to do 'Lil' Wallet Picture.'" He grabbed his guitar, went into the vocal booth, we hooked up the 4050 and the 460 and away he went. That's the version on the record, they just added some steel and other instruments in Austin.

Have you been experimenting with any studio trickery lately?

I guess one thing I've discovered about myself and my philosophy and what Wavelab does best is that I really try to capture the natural acoustic of the instrument, good or bad. I don't use many effects although I've started getting into compression a bit more probably because I've got better compressors now. I now have a couple of LA4s and LA3s. I don't think I could do a vocal track on mix without reaching for an LA3.

What were you using before that?

I had a Behringer or something like that. I still have it in my rack, but you know...

Do you have any formal training?

No. I started in my garage with a 1/2" 8-track. I was a MIDI freak with keyboards! I didn't know what I was doing but I was really enamored by the whole keyboard explosion of the early '80s and all of the possibilities.

And now you've flushed it all down the toilet.

Yeah, give me a Fender Rhodes, give me a Wurlitzer, give me a Hammond organ. I went full circle. I still have my Casio CZ101 – it's got that crazy sound everyone likes – it's got that wheel that makes it sound nuts! I used to have a Mini-Moog here, but the guy took it back which is a shame because we used to use it for bass a lot. I want to get my hands on one of those again because they're great for bass. JD taught me that trick, using the little zip strip for the pitch wheel.

How are you recording the bass now, without the Mini-Moog?

I just purchased one of those SansAmp boxes for bass DI. It's really cool! For one session I did recently I took the recorded DI sound out from the board plugged that into an amp and mic'd the amp and recorded it onto another track. I only have 16 tracks so I have to be careful about using them but on that particular session we were borrowing a Studer 24-track with a Neve sidecar.

It makes it kind of hard to go back doesn't it?

It really does, but you know, in this business it's easy to get caught up in wanting the things you don't have and telling yourself that you would be better if you had them. But you have to remember, that if you can be good with what you have, imagine how much better you will be when you do get that stuff. I look at it like this: if you were a professional runner and everyday you went out and ran with army boots on, imagine what will happen when you finally take off the boots and put on running shoes. I read *Mix* magazine and I go through it and sometimes I'm full of gear lust, and other times I just think, well, I'll never get there. Recently I was out in LA with an up and coming producer from Tucson named Harvey Mason, we were visiting his uncle who is a famous jazz drummer at this studio, I don't even know the name of it if it even had one but it was amazing - two Neve rooms, Studers, Neumanns everywhere. There was a Leslie cabinet mic'd up with three Neumanns; it was that kind of deal. Me, I'm using a 58 or a 57 or whatever. It was funny, my emotions ranged from being totally disgusted because I'll never get there, to feeling fine about it because I don't know if I really want to.

I think your recordings sound great the way you're doing it - they always have such a unique vibe.

I think vibe is really important. In this day and age, vibe has been passed over in the name of tech, and I think that's the downfall for a lot of music. You gotta know how to capture the vibe. I've learned a lot from guys like Howe Gelb, he's been a huge influence. He's a firm believer in the idea of always rolling tape because you never know. JD is also one of these people. So lately when I've been recording I'll always keep a DAT running in the background just in case. So often you get this great feeling on a demo and you never get it back on a record, it's part of that philosophy. I always monitor in record; I want to hear what's happening on tape. A lot of people won't know I'm recording and I'll play what they thought was a practice run and it turns out great. There's something to be said for that first take vibe. It goes both ways. I also like to produce, which involves lifting people to the magical take after relentless unsuccessful attempts. That will always take more time and you have to have a player that is willing to let you do that, to guide and refine them. "Right there when you hit that note, that was really close but if you could just dig in a bit deeper..."

Do you have an easy time relating to people on that level?

I seem to if someone lets me. I don't really enjoy the role of the engineer who sits passively by and just engineers. I'm a frustrated guitar player so I hear things in my head, I can explain things and play them on a piano, I can sort of show you, and most guitar players will say, "Oh, like this?" and I'll say, "Yeah, that."

That's probably why we all got into recording.

Exactly. I also think that by me being a harmonica player, because it's so limited, its taught me the 'less is more' philosophy. I do like to get nutty sometimes, as is evident in some of the recordings. There's a track on the Barbara Manning record called "Joan of Arc" that if you were to hear the basics it's as gooped up as possible. It has accordion, cello, vibes, thunder drums, mandolin, you name it. We went to mix it and no one knew what to do with it. So I said, "Let me have at it here for a while" so she left me alone and it was one of those rare inspired things. I just sort of set up some sub-bussing of things and literally did this sort of DJ mix of it, bringing instruments in and out. I left the drums out until the very end for the last 16 bars. I don't want to blow my own horn, but it's a pretty brilliant mix.

CALEXICO
Spoke (Quarterstick)

Spoke appears to be more of a sketch pad for musical inspirations rather than a complete project which in turn makes it come across as unassuming and inviting. Calexico is mainly John Convertino and Joey Burns who have recently produced and/or played with many distinguished artists such as OP8, Giant Sand, Vic Chesnutt, Richard Buckner, Friends of Dean Martinez, and Barbara Manning, all of with whom they manage to incorporate their unique *desert* sound while utilizing diverse instrumentation. Most songs are somewhat folky, based around acoustic guitar, but there are also a couple of ethnic sounding numbers [in the Camper Van Beethoven vein], and a surf tune as well as some 'uncatagorizable' sounds. Burns and Convertino usually work out of Wavelab Studios in Tuscon, but this assemblage was, given the nature of the project, appropriately recorded in their homes on 8-tracks which seems to have given them the freedom to record creatively many of the sounds appearing uniquely experimental and spontaneous, including the instrumentation which includes vibes, marimba, accordion, cello, mandolin, and violin. As a whole, the record comes across as a fun, homemade project which, incidentally, contrasts the alluring industrial, working class photos and artwork printed by One Ton Press. But somehow, in this case, it works. –*Adam Selzer*

Don Zientara

by Curtis Settino

Don Zientara is a name I became familiar with simply by seeing it over and over again on record, and then CD, liner notes. From his Inner Ear Studios, he's been engineering and producing Washington, D.C., area bands for more than 20 years. His most famous credits include Minor Threat, Scream, Dag Nasty and Fugazi. He was kind enough to sacrifice his in-between-sessions downtime for a lengthy and informative phone interview. I was pleased to discover that Don was yet another mad scientist whose laboratory is his studio and whose creations are the shining results of creative experiments and hard work.

How did you get into recording and being an engineer? Did you go to school?

No I didn't. I was intrigued with electric guitars... we're talking mid to late '50s... and I was wanting guitar amplifiers and things like that. One of my friends in grammar school used to work at a hi-fi repair shop. The guy was just a genius in terms of putting stuff together. I had an old tape recorder and he helped me rig it so I could play the guitar into it and actually use the tape recorder and the speaker...

As a little amp?

Exactly! I couldn't afford an amplifier, so I used the little amp in there, and that got me into fooling around with wires and stuff like that. I was in bands all the way through high school, college and afterwards. In the early to mid-'70s I was in a group, and we needed to record our own demo. So I got my trusty stereo tape recorder together, which I always had around, and a crude mixer. We sort of pulled together equipment and recorded the demo. But we needed to buy a Shure mixer and a few other pieces of equipment. Once we started gathering some of that stuff, word got around and other people asked us to record their demos. I helped out some friends of mine who were in The Look. The first time I recorded them I think it was in the basement.

Then they wanted me to do a live show, in hopes of getting a better recording. If you can imagine: a Shure mixer with four microphone inputs with very, very cheap microphones. Usually, one microphone would be propped up in front of the PA speaker for the vocals, then three other microphones: one for the drums, or somewhere between the drums and the bass amp, and the other two for guitars. We put the vocals on one stereo channel and everything else on the other. At that particular show, there was a group called the Slickee Boys who were playing too, and they asked me to record them since I was there. They were an underground band of some renown in the city. So I recorded them, and it turned out... oh I guess reasonably good. Most of the stuff from those days... if you really go back and listen hard... really sucks. But for the time, I guess it was all right. And also for the price, it was all right [laughs].

And what year was this?

About '75 or '76, maybe '77 with The Slickee Boys, I recorded a bunch of other albums, of equal fidelity, probably, and through them got to know Skip Groff, who put out a couple of their records on Limp Records. Skip was really in touch with a lot of the bands who were on the forefront of music like The Slickee Boys, Bad Brains, The Urban Verbs and a bunch of others. So, he brought a few of these bands in to record. Then he brought Minor Threat in. He thought they'd be a good try since they were so raucous and brash. And all of a sudden, I was doing a lot of this punk music recording. This was going on in the evenings. In the daytime, I was working at the National Gallery of Art in Prints and Drawings. Because, basically, my background is in art. So this [recording] is all going on as sort of a life outside my life kind of thing. Eventually, the National Gallery built a studio. This was in the early '80s. But they had problems getting the patchbay together. Since I'd been messing around with this stuff, I said, "I can help you guys connect this thing up and get it going." I think they had two 2-track recorders, and that's about it. The mixing board had about four channels. But it was high-quality stuff. [It was used] for narration, mainly, for their programs on tape, audio visual shows, slide shows and things like that. So, I connected that up for them. And immediately after that was done, they didn't have an engineer to run the thing, so I said, "Heck, I wouldn't mind running the thing if you want." So I flipped over into the whole recording side of things as an actual profession. I did that for about five or six years. Then I went to manage a private studio for a while and got out of actual hands-on engineering. I didn't like it at all. I liked fooling with the dials and moving the patches all around the place. After less than a year, I quit there and started my own studio.

Was that when you moved the studio out of your house to another space?

Yes. It's in a separate building a couple miles away. It was a warehouse before, and we built it up as a studio inside. It's got two control rooms. J. Robbins, of Jawbox, engineers in the 16-track control room. And I do the recording in the 24-track room. There are a couple of other engineers who do things in here every once in a while, too.

What kind of machine do you have in there right now?

It's an Otari MTR-90 (24-track).

And what kind of board and mics are you using most often?

We have an AMEK Angela board. It's one of the original Angelas, which I like very, very much. I have a Fostex E-22 (1/2" 2-track) to mix down to... that or a Tascam DA-30 DAT, the MKII thing. Other than that, there are bunches of outboard gear. The reason I got into recording and the reason I like electronics in general is because it's sort of an experiment, a laboratory. And that's where the fun comes in really. I build electronics myself too. I've built some compressors and some mixers. And I've built noise gates and a lot of things like that. Some of them are more successful than others. I have a (Fostex) B-16, which is now in the 16-track studio, that we modified/hot rodded. Getting something like that tweaked is very satisfying because those machines can be very mundane and pedestrian unless they're really pushed. And when they're really pushed, they can sound quite interesting. J.'s done some fantastic recording on it. My mouth has hung open a few times. And mics, I've got a pretty big collection. Boy, where do I start?

Well, what do you use frequently for snares or for guitars?

For snares, I have the Shure Beta 56 I believe it is. It's their new small one. The (Shure Beta) 57 I use. I use the EV N/D 408. Those are primary things. On kick drum, the (Shure) Beta 52 I like a lot. I use the Equitek E-100 a lot. But there are a lot of different things we've played around with. I've taken the Audio Technica 4033 and laid it, literally without a stand or anything, inside the bass drum and covered it with a pillow. And it has some interesting results, not as a primary kick sound, but as a nice thickener for the whole thing.

So you'd have another mic that you'd submix that with or put it onto a separate track?

We just throw it on another track. And then, if we decide that it's really bad, we just record over it. A lot of times they do turn out kind of bad. We just did a project with a group called Boom where I threw up a room mic. I think it was a (Neumann) U-87. We put a good deal of delay in, about 70 milliseconds, and had it right in the middle of the guitars and the bass and the drums. It got a good mish-mosh of the music, which sounded very blocky if you listened to it alone, but in with the mix itself, it was the perfect alternative to just listening to a lot of close mics. Instead of distance mic'ing things, I'd rather use a separate mic that's really way out and not even connected with an instrument.

It seems, with close mic recordings, instruments don't always sit well with each other in the mix. But when you capture the room sound of everything bouncing off of each other, it can tie things together really well.

Sure. It plays into the fact that your ears are hearing from one source [your stereo speakers]. And your mind wants to hear it the same way. If everything is close mic'd, you're hearing it from a lot of different places, and it just doesn't gel quite as well. But when you have this one mic that's picking it up as one source, even if it's in the mix a little bit, it lets the mind anchor itself somewhere so that it has a viewpoint. It really pulls it together.

So then do most of the bands that come in there record live?

I try to get them to do it live. I really don't like doing things one at a time. I guess you have to go logically into the whole thing. If you're listening to a band live and the interesting part is the way they perform, then why shouldn't recording try its best to get that side of it? I think every recording engineer knows it's the energy of a performance and the nuances that go on that really make things interesting. So I try to do it that way. And also, it probably saves the bands a lot of money too. They can get things much earlier on. It usually doesn't take a million takes because they're all looking at each other like they would in a rehearsal space, and they know instantly if something's good or bad. It gives the band a good perspective on the song. And it gives them a good perspective on the whole project too, because they know what they're playing is going to matter. It's something that's going to be there. It's not something a producer or an engineer is going to be able to press the mute switch on and take out completely. It's going to make its mark permanently!

Do you have things baffled off, amps stashed in corners and people playing with headphones on?

No. It's just a big room. We've got 18-foot ceilings. It's about 30 feet long and about 18 or 20 feet wide. There's a vocal booth towards the center part of it on the wall. And, actually, the drum area is raised off the floor. I built a platform that's like a stage. It has that thumping sound like a stage. Everything just sort of plays off of each other. For the last band I did, we set up the bass facing right at the drums. When the bass player played a note, the snare just went crazy. I really don't care if there's bleed into other mics, as long as the musicians understand that what they're doing is permanent. If you're going to have a lot of punch-ins, it may not be the thing for you. You can certainly do lots of fixes. We've done fixes, even though things were bleeding all over the place. As long as you know that there are certain little areas where you can't fix. Like if everything comes to a complete stop and the cymbals are dying away and a guitar plays a loud note, that's always going to be there, because it's going to be on the cymbal mics. But other than something like that, there are usually no problems whatsoever. As a matter of fact, it yields fantastic results. The problems [of live recording in the studio], I think, have really been overrated.

I think, from listening to the things you've recorded, it's apparent that the results are fantastic. You seem to have been able to let that live element happen while still keeping things coherent. You also hear bass guitar and kick drums prominently in your recordings, which isn't the case with lots of other punk rock recordings.

Those are the points I try to hit on. I'm glad to hear you say that. A lot of that comes from simply routing stuff. Right now, we're in the middle of a mix, and I've got the kick drum triggering an old Tama drum module... it has that analog "boOOom" sound. The bass guitar is being run through a distortion box and then fed back into the mix just to get a little edge. People ought to try a lot more different things than they do. A lot of new products are being presented to the people who record, but there's really so much equipment out there already, and so many pedals! You can run things through those. There's no reason why you shouldn't try absolutely anything! Take a snare drum or a guitar and run it through any effect or device and see how the thing sounds. You might get some marvelous results. There's no reason to buy lots of new equipment, really! One of the best reverbs... the one I come back to time after time... is the Alesis Midiverb II, and I have a lot of the Lexicon reverbs and some of the higher priced ones too. It (the Midiverb) is one of the original reverbs. It just has the numbers, no parameters whatsoever. You can't change anything on it, other than go to another preset reverb, and the reverbs are great! When you find something like that, it's a gold mine. Then there are things like wah-wah pedals. You can run a guitar through a wah-wah pedal and bring it back in. Just let the wah-wah sit in one position, find the right tone for it, and put the guitar on one side and the wah-ed sound on the other side. You can get some amazing things going on! Echo units are the same way. There's some analog echo units that are really dirty and scratchy and hissy, but you can get a nice, almost reverby type of an effect because there's so much hiss in them [laughs].

Do you ever use your room as a reverb when mixing?

Yes, I have a couple of times. But there were so many alternatives, in terms of what mic to mic it with and which amp to play it through, that I found, truly, the best results come from using a reverb in a box and processing it before it hits that reverb. You can almost do more wacky things that way. A lot of bands simply don't have the money to spend hours getting a room reverb set. So we'll send it through an effects box and then from that box through a regular digital reverb, or actually, a guitar reverb. We have sent things through spring reverbs too.

Are there any unorthodox approaches you've taken?

Well, there's a lot that can be done in the mic'ing when you're recording. I would suggest recording with some mics that are lying on the ground or on shelves and mixing them with the regular signal. I've found that that's very, very helpful. I think another engineer called it a "mechanical filter." That's basically what a floor or a shelf is. You're getting a very weird sound going into the mic because of the bounce off of the shelf or floor. A lot of times, it fills up an area that sounds quite nice, for guitar especially. Just set up your regular guitar mic, then lay a directional microphone right there, a couple inches from the cabinet, but on the ground. Or for the drums: instead of putting the room mic on a stand, just lay it on the ground or in the corner of the room stuffed as closely to the corner as you can get it. You'll get some interesting results.

Do you think that it reacts with the environment a little better when it's on the floor?

Yeah. But it certainly has a lot to do with the room, of course.

What do you do differently when you're producing and engineering versus just engineering? What does being the producer mean to you?

I don't know. I guess the producer sort of fills in the gaps where the musicians can't do the job. In other words, it's their responsibility to put the whole thing together into a cohesive unit. Musicians may be able to do this, or they may be able to do different phases of this, but the producer has to fill in the rest. And this filling in requires a lot. It means arrangement at times. It means actually playing parts at times. It means mixing the thing, giving any support. There's one great producer I worked with who sat in a chair the entire time in the back of the room and really didn't say a whole lot. But he was a fantastic producer in my eyes, because he had the good sense to take a look and see how the musicians were doing. And they were hopping along. But every once in a while, they'd hit a snag where they'd need a couple words of wisdom and he would provide them! Then he would go back and sit down. At the end of it all, the project was very together, very united in terms of all the songs. It just had a nice feel to it, and it was all his doing.

So you've found yourself drawing upon your musical past to help with arrangements here and there?

Yeah, I try if they need it. If they don't, I don't say a thing. I think the area where younger bands are most needy is in getting their thoughts together on the vocals, in terms of really looking at the vocal and the vocal structure, just working through it, critiquing it. A lot of times, they'll just want to get the vocals sung and that's it and forget it. They don't even want to listen to it.

I've seen bands treating vocals as an afterthought, and then they get into the studio and realize that they're not going to be buried in the mix anymore; people are going to be hearing what they're saying, and they should probably think about what they're saying.

Yeah, and a lot of times, the bands will not want the vocal to be up front, which is a very big mistake in my estimation. Because you latch onto the vocals in a song.

That's another thing about your older recordings, the vocals are surprisingly understandable despite the flurry of music that often surrounded them.

Well, we were probably very lucky [laugh]. No, really! A lot of those days, we tried hard and hoped it hit. But our monitoring systems were flawed, so we never knew where things were going to sit.

What do you monitor through now?

Monitoring for me is the most important thing in the world, even beyond tape recorders and microphones. Microphones come in second. I have Westlake (Audio BBSM-12) monitors, and I use QSC and Hafler amps. I have (Yamaha) NS-10Ms. I also have some nearfields from a company called Digital Phase 8 that are very good.

That's about it.

Brendan Bell

ON BÜGSKÜLL AND BASEMENT STUDIOS

by Larry Crane

's Robin Ford

Ahh, the saga of Brendan Bell: A British expatriate who somehow ended up in Portland, and later became a member of the elusive Bügsküll to boot. In Bügsküll he managed to hone his recording skills, and as a long-term "temporary" member of Sone, got to play with more recording toys. Along the way he's worked on records by the Irving Klaw Trio, Kaia, Pete Krebs and New Bad Things along with many others. His open-book recording technique has helped many musicians get a grasp on the recording process and should stand as a good example to other engineers who'd like to keep us all in the dark. Anyway, we met at the *Tape Op* headquarters and after a quick tour of the basement recording facilities we retired to the front porch with a few pints of water and had a nice long chat.

How did you get started in recording?

Well, I first got a guitar when I was 10, I was really into the Beatles, and I had these two little mono, shitty tape recorders and I would just go back and forth through one of those little Realistic 4-channel mixers. I would do all these things live; I had a drum machine, guitar and a vocal all going live and I'd sorta bounce back, play along with...

The cassette? Would you play along with yourself then?

Yeah, I would record along with the backing track onto another tape recorder. It was very primitive and I was getting an awful lot of hiss. My mom's a piano teacher and she was always trying to figure out how to record her students and so I would help her out. She got some okay gear, like fancier boom-boxes, and I got to use those. I gradually got some better gear... guitars and pedals. I got my first pedal for Christmas, a DOD stereo chorus; my parents got me one for Christmas. From then, I went into a few studios and saw how things were done and was never really that happy with the way things came out of there. They were just 8-track studios, very cheap.

Were you playing in a band?

I was. I played in half a dozen bands, in England, from age 14 on. The first studio I ever went to was in this old railway station, this 8-track in the basement, the trains still came by and so every time they did you'd have to scratch that take. It was a really fancy studio, the room was suspended, but of course it would just shake when the trains went by. Other than that, I didn't start multi-tracking or using a 4-track until Bügsküll in '91. Sean had this 4-track and he'd just been sort of goofing around with tape loops and doing things straight in.

Like a reel-to-reel 4-track?

No, it was a Fostex X-15, one you could only record two tracks at once, but a really great machine. We still have it and it still works really well, somehow. We've put thousands of hours on it and it's working great. We had this god-awful Tapco mixer which was just a nightmare, a real pain in the ass, and various cheap, shitty microphones. I'm amazed, listening to that stuff now, like the early tape *Garbled Melodies* and the early singles, that they were all done on that little 4-track. We had this basement room that we built.

And you'd practice down there and record a bunch?

It was very nice 'cause Bügsküll was always very organic and we could just make a song. There's tons of stuff that's been discarded. We're pretty selective about what we've given out. There's an awful lot of really dodgy stuff and stuff that was never finished. One of these days we're gonna get through it. *From the Vaults*, Bügsküll!

A four CD retrospective.

Box set! Oh my god.

With Bügsküll, did you ever record with anyone else?

The only times we've recorded on other equipment was for live things we did. Dean Fletcher, who did the live X-Ray recordings, really liked Bügsküll so he recorded us a few times. I have 3 or 4 tapes of us live from various different places and they sound pretty good. Dean had his own idea of how things should sound and we would just go over and mix it, just listen to it once through and get something approximate. Anyway, we had this one room in the basement which was all carpet and stuff and we tore that out and we built a proper room with insulation and drywall, a door, a window and tried to seal it off a little.

Did you take turns engineering on stuff?

Mostly me. Sean [Byrne—Bügsküll guitarist] did some of it. A lot of the Bügsküll stuff was done a track at a time. A sort of layering of ideas. Particularly the more out-there stuff. Usually it was like when the mood striked you'd go down and listen to the new tape and if you're inspired, lay down something. It was all very individual, but then we would come together for the last track and decide what would bring this whole thing together. It was a really fun way to work.

What kind of mic'ing do you use for things?

I generally mic things individually. It's only in the last couple of years that I've really experimented with lots of different mic'ing techniques. I've used PZMs a bunch and DI [direct injecting] things. Running guitars into weird compressors and reverbs and whatever. We had a lot of access with our pretty close relationship with Sone, and they had lots of neat toys. I also got a 4-track open reel, Teac 3440.

When did you start using that?

Three years ago, maybe. It's a great, really solid machine.

Did you notice a big jump in sound quality?

Totally. From running at 1 7/8 [inches per second] to 7 1/2 ips. I also got a mixer at the same time. An old Studiomaster 16-channel board.

A little better than the Tapco?

Oh man! So much better. The Tapco had bass and treble [EQ] and this has sweepable mids and shelving and phantom power.

Where have you found your gear?

Generally I always buy things used. I bought a bunch of gear from SuperDigital [a local studio-supply shop] and yard sales and through the paper. I often check the *Nickel Ads* [local want ad paper].

I always call people in the *Nickel Ads*. "You still got that microphone? ...No."

That's the thing, getting microphones. Everyone's picking up on the buyer's market, especially in this town where there's a lot of people in basements.

There's a lot of basements in Portland.

There's a lot of basements around here.

There's a lot of people who have setups like this where they record downstairs.

I think it adds such a healthy thing. It really encourages collaborative things and a sharing of ideas.

It makes recording more casual. It'd be hard for me to imagine Bügsküll "working up" your set and then going to some 16-track studio and paying $25 an hour!

I could never do that. Without all that hiss and bum notes. Being able to capture the moment, that magical moment...so many recordings done in "big" studios are *clean*, but they're sterile, they have no life. Who cares if there's a couple of pops in there? It's the feeling that matters! I think people have realized that slick sounding rock is not the be all of recorded music.

We were talking about microphones. What kind of microphones do you like using?

My PZM is broken. I don't have anything extraordinary or odd. I have [Shure] 57s and a 58 and an SM 81, which is really nice. It's a Shure condenser, a long silver thing, and an excellent overhead mic and I use that on vocals a lot, too.

Is it real crisp?

Really crisp. It has a low cut and a pad on it. You can do lots of different stuff with it, like distant mic'ing. It's just so clean and sensitive. I have a bass drum mic. I have a bunch of old, fucked up mics, like this old Beyer which sounds really interesting.

Do you have any kind of preamps or anything?

I don't have any of my own. I borrowed this great tube preamp and I can't remember what it's called, but it might be from a kit. It just had this on-off [switch], a big knob and a 1/4" out with an XLR in. I just ran everything in there. All the vocals were done on a 58, 57 or an EV all run through this preamp and they sound so good. They're kind of dull, compared to a condenser mic, but they're just so middley and warm.

It seems, on those sorts of mics, that a mic preamp brings it out a lot more.

I guess it's the difference between running your fancy guitar through a Peavey solid state amp or a really nice Fender.

True. When you do vocals do you use pop filters?

I do if I have one!

You can make one, you know!

I know I can make one, I'm just a little lazy. I generally use them and they make things a lot easier. I like to do as much first take as possible and I actually use a fair amount of compression. It depends who it is. Like John [Vehicle guitarist], he has a really nice voice, but his dynamic range is HUGE! For a lot of vocals I usually have the ratio really low with a fast attack and fast release, but with him I totally had to crank the ratio to about 8:1 or so.

Ow. That's pretty high.

Yeah, but that's the one thing that I do have is a really nice compressor. It's an Ashley, a beautiful thing, and it's really simple to use, but it's so transparent, fast and smooth. You never hear it. Compression is a dangerous thing. I want to find the guy who invented compression and rip his liver out. I use it a lot. If you don't have really nice microphones and great separation you have to use it if you want to capture a lot of things. I record things really hot. With modern tape and a [Tascam] 38 you can just crank it.

I've never found any tape distortion and I peg the meters constantly. Have you ever used any noise reduction?

Unless it's a really high quality noise reduction I don't like using it. On our LPs, when we mastered them onto 1/4" tape we used Dolby SR which is amazing. Dolby SR is great.

You said you were doing recordings with Vehicle all over their house.

We were doing it in their house and they all live together so I used their practice place as an engineering room and we used various different rooms in the house and we had a couple of snakes so we could send cables a ways away.

How did you talk to the band while recording?

That was a problem. I had this Dynaco amp that I rigged up, but it would constantly distort stuff through the headphones. I really need to get myself a headphone amp. It was really only necessary on the overdubs for which I got it down, distorting the least. Using the different rooms in their house was really fun. We tried the drums in the kitchen and the living room. Vocals on the porch and in the stairs.

No way.

Yeah, on the porch. We did several takes.

Were there background noises?

Like wind. We did it late at night so it was fairly quiet, but there were cars going by. For one song it fits really beautifully. It's nice to have some ambient sounds.

They make you have pictures in your head.

Absolutely.

Did you try any bathrooms?

They had this upstairs hallway which was long. We did some bass up there and tried a vocal track up there which I really liked, but it didn't quite fit the song so we changed that. I did 6 foot mic'ing on the vocals so we had this weird slapback, echo thing going on. We did the bass in the kitchen.

To give it some presence?

Yeah, just messing around.

When you're recording something like that do you use a couple of mics?

It depends on what sort of amp it is. He had a 4-ten [inch speaker] cabinet which I mic'd. Sometimes I ran it into the tube preamp, but it was harder, it distorted a lot. He also had this really neat tube direct box and I used that quite a bit, just ran the instrument straight in there and then into the compressor. The one thing I'm so happy with-that I got to be involved in-is the Irving Klaw Trio record [on Silly Bird and Imp records]. That was a dream to record. Jason is a brilliant, consistent drummer and has a well-tuned drum kit and I was really lucky mic'ing it. I did that in the old house where we had a super-live room and I turned the amps away from the drums, but didn't use much isolation. Everyone in the same room, two guitar amps and drums.

Did the amps rattle the snare and make it buzz a lot?

Maybe it did a little bit. He had a pretty well-tuned snare which didn't seem to rattle. I'd record the drums on 4 tracks [of an 8-track] and the guitars on 2 and then mix the drums down to a stereo mix and then we'd have 4 tracks to play with. They had Michael Griffin from Noggin come in and play on a couple of tracks and they did various different tape splices here and there.

With their material?

Yeah, their weird little boom-box recordings, drop them in. We did that from the source onto the reel 'cause it was usually part of the song. Like a radio through a phaser with tremolo. Jeff has a really good vision of how he wants things to be so it was a relatively easy thing to do. And it was fun, I love those guys.

What other things have you worked on?

I've done a lot of recordings and some of them have not turned out so great, even though the bands have been great. I did this one thing with Third Sex when they were fairly young and the songs are great, but it didn't really happen onto tape very well. I did a bunch of the first Sone tape, which was all done on the PortaStudio 4-track, and I'm pretty happy with that. I worked on a bunch of different Sone things on their two full-length CDs as an engineer and I played bass on a few things, too. I did a Pete Krebs [of Hazel/Golden Delicious] record. The most recent thing that just came out is the new Kaia [of Team Dresch] record, which I'm very happy with. That came out great. I helped a lot with the New Bad Things on their first

record. I engineered a bunch of it. They had an 8-track and I had a board and we came together and had this studio. I started off engineering and encouraged them to learn and by the end of it they were very competent.

That's a nice approach as opposed to the, "You won't understand what I'm doing here."

Definitely. Have you ever been to Smegma Studios [in Portland]? He [Mike Lastra] has a really good studio and he's one of the most "hands off" engineers I've ever met. He really encourages you to go to the board and do it yourself which can be good. Sometimes it's best, depending on the band, to let the engineer do things 'cause otherwise you can spend eons farting around.

It seems like you help people learn and explain things.

Having a studio in a basement is so non intimidating and people feel really comfortable there and it's not such an out-there concept, it's real and it's not intimidating. When you have a studio that only charge a few dollars an hour people feel they can take their time. Sometimes I get kinda lazy and I tend to rush things when it gets near the end of a project. I'm getting much better, just learning what's a wrong shortcut to take.

Does that have anything to do with studio fatigue?

I'm pretty good about taking breaks. I think it's really important when taking a break to get away and not think about it. "Let's not think about it right now."

I like to send people home with rough-mixed cassettes of what they're working on and tell them to listen to it and think about what it needs.

Also, during a session, I like to change things around between songs. Change a microphone.

That's a good idea and that's where I get lazy.

You run the risk of, "Oh that was such a great sound on that song, why didn't I use it here."

But every time you mix something it sounds different. We're not using automated mixers!

Thank god!

VEHICLE

Can't Get to Memphis (Schizophonic)

Recorded on an 8-track in various rooms of the band's house by Brendan Bell, this is another fine example of sweat taking the place of fancy studios. The production reminds me of Badfinger, vocals a bit louder than I'd place them, some tasty double-tracking, hooky guitar parts and a clear, but not over trebly, pop sound. It's a good example of Brendan's recording prowess, and be on the lookout for more stuff he's worked on, including a mind-blowing CD by the Irving Klaw Trio (*Utek Pahtoo Mogoi* on Road Cone). –*Larry Crane*

Steve Fisk

PELL MELL/HALO BENDERS MEMBER, SOLO ARTIST & NOTED PRODUCER

by Larry Crane

© Arthur S. Aubry

Umm, Steve Fisk has been playing and recording music longer that some of you have been out of diapers. It's a bit of a tale, but we'll trudge through some of it here. Lately, he's been a producer for many of the finer bands in that "alternative" scene, like Low, Wedding Present, Geraldine Fibbers, Boss Hog, Unwound and Three Mile Pilot. His earlier productions for the Screaming Trees, Beat Happening, Girl Trouble and even Nirvana set the stage for his adeptness at recording different styles of music and a sure grasp of "capturing" a band to sound like themselves. We chatted on the phone for over two hours while Steve was in San Francisco working with Pell Mell on a soundtrack to a documentary. Really!

You went to Evergreen, in Olympia, WA, and studied recording there, didn't you?

Yeah.

Was that where you first got into recording?

No, I was playing with synthesizers and things that required tape decks way before then. An older friend of mine used to smuggle me into the Moog studio at USC when I was 17. Once and a while we had an 8-track in there, but the rest of the time we had a huge Tascam 4-track. I remember that it was bigger than a regular 4-track; I had friends that had 4-tracks when I was a kid. I did a science-fiction-y kind of sample and hold thing on a 4-track when I was 16 with this other friend of mine that had a connection with somebody that had a 3D fish-eye lens that would make 3D films and stuff. We were making a mock-up for the porno sequence in this 3D-porno movie the space/porno scene. I was doing that in the garage when I was real young. I had this other friend, who was a lot older, that had two Sony 1/4" decks, semi-pro machines. When I first got my synthesizer we would go over to his place and just do sound-on-sound, going back and forth between the decks making this hideous, useless, noisy Todd Rundgren synthesizer shit. So synthesizers first got

me into recording. Evergreen was the first time I got into using microphones. Everything else was just 1/4" plugs.

Were you thinking of a career in recording when you went to Evergreen?

I wasn't thinking of a career as much as I wanted to be a composer. Once again, synthesizers were the main point and then it was; we have quad and 8-track and 16-track here. My friend Peter Randelette was sort of my entry into all that. He did all the production and engineering on stuff that I wrote when I was in college. He played on a bunch of it and helped me write songs. It wasn't really songs, it was more like a 6/8 quadraphonic salsa/fugue jam that was sort of my thesis piece (if there ever was such a thing at Evergreen). I worked on it for about a year and it was set up for quadraphonic tape playback that was on 16-track so it had things flying around the room. Congas and tympani set up in a serialized pattern. It was very *intellectual*. Then there was live shit that me and Peter did on top of it. I did tons and tons of Fripp and Eno tape loop shit. It's a cool trick and it's nice. Have you ever listened to *Wonderwall Music*, the George Harrison record?

I've never heard that.

He does the Fripp and Eno thing way early. He does the Eno ambient synthesizer with too much echo way early in the game. It was all stuff he'd offered the Beatles and they didn't want to have anything to do with it. He was the smart Beatle. He was a lame singer so everyone just sort of wrote him off. The *Wonderwall* album is like a Beatles instrumental record. Ringo plays all over it and what bass playing there is, is George or Klaus Voorman, who played like Paul McCartney back then, so it was sort of the Beatles' instrumental album with Paul and John out of the way. It's on CD now and it sounds great. It was recorded when all the great Beatles' stuff was recorded, but nobody gave a shit 'cause it was George's side project. So he's doing all kinds of abstract stuff with wonderful Indian musicians and putting it through flanger and phaser and compressing the living crap out of it. Plus the most blown up Ringo drum sounds ever and Eric Clapton, right out of *Disraelie Gears,* doing really groovy backwards guitar solos. When Eric Clapton was good. Back when all these people were good!

So how did you end up doing what you do now?

You don't have time for a Steve Fisk history! When people get it, they print it all wrong. Don't worry about that. People don't care about it anyway, and it's certainly not how anybody else would do it. I'd done a lot of "punk rock" 4-track stuff in Olympia, aside from the synthesizer work at Evergreen. I recorded Calvin Johnson's first band on a 4-track in a basement of the college. I recorded the Beakers on a 4-track in a basement in Seattle; that's one of the 45s I helped put out. We used one of those really rancid Tascam mixers that had little switches instead of dials for the EQs and six inputs and two outs. That was my mixing board. Once and a while I'd get to take stuff up to the synthesizer studio. I'd put the tracks through quad panning and weird filters. Back then there was really wonderful 4-track stuff coming out, like Chrome, Half Japanese and The Normal. So anyway, that's the kind of shit I was doing when I didn't know what I was doing. Then I went down to San Francisco and got called a producer a few times when I was in Pell Mell. I got to sit around and make aesthetic calls at the top of a ship of fools in a few studios. Fantasy [Studios] being the notable ship of fools. A friend of mine smuggled me in there and I got to pretend to be a producer on a record that was way too ambitious and recorded way too much material in three days.

What was it?
It was called Paris Working, one of those San Francisco new wave bands. They were contemporaries of Wire Train. They were good, but their record isn't any good, although it does have a dub mix on it that's kind of groovy. Phil Hertz played drums in that band, if you remember who he is.

I don't.
He works for Cargo now, but he was an Evergreener. There was a house on the west side that Bruce [Pavitt] always brought the tapes to whenever he'd get the old Sub Pop stuff. Me and Phil and about 3 or 4 other people had all of our gear in one house. We had two 4-tracks, some synthesizers and a bunch of mics and cables. When Bruce was putting together the original Sub Pop cassettes, which back then were new wave and experimental and hardcore, he was always coming up the hill with the mail saying, "Oh, let's check this one out." The home studio that me and my friends had in college was also sort of the launching point for the Sub Pop empire! So what I've been trying to say for 10 minutes is that when Pell Mell broke up in '85 I moved to Ellensburg and my friend Sam Albright had built this gorgeous 8-track studio over there in a huge room. Velvetone Studios. Named after Jimi Hendrix's first band. That's where I was the house engineer, forever, with a beautiful Otari 8-track.

A 1/2"?
Yeah, and a huge room which would've accommodated a 24-track beautifully and Sam had hopes that if the studio took off... but as it was it was just this gorgeous, acoustically crazy, but kind of cool room. We had 5 [Shure] SM 57s, 2 AKG 460Bs, a Neumann KM83 and that was it.

You did all the early Screaming Trees' stuff there?
Yeah, Beat Happening, the Soundgarden *Fopp* remix and bands that nobody knows about!

So after that you moved to Seattle and worked on more stuff. What's been some of the latest projects?

Crowsdell. They're a 3-piece from Florida and they just moved to Brooklyn. I did their second record for Big Cat Records. Damien Jurardo. He's put out a few singles on Sub Pop. I recorded his first LP at Avast.

That's a cool space.
Yeah. They're getting ready to put an API mixing board in there. I'm getting ready to jump into the second Violent Green album. I'm gonna do that when I get back. The Low record just came out. The new Unwound record came out a month ago.

Have you done all the Unwound records?
All five. They're still very young.

They're pretty darn good, too.
They rock! The new record is... do I dare say it... Beatle-y. They called for many things to be brought to them and they played them all themselves. We had tympani and vibraphones... all kinds of shit on the record.

How do you select what stuff you work on? Are you selective?
Yeah. There's certain kinds of music that I'm just not good at recording anyway 'cause I don't have any interest in it. I couldn't spend a week on it without getting really antsy. For being as cynical and hateful as I am, I actually like a lot of different music. It's a combination of what the dynamics of it are gonna be and what the expectations of the band are. Some people have such stupid expectations you just really don't want to get involved with them.

Like in what way?
"Hi. I want to make a killer record. We've got three weeks in an ADAT studio and I've got a friend that knows some string players and I want to add strings and I want to add horns. Yeah, it's a Mackie board, but we got a deal on it." I'm not gonna help that guy. He's gonna find out the hard way that you can't do that. I don't do metally shit. I guess some people might think Unwound is metally, but I don't do metal shit at all. I'm waiting for somebody to bring me something metally I'd like to do. I stay away from that. When I get demos... I guess I sound like some politically correct fascist or something... I try hard to listen to the lyrics. I don't want to record a song that's got something I don't endorse like, "She's a Hurricane," "Hot Blooded," you know, woman as natural force-of-nature kind of song.

Those cliche's and sexism have been driven into the ground already.
Once somebody sent me this band, they had money to spend—they were on a major label, and the first song on the demo was just this idiotic, stupid diatribe about Courtney Love. It was all a first-person fuck you to Courtney Love. I thought, "Well, even if I was mad at her why would I do this?" It was just stupid. This band has no place to take on Courtney Love in a song and I don't want to help them. That would just be pointless. So, you sort of listen for stupid-factor.

Plus you're gonna have to spend weeks cooped up in a room with these people.
There have been some people that I have at least gotten into conversation with where I thought there were some things that I really wanted to help alter or obliterate from their previous album. "I'll take this on, but we can't do horns like you did the last time around." Things that weren't executed right or things that they were trying to do stylistically where they got it wrong. If I find out that they think they got it right or they're not interested in what I'm doing, I'll say, "Great, there isn't anything to talk about. You just keep doing your stupid records."

Does where you can record affect your decision?
I'm lucky 'cause Seattle's got two really cool medium to cheap priced studios. They have all the gear I need to record guitar, bass and drums properly. Basically, it's not rocket science. I spent years working with the right mic, the [Shure] SM 57. When I finally got through the Logics 8 board to the goddamn MCI board to finally a Neve module I was, "Wow, this sounds great on drums and good on guitar." Then I got to work with the API and it is really good too. Even Trident

rocks. There's a reason why these songs sound right through older gear. It's because the bulk of the historical information we have in the 20th century is a vibrating guitar string through a pickup that had something to do with Leo Fender, Gibson or someone, going through an amplifier that has something to do with Leo Fender going through a Neve, API or Trident console onto a piece of regular analog tape. That's how that sound happened. You can't make that happen on a Tascam console and you can't make that happen on an ADAT. You can't even hope to make that happen on a Mackie. If somebody can, bless their hearts. I've been forced to use things like that, in demo situations, and it's so demoralizing. Greg Freeman's [Pell Mell member] got a great way around a bunch of this by using the EQ as little as possible and using mic preamps. He's still got a Mackie in the back end. It's interesting though; his Mackie upgrade was a good one because his console before wasn't really giving him a clear picture of his tape deck. Now that he's got a Mackie in there he can actually hear what's glorious about his tape deck. He's also got all this hot-rod signal path TLA gear. I brought along my rack so we can use the Joe Meek for drum sounds. That studio, with the concrete walls, it just sounds great with program compression and all that.

Do you find that you'll choose projects that you know will get a good label push and be heard?

Some of my favorite things I've worked on are totally unheard. Ask that one more time before I answer that one 'cause that's political.

I'm sorry. I do that, on a much smaller level. I'd rather work on something that's gonna get released than someone's damn demo cassette.

Well, yeah. I've got to stand behind what I record, at least at this point in my life. Five years from now I may not be able to answer that question the same way. I kind of endorse what I record.

The Steve Fisk stamp of approval.

I certainly recorded some major label stuff that I was quite passionate about that disappeared. A majority of it, actually.

Does that bum you out?

Yeah. It's pretty demoralizing and there's people tied to all that and they all have lives. The 360s had a very bad relationship with what their thing turned into and that's a record I cared a lot about. Wedding Present, for god's sake, they were bungled completely.

And the production on that record has been called brilliant.

I still get a lot of work based on that record. That's a record where the band was radically involved with their sound even if they didn't even know what they were fucking talking about. "Oh. Double skin on the kick drum. Well, it's just gonna sound like a giant tom-tom." I'd put a little muting on it and they're all, "Steve Albini didn't put muting on it." Well, Steve was doing a different kind of mic'ing configuration in that studio. We did it anyway and

I thought we made some fun stuff. The Wedding Present is one of the only bands I've worked with that's done 8 albums. It's a band that people are passionate about and it's a "song" band so what the producer does is pretty obvious from record to record. I can't talk about that record without throwing down props at John Goodmanson, my trusty engineer/co-producer. He's all over it and has a good deal to do with why that record rocks and why the guitars sound the way they do. John's really great.

How would you describe his role when you two work together?

We have a lot of shit in common and he knows what I'm trying to do. At the beginning we did a lot of talking about things, which mics on which, which mic pres and what to compress and what not to. The more we work the more there's less spoken. Now, it's more like I turn around and everything's going how I would expect it to go anyway and, unless I've got something to fuck with him about, he takes care of a lot of the stuff himself. A lot of times I don't touch a lot of knobs. It's really great and gives me time to deal with the musicians and answer their questions and run off on a piano and bang out parts with them. It definitely puts John in co-producer territory. I would really love to keep working with him for a long time in a situation where he's getting his props, more or less, 'cause he's really great. He's doing major label production now and he's been doing independent production for years and really making some incredible records.

He did that last Juned album, didn't he? It sounds great

I like his Bikini Kill records and his Team Dresch records. He does record more metally rock bands that I'm not into. He's a guitar player.

You guys end up working in a lot of the old studios from the seventies.

If you work on major label records you end up using the studios that the Romans left behind. I just got through working at the Village down in California. Fleetwood Mac, Steely Dan. I got to say "Hi" to "Skunk" Baxter [Steely Dan/Doobie Brothers] in the parking lot.

When you work in a place like that do you find some good sounding rooms?

Oh, they sound incredible. The Village has got this one room that's the echo chamber that everybody liked to use, like Eric Clapton and George Harrison. So when you're running Three Mile Pilot flying tympanis and weird whirling horns through it you go, "Well, there's got to be something right about this reverb." There's some kind of justice in that. Old studios are great. You find crazy shit, like, "Here's the piano they recorded 'Ricky Don't Lose That Number' on." Up at Sear Sound, the piano there is from 1910. I worked with Soul Coughing and the piano player and I were talking about the John Lennon and Yoko Ono *Double Fantasy* record that was done there and he knew all the parts and started playing them on the piano. That's really cool working in historical places because they're historical for a reason. Hundreds of things have been tweaked over 15 or 20 years and they're all tweaked a certain way and a certain thing happens. That's why Power Station and Hit Factory are so lame to record at because so much music is done there that you recognize the sound even though it's all the right gear. "Oh yeah, that sound!"

Have there ever been any sessions you've done that have been excruciating?

I once recorded in a part of the world where the electricity was very undependable. It was a 220 [volt] country and putting a SM 57 on a guitar amp... it was really funny... by the time you got into the control room, the 'crackle' sound of the guitar would be 3 dBs louder. We're getting fluctuations in voltage over the course of the day. The guitar sounds would be shitty, then the guitar sounds would be great. That was pretty hateful. I've been at another studio in England that was very badly maintained. It looked like it was gonna work for the first day and then about three or four days into it I realized we'd been waiting around hours for nothing.

As far as gear breaking down?

Yeah, and being able to trust the monitors. Something would sound wrong and then you'd throw on a reference CD and realize the monitors are fucked up. Then you start fixing the monitors and they'd get them half together, but things are still wrong.

Ouch.

Yeah. That's a place where they're charging the equivalent of a thousand a day. It's pretty horrible.

Have you had trouble with people in the studio?

Well, I don't work with junkies. Drunks are fucked. They get all drunk and they think their mix is good and they go home and it's not how they wanted it.

It's your fault.

"But you were drunk and you said it was good. I told you not to drink, then you got drunk and now you want me to do it again." That's a drag. People dying. It sort of evened out a bit, but just with people dying... John and I were doing all kinds of work and it seemed like every other session the phone would ring and somebody's dead. If it wasn't somebody you knew it was somebody all your friends knew. Now we've got to work on a record and somebody that a lot of people loved is dead and it's gonna be part of that dynamic. If you're from LA or Manhattan or San Francisco, a lot of original punk rockers died real hard. In Seattle it's just kind of a new thing. It's really sad that people in their early 20s are now writing songs about dead friends. So yeah, death is a real drag. Heroin's a real drag. Suicide's a real drag. It really can fuck up sessions, even if they don't happen to anybody in the band.

It'll cast a mood over everything...

Or, "Oh wow, this song now changed. It's now more important than it ever was before because it happened when the phone call came in." It's getting better now. There will still be more people dying, you can count on that. The universe is kind of strange. What else? Brothers and sisters have one kind of problem. Couples *always* have problems! Something starts at the breakfast table and you carry it into the session and everyone's wondering why you're getting so pissed off.

Anyway... You said you had a Joe Meek box.

You know what sounds better than any tube compressor? The Joe Meek. It is expensive, but it's paid for itself for me. I bought it when I did the Boss Hog session. They had one lying around there and I didn't know who Joe Meek was. I'd seen references once and a while, but it never really clicked who he was. Jon Spencer was, "You gotta know about Joe Meek." I asked Ray Farrell [former Pell Mell mgr./DGC employee] about him and he made me a cassette. I bought a bunch of CDs and became a full on Meek-o-phile. We've got a Clavoline down here at the Pell Mell studio.

Are you gonna put a reverb chamber in your attic? [Like Joe Meek was rumored to have done]

We don't have an attic here. These guys [the city of San Francisco] are building a ballpark.

Are they knocking down Greg's studio [Lowdown]?

Sometime in the next couple of years.

Oh man. That's a piece of history.

I know. You'll be able to look out the third base dugout. That's the drum sound, right there in the dugout. In Japan when they do that they allow you to keep your business in the new building they put up. It'd be great. Happy Donuts [infamous local eatery] would be over in centerfield. Some stoned rock band will be wandering around buying hot dogs on their break. I don't think we'll see that. I'm rambling; you got any more questions?

Umm, yeah. I think this will be a good interview 'cause a lot of these dorks think I'm promoting the 4-track revolution or something and I'm just looking for where good records come from.

I'm waiting to find out that there's some record I love that was done on a Tascam DA-88 and a Mackie board, but I haven't heard it yet. I love Guided By Voices; they sound great. When some band comes to me and wants to do a 4-track record I say, "Well, can we use 4 channels of a 24-track?" Why put it on a Fostex cassette deck? It's not the same thing the Beatles had.

No. And they had 7 or 8 of the best 4-track reel-to-reel decks in the world sitting around...

And a staff of 4 or 5 people operating everything and plugging it in for them.

And great tube consoles with giant round fader, knobs and rooms that sound really good.

And a radical, bad-ass producer that was gonna become very important later on, but no one realized it when they were starting. You can't really say that Beatles rocked on 4-tracks. Well... no. There's a guy in Seattle that's got some well-maintained Ampex tube 4-tracks that I'm interested in using at some point or another.

I hear a lot of times that even just using the input stages on those works real well as tube preamps.

I've never been lucky enough to have one of those lying around. Sear Sound's got some crazy decks. They've got an Ampex 300, 1/2 " tube mastering deck. The only functional one in the country. It poses interesting problems since, when you take the tape out of there it's not the same on a regular deck. They've got a Studer 1" 2-track that they're restoring and getting ready to hook up.

That gives you plenty of track room.

Yeah. Once again, mastering becomes a problem. I think they burn all of them onto CDR and take that into mastering.

Just use that to get the nice sound.

Right, then get some very expensive A to D converters.

I'm enthused to see that people are realizing that DATs and ADATs are not the end-all answer to everything in music recording.

They're not even a storage medium. Anything that has to have 2 backups isn't a storage medium.

It seems like a stopgap measure, to me. You're working in digital, so why bother having this little tape moving along? Why not go direct to a hard drive?

The dependable thing.

I think we're gonna be seeing these things in thrift stores soon.

It's a complete ream and they're dying. Projects that were started 6 years ago don't play back on them now. It's unfortunate. How many records have been recorded on an ADAT that you and I like?

I can't think of any that I know of.

Yeah, and I'm ready to find out that one I really like was done on an ADAT. I'm morally opposed to a lot of the digital workstations 'cause they've got shitty D to A converters. It's great for Pigeonhed [Steve's "techno" side project with Shawn from Satchel/Brad...] and loop kind of stuff, but guitars, they don't come back the same way. That's cool if people want to do it, but I really worry about that and Seattle people quit using those for mastering about 2 years ago. Originally everybody was all down with it. "Oh this is great, we can do back ups and sequence our record." Then D to A converters got better. "Oh, I can send this off to LA." It's interesting... in Ellensburg when the F-1 got over there I just started using it exclusively 'cause it really sounded great; it sounded like the board. Those F-1 tapes don't play back anymore. Try to find an F-1 playback system someplace in Seattle... forget it. My whole Ellensburg history is all in these weird little Beta tapes.

It was a digital system that recorded on Beta tapes?

We tried to put out the Pell Mell cassette again, the one that Calvin [Johnson, K Records] put out, but the tapes are all gone. The F-1s won't play back. It was an assemblage of a bunch of really groovy mixes that Tom Mallon made that became part of *Bumper Crop* later on and a bunch of great live shit. It was all recorded on an F-1 and it's gone.

Oops. That kind of worries you. I was compiling a CD that was on all kinds of formats.

What's wrong with all these oddball formats is that people end up in one-of-a-kind studios that somebody set up and it can only be produced and mixed there. You can't take it anywhere else.

Yeah, but if you have a small studio maybe it's better to have a format that only you have and they have to keep coming back to you.

Oh sure. The first Pigeonhed record, they talked about doing remixes of that. For god's sakes, we've got the vocals on a 1" 8-track that got transferred to an ADAT and fucked up with a MIDI configuration. C/Z [records] just asked me to do a remix of this band Moonshake and everybody's doing remixes of it. All they sent are these component mixes of DATs. Like the vocals by themselves, on a DAT.

And you have to sync it all up?

To me, it's like, "I'm sorry." The remixes I've learned to love are mixed from a 24-track so you get the nuance of the vocalist and the nuance of the playing and you're turning it on and off. You're not reinventing the time frame for the band. I felt really bad for them 'cause they're doing all this stuff now and I can't get into it. I'm sorry... I need a real recording studio and I need a copy of the 24-track and I'll do a remix. Then we might have a bunch of samplers and looping and it might all end up in a computer but I gotta know how it was done.

All the cool reggae dub mixing was done like that.

You take out the vocals and guitar and you can hear what's right about the bass and drums. You can't do that if you're reconstructing bass and drums from DAT. Even if they're sequenced there's still some musicality in there someplace.

Maybe you should just dump it to a 4-track cassette.

I'm sure the record's gonna be great and I'll be blown away by it. I feel like a retard. I'm sorry, I don't know how to work the way these people are working. I've always thought remixes are great, a recomposition of the song. I love to go and radically alter shit, but this was like, "I wanted to go dancing and you sent me a bunch of arms, legs and feet in boxes."

It sounds like more work, putting it back together.

That's the other part of it too.

So... what kind of cool gear do you use lately? You mentioned the Joe Meek compressor.

I use that a lot. I own a Summit tube preamplifier, the TPA 200A, that's really great. I'd like to have one of their fake Pultech EQs.

Are these things you usually haul around when you work in different studios?

I have a rack that's got the Meek, the Summit and a MicMix Master Room reverb, which has sort of become a new toy up here. Calvin [Johnson] found a bunch of them, but I fell in love with this one they had at Bad Animals, a little tiny spring reverb unit. Those are really cool and they're all made differently so they all sound different. It's not a natural spring, it's a hyperbolic spring... more like a Lee Hazlewood spring or something. I use those DBX 120s sparingly, but I like those... those are the sub-harmonic bass synthesizers. You can make weird kick and bass sounds with that although they're really easy to overdose. I have a rackmount version of EPS in the rack as well. That's the rack that travels. In the Northwest when I can move around and do things right I've got an AKG BX-20 spring reverb. I put that in the backseat of the car. That's another score from Bad Animals when they closed. I got that for $200. That's a $7000 unit. You see them for $500 or $800 and you see BX-10s around. Those are great. We had those at Evergreen... Quad! We had two BX-10's for 4 channels of reverb. Not very discrete, but just lovely. And you can kick them.

Good sounds!

Yeah. That's about it. I have a lot of keyboard toys that are patented Steve Fisk things that I haul around.

Do you still have an Optigan?

Yeah, it sees regular duty. It's on Unwound records, the Crowsdell record and Pigeonhed's got Optigan all over it.

Do you have any microphones you haul around for sessions?

I'm really hurting on mics. I know what I like to use and I suppose in the next few years I should probably throw down for some tube mics 'cause those are all different and you have to take care of them. I'd love to have a [Neumann] U47 tube. I like those a lot. I like Sony C237 As. Those are cool. Old ribbon mics are fun. Most studios don't have them. If you've got a great, special, bad-ass singer it's really wonderful to try to find different mics and see which ones work. The woman in Crowsdell had a very strange voice that would get brighter as it got louder and duller when she was quieter. We were trying all kinds of things to get that to work and all the regular tricks weren't happening. On the record that had been recorded before, by Brian Paulson, he'd had her on some fat tube mic, I can't remember which one. It was EQ-able, but you could hear what was wrong with it. By the time we were done we had a 414 and an Audix placed next to each other and mixed them together.

Did you get any phasing?

That's John's job and he does everything well. When you put them really close together you don't get any phasing. The record sounds hell-a vocal loud. She's got a really wonderful voice and we've got it turned way, way up.

Do you listen to a lot of music for production ideas?

I don't listen to very much contemporary music at all. About 6 years ago, most of what I was listening to was shit I was working on. I'm in the middle of the record and I'd drag it home and listen to it. Now it's more like, when I get hooked up with a band, I kind of figure out what I think they're trying to do. For some reason, there's not much new about music anyway. How you'd record a punk rock band versus how you'd record this kind of band... I don't know; I'm not answering this question very well.

It's a tough question.

I'm aware of contemporary stuff. Periodically people say, "Steve, you have to listen to this." I'll go out and listen to it and decide what I think about it. There's certain things that are inspiring, but that's more personal than how it affects bands I work with. Tchad Blake and Mitchell Froom are very inspiring producers to listen to, though sometimes I don't like the music they record.

They leave a stamp on it.

Oh yeah. Their collaboration with Los Lobos continues to be a very wonderful thing. I just heard the new instrumental record, the jam thing, and it's really good. If somebody wants to sound like Steve Albini I say go to Steve Albini.

Well that's why people are labeled producers, because they have a sound...

But at the same time if all a producer does is leave an imprint, that producer's not gonna be working very long. Seriously. It's like, "Hi. How do you fit in my little slide show? What backdrop do you want?" I never use drum replacement stuff unless I'm trying to do something strange or if there's something where the drummer has fucked up and he hasn't hit the drum hard enough. I don't get involved in that one. Most of my drum sounds are 99% as recorded. A lot of them are dry.

As far as room sounds that are there or digital stuff?

First off, digital stuff sucks on drums 9 out of 10 times anyway. That's why you use plates, springs, room sounds and chamber reverbs, if you're lucky enough to work in a studio with something like that. The records that John Goodmanson works on, the drum aesthetics' part of what he's good at too. You've got to love it if you can make the drum sound out of the natural sound of the drums. The minute you start putting digital reverb on, it starts making it like other people's records, but if it's the right thing you got to do it. Some records should sound like low-budget Martin Hannett. Spring reverb all over the overheads. But... You do a lot of listening to the musicians, finding out what they like and where they're coming from. A lot of times you can't really tell what motivated somebody to get to point A without really understanding what records inspired them or something. At the beginning of the Geraldine Fibbers session I brought in some Pink Floyd compilations 'cause Carla wanted to talk about them and we found out she's really passionate about this vintage Pink Floyd stuff.

So you're almost researching the people you're working with?

Sure. I don't like recording people that like Metallica!

You'll find that you'll have no common ground.

People that like Kiss can make good records and you can find things in common. They'll say, "You know, like that Kiss song." Ah, shit. "Not like that Kiss song." Like the Police. I always thought the Police were complete shit and I hated the Police. They've inspired some really good musicians, but I'm busy explaining to them that Sting was a jazz-fusion head from the beginning. They were laughed off as old men with dye jobs in England. It was the guitar player from Soft Machine and the idea that they were youthful new-wavers... I don't want to hear anybody talkin' about punk rock sellouts and tell me they like the Police at the same time. The only thing that distinguishes the Police from the Stone Temple Pilots is that the Police could write their own songs. They were just a complete distillation made out of the crap that was happening in that time frame and I was of an age and a temperament where I called bullshit. But, you know, if you were 13 you're running around singing "Roxanne" while your voice is breaking. Anyway. Sure, I don't go looking for like-minded people that have all the same records [as me] or anything like that.

You might not find anyone like that.

You work with the 360s. They're archivists in a really beautiful sense. They're reminding you of things you'd forgotten about. "Whoa! Have you heard this bootleg?" And you're, "That is a really good Cream bootleg." I'm 41 years old. I don't listen to Cream. I got through with that a long time ago.

It's cool to see how turned on people are by music.

What they bring to it and what they take out of it are different than what you'd do anyway. As a keyboard player I don't take anything out of music the same way a guitar player does. I was trying to explain to Jon Spencer that I was part of the original blues explosion, which was a bunch of white guys with long hair and t-shirts playing 3 bar chords over and over again in LA in the early '70s. The black people invented the blues. The English white people brought it to America. At least back then the English were saying, "No it's Muddy Waters. No it's Howlin' Wolf. This is where I got the licks." So all the young white kids could go figure it out.

Do you find that there are only a few things you've recorded that you keep listening to?

I listened to Screaming Trees a lot when I was working on that. As weird as those records were I kind of loved what they were and how they flowed in between songs. I like Geraldine Fibbers, although, I worked so hard on that when it was coming together it was hard to muster up some fresh enthusiasm for it when it was done. I like the Boss Hog record. That's one of the rock records I like. It's bassy and rad and strong. The drummer doesn't have any cymbals so the top end is all guitar and vocals. Like Peter Gabriel's 3rd album! The Treepeople stuff, I listen to that. *Something Vicious for Tomorrow* and the "lost" Treepeople album [*Guilt, Regret, and Embarrassment*], it was on Toxic shock and they managed to release it and bury it two or three times on the CD, cassette and vinyl formats. The world doesn't have a lot of Dougs. The *Guilt, Regret, and Embarrassment* record's filled with all kinds of really great Doug and Scott stuff. It's when they were working together instead of writing their own songs.

Are there any good influences you've had over the years?

There were people who set me to thinking, where I didn't necessarily adopt how they thought about it, but what they had to say on it was very interesting. There was a period of time where you couldn't open up a magazine without hearing Robert Fripp talking about the end of the world. I read most of those articles. Your standard pothead Evergreener Fripp/Eno fan.

I think a lot of the concepts he had are still really valid.

He would also dismiss a lot of the crap. Saying, "Don't think about it that way. Try to think about it this way." That's what those stupid cards were all about.

Oblique Strategies.

Yeah. And George Martin, obviously. George Martin I absorbed by listening and listening. There are several George Martin books that are very entertaining.

I read *All You Need is Ears.*

There's also the *Sgt. Pepper's* book. It's about the recording of it, but it references back and forward to different records so it's not just about *Sgt. Peppers.* Like why we did this on one song and that became something that was on *Sgt. Pepper's.* Lee Hazlewood [produced and sang with Nancy Sinatra]. Just from what he sounded like. I never heard the guy talk, but sonically, he's very important to me. Someone I've been hearing since before I even knew what a record was.

Billy Strange had a lot to do with that too, as far as arrangements and guitar playing. Like plate reverb on a bass guitar and stuff like that.

"Boots..." has two basses, an acoustic and an electric through a plate and they're panned in stereo.

Ah ha. In '88 I picked up the Nancy and Lee record on a lark and by the end of the summer I was hooked on the amazing production stuff.

When I was living in Ellensburg me and Mark Pickerel [former Screaming Trees drummer] were talking about Lee Hazlewood and Mark was talking about how passionate he was and how he loved Nancy Sinatra. When he was a kid, his parents had the Nancy and Lee record and it was his favorite record and he didn't have it anymore and he was really bummed out. The next day I was in a thrift store and I found it. I went over and gave it to him and he was almost crying. Martin Hanett [Joy Division pruducer], you know, you never heard a thing he said, you just listened to him. I guess he's dead now. The guy's from Chic [Nile Rogers, Bernard Edwards] are pretty incredible. Another guy who just passed on. That's different, they're players and producers. I can't say I've figured out what David Byrne is trying to do. Producers don't write or talk a lot. When I finally started getting called a producer I really got an idea of how little people even understood what the role was. "What do you do?" It's like being a movie director; you assemble technical and artistic people at a certain place at a certain time and hope you get something real or tangible or engaging. Then you have to take it someplace else and finish it.

It is a hidden job. People don't understand.

Sly Stone was really involved in all of his stuff. He had a degree in music theory. I'm way into Sly.

The layering on that stuff is amazing.

Yeah, and when it's dry, it's so goddamn radically dry it's crazy. When something's in your face it's really...

Everything sounds like it's on the edge of the speaker.

Those were kind of radical records. It was radical to see this mixed-race, hippie-freak band. The best band at Woodstock for gods-sakes! It made the Who look bad.

And Crosby, Stills and Nash blow...

Yeah, can't even get it together to do weepy acoustic music live. Country Joe and the Fish were an abomination. Canned Heat was terrible. Hendrix sucked at Woodstock. That's way the hell back. You know what record sees the most play at the house now? It's a badly put together nature record from the '70s on an independent label. Side one is a narration of all the various flora and fauna that you find in your average Florida swampland and side two is just the effects. Side one, the effects all come off separate sources... "Now we see a flock of Canadian geese as they migrate south" and they come up on the right side of the speaker and migrate south to the left side of the speakers. Then the bullfrog sounds start happening all over it. This completely artificial marsh environment made out of tapes.

They run all the tapes at once?

Yeah. Side one's funny because it's two guys in a boat pointing at things, but side two's a crappy marsh being run like a mixing console. It was an instructive record in field recording, but it's not a field recording, it's an abomination. Instead of playing an environmental tape I'm so post-modern that I'm playing this deconstructed lie of what a marsh sounds like. I listen to that and I listen to Low, 'cause I like Low so much and it's so fun to listen to.

P.102/103

This is an excerpt from an interview with Steve Fisk by Seymore Glass in *Bananafish* #2. You can find it in the **Bananafish** compendium book featuring issues 1-4. It's recommended reading for all.

Bananafish: Tell a little bit about the Optigan, what it is, how it works.

It's a weird old home organ that plays flexi-discs. It uses the same technology with which you would record cheesy soundtracks for a 16-mm film. Since it reads optically, the discs are subject to scratches incurred during handling. Screws up the fidelity. I read an interview with Tom Waits, who's using the Optigan now. He said this great poetic thing, "It's an early synthesizer home organ that creates its own music universes." It comes with a whole selection of "musical universes," like "Tahitian Lounge," "Banjo Singalong," "Easy Does It with Vibes," and my personal favorite, "Big Organ With Drums." He didn't talk about anything technical, but essentially it plays tape loops.

Bananafish: I saw one in Portland at the house of Jackie and Ric from Smegma. You insert huge, clear plastic discs with concentric black circles on them.

Those are the loops. They can be maddening if you leave them going. There's a tape loop for each key. One for the key of G, one for the key of F, and so on. You just keep pushing buttons.

Bananafish c/o Tedium House Publications, PO Box 424762, San Francisco, CA 94142

UNWOUND
Repetition (Kill Rock Stars)

Unwound, Unwound, Unwound. The last great unsung heroes of the exploding universe. The final flash of brilliance before the dying of the light. The Hermes of Athena's temple, banging away at the iron doors erected against truth and beauty. *Repetition* is without a doubt their best since the immortal epic *Fake Train*, and while the music isn't quite as immediate as on that original masterpiece, it is nonetheless refined to the exact point of a diamond. Once again Steve Fisk mans the boards as though he were the invisible fourth member of the group, playing his instrument. More than any of their previous releases, this record perfectly captures the ecstatic live feel of Unwound – raw, angry, poetic and absolutely sublime. From punk to dub and free jazz, Unwound and Fisk go places that are beyond most of our dreams. Much like the Minutemen's *Double* *Nickels on the Dime*, and Sonic Youth's *Daydream Nation*, *Repetition* is the product of a band at the height of its musical prowess, who through the physicality of their sound define an exact moment in time. —Dewey Mahood

Hillary Johnson

by Larry Crane

Hillary first came to *Tape Op's* attention when she e-mailed us, from New York, with some hot "snapple-mic'ing" tips. I was impressed with her rockin' producer/engineer résumé, which included the Ramones, the Godrays, Murphy's Law, Tribe 8, L.E.S. Stitches, Spook Engine, and more. We managed to meet up face-to-face for an interview at the palatial *Tape Op* digs while she was in Portland visiting for the holidays.

So how did you get started in recording? Were you in a band?

I've never played music. I've always just listened to music. When I was in grade school I wanted to take up trombone lessons and the teacher said, "Your arms aren't long enough." I know now that it's more like, "You're a girl, you can't do that." I was kinda discouraged. I just loved music and when I was in college. I was studying communications and I took a sound production class, like razor blade editing and that kinda stuff. I read chapter one of the book about what a producer is and I thought, "This is what I want to do."

Did you study all that stuff at school?

Not in college. I got a degree which was more production orientated and I did a lot of video. After I graduated college I took a short 8-week basic course on the theory of recording. It wasn't even that technical. It was more like

there are these steps in recording and this is how it's done. I was living in Maryland and I got a chance to run a studio in New York, turn it into a business, and learn engineering at the same time. I just jumped at it 'cause I wasn't doing anything exciting in Maryland.

How did you end up with the chance to do this?

Friends of mine had recorded at the studio [Spa], where I'm working now, and the guy who was the assistant engineer at the time ended up clicking with the band and they needed a soundman - so they took him. The studio owner, who was friends with the band's manager, said, "If you take him you need to give me somebody." The manager knew that I wanted to get into recording and said, "Well, go up for six weeks." It ended up being more than six weeks.

How long have you been there now?

Three and a half years. After I was there for six months I started engineering - just small bands. The studio is a small 24-track; a midsize studio for Manhattan. It's pretty much a word-of-mouth kind of place. I was doing real assisting: answering phones, making coffee, emptying the trash and also setting up mics. All the stuff an assistant does. At the same time I was running the studio I was learning about where to buy equipment... if something breaks, who to call.

So they gradually eased you into recording.

It was just me and the owner and one engineer but he wasn't involved in the business aspect. I pretty much taught myself all the aspects of the business of recording.

What was the first session you recorded?

A lot of the times there's a crossover, when you're still assisting, of when you're assisting and when you're actually engineering. "You want me to get the sound? I'm just the assistant." It might have actually been D-Generation. They just came in to do one song for a demo. They're a big, New York based rock band. They opened for Kiss! I pretty much just started engineering, not really working with a separate producer but working with the band, just giving them suggestions. Not even really co-producing. I just worked with a lot of New York local bands that I liked. "Come in and record. I'll get you a good rate on the studio and I'll do it for free."

You were coaxing people that you knew or had seen?

A lot of the bands hadn't recorded before - or if they had it was just 4-track stuff. I thought, "This will be great for them. They'd be able to learn what all these other bands are doing out there." It was a way for me to get more experience doing it. We'd go in, off-hours, late at night or in between two lockout sessions or something.

For cheap. Has the studio always had a 24-track there? I assume it's a 2" Studer.

Yeah. We also have an 8-track digital (Roland DM-80).

Hard drive?

Yeah, the Spook Engine record was done on that. An experiment on how to make 8-tracks work. A couple of songs were done on the multitrack and then were bounced.

Was that a neat experience?

That was a very long process. That record took 3 or 4 months to make. I'm used to doing a 4-song demo of a band in two days. It might sound like a long time to some people who think, "We can just go to the studio and record and be done in four hours."

They're usually kidding themselves. You did some stuff with the Ramones?

Daniel Rey is their producer. He's done the Ramones' records for the past zillion years and he produced the last Murphy's Law record. I think he first came to the studio to do a couple of 7" singles with Murphy's Law. He usually just uses the engineer at the studio where he is working. I worked with him and he liked the studio and he liked working with me. We did the Murphy's Law record, which is supposed to be their big comeback record, and then he came back and we did some stuff with the Ramones. We did one song for a record that was a live compilation record with a couple of studio tracks. Then we did basic tracks for a Dee Dee Ramone record that I think still has to be mixed. I like working with Daniel. He's a great producer. He gets the band in such a good mood.

Do you feel like you learn a lot, watching someone like that working?

I learn a lot, production wise. I get more confidence engineering wise 'cause he's the kind of producer who'll be out in the lounge or the hallway when you're getting sounds. He'll come in and say, "Great, cool." The same with mixing. He'll say, "Okay, do your thing" and he'll leave.

Was there a period where you didn't feel quite knowledgeable enough about recording?

I always thought, "I'm never gonna figure out this EQ thing." I actually spend a lot of time now teaching friends of mine the basics of recording. It's a lot of females – a lot of girlfriends will come and say, "I'm interested in this. Can you teach me?" It's something you'll learn; you'll figure it out. Every day I still learn from people. A band will come in and they might have their own producer. There are two assistant engineers that work for me and if neither of them is available then I'll assist. I'll be able to step back - it's really hard though - and see how someone else is doing things a little different. I pretty much learned from just two or three people. The first studio I went to, outside of Spa, was when I did the Godrays' demo. We went to a 16-track studio. That was a great experience 'cause I didn't have to worry about answering the phone or if somebody was gonna call about scheduling.

Did you find that you were pretty familiar with everything there too?

Oh yeah. It was actually good 'cause there's a lot of things that I found I took for granted. I knew which buttons had to be pushed but I wasn't really reading what this was doing what. Maybe on a gate, I knew if I turned it to 10 o' clock it would give me that specific effect. If they had different gates at this other studio I would actually have to think about it.

It might even help you rethink what you were doing back at Spa. There's not very many women doing engineering. Did you ever encounter anything weird about that?

I always knew that most engineers were men. When I was taking the short recording class there were a couple of girls in there that seemed to be technically orientated and that gave me confidence. When I started working at the studio there weren't any other female engineers but it was never like, "Oh, you're an engineer?" I don't think that ever was an issue. I worked with this artist once who said, "I think you're really great and do a great job." She would be interviewed by a magazine and she would say, "Hillary's the best female producer..." Don't do that! I don't want to get pigeonholed! I do what I do and it doesn't really matter that I'm a girl.

It shouldn't be a matter of consideration.

There was a point where I thought there were a lot of female artists out there that were afraid to get their songs out there. I wanted to get them all. I wanted to work with all these female bands. Then I was like, "Who am I kidding?" There are guy bands that are just as good that have just as much potential that I would want to work with. It was a stupid thing to think.

But on the other hand it's good for people to see a female working as an engineer/producer.

When I first started engineering pretty much every band, whether they were male or female, would say to me, "How did you get into this?" It got to the point where I got tired of telling the story. Now, the bands that come to work with me have come from word-of-mouth. It's not even an issue anymore.

Do you find that word-of-mouth works well?

When I first started running the studio we took out an ad in the *Village Voice*. It was a really dumb ad. We didn't have a clientele; we didn't have anything. We just got the worst calls. I didn't know. We got ripped off and stuff. But now we're advertising and we have a clientele – I have a clientele.

Was it pretty new when you first started working there?

Well, physically it was 2 1/2 years old but it wasn't a business It was just a hobby studio.

So you kind of took it from there...

The owner and I are kind of like partners, even though he's definitely the owner. He's trying to get involved more, now, in the business aspect of it. I understand the whole point of the studio – which is important. It's weird, 'cause a lot of times bands will come in and I'll want to work with them and they'll have their own engineer. "No! Work with me!"

Do they bring them in for a certain reason?

Usually when that happens the engineer's also the producer. It's a combo deal. They've either worked with them before or they're trying this person out. That's happened a few times. At least I get to see the qualities they're looking for in a producer or an engineer. I get a feel for other kind of people that are out there. There's some mean people out there.

What?

I've come across a couple of producers that treat singers really badly without realizing it. They don't give them any confidence and end up getting a really bad take and don't know why. I've come across producers that are just the opposite that are like cheerleaders and they keep the people happy and they get a really good take.

What do you think causes a producer to treat the musicians badly?

Arrogance. They get to a point where they think, "They're listening to me." They get a little cocky. "I know what I'm talking about."

What things help make a session comfortable?

Usually the people I work with I like as people. I try and make them feel comfortable as people and make sure and tell them what we're gonna do ahead of time. Get them involved. If they haven't recorded explain how it works. If they have, and I'm just hired help, I might ask the singer, "What kind of mics have you used before?" Just get them involved in the whole process. We have a carpet in the studio that, if it's rolled up, the room's live. That's the first thing I say. "What are you looking for?" I'll ask the drummer. Than I'll ask the band what they're looking for. Just so I know how to mic everything. Then, get the sounds, put it on tape, and have them come in and listen. It's important that everything on tape is really close to what they want. They'll be, "Don't worry about that; We'll fix it in the mix." I don't like that! You never know who's gonna be mixing it.

Have you had that happen?

I've had to mix stuff that other people recorded and usually you end up criticizing something. You're like, "What did they...?" I feel so bad...

Someone could be doing that to you.

Or it could be on purpose. That could've been the intention. You just don't know. On the Tribe 8 record I did mixes, we were kinda rushed as usual, and then Jello Biafra [who runs Alternative Tentacles, the label they are on] was like, "I don't like the mixes. Let's remix." The band was wanting to record some more stuff and they couldn't get back to New York, since they live in San Francisco. They just had to do everything in San Francisco with the guy they had been doing their last couple of records with. Everything sounds fine, it's just kind of like an insult. I know it's not intentional but...

Did it mess up your relationship with the band?

It was an insult at first, but it shouldn't have been. It was only in my mind. I knew why and the guitar player was always calling me, "We're really sorry. We don't have the money. We really like working with you and we want to do it again. We're here and you're there."

Did you check out the record?

Oh yeah. It was pretty close to what was there on the tape. They also recorded a lot of newer songs, which I think, overall, made the record a good record. I really wanted them to go further, 'cause at that point the press was really picking up on them. I was like, "What do you guys want to do? Do you want to go out and be L7 or do you want to have the reputation you have now and do it more?" They didn't know. I also like having other people mix my stuff 'cause then I can step back.

So when you record you're trying to have the best sounds you can on every track?

Not necessarily. I'm a person who really likes clarity. I hate muddiness. That's just me being anal-retentive. I like everything to be "correct" I guess. If you're gonna mess with the sound or make it perfectly distorted do it in the mix, unless that's part of the sound and you know for sure, 100%. I hate trying to get rid of hum from a direct bass sound, or something, after the fact. I want to get rid of it now.

What would you like to do with your future in recording?

[Sarcastically] Be a millionaire, of course. Make one record a year...

Are you pretty comfortable working at Spa?

Yeah. I'm a stress freak. I like being busy all the time. I like helping people learn stuff about recording. With a band, I like teaching them about recording and I like helping them make a good record. I kind of like where I am now. The studio that I'm running is a good place.

You were saying, when we talked earlier on the phone, that you'd been doing a lot of punkier/hard edged stuff and you felt like you were getting pigeonholed as a producer who did that kind of stuff.

I've been getting a lot of work from people that come in and kinda want a co-producer, and it tends to be a word-of-mouth thing. It's a lot of the New York hardcore and punk bands. I love it, but I like everything equally, so I tend to go out and see bands and I'll find somebody I like and try and develop an artist that way. I wouldn't necessarily go up to a punk band that I liked and say, "Do you wanna record?" I don't think that it's commonplace to ask a band like that. It's not like you're trying to develop them. With the harder stuff that I've been doing, either co-producing or producing, it's more like just getting a really good take or capture the energy of that band.

You don't go changing songs around...

That's them; they know what they want. I might suggest doubling a guitar or something like that. I wish I could do more experimental stuff because I'm really into that.

What kind of stuff?

Like Neu bauten. Not necessarily noise experimentation but just techniques of recording. Unlike a band that says, "I want the drums to sound like Metallica." You know, a band that wants to come in and play around. The Godrays were really fun to work with. We ended up recording background vocals on hand-held U87s. They ended up doing that on the record too.

Did you work with them on their record?

No. Well, I played tambourine on one track.

You said you weren't a musician.

I'm a percussionist! Egg shaker and tambourine.

Who produced their record?

Adam Lasus. He's a super nice guy and he's the kind of person who gets the band in the right state of mind.

They had to deliver some demos first to get a deal?

Yeah, and I didn't know them. I ended up working with them through Greg Griffith, who is in Vitapup, who had been a friend of Alex's [of the Godrays] and he ended up playing with them, on the demos and on the record.

Do you have any experimental stuff on the horizon?

I'm still working with Jane Hoenberger [of Spook Engine]. We're supposed to be doing a split 7" with John S. Hall. That's with a full band, so I want to play around with that a little bit. Next, I'm going to be working with Daniel Rey recording the Misfits next month.

The original Misfits?

I have no idea. It's not gonna be that experimental. Maybe it will – I have no idea! I'm still working with a lot of other local bands.

Are you still grabbing bands off the street?

I'm really scared to now.

Are you too busy?

No. Personally, there's bands I'll see and like but I'll be, "They don't care - they've got their own thing going on." They don't need me coming up to them and going, "Oh, I really like you. Let's work together." I'm just really freaked out about it now.

In what way?

Like the other night, I saw this band, and I thought they were really good, but they seemed like they'd been around or whatever. They finished a set and I was like, "I should go up and talk to them," but I felt like such a cheeseball. It just seems cheesy 'cause now I know what I'm doing. I've got a discography that's relatively decent looking and I just feel like I'm looking for business, and I hate that. That's not what it is, but it's how it comes across.

Smarmy. Have you ever had any awful studio sessions?

I'm not the kind of person who is a super feminist. If I'm working with a guy band I try to just be a person and not be all, "You shouldn't say that." Every once and a while there's a band that comes in and they'll really offend me and I'm stuck between a rock and a hard place.

"Should I just kick them out?"

Yeah. It's not like they're doing it consciously, but at the same time...

Do you mean how they're acting or what they're recording?

Oh no. It's what they're saying or doing. Lyrically, I would know ahead of time that I wouldn't want to work with that band. But sometimes the guitar player will be the rep for the band. He'll call me, "We want to record some songs," and then they come in and the drummer will be a dick. Ohhh...

Do they treat you bad, personally?

No. Somethings they say... I can't understand why they would even think it. Another problem is when someone is not 100% comfortable that there's a female recording them. The way it comes across is them saying, "Oh I'm sorry... I shouldn't say that," or being aware that they're saying something that could possibly offend me. It takes away from them being a person.

They're trying to be careful?

Yeah. Then it's too personal and you can't really get a good take.

It's strange that a person would put themselves in that position.

A lot of people I've worked with are very aware that I'm a female and I'm not gonna take crap from them. They may get feisty and want to fight about it. This has happened maybe two or three times.

Yikes. Do you ever find it difficult not being more of a musician?

It makes me feel stupid. The only thing I will usually do is say, "That note needs to be higher." It's hard when the band is really in tune, musically, and they'll talk in those terms. "Punch in on the E." Then I feel stupid.

But you probably know enough from just listening to music.

I've never tried to mess with song structures.

Do you foresee yourself thinking that way?

I'm more of a sound person than a music person. Sometimes that's a problem. Friends of mine will say to me, "Oh, this is such a great song," and what they're thinking is the lyrics. I'm like, "Oh, I love the way everything sounds." I end up hearing bass drum sounds before I ever hear what the singer is saying. It's sometimes a problem! I was just listening to a Joy Division record recently and I was trying really hard to listen to just the lyrics and I was thinking, "This song, lyrically, is exactly how this song made me feel."

Hillary now works as a freelance engineer in New York.
www.hillaryjohnson.com

HEY TAPE OP-

When I recorded the Godrays (ex-Small Factory) I put a Snapple bottle (one of those bigger ones) about 6 feet away from the guitar amp (mouthhole facing the amp). I put a 452 or something about an inch or so into the mouth of the bottle and got this crazy phase-y thingy happening...combine it with the normal close-mic and presto-the "snapple" sound...

—Hillary Johnson, NY

Rob Schnapf and Tom Rothrock

THE DYNAMIC PRODUCTION TEAM OF ROB AND TOM TELLS US OF THEIR TRICKS, HISTORY, DISTORTION, AND STOMP BOXES **by Larry Crane**

Rob and Tom have been recording records together for 10 years or so. Some of them, like Beck's *Mellow Gold* or the Foo Fighters debut [which they mixed] have done very well. Others like Elliott Smith's *Either/Or* [which they partially tracked and mixed] and Mary Lou Lord's are critical successes and stepping stones to bigger careers. All these records work because Rob and Tom do a great job, focusing on the songs, the overall album and bringing out the most of what's there while making something that is a treat to listen to. I got a chance to spend a week with them in Los Angeles while they were working on Elliott Smith's fourth solo record (*XO*). They were fun to be around and took me under their wing, giving me a lot of advice on how I should consider my "career" in recording, avoiding studio owner burnout, and tons of great recording tips, concepts and techniques. It was also refreshing to see how they worked together in the studio and how much importance they placed on the *song* and the performance/feel thereof. It was a blast to observe, and I even felt a part of the whole process at points when we'd toss album order ideas around and such. Anyway, after getting a kick out of the copies of *Tape Op* I brought down, they agreed to sit down for an interview. Thanks to Elliott Smith for bringing me to LA for the week and letting me sit in on the making of his record...

How did you guys end up working together?

T: I was working at a car wash.

R: And I had to get my Mercedes cleaned.

T: And I was wiping it down and putting the fake ArmorAll on the tires and I thought, "Man, I gotta get me one of these cars." So I asked Rob how he got the car.

R: So I told him, "It's from doing publishing deals with artists and taking all their money."

T: And I said, "Wow. That doesn't seem right. Yet you have this very big car."

R: And I said, "That's what makes it right."

T: The end always justifies the debauchery.

Uhhhhhh...

R: Any other questions? No, we met at the Record Plant [long-time LA studio]. We were both working there.

T: 1988

R: And we were both runners, broom pushers and it was pointless and stupid.

T: When Robin Crosby from Ratt would throw up I'd have to clean it up.

Cool.

T: That was my job. That was at the first studio I worked at, Cherokee, just months before I met Rob. Robin would come in and say, "Tom, I got sick in the bathroom." It was really kinda nice of him.

Did you guys have recording school backgrounds?

T: No. I took one course at Humboldt State University. The closest they had was an audio for film class so it was taught by film people who are inherently, *masterfully knowledgeable* of all recording techniques. That, of course, confused the hell out of me. I spent the whole quarter trying to figure out what a buss was.

R: Other than what you take to college.

T: Yeah, I didn't know what a buss was...

R: I was working in a studio in D.C. and I had gone to a college that had a studio there but basically they taught you physics and electronics. The studio kinda sucked. I got in there, and that's the last three years of college... that's what I did. I blew a lot of stuff off.

And recorded?

R: Yeah. Just made bad recordings as often as I could.

T: That's why I took that course in film. To get into the studio.

R: You gotta make the bad ones before you make the good ones. Just like you gotta write the bad songs before you write the good ones. Sometimes you have to revisit the bad.

So you were working shit jobs at Record Plant...

T: That's where we met and I was doing this project at this studio I'd worked at before. I'd found this band through my girlfriend, and they had a lot of money, so I went to this studio that I used to work at and we made this tape. Rob heard the tape and said, "Oh, that's cool." And then we just skipped to producing together. That started on Christmas day, 1988. We've been working ever since.

Have either of you done projects on your own since then?

T: Projects, we're pretty much all together. We both record stuff at home all the time.

Sometimes we collaborate with other people as well as ourselves. Whether they are artists or bands, or other producers or engineers. There's lots of great people out there to work with.

When I watch you work in the studio I'm trying to figure out who delegates what. It switches back and forth.

T: As the Dust Brothers say... We like to use nonverbal communication in the studio. That evolves.

It seems like sometimes you can work faster. You've got the setup in the back here with the digital editing.

T: That happens a lot through every project we do... splitting off into two rooms. Sometimes when it's a traditional band setup with a tracking scenario we've set up another 24-track deck in a closet or a storage area and one guy will keep tracking and the other guy will be cutting the tape to pieces.

R: Or it can even be that one person keeps recording while the other is attending to the psychological warfare aspect.

T: Or one person's on the phone getting the string section together. When you're making a record that's not gonna be a compromise in terms of time or technical limitations and you're gonna have whatever you need at your disposal... That sounds easy but the reality is you have to build yourself in parameters and limitations or it just immediately falls apart. There's an incredible amount of coordination and stuff that doesn't have to do with moving a fader or pushing play. That's where the "two" thing is really great.

There isn't a set pattern of who does what?

T: No. We're just always going back and forth. Sometimes somebody will give one of us a number so we'll just start following up on it.

R: Or, "I really hate that person. Could you talk to them?"

That could be handy. Do you think that there are any areas that one of you has more expertise in?

R: It's different personalities.

T: See who's jelling with who and get out of the way. Rob has a really extensive collection of guitars from being a guitar player so that's an area of expertise.

Do you play any instrument?

T: I play guitar a little bit. At the point where one would usually be in a garage band, I was in a garage with my buddies recording them.

But you really had an interest in recording...

T: Since I was a kid. It never stopped. I got really into records and record collecting. I'd buy a record and obsess about it for months. I was into it but it wasn't like I was buying records every day.

Rob, what kind of background did you have? Was it more from being a musician?

R: Well, it's been in the family. My father and uncle had a studio in New York City. I was always more into the music and my dad was more technical.

T: Yeah, your dad didn't seem so into the art of music...

R: He's not really into the bullshit, intangible stuff. He was really pragmatic so he was just into getting stuff onto tape. When I was a little kid he used to take me to the studio. It was always sort of, "Well, that's pretty much what I'm gonna do."

So now you guys are at the point that you get to pick and choose what you're gonna work on...

T: We kind of always have...

And now you can spend longer working on a record?

T: We've always found ways to spend the time.

R: Sometimes you're compacting a month into a week, but we've always worked on stuff until it was right.

T: It doesn't mean you have to work in big ostentatious, elaborate studios.

R: Yeah. Beck's *Mellow Gold* was done at Karl [Stephenson]'s house and my house.

T: In a series of living rooms! The lead vocal on "Loser" is a hand-held Radio Shack PZM. And the slide guitar. I held the PZM up to the acoustic.

Was that out of necessity?

T: That's what we had that day.

R: Fostex 1/4" 8-track.

T: And a Roland DM 80 hard disc recorder and Mackie mixers. Technology is to the point where there's enough cheap, transparent stuff that anybody can have the tools. It seems like a lot of people go down the path of thinking they're limited by their tools. It doesn't matter what you have.

R: It's about documenting a performance... whatever that may be.

T: Wherever that leads you.

R: You don't need to document a performance in a $1200 a day room. You can do it in your living room. It's just a lot cooler to do it in a $1200 a day room if you've got two guys with Marshalls! In your living room you'll bum out the neighbors!

True. You can see with something like "Loser" where it could be recorded in an apartment and you're not gonna bug anybody.

T: Or the back room of a dilapidated mansion off of Wilcox.

You mentioned before that you worked with a guy that had a studio and let you use the downtime.

R: That's how we got started. He had this studio up above the Record Plant called the Microplant.

T: Steve Deutsch. That's why, from the very first thing we did together [which was there], we weren't compromised for time. It might take a while but we'd get as many evenings in until we felt it was done. I don't know if that's good or bad but it's always been that way. Leaving Microplant, it was clear that we were gonna have to have our own studio. Being able to work with people who didn't have money was the key. That's why we've always had a studio, so we could just do it.

So you built a studio up in Northern California in the woods. What is it called?

T: The Shop.

What year did that happen?

R: In '91.

T: It was in the works for a long time.

You were probably assembling gear...

T: Yep. We had all the gear down here in LA.

You were saying that you only use that part of the year but you have a very low overhead when it's not being used.

R: The key to all this stuff is: If you can, buy it outright with cash.

T: Or don't buy it.

R: Rent is one thing, but loans on gear are a bummer. That makes you worry.

Yeah, yeah... I know.

T: If you have debt it means that a certain amount of the time you're gonna be doing a day job or something to just cover that bill every month.

R: Or it makes you have to be in your studio having to do something you don't want to do.

T: You're gonna be spending a lot of time to cover that debt doing shit that's not gonna further you. If you're out of debt you're gonna spend a lot more time doing things that are gonna further what you're trying to do.

Like dragging people in to record that might not be getting around to it. With Beck, was that someone you'd seen around?

T: Yep. Saw him once and said, "Wow. We should record." That only happens every two years.

R: Y'know, Elliott was sort of the same way. "Woo, this guy's good." And y'know, *Either/Or*...

Did you just kind of offer to mix that for him?

T: It was a lot more than mixing it.

I was never sure what was done at The Shop.

T: It's not clear in the liner notes.

It's not clear what was done at my place [Laundry Rules] either!

T: Everything he brought in was on 1/2" 8-track. Some things were done entirely at The Shop but the bulk of it was half-and-half.

R: We bumped it [the 8-track] over to 16-track...

T: And added more stuff and then mixed it.

How long did you spend up there?

R: Ten days or something.

T: There were two trips up there to do it so I don't know the total time. One session to collect all the stuff and another session to mix it.

I was always amazed because I'd tracked the vocals on "Pictures of Me" and when I heard the record there were little things added. That record is rather unclear about where things were recorded...

T: That's important too, when you're working on stuff, be sure people can't really tell what you've done. Never be clearly credited. That helps you out! If too many people want to hire you it's a headache. [much laughter]

Yeah, I've done a number of records where there's no recording credit on them.

T: Great! That's good. You're already on top of it! Really, it's good to discuss all that stuff. You don't have to make a contract, but just put it on a piece of paper. "This is how my name should be." Ross from Sukia did a remix for Bongload the other day and the last thing he did when leaving was... I said, "Ross, write on this piece of paper how you want your name to appear." He wrote down something that we would've been way off on. We didn't have any of those conversations on *Either/Or*.

What records were you working on before taking on Elliott's new one here?

R: Lutefisk... Mary Lou Lord...

T: Plastilina Mosh...

How does the work come to you these days? Do you have an agent or do people come to you?

R: We have management. It's a little bit of both.

T: Over time we've certainly picked our own stuff and we found most of it. The one act that came to us, based on someone we'd found and worked with.... We'd worked with this band Wool, which was the outcome of the D.C. band Scream. Then some people at a record company heard that and got excited and...

R: From doing Wool we did the Toadies and the Foo Fighters.

T: That was the direct outcome of that work. You never know by doing one thing, no matter how unrelated they are. That was neat. That was the first project that came directly to us that we would have never known about had we not done some work before that. That was an exciting thing, the Toadies record.

R: And Wool was a band that we found, recorded and did a single with them on Bongload and then they got signed and we did their EP and then their album. From that we did the Toadies record and the Foo Fighters. That's a cool little illustration of finding something before anyone knows about it and how it can turn into other things. It's like the time you invest into it ends up reaping more.

For the Wool single did you do it after hours at Microplant?

R: Tom had this studio in Van Nuys that was 300 square feet...

T: But it had six rooms!

R: We had our main room, we had our drum room...

T: A control room, our bass booth, a vocal booth, a bathroom [which we used]...

R: Our live chamber...

T: We did a lot of great stuff there. That was the early '90s. The Pleasuredome! The first three releases on Bongload were all Pleasuredome recordings.

R: It was like this... the console and the wall [right behind]. After a while you'd be like, "Ugghh".

T: "We gotta get out of here!" You'd be in there for-fuckin'-ever.

T: We kept go-peds there, these motorized skateboards, and it was off an alley and we'd just blow out of there, jump on the skateboards and race around the alleys of Van Nuys. We'd go to the hot dog stand and get hot dogs and take off. The hot dog stand down the alley was right across the street from the jail so the first place people would go when they got out of jail was to Happy Dog.

R: They'd be taking their wallet out of the plastic bag.

T: Happy Dog!

How long did you run The Pleasuredome?

T: It was about two years.

R: Really? Wow.

When I first heard about you I couldn't believe you guys were doing all this production and running a record label. How did that start up?

R: One of the things was... you'd make these tapes, and if they stay in cassette form they're a demo.

T: If you press it up, it's a record. We got hip to that.

R: "Okay, we're making records."

T: We even talked to another independent label, "Hey, let's find somebody to put these out." We had a bunch of single songs by different bands and the guy was like, "Oh, that costs too much and compilation records don't sell". Another few months went by and we said, "We'll just do this ourselves."

What was the first release?

T: Grimace. *Quagmire* CD. They're from Humboldt [County]. Excellent band, got great press.

R: There's also a Grimace from Denver.

T: When Bongload got more noticeable, they wrote us a letter and said, "Hey, we're

Grimace too. You're not gonna sue us are you?" We said, "No, the other one broke up. Keep going."

"And I'll sell you some back catalog to sell at your gigs!"

T: Our Grimace sales did pick up when those guys started putting stuff out!

So you just started putting out stuff that you'd been recording. At this point you're not doing all the recording for the label, although I saw you listed as executive producers on the Lutefisk record...

R: That was their idea, not ours! [laughing ensues] That was just because they would come over and say, "What do you think?"

T: They wanted to put that on there. It was nice of them. The joke is that, in the liner notes, it also says it was recorded on a 4-track. Then you have "executive producers" of a 4-track cassette production. It's clearly beautiful!

It does shock me how good that record [*Burn in Hell Fuckers*] sounds...

T: It took them over a year to do it.

R: We spent 7 months on the new record.

T: That may or may not come out...

So you have people running the label for you...

T: Since the first pressing, there's always been a day-to-day person. Neither one of us wanted to stop recording to do it. Somebody had to do it. That's how it is able to stay active and be an outlet for stuff we come across.

It was funny; I think Poolside [recently recording for Bongload] seemed to expect that you guys would jump in and produce their record for them. I told them it made more sense for you two to record someone else for money and delegate the recording of their record to someone that you trust.

T: We don't make a living off the label or the bands on the label. We make our living off of recording. The more recording we do, whether it's for the label or not, the more it helps the label and the bands on the label. Poolside is better off with us recording Elliott Smith this month while they record their record with Dave Bassett (who also worked at the Record Plant with us). Here's a guy we've known a long time and know well and it's perfect. It's a much better situation. The reality, at this point, is that we can only do a couple of things a year on the label.

R: And they also have to fit into the schedule at the right time.

T: If we were to record Poolside, which would have been great, they would have had to wait until June and they're recording right now, in the beginning of February. They're one of the first new bands to be involved in this new mentality... we started the label as an outlet for stuff we recorded. At a certain point, when we got busier, bands would end up sitting around for months waiting for us. And we know great producers with great studios.

In the past you've had the time to go watch people play and check stuff out. I would gather that it's been hard to do that lately.

T: Very good point.

R: It's not as regular.

T: That's the thing about recording music for a living... a lot of it isn't even about being in a studio. You also have to be your own A&R person. It's very important what you decide to work on and you have to put a lot of time into that. Going out and getting inspired by other bands.

R: Or whatever it is.

T: You can't stay in your little cocoon in the studio all the time.

R: Books and art...

T: Whatever it is that turns you on. I like working on cars and I don't get enough time to do it. You have to schedule it. Build it in.

Do you ever find yourselves burned out on music in general?

T: It happens. Only in the middle of something I think. It's not so much that you're burnt out and sick of music but that you're so burnt out that you don't know anymore.

R: It's usually on the projects that are obnoxiously trying on many different levels. When it should just not be that hard. "Okay, we've got these songs and you should show up and we should work on them." Sometimes all this other stuff comes into play.

T: The external things aren't necessarily as simple as people being difficult with each other either. There's a lot of forces that can come in. Working with Elliott and then the Academy Award nomination coming up was a huge positive, but it was extremely disruptive to the session.

It seems to be taking a toll on his concentration.

T: And ours too, at times. Sometimes the universe throws a lot of fuckin' curve balls at ya'. If you get enough of them thrown at you and you end up working on this record, five months in, and you could have been done in two months. That can be tough.

R: With making records, whether you admit it or not, you only have so much energy per project. And it's one way.

T: When we start a project, a band usually wants to record 15 or 20 songs. Well, "That's a great idea. Then we'll pick the best ones and put them on the record." Great on paper, but the problem is, if you only have a certain amount of energy per project it becomes simple mathematics. That's part of the corralling in. Technically we're not gonna compromise, but there is still a finite amount of energy.

Do you find yourselves reining a band in?

T: It depends. Sometimes the band or artist really get that. Other times they're clueless to that fact. "We wrote 20 songs so we should put 20 on." It's not about that... It's about making the best record. The best record benefits *you* the artist. Having 72 minutes of music is rarely a good idea.

R: But there's an exception to every rule.

T: Yeah. But just because you can doesn't mean you should. A lot of that can get sorted out in good pre-production. Hanging out at rehearsal and just going over stuff. That's another thing we were able to do early on was to go into people's rehearsal places. When you have your own studio and you're the recording guy, people just come to you, theoretically ready to go. If you can back it up and go into their environment it's helpful to everybody. You get a much better concept of where they're coming from and watch them interact in rehearsal, so you'll understand the dynamic of the band before you're in the middle of trying to get great drum takes.

It's nice to be in a position where you can work that way.

T: Anybody can put themselves in that position... The trick is defining what position you think you need to be in. If you think you need to be in it, go for it.

Any tricks or gear you've been using lately?

T: Some you don't notice. You get these basic ideas and you keep building on them.

R: Different ways of doing distortion. The one thing we did on this record was that we'd bounce a bunch of vocals to one track and then we'd bounce them around about nine times, kinda hot to the tape. Then get that and blend it in with the original again.

T: You started getting this high-end thing.

R: Sort of a sibilant thing, just sort of this weird thing happening. It wasn't really good all on its own, but it was really cool when we combined it.

T: We thought we'd bounce it a million times and just use the bounce, but by the end Rob discovered that it was better to go back and blend the 10th one with the first one.

R: That's something you can try with drums and stuff.

I did some stuff like that with vocal comps. It made me think of the sound of vocals on Beatles records.

R: A lot of that old sound is the old tape.

T: It was like the quality of a cassette tape.

R: So you go into tape compression real quick and print through.

Hey Elliott! What kind of tricks have you seen these guys use?

E: Tricks? I saw them record the drums with very few mics. I don't know.

T: I think a good trick is not getting comfortable with something. Continually changing things up. On one song use two mics on the drums if you can. See how little you can get away with and how much you can get away with.

R: Also changing the environment. There you are in the room and you've got these drums. "Okay, let's make it dead." What does that do?

What kinds of effects do you guys like?

R: Analog effects. Or the early digital delays that can get you that analog feedback.

T: When it recycles and collapses in on itself.

R: Like the old Yamaha delays.

T: The black ones with the round knobs that are recessed. Those are cool.

R: There were Ibanez ones too.

We've got one of those Ibanez analog ones at the studio.

T: Rackmount analog? Oh yeah.

It's Elliott's. It will regenerate into oblivion.

R: Nothing like tape delay. Run it to the Echoplex.

T: Echoplexes are great. Nothing's better than having a big complement of analog stuff.

R: With tape delay, if you have a 4-track you can run it through all four tracks and keep building up delay.

T: You could use your 1/2" 8-track as an analog delay unit. Go crazy. You never know what you've got.

We were talking about setting up the two 8-tracks and making a delay line between them.

R: Frippertronics.

T: Nick Saloman [Bevis Frond] is really into that. He'll make tape loops on his reel-to-reel and put them all around his room with mic stands up so the tape rests on corners of mic stands.

What kind of stomp boxes do you use in the studio?

R: The Boss delay. The red one. That's a really cool delay.

T: Just use it as an outboard effect when you mix down.

R: There's these little boxes called a Reamp that's like a...

T: Backwards DI.

R: You come off tape and it gets the level back down and has a volume control and you can send it into your stomp boxes without exploding them. Or you can run it back through an amp.

T: That's why they call it Reamp. There's no better way to get a thick flange than a Boss flanger pedal or something. Rack mount shit for flange and chorus always sucks - go to a stomp box, Small Stone or whatever you need. All the stomp boxes are great because: A) they're cheesy which is great, and B) they're single task devices. They don't try to be clean and that's why they sound good.

R: You get that distortion, once again. Distortion is usually your friend.

T: I can't tell you the hours we've spent in studios with H3000s trying to get a flange.

R: And the flange just sucks.

T: And the whole time you just picture in your head, "When I put that one on my guitar it's so thick." Grab that one and use it.

R: Running drums through the Phase 90 or the Small Stone.

T: Buss it on through.

R: That's a cool sound. Doing that with compression, multing out the kick and snare, sweeping them till they have a sound and then blending those elements back in. Or you can do that with a good stereo compressor. You can lean on the room a little more, put in some of the drums, squash, and blend back in.

T: A great thing when you mix is if you've got a couple of stereo compressors, just put them on buss buttons. So you've got your mix going, and then you return them on faders just like they were reverb. When you're mixing and you need more kick and snare you just hit the buss buttons and boom. The second one you can use for other shit. "Let's put the bass and the vocals in the second one." You'd be amazed at how everything gets thumping and glued together in a cool way.

R: Cause then you have this thing that's sort of like the core and then you have the other, less compressed, track that still lets things poke out.

T: The compressor will kill all the transients.

R: Yet you get that smack that the compressor gives you.

Do you guys use that trick where you mult the signal out to several faders to bring out a sound?

T: Never more than two faders. Sure, you want another EQ on it. I had a friend that would always do that on bass drums.

R: If there was a problem for some reason, if the kick drum wasn't thumping, that's what he would do.

I do that a lot.

R: With bass, if it's in E or A, if you do EQ around 200 Hz you're in a harmonic zone and it helps it "speak". Remember frequencies and keys...

T: There's a correlation.

It'd be nice to have a chart...

R: Well, you know A is 440 Hz so 220 Hz is a lower octave.

T: That's a good way to look at your equalization too. Start thinking about it in octaves. Look at the numbers and think what they actually mean. You start to look at the sonics of your mix in a more musical sense perhaps.

Zero Return for Man or Astroman?

JIM MARRER OF ZERO RETURN STUDIOS AND BRIAN TEASLEY OF MAN OR ASTROMAN? ON TECHNOLOGY AND TECHNETIUM

by Henry Owings

Brian Teasley, better known to most of the civilized world as either Man or Astroman?'s "Birdstuff" or Servotron's "Z4OBX", had bandied the idea back and forth with me of doing an interview with him and Jim Marrer from the Zero Return Studio in Alabama for TAPE OP for almost a year. And seeing as how I just love spending countless hours transcribing, I said "sure." For an explanation of why Man or Astroman?'s recording career is worthy to TAPE OP readers, please do the following: Listen to a copy of MOA?s first full length *Is It...* alongside a recording of their newest release *Made from Technetium*. Even to my untrained ear, the amount of recording knowledge that has been accumulated and implemented by the band and Jim has grown exponentially in the five years they have been working together. On top of this, when you consider that their recordings have all been done within the four walls of a hundred year old house [rented for the unheard of price of $75/mo] at the end of a dirt road, right off the train tracks, 2 miles down from Raper Prison [yes, a real prison], and well outside the Montgomery, Alabama, city limits; Zero Return automatically leaves the parameters of "Yet Another [Boring] Studio Profile" and enters the realm of "Deliverance Meets Sci-Fi Geeks Head On In A Blender." Really quite fascinating. The timing of this interview could not have landed at a more opportune point in their respective lives, either. With the help of Man or Astroman?, Jim will have moved Zero Return within the Atlanta city limits by the time you read this. It will be Jim's first time living outside of Alabama in almost 30 years. Jim was visiting Brian at his home in the Georgia outback when we all decided to sit down and do an interview proper.

So...1992, the band just started. How did you find Zero Return?

BT: Actually, it was kind of a strange story. There was a fellow who will remain nameless, who promoted shows in Montgomery, and got us a cassette tape of all these terrible, but well recorded Montgomery bands called

Offerings. Brian Causey [Starcrunch] and I were listening to this tape and commenting on how terrible a lot of the bands were. And then we were like "God, the drums sound really good on this stuff." And we were looking for a place to record what was going to be a self-produced record at the time that we were going to put out on what turned out to be our record label.

JM: *You all wanted to put it out on 8-track cartridge.*

BT: That was the start of many failed MOA? ideas for strange 78 or reel-to-reel formats. So I got in touch with Jim and he said, "Sure, come on down. I got a couple different formats we can record on.' There's a funny story about the first recording we did about the 4-track thing. He didn't tell me this until a year ago.

JM: *I had a Trashcam, or Tascam, 8-track that was always broke down. It was a piece of crap. Japanese junk. It broke down right before they showed up and I didn't tell them. So I pulled out the old Scully 1/2" 4-track. In retrospect, I'm glad we did do it because track-for-track it's so much better. 1/2" is 30 ips and pretty good sound quality.*

BT: We didn't think anything of it.

JM: *I looked at those guys and thought they'd never know the difference between 4-track and 8-track. Besides, the 4-track is five times larger than the 8-track so it looked a lot more impressive.*

BT: So we were doing what was to be the first record that Estrus ended up putting out on 4-track from this Scully machine and we did the majority of it live to 2-track, right and left. Then we did samples on track three and vocals on track four if we needed them.

JM: *We did all the music live stereo to 2-track then whatever else we had to do we just did on the other two tracks.*

BT: And ever since then, we've been bugging Jim and he's been adapting with us and obtaining new apparatus to give the illusion that we actually sound good.

JM: *No, I think y'all sound good in spite of what I do. The next machine we got was an ancient 1" 8-track that was dated 1968, which has to be real early for the Ampex 1000. It weighs about 600 pounds. It broke a red headed guitar player's arm, so it's got some good karma going there.*

BT: I think on that machine we did most of *Destroy All Astromen* and some of *Project Infinity* on that one. Then we've been getting greedier and greedier and getting more and more tracks, but I can't really see going past sixteen tracks. 16 tracks serves as a pretty nice natural editor. Like right when you're on the phone calling the string section, you say, "Ah, we're out of tracks!"

JM: I had a brief stint with the digital thing before I realized it was a load of crap.

BT: We've done one or two things on ADAT and that's it.

What was your feeling about it?

JM: Um, I really didn't like it too much. I'm definitely what they call a "Loghead." I'm pretty much a digital hater. I can see some merits to it. They are cheap, and for people who can't deal with a 20-25 year old machine that's constantly catching fire, it's...

BT: The biggest problem I've had with recording on ADAT, is that the sound is just so flattened out. Every band that records on ADAT, you can totally hear and perceive it was recorded on ADAT. And all those records tend to sound the same. So many pop punk bands have that clean sound, but it's so ADAT. It has no characteristics. I think a lot of old analog machines had different tendencies in how they captured sound and the way things were laid to tape depending on what machine you were using. I think that gave records a lot more individual characteristics instead of everything sounding exactly the same. The main difference in a lot of things now is just stylistic differences and not recording techniques.

JM: I think the greatest thing about digital is that when it came out and everybody started buying into it hook, line and sinker, all this old analog equipment started dropping in price. Those are the great machines.

BT: Especially like 8-track 1" machines.

JM: Those are great, they just sound so much better - the quality that went into them. There's no way with modern technology, and the way things cost now, that those machines could be built again without costing $100,000.

So lead me through this, you started on 4-track, went to eight and now are working with sixteen?

BT: Yeah, we started with 4-track.

Then lead me up to how things ended up the way they are today. It just seems like things have more of an air of credibility to it now. It's more of a "studio" studio.

JM: Yeah, it used to be more of a home/studio, now it's a studio/home. I've got some straw in some Kroger sacks over in the corner that I sleep on.

BT: It used to be a house, now it's a house with a lot of expensive stuff in it.

JM: I'm kind of like the Fred Sanford of the recording world. You walk into my house, on the back porch; the first thing you see is...

Lamont! [all laugh]

JM: But the first thing you see on the back porch is the two sections of the board from the Neve console with parts and pieces just lying around. Speakers are hanging on a wall, and when you walk in the house there's two huge boxes full of electronic parts. I don't even have any closet space. My closets are like those cartoon closets. Seriously! Where you open them up and it doesn't fall out, but it could easily. Just from the floor to the ceiling it's electronic junk.

[In gruff Fred Sanford voice] Lamont! Don't touch it!

BT: It's really awe inspiring to go out to Jim's. The first time we ever went out there, Jim gave me directions on the phone. We were about ten to fifteen minutes outside of Montgomery. At the point he said, "Then you hit the dirt road..." I knew we were in for something special. There's all these spare crates filled with undefined electrical components everywhere on the porch. Jim showed up at the door with the sweet tea on the oven. Jim makes the world's finest and sweetest tea.

JM: They come to record, but they stay for the tea.

BT: Exactly right. What I love about the whole situation is that any band that has ever come up there [intending] to record in your typical modern dentist office type environment where everything is state of the art and is totally into getting that kind of vibe, don't last fifteen minutes out there if they're just not used to having just anything and everything goes. And the thing is, Jim's amassed some really amazing stuff with the Neve console and the Neve mic preamps. Stuff you can't find in modern studios, especially around Alabama.

JM: Everywhere else is either ADAT or Mackie. I'm pretty much a non-computer person. I don't have any MIDI stuff. No computers. I got a rotary phone. I'm ate up with it.

Brian has told me about all of this really sophisticated equipment you've acquired through some guy who did a Depeche Mode movie?

JM: That actually started before MOA? I started getting some nice microphones, which I think is the key to any recording. I started collecting them and basically never threw anything away. I guess that was my motto. I never really had a lot of money to spend, but whatever money I did have, I'd buy one piece of equipment, like one microphone. The first good microphones I bought were a pair of RCA 77 DXs, which are really nice old ribbon microphones. But when I bought the 77s, they also had a Neumann U47 tube microphone [in the shop] and it looked really neat. Big phallic looking mic. I asked how much it was and they said $500. I thought that was just way too much to spend on a microphone so I bought two 77s. Now if you can find a 47 for $4000, it's great. Most people try to get $6500 for them. That was the one that got away.

But from what I've gathered from Brian, it's almost like there's an arsenal of microphones.

BT: I think it's mainly come of Jim's ability to spot a good deal and amass stuff over the years since there's a lot of weird sources for stuff in Alabama. It might be more different now, but there's always some weird studio that's shutting down or some old guy who doesn't know what he has. The bulletin board down there has been the provider of many finds.

JM: Yeah, the bulletin board. You find somebody selling a 1954 Stratocaster, you go look at it, and it's got like a 3-bolt neck and the guy's saying "Yeah, my granddaddy got that for me way back in the '70s."

BT: What do you think is the strangest piece of studio equipment, be it microphone or preamp or outboard unit, that you've actually gotten through a source like that?

JM: Probably not a real valuable thing, but a real great piece of gear, a mid-'50s GE tube compressor that this TV station just gave to me. They were just going to throw it out. It's a great sounding compressor. Also, I bought an Altec 639 microphone which looks like a giant birdcage. It's a pretty neat microphone. I got it from somebody for next to nothing. They actually sound pretty good sometimes.

BT: I think there's a weird concept in places that aren't part of a large metropolis area like Alabama. A lot of times, a studio in Alabama will be trying to keep up with the latest, most insane piece of technology they can get their hands on. There are studios out there that have spent tens of thousands of dollars on the latest digital crap. And as far as really cool tube and analog stuff, they ignore it and it's really opened up a lot of outlets. Like maybe if you were in Chicago or some place where people would jump on that stuff, but a lot of times, it leaves things open.

So do you thank the digital revolution for Zero Return's arsenal of equipment?

JM: *In that aspect, digital's great. People said, "Oh, we don't need this old stuff..."*

Good!

JM: *A friend of mine from Chicago told me, "Never buy new." As soon as you buy it, it's worth half the money. Go out and buy something old. Go ahead and wait and buy something of really good quality instead of buying something with a lot of whistles and bells on it.*

BT: We often talk about a lot of those old tube compressors. What's so great about them is that they're built so durable and there will be two knobs on it so you can't fuck anything up.

JM: *The GE compressor I was telling you about, all it is is a two or three rack space box with an on/off switch and a big red light right in the middle of it. You just plug into it and it sounds great. You can't fuck with it. The new stuff has fifty buttons, and has so many parameters and functions, and layers and you can never figure out what's goin' on in it.*

BT: It's so far removed from the original signal.

JM: *The best guitar amps have "volume" and "tone." They have a sound and that's it. All these new amps have 20 knobs across them.*

BT: I think the biggest improvements on music in general hasn't made anything sound better. It's made things be quicker or more convenient or you can have more options with something, but none of the advancements have been technically superior to anything from the '50s or '60s.

JM: *I try to recreate that sound from the '50s and '60s. I'm using a lot of the same equipment. I don't know what it is, but people really knew what they were doing. I think a big part of how well things sounded then was due in large part to the people who were involved. It still sounds too new to me sometimes.*

BT: Bands don't take that into consideration when doing a recording project. There's a whole mentality out there that everything can be fixed or made to sound different or manipulated in the studio. Very few bands I've been involved with outside of the ones I've recorded get into the studio and hear that the guitar sounds a little weird or timid, and will get in there and just play it harder or just...

Now for the tech-heads, what's the equipment you use now? What's the board, the tape machine, all of that?

JM: *The tape machine is a 1971 3M M56 with a 2"16-track, all transistor. Pretty much stone age type stuff. We then mix down to a 1/2" MCI machine that is somewhat more modern. I think that it's early '80s. The board is not what would be called a vintage Neve. It's a broadcast console from the early '80s. Weighs about 700 pounds. About eighteen channels. It's a nice board. It definitely has that Neve bottom end sound that Neve has been famous for. I pretty much use the board for monitor and mixing.*

Everything else we record right into Telefunken and RCA preamps. I do have some Neve 1066 preamps, which are great. API preamps, Altec stuff. Various microphones, RCAs and Neumanns. I just noticed that I don't even have a Shure SM57 anymore. When it comes to guitar sound, you can get just as good a guitar sound out of a $4000 mic, where a $90 mic gets a better sound some times. Guitars are funny. Mics are funny. It's like a tool.

It's only as competent as the person who's using it.

BT: Or the luck therein.

Which ain't much of a stretch.

BT: We've had some great success with equipment working out or doing weird stuff. Some of our coolest, strangest space warbles have been like one track acting up, and we go back and listen to a pre-mix and we say "What the hell? Who put a Moog on here?" And it'll be mysterious Track Ten. Actually, the single we did for Drug Racer, at the beginning of the Pylon song, that's one of those tracks.

JM: *It also happens on one of the songs on 'Experiment Zero.'*

BT: There's one song where we had tape, and the test tones start one of the songs off *1000X* "100 Individual Magnets." We just left it on there and let it fly with the track.

JM: *I've had to do sessions where I had to have the top of the transport jacked up and had a big stick wedged down into the bowels of the electronics. Then I have to go over and wiggle the stick. Remember the old Warner Brothers cartoon where Foghorn Leghorn had the clown head on a stick and he'd go wake up the dog? That's my level of expertise basically. A clown head on a stick.*

BT: There's nothing better than being in a session and getting close to the end of mixing a pretty important song and something will sound a little weird or there's a little whizzing noise in the machine. Jim has a very Fonzie-like approach to maintenance. Jim will get kind of pensive, think about it for a second and then flip open the hood of the machine and give it a nice blow in there, or stick a vacuum cleaner nozzle in there, spray a little cleaner in there, and next thing you know we're rollin' again. I don't think we've ever had a set back that's ever cost us more than an hour or so.

JM: *Nah, an hour's really pushing it. I really start sweatin' it if it's down an hour. Amazingly enough, it's never really burned up a part, it's always like a wire breaks loose and starts arcing off the frame. Those 3M machines, they take a lot of physical abuse, and this one's taken a lot of verbal abuse.*

BT: I think one of the amazing things, outside of the actual equipment, is the big change that happened when we started recording drums in the foyer of the house.

JM: *Yeah, it's like recording in a big wooden box. It has a 12-foot ceiling. You would think that a perfectly square room wouldn't sound that good, but back then when they built those houses, they're all out of square. The door to the drum room looks like one of those things you see in the Midwest where water runs uphill. The room's all cock-sided one way, but the door swings shut the other way so it looks like the door is swinging shut up hill. People come from miles around just to see the door shut.*

Maybe the building was actually designed 100 years ago to be a modern studio. They definitely had foresight.

JM: *You open up the door to the drum room and there's a toilet right there.*

BT: You have to go through the bathroom to get anywhere. So if you've got to do a Mr. Dookie, you're in bad news because there will be some traffic coming through.

JM: *[During the 'Experiment Zero' session] Steve [Albini] went to the bathroom. I do have a sign up that says, "Steve shat here." But he came back and sat down and started recording again and said "Jim, you didn't have any toilet paper." I said, "What did you do?" He said, "Ben Grimm." I said, "Who's Ben Grimm."*

BT: The Comic Book Hall of Fame?

JM: He was the guy in the Fantastic Four who was just piles of rock. That gets my respect. Anybody who can walk out of a bathroom after something like that and not wipe, that's a man's man right there.

BT: Then there's when the plate moved from the kitchen to the foyer.

JM: Plate reverbs weigh 4-500 pounds. Big wooden box. Servotron came over to record one day and I said, "Hey, would y'all like to try the plate on this recording?" They said, "Yeah, let's do it." All we had to do was move it.

BT: We didn't know what we were suckered in to. A lot of times Jim says, "Yeah, you guys should record a new single just so he can get his equipment shifted around.

JM: Yeah, we had to knock all of the partitions out of the drum room to get the plate through the doorway.

Brian, did Jim have anything to do with your mastery of production?

JM: We used a method that works pretty well. I just ball park everything and get the levels up and...

BT: Then we ruin it.

JM: It's kinda like tag team wrestling. I'll wrassle with the board, then I'll slap Brian's hand and...

BT: I'll get on the top rope. It's more like a Texas Chain Death Match.

But you didn't walk into Zero Return the first time and know what to do.

BT: We've been really lucky... we started off as these stupid sci-fi geeks coming over from Auburn to record with Jim. In the band, we always had a decent musical vocabulary as far as knowing what we wanted to do, but we were always at a handicap technically. Which is why it was always amazing to have Jim there holding our hand when we knew what we wanted to do, but didn't know technically how to patch it in. It's all been a learning process. Even recording backward stuff, and flipping the tape over. I'm counting the tracks on my hand to make sure we don't record over something. We've learned everything there and luckily with what knowledge we do have; Jim's been really helpful. Zero Return is totally the kind of environment where Jim wants you to learn what's going on. He wants you to experiment with the EQs. A lot of times Jim will get the most excited when we have a stupid idea that doesn't really make sense. There was one song "Junk Satellite" and I bumped the left fader down with my elbow. I realized after about two bars what I had done, and kicked it back up. We decided that it sounded pretty cool, and we didn't go back in there, which was technically pretty stupid.

JM: It's the kind of thing that when I hear that, I think the machine is tore up.

BT: Jim's always tearing into us about balance and phase. I'm always pushing things on the edge of getting way out of balance.

JM: "Change the polarity!" That's the answer for all sci-fi problems.

BT: Even at Zero Return. But sometimes we'll get a nice little thump to the back of the head and Jim will point up to the meter. But it's a really great environment for us to have total access to. Plus, it's been a second home. I think last year I spent about two months of my year there. It's really been amazing. When we did *Made From Technetium*, it was every morning waking up at 9 and working until 3 AM. Eleven straight days like that.

JM: Was it eleven?

BT: Well, it probably felt like thirty. But yeah, we just have this system, somebody goes to get the ice, Jim makes tea and we make a record. It's probably the most hi-fi of any of the records we've done so far. It's interesting because some tracks sound really hi-fi and large and spacious, and others like what Brian [Causey/Starcrunch] did through the Mr. Microphone sound really dirtied up.

JM: That kind of goes back to what I was saying about microphones on guitar amps. On "Structo" we used a Mr. Microphone on the guitar then picked it up on the Kenwood FM receiver. We were kind of disappointed that it sounded so good.

BT: We've had the weirdest experimentation with guitars. There's been some tracks that are with the bathroom door open and some sounded better with it closed. Depending on the track.

JM: And what was going on in the bathroom.

BT: I really enjoyed this record because we got to do anything we wanted to do.

But it's always like that, isn't it?

JM: This one and '1000X,' they basically came in without any songs.

BT: We would totally have a certain portion we'd work on and see what would happen. We had a decent amount of material to fall back on, but some of the best stuff on the record was totally made up. Like "Lo Batt" was one of my favorites that was done that way.

JM: They pirated my talkback jargon on the last record. They got all this stuff I say back on the talkback system. They recorded it and then spliced it in as samples in a song. "Wait a minute, I think you're standing in cat piss."

BT: The cats do add a very interesting element to the studio and actually a lot of times we've had things spawn directly from the cats. That song being one thing, but there's no telling what you'll hear over the talkback mics. We actually got Jim to record some of the great sayings we do hear at Zero Return. I personally like the one, "Can somebody go get ice at Doziers?" or "Wait a minute, something's not working," or "The machine's messin' up, hold on" or "Something's screwed up again."

JM: But that machine has been an absolute workhorse. I have been in the middle of a session where the room's not very well lit and all of a sudden it looks like there's somebody arcwelding inside the machine. This blue light shines out from the cracks and crevices of the machine. It just keeps rolling.

So now you've signed off on some property in Atlanta with Rob [DelBueno/Coco] and Brian and Zero Return is moving out of Alabama. I guess this will lead to a much closer, tight-knit relationship with Brian and Rob?

JM: There better be because I definitely don't know anybody in Atlanta. I really am a country boy.

BT: I think in Atlanta, the biggest endeavor will be not to lose that environment that Jim has out there now. We're gonna be building two small brand new buildings that Rob has designed that will be designed specifically for the studio. The greatest thing is when Jim and Rob conversed on what the studio would be like, their ideas were extremely similar, and they came up with the same plan 200 miles apart.

JM: I just hope with the overhead, we'll still be able to record bands that don't have a lot of money and if a band wants to do a CD for $1000, we can do it. A lot of my favorite CDs I've done were recorded for $500-600. I like doing that kind of stuff.

BT: Most of the bands that are worth recording haven't gotten to that level of pretension or are bands without any money who come in and record. I know that's a lot of times why Steve takes on like the Page and Plant project. As crazy as that is, it allows the bands to come in and record really cheap. I think that's something we have to keep in mind, too. It needs to be affordable. Guys that are working ten hours a day at some crap job and are trying to make their band happen an hour or two a week need to have an outlet where they can record amazing records that don't cost much without having to go to ADAT.

Trent Bell

by Larry Crane

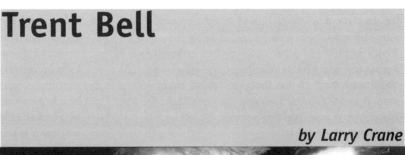

Craig S. Smith

Mr. Trent Bell is the proprietor of Bell Labs, a fine recording establishment in Norman, Oklahoma, a member of the preeminent pop combo known as the Chainsaw Kittens and a soundman for the Flaming Lips. We caught Mr. Bell as he was on a short tour with the Kittens supporting their self titled CD. Not coincidentally, the said recording had been created, written and recorded at Bell Labs in a wonderful, low-pressure environment and it shows. Yes, the record is a treat to listen to. Well, anyway, we whisked Mr. Bell off to the colorful Jackpot! Recording Studios for a quick tour of the facilities and an informative little chat.

So have you been in the Chainsaw Kittens all along?

I played guitar on the very first record, but I wasn't actually in the band. After it was done they were like, "Hey, you want to be in the band?" So I did. It's been a while now. I'm only 26 years old, but it seems like we've been around forever. The Chainsaw Kittens formed when I was a senior in High School and they had another guitar player at the time. They had just signed to Mammoth and at that point, bands like us weren't really getting signed.

Wasn't that in the late '8os?

This was around '89-'90. That was before Nirvana. I think we got $3000 to record the first record and we were like, "Oh my god! We're in the big time now." Have you ever heard of that country band that has sold 3 million records called the Tractors?

Yeah.

The singer, before he was in the Tractors, recorded our first record and he hated it.

Really? Why?

He just thought we were so weird. A couple of years ago we saw a Tractors video and we were like, "Oh my god that's him!" We thought it'd be really funny to re-release that record. It's a really weird record as far as lyrical content and stuff. Re-release it and put real big, "PRODUCED BY STEVE RIPLEY OF THE TRACTORS!" Just ruin his life.

Where was that done?

In Tulsa, at Leon Russell's old studio. A big church.

Did it have good acoustics?

Yeah it did, but the album doesn't really sound that great 'cause he didn't really do that great of a job on it. He had a Neve board and all these Neumann microphones, but thinking back, he didn't use any of the Neumann mics. He used all 57s and stuff. I think he really didn't like us.

Ouch. Do you ever think about that kind of experience when you're working with someone?

Oh yeah, totally. We did a record with Butch Vig and he's such a good guy. He practically did our record for free. We worked with a guy named John Agnello, who I learned a lot from. Working with a lot of these people, I'd just sit back and watch what they were doing. Whenever we had some time off I was like, "I'm gonna put a studio together." When we got signed to Scratchie, the first thing we said to them was we're not gonna do demos for our record and we're gonna record it ourselves. They were like, "Cool."

It's nice to know a label will allow that. So that was about two years ago that you got the studio going?

Yeah.

And that all started 'cause of the Scratchie deal?

We had some time off and this guy in Norman was selling his 16-track and an AudioArts board together. I had saved up some money so I thought I might as well get it. I bought it and I had it in my house for a while, I eventually got mics and outboard gear, two DAT machines and stuff like that and moved it out into a barn. Over the two years we've gotten new stuff. The new board I got I just love, the Neotek.

How many channels?

28 by 28.

28 assignable busses for each one?

Each channel has 28 little buttons. Very flexible. It's huge. It's 7 feet long, 3 feet deep. It has a hundred something point patch bay.

Can you pull out individual channel strips?

Yeah, but all the mic connectors and stuff you have to solder. It's a pain, but it's a good board.

What did you do with the old board?

I still have it. I think what I'd like to do is if I could get a 24-track 2" I could have a studio A and B. But in Norman, there's not a hell of a demand for that!

So this is all set up in a barn on your friend's property.

It's a big, metal, prefab building. What we did is we went in and built a building inside that building. We built it so it's kind of a chapel. We have one ceiling that goes up, at the top point it's about 16 feet. Good for drums.

It sounds like a hell of a project having to make a whole building.

It's Carl's (the guy who's playing keyboards for us) parent's property. I shattered my wrist playing softball right when we were getting ready to build it. I was there for moral support, but I couldn't really help a whole lot.

What inspired you to start a studio?

We recorded all these records with people. One of our records we did out in Los Angeles and we spent five weeks in all these huge studios and spent an outrageous amount of money. We mixed at Ocean Way where the Beach Boys had worked, which was really cool, but we were spending so much money. When we were done, I wasn't that happy with the way that record sounded. I was thinking, "God, if I had my own studio there would be no one to blame except ourselves." I like that.

When you feel like something's being rushed you can stop...

Yeah. We took a really long time to make our new record and we could do that because it was my studio. Plus, since we were in Norman, we were in our own environment. It just worked out a lot better. I think it's our best record by far and I'm happy with the way it turned out.

If I didn't know where it was recorded I wouldn't say, "Oh, it sounds like the band went out to their friend's barn and knocked it out!"

In all the reviews and everything, I've never heard anything bad.

No. It sounds like the kind of record where the band got to spend the right amount of time.

We put strings on everything we did.

And lots of keyboards.

I love old keyboards. We have an old Acetone organ. I did all the keyboards on the record. I'm the guitar player who hates guitar. I like them but I hate guitar solos. I did an interview with *Guitar Player* magazine and the whole thing was about recording. I never even talked about the guitar.

I think people get a good perspective when they've done a lot of recording. When you've watched a lot of bands work you become a little less self-involved as a player.

Definitely, I know we'll never not record on our own anymore.

What other stuff have you worked on?

I've done a bunch of stuff with the Flaming Lips. There's been a couple of things on b-sides. I just recorded a song for the new Batman soundtrack, but I don't think they accepted it. I don't think the song is what they were looking for! I did this thing for Steve, the drummer of the Flaming Lips. He did this song on a record coming out on Hollywood records that has nothing but drummers on it. There's a lot of bands from Kansas and stuff like that. Hopefully, I'd like to start doing more, mostly mid-west bands. There hasn't been a ton of major label CDs there! There's been some good stuff. The way I look at is that you learn by doing that stuff. You don't want to get thrown into a $100,000 budget record... you want to make sure you know exactly what you're doing before you do something like that.

It's not like you're experimenting on people but you're honing your craft.

Exactly. It's mainly CDs for bands from around the mid-west.

At a reasonable price?

I charge $25 an hour. Considering the equipment that I have... Most of the studios in Oklahoma are ADAT and Mackie boards. This Neotek I just got has a four band parametric EQ that's just awesome.

Four of them?

Yeah, that's a great thing to have.

You use a 1" 16-track. What kind of deck is that?

A Tascam. It has DBX noise reduction.

Do you use it?

No.

Good. Did you try it at all?

Yeah, when I first got it I tried it but it just made everything sound kinda weird.

A little compressed?

Exactly. One day I was recording some friends and I said, "Do you mind if I try something?" I wasn't sure if it was gonna work or not. I took it out and sent the signals really hot to tape and it sounded so much better.

What kind of tape do you use?

I use [Ampex] 456.

And you run it at 30 ips?

Yeah. Whenever people find that we did our record on 16-track 1" they're pretty surprised. It's a 1982 machine and I've never had the thing worked on once.

That's nice. Nothing weird at all?

Nothing. I should probably get my heads relapped.

You said something earlier about getting a Neumann U 87 for $600.

Well, being in Oklahoma, you run into people who don't know what they have. What's really crazy (and this is one of the dumbest things I've ever done), is that I actually found a U 87 for $250 once. The capsule was busted, and it would have been $1000 to get it fixed, but it still would have been worth it. I traded it for an AKG 414 that worked, which isn't too bad. Then I was in a music store in Norman and they said, "Oh, this guy was in earlier trying to sell a Neumann U 87." He gave me this number and I called him and he was like, "I gotta go on this cruise ship and I have to put together this little PA for the cruise ship and I have this Neumann that I'm trying to sell." I told him I'd give him $600 cash right now and he said, "Okay." Everyone I tell that too cringes. That's nothing for that microphone.

We all want to find those deals.

I like that mic a lot. I really like the 414s a lot. I use those for room mics for drums. I use Shure SM 81s as overheads but I really end up using the room mics more than anything. I pretty much never put any kind of muffling in the kick drum. I usually use an AKG D112 inside. Outside of the kick drum, I put the Neumann.

Do you mix those together to one track?

Yeah, you get the big bassy attack from the D112 and then you get the space from the Neumann. I love Ringo-type sounding drums and John Bonham sounding drums. I just love that kind of drum sound – I learned a lot of that from the Lips. They really do that a lot. The guy who does their records, Dave Fridmann, I really like the way he does that stuff a lot. I like the way a kick drum sounds without muffling.

It's definitely the way Bonham sounded.

I read an interview with a guy who engineered a bunch of stuff for Led Zeppelin and he said that they'd just put one microphone above the drums and he would play and then listen to the drums and whatever needed to be louder he would just hit harder.

That makes life easier. I wish more people could do that.

I know. That kind of inspired me to use less mics on the drums. I always put mics on the toms and I use a top and bottom snare mic, but if I can get away without using a lot of stuff I'll take it out. I like SM 57s on snares. For my toms, I bought these little Sennheiser 504s and they sound pretty good. Then, I actually use a BBE Sonic Maximizer on the toms. They cut through.

How much EQ do you do on the toms? I find myself pushing them more than I think I should.

That BBE helps 'cause it brings it all out. I tend to roll some high end into the toms. With a room mic you hear the toms pretty loud, but then I use the close mics to get the attack.

You really ought to check those BBE Sonic Maximizers out. I wouldn't use them on everything, but on toms they sound cool and they're cheap, like $150 or so.

What other kind of outboard stuff do you have?

I have a Yamaha SPX 90 and SPX 990. I want to make the jump to an Eventide reverb. There's a company in Oklahoma called PAIA. You know about them?

I've got one of their mic pres.

I have one of those and I like that. I use it as an effect more than anything.

It's really gritty.

I use it if someone wants to have that "John Lennon vocal thing." Distort it out a little bit.

And put a gate on it. It's noisier than hell.

Yeah it is! I also have, well it's actually the Lips, the TL Audio tube preamp. Those are really nice. I have a few DBX compressors.

So some pretty straightforward gear. It doesn't seem like you have anything really outrageous.

No, not really. I would love to find some old, weird stuff, but right now I need stuff that works. Sometimes things looks cooler than they sound. I've got a couple of DA 30 DAT machines. My secret weapon (and I don't know if I should even tell people this) is the DBX subharmonic synthesizer. Those things are awesome, put it on the kick drum and it'll make it huge. Put it on the bass guitar and you get some crazy low end.

Do you have to be really careful how you use the thing?

You can totally overuse it if you're not careful. Sometimes I'll put it on the kick drum and you won't even hear it but you'll see the meters on the board going crazy.

You could drive the mastering engineer insane.

I've blown my NS 10s four times with that thing. If you're ever lacking in bass, put that thing on. They're only about $300. I don't compress stuff a whole lot. I never really compress drums, I compress bass guitar and vocals and I never compress the whole mix. I figure whoever's doing the mastering should have the most kick-ass compressors around. There's no reason to compress the whole mix.

It seems that you'll read about how you should compress your mix in some of those "project studio" type mags.

Sometimes compressing room mics on the drums can be a neat sound.

What's that sound at the beginning of your record?

That's a Moog going through an amp with the distortion on full.

Was that fun having people come in and do strings?

Oh yeah.

Was it just two people? Did you double them up at all?

Yeah, on some of them.

Was this the first record you used strings on?

For the most part. It's the first record where we went over the top and put them on every song. They're just little embellishments. When I was thinking of strings I was thinking of the way T-Rex would use them. We're still just a guitar rock band, but we wanted to put all these other things on.

That last song, "Speedway Oklahoma" has some great piano on it.

Steven [Drozd], the drummer for the Flaming Lips, plays all the piano on it. We're using backwards reverb on it and while we were mixing I did it off of a tape delay. The piano on the record isn't even a real piano. Steven has a Roland piano thing and we compressed it quite a bit to try to make it sound like a weird old piano. For our next record I'm gonna try to get a real piano in the studio.

We got ours for $500. The tuning guy was just here and complained about how my room has uneven humidity.

I think what inspired me so much as far as not having to use real piano sounds was that Cardinal record. A lot of the stuff on that record is just keyboards. If you use them right they sound cool.

You hear a lot of music where you know it's a drum machine or a cheesy sample. If you use things the right way people don't have any idea.

If it sounds good, who cares how you got it.

What stuff have you been listening to lately? You brought up that Cardinal record.

I love the way that record sounds. I just saw Beck live. I dig his new record quite a bit... *Hunky Dory* and *Transformer,* I love Lou Reed's *Transformer.*

There was some review of your record that mentioned Bowie and Lou Reed.

When we did our record I listened to *Transformer* a lot. I think Bowie, Lou Reed and Mick Ronson were a pretty good team.

I think Mick Ronson had a lot to do with it.

I think he had a lot to do with everything good that Bowie did. I'm trying to think of good sounding records...

There aren't any!

That's true. There aren't that many.

Do you have enough time to listen to stuff?

Sometimes I don't get a chance to listen to as much stuff as I'd like.

I was watching your soundcheck and I was wondering how you keep your ears intact playing in your own band and doing live sound for the Flaming Lips.

I bought those earplugs that mold into your ear and haven't used them once! I'm lucky. I had my ears checked two months ago and I hadn't lost any hearing. The Flaming Lips are ridiculously loud. I'm starting to worry about that 'cause I don't want to lose any hearing. I've been pretty irresponsible about that stuff so far, but I don't listen to headphones a lot. I think that can really do a lot of damage. I think one of the things that saves my ears is that we don't practice!

Yeah. My old studio was in a little room that we practice in. You walk out of there with your ears ringing. How do you avoid practicing?

When we did our record, we wrote everything as we recorded. I would walk in with what I thought would be the guitar part and Eric, our drummer, would come in and we'd go over it for about two hours and work out the arrangement. Then I'd roll tape and just build on top of that. I'd pretty much get all the music done and then give it to Tyson and he'd take it home and come up with the words. There's one song on there, "Tongue Trick," that took him ten tries of coming up with words and melodies. At one point he was like, "I don't think this song's gonna work out." Then one day he came in and said, "I think I've got it." He did what ended up being on the record.

It's kind of cool that the studio's an extension of your band.

When we started recording our record we had one song written. It's fun to do it that way.

How long did it take?

Probably about three months. Some days, if we didn't feel like being in the studio for ten hours, we'd mess with some vocals for two hours. Not having to watch the clock in the studio is a good thing. My ultimate goal is to record records with bands that I love. I wouldn't mind travelling to New York or somewhere and work in different studios. I hate the way so many records sound that come out today.

I understand.

All the Better Than Ezra's of the world... those records just bug me so bad.

I think there's a lot of fucked up production going on in the "alternative top-40 radio" or whatever that stuff is. Even if it's something that was recorded well, somebody went and compressed the hell out of it for radio play.

I don't know if people listen to sounds that much. Do people know if it's a good drum sound or a bad drum sound?

Bell Labs 405-364-7458

Scott Henderson

LIVING THE LIFE OF HENDERSON

by Graeme McIntye

Whether they know it or not, anyone roaming the streets of Victoria, BC, will have brushed by Scott Henderson at some point. He is easily spotted, usually clad in his ubiquitous green Minnesota North Stars jacket and baseball cap. He has worked in just about all of the record stores in Victoria [including a few which have long since disappeared], and as one might imagine, he houses a massive collection of records, with genres too numerous to mention. His aptly titled studio, S.O.S. (Sea of Shit), resides in the basement of his house on the outskirts of Victoria. The basement is basically split up into three rooms; one for recording, one for his personal collection of music, and one for the control room. The studio exists largely for Scott to document his own ideas. With that being said, a plethora of Victoria bands have called S.O.S. home for a couple of days. His close association and numerous recordings with NoMeansNo [now based in Vancouver], as well as his membership in the group, the Show Business Giants [who recently returned from a tour of Europe], Shovlhead, and his most recent project, Hissanol, have allowed Scott's music and recording acumen to flourish internationally as well as locally. If one needs further proof that the digital age has arrived, look no further than *The Making of Him*, the new Hissanol record released on Alternative Tentacles. His collaborator, Andy Kerr [formerly of NoMeansNo], lives in Amsterdam. The distance between the two was easily bridged [or not so easily at times, according to Scott] with the continual exchange of R-DAT tapes through the mail. The result is a testament to everything that Scott is: composer/musician/engineer/producer/mildly psychotic and furiously creative. What follows below are mere shards of our two hour conversation which was interrupted only by the occasional exchange of a barbecue chip or two. It was terminated when the hockey highlights came on.

What was your first studio setup?

I used to have a house on this welfare strip. The studio was called "Hole in the Wall." I had this 4-track 1/2" Tascam series 70 monstrosity tape machine with an old M & M board [shows me photo]. It was a British thing with a four band fixed EQ. I used to drag it all over town in this cabinet. You could barely lift the thing.

What year was that?

It was about '80 or '81. It was a great studio. You'd open the back door in the winter and this flood of water would just wash through the studio.

So it was all in one room?

Yeah. I had fruit packing for soundproofing. I didn't even have egg cartons [laughs]. I got a little 4-track PortaStudio after that... The best cassette one they made in the first few years.

Did it have any noise reduction?

It had DBX and two notch filters like all Tascams. It was a great machine and it's still being used.

Does it have the original heads on it?

I think so. The guy who has it now isn't the type to be changing them.

What were you using for mics?

Mostly crap. Whenever anyone gets started recording you have about eight mics and [takes on a holy tone] and they're all, save one, Shure SM57s. In my case it was an AKG 125. I still to this day don't know exactly what it was. I had a couple of AKG 330 mics which in those days were pretty cool. They were bulbous mics with the vents and had a couple of roll-off filters on the bottom. They were really popular for live use. I had a whole bunch of miscellaneous garbage I picked up. I never had a decent collection of mics until I moved out here [to Sea of Shit].

Any other locations of note?

Well, for a while I had a studio on the second floor of a building downtown. Basically, I had a whole corner block. The place would've made a huge night club. Red Tide [early Victoria punk band] brought in the first Fostex 8-track. It was the worst shit I've ever used in my life. It was upright reel-to-reel with the microscopic VU meters hooked up to the special board that came with it. The board was about the size of a large book and was the most amazingly hissy crapola. It had 1/4" tape running at 7/1/2 ips. All I remember is that I really wanted to throw the thing out the window. Horrible gear... it scarred me for life. I'll never use Fostex gear again. I haven't used so much as a pair of Fostex headphones since then. I always go for the Tascam stuff because it's bulletproof. It's never the best, but it runs forever. My Tascam 8-track reel-to-reel was outside for a whole winter [after being sold] in a shed open to all of the elements and it still works. I bought it back for $100. When I first bought it in 1985, that was the big step up. That was around the same time I discovered that gated reverb sounded good on drums, so there's all this gated reverb on everything from those years. I had a Yamaha REV-7. I've still got it. It's the noisiest effect in my rack by a mile.

What was the first piece of outboard gear you ever got?

When I needed an echo at my first place, I used to use this old Sony tape deck hooked up with a three speed echo. You know, slow-medium-fast. It was really noisy. I also had a Binson disk echo. It was a freakish looking thing. It had to be from the early '60s from England. It had a metal magnetized disk with heads against it. It had four playback heads and you could only turn one of them off at a time. You couldn't change the speed of the disk, but you could adjust the volume of each echo. It had a cathode tube in it for a level display. The louder the sound, the hotter the tube would get. It weighed a ton and was about two feet by one foot. Hank Marvin [of the Shadows] used to use them in the '60s. I had a Roland spring reverb that you had to severely beat in order for it to work. You really had to whack the thing.

Did you buy anything else when you jumped up to the Tascam 8-track?

When I bought that I went on a binge. I bought a Yamaha RX-5 drum machine which was a fortune then... it was $1500 or something. I got the REV-7 too. I still have the RX-5.

Any mics?

I think I bought a new 421 [Sennheiser], but I still had mostly shit. I was mixing straight to a cassette deck then.

At what point did you switch from doing friend's bands to bands you'd never heard of?

Hmmm... [thinks ponderously]

At what point did you think "I'm just going to stop recording my friends and try to make some money at this..."

Oh god, I've never thought that! [laughter]

You know what I mean.

The first "money" thing I did was this blues guy who was a caddy at a local golf club. He hired some born-again guys who worked at a Christian music store to come in and play the bass and drums. They were good, but really bad at the same time, you know?

Any strange forms of payment for studio time?

Pigment Vehicle [frenetic Victoria band] wanted to mix their last album and they're like... "We just need a couple of days to do the mix." I know this means two weeks. They also needed to "touch up the vocals" which, for them, means write the lyrics. Jason [PV drummer/vocalist] gave me this really nice saxophone. Colin [PV bassist] built me a rock wall out in my yard. It was about two weeks of studio time, too. I've never done it for a car, but I came close once. A vocalist came in and I got a sampler and a 441 [Sennheiser mic]. She was also kind of our nanny for a while. Another band didn't have any money to pay me, so I got an amp and a bass drum mic.

Is there any gear you had in the past you wish you hadn't gotten rid of?

I had a twin manual drawbar Farfisa organ that was sort of like a Hammond. I sold it to a mod, which of course, means I didn't get paid for it. I sold my roommate my beautiful canary yellow Premier drum kit with Paiste cymbals. I must have spent about $2500 on it in 1982. He was a loans manager for CIBC [Canadian bank] and was about 3/4 deaf. I was supposed to get about $2000... I think I got $100.

Have you heard from him since?

No, he disappeared into the ozone! Later, some guy in Duncan [north of Victoria] told me, "I know that drumkit! I traded a motorbike for it!"

Is there a piece of gear you don't have that you'd love to have?

Oh god, there's always stuff...

Mics, board, monitors?

Actually, you know what I need more than anything is a new room [laughs]. To hell with the gear!

So you could have more room for records?

Well, that, and I need a higher ceiling. My studio is the kind of studio where you try to negate the room. You just don't want the room to come into it ! [laughs]... which is fine for hard rock, but if I brought a string quartet in here, things would get ugly fast. I'd love to have a spare DA88 [Tascam R-DAT 8-track]. Once they get long in the tooth like mine, there's always one that's kind of not working right.

Are you happy with the DA88s?

Yeah, they've been quite reliable. My place is as dirty as a studio should ever be, too.

Are there certain tapes that work better than others?

At first, it was like a black art getting tapes for that thing. I just use the regular Sonys... they're about $10 bucks a piece. I used to get glitches all the time, but that was because Tascam told me to get metal evaporated tapes. Then, about a year later, I called them and they said, "Did I say metal evaporated? I meant metal particle." So, I've got a whole archive of metal evaporated tapes that glitch out like crazy. The thing I worry about with digital is archiving stuff.

Is it any worse than analog tape?

Yeah, it is because if the tape crashes, it's gone completely. If the analog tape starts to deteriorate, you've still got something there.

I was just reading about a band that dug up some old 16-track analog tape that was beyond repair and they put it in the oven for three hours and fixed it.

Yeah. You can bake the tape. I've heard this fable from somewhere else. It's a prescribed ritual. You can get soggy tape to work, but you'd better run it once and copy it. I don't think I'd want to play the tape very much.

I think it was sticky...

Yeah, the tape will stick together and pull all of the oxide off [just as he says this an analog tape anecdote flashes through his brain]. This will make you shudder. When I was in Amsterdam for a vacation, John Wright [NoMeansNo drummer] and Tom Holliston [Show Business Giants] were watching my place and using the studio. Well, the sewer main broke and soaked all of the old NoMeansNo demos – stuff from around 1980. Some of the tape was salvageable, but the boxes had to go. They really stunk bad. A bunch of my records got fucked, too.

Where do you stand on analog vs. digital?

Well, that's simple. I figure if you can hear the difference between analog and digital recording, then you're not listening to the music hard enough. The thing you'll find in common with almost all analog people is the vast majority of them seem to be older and listen to either classical or jazz and consider themselves a notch above everybody else. When you boil it down, they really seem to miss the even-ordered distortion in analog. I like analog as much as the next guy, but it's just not cost effective anymore to use it. Have you ever seen the Metallica video of the making of the black album? They show them loading the reels into a van. There's about $40,000 in raw tape there. The average band just can't afford that. The cost savings of digital are enormous and you can make digital sound less digital. You just make sure there's lots of dirt in it. If cost was no object, I'd probably stick with analog. Rock music is such a moot point. Would Aphex Twin sound better on analog? I don't think so. I think the young rock n' roller guys prefer analog because they're so used to hitting the tape hard. I'd love to have a Scully 16-track 2" machine with Dolby A on it, so I could just whack it. It's like having 16 compressors built into your tape deck. You really have to learn to use an outboard compressor well with digital.

One of the myths when digital first came out was that everything would automatically sound great. Really, it's just as easy to make a bad sounding record.

Especially in the days before they realized that mastering for digital is not like mastering for vinyl. Mastering for vinyl you have to take into consideration the physical characteristics of the needle in the groove, groove distortion, and on and on. With the first CD I heard... you know, as is always the case when a new format comes out, there was nothing but wretched music. They had *Marathon* by Santana and a bunch of crap-ola classical. They also had this Archie Shepp/Dollar Brand record. It sounded like the piano was made out of stainless steel and the sax was a giant kazoo. It was a Denon 14-bit PCM recording. I was working at a record store at the time and everyone was standing around me smiling and I was thinking, "Wow, this sounds really awful." They all said, "Wow! No distortion!" and I said, "But it sounds like shit!" The Santana recording was excruciating... no mids or warmth at all. So, the analog people went crazy and said, "See! It sounds like shit! I told you!" I knew once they figured out how to master the stuff, it would be better. The things that are bad about digital most people, I'm sure, can't hear. It starts at about 20,000 cycles. Piano harmonics get sawed off. My dog might be able to hear that. I bought Colin Newman's record *Not To*. There's points where any extra noise just ruins it. I think for the average punter, CD is the way to go. One of the things I like [with digital] is that you don't have to compensate as the needle moves towards the middle of the fucking record. *On Chairs Missing* by Wire, the last song on Side 2 is a blitzkrieg of noise and I've yet to hear a record that didn't crap out. The physical limitations of analog are really frustrating sometimes.

So you think mastering is the weak link with digital?

Yes, but most of the problems were solved quite a while ago. Some companies still use analog masters for CD, but they're usually death metal or punk rock.

Do you have any recording tricks you'd like to impart?

The funny thing is I've never worked with "professional engineers," so every time I come across one, I watch what they do. I'll ask them, "Why do you do this?" and they'll say, "I dunno..."

Everybody just learns their own way I guess...

Yeah, I guess. Especially drum mic'ing. I picked up a lot of things from John [Wright of NoMeansNo]. I don't do too many arcane things for the simple reason that I usually don't have time to experiment.

Most want it fast and good I suppose.

Most experiments don't work the way you think they're going to work. More often than not they don't work. Once I mic'd these guitar cabinets with mics all over the place and I ended up in phase hell. I had a mic under my stairs, one on an open Pignose [amp]. I read about Zappa doing the Pignose thing. All I ended up with was a big mushy sound. I used to use two mics on guitar cabinets – one jammed against the cone and one behind the cabinet with the phase flipped... lots of stuff. Nothing worked very well and then I just said, "fuck it" and stuck a 57 in front of the thing. Sometimes I'll stick a condenser mic in front if I want a little more crunch. The more basic I got, the better it sounded. You know, with a bass, I always do a DI with a mic on the cabinet. If guys want a little more dirt on their bass setup, then I'll use my Sunn amp. It's 75 watts with big Sylvania tubes. You can crank it without shaking the whole house down.

What about vocals? I noticed when Treecrusher [Victoria pop-punk band] was here, you didn't use the swank 414 mic for vocals. You just stuck them in front of a Shure SM 58... why?

I can use the 414 through my wonderful tube preamp. It's just the cleanest, most beautiful sound. I also started to discover that it was no bloody good for rock music. I didn't even use a Beta 58! Use a dynamic mic, and let 'em scream their heads off. Especially for people who have no mic technique. They'll just walk up to your $1500 414 mic and go "YAAAA!" You can hear the plates going clack-clack-clack. It's usually about 200 decibels coming out of the speakers, too.

What's the most non-rock thing you've recorded?

I did a jazz quartet one night at midnight live to DAT. It sounded great. Also, I did the incidental music for a local production of Shakespeare's "Twelfth Night" with a violist from the symphony.

What did you mic the viola with?

I think I used the 414. I've got a couple of AKG C-1000 mics for anything that requires any detail. Good cheap condenser mics. For drums, I'll use one of the C-1000 mics under the hi-hat and sort of pointed at the snare. I almost bought a Calrec mic - one of those 4-capsule quadraphonic ambisonic mics for $6000 bucks. I just kept thinking, "Am I going to get $6000 of use out of this thing?"

You really have to have tuned rooms if you're going to be using a swank mic like that.

Exactly. You also have to charge people for the swank mic. I'm just too nice a guy to say [assumes a snotty tone] "Oh, if you want to use the good mic, it'll cost you an extra $150."

Pull it out of the glass case...

Yeah. The difference between that and my 414 is $4500. You can buy a lot of gear for $4500. I've really gotten the most bang for my buck out of my gear. I never built a patch bay and I've yet to have a problem because of that. If you don't mind the inconvenience, you can save yourself bags of money. I'll bet I'd spend $1500 putting it together. Then there's millions of connections there just waiting to die on you. I'm not a very good solderer either. Somebody else in my studio would be lost, but that's just as well! [laughs]

That's the way you like it.

Keep 'em outta here! I spent my money on good monitor speakers [B&W 803s]. My power amp was a bit of a frill at $1400. It's a 120 watts a side Tugden AU-41 which is sitting idle right now because someone blew it up for me. I bought this Harman/Kardon monstrosity which has turned out to be a really good amp. I can hear the difference between them, though. The Tugden has a lot more refinement to it... especially for acoustic stuff. The B&W's are really clean too.

When you're recording solid over, say, two days, how do you avoid ear fatigue?

I don't turn it up very loud. When I get my sounds, I make sure I'm in the right ball park getting them to tape and then I turn the volume way down when I'm doing tracking. You can talk over it easy. Why listen to it loud 15 times while the band learns to play it? I hate to mix the day I track. I've had to do it lots of times. You just have to stay away from it to keep your objectivity. Otherwise, you're just brainwashed when it's time to mix. It gets terrible, especially when you're pushing 40 like me. I tell people, "Just go away and come back tomorrow and you'll have twice as good a mix."

Sea of Shit Studios 250-474-8948

Kyle Statham of Fuck

by Larry Crane

Okay, here's the story. I saw Fuck play a show a while before this interview. I was unimpressed, but several people said they loved their records and that the show was great after "getting into" said records. "Okay," I said, and filed that away. Not much later, *Pardon My French*, a new CD on Matador, arrives at *Tape Op* world headquarters and it's pretty damn great. The big bonus is that Kyle Statham, drummer, etc. for Fuck, owns a recording studio and has recorded all the Fuck material plus some other fine artists [like Snowmen, Sonya Hunter]. And, as it turns out, Fuck began as a recording project, and still build all their songs in the studio. A definite *Tape Op* kind of band. I cornered Kyle before a recent show in Portland where they played with the magnificent Two-Dollar Guitar and put on a show themselves that I was much more "into." Rock on!

So, your studio's name is Black-Eyed Pig. How did it come about that you were recording bands?

Probably the same way a lot of people get started. I played in bands for a while and had a little cassette 4-track pretty early on. Then I got a couple of these 1/4" Dokoder reel-to-reel machines. I had two of those and was recording whatever band I was in and started recording some other friends. I was moving out of an apartment in the Mission into North Beach and both tape decks were stolen out of the car. I had renter's insurance, which covered them! They were both made in the mid-'70s, I would guess, and when they were made they were very expensive, a couple of thousand dollars. The clause they had was for replacement costs, so they take how much they were worth then and they increase it by the cost-of-living index for twenty years.

So you decided you'd better buy some real equipment then.

Right! The option is that you can take cash for them for the depreciated value of the objects, which meant the decks were worth $25 each, or I could go out and buy something new, up to a certain level. The problem was that I had to buy something brand new and I couldn't go over this limit. It put me in an awkward position, machine wise. I ended up getting a machine that I don't like. I got a 1/4" Tascam that I do like – it's a BR 20 – that I do like. It's a 1/4" 2-track. I got a mixdown deck first 'cause I knew I wanted one of those. Then I got a 1/2" 16-track that I don't like at all. It's also a Tascam. It's the DBX which is the problem. The narrow format you just can't run without noise reduction and the noise reduction doesn't sound very good.

It's got that sorta weird compression on it.

It just kills the high end. I think those machines were originally made to do post-production, dialog for movies and such, so to actually do music on them you gotta really battle them. This was all pre-ADAT and all that stuff.

I don't know if you're better off one way or the other with that.

It's hard to say. It'd have been nice to have kicked in some of my own money and get something decent.

You couldn't buy anything used? You should have worked out a deal with a friend at a music store... buy something and bring it right back. So when was that?

That would have been seven years ago.

So you had that stuff...

Yeah, and a crappy, old piece-of-shit mixer, one reverb and two mics. So I had a brand new 16-track, a brand new 2-track, and 2 microphones. I was in the process of moving into this little place in North Beach that had been built after the earthquake as temporary housing and they never tore it down. The place had no foundation, it was just sitting on pilings, and you could go under the house and you could see that there were just beams sitting on stacks of bricks. Over the years the thing had settled so much you couldn't open any of the doors or the windows. It was this little-bitty four-room place. It had a kitchen and every other room was all about the same size, 9 by 12. I lived in one and turned one into a control room and one into a studio. It was so cramped. We made a lot of records there.

Did you ever have a noise problem there?

Yeah, but I tried to do mostly quiet stuff. Sometimes on the weekend we'd have one loud band track.

What bands did you work with there?

There's this woman, Sonya Hunter – kind of a singer-songwriter- and we did a lot of her stuff. Lots of local bands demos. A friend of mine had a studio that went out of business and he wanted to do some recording after that and instead of him paying me I took it all in gear. I got a whole bunch of good mics, some decent outboard gear and a ton of mic stands. Then we were rolling. Then I got the Mackie board. A 24 by 8 bus, I don't use it for in-line tracking very often. There's lots of good things about the board, but if you do it in-line there's no mutes on the mix-B path.

I've only used that for a couple of headphone mixes.

If you run it in-line and use that for tape playback... sometimes it's hard. So I had that place in North Beach for about three years and then I moved to an actual commercial workspace down in the Tenderloin in S.F. It has a storefront at street level and then a basement of this apartment building. It's about 2500 square feet or so. It's pretty big. It had been abandoned and was just a mess down there. It was full of shit. The landlord had owned a couple of other buildings and every time something broke, or didn't work, instead of paying to get rid of it he just threw it in the basement. We cleaned it all up and soundproofed the room. We put in some great big windows. I didn't have any windows for the control room in my other place. I still have some problems, leakage wise, with the bass cabinets, but everything else seems to be pretty contained.

Are there people upstairs from where you record?

Yeah. I'm in the basement and on the first floor there are offices. Above that is where people live.

But you don't rent the offices or stuff.

I have just one of them. The other half is a lawyer's office, but he's hardly ever there. Almost all the work that we do is on weekends or the evening anyhow. There's only one guy we ever get noise complaints from and he lives two floors up and he can't hear us, but he sleeps on the floor and he can feel the bass.

Did you ever think about buying him a futon?

I've thought about a lot of things... He's wrecked a bunch of people's sessions.

He's come down and said to stop?

Yeah, and I basically have to. He's had some problems with other people in the building too. At the new place we've done a bunch of cool stuff. We did a bunch of Snowmen stuff. There's a record that is finished. It's one of the favorite things I've ever worked on. We did a deal for Richard Buckner that turned out really good. He came in for a whole day and wanted to catalog his songs. He did about 20 songs. It was really fun.

Is there any other CD releases you've worked on?

There's a woman, her name is Alice Beirhorst, and we did some records for her. She plays a lot in San Francisco. We did some more things for Sonya. We did these Pat Thomas records that have been coming out in Germany. Pat's an archive now. He collects everything. Rich [Avella] and I did something the other day that was really fun. It was this Little Princess 7". It's an 8 song 7".

You've got other people working out of there?

Rich has done some pretty cool stuff. He did this Skypark 7" which is coming out on the Mod Lang label. This guy, Rick Wilson, has done a lot of stuff. He's doing a new Sonya Hunter record down there right now.

So the place is busy.

It stays pretty busy.

So you like where it's at now?

Yeah, it got easier and easier and the truth is I don't have time to do it. If someone else wasn't working down there I would have a hard time justifying keeping it open. I'm only there less than six months a year. This tour is 10 or 12 weeks, but there's a week or two ahead of time just getting ready for it and already there's talk of it getting extended. I actually start to feel guilty, sometimes, if I'm not using it enough. It's a shame to have it all and not be cranking on it.

But now you've got two people in there working. Are they watching the books and paying the bills while you're gone?

I do it from here. I kind of have all my bills consolidated in a few places so I can just call up and say, "What do I owe you?"

What's Fuck's process of working in the studio?

Tim lives in New York, Ted and Geoff live in Oakland and I live in San Francisco. Even Ted and Geoff; I don't see those guys until it's time to go out and tour or it's time to record. Most of the songs; someone has the basic idea. They have a boom-box tape of it or something that they recorded at home. We'll swap tapes a couple of weeks before we're supposed to get together to record, listen to each other's stuff, assemble at my place, and compare notes. First, we'll set up everything to record that we think we're gonna need. Set up the drums and mic them up. Mic up all the guitars... set up some keyboards and mic those up. We'll pick the songs. When we start playing we'll kind of jam through them a bit and as soon as it comes into a place we would be happy to work from we'll record it. Sometimes it takes 10 or 20 minutes and sometimes it takes a couple of hours. If anyone's got any specific ideas we'll go from there or we'll just say, "That's fine. What's next?"

Do you do overdubs right away while you're working on the song?

Guitar overdubs or backing vocals. We usually do a lot of those in one session. 25 or 30. Everyone will take those tapes home and we'll decide which ones are worth pursuing. The first few records we put out ourselves so we really took our time. Some of those, from the time a song was recorded to the time it came out, took a year. Now we work a little faster. We'll get back together the next time, maybe at the end of a tour. We have all this stuff, and we'll focus on ten songs and these other two, where the song is right but we got bad versions so we need to re-record the basics. We'll pick one, usually, and work it all the way to the end; mix it and everything. Then we'll pick another song...

So it's much different than your typical studio assembly line process.

We kind of do it backwards in some sense.

When you do this stuff are you doing a lot of the engineering?

We've never had anybody outside in. It would be a trying process for someone. It's actually boring to watch people write songs. From an engineering standpoint, my least favorite sessions are when bands come in and are not prepared and do not know what they want to do. When we record that's exactly how I'd describe it. We have no idea. For someone who's not in the band and doesn't have a vested interest... they would just be bored to tears. We could probably chart a suicide rate here. I've been doing most of the engineering. If I need to do an overdub or something, I can tell one of those guys what to do. As far as patching stuff in, loading reels, dialing up reverb programs and understanding parametric EQ... They aren't very interested I don't think. They are at first, but if you don't use what you've learned it kind of goes away.

It seems like kind of a spontaneous band. It doesn't feel like things were labored over and played for two years.

A lot of us aren't very good musicians, and we knew that from the beginning, so there's no point trying to spend two days to try and get a guitar solo "perfect" because we never could. The same thing with a vocal. We understand what our limitations are and we try and spend our time wisely. When I first met Tim, and we first started working on this, we'd been in bands before and neither of us liked to practice. It seems like bands go through this cycle. You get a bunch of people who are into something, you jam and rehearse through some stuff and learn some songs, six

months later it's time for the first show, another half a year and then it's time to record... It's a long time to wait. We said, "Well, we'll do it the opposite. We won't rehearse and we won't play any shows... We'll just record." He would come over one day a week to my house after we met. He'd call in sick every Tuesday. One of us would pick a song and we'd learn it, record it, overdub and mix it and it'd be done. We did that for a few months until we had enough for a whole record. We started thinking about playing live and that's when we got Ted to come be a part of it. This idea of not really rehearsing and spending a lot of time deciding what we wanted to do... it's been like that from the beginning. Sometimes it's good and sometimes it's bad. Some stinker stuff gets done just because we don't do our homework.

Stinky in a writing way?

Yeah. There's some stuff where the basic song idea doesn't get the treatment it deserves. Some where I think, "All the elements are here but we just fell down on the job."

Do you end up working stuff up differently live?

Definitely. Also, when we record, everybody has different work schedules. Usually Tim and I are always there but Ted and Geoff... sometimes they can make it and sometimes they can't. So maybe on one song Tim and I play all the instruments and when we play it live some of the instrumentation might get dropped for something else. We don't concentrate too hard on trying to reproduce the record live. The decision we made not to practice and not to play too many shows... maybe it makes for some fresh recordings but it makes for some pretty beautiful live experiences. The beginnings of our tours are not something you want to be a part of. We never play together, ever. We practice twice before a tour. Hopefully by the 5th or 6th show it's getting close!

Have you ever thought about recording your band live when you come off the end of a tour?

We did a press tour in May and June and we did a Peel session while we were there. We played everything live, no overdubs. It was mostly songs off the new record but the funny part is, except for one or two of them, we'd never played any of them before. They were recorded in such a piecemeal way. A lot of them, some people hadn't even played on yet.

It's funny. Pavement started out in a similar way.

That's what I've heard.

And "big" bands seem to work that way, where they no longer tour the new, unrecorded, songs live but instead work them up in the studio.

You have to be careful. Some of the stuff can be half-baked and you have to edit yourself very hard.

I imagine with a process like that you're always gonna be throwing stuff out.

It's hard. I can think of a couple of songs where it was as good as anything we've done but it's a bad version of it. Usually the best ones get revisited. That's a really hard decision to make when you really believe in the song but this isn't the right take and you know it's a gamble, "Well, if we don't put it on this record it may not get on another record." It's hard to edit yourself.

What kind of gear and mics have you been using at the studio?

I have an older pair of Sony C500s. They look like giant ice cream cones! It's a large diaphragm single pattern condenser mic. There's a really hefty pad built into them and you can mic kick drums and floor toms. It never craps out. It's really good on really loud low-end stuff. They're old mics so they need a lot of gain. If you've got someone who's a quiet singer they're not very good. If you've got someone with a lot of sibilance problems, like me, it's a good mic because it's not as detailed on top.

Are they from the '70s?

I think so. I have one of those Audio Technica 4050s that I like a lot. There's one of those Groove Tube mics in the studio that I really enjoy. They aren't very transparent but I really enjoy their character. They have their own sound, but everybody always likes them a lot. Rick just got one of those Rode tube mics that sounds really good.

What kind of outboard gear do you have? Do you have any mic pres?

We use the board a lot. I can't think of anything interesting, really. We have an old Lexicon model 200 reverb. Only one input works, but it sounds pretty good! We have one of those Ensoniq DP4s that is really fun to play with but it has kind of a steep learning curve.

Some of that gear is too much. You don't have the time to learn all the tricks.

Not too much. We have a 1/4" 2-track, which I really enjoy to mix to. And then we go to DAT player and we have a Digidesign rig to do 2-track editing on the Macintosh. And I have a CD burner.

No way.

It's helpful for a lot of reasons. We can make the CDs that they'll actually send to the plant and master from. What we use it for a lot, also, is like when we did the Snowmen record those guys had 30 songs or something. How do you pick and then come up with an order. So we make everybody a CD. They can take it home and test it out. They can just call each other up and say, "Try this: 11, 5, 9…" We do that in Fuck a lot too. We never have time to do the editing while everyone's together. We finish the recording and all the mixing, hopefully, and we do all the other work over the phone. At first it seemed like a luxury, but now I don't know how I'd get a lot of the stuff done without it.

I really wish I had one. I don't have any computer editing either. There's the stand-alone's but…

If you want to get a stand-alone get one that you can burn masters off of, you can get these really cheap ones but you can't use the discs they produce for mastering. It's a good safety of the DAT. For important stuff I'll usually mix to 1/4" and DAT at the same time. Then I'll make a safety copy of the 1/4" on DAT.

What do you end up using for CD masters?

The analog, 2-track stuff.

You like the sound of that?

Yeah. Most of the stuff I record we really hit the machine hard. I hit it a little too hard on this last Fuck record on a few songs. Usually you can really nail it.

How hard?

If the meters go all the way down and never go back up… I've recorded like that. On some songs you get it where it's just moving an 1/8 of an inch off the peg. I don't know but it sounds really good. It's a Tascam of all things. You can probably buy one of these things new for $1000. It's a

great machine. The transport is solid. If the 1/2" 16-track I have were half as good as the 2-track I sure would like it a lot more.

Are you thinking of getting a new tape deck?

Yep. I've been searching and searching. I thought I had a 2" 16-track. This guy has this studio and he switched over to 2" 24-track a long time ago and he kept this 16-track as a backup if the 24-track goes down. Which doesn't make any sense. He was gonna sell it and it was a pretty good deal, only a couple of thousand bucks, and it needed a couple of thousand in work. It was a really solid machine and it had an interesting history. They'd done some Neil Young records on it. But at the last minute, he changed his mind. It was an old Ampex MM1000.

They sound great. Have you ever recorded on a 2" 16-track before?

I don't think I have. I've heard a lot of stuff that was done on them and I've really got my heart set on one.

Just the detail that it captures is so much more interesting. Have you ever had any weird studio experiences?

I've only had to ask one guy to leave. It was a long-term project and he was nuts. Even when he wasn't recording this guy was just bananas. It was gonna be an 18 month project and after a few months I just said, "Look, this isn't gonna work." I found another studio, brought him over, I paid to transfer all the tapes from my format to the format they were using at this place and then I said, "He's all yours."

What was he gonna do for 18 months?

He was putting together a record one track at a time. He would start off and record the bass, guitar, scratch vocal and drums and then he'd throw away everything but the drum track and he'd go and replace everything one-at-a-time.

Was he sloppy, but a perfectionist?

I don't know if perfectionist is right. He didn't have any really solid ideas. He would set click tracks so he could put down bass and guitar parts. On this one song he couldn't tell if it was supposed to be 89 or 90 beats per minute. So what he did was he played it both ways and he had his girlfriend dance to it and he watched her dance and he said, "89."

It's hard to say "no" to work, but when you're gonna lose your mind…

That's the best part about the studio getting established and taking off is being able to say "no" to stuff. A lot of it is really horrible and it makes you not want to record anymore. I tell people that I'm retired and I don't do it anymore. "I just do it for fun." That way if they bought some record I made I can say, "Those were just my friends." It can be extra-depressing to have someone leave such a foul taste in your mouth that you don't want to do the one thing you love.

RICH AVELLA
by Larry Crane

Rich Avella works out of Black Eyed Pig Studio. He's also a member of Snowmen, one of my favorite San Francisco combos these days. I was curious how he had ended up working out of a studio part time and what his plans were. Plus, I wanted to plug the fact that there's an amazing Snowmen record [*Last days of the Central Freeway*].

So how did you get started working at the studio there?

The way we met Kyle was that he was having a party at the studio, and he asked us to play a few songs there. A while passed and he asked us to come to the studio and do some recording.

He asked you to come to the studio and record?

Yeah. He said, "Hey, I'll give you a little bit of free time." The tracking and everything was free. He wanted to record us and that was great. We did a demo with him. While hanging out with him, me and Mike [Ehrhardt from Snowmen] told him how we'd studied recording at school at San Francisco State.

Was that what you majored in?

Pretty much. We were in the broadcasting department and our emphasis was audio.

Did you get a degree?

Yes, we did. It wasn't like the whole degree was focused on recording but we got to hang out in the studio and record bands occasionally. We learned a good bit but not as much as you do when you're doing it hands on. I guess just through hanging out with Kyle, we just expressed interest, me and Mike, in helping out on a session. He basically said, "Well, I really don't need help, I pretty much run sessions by myself." But what he did is he offered to set something up with a band to come in and he would run Mike and I through the setup, how the studio worked, the patchbay and all of that.

And then leave you?

Basically... it went in that direction. That's kind of how it started. The studio is below his house so he was always available if I had a question or anything. He just let me book sessions and bring bands in. It's been really nice. As I said, Mike did some of the sessions with me.

Has Mike done sessions on his own?

He's done them with me but Mike's done a lot of recording on 4-track. I don't know if you've heard the 23 Aorta.

Yeah, he gave me a tape a year ago or so. It's pretty cool.

Yeah, he did that stuff on a 4-track with a couple of mics.

And it sounds really clear. It didn't sound like 4-track recordings!

But anyway, that's how it happened and Kyle was kind enough to show me the ropes at his studio. I don't know if anyone would know any of the bands I've recorded. One of them was a cool instrumental band called Apollos of the Ozarks. I don't think they're still around. We did some of the engineering on the Snowmen album we recorded with Kyle.

He did the majority of it?

He mixed all of it. He engineered the basic tracks and then Mike and I did the overdubs. I did some mixes and Kyle came and mixed some stuff and we liked what he was doing better so we just had him mix the whole thing.

It's probably good having another opinion.

It was a weird position to be in, mixing. I felt better handing it over to Kyle.

If you're the person in the band it's hard to put your parts up as loud as they should be.

Or push them down!

Oh, is that your problem?

Front and center, there's my part! The one thing that Kyle was really good at, I think, was that he was able to listen to a song and bring parts out, like down to guitar, bass, drums and then bring a part back in. He would mute things.

That's a definite outside opinion sort of thing. You would find it really hard to mute Cole's guitar part. You'd feel kind of guilty. What else have you done?

I recorded this indie-pop band called Skypark. That was fun. I haven't seen either of the singles yet. Kyle probably told you about Little Princess. They could become legendary. They're just hilarious. Their whole concept is that they're from some other planet and their spaceship broke down so they started a band to make money... They're these three young Japanese women who just started the band in January. They're basically doing 15 or 20 second speed-metal songs with really deep "Raargh" vocals. It's so funny. They have a 7" of that stuff out. They have matching little costumes and little tiaras. As far as recording out of Kyle's... I do occasionally. I keep my ear to the ground.

Do you ever see yourself doing more or trying to do it as a full-time job?

I've definitely thought about it but my current job has a steadier income!

Oh... yeah... uh. Recording bands is not the steadiest income at this level I can assure you...

Contact Rich and Snowmen at 826 Diamond St., San Francisco, CA 94114.

Studio .45

by Liz Bustamanante

Drive through Hartford, Connecticut, and you can't help but notice the giant blue onion sitting atop a tower in an industrial complex. The onion was a gift from Czar Nicholas to Samual Colt in exchange for two engraved dueling pistols during a tour of Russia. The building was originally created to house the old Colt Firearms factory. Today that space is home to artists, dancers, and a cozy, but spacious 24-track analog recording studio. The first interview was conducted with Dave Shuman, the owner, who explains the origins of Studio .45. The second allows Michael Deming, the chief engineer, to discuss some of his techniques and equipment. Together these are the gentlemen that make Studio .45 go.

DAVE SHUMAN

Did the studio get started when you and Michael met in college?

Well actually, Michael and I went to the same music school, but we went several years apart. We didn't know each other at that point. Michael had several friends, who now are great friends of mine, and each person had a certain amount of gear that, by itself, wasn't anything in particular. A couple of people had leftovers from PAs. Two people were in a band together and one of them had a 1/2" 16-track machine. Someone else had a small board and some monitors. Michael had scouted the space for the studio because he was living across the hall in an apartment, which is now our B studio. When he saw the space in its raw form, he thought it would make a wonderful studio. He gathered up a couple roommates to help defray the expenses and convinced a few people to drop off their unused gear there. It got wired together just like that.

What was the first board you started out using?

The first main board was a Tascam M520, which is a 20 x 8 Tascam board that the Mackie boards now replace these days. It was a muddy sounding thing. I barely remember.

It was so many studio hours ago. We would run it with a series of sidecars, depending on what we were doing. The last installation had a Hill mixer, which was configurable to either 16 x 2 or 12 x 4 x 2. And that was a really good mixer. I still have it in a rack. There was also an old AudioArts 2k, which was another 16 x 2 mixer. There was another Tascam mixer before I was involved. But usually it was used with a monitor attached to it, along with whatever could be wired for extra inputs and was available at the time. When the studio started, it didn't have much in the way of patchbays. There were cheap patchbays and Hosa, which is horrible cheap cable. It was very noisy and hissy. Michael and I would do searches for noise every time we would come in. The old patchbays would act like antennas for whatever noise they could suck in. You'd crank up your levels for testing to see what was making the most noise and figure out how to make it quieter before you'd start working.

How much engineering experience had either one of you had at this point?

I'm not really sure exactly how much Michael had. I know he had done some work at Kramer's Noise New Jersey studio with Giant Metal Insects. In a related vein, he was booking shows at a small venue in Hartford and having to be the promoter and sometimes door-person and sound person all at the same time. He had a lot of cool bands, but Hartford didn't have an audience for those bands at the time. He had various friends and people in the Hartford area who would ask him to help out with the recording, production, or some engineering. I don't think he had a solid studio background before the studio came into existence. For me it had been mostly 4-track cassette-based recording with friends. One band I was in had a very elaborate 4-track setup. Two 4-tracks were used, one as a sub-mixer for the other in a permanently wired rehearsal space for recording every rehearsal. When I was in college, I ended up doing demos for people on my own 4-track. I'd spent time screwing around in the college recording studio, which wasn't very extensive. A little bit of work in smaller 16-track studios - more as a musician than as an engineer. I had read quite a bit about what it all did and as an electric bass player, I'd used amplifiers and effects units and they're all very basically the same. I mean, there's not a lot you can do with a signal at this point. There are endless ways to combine effects, but when you think about it there are things you do with volume and things you do with tone and things you do with time. I think that's about it unless I'm forgetting something. It's just those three elements.

That's an interesting way to think about it. It's an incredibly simple view that is often overlooked.

Some of your more involved guitar amps have more complicated EQs than your basic mixing boards. The basics are there. If you understand how they work, then it's the same principles. Obviously, how you process your information and how you use it is different, but your basic building blocks are the same.

How long has it been since the studio has been open?

It's been Studio .45 since March of '93; Michael had started the studio about a year earlier. At that point I became involved as the owner of the studio and the studio got a name for the first time. About a month later, we got a 2" 24-track. I think that point was the start of the studio as most people know it today. There were some interesting releases and odds and ends recorded during that first year. I think a couple are still bouncing around and have been released on 7 inches and compilations. There have been some interesting things that have had some attention paid to them.

Who were some of the more interesting bands?

G'nu Fuzz, China Pig, a band called Freak Baby, a band from Danbury called Head that was really cool, but is now defunct. Except for G'nu Fuzz, probably most of those bands aren't around anymore.

Who have you been recording lately?

The Apples In Stereo. Lilys are going to be doing a big project very soon. A few Sub Pop things here and there. We're doing a group called Holler, which is a country thing. I've been recording some interesting bands like Wampeter, a cool band from Southern Connecticut called Deep Banana Blackout, and Aboriginal Bluegrass. Late summer was kind of a dead period as it always it. Usually we're always booked, but right about now we're coming into almost more sessions than we can handle. Which is interesting, because we built a second room last year to handle that demand, and almost as soon as it was finished it seemed impossible to imagine how we functioned without it beforehand. Often Michael and I will be working on two different projects at the same time. There has been interest from bands that have wanted to book the whole facility. Which would be the best way to do things because there are so many different sounds, not only in gear, but in rooms as well. That's probably one of our most important assets here, the sounds of the big rooms here in the former Colt Firearms factory.

MICHAEL DEMING

Would you like to clear the air about your oscilloscope and the role it plays in recording?

We use the oscilloscopes for numbers of different things. It's used for everything from setting up the tape machine to looking at the phase correlation between left and right sides. It's just a piece of test equipment used for looking at any audio signal and measuring voltage. You certainly need it to be able to set the tape machine up so that you can check that the azimuth and zenith are correct and that the phase between the outer tracks is correct. In other words, you cannot be without an oscilloscope in the studio.

In the Lilys song "Shovel into Spade Kit" there's a section that features an orchestra. I want to know how you found that piece.

We had many de Wolff records sitting around the studio. They are samplers of orchestral passages in different styles. I listened through them all and was able to find solo bits of instruments that I wanted to use in that passage. Trumpet, bass clarinet and clarinet. Those are the three instruments you hear in that passage.

No oboe?

No oboe, just trumpet, bass clarinet and clarinet. I was able to transfer that material from vinyl to 1/2" 2-track and then Varispeed the parts by using the Ampex ATR102. I would Varispeed the segments into the song the way I wanted them to appear in the piece.

And it was all done by sound?

By ear, yeah. But it would have been easier with a more modern tape machine, with more fine control over a capstan motor.

Couldn't you have just sampled it more easily?

But the sound quality would suffer. If I used the best sampler, I would have had to sample it in real time and it would have lost a lot of sound quality, I would imagine, by changing the pitch. It was simpler to put it straight from vinyl to tape, all along fully preserving the analog signal path. In the making of that record we used no digital devices at all at any time. There probably are hardly any records made these days in which there isn't one digital device.

The Apples in Stereo are known for their extensive usage of home recording for their records. How did they get hooked up with Studio .45?

Robert heard the Lilys' record and liked it. That had a lot to do with why I wound up working with him. As time went on, Robert started to realize the limitations of his set-up and realized that what he really wanted to hear wasn't always achievable all of the time. If he had 50 overdubs, it was going to become increasingly difficult to submix all of that material and have it still sound clear.

Especially if he's doing all of the engineering.

There's a huge difference between a 1/2" 8-track and Brian Wilson making *Pet Sounds* on an 8-track. There's a huge difference and people have to realize that.

Everybody references the recording of *Sgt. Pepper's* on a 4-track, and forgets that the Beatles weren't using a Porta One.

Yeah. The 4-track was probably a Scully or a Studer and it was probably a 1/2" 4-track that was aligned every minute of the day by engineers who really knew what they were doing. They treated the tape machines like we treat them here. We line them up every day. Every day an MRL is put on the machines. The entire calibration procedure is gone through every single day. I know of big commercial studios where that isn't even done these days. People use these new Studer A 827s and they align themselves. They are supposedly auto-aligning and auto-biasing and I don't particularly trust them. To me, there's too much electronics in there to have to accomplish all that. I'd rather have an old MCI machine like we have that might be a little bit harder to handle. It might be a pain to keep calibrated all the time, but the sound is certainly worth the effort.

When The Apples were here recording, Robert took some of the tapes back home with him to record more overdubs on his 8-track. What'd you do?

They came out here for a few weeks the first time and we recorded the basics live, which was quite a lot of fun. We set up in the main room, real old-fashioned, guitar amps and drums and everything in the same room. I gave everybody a fully discreet monitor mix so that each musician could hear the balance the way that they wanted to hear it. And then we proceeded to go through the basics. We got everything on to 2". Drums, bass, and two guitars. Then we went through and got rid of some of the original rhythm guitars. We treated them as being scratch. But there were some good performances in that first pass which were saved. Then we did as much overdubbing as we had time for in their first trip out here. I mixed a reference mix to two tracks on a 1/2" 8-track player, because that's the multitrack machine in Robert's studio, He has two Otari 5050 1/2" 8-tracks. We put SMPTE time code on one track of the 24-track and on one track of the 8-track and I mixed a stereo guide mix. That way they could take the 1/2" tape and continue overdubbing at home. There they were actually able to use two 1/2" 8-track machines and do two runs of overdubs that I was able to sync to the 2" later when they came back. We synced that material up and transferred it all back to the 2" tape.

There's a song recorded at Studio .45 in which an entire Can song was recorded on one track. Apparently it's inaudible until someone points out that it's there and then you can't hear the song without noticing the Can track. Do you remember who that was?

Flying in the Can tape, I believe that was on Flowchart. That was the first record I did for them and that was about two years ago. It was just a cassette that we wild synced in. We started it up at a certain point and it just bubbles along below the level of the program. It's in "Metro Survey", I think. That's the name of the song.

Could they get into trouble for that one?

I don't think anyone's going to notice to be honest with you. We've done quite a lot of that. Wild-syncing little things in to the program. It's fun to see how that stuff will come up in a random way. Sometimes it's great, it comes up so good that you could never recreate it. It's a lot of fun to just let it happen. Sometimes it's not usable at all. And then sometimes it's very calculated and predetermined like in the Lilys' song; where I sat there for hours overdubbing, marking the tape with a grease pencil, and starting the tape at a certain point... Hoping it'll run up to speed by the time I'd punch in on the 2" machine.

Is there a standard way that you mic drums?

Not really. I really try to do what's going to suit the music or what I think is going to suit the music. I never put a mic in front of anything until I've heard it with my own ears first. I'm definitely not one of these people that talks about these things that they always do as a matter of course. I read in audio trade magazines all the time that an engineer will be asked about what he does with compression or EQ, and he'll immediately start rattling off things that he always does. I'm always so amazed by that.

I wonder how he knows he's going to use 3:1 compression and this and that EQ until he's heard what he's about to record. Or is he just in the habit of doing that no matter what it is? It's confusing to me. Basically, I really have to hear what it is that I'm going to take in with a microphone and get to tape before I start making any kind of valuable judgement on how I'm going to do it. I know the sounds of certain mics. I know their EQs and how they color sound. If I have a really bright source, I might pick a dull mic. I basically have to hear it before I decide what I'm going to put in front of it. Each piece of electronic gear colors the sound in some way, or it's designed to not color the sound at all and I'm going to pick it based on how I know it sounds.

Tell me about the more unusual pieces of equipment that you use in the studio like the older microphones that were initially intended to be used in a courtroom.

We have these old dynamic omnidirectional mics that were taken out of the Illinois statehouse. They're Shures, and a friend of mine who has a studio across town bought a bunch, and has given me a few to listen to. Basically, I've been rediscovering a lot of really old dynamic microphones that don't have much gain. A lot of people don't even consider using these mics, because they're really low gain. I've been experimenting with them using really high gain microphone preamps – Telefunken V76s – and dumping that out and putting it into a really clean sounding line driver on the console. You really get to hear close up the character of some of these old microphones. These old mics have really unique EQ curves. Frequency response wasn't very good back then out of any electronic device. To get something to go 20hz to 20K was a huge feat. Some of these microphones start cutting out at 9K, so you hear all these different slopes of attenuation in the top end. Some of them are so great on certain sources. We have to hear what we're about to record and then pick a microphone. If I hear that something sounds a certain way and know that the sound of a microphone will complement it, or add something to the music, then I'm into that. Some of these old dynamic microphones, they definitely have their use when you have a high gain mic pre and really good line amps on your console. Otherwise, they're pretty much useless compared to modern condenser mics that have tons of gain. When you can buy an AT4033 in the store for $500, there's not much use for an old 55S or some old dynamic mic.

Which other mics have you preferred lately?

I use a lot of condensers on everything. I like to choose things that are going to add something to the sound. I'm not one who likes electronic gear of any kind just designed to measure out nicely. THD and low distortion, those things are all good, and we like our audio gear to measure out. But there are a lot of things these days that are designed for utter clarity and it just adds nothing to the sound. It's like passing the signal through nothing. It doesn't add any magic to the music, because it's not designed with that kind of passion. It's not designed by ear. It's not a case where people are listening and designing. It's a case where people are measuring out frequency response, distortion, noise and using that to design. I use a lot of mics that color the sound greatly, mics that are high quality – not noisy and very clear. I like to use Microtech Geffel UM70s. I like a 30-year-old Neumann condenser U67 that I use a lot.

Greg Freeman

by Larry Crane

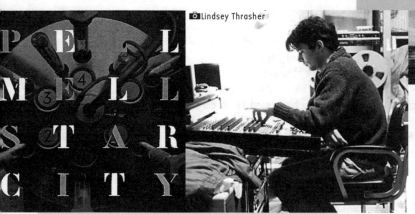
Lindsey Thrasher

Mr. Greg Freeman may be best known to you as a member of Pell Mell, the fine instrumental band with 3 lives... or maybe as a former bass player for the Call. Check out the first 2 LPs to embarrass him... but one would hope he is best referred to as a fine producer. From his scratch-built Lowdown Recording Studio (which shut down in 1997) in San Francisco, Greg worked on albums for Barbara Manning, Thinking Fellers Union Local 282, Faust, Gate, X-Tal, Donner Party, Frightwig, the Dwarves, Royal Trux, Ovarian Trolley, Vomit Launch and many others. He's a talented, creative person to work with, and as Barbara says, "I can tell him a song is a color and he knows what I mean." And as if he needs any other acclaim, his studio once featured a mixing board previously used for sound on the Gumby claymation show. Now that's cool!

How did you get into production, studio work, etc.?

My friend Dave Spaulding and I were goofin' around, doing music together after Pell Mell broke up in '84 and he sort of, on a whim, bought a 1/2" 8-track. He saw one for sale and went and bought it, and then it just kind of sat there at his house and we looked at it and went, "Wow, 1/2" 8-track!" He had a mixing board left over from his band, from their live setup, so he had a board, some mics, some mic stands and I had a 4-track reel to reel. So we thought, "Hey, let's put together a studio." This space came along, Dave was in a band with this woman who was also in this other band, Typhoon. We split the space, they rehearsed there and we would, the rest of the time, set it up for recording. It was really shoestring, we didn't have anything. Then he bought a real board, a Tascam board... it was pretty much all his stuff when we started. I would buy stuff as time went on.

When you were in the Call, I remember stories about them spending a week doing the kick drum sound...

Right!

When you were recording with other bands and seeing how it went, did that kinda turn you on to the recording side of it?

Oh yeah, definitely. I was always kind of into it, though at the time I didn't know as much or I wasn't really that involved. The most valuable stuff I retained was the procedure, like what you do first; setting up to record, getting sounds, getting the headphone mix. The logistics I picked up 'cause we did it so many times. Basic concepts like EQ and compression, and how that stuff works I picked up. I wish I'd known more about what kinds of mics and exactly what the boards were doing. In a way, if you know the basic stuff, you don't really need to know that right away. The more important thing is knowing how things go together, just trying to get things to sound good.

Having ears.

Right. That's the thing.

It's true. Maybe you'll come across things that maybe you wouldn't have picked up anywhere else.

I just comes down to what sounds good... There's other things I just learned 'cause I spent so much time in all these different studios and a lot of them are pretty big-deal studios, but even so, they had problems or they would deceive you into thinking you had really good sound when you didn't, because of various things. It teaches you that you've got to compare what you're listening to against other things that you know or listen to on different systems. It was also before every studio had Yamaha NS-10s... you'd just have these huge custom monitors or you had Auratones.

There wasn't some sort of reference you could use everywhere.

Yeah, I remember at the Record Plant [big L.A. studio] we would do stuff and we would listen on these huge monitors and the engineer would just crank it and it was like, "Yeah, it sounds great!" But then later you'd listen to it and say, "Jeez, it doesn't sound so great." It's like anything; if you're used to it I guess you could use it.

What's some of the latest stuff you've done?

I did an album for this band, Granfaloon Bus. They're great, I like them a lot. I think a small label in Texas or someplace is gonna put it out. They're a lot of fun. There's just been a ton of stuff.

What's the latest thing that's been released that you've done?

There's the Ovarian Trolley album which is pretty recent. I did this band called Couch from Eureka, an EP for Lookout Records. They're more Thinking Fellers-ish than punk rock... that's not out yet, that'll be out in a little while. This guy, Ian Brennan; did his solo album. I just did something for Pony Ride.

Do you still do a lot of stuff that ends up like "demo-tape" type stuff?

Yeah, a fair amount of stuff. It's been more like stuff that's planned for a single or a record. I still do a fair amount of demos.

Do you feel better when you're doing stuff that's going to be released?

Yeah! [Laughs] Oh no! I try to do the same job. Actually, my new scheme, which I'm just now beginning to enact is, I'm trying to only do projects where I've got a creative hand in, where I'm either producing or co-producing. In the past I've pretty much taken on everybody, which has been fine, but it's at the point now where I've done it for so long I have just too many people wanting to record. Besides, I would rather do stuff I'm into or people I've done before that I know I would have a good time with. Stuff that I would enjoy rather than getting calls from some band I've never heard and they come in and it's some god-awful fusion/prog band and I'm miserable. So that's my new thing and I think it's starting to work out. It's not fair for a band to come in and I'm not really into it. I try to do as good a job for everyone, but still, if someone's doing some... if they want to sound like Helmet or something, I'm not gonna care.

Do you feel kinda happy to be in the position you're in?

Well, if it works I'll be happy. If I end up with no business then I guess I'll have to change back!

What's some of your favorite things you've recorded over the last 10 years?

Oh god, I guess the stuff that's come out the best, like some of the later Thinking Fellers stuff, was probably some of my favorite stuff. The very last song we recorded is probably one of my all time favorites. It ended up on a single on Amarillo Records, it's called "Every Day". Have you heard that?

No.

Well, the single doesn't sound so great 'cause it got mastered shitty or something but the original mix was, I thought, really good and I was pretty happy with it.

What about Barbara Manning's *Truth Walks in Sleepy Shadows* album?

Some of that came out pretty good, I thought. That was kind of a handful 'cause Barbara got really into inviting all these people to add stuff to it and it was sort of my job to go, "Holy cow, take something away!" It was too much and she had the whole band doing their band version and on top of that would be strings and piano.

It's pretty layered but it's also mixed sparingly, it's got a lot of stuff going on but it's not mush.

That's good. Thanks, that's the idea. It was tough. Some of the stuff, I thought, came out real good. There's this band called Package, they have a single out. They're more Minutemen, popish, hard rock... very cool songs, interesting lyrics, they're real nice guys, too. We're working on a bunch of stuff, I don't know what's gonna happen to it. I guess they're gonna do an EP. That stuff I thought sounded really good.

What kind of gear are you using now? Do you still have the Gumby mixing board?

It's for sale... cheap! Now I've got a Mackie, 24-channel, 8-buss. It's good. In general I like it, and I have my 2" 16-track Ampex.

Where was that from?

I bought it from a guy who got it from Fantasy [Studios]. Yeah the Mackie is decent. The worse thing about it, I think, is the EQ, but the virtue of it is that it's really clean, the routing's really good... for people recording, their headphones sound so much better, it's really phenomenal. I got one of those TL Audio 2 channel tube EQs to make up for the lousy EQ on the Mackie. There's four switchable frequency ranges for each channel, it's basically a really good mid-range; the Mackie's got a decent low-end but the mid-range is awful. If you try to make a snare sound good it's just awful. The next thing I'm gonna get is some kind of Neve mic pre-amp. I tried one out and I was just blown away, it really sounded so good. It'll cost me another $1500 but it'll be worth it. So that's the way I get around the board.

With the 2" tape on the 16-track do you find you can really crank the sound onto the tape?

Oh, yeah!

Do you use any noise reduction?

No, with the new, higher output tape, like Ampex 499 or 3M 996, it's pretty darn quiet. Because the tape is so huge, you get a lot more "juice" per track, a lot more magnetic "ju ju" going on so it's really quiet and the bottom end is really amazing.

Does anyone ever complain about the tape cost?

No. I present myself as, this is what I have, this is what it's gonna cost. I've had a lot of people who've come in and said, "God, Greg, we did our last band on ADAT in the studio... it sucks. We like analog." I'll notice that after I mix to the 1/4" reel-to-reel it gets even more bottom end.

Do you do a lot of your mixing to that?

Yeah, I usually tell people to do both, to run 1/4" and a DAT and use the 1/4" for the master and the DAT as a backup.

Do you have any old, cool gear or strange stuff you use?

Well, most of my studio's old and strange! Nothing too weird... I've got an AKG BX-10 spring reverb, which is more of a hi-fi, older spring reverb; it's pretty cool. I have this Mutron delay that's broken and sounds really weird.

Do you still use the Yamaha SPX 90?

Yeah, not very often. I've got an LXP 5 (Lexicon) and a Roland SRV 2000 which is pretty nice. I have this weird ribbon mic, it's called a Mercury, and it looks like a taxi dispatcher's mic. It's got a grill. I tried it out, putting it behind the drummer's seat, facing the corner, a cement corner, and it sounds real weird. There's the old SansAmp trick, too. That's sort of the hip thing to do, use the SansAmp on an effects send. I use it on snare drums a lot, and it comes back all messed up and you mix a little of that back in for your extra chaos factor. Flood, he does that. I picked it up from Tchad Blake.

What kind of books or magazines were you able to find good info from when you were starting your studio?

I would read *Mix* magazine. There's a couple of recording books that I think are really good. There's *Practical Techniques for the Recording Engineer* by Sherman Keene. I highly recommend it. It's the best one I've found. It's more like a procedural thing; how to record stuff. It doesn't talk so much about gear and how microphones work, although it does cover some of that. It has some physics in there and stuff, like Ohm's law, the dB scale and stuff. It is, like it says, practical. It talks about how to edit tape, which is a dying art. It's really good. There's also John Woram's book, *The Sound Recording Handbook*. It's got a microphone section; he has different examples of mics and explains how they work. He's got a really good bit on mid-side stereo, which is neat. It's got a bunch of math, too, if you really want to get into it you can read the math. He's really good, it's very well written. Those two books I think are the best ones. Other than that, I just read the magazines every month and try to pick up info here and there.

Are there any plans for Pell Mell?

We're trying to get this tour together for Europe, I don't know when that'll happen. We're hopin' to get this next record going, too. We gotta make plans still about it, but if all goes well, we'll record it this summer and it'll be out next year. In the meantime, we've got a couple of little song-

snippets in this new Kids in the Hall movie [*Brain Candy*]. We did some music for it. And we've been poppin' up on MTV on Road Rules, y'know that show?

I've never seen it.

They used a bunch of *Interstate*. Also NPR, All Things Considered. We just got this last BMI check but radio doesn't pay anything. We had a couple of network TV broadcasts and those pay a lot. Well, relatively a lot, not a whole lot. It's cool.

PRACTICAL TECHNIQUES FOR THE RECORDING ENGINEER
By Sherman Keene (SKE Publishing)

It took me a while, but I finally found a copy of this book and it was at our local library! It's as good as Greg implied. Sherman worked on records with Zappa, Ike and Tina Turner, and others doing some cool rock and R & B stuff, and he approaches everything from that sort of perspective as opposed to classical recording or mathematical theories of tape properties. There's a million great ideas, ways of working, and practical tips in this thing. I think one of the problems I've had with many books is that they don't really help you... they just give you explanations for why stuff works the way it does but no real ways to work with it. This book counterbalances all that. I think it's out of print, but look hard and you'll find it! –*Larry Crane*

Dan Rathbun

"TAMER OF DANGEROUS SOUNDS"

by Curtis Settino

📷 Katherine Copenhauer

For the last 10 years Dan Rathbun has been writing, performing, producing and recording some of the most distinctive music around. He co-owns and operates Polymorph Recording, in Oakland, CA, with fellow musician/engineer Mark Stichman and electronics maven Lawrence "Rance" Fellows-Mannion. The studio has seen many well-known San Francisco Bay-Area artists [The Mommy Heads, Ralph Carney, Papa's Culture], plus countless punk rock and avant-garde bands [many on Vaccination Records, also based in Oakland]. Several

of Dan's personal projects have also been tracked, mixed and mastered there, including CDs by the late Idiot Flesh *Nobody Rocks Harder... three to seven measures at a time*, the current Charming Hostess *Bulgaria-go-go with brains, brawn and beauty*, and compilation and mastering of the first ever Residents tribute CD *Eyesore: A Stab at the Residents*. The studio itself features a Trident 65 series board, a Tascam 58 8-track and a Tascam MS-16 16-track synched for 22 tracks (both of these are slated for replacement with a 2" machine), many "warm and fuzzy" electronic devices, and a few "cold and clean" ones. Among the many microphones Dan finds himself using an AKG C-414 and a Neumann U87 the most. The recording room and

So, ready to talk some shop?
I'll just lay some groundwork first. It'll be like a lecture.

Split-Spectrum Compression

Most of the music I'm working with is made by vibrating membranes – be it a metal string or a vocal chord or a drum head, it's a vibrating membrane of some sort. And a universal characteristic of vibrating membranes is that they vibrate more strongly at some frequency ranges than others and that intensifies as you play louder, which, in effect, means that any instrument you play louder tends to gets more midrangey.

Because the upper harmonics are coming out more?
Just because some frequency ranges are easier to reproduce for a vibrating membrane. You know this intuitively if you play a bass string really lightly. It has this huge, fat sound, but then if you lay into it, it sounds like "clank, clank." When somebody's talking really quietly, you can hear all of these highs and lows, and then if they start yelling, it becomes more midrangey. To some extent, this is present in every instrument. You know how drums being played hard sound when you hear them through a mic? It's always struck me as not quite right. It's not what you want to hear. When things get louder you don't want more midrange, you want more of everything. The idea, therefore, being to compress the midrange frequencies more than you compress the highs and lows so that, as an instrument gets louder, the spectral balance remains pleasing. You can really just divide a lot of instruments into highs and lows then compress the highs one way and the lows another way. It's not always the mids that pop out, sometimes it's the highs and the mids. It's not universal. A typical application is a bass guitar. Every time a player goes up to the high strings, the bottom drops out, and every time they hit the low E, the thing just gets outrageously fat. It's annoying! You can't get a consistent low-end picture. So in my studio I have a crossover, which is like what you'd use for a public address system to separate the lows, mids and highs. I can either use it as a mono three-way or a stereo two-way. So the first thing I do when the bass leaves the tape deck is run it through the crossover, and then I run each of those signals, the highs and the lows, through their own compressor. Then I bring those up on the board so I have a high-end portion and a low-end portion. The advantage of using a crossover is that when they recombine, there's minimal overlap.

You don't have phase problems?
You have less phase problems.

So your crossover is pretty discerning?
I have one that has a pretty high slope... 24 dB per octave, which means that one octave away from the crossover frequency the signal is attenuated by 24 dB. In a normal mix this is inaudible. Some times a gentler slope is preferable. I have one of those too. But then you've got to choose the right compressor for the high-end and the low-end. Typically you want different compressors. The one that you're going to compress the low-end with has got to have much slower attack and release characteristics and be something that sounds punchy with low-end. Whereas the one for the high-end wants to have a lot faster response. I like the Urei 1178 for the low-end. But there are many that will work. You've just got to know your collection of compressors to make the right choice. Now let me give you another example of the power of this technique.

You sound like a barker.
[Laughs] It's the gong/kick drum sound, which you get if you put a nice coated Ambassador head on a kick drum, tune it so it rings and maybe play it with a mallet, sort of like a timpani. You know, you're doing a marching band kind of thing where you want a big "BOOM, BOOM, BOOM." But if you just put that in the mix and say, "I want some low-end on that thing," it just goes "wooom, wooom." It just clutters up your mix. So what you do is send it through a crossover. And then, because it's a drum, you gate it so that the high-end portion and the low-end portion have different release times. Then you compress them also, of course, to keep things in control. But you gate the low-end portion with a fast release time so the low-end is now going "wup, wup." But you leave the high-end gate open for a long time, maybe you don't even gate the high-end. Maybe you compress the hell out of it with a really fast-release compressor so that it accentuates the "kaaahhh" sound.

The tail of it?
The tail of it. If the compressor's release is really fast, it goes in and follows the tail down. In doing that you can get all of this personality, which is, in a drum like that, above 500 Hz. The "boom" is down below 200 Hz. I often end up crossing over around 200 Hz. Sometimes what I'll do with a bass guitar is record through an amp that is a little overdriven and fuzzy sounding, without much low-end, and also record a direct signal. Then, instead of taking just one of those and crossing it over, I'll take them both, cross them over at exactly the same point and use just the low-end from the direct signal and just the high-end from the amp. That way, not only do you have individual controls over the lows and highs, but the lows are clean and punchy and the highs are gritty and a little distorted, which makes them more interesting under a lot of conditions.

It gives you a lot more information up there.
Yeah, information! Like on the Nine Wood CD [two basses, drums and a vocal], it was crucial. On my first attempt to record those guys, I wanted high-end in the mix, but the high-end on the basses was all "ping, ping, ping". I wanted some "szhhh". So I tried a different approach and said, "Okay, you're going to play through this amp, and I'm going to turn it up so it's gritting out and then I'll record that on a track. I'm also going to have a direct box and a track where I'm recording your regular amps with more lower mids, so I'll have a few different degrees of edginess and distortedness and high-endiness. Then I'll recombine those as I mix it to get a nice full high-end, which is the hardest thing to get without a guitar." I realized that I sort of count on guitars to fill out the high-end of the spectrum. So with a band like Nine Wood, I needed to treat the basses more like guitars.

Do you ever do this with vocals?

No, I never do. I never have. I might some day. Vocals I consider much more of a voodoo area of recording. Basically, I've got my Neumann U87 and I've got my Urei 1176 and an old East-German tube mic, and, you know, you put them up and you hope for the best. You can reposition the mic, but if you try adding low-end with EQ, it can sound really bad. But that brings me to another thing that I do. It's called frequency-dependent compression or dynamic notch-filtering.

Frequency-Dependent Compression

There are only a couple of units on the market that do this, and they're not too popular because they're kind of complicated and confusing to use. The ones I have are the Urei LA22 and the Brook Sirens DPR901. These are compressors that will compress just a narrow band of frequencies. For instance, if a vocal is going to get piercing, it's usually going to be around 2.5K, 3K. So if you've got a problem, you just set this compressor for that little range, and then every time the vocalist honks in that range the honk, and only the honk, is pulled back. This allows you to really crank up the high-end on a vocal and get this really shimmery present tone, which is nice, but without getting so much piercing midrange.

Can you dial in more than one frequency?
With the Brook Sirens you can. It's got four separate bands, each with its own frequency, threshold and bandwidth. I usually use one band around 3K and another, to de-ess, at 9 or 10K. The only thing I don't like about the Brook Sirens is that it's a little slow. It's an excellent vocal box. If I want to do this type of compression with instruments, instead of vocals, I'll usually go for the LA22 because it's faster. But with the LA22, each channel just does one frequency. These are units with two channels, one frequency each. They're great for toms and kick drums if the player is using too much dynamic range. You can do normal compression, but you can't keep the hard hits from being really attack heavy. You've experienced this probably.

Oh, yeah!
You can compress the hard kick drum hits until they stay in one place, but then they go "ATTACK," and the soft ones are just "thump, thump" and you're going, "Jesus, this is frustrating!" So you can use the crossover technique to control the high and low-end independently. What I often do now is compress the whole kick drum and then run it through an LA22 just compressing the area from around 1K to 4K or 1K to 8K, all the attack areas. I hold those in place independent of holding the whole thing in place. Then if I want more high-end on the kick drum, I move the threshold up and if I want a little less, I move the threshold down. It really allows me to sit the kick drum right back in the mix. If you don't have one of these esoteric boxes, you can compress your kick drum as usual,

then cross it over at, say, 500 Hz, then run the highs through a second compressor. Since we're trying to affect the attack, we're going to need a very fast attack time. A much slower release time will help you avoid unwanted clatter. A SpectraSonics 610 would be my choice.

So are you doing a lot of this application during tracking?
No. This is all done during mixing.

Couldn't you do a light application while tracking, just to get your levels to the deck a little hotter.
That's true, I could. What do I do when I'm tracking? I always compress vocals. I always run them through the 1176, usually slow-attack, fast-release. What else do I compress to tape? I'll do some high-end percussion, like shakers and tambourine stuff, again with the SS610. I'll compress those just to tame the transients a little. For the most, part though, I don't compress things to tape. I just try to be careful to get the right levels. It always makes me uncomfortable to do too much as you're going down to tape because you're never quite sure what the mix is going to turn out like. So as much as I can, I focus on getting good sounds and then leave the rest of it for the mix.

That reminds me of some technical liner notes I just saw. They listed a couple of microphones, and then they asserted, "Individual microphone equalization is not permitted!"
There's this album by Jerry Garcia and David Grisman where they did the same thing, there was no EQ, just the mic. And of course, the Shellac [engineer Steve Albini's band] albums. He does all this stuff where he records right onto lacquer or whatever, the whole band with only four mics. But he does incredibly minimal processing.

He's also got a great collection of microphones.
He's got incredible stuff. And let's not forget that he's using certain kinds of natural compression. He's using old tube preamps that will compress a little bit, and he's using guitar and bass sounds that are distorted. Distortion is a kind of compression. So he says he doesn't use any compression, but it's sort of a question of semantics.

Yeah. Well I was just reading this article about getting, "in your face" mixes. They started off by knocking compression, but then they went on to say how much they use it in all these different ways. I think they were trying to warn against over doing it, because there is so much squashed stuff out there, but it came off kind of funny.
Would you say that my stuff sounds "in your face"?

Oh, yeah.
Good.

One of the things that really stands out about your recordings is that they are "in your face," but they're not painful, and they're also incredibly clear. A lot of people think that the way to achieve "in your face" mixes is through multiple sound sources and volume. A lot of current movies are like this. They're becoming cluttered and really loud in an attempt to overwhelm you, instead of through orchestration or by having a few choice things louder. It's a different issue, but I think it relates, because you're talking about delivering intense information and doing it in a way that's enjoyable to experience.
It's like being at the zoo and you have a lion there. If the lion is presented correctly you can get really close. You see the markings on its nose. You see its mouth full of teeth. You can really appreciate the lion without fearing that at any moment he's going to reach out and slash your face! That's sort of a mandate for me, especially for Idiot Flesh, since it's not easy music.

You mean it's not easy to get into because of the type of compositions?

Yeah. Compositionally it's not easy. And a lot of the sounds are basically harsh and nonmusical, at least not musical in the traditional sense.

It takes more than a few listens to absorb it.

Yes. And a lot of production to tame it. So for those albums, I've bent over backwards to make them friendly. I've really cut down on the dynamic range. The literal dynamic range is very small. But the dynamic range that you hear is implied through orchestration. I've done everything I can to make those records submit to the automobile test and stuff.* That music doesn't need any more strikes against it.

It's a wise way to go. It always makes me laugh when people go the lo-fi route, strictly out of rebellion. "Why should I have to bother to make it sound good?" I think very few people will tolerate, let alone enjoy, music that makes them wince.

Well, let's remember why we got into rock-n-roll in the first place. Rock music is a music that's about tone. You know, the feel of the music washing over you. You know, that's as important as composition and lyrical content. Teenagers like this music. You dig it because of the way it feels as it hits you, it's got this sound picture. Now that's ALL about production.

But for music that is more, I guess avant-garde... those artists usually can't afford to make it sound amazing. And that kind of music usually needs more care.

Right. That's one of the tragedies of economics.

Yeah. And then there are a lot of things out there that sound amazing but the music...

There's no content. I love working on pop music, but a lot of it is really insipid. I also end up recording a lot of punk bands. You learn a lot from having to record and mix an entire album in two days. My leaning, however, is toward more avant-garde artsy music with nonstandard sound sources and more involved compositions. I love the experimentation in trying to record a bucket of water or a squeaky guitar strap. Obviously, Einsteurtzende Neubauten [considered the beginning of industrial music by many] has been a big inspiration for me.

Poor Man's Automation

Oh! Here's a cool production move I just did. It was for this Ether [from Salt Lake City] song with a sort of cyclical drum beat. I took an extra track and put a test tone on it, a little blip, at beat one of every measure. Then I ran the room mic through a ducker**, heavily compressed, of course. I set up the ducker so that every time it detected the blip at the control/sidechain input it closed the gate. So at beat one the room mic would be almost off,

then during the rest of the measure it would fade up to full volume, and then at beat one again it would duck back. This way the whole drum mix would sort of rush toward you and then jump back.

Did you manually apply this blip through the whole song?

Yeah. I went through a couple of times, pushing the button on the tone generator until I got it just right. It's like a poor man's automation, which I do a lot of, recording control tones on empty tracks to trigger gates. It's just what I have available.

Well, you guys aren't doing anything digital, recording-wise.

Yeah. In fact, almost none of my current recordings have digital sound sources, no sampled sounds. I prefer chasing down the sounds on an actual instrument, even if it's available on a sampler. I just don't want that sampler around! It has so much more meaning for me if it comes from someone hitting something with a stick.

There are certain qualities to that that you'll never be able to replicate with a sampler. But how do you feel about sampling performances, rather than notes? If someone's struggling with playing a repeating pattern, they can play it once and then trigger it.

Yes, assuming that the tempo of the song remains constant. One of the things that has made me a good engineer is having to deal with players whose ideas are way ahead of their ability. I try to make them sound good. You learn a lot about dynamics processing. Some times you punch in every three notes.

Mixing

Do you have a favorite recording of yours?

Nine Wood is probably my best recent work. The mixes took four to eight hours each which was great. One of my pet peeves is bands that labor for days to get perfect performances and then expect me to mix ten songs in a day. I like to think of mixing as half the total studio time. My main criticism of the Nine Wood CD is that it may be a little bass heavy.

But it's only basses!

What I mean is, not so much bass guitar heavy but, spectrally low-end heavy. On some systems, if you turn the loudness on, it clouds a little bit. The place were it breaks down is on a fat stereo with the loudness on, or on nightclub stereos where the bass is pumped.

I really hate that exaggerated bass playback.

I do too, but you have to take that into consideration. I gave some high dollar albums a listen recently with that in mind, things like *Nevermind* [by Nirvana] and other modern pop. And I realized these things are all a little bass light to me. The conclusion is that a lot of people are mixing things with modest low-end, so when people turn it up it's there. But not so much that when people turn it up it's overwhelming. So I'm going to change my approach a little bit, and try and lighten my mixes up. You want to make it sound full. But a lot of people are going to leave their loudness on all the time. And I don't want things to fart-out under those circumstances. I think in the past I've subjected things too heavily to high volume listening. But the fact is 80 percent of your listeners are listening quite quietly.

You think?

Yeah. Really, how often do you listen to music really loud?

Well, I know better.

[Laughs] So this is another one of my new philosophies that I've adopted in the last six months: to really stress the sound picture at low volumes. If you make it sound perfect at high volumes, then at low volumes things sound dull. I've started mixing really quietly, almost annoyingly quiet. It really helps when you are mixing 14 hours at a stretch.

Have you had any trouble with bands wanting to rock out while mixing?

Yeah. I have to turn it up for them sometimes. But they understand. They're dealing with it and getting used to it.

I know some people end up mixing a little louder just to be able to hear what's going on above the control room chatter.

I know what you mean about that!

Have you ever had to send anybody out of the room?

Sometimes I have. Or sometimes, for a moment, I'll turn it up deafeningly loud to shut everyone up! [Laughter]

* The automobile test is just that, checking out your mixes on a car stereo. It gives you an example of what your mixes sound like in less than optimal conditions. Many studios have Auratone speakers for the same reason.

** A ducker is the opposite of a gate. When triggered, it will turn the output volume down on a signal. It's used a lot in radio so that DJs can talk over the beginnings of songs.

Dave Doughman

by Larry Crane

"Who the hell is Dave Doughman?" you might say. Well, I didn't quite know who he was until I stumbled across him running sound for Guided By Voices and Thomas Jefferson Slave Apartments on tour. In some ways, maybe, Dave's not a name you may have come across, but on the other hand he has worked with Kim Deal's Amps, has recorded demos for Robert Pollard, and has his own fine combo known as Swearing at Motorists. I just felt that our conversation touched upon a lot of the stuff of recording, and that Dave was another guy who had thought about this *Tape Op* stuff quite a bit. Enjoy.

How did you get into recording?

As a kid we had this little, flat Panasonic tape recorder. I would go around and make up songs. I would tape soundtracks off of television and then I'd listen to them. I would make up plays, like do *Star Wars*, on tape. But very few songs at first. Mostly I was using it to spy on people. I'd record something and listen to it later. I got into doing music from hanging out with bands. I had a Walkman with a good stereo microphone and I'd just find a good sweet-spot. It was an

Aiwa and I wish I still had it. It got the greatest sound. From that I went to 4-track. Then I went to the EVIL Full Sail Center for the Recording Arts.

You did?!! Oh my god. Elaborate please!

It's a lot of money and it's a good program, but in retrospect, I would have purchased a 4-track and saved myself $20,000. Here's the thing: There's nothing like walking in on your first day and being on a Neve console. But then again, you're not going to walk in on a Neve console out of school. Yeah, it's nice to learn on all the bells and whistles and to have the chance to see what it's like to record huge sounding stuff. I basically went there because I was really interested in doing it, and I had been doing it on 2 and 4-track, but I wanted to know all the laws and reasons and theories... so I could break them! And that's basically what happened. I went there and everyone that was there was either into hip-hop or metal and I was kind of into my own thing. Really into the Beach Boys, Neil Young, Guided By Voices and stuff. So I'm in there getting weird in a totally different way and they're going, "You can't do that. That's not the way it's supposed to be." I'm like, "But it sounds great." There's no rights or wrongs, there's just good and bad.

Did the instructors really tell you...?

There were times where they were, "Well, that's just not the way we do it."

But if you're achieving an end...

They didn't understand the times where I wanted to overload a channel on the board to rip the vocals up. "You're distorting!" "I know. Thanks! If you want to give me a preamp I can rip up instead of the board preamp I'd be more than happy to, but that's the sound I want." It really helps when you get to understand how frequencies work with each other. That is insane. A lot of people don't realize how muddy their tapes get because there's too much in there. If you would just EQ in the negative a little bit. Just take a little bit out here and there. That's all you have to do. I rarely ever add on EQ, but I love to take things out. That frequency may not be something that's all that great about that instrument, but it washes out the part that is great about another instrument. Toms and bass drums - I do it all the time. Upper range vocals and guitar. Snare and guitar. There's different places where they overlap. You really have to get in there and make room at times. If you have time, whether it be because you're doing it at your house or you're doing it in a studio where there's more budget, money wise. Ideally, you'll move your microphones until you've done it. Sometimes people will look too much at one thing. "We have to get the snare just right." Put the guitar in and pop the EQ in and out and see whether you like it better or not. It may not have any effect. You may sit there and tweak on a frequency that's buried by the guitar. You always gotta look at the big picture. How's this gonna sound at the end? Think about it. "I want this, in itself, to be a really good sound." How's it gonna sound with everything else? You don't want it to sound layered; you want it to sound like it happened all at once. That's the hardest thing. It's like this live thing; explaining to the guys that you really need to turn down so I can make it louder.

So you're doing sound on this tour. That sounds like fun.

It is fun. It's a challenge going into a different room every night.

Are you bringing any stuff with you?

I brought no gear. We have a tech rider, and every place pretty much has what we ask for. You walk in, you don't know what the mics are, but you know you're gonna get one of three or four different units. The boards are different everywhere. One night you're reaching down here for the pan and the next night that's not the pan, it's the gain. Soundcraft boards have the gain right above the fader where most boards have it at the top. On top of theirs is the pan.

I try to avoid doing live sound as much as I can. It's hard.

It's way hard and it burns your ears. I like Bob and the band a lot. Any opportunity to work with them is great. We just recorded some demos that went really well at my house. Bob and I recorded 25 songs in ten hours.

He said he had a bunch of stuff.

He came over to the house at noon and at ten o'clock he left my house with a tape of 25 songs. It's incredible. The guy's no joke. He just sits down and bangs them out. He wrote 16 of the songs in one day.

Were they just guitar and vocal?

Yeah, guitar and vocal. I play the e-bow guitar on one track but that's it. Some guitars we'd do a couple of tracks.

So you worked with the Amps a little bit?

I recorded some stuff on the Amps' record, *Pacer*.

Where were you doing that?

We did that at Cybertechnics in Dayton, Ohio. That's the place that Kim [Deal] and I did the Brainiac *Internationale* EP.

How did you get into all that?

Timmy Taylor [of Brainiac] is my roommate and I'd been working around town doing records and stuff with different people. The Brainiac thing they wanted to record with a few different people and it kept falling through. It makes me sound real bad but it's the truth. The deadline for that single was creeping up and their first choice, Albini, was booked. So Tim's like, "Hey, do you and Kim want to do it?" and I'm like, "Yeah, sure." That's the first time I ever worked with Kim. Now, being a small town and everyone in town has jammed and hung out and 4-tracked with each other, but that's the first time that we officially worked together. Most of our first record was recorded at her house.

What's it called?

Swearing at Motorists. Myself and Don Thrasher. We 4-tracked a lot of stuff off of that in Kim's basement when the Amps were in Europe that year. They were finishing the record in Ireland and we were using their gear.

I heard she had a home studio of some sort...

She has two 4-tracks. She has a monitor system, like a little PA that she uses for monitors, and then she has all their stage gear, in the basement. It sounds cool down there.

What studios are there in Dayton?

I would say for certain, and this is gonna hurt some feelings, the number one studio in Dayton is definitely Cybertechnics. The guy who runs it is just nuts. If you can deal with Phil, it's $35 an hour and you've got 2" 24-track and you can even go down to 16-track if you want a fatter sound.

Does he switch out heads?

Yeah. He's got 1" 4-tracks. He's got all the vintage gear you want. He even has an electric harpsichord. It's got a nice big room and the isolation rooms are really nice. His board is really clean. You get a nice warm sound. He has a great mic selection so you're able to use anything you want. You can put tube mics on drums if you want. If you break it you pay for it, but he's not afraid to let you use it. That place is number one. I always liked Cro-Magnon because of the room. They don't have analog... they only have digital, the ADAT. You could always take your own machine in there. Houses though, you can't beat. I've recorded a bunch of different seven inches and full lengths out of my basement and living room. You get a good sounding room and people that can play their instruments and it's not that hard. Then just pay attention. The real cool thing about 4-track is you need to take a lot of time doing it and I think 4-tracking has made me a way better studio engineer. You've taken so much time to find out how to do something at your house that when you get there, to the big studio, you kind of know what kind of things are gonna pop up. You have all the time in the world, at home, to fiddle around with mic placement and placing the amps differently or where you put the drums in a room. Even like when you're singing; maybe standing closer to a wall or laying on the floor. Weird shit like that. Then, when you get into a studio, you have that groundwork already laid out. When you want certain sounds you already know where to go for it. The other thing is... once you start taking that much time with it, you can make 4-track stuff sound better than 4-track "quality." You'd be hard pressed to make someone believe that it's a full-blown 24-track studio but no one would ever guess it was 4-track. A lot of the Swearing at Motorists you'd never know. A lot of it, you could tell it was 4-track, but some of the other stuff doesn't sound like four at all. It sounds like at least an 8 or 16. That all comes from listening. Less is more, definitely. Ideally, if you could use one microphone to record everything at once it'd be perfect. My ideal drum setup is two microphones.

Where at?

Basically, I like to hang one, either a 57 or a condenser, about 6 inches above where the drummers head would be and out, a little bit over the snare so it's in front of what he's hearing. Let it point straight down. The other one is really strange. You go about two feet out from the kick but in between the kick and the first rack tom. Point it at a slanted angle so it's shooting towards your rack tom. So what's happening is you're getting the kick blowing across the mic and you're getting the top with the other. The easiest and hardest thing to do is think about a microphone as an ear. Would you listen to a guitar with your fuckin' ear right up on it? But then again, if you don't put the mic right up on it, you might get a little too much space. That's why it's nice to be able to record with more than one mic on things like guitars. You can get one thing really close, to get your attack and your drive, and then you can put one mic further back to get the room sound and capture the actual depth and the sound of the instrument... where you would hear it as a real person.

Do you do that on 4-track stuff? Do you mix it in a mixer to tape?

I have a Porta 2, which is basically a Porta 1 with two extra inputs, so you have six inputs to four channels at once. What I'll do is I'll take something really close, put that way down in the mix and even EQ out some of the low end of it. All I want is the bite and the push. Then use the room mic to get more of a full sound. It also depends on what you're doing too, but I'm really into natural sound. I would much rather spend an hour moving a mic around than getting one basic sound and then EQing it. I use very little EQ and when I do it's very deliberate. The first thing I do is go in and listen to the band and listen to how they're playing right there live. Then thinking, "How can I make it sound like that on tape?" Then, if anyone wants to do anything weird with effects, you do it from there.

That's a good thing to have, a grounding, as far as what things sound like to you.

That's another thing about going to a studio that sucks. You're getting that engineer's perception of what your drum and guitar sound is. You're just another guy on his schedule. That's not slagging him; that's the truth. He's gonna go for what he knows, not what the band needs. Sometimes that's good 'cause the band doesn't really know and they'll go to a place and kind of get

straightened out. That's another thing about the home recording thing is that you get so accustomed and so comfortable with what you're doing that you just do it.

I think a lot of times that a band might have a certain charm, and they go and record somewhere and the guy has no idea what the "good' aspects of the band are. It might not even be anything musical, but even just the personalities that carry across in the way they play. It's so hard to convey that when you start setting up a band to record and make them sound "clean". I find that a lot... and I'll just have to backtrack. Like using just overheads on somebody's drums if they can't play, and make it feel more like a practice tape.

Drums are hard to fool. Live and on tape.

There's no such thing as a perfect kick drum mic.

It's all in using big diaphragm microphones really far away.

I've been using an RE 20.

Those are the standard, but I'm talking about U 87's. I like to put the big Neumanns or Telefunken tubes up there, but it's hard to find places that'll let you do that!

Tiny Telephone

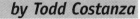

by Todd Costanza

mk ultra

TINY TELEPHONE

the dream is over

TINY TELEPHONE

Tiny Telephone is a studio set up by John Vanderslice, a former member of MK Ultra. Todd Costanza is a member of Granfalloon Bus and interviewed John. Oh yeah, Todd's also the brother of David Costanza ["The Barn"]. Read on...

John, I've heard you play quite a few times over the years and I've heard your recordings. I think you have a definite sound, that you know what you're going for, you know what you want. If I'm correct in saying there is a sound that you're after, what albums do you have that typify that sound?

David Bowie's *Diamond Dogs*, which is a fairly experimental record. I think he did it in 1974. A wide range of sounds – it's kind of out of genre, you know, it really shifts. There's even hints of disco, like in the song "1984." Many original sounds and textures, many acoustic instruments treated with effects or distorted. That appeals to me. And the underpinning is hi-fi. It's a good sounding record; the drums, the bass, everything sounds natural and real, and that's a key for me, that it has to start out hi-fi. I don't mind if the recording or the mix is pushed in a lo-fi direction, meaning maybe everything is heated up through a preamp or distorted, or kind of crunched through a compressor. I don't mind that as long as the signal starts out hi-fi and the initial sounds are good. I think on all the early '70s Bowie stuff they started out with great sounds and then really pushed it in the mix.

In terms of fidelity, I was going to bring up the supposed lo-fi thing that's going on. To me it seems like sort of a marketing scheme, because when I hear it I think of musicians working within their means. You have so much money to work with, you make an album and then somebody hears it and they call it lo-fi.

It's a cover up, isn't it? I mean people are afraid, and they're rightly afraid of being overproduced. The thing is that many bands have no control over their sound or their recording because they don't know enough, and everyone falls into that. I mean, it took me ten years of fidgeting around with microphones and guitars to wake up and start to listen to initial sounds. It takes a long time to learn it, and I think, just like it's against [a musician's natural instinct] to deal with money and the business side of it, it's also against a musician's kind of natural intuition to be too obsessed with tones and recording techniques. So the default is lo-fi, because then you don't have to be embarrassed about making an overproduced or slick record. But really, the best thing is for a band to have enough experience in recording, like you guys, you know. You've been in the studio, you know engineers, and you pay attention to what engineers are doing. So if you work with a particular engineer you're not going to be surprised at the sounds they are getting. You'll know that that's a fit for you. In your case Granfalloon Bus works with Greg Freeman and that's a perfect match. Many bands hook up with engineers not really thinking about what kinds of sounds the engineers are going to get for them. It's more of a personal connection. I think that the best thing for any band is to start out listening to their guitars, listening to their amps. Actually getting down and sitting in front of their amps and listening to their signal. That's really... that is rare. It took me six years. And finding out about equipment... You know, I had an Ampeg VT40 amp for five years, and I was embarrassed, I thought Ampeg was just some dumb company. So I put a sticker over the Ampeg logo. It wasn't until I got a good guitar that I realized that the amp was actually fantastic and that it was this classic '78 Ampeg VT40 tube amp, and then I kind of started fooling around with the EQ on it. You know, just fooling around: "What happens if I use this 20 dB cut?" "Well, it destroys your signal." So then I decided just to run it at 0 dB, no cut off, no roll off. Anytime you roll off anything on a mic or an amp you might cause trouble, you know. So I sat down in front of my amp and realized that I had a really good amp, but that my settings were poorly chosen.

We went a little astray there...

Sorry, that's me. [laughs]

I guess what I'm trying to find is the difference with a lo-fi band, someone like Pavement, who's considered a lo-fi band, they come out with a new album, spend more money on it, and then you hear people say, "Oh, it's too slick." So

if you're the engineer or if you're the musician, what does "too slick" mean to you, how do you avoid it?

Well, I think that it's signal processing that makes records sound too slick. I think adding delay and reverb and chorus, in the mix, especially, I think that if you're just going straight to tape... Let's say you have the best of everything. Let's say you have a brand new Studer 24-track. You have extremely good preamps, and good compressors and you just run your signal direct to tape without fooling around with aural exciters or any other B.S., that you do no EQing. If you bring that stuff straight to tape, get a good drum sound and then mix it back, get a rough mix of everything without processing anything, adding no reverb, adding no EQ, or very minimal EQ, maybe EQing the kick and snare to tape, but maybe that's all you need to EQ. If you have good guitars and good amps, and you choose your mics well, you won't need to EQ guitars. And the same with bass. If you bring that stuff up, do a rough mix without adding any effects; I think it would be impossible to find a slick recording there. It just won't happen. What happens is an engineer will compress an overall mix. That's a fast way to make things sound real radio and slick. It takes out all the rough spots, which can be good, but if you over-compress it just makes everything soft and in the pocket. And adding reverb on drums and reverb and delay on vocals. Very quickly these effects add up and put a cushion between the ear and the band. And it makes it soft.

So there's a fine line between lush and shit.

Oh yeah. Generally I like everything close mic'd and with very little effects, but with the initial signal there, so you hear a drum and it's a kick drum and it's a snare and it's a drum set in a room and you can feel it. But I think that that's a way to avoid slickness.

Now that you're starting the studio, what does technology offer that could really work now for continuing with analog recording but including digital?

Just right now, the state of digital, where it is right now, I wouldn't touch it. I wouldn't record using a digital deck and I wouldn't record using a digital board. I also wouldn't do any editing with Pro Tools. That's my personal, intuitive feel, and digital people would certainly argue with me, but that's fine, that's why I've got my own studio. Our thing is that we're in 1973; we have a deck from '73 and we have a board from '75. You could stop at '73 and just have gear, that's in good shape, made before '73 and you could make the best sounding records, if you had the money. And that's a long process of buying gear, but I think that, just from my experience, I would avoid going to digital until you make a 1630, which is the tape you send into the CD manufacturer to make a glass master from. Or the CD-R. In other words, I would absolutely avoid going to digital until that point. I personally prefer vinyl. Our next record is going to be pressed to vinyl and CD. I like vinyl, but if a CD is recorded in analog, mixed in analog and is well mastered and not fooled around with too much in the mastering process, in the digital realm, then it can sound great. It really can sound very good. So I'm not totally anti-digital, but I would say that you absolutely, 'til the last second, have to stay in analog. And I've never, honestly never, heard a good ADAT recording in my life. We had ADATs for three years and it's a long... it's like coming out of the closet. It's like waking up. You have to face the music that you hate digital, but if you've invested money in it it's very hard.

You did your early albums in digital, right?

Well, we did our first CD in a mixture of 8-track tapes and ADATs. And I wasn't happy with it, definitely. The second CD we decided to record at Dancing Dog and they had a 1" 16-track and about $100,000 worth of vintage gear. It was owned by Dave Bryson of the Counting Crows. He had a tremendous amount of old vintage gear that he was just stockpiling.

I want to switch over to how you record as a band. Let's say there's a continuum going from completely live, just mic'ing everything, even though they're on separate tracks or whatever, and just playing live. Say that's one extreme. And the other extreme is say, just setting a click track and doing one instrument at a time and doing everything piece by piece. Where is your preference and where do MK Ultra fit in that.

Well, for the second record, *Original Motion Picture Soundtrack,* we isolated everything. We stood in one room, but the two guitar amps were in different rooms and the bass amp was direct. We had a DI signal only. The drums were recorded in a very small room, a very dry room, and we didn't use a click track on anything, but we were going for a very separate feel. No bleed whatsoever. So on this CD we decided, "Well, why don't we stand in a room. Let's not use headphones, let's just have our amps and have a little bit of bleed. We'll use baffling, but we'll do, you know, what Led Zeppelin used to do. They'd just sit in a room. They'd use some baffles. They'd use small amps, generally, and we'll deal with the bleed later and we'll play live. We're not going to worry about mistakes, we're not going to do punch-ins, and we're just going let the tape roll. But we're going to make sure we borrow a lot of gear, get really good microphones in here and get everything just direct to tape sounding good. And we'll deal with it later." That's what we did and I think that it's good, but there are limitations to it also. I think it's a good way to work, but on a CD you might want to have different sounds. I think it would be great to have a click going and have the drummer play alone. Do some kind of inventive baffling. You know maybe putting a mic behind a baffle so you're getting the refraction of the drum off of a wall. That might be a half a second delay, who knows, depending on how big your room is. Maybe just have the drummer play and have things added on later. I think that it's good to mix it up. I regret now that we didn't mix it up, but you don't always have enough time.

Mix it up from song to song within an album.

Yeah.

Yeah, I agree with that.

I think it's really important to mix it up.

Last time I was in here we were talking about the direction of this studio and you referred to it as a guerrilla studio.

It definitely started out as a guerrilla studio. Meaning you just come in here and do fast and cheap recording and it's exposed drywall, it wasn't clean, and probably your playing and recording would reflect that, you know. You just come in here. You wouldn't worry about much. That's when we had ADATs in here and it was pretty much a demo studio. Then last year we went to a Bay Area studio, a 24-track 2" studio, and we actually got some money from Discovery and Adam from the Mommyheads produced a demo of ours.

What's Discovery?

They're a Warner label. So, we got some money and we felt pretty snazzy, you know, and of course you're going to get mowed down whenever you feel snazzy. So we went to this studio and it was pretty expensive but we bargained on the rates; they were slow. We brought our own engineer, and we made the worst recordings we've ever made in our lives. We were pretty confident. We felt you can't go wrong. You go into a big studio, sure, you know, but the vibe wasn't quite right and who knows what was going on with the board and the wiring... They were worse recordings than the demos we were making in here, as far as feel and even sonically they were dismal.

Was it a $1000-a-day studio?

It was about $350 without engineer.

What made it dismal?

I think there was something in the chain, possibly the board, in the signal chain that was just screwy.

Did you say the name of the studio? Are we allowed to?

No, I can't because I want to bash it even more. [laughter] But anyway, I decided at that point, after we got these recordings and dropped $3,500 for three days or four days of recording, that I was going to have to control the recordings. This was the first idea I had. I thought I really should convert the studio I had, which is really just a 17,000 square foot warehouse that is not even complete, not even built yet. That I should borrow some money and complete it and have a place for my own band, MK Ultra, to do recording in, because we were getting ready to make a new recording. So that was my initial impulse, after going to another studio and getting burned and going, "Shit, I 'd rather be in my own place and know the walls, know the room, know the board, know the deck and own it. And that way, maybe when we get some more money from a label, we're not going to piss it away. It's actually going to go into our own pockets." There were many precursors, you know. Kyle, from Fuck, who opened his own studio, that was certainly in our mind. We thought, "Look at these people. They're controlling their own recordings and they're putting their money into actual capital." It's stuff that generally, if they choose wisely, it's going to appreciate. So that was the immediate impulse, to convert this place from, at that point, just a guerrilla studio. We borrowed some money and bought an old Ampex MM1000, which was Greg Freeman's, the same deck that Greg Freeman had at Lowdown. It's the best 16-track ever made. It's the one, you know. You can pick one up for $3,000. People are going out and spending $4,000 or $5,000 on ADATs and they can go and get an 850lb analog deck that's the shit. It's the one. It's the best. Many, many techs and engineers will say it's the best sounding analog deck ever made. And it certainly was responsible for every multitrack recording from '68 to '73, you know. So we bought a few choice, kind of antiquated pieces of gear

that no one wanted anymore because big studios have to have new gear and most smaller studios are going digital or buying smaller stuff.

So a bad experience in a "good" studio turned you out on your own here and now it looks like you are going to be recording other bands as well, besides MK Ultra. What are you going to do in here to give it a feel where a band can come in, maybe a band you like, someone who is local, and give them the confidence and feel to put out a good album.

Well, there are two things for us. One is to have very good hi-fi or near hi-fi gear here for people to access. We generally just go direct to tape, very little EQing, we try to use good microphones, we have two Neumann M582 tube mics. They're small diaphragm, all-purpose mics. We use them as drum overheads. We encourage people to borrow microphones, like when Granfalloon Bus was in here you guys borrowed the C12A, and there you have three great tube microphones that can be responsible for 80% of your signal on the record. You know, you're doing all your vocals, acoustic guitar, drum overheads, which is most of the drum sound. And good mic pre's.

What are your mic pres?

We have the Neve 1272s, which are pretty much the poor man's Neve modules that you can get from Brent Averill, who's in Sherman Oaks, CA. They're $1500 a pair. They're great. They're fantastic. I mean, if you can't get a good tone out of there you are in trouble, you know. You better just get out of town.

You're getting a new board...

Yeah. It's a Quantum AudioArts board from 1976. It was hand built. It's a 31 x 8 board. It's actually a quadraphonic board. It was made for quadraphonic recordings. It came from Studio 55 in Los Angeles. A big mainstream studio. At the time it was a primo boutique board, it's discrete mic pres, very good Neve-style usable EQs, four band parametric, all the way to 20,000 cycles. I mean, you've got to love that.

Who advised you on this board?

Well, I actually talked to a number of people about the board. The first thing I did after finding out it was for sale was I got the number of the engineer that worked at Studio 55 on the board for 12 years. His name is Gabe Veltree. And he had no financial interest in talking to me about the board. He has no financial connection to whether the board is sold or not, so I knew he was a totally disinterested third party. So I just called him and said, "This board you used to work on is for sale through a third person, and what do you think of the board? You worked on it for 12 years." He's a big name guy.

You just rang him up?

I just called him up. On a Sunday. That's pretty ballsy. Anyway, he was incredibly nice to me, and he vouched for the board. He said "$7000 is a steal, you should grab that thing. It's a great board. We did so many records on that thing." Twelve years he worked on that thing. He did the first Tom Petty record, he did Pointer Sisters, like "He's So Shy," "I'm So Excited," Barbara Streisand, a bunch of stuff.

There'll be ghosts in that board.

There are going be ghosts in that board. Barbara's going to be fucking screaming in that board: "Get me my coffee!" So, that's the idea. What you want to do is call up like a 50 or 60-year-old engineer whose been working for forty years, you know, maybe he's mastered records at CBS, maybe he's worked at Ocean Way. Find out the pros and just say, "Hey, I'm a young guy and I need some advice." They will keep you on the phone longer than you want to stay on the phone, because they are just impressed that anyone cares anymore and that you respect them. So that's what I did. Just called up local people. Steven Jarvis. Engineers. John Croslin, who recorded Spoon, he's a brilliant engineer. He did Spoon's *Soft Effects* EP, which, if anyone hasn't heard that, sonically it's totally original. It's a very,

very good recording. I called up these engineers and I said "Tell me, what do you use, what kind of mics, what kind of compressors, what kind of mic pres." The same stuff comes up. Urei 1176s. Summit tube pres and compressors. Manley. Same kind of gear. Neumann tube mics, you know, pre-'74.

You said you called up Dan Alexander as well.

Called up Dan Alexander. He's the owner of Coast Recorders.

I just brought him up because I've been to his studios and seen his stuff and he kind of has a warehouse full of this gear like you are talking about. He's a wheeler dealer.

He buys and sells gear and he will talk to you. He will tell you what he knows, and that's good, you know.

But he told you something.

Oh, "Go digital." He said, "Go digital." Well, you know...

Does he mean either you have to have half a million dollars or go digital? What was his point with that?

Well, his point was that he didn't think it was worth it for a young studio to buy an old Ampex deck because there's upkeep on the deck and it's funky. It's not punch-in friendly, which I personally like. I think that anything that discourages bands from doing punch-ins is good. Including vocal takes. I think that you really should rethink the idea of punching in parts and making every word perfect. I think that's a major, major mistake. So he wants to do digital editing. He wants crystal clear recording. See, all the problems with analog are actually, and people should realize this, all the problems with analog are the best things about analog. Noise. The suppression of high end and the multiplication of low frequencies, not to mention tape compression, which is everything. You compress to tape and it's some of the best compression you can get. It's very smooth and natural and subtle and it keeps everything in line.

You mentioned it discourages punch-ins, but it seems kind of studio standard to have someone do 100 vocal takes. I was just hearing this from Adam of the Mommyheads. Do a bunch of takes and then piece the whole thing together.

Well, I'm trying to get the Mommyheads in here to do their next record and I'd love to see Adam try and punch-in on this deck.

I agree with you on that. If you can't sing the song all the way through then get out of the studio. [laughter]

Well, in the end it's all personal preference. It's not like I'm going to challenge someone to a duel if they want to do 100 vocal takes. But just for me, personally, I found it to be a revelation when I had to keep continuous takes down and not fool with them and then you come to the studio the next day and everything sounds good again. It's like, "Wow. You know, there's something about this mistake here that's very, very pleasant." And if you take out all the mistakes, just like with digital, the whole thing with digital is it's mistake-free, you can put that thing up on the Mac and hack those tracks to death, you know, and it's lifeless.

I love mistakes. We had a great one here when we were recording. The Blue Angels. Did you hear that on the track?

Yeah, the Blue Angel jets come right in at the end of the song. The Blue Angels are Navy fighter pilots who fly over San Francisco. So that bled on the microphone when Granfalloon Bus were recording in here.

Of course that's not a mistake of analog.

But it's a state of mind to be open to that. So yeah, I think anything that discourages punch-ins and encourages takes as they are is good. That's my stand.

That's good. I hope you carry that on here.

Yeah, we will.

So are you in a desperate business state where you'll do anybody's demo or are you trying to hand pick some bands to come in here? What do you hope for?

Our whole thing was that this was our rehearsal hall before it was our studio. We still rehearse here. The rent is low. It's rent controlled. We decided that the studio was never going to be seen as a money making venture, that's a major mistake and it's going to make everyone neurotic. So we decided to borrow some money. We'll charge pretty low rates and we won't look for business. We're never going to advertise. It's word of mouth. We've been discouraging people recently because it's been too busy and also we're trying to finish our record. So that takes up a lot of time. But the goal right from the start was to have house engineers. Greg Freeman, primarily, is our house engineer. I wooed him. I mean, in a way, this place was built to woo him over here. So Greg Freeman, Damian Rassmussen, who used to manage Dancing Dog and work there, and did our second record. Two very, very good engineers. Also, Rick Stone, another good engineer who used to work at Dancing Dog. Those are the three engineers who work here.

Do you encourage bands to bring other engineers in?

Actually, we probably won't. I'm not even sure if we will allow it, at this point. I don't want a lot of people passing through here. The gear is relatively delicate, you know. We'd rather keep it down to being blocked out 15 days a month and having all the engineers, who we know, have keys to the place. We're friends with them, we've known them for years and we know they're responsible. It's going to be kind of a family affair. And we do really hand pick bands that come in. If we like a band we will approach them and say, "Listen, we'll cut you a deal, we'd like to be part of your next recording," as in the case of Granfalloon Bus. There's been many other bands that we've encouraged to come in here. The Keeners, Action Slacks, a whole bunch. The Mommyheads right now. Engine 88, you know. We got them to do almost a CDs worth of material in here. That was great for me. So yeah, we're going to be hand picking bands and probably discouraging bands that we don't know from coming in here, just because it's going to be too busy as it is.

That's good. I'm happy for you. Let's just do one last thing. We've talked before about headphone treats, a personal favorite of mine, for the stoners who like to put on the headphones and go, "Wow". Do you have any good headphone treat ideas?

Well, I think that I rely on nonstandard instruments, generally, for those kind of sonic treats. We have a Moog Source, which is the first programmable Moog. It's a very simple, late Moog synth. You can pick one up for $500. If you ever find one, buy it. They're incredible. Two oscillators and a noise generator. You can make some incredible tones with that synth. We wrote a lot of patches on that and it has an incredible range. You can get very high tones and very low tones and if you mix them down very low and you pan them you can barely hear them.

Until you put them on headphones, then they're there. Also, we have a very early Roland guitar synthesizer that we use a lot, and again, you can make sounds that are totally original. Tones that you've never heard before. We use a lot of samples. I've sampled a lot from classical CDs, like early 20th century Schoenberg and Weburn and a lot of Hafler Trio. I probably shouldn't say this, but a lot of more avant-garde, experimental cut and paste music. And then we drop those samples in more as kind of a texture feel. Can I add, and this isn't really a sonic treat, but the one thing that I've discovered in the past two weeks, that's been the most important discovery for me personally? It's not my idea; it was suggested to me by Brent Averill, who sold us the Neve 1272 mic pres. The idea is to put the whole mix directly through the 1272s. Up the gain, lower the output and get a little bit of amp distortion. This is when you're mixing down, instead of compressing, to warm up the signal. I have to say that this is the sound I was looking for my whole life. It's that kind of crunched, heated, and slightly broken up sound that I've been looking for. Talk about getting away from overproduced.

You put anything through 1272s and crunch them hard and they will begin to sound, well, slightly metallic, crunchy...

Does it take away the dynamic range?

It does. It compresses. As you know, compression is distortion. If you're getting some distortion you will be compressing, but sometimes you have to compress a bit to get everything in line. But you can always back up from the gain, and it was the sound, it was what I was looking for. It converted some good recordings into something that I would feel comfortable mixing direct to a disc.

So you've found the exact sound you're looking for.

Yeah. Totally.

You can quit now.

Yeah, I can quit. I'm just going to do that for every damn song we do. It's amazing what it does. It tightens up everything. The kick and the low end, everything comes together. And in a way it makes everything more monochromatic and unidimensional, but in a good way. In the end it makes the sound more focused. It's a trick. It's worth spending $1500 to get two of those things.

So are the kids allowed to try this at home?

Yeah, it's the way. It's the thing to do.
Tiny Telephone 415-695-9288

www.tinytelephone.com

Darron Burke

SLEPT AND THE COLD ROOM...

by David Ackerman

From 1992 to 1997 Darron Burke's Cold Room Studio was a haven for young Boston bands. Many singles came out of his 8-track room like Cardinal [featuring Richard Davies and Eric Matthews], Gigolo Aunts, Sugar Plant (from Japan), Lou Barlow, and Kudgel [purveyors of "chimp" rock]. A collector of weirder recording equipment, Darron owns an original Studer J-37 1/2" 4-track from the Beatles *Sgt. Pepper's* era and the Troisi mixing board that recorded George Thorogood's *Bad to the Bone* LP. Darron is currently constructing a 1960's style studio just outside of Boston and plays drums for Ultrabreakfast.

Dave Ackerman's history includes recording and mixing the Lyres, The Allstonians, African pop star Tabu-Ley Rochereau, Derrick Morgan (1960s Jamaican singer) and The Diary of Anne Frank String Quartet. Dave works at Harvard Universities Music Library as an audio preservation engineer where he restores old recordings using Sonic Solutions No Noise processing. Over the last few years Dave has been providing mastering services for clients in his home studio, which is based around a TDM Pro Tools system.

What follows is an informal self-interview between Dave and Darron about the recording and subsequent mastering of a full length CD, *Guy Trapped in a Situation*, by the Boston band Slept.

Darron: Rolling? I'm shy, can you turn this off?

Dave: Darron Burke doesn't like being on the mic. Huh? That's not true, right?

Yeah, but only in falsetto, aaahhhhhh. [in a heavy metal shriek]

Who is Slept?

Slept is a 3 piece band; bass, drums and guitar originally from Little Rock, Arkansas. The guitarist, Aaron Sarlo, used to be in a band called Technosquid Eats Parliament, the drummer is Phil Ouellette and the bass player is known as "The Chris" Schutte. They're a young band, they don't have that much money but they had a friend named Terry who is a fan of the band and she gave them five thousand dollars. They actually had planned to do the record before they had the money but she really got things going. I had done stuff with Slept on 8-track a couple of times in my old studio [The Cold Room] before it closed down. We did a session in the middle of winter once and we were heating the studio with a Coleman stove.

And how did that work out?

The room was full of fumes but we could make tea all day. There were a lot of jokes about marshmallows and hot dogs.

Now, isn't Slept the fire starting band?

Yeah. Every time I record Slept, something catches on fire. I had a tube mic pre that I built and I hooked up the power supply wrong. It just started smoking and going crazy. It turned out only to be a resistor so I easily got it working again. Another time we used a weird mic pre-thing I got at the MIT flea market and smoke was seen on that occasion as well. While tracking this record, we were trying out some Event 20/20 powered monitors; I was blasting them pretty loud to see what they could do and one of them started smoking and burning. Event was pretty cool and shipped us out another pair.

So were you excited to make a full length record with Slept?

I always saw them as a creative band, but I wasn't completely happy with the stuff we had done in the past. I thought Phil's drums were kinda sloppy, Chris was playing too many bass chords, and Aaron didn't always have the lyrics ready and was writing them in the studio. I saw this as a chance to make it up. I always wanted just a little more refinement out of them. When they said, "let's make a record," I explained to them that I was going to kick their asses! We were going to work really hard... I wanted to get some really good drums down on tape, to get tight bass parts... I just wanted everything to be in place and thought out. I decided to take a free day at Supersonic Studio [where I worked for a year and a half], to do a pre-production tape. We recorded live-to 2-track so we could to listen to the songs and also they could get a sense of the new studio since we were going to be spending a lot of time there.

When they heard the playback they were like... "Why do we need to do anything more? This could be our record!" And I was like, "No no no no!" [laughs] Because I knew they were capable of so much more. There were 3 songs that I really liked ["Radio Death Gear", "I H8 The Dead" and "Apollo"], and there were other songs that were good, but honestly they sounded like filler at the time.

It certainly didn't come out sounding like filler. It really stands up and holds its own in my opinion. Do you have any stories to tell about tracking the album?

The first day was devoted to getting sounds. I didn't want to proceed until we got the drums right. I just couldn't get a bass drum sound. We had brand new heads and it was a 20" bass drum, but it wasn't happening. I'd get a sound and on loud hits it would totally glitch out and sound like this clicky smack. It was awful, with no tone and no thump. We tried everything: combinations of mics near the head, away from the head, we moved it across the room, cement floor, wood floor... nothing. So, we went down the hall to the Gigolo Aunts space to borrow Fred's bass drum, but we ended up taking the whole kit. It's an old Ludwig swirly-look. I've seen pictures of Ringo using them. That was the magic bass drum! It sounded great with one AKG D-112 just outside of the hole. The rest of the drums were mic'd with 57s and Peavey (PVR-1) omni cardioid mics for overheads. They are cool. They capture the room in addition to the direct sound. I got frustrated trying to get a good room mic set up that day, but the bleed through the scratch vocal mic sounded pretty cool, so I used that in a couple of final mixes. We recorded bass, guitar, drums and scratch vocals live. I had the bass amp isolated in a small room. We used an Ampeg B-12 Flip-top tube amp and a Precision bass. We tracked "Apollo" at the end of the first day and it was slow going and nervy. We were starting with, to me - the most important song on the record... maybe that was a mistake. It was a 12 hour day. AHHH, day one! We spent 4 full days tracking, took a break, and then spent 4 more days for overdubs. From this point it all becomes a blur, but recording and mixing took at least 16 full days. There's one song where I suggested a kick drum pattern because I thought it fit more with the bass. Phil used it in the first part of the song and it worked. Later, when we were overdubbing the guitars, I was saying to Aaron, "Hey you're not playing it the same way you did in the first chorus." We'd go through the part and punch the guitar, and then I realized it wasn't him, it was the kick drum. Phil had forgot to play that pattern in the second part of the song and it really made a difference in the feel.

Which song was that?

[sings a bit trying to remember] "Bring Back GKW." [The song title refers to the episode of "The Simpsons" when Groundskeeper Willie got deported as an illegal alien.]

Did you guys go back and fix the kick drum?

Nope. It's still there.

So guitar sounds, what did you do for that?

We didn't keep the basics. For overdubs we used a Marshal Bluesbreaker reissue, the Ampeg bass amp and the Vibrochamp. For some stuff, we used your idea and took ceramic floor tiles that are on mesh. They are like 1' x 2' or so and are flexible, so we could make little channels coming away from the guitar amp. We'd have it sitting on its edge in an "s" shape coming from the speaker and another one about 4 or 5 inches away in the same shape with a microphone at the end so that the sound is bending and bouncing through this channel of ceramic tile. We were able to squeeze the sound and get a really interesting squeaky midrange... we were inspired by engineer Tchad Blake from an article in which he spoke of acoustic filtering. We took the Vibrochamp and just put it on 10 with no distortion box. We used an EQ pedal before the amp to bump up the signal to hit that first tube a little hotter. Vibrochamps use one 6V6 tube and have a lot of harmonic distortion so we just used the natural amp distortion. We mic'd it with a 57, a borrowed Neumann 149 ,and an old Shure ribbon mic model #300.

Did Aaron play a bunch of different guitars on the record?

Yeah. There was a '70s Telecaster that we used, and your Gibson L6, his Rickenbacker another Gibson thing, a Yamaha 12-string and an acoustic. We did a lot of effects to tape and sculpted the sound to fit the idea of the song. We had a Roland tape delay that we would plug the guitar into and then that into the amp and sometimes it would distort a little bit in itself. We used it mostly for the clear and clean sounds. They're kinda sparkly and a little bent sounding because of the tape. And the Bluesbreaker amp was really good for that. A lot of clean power. We did a lot of doubling with the idea of panning them left and right just to see if we could kinda widen up the field. We'd do all the verses and we wouldn't play in the choruses at all. Then we'd get a different sound and play the choruses, then do stereo verses, then stereo choruses, so then we'd have four tracks. And then we'd have another idea, say to do a little build-up thing before the chorus. Then double that so then we have six tracks, then we'd add a couple more parts and we might end up with 12 guitar tracks. When I hear about someone using 12 guitar tracks, I always imagine them all blaring away at once but in our case they were just a bunch of little parts taking over where the other left off.

It's funny that you mention that. One of the things that really struck me was the amount of attention to arrangement. It is clearly a record that you spent a lot of time thinking about. Maybe not pre-planned, maybe it all came together as it went. But, so many records end up sounding like expensive demos. I think that part of that is somebody just plays their guitar part that they always play, and someone plays the bass part they always play, and the singer sings it just like he or she always does in the rehearsal space. That's fine, if you just need a demo that will get you local gigs or whatever. But this is something that sounded like a record, somebody really put some thought into what they could do to make it interesting. It was obvious to me that those guys listened to a lot of Pink Floyd. [lots of laughter]

I don't know if they did or not. But I was thinking, "Oh my god this sounds a lot like Pink Floyd. I feel like I'm making *Dark Side Of The Moon*!" One of the things about this record is that these are three guys that haven't been approached by a record company, don't play live all that much, and by today's standards and money constraints, they shouldn't be able to make a record this good. And that's why we did it. It was really fun... we came out with something like that as a once in a lifetime thing.

You went for it.

Yeah, we went for it. We recorded this as if the world was waiting to hear it. We put all of our energy into it, and we're really happy with the result. We didn't want to record it if it was going to be another demo, so we worked hard.

It's hard to find people you can do that with, and it sounds great, and it really shows.

There were times when it seemed like we were never going to finish. I think they all wanted to have a really fun, creative, exciting studio experience, but we were working really hard, day in and day out. I was really tapped and all three of them were looking at me going, "What next, what next?". It started to get fun around the time of the mastering because we could see the finished product emerging.

You know, I've read a lot of those interviews in *Mix* magazine and the producers are always saying things like, "You just have to cheer the band on and inspire them and tell them they're great." I always wonder if they are lying because sometimes I just run out steam and get so frustrated and I can't pretend that I'm the most positive, happy guy on the globe. But it's usually when the band is getting antsy, so if I admit my frustration to them it often puts us back on the path. Hey, what's so bad about honest human emotion? It's part of the creative process, right?

For tracking and recording we used a 2" 16-track Studer A80 MKII at 15 ips, a Neotek Elan console, my Peavey omnidirectional mics, SM 57s [of course], AKG D-12 and D-112, Shure ribbon mic, the API mic preamps I got in a milk crate from a radio station [thanks to Andy Hong at WMBR], and old Ampex tube mic pres (model #601)... we put keyboards and bass through these to get a highly sustained fuzz sound. The mic pres come from old suitcase tape recorders. A Distressor compressor was used on the bass drum while tracking. Later it was used for mixing top and bottom snare mics and bouncing to another track. [I did this on the Sleepyhead record too]. It was also used on guitars and vocals while overdubbing. I now confess... I went totally crazy using the Distressor. I bought an old syndrum in New Jersey which we used that for super-low frequency sweeps in "Tip Of The Style." We also used a Hewlett Packard (tube) tone generator through a delay with square wave oscillator... kinda like a homemade analog tube synth! [drooling]

And you had 2 DA-88s locked up to the 16-track, right?

Yeah. It was kinda like an afterthought, really. We were going to make the record on 2" 16-track, and they had a lot of ideas for overdubs. I thought we should try synching up the DA-88s the studio had sitting there. I forgot what I was doing and got all excited and started splicing up the tape and the DA-88 couldn't sync up to it.

Oh, because you had timecode on the tape and you lost continuity and the DA-88 would freak out?

Right, it would hiccup, stop and go off-line. For some reason the vocals were actually coming before the song, they were pre-delayed. So I had to run a lot of vocals through delays. When there were backup vocals I had to figure out schemes for delaying 4 or 5 vocals... do I want to go through 3 delays or have just one delay and have one buss for all vocals?

So, what happened with "Apollo?"

After we finished basics we tried to get a better version of "Apollo." It seemed to be the best yet, but I was still a little leery about it. We put guitars and vocals on it anyway. Then after mixing the whole album except for "Apollo", I told the band I was unhappy with it and I just couldn't see putting it on the record. There were lots of drum lags and rushes that we couldn't hide with guitars and other noises. I suggested that we re-record it but they were out of money so we waited until they were ready, then recorded the song on a Tascam 388 1/4" machine down the hall in my friend Greg's practice space. The day before the recording Aaron told me that they were having a piano delivered. I was kinda unnerved a bit because my vision was to make a more homespun version of the song and the piano implied something more grandiose. We couldn't fit the piano into the space, so we left it in the hall and stretched headphones out there. The drums were recorded before piano with scratch guitar (no cymbals) with a D112 on kick, a 57 on snare and one Peavey Omni through the Distressor at 20:1 for tom and ambience. A guy named Sid did the main piano part then Aaron did some random tinklings on top. We kept the first take and mixed it in. You can hear some giggling and other sounds on that track. For piano I used two Omni mics, one looking at the strings a foot from the top opening [upright piano] and one behind the piano [the soundboard]. The tapedeck was a little shoddy so you can hear the piano track dropping-out, especially in the beginning. I compressed with the Distressor and a DBX 160a and mixed them together on one channel. The vocals were through an Equitek E-100 mic and Distressor. Guitar was the same mic, same comp and the Vibrochamp and a Daddy-o distortion pedal. We love the way the song came out, so different from the other songs.

How about mixing? You mixed a lot of songs in little pieces?

Yeah. I guess I mixed with the mastering process in mind. Some of the songs were up to 30-tracks. There was no automation, so when I got overwhelmed, missed a fader move or couldn't mute something in time, I would just stop the DAT and start over again with a little overlap and say... ha ha ha! We'll piece it together in the mastering. I knew we were going to be throwing a lot of stuff at you and I assumed you might get mad or irritated, but I figured in the end we would all be pretty happy.

Yeah right! As I recall most of the songs on the record, you hadn't heard as complete mixes until we got into the mastering sessions.

Some songs were like three to five parts that needed to be edited together. There was one song with tracks that I missed while mixing and the band said, "Hey where's that warbley tone thing" and I'd go oops, "I know, mastering!" So we took those sounds and laid them down on the DAT and had you load them into Pro Tools, sync them up and mix them in. We didn't know how it was going to come out.

Pretty wild. Were there any songs that you had heard complete?

Yeah there were 2 songs, "Radio Deth Gear" and "I H8 The Dead". I mixed them before we were even done tracking other songs. We immediately mastered them and burned CDs so we could listen at home to see if we liked them. We needed to feel like we could complete something. After months of work it seemed like we were never going to finish and we all wanted to know if it was worth it.

It's funny. I stopped by the studio a couple of times when you guys were mixing, knowing that I was going to be mastering the record. One time, you were working on "321 Contact" and you were mixing it in

LOTS of little pieces. You laid down this chorus or something and I was hearing a little bleed from a click track, I think, and I asked you guys, "what's up with that?" Aaron, [the guitar player] looked at me, totally straight faced and said, "We're going to overdub another guitar to cover that." And I thought to myself, "You're mixing the fucking song! What the hell are you talking about?" And he was like, "We're going to do that in mastering"... that's when I knew I was in for it. Right at that moment.

I wanted to say, "SHHH, don't tell him. Don't tell him."

So, suddenly a big red light started flashing in my mind like a warning siren. I was like, "Wow, this is crazy." You know, "Like oh shit, I wonder what else we're going to do?" You know, we actually didn't do as much as I was afraid of. Probably because I just psyched myself out. I thought that I was going to spend the rest of my life mastering the Slept record.

I'm happy that I did leave so much to be done in the mastering, cause it proved to me how important mastering is. I feel like we were re-recording the record or like we were recreating it. The record was supposedly done and mixed. I don't know how to describe that.

I know what you mean. And this was definitely an exceptional mastering session in that the record really wasn't complete when it came in, we did guitars, we did vocals, we did some crazy stuff with the syndrum, and overdubbing cymbal crashes. It's one of the only mastering sessions I've done where we have gotten so involved in adding parts. It was cool to have that flexibility.

We were able to hold to the original concept of the record. So often bands have ideas about funny little sounds and wiky-wiky tweaky things that they could put on their record and something happens. You know, "We didn't have time" or "We ran out of money." We pushed ourselves to make sure we got them on there and the mastering was one of the places where we could do it. If Phil forgot a cymbal in one of the songs we added it later and it sounds like it was always there.

Yep.

When we were recording we did this thing on the first song where we slowed the tape down really slow, played the drums and then sped back up to normal. So it would sound like a hyperactive drum machine. And it doesn't really fit all that well. It felt like the song dropped out there. We asked you to center it a little more so that it had more body and you did it.

Right. I edited out a little in the beginning which seemed to make it feel better and then used the automation in Pro Tools to pan those tracks to the center and then back out, just for those two seconds. It's really neat; you can hear the stereo field expanding as that drum riff ends, its kinda crazy sounding. Sometimes we would use the computer to time-stretch parts without changing the pitch and drag-out a vocal. On one song, "Radio Deth Gear," Aaron did some backing vocals and then without changing the timing we changed the pitch on him and added a pseudo female vocal harmony.

So, all the overdubbing and stuff aside, when you sit down to master a project like this, what are you trying to achieve?

Well first off, I listened to the songs and try to get a sense of what you guys were going for. I also keep an ear out for any problems that might have made it past the mixing, and look for ways to correct them. I guess I try to take the

project as far to the next level as I can while retaining the artists' and producer's vision. To make it sound like a record and not just a collection of songs. To create continuity while emphasizing what is great about each individual track.

Maybe we should talk a little about the equipment that was used.

Well, this is one of the first records where I experimented with mixing analog and digital signal processing in the mastering. You know, a lot of people say that once it's digital you should keep it digital, and while there is some truth to that, I've found that sometimes things can start to sound kinda glassy. So this time we went through Distressors, from the DAT master, on the way into Pro Tools and it really made a huge difference.

The Distressor compressor is microprocessor controlled with a totally analog signal path and incredible flexibility. You have the choice to dial in either 2nd order harmonic distortion, which is what tubes do, or 3rd order harmonic distortion, which is what tape does when you drive it hard. It's like a fuzz box, but a lot more subtle. It's really hard to

drive it so hard that it sounds like a Rat, but I think it is possible. [laughs] It helped to mush-up our sound a little.

It definitely adds a whole new flavor to the sound. We also used a TC Finalizer, which is cool because it's a multiband compressor. It lets you split the mix into 3 different frequency bands, process each differently, and rebalance them. So if a track is a little too dark or bright, you can pick two crossover points and bring up or down whichever of the 3 frequency bands that needs adjusting.

In closing... something I learned recording this record is that those who wait for permission from some magical record label to make an album may be cheating themselves out of a valuable life experience. By skimping on your recording and making just a demo, you may end up looking back years later to a pile of embarrassing cassettes or singles. But committing yourself to making the record of your dreams right in your own area, not fantasizing about being whisked off to the Bahamas, takes a lot of guts [and work]. Recording is not magic, it's not a mystery held only in the vaults of Jimmy Page and George Martin. These guys are still alive! There's still time to ask them questions! Start recording seriously now! If all you have is a 4-track, exploit it for what it is. Load those songs in hot with gusto and ferocity and stop making excuses. People are launching careers on 4-tracks these days. Hook up with a cool engineer and stay with them as you both learn your craft. That type of loyalty goes a long way. I've seen people make their move to the greatmajorlabelinthesky and find they wished they had spent more time recording and defining their music before they made that move.

Jason Cox

WILL PRODUCE FOR FOOD

by Brian McTear

When Larry first mentioned the possibility of interviewing my friend Jason Cox, former Studio Red producer/engineer for bands like Bardo Pond, Varnaline, Space Needle and others, I had to think long and hard about how I would ever come close to capturing this character in print. I've known Jason since I worked at Studio Red, and I could always do my impression of him if I needed to describe him to someone. I'd raise my eyebrows, squint a little, hold my head with both hands and say, "Oh my god, Bri, that is the sickest, most excellent thing I've ever heard, ever. You rule! That's all I can say, you rule like it's nobody's business! Don't change a thing!" (This would be if he were walking in while I was working in the studio or doing live sound somewhere.) So I guess the best way to describe him then would be in his own terms using his language That is, in one high pitch energetic blast, J Cox is the world's sickest, most killer fucking engineer, producer, and/or anything there ever was... ever!

And it's the truth. Since the demise of Studio Red, he has been working at Cycle Sound Studios across the street from my place [Miner Street] here in Manayunk, Philadelphia. I see him every few days either taking a break outside the studio, or riding to work. At a recent Varnaline show here, I couldn't help but notice that the first voice from the crowd after every song was a boisterous Marine's roar from J huddled up in the corner... manning the sound booth! (I have to say I was a little embarrassed for him) But it seems to be true that every single person who is around J, let alone records with him, has a great time. When you are working in the studio with him he exudes energy and this sort of "ultra-hyper positiveness" that could make three days of re-attempting the same guitar overdub seem like a few hours at the park... but playing Australian Rules Football, or something like that.

I spoke with J the first day he was back from a several week tour with Reservoir, the one-man ambient show featuring Jud Ehrbar of Varnaline and Space Needle. Each night's performance was taped to DAT, including one spontaneous night in Ann Arbor, MI when Jason busted out from behind the console to join Jud on stage with a rap performance. I haven't heard the tape, but I believe him when he says it is twisted. (The event was staged again in Philadelphia on the tour's final night.)

What follows is more like outtakes from a conversation than a formal interview. To start off, though, I wanted to hear his distinction between the words "producer" and "engineer." Luckily that was enough to get us rolling.

He began by quoting Steve Albini equating the word "Producer" with "Nigger" and "Faggot," derogatory terms Albini feels shouldn't be uttered, let alone used in reference to him (he prefers the title "Engineer"). Of course J's take is a little more sarcastically lighthearted.

The only reason the "producer"/"engineer" thing is weird, Bri, is because fucking higher-ups in the music industry made it weird. As this bunch of people gets paid more and more money, they trick up-and-coming bands into thinking that they absolutely need a producer. There's a very specific track for bands these days. A manager gets a band, gets them in the studio... lets them record, produce... whatever. You know, waste a few months on some label's money. Then they pick one song, knowing the whole time that the one they pick, they're going to send off to be remixed or even recut by a big name producer-guy and get on MTV. It's the "one-hit wonder" thing. That's why you have a band like Weezer, who was huge as fuck last year, now opening for No Doubt, who is huge as fuck this year, who next year is gonna be opening for someone else. The 22 Brides thing Red and I did... They took the single and sent it off to this guy, Tim... Tim O'Heir I think his name is... I could be wrong, actually. I really don't know who it was... but they went into his studio, probably recut it on 48 tracks or something, quantized shit, double and triple tracked instruments... I don't know... and now the CD single that came out is that take. That's just how it seems to be now.

Does that bother you a lot?

Yeah, it does bother me, actually. I made no mistakes with that recording. It was done when it left the studio. The way it was, was the way we intended for it to be. The only reason it was redone is because somebody higher up in the music industry thought it should be redone... and you already know how much disdain we have for people like that.

So I guess that seems to set things off balance as far as the commercial weight that one song carries verses the value of the album as a whole.

Well, it's not even that. That song is actually not on the album. The album cut was called "Lullabye. But the version they redid was for radio only. It was on a CD single and it was named "Lullabye '97" or something like that. So it's not even about the album. It's about having a radio hit.

Do you think that's going to be a lasting trend? Or do you think that it's always been like that? Because I think that for the last few years this lo-fi/DIY/independent rock thing has made it possible for beginners like us to record someone and actually hear it played on the radio, no matter how crappy it sounds.

Well, I would like to say it could be like that again, but I think really what is happening is that our peers, who we were lucky enough to record back then at that stage, are coming up and getting caught up in it all too. But hey, I might get caught up in it too. [He smiles and begins to pick up speed] If I were getting paid to take four months to make a record, I might just be an editing, cocaine-snorting fool – me and Billy Corgan sitting around doing nothing but wiping our asses a few weeks at a time. [He breaks out in a roar of laughter. A few seconds passes, he looks around.] We're not being very technical are we... hmm

But I seem to think that lots of bands don't want to call us producers, they'd rather say "recorded by..." or "mixed by..." And I think that in a backward sort of way that it's because we're not getting paid a shitload of money.

I talk about how hypothetically I'd walk into Cycle Sound during the Bardo sessions and there'd be a bunch of people mostly on a couch reading, and one guy's saying they want another guitar in this or that song. From there J would go to work. He'd get really excited and say, *"Yeeeeah, cool. Let's take the Marshall... or something huuuuge like that... and,"* his eyes getting wider the whole time, *"we'll hang a 414 from the ceiling in the Warehouse, like 30 ft. up... something fucking totally sick like that."* The band would look around, until someone let out a half-stuttered, marijuana-toned, *"Yea... Yeeeeaahh!"*

In that situation, I think, the album's a little bit of your art as well, J. I always picture that to be the role of the producer. Don't you think that right there, by being so genuinely involved and creative, you're doing as much, if not more, for an artist than someone whose biggest contribution is their name and a big hole in the label's bank account?"

Exactly, Bri... [He smiles as I'm getting just a bit overly passionate, and puts his fist on the coffee table], I want to be that guy... the one who does less for bands, and takes most of the money! [Another burst of laughter.]

I figure I should drop the subject for fear he was starting to get too much of a kick out of me. In an attempt to talk technical, I ask him his opinion of the recent outburst of "retro-'60s style" recordings. I mention Olivia Tremor Control, the

Apples, etc., all of whom he seemed to know very little about. But he does have something to say.

Clothes, bikes, cars, music... everything, it seems, has to be retro. [He mentions that he, on the other hand, feels the bulk of these recordings are just poorer quality.] I don't know, Bri. I'll say two things... First of all, I'm a '90s-guy. I hate the '80s, I hate the '70s, '60s, '50s.. I just want to look ahead. [He trails off to talking about Aphex Twin, but I'm not sure that his second point ever got made.] Now that [Aphex Twin] is THE BEST shit! It really is something new... drill sounds and shit... ambient, fantasy – J.R.R. Tolkien kind of background stuff. This guy is a super-genius. Jud and I listened to it the whole tour. We've got to get a sampler for the studio, Bri, [talking about Cycle Sound]. You can just do the sickest shit... really!

What kind does Jud use for Reservoir?

It's about the $1000-range Akai. I don't know much about it, but it fucking rules.

Do you have any plans to record with him soon, or is Reservoir going to be all self-recorded by him?

He talked a little about doing some drum samples here at Cycle, and up at Red's [Adam Lasus] in New York, and then just choosing his favorite segments to sample from... He's a sick drummer, though, you know it? Whatever comes of it, I'm sure will be crazy. The last album was done all on 4-track, but I'm not sure what this one's gonna be like. Probably more digital stuff, I don't know.

I don't think I have ever heard you say anything about 4-tracks, or home recording experience. How were you first introduced to recording music?

In general, I have about five minutes of experience with 4-tracks.. No, not even that much. But I remember when I was little, in like third grade... listening to like, "Reunited" and "Hot Child in the City." I'd make tapes using the three-band EQ. It sounds hokey, but I remember that shit. I was the kid at school who always carried around the tape recorder... you remember, the kind where the record button is a little red dot in the play button." [That, he finds particularly funny and laughs for a while.] I had one of those. And, you know, fuckers would be following me around the school yard... I'd be playing 'Life in the Fast Lane,' and like, Three Dog Night, and shit. [He really cannot stop laughing.] So I always wanted to be into that shit. When I was in college, I was bored... went into the Marine Corps, and after about a year I realized I had to go to recording school. [Note: he spent another three and a half in the Marines, one of which he was at Desert Storm.] I enrolled when I got out at Full Sail Center for the Recording Arts in Florida. It was basically overpriced... like $20,000 for a one-year Associate's Degree. There were some great classes, but a lot of throw-away shit too... like a music video course I couldn't give a shit about. I interned at Third Story Recording in West Philly, making

DAT copies was about all I did. I was looking around. I needed something, and I heard Red's place got flooded, and he was going to be opening a new place [by this he's referring to Adam Lasus' basement studio in Queens Village, Philadelphia]. I didn't know him, but I gave my resume to Dave Frank the manager. We all met and that's when I really got started. I started out assisting with Red mostly in the beginning. Later with Kittywinder, Sugarplant, Varnaline and all that, it was pretty much equal, at least that's how I approached it. And that was nice of Red. He definitely didn't have to do that.

So you were getting "producer's" credits then, even though... [laugh] you probably weren't getting paid like one...

Yeah... well, you see, Bri... [stretching his arms out], isn't that the basic rule? "NOBODY GETS PAID!" I mean, it's not "getting paid" unless you can just like... do nothing for six months at a time, but... take drugs and go around the world, or something. [He laughs for a second.] But I'm sure... that if eventually we were making a little money, there'd be a whole bunch of shit that'd come with it anyway. You start becoming a little crazy. You feel cheated. You feel like you're always getting screwed. I mean, listen to Jello Biafra... that guy just sounds like a sniveling, sneezing... bitch. To him everything's a conspiracy. He's always saying how much he's been fucked. And it's probably true. But that's true on all levels, whether it's the state, government... everyday life! You just gotta walk the line, and if you don't make a few bucks, at least have fun and try some different shit along the way.

The set-up at Cycle Sound, where Jason records, is simple yet very classy. They record to a 16-track, 1" Tascam normally, and recently they picked up an Otari 1" 8-track machine. The main focal point of the studio, however, is the console. It's a 32-channel MCI that was custom built for Philadelphia's legendary Sigma Sound in 1978. It has seen the likes of The Talking Heads, Madonna, Steely Dan, and a lot more. The sound, like lots of consoles in its class from that time period, is beautifully warm and huge, and although it has its scratchy knobs here and there, it is a delight to use. I know from the times I have worked on it. As for the environment at Cycle, well, all I have to say is that the warehouse opens up to a large motorcycle restoration garage lined with rows and rows of bikes [how cool is that?], and in addition to that, somebody there... I haven't been able to find out who yet... has this thing for collecting what is truly the most terrifyingly awful artwork I have ever seen. The collection is mostly nudes that seem to have come from some College Painting 101 class or something [the elective section]. They are mostly very bad, but the collection as a whole is hilarious, a moniker of bad taste. For the past year and a half Jason has been working with a band called Burn Witch Burn. Their music is sort of Celtic-bluegrass meets Zappa, and the lead character in the band is none other than former Dead Milkman, Rodney Anonymous. For an engineer they present somewhat of a challenge, since they, like Bardo Pond, insist on performing all their takes live... drums, mandolin/bozuki, acoustic guitar, violin, bass and vocals. I heard the recording and it sounds excellent. So I had some questions.

Okay, give me the low-down on the Burn Witch Burn sessions. I understand they wanted to play live. How did you make it work?

Yeah, the whole band played live... drums, acoustic instruments, everything. They even had a recorder and/or harmonica in some songs, so I put the drummer in one closet [i.e. isolation room] and the bassist in another closet. Those two wore headphones, but everybody else was just out in the main room, even vocals.

How were things mic'd up?

SM 57s. The way the gain is, you have to put them millimeters from the strings. But if you can get the gain up, the frequency range on them is great. It seriously is. We also used a few [Sennheiser] 421s. I think there's four or five settings, the extremes are S for "Speaking" and M for "Music", that might not be what they stand for, but whatever... we had one at Studio Red for years and I never knew it had the different settings, but anyway, if you put them on the S setting those things transduce as much gain as a 414 [AKG] or more, no shit.

It sounds like you didn't use any condenser mics.

We didn't. Well, the truth is, we didn't have any. We have all dynamic mics in the closet at Cycle. When we need condensers, we just rent them, but I've become pretty proficient without them.

So having worked at Cycle Sound, and Studio Red before... two really nice places, how do you feel about the word "demo"?

Uughh! Another four letter word, in my book.

Do people still talk to you about doing demos?

Sure, and I laugh. I say I am not into demos. Because, when you say "demo" you are automatically sellin' yourself short. 'If you want to record songs... and have them sound great, then I'm into that. But I'm not into demos'... Seriously. I really think when you've done a recording; it is what it is. Even if it sounds like shit, it's not a shade of what it is, it is what it is. If it is a bad recording, then that's that. But it is a recording ...therefore it is. [he laughs]

What do you say to musicians out there about how to make a good recording great?

Well, effects... DON'T BE AFRAID TO USE EFFECTS! I hear so many bands say, "We don't to do that, because we can't do it live." Well, there is a difference between live and in the studio. And you can do shit in the studio if you want to. People are so scared. They say that as far as any effects they want "just a little reverb, just sit it in the mix." Then you ask them their favorite records and they are usually crazy, sick mixes with lots going on. Effects can be too much sometimes, but used properly in a tastefully noticeable way they can make a record twice as good.

Are you talking about blanket effects like reverb and echo, or things like a one time echo on a lyric, a phaser on one bar of the drums... little accents here and there?

Either, really. They both can be used tastefully. Even just a nice plate reverb on a few things. The problem is a lot of times you can't even get around to doing things like that in the studio, because musicians just have a conniption about using effects.

What was the effects situation like with Bardo Pond?

Well, that's different, really. *Lapsed*, like *Amanita*, was recorded completely live, just like Burn Witch Burn's stuff. But those songs were cut with over 40 effect pedals right to the tape to begin with. There were pedal effects on two guitars, bass and vocals already.

Then did that make mixing easier or more difficult?

Well, it's crazy. The majority of that record, again like *Amanita*, is the original rough mixes, the actual takes I did for them to take home and listen to when we finished cutting. We came back the next couple of weekends to mix, and spent hours working on each song, because, you know, everyone thinks that you are supposed to do that (including me sometimes). They'd eventually become frustrated, so we'd either stick with the rough mix from before, or I'd start everything from scratch, go through the normal adjustments that I make every time just to get started (like the rough mixes) and take one or two suggestions on top of that. Then we'd go to tape.

So I hear a lot of people are already commenting on the production of this album. Does that make you laugh?

Well, yeah, actually. It does. It's a sick recording, but that's them, not me. [he's being modest]

After our conversation, I realized that J was much more interested in talking about the creative aspects of the music he was recording than the specifics of the recording process. He would talk about the quality of the sounds much more readily than the technical route to getting it. Speaking of favorite recordings of his own, he praised J. Mascis for how dramatic the Dinosaur Jr. albums are. "The guitar solos just pop in loud as fuck, like 'here I am!'"... Kind of like J himself [just kidding, J]. I think for any band he's the perfect mix of "big studio engineer meets the kid who'll try anything." If there was anything I learned at Studio Red watching Jason and Red, it was that anything goes. You could use a converted Walkman as a room mic, or you could record vocals out in the street [like they did with Varnaline]. But in the end, the sound from Jason, best heard recently in Bardo Pond's albums Amanita *and the upcoming* Lapsed, *both on Matador Records, is big, rich and, yes, dramatic [like him].*

Don Depew

HE'S THE MAIN GUY AT CLEVELANDS 609 RECORDING, AND A MEMBER OF COBRA VERDE

by Mike McDonald

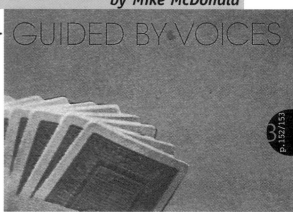

When I moved into Cleveland a little over a year ago, I had a limited knowledge of the current music scene. Most of the local music I picked up was the usual crap you'd find in any other city. However, just like any other city, there were a handful of releases of varying styles that were phenomenal. Without fail, when I looked for the recording credit, Don Depew's name popped up. Don owns 609 Recording, a 16-track facility located in a sleepy suburb of Cleveland. He also plays bass for Cobra Verde and was guitarist for a local metal act, Breaker. He's recorded some great bands like My Dad Is Dead, The New Bomb Turks, Guided By Voices [who he played bass for too], Gem, Monster Truck 5, Cruel, Cruel Moon, QuaziModo, The New Salem Witch Hunters, Cobra Verde, and many, many more.

So Don, how'd you get into recording?

I don't know... It's been so long. There was this studio... Mark [Klein 609 Recording co-conspirator] and I took a class at this studio. We were into doing that kind of stuff and for some reason it seemed like a good idea. It was just the usual kind of recording class. Guinea pigs would come in, and we'd work on them. Geez... That's like 20 years ago. Mark had a Teac 4-track and he eventually wound up getting a Peavey mixer. We'd use whatever mics were lying around and weren't broken. We'd use whatever practice space we had at the time. It's been this place since about 1982.

Were you recording Breaker with that?

Yeah... Well, with the heavy metal stuff, it was a whole different thing, especially back then. The first place we went with Breaker was Suma [a top-of-the-line 24-track facility in the Cleveland area]. Mark saw a special advertised for $32 an hour which, at the time, was a really good rate, you know? The only stuff we'd recorded up to that point was the 4-track stuff. Some of that stuff sounded decent, considering what we were working with. So we were going to do a single and there were no such things as project studios back then, there were just, you know, big time

studios. Back then, people didn't make records. Now, it's like everybody will crank out records. Kids, 15-year-old kids, put out records. To us, making a record was like... You can't understand how different things were back then.

It just wasn't available?

No! Making a record was something that was very expensive. It was a really big deal. We'd know people who'd go their whole life, years and years, and they'd recorded one time or something. Or never play on a record.

That sounds almost better than now. I wish it were more like that now.

[laughs] It had its good points.

That would be so much better. The people who had the studios actually knew what they were doing. I mean, how many studios are in Cleveland, and how many of them actually know what they're doing?

Like anything else, it had its good points and bad points. Anyway, then Michael [Klein, Mark's brother] got an 8-track, a Tascam 80-8, and a Biamp mixer. Around then, it started to hit me. I never had any money, but at least I could weasel enough to go see bands. I'd come across bands and I'd think, "The coolest thing in the world would be to be able to make a record with these guys." Just because I liked them, not because I wanted to scam a bunch of money off them, because they didn't have any money either.

That seems to be a recurring theme.

After awhile, people just assumed they didn't know anything because they hadn't really been in a studio, and [pointing] THAT guy has been in a studio a couple of times so he must know something. THAT guy was me. [Laughs]

What is your favorite project you've worked on?

The New Bomb Turks. They were fun.

I remember you telling me that the drummer [Bill Randt] didn't use headphones while tracking. What did you do?

Got a guitar amp and aimed it at his head.

Didn't you have a problem with bleed into the drum mics?

No. It's the New Bomb Turks!

What was recording the GBV thing like?

Weird.

Why?

'Cuz it wasn't GBV, it was Cobra Verde with Bob.

How'd that all get started anyway?

Well, because of the "Insects of Rock" thing. GBV was on Scat, who also put out Cobra Verde's record. We did some shows with Prisonshake and GBV, and Bob was into Death of Samantha, so one thing led to another... It was weird because it's one thing to record people who just come in and you can look at them objectively and try to make a record of this object that just walked in. It's another thing when you're participating in the thing too. And it's an even harder thing when you've got to be a participant, record it, and it's somebody you liked before and it sounded a lot different then. Bob's easy to get along with, but it was still a weird thing. I think the next one will be a lot better.

How did you do the tracking? Did you do it live or did you piece it all together?

We didn't really know the songs. We just had a cassette of Bob singing and playing an acoustic guitar. We never played the songs before. Bob basically ran through them with Dave [Swanson, drummer extraordinaire], and then we put everything else on it later.

Are you going to try to approach it more live next time?

Supposedly that is going to be the case. Some of the older stuff is real established in what it sounds like. They sound one way on the record and then plenty of people, ourselves included, have already heard what those songs sounded like when the other band was playing them, which was great. What are we going to add to that? But some of the stuff, like off the solo record, where it had never gotten played out, we had a little bit more of an opportunity to expand on it. Sometimes that worked out pretty well and Bob was pretty happy with that, like, "Man, I wish we would've recorded some of these songs this way instead of doing it like that," or "Some of the songs on the solo record, I wish I could've saved them and done them with you guys playing on it." Great! Because after awhile, we were kind of getting into doing it. We look forward to actually doing less of a piece together thing. You know, working on the songs together and making them sound like a unique lump rather than tweaking parts.

You piece together stuff with Cobra Verde a lot.

Oh yeah.

Man, that's hard. It's a totally different way of recording than what I'm used to.

A lot of times, it's hard to finish stuff like that. How do you know it's done when you don't know what it's supposed to sound like? Sometimes when you're doing songs for a single or something, that's great. It'll be like, we need to get one song done, and we got a couple of nights to do it. Bam, do it, that's fine. But to do whole records, just fill up reels of tape with stuff. Some things are more defined, okay, you can get that done. But some things start out one way and a couple of years later, after you're done fiddling around with it and doing it so many different ways, it's an entirely different thing so why not...

Just re-record it?

Yeah! Sometimes I think it winds up with this kind of butchered feel to it or like a halfway done thing because you're trying to get it to be something that it wasn't. Not even just something slightly different. I'm talking something A LOT different than what it started off as.

That's another thing I don't like about people having so much access to studios.

I know, it can be a bad thing in a way.

It used to be you had a band, you put some songs together, you went on the road, and when you were ready, you went into a studio.

Okay, yeah, which can still happen. It can work both ways. There are no absolutes.

609 Recording, PO Box 46508, Cleveland, OH 44146, (216) 439-6180

Recording in New Zealand

by Larry Crane and Barbara Manning

New Zealand music experienced a bit of popularity in the late '80s and early '90s. Then things changed. Barbara, who had recently recorded an album while travelling around New Zealand, and I sat down for breakfast with Tex Houston, who used to engineer at Fish Street Studios, and Brendan Hoffman, former owner of Volt Studios and IMD records. Both had defected to the US doing live sound and looking for recording work since the NZ music scene was on the wane. Barbara starts off with her appraisal of Tex's output.

Barbara: I think one of the greatest albums you've recorded would be *The Venus Trail* by the 3D's. That record sounds amazing. You participated in some of *Modern Rock* [The Clean] but had to fly out of town and leave it all in Stephen Kilroy's hands. You did the newest Verlaines record, which never was released in America, although it's on Sony/Columbia – that record sounds absolutely amazing, sparkling, gorgeous – but they didn't have you mix it down. I think the person who puts the musician's stuff on tape should be the one who serves it out.

Tex: Yeah. It's kind of weird when someone else mixes it.

Barbara: You also did several Magic Heads' recordings, including a song that I recorded previously, but we did it way better.

Larry: Recording wise?

Barbara: Yeah, the sound of it in every way. Oh, you did lots of the Chug records and Barbara Manning.

Tex: I've done a little Barbara Manning, a little bit.

Barbara: He used to say, "We'll spend all this time on the vocals" whereas every album I've done, the vocals were the last priority, you know done at four in the morning.

Tex: They have you do all of them in one day.

Larry: The vocals?

Tex: Yeah, it's crazy. People spend two weeks doing the recording. Why do the vocals in one day?

Larry: That's the thing listeners focus in on usually.

Tex: Well, I have been accused of being a vocal nazi in the past.

Larry: Like making people work a little too hard on it?

Tex: I don't like listening back to the CD and your like, "Shit, that's out of tune." It's always a consensus; if three people out of five like it, then it's in.

Larry: When you say you're a vocal nazi, are you looking for pitch and performance, or both? I guess both probably, but....

Tex: Yeah, in general. Barbara was scared of coming to do some things with me, weren't you?

Barbara: I was terrified, that's why I drank all that whiskey.

Tex: But they stood out all right in the end, didn't they?

Barbara: I was warned about Tex way before I recorded with him.

Larry: That he didn't have any ethics?

Barbara: No, that he would say, "Everything sounds fucked!" Everybody would tell me, "When you record with him he's going to end up being really negative about it." He did, he was great. The night we recorded, we got four songs recorded - three of which we kept. It was all improv too. It went really fast, we only had the evening, and it was excellent. All the songs just kind of poured out.

Tex: It was a good mix of things on that record, because it goes from 4-track, 8-track to 16-track. So there's a lot of different stuff on there, recording wise.

Larry: I always enjoy records like that, because they feel like a good compilation album.

Barbara: Brendan, you said he taught you some things.

Brendan: Yeah...

Barbara: But, was it about music or life? [Laughter]

Tex: I think the first time I met Brendan I moaned to him about a PA he had set up for me.

Barbara: So what did Tex show you?

Tex: I let you do any thing you wanted, didn't I?

Brendan: Yeah, you did.

Barbara: What bands were you with?

Brendan: Tex was working with MVPs, and I was working with a band called London Bellyflop.

Larry: So you guys had both been doing live sound long before you ever did recording?

Brendan: Basically.

Tex: Stephen Kilroy was starting a studio and he asked me to join in, which I did.

Larry: Stephen started Fish Street?

Tex: Yes, he got an 8-track from the television museum. He didn't know much about the 8-track either. We learned everything from scratch, really.

Larry: Fish Street had been around awhile before you started your own studio [Volt], right?

Brendan: Yes. It started in '92 or '93. There's two or three people who've taught me a lot and Tex is one of them.

Larry: Who are the other people?

Brendan: I learned a lot from [Stephen] Kilroy.

Larry: Is their any mastering place anywhere in New Zealand?

Tex: Not a specific one.

Larry: Do you play music?

Tex: No, I've never really done... I'm not a musician.

Barbara: What's your favorite recording project that you've done? What are you most proud of?

Tex: Nothing in particular. I like bits of all of the stuff. Instead of mixing at Fish Street for the Helzer Pump record, I brought some of the equipment to my house and set it up in my living room and it sounded nicer there than it did at the studio. The studio wasn't really a studio; it was just a space. That was fun because it was in my home environment. I sat up all night and mixed "Spooky" and that was really good fun.

Barbara: And what was your impression when Barbara and Joey and John [Calexico] walked into your studio and started to...

Larry: Get these fuckin' Americans out of here! [laughter]

Tex: I really enjoyed that day; that was great.

Larry: How did Joey and John end up going down that way?

Barbara: I paid their way, I paid for everything except for studio time.

Larry: Who did that?

Barbara: Nobody did.

Larry: Ouch.

Tex: I did it for free.

Barbara: Yeah, but I've taken him around the world.

Larry: That's true.

Tex: This was before that.

Barbara: Yeah, but somehow, instinctively, you knew you were going to get paid back in full. At the time I had spent all of this money trying to get these boys there and I paid Graeme Downes [The Verlaines] and David Kilgour [The Clean] to join me in my band so I gave them $600 each. I paid for the rental van to do the tour and by that time I realized I didn't have any money left over. Tex said the studio was still set up for another week and to come on down. We didn't waste time.

Tex: I wanted to try out my new recorder. The 1" Otari. I hadn't hooked up the noise reduction so it was kind of noisy. It was good fun to play with and it works real nicely compared to the 3M. You drop in and drop out and it's just so nice.

Larry: Have you guys ever kicked someone out of the studio?

Brendan: I've hit someone.

Larry: What did he do?

Brendan: Just fucking around and pissing me off.

Tex: I think in the control room a couple of times... there's like ten people in there while your mixing songs and six of them drunk and talking really loud. You're like, "Can you go into the other room?"

Barbara: Do you boys think that there is any hope for resurgence in the New Zealand scene?

Tex: Maybe in ten years.

Brendan Hoffman

We found Brendan doing sound for the Chills on tour in 1996. When he got a look at *Tape Op*, he wanted to sit in on the interview – and when Martin got called out to autograph a female fan's shirt ["Well, she can't take it off for you to sign"] we chatted with Brendan for a moment.

So what's your background, what brings you here?

I used to run Volt studios in Dunedin and I used to run IMD [Records]. I started off with King Loser and Trash and eventually it evolved into a studio and a label. In the course of running Volt I started working with Martin Phillipps doing demos for the new album, plus his track on *Disturbed* [a compilation album on IMD]. He was working with lots of various people there, which was cool, and he was still into working with me.

Apparently. So you recorded with King Loser?

Yeah. I did the first album. That was quite an interesting one 'cause it was recorded on 4-track all over the country. We brought it to Fish Street [Studios], dumped it across to 16-track and at the same time added the vocals, put some pieces in and it was done in one day, starting at mid-day and finishing at 6 the next morning; then driving home in the snow. It was a bit of a budget one. The whole album ended up costing $350.

New Zealand or US money?

It was New Zealand money.

What kind of setup was the Volt Studio?

Initially, it was a really old, crappy Soundtracs desk [mixer, yankee] and a Tascam 8-track. The King Loser single was done on that. Sandra Bell, the double single that she had, and the Bilders album, *Cut*, was done on that as well. We upgraded at that point and got a 16-track, once again a Tascam, and it was an MSR 16S. It was a 1/2" with Dolby S [noise reduction], which I really liked.

One of the few Dolbys that work.

Yes. I got a Mackie 32 x 8 buss, which was very reasonably priced and sounded okay. That was the basic setup.

Is that studio still going?

It doesn't exist anymore. Gone.

Don Dixon

by Kevin Coral and Scott Bennett

©Catherine Bauknight

Don Dixon is probably best known for his work with REM on *Murmur* and *Reckoning*, but his other production credits include such great albums and artists as the Smithereens [*Green Thoughts* being the best, in my opinion], Let's Active, Marti Jones and his own critically lauded solo albums. We got to meet him when he came into our studio to do some tape transfers and such and we were immediately struck by how friendly and open he was. He was very giving of information and very tolerant of our questions. In other words, for a guy who's recorded all over the world, got gold records, and almost ended up producing *Nevermind*, he was super cool. When we collared him to do an interview a couple of weeks ago he was open and very forthcoming with anecdotes AND recording/production insights, including what is probably the first in-depth discussion of the recording techniques used during the making of REM's seminal first album, *Murmur*. We also talked about some of his recent projects including a great sounding solo record by the lead singer of the Smithereens, Pat Dinizio... some of which was recorded in Don's home studio. We got to hear some of the tracks and they sounded amazing. And we're not just saying that...

Let's talk about how you got into this, and why. I mean, because obviously you started out as a musician...

Well, I still am. I don't think of myself as a producer, that's like way down the list of things that I think about.

Well how did you even fall into knowing how to even run a tape machine?

Oh, just always interested as a kid, just like a lot of people are, you know. I bought a little Pintron tape recorder, it was before cassettes had been invented, so it was like one of these little tape recorders with tiny little reels, and make little tapes. I always loved to sing. I went out to California between my junior and senior years in high school, worked on a wildlife refuge, and made a bunch of money, like

$2.70 and hour which was a lot back then! This was in the summer of '68. I came home with all the money I'd saved up and bought a Panasonic sound-on-sound tape recorder. When I was in junior high school, I chose to play bass because of the control that it offered. I played a little guitar; played a lot of things by ear. There was the coolest band in town, where the organ player played bass on pedals, and I knew they needed a bass player. I like the fact that, if somebody's playing a C-chord, and I'm playing an A, it was an A minor seven. That's something that I figured out on piano. I like the compositional control of the bass. I bought a bass, one of those great Danelectro Silvertones, and I wish I had it back. From Sears for $79. Then a few months later I really liked upright, so I found an old upright in a church in Charlotte, and just was sort of self-taught on those things, but I could read music. I began doing some sessions, there was a jazz guy named Louis McGloughn in Charlotte, which was the closest big town to where I grew up. He had seen our band and he was always looking for a young guy who could play upright to do sessions and stuff so I started doing sessions with him. That was sort of my introduction, when I was 15 or 16, to the studio. And I was interested in recording, so I'd sit around and make up my own Jimi Hendrix songs in funny tunings, and record that stuff on my old Pintron that I had bought for $30, and then I saved up and bought that nice Panasonic... So I was always just interested in the sound of things, and was working on sessions and doing things...

So you were around studio stuff...

Yeah, there were a couple of decent studios in Charlotte. Charlotte had been in the '30s like a little Nashville, with a lot of bluegrass and blues recorded there in the '30s. And then there was a guy named Arthur Smith who had a really nice studio, a real professional studio there in Charlotte, which is where I did most of my recording.

What kind of stuff are we talking about?

Well, you know, he probably had a Scully 8-track...

Which was 1/4" or 1/2"?

Oh no, the Scully would have been a 1". The formats went this way: everything was on 1", those 1" 4-tracks that were used for all the Beatles records, and then the 4-track standard in the United States was 1/2", and then they did the 1" eight. Later the 2" technology was really picked up from the 2" video transport technology, the MM1000 Ampex machines, which were basically a whole bunch of 440 electronics on this bed that had been made as a video transport. Because video went from 2" to 1" pretty fast, less than probably five years, they used those old 2" transports to build their 16-track machines. It all kind of happened real fast and then it just stopped there. I mean, they tried to come out with a 3" machine for a while, and that Stevens guy came out with that 40-track 2" machine, which was a nightmare for alignment. The Stevens electronics actually sound pretty good because they're very simple. You can't do much to it, but you can put something on tape that's got a lot of juice to it.

So he [Smith] probably had some U-47's or something?

He had great mics. Everybody back then always had great mics.

Well you could probably go buy a Neumann for about $200 at that point or something?

But again, people worked all day in a factory for about $30, so that was still a lot of money by any standards.

But it just seems like everyone had them back then.

There were no budget microphones. The budget microphones were CB/Turner mics, and then the good microphones were good microphones. You bought Telefunkens or Neumanns. AKG was not even really in the big-time ballgame here in the United States. They were in Europe.

EV to an extent at that point, right?

Well, EV was good, I mean EV had the RE 20 which was a great mic. Shure had a couple of good mics...

Like the 545, was that one of the early ones?

Yeah, and the RCA 77DX.

And they had the 44, which was a smaller version of that. So, um, you're at that point, you're a teenager, and you're out of high school at this point, then...

I went to college in Chapel Hill, and we got a band together, that turned into Arrogance, and we learned all of the first Black Sabbath album, which was an import only. That kind of metal, they really invented it. And then we would do most of the Beatles' *Abbey Road*. An interesting combination of stuff. And lots of heavy blues songs, like a few Ten Years After versions of songs.

So that would have been when?

About '69. And we recorded out first single... at a pretty nice studio in Greensboro that was another real place; they had a lathe and everything, where you could cut the actual acetate. That came out as Arrogance, it was a single called "Black Death," it was anti-war, [sings]: "Dressed in crimson shadows, caught in shades of dark despair." [Laughs] So that was cool, we had a great guitar player who didn't stay in the band very long.

What were you playing bass-wise at this point?

I played an EBO with red, white, and blue tapewound strings...

Oh man! What kind of a stage rig did you have?

Four giant cabinets, each with one 15" [speaker] in it, but each cabinet was like as big as this room, and two Sunn 200s. The Sunn 200s aren't really that loud, but I loved the way they sounded, I'd love to get any of that. A little-known fact about Sunn: one of my heroes when I was growing up Norm Sundholm, who was the bass player for the Kingsmen, the bass player on "Louie Louie," and he played an EBO, so I bought and EBO. And he and his brother went on to start the company Sunn amps, right there out of Portland. And I didn't know that till a few years ago, otherwise I would have tried to find him. The Sunn amps were great...

Okay, so you're cutting and this point and you release the first single as Arrogance...

Yeah, we released "Black Death"... I kind of ended up producing that, it was a little 4-track thing, but we did three songs.

What was the board at this point?

I don't remember what they had in there. It was probably a Neotek, but that is a very filtered memory.

Are we talking four inputs? Eight?

I don't know, it was a pretty big console. This guy knew what was going on, I mean he had a lathe in his place.

Oh, I forgot it's like 1969. I forgot that by that point things had jumped ahead pretty fast.

Well, the Reflection console was a homemade one, but it was a pretty good one. It had some Fairchild EQs and it was a pretty clean console. The records we made on that original console sound pretty good now.

Were you working with any outside bands at this time? Anyone other than yourself?

Not really, I mean I was just some dumb-ass draft-dodging freshman in college. And I was playing in several bands, still playing jazz with some people. I did audition my sophomore year for Buddy Rich, and he wasn't real happy about my hair. They offered me a job, but I was going to have to lose a whole semester in college and everybody warned me that I would probably get fired and left in Belgium, you know, that he went through bass players really fast. But there were a lot of things still going on, and I didn't want to leave the band. In a nutshell, that band turned into more of an acoustic version with me and the other guy who did most of the singing and writing. We'd just play and sing. It was mostly designed to write these new songs and work out vocal stuff. We did an album with that version of the band, the acoustic version. We have an album called *Give Us A Break* that came out in '72, that was the acoustic version where we had a conga player, and guitar, bass, and piano. Then that band did another independent record like that, more of that odd kind of blend of acoustic-y Beatles things.

So you were learning more about the studio as all this was happening?

Yeah, we're recording these records in Reflection; we had a production deal with them. Recording there and releasing them on our own little independent label. Meanwhile, we're getting a really good following in Chapel Hill, and creating sort of an environment that is receptive to original music. So we're sort of helping to create this; there are clubs popping up and we're filling them up, we're playing a lot, like 150 nights a year. We're doing this for a living. And then we get a lot of interest for this woman at Elektra, by now the PBS station is doing a special on us, we can fill up the big clubs, we do a special for a big theater there. And this woman comes and sees us, and then she quits her Elektra job and ends up at Vanguard. We signed with Vanguard, went and made a record in New York, lived in the Chelsea Hotel, and we made this record with a guy named John Anthony who had produced Ace. He was a coke freak, nice guy, but he made a bad record with us. And we tried, and I learned a lot during our first record. I did my first string writing, and got to record it with real New York guys, which was a little nerve-wracking.

How big a place are we talking studio-wise?

The Vanguard studios were really nice. We were working days and Elvin Jones was making a record at night, so we had to break down and setup every day during a week and a half of that record. It was huge, giant, not like your typical New York studios. Most New York studios aren't that big, because space is a premium there. These old places were big, still one big room. Most of these rooms were big because they were doing a lot of soundstage stuff in New York in the '30s and '40s. They needed to put the whole orchestra in and do radio shows at these places. It was a giant room.

You always see pictures of places in the '60s with about a thousand goboes there! It's like, let's reduce this room a little, it's rock and roll!

Well, they needed all the goboes to do the radio shows. And since everything was live, they needed to create little dead areas for the vocalists, dead areas for the percussion.

So that was probably the biggest place you'd worked in?

Up to that point. It was a big room, I mean you gotta remember, the room in Charlotte was gigantic, the Arthur Smith room was huge. And Reflection was more your typical kind of Memphis size, the original version was a nice, small little place. But it was still a real studio, they went to a lot of trouble to make round things that they saw. The guy who owned Reflection had played on hits for Ernest Tubb, he was a troubadour, so he'd played on "Sweet Thing" and stuff like that and he'd been in Nashville for years. I mean he knew what the stuff looked like, he knew that they had round things, there were no real signs like "This will help break up standing waves." [laughter] And it did.

Were you intimidated going in there at all? Were you the producer at this point?

I was just trying to be a guy in the band. By then I had already produced a few things, but again the producing stuff was all by accident. The first thing, in 1972, was this package record deal. They would come through Reflection. There was this guy named Toby King, who had his own band, and he bought the typical thing, which is four hours of time, and you get 500 singles for $500, which we'd send out in about three weeks. That was kind of the deal. People would really respond to those deals, they think they don't have to do anything, like some Crackerjack surprise in the mail. They did a lot of gospel records, a lot of things under these packages. And then they would just work out a deal with the local guys to print, do the mastering, all that shit. And this [Toby King] thing kind of had potential, it was a song called "Operator," and I was just sort of there helping engineer. After they'd spent a couple of hours, the band kind of sucked, but the singer was really good and the song had some potential. We took him in the back and said, "Look, we'll put some more time and money and effort into this if you sign on the dotted line." Well, I didn't have anything to do with that, I still got my $25. So I went back in and replayed a lot of the stuff after the band left. We kept the vocals, and there was a girl singer and she and I came up with a background vocal. It got picked up by Delight or one of those labels at the time. And it did okay. And that was the first thing I kind of co-produced. That was '72. The reason we did *Give Me A Break* was... I sat up in bed one night and said, you know, these assholes [gospel producers] come with $1500 and put out a thousand records - why don't we do that? So that's why we started doing our independent records. We'd collect $200 from five friends, pitch in the other $500 ourselves, and split the money out when we sold them. We never tried to make a big deal out of those records, never sold more than a couple thousand of them, we just wanted them to perpetuate what was going on until we could get a *real* deal.

So you weren't looking for national distribution?

No, which is where we made a mistake, because we didn't know... and I also didn't want to become a businessman.

Well, I find it very interesting, because I think a lot of us think that the independent records scene has been relatively new, like it started in the '80s or something. This has been going on since rock and roll started.

Well, yeah, we did our first single in '69, we put it out and we sold some. So it wasn't totally unprecedented for me to say, "Well, we can do this," because we'd already done it. But we had been chasing the major label golden apple after that. Well, actually, we hadn't really, we just tried to be able to make a living, open up the club scene, and have places to play. And we succeeded. And it was very hard, you know! Well, anyway, after that experience with Vanguard, we asked to be released, because somebody at Elektra or Epic had expressed some interest in us, and there was this new manager guy hanging around, and it ended up taking quite a few years before we got another deal, but we ended up getting a deal with Warner Brothers through this guy. Meanwhile I was recording other stuff, like that Sneakers EP which was done on my 4-track (or maybe Chris Stamey's) in '75... we did the first half of that at Cat's Cradle, but got kicked out because we were too loud for the dinner crowd, and had to finish it up at the bass player's girlfriend's apartment. Which was hell, the console on the bed. I had this cool little Valvetech console, really nice with a compressor built in.

So were you aware of Big Star at that point?

Chris and Mitch [Easter] used to try and get me to give a shit about Big Star, and I just never could, still can't hardly. I like Jody, and Alex is kind of an asshole, but personality aside, it never meant as much to me as it did to them. I was listening to Mingus and stuff. I went through periods, even in high school, of casting it all aside. And for whatever reasons, what they were trying to do was a lot of what I felt like I never liked about the Replacements, just too much unfinished ideas and debauched drunkery on tape.

Is part of it just because you considered it retro at the time?

It's very hard for me to put it back into context. I remember Mitch and Chris coming over, and I remember them trying to get me to like them.

Did you genuinely like the Sneakers at the time?

I truly loved what they were doing.

Because it's not very far removed...

I understand, but there's a big difference when you're recording and when you're just listening to some finished thing. And in knowing these guys since the eighth grade. And there's a big difference between a freshman in college and a freshman in high school, so it took a long time for that to balance out, for me not to just be the old guy who knew everything or was an asshole or whatever.

See I guess a lot of people who know that history are kind of hoping that there's some secret Southern power-pop Mafia syndicate, that you all were interrelated, that you all knew everybody...

Well, I think the secret to a lot of those bands, a lot of those people still being interested in music, was the Winston-Salem [NC] Parks and Recreation department and the churches at the time being in collusion to keep the kids off the streets. So they were trying to give the kids someplace to go. Everybody was worried about kids taking acid and jumping off buildings... they didn't know they were taking acid and going to the church buildings. Ask Peter Holsapple, he was coming to see Arrogance on acid at this church. So when you've got places to play, we could go be a six-month old band and be gods to 300 kids in a church basement. Every week! One of the first gigs we ever played was in Winston-Salem, at a battle of the bands, where Mitch's band Sacred Irony also played; they let us use some equipment and stuff.

What a horrible name.

They had a hearse; we were dragging in our little crap amps. But compared to these guys in the eighth grade, we were mean, loud and screaming... there was some serious energy being put out by this band. So we got real popular, real known right away. And then at Chapel Hill, that was the year of the Kent State killings, and all the colleges shut down, so we had lots of opportunities that spring to play outside. The reason guys like Chris and Peter Holsapple, Mitch and Gene Holder and all those guys have stayed in the music business is that they had this early sense of success, and they had venues in which to become good. Peter, out of attrition, has stayed in the music business, not because there's not other things he could be doing.

It's interesting though, that out of those guys, you're the only one who didn't like Big Star.

Well, it's not that I didn't like them – they were just not remotely an influence on me.

But it's interesting that you're connected with all those guys, you have a big part in the Southern power-pop history there, that mythical... but as you explained, you were older than these guys, they were kids.

I was a lot older, I had been exposed to jazz in a way that they weren't, from a very early age. From the time I was fifteen and on, I was playing in bands that were doing Cole Porter, not really heavy stuff, but "Night and Day," "Take 5," some Dave Brubeck stuff.

Did you get into it as jazz got more out-there, like the Impulse stuff of the mid '60s?

The Impulse stuff was pretty good, but I was not a fusion fan, and still am not a fusion fan. I was a big Miles Davis fan, a huge Cannonball Adderly fan. I always loved Coltrane, even as he got more out. I mean I like Sun Ra. That's not fusion, see fusion was Chick Corea... chops for chops' sake that seemed to have missed the whole idea of what be-bop was about, which was *some* chops for chops' sake. So I worked very hard at jazz, ignored the Beatles for a time and only later went back to them. So I missed some stuff

in there and Big Star is just something that never meant anything to me. I missed it first time around, and if you miss something like that the first time around, I think it's harder for it to have the same impact.

When did you start working with Mitch Easter in the studio? Was he into recording as long as you knew him, or did you introduce him to that?

I think for a lot of these guys who were significantly younger than us, we were the first direct contact they'd had with people that were making a living at music. They did things that we never had the balls to do. They went with their tapes and had meetings with A & R guys in New York that I would never have dreamed of. They sat around and made tapes that were real good. I helped them with their first real recording, but they were doing some stuff before that...

Did you do any cool tricks when you were working with the Sneakers? Did you have them in the basement or the garage or whatever?

The first Sneakers records, there's no tricks to that. It's live to two tracks [of a 4-track], mixed through a ten input console. There was a drummer, percussionist, bass, guitar, some piano, then Mitch playing a gut-string guitar off in a bathroom somewhere. Basically just trying to get a performance all the way through, because we really couldn't do much editing. And nobody could really sing, because it would have been too much leakage. And then we had two tracks to overdub a solo and do vocals.

Did you have a collection of mics at this point? Or were you borrowing some from Reflection?

No, there was nothing better than an SM57 on that. Just whatever we had. I think we had some AKG 57-style mics, some 57s, probably a couple of 635As, which are great mics, you need to have one of those.

How old were these guys at this point?

They were freshman in college, 18 or so.

So was this the board that had the compressor in it?

It was an Altec PA board that they made for a while that was just treble and bass control, an effects send, a monitor send.

Did you use any outboard stuff?

No, just straight through. I might have had slap on the vocal in the mix, but things like inexpensive Lexicon boxes, that stuff didn't even exist. There were no really good sounding digital things at all. You had spring reverbs - I had a Fisher Space Expander I would use on things - and you'd use tape slap. I don't think Loft had come out with one of those analog delay lines yet. Those were expensive when they came out, like $400-$500. The very first Lexicon delay line that would go all the way up to 120 ms was $1400. Delta Digital, even Mount PCM60s were $1500. And I bought them for that, and I still carry them around.

Who else were you working with at the time? Any more prominent names?

I would do guys who were big in the region, like Motorcross. His records were relatively expensive, which meant you got to record them at Reflection, got to put real strings on it and stuff.

How were you recording strings at that point?

Well, you record them the same way you always record them, with mics over them. [Laughter]

Okay, that was dumb, but I mean, you were doing them in stereo, so you'd put like two 47s up over them, or...? How many pieces are we talking here?

It depended on what kind of sound I was trying to get. The biggest group of strings that I would typically try to record was about seven. Which was usually about 3 violins, 2 violas, and 2 cellos. Lots of times you would just record a quartet. And I'd ask the players to bring their spare instruments, so they could switch when we doubled it, so it wouldn't glass up too much. Because each of the instruments sounds slightly different.

Okay, so they're sitting down, are they in a circle?

In a curve, like at a recital. Just a slight curve, so everybody can see each other.

Are you coming over their shoulders, on the far outside...? How high of a ceiling were you recording in?

About eighteen feet in Charlotte. What I would sometimes do is a nice stereo pass and then a couple of mono passes. It just depends on what you're trying to do. If you want it to be real slick and glossy it needs to be a little more distant.

Are you compressing this stuff?

Typically not when you put in down, but that varies sometimes. What kills string sounds more than anything is if you lose phase. If you lose your phase field, it's just like drones. I would be more specific if we were talking about a particular project...

See, I want to get more detailed with things, because that's the most frustrating thing, when I'm reading an interview with someone really interesting, and they just talk about stuff but they don't give any detail.

Well, okay, here's my theory that I use on anything. When I'm making a record, when I'm recording the very first instrument, I'm thinking about the proscenium effect that I want this instrument to have. I'm thinking about where it wants to be in the song, where it needs to be in the mix, so that I don't have to artificially put it there. If I can record it there, with the microphones in the room. You try to get the right mic, but many of my favorite sounds are because they took the treble control and turned it up twice, ran it through another one.

So you don't get hung up on it being just the microphone on the thing?

No, I've been that way in my life, much to my regret. But as I find out more about what's going on, the thing that matters is that it works. The road you take to the Emerald City is less important than how well you get brushed up at the end before you see the wizard. There are sounds you cannot get if you don't mic them correctly. So if you're looking for something that has true front-to-back sound, you can fake that with boxes, but it's not the same thing as if you record it. A lot of the background vocals on *Reckoning* were recorded 25 feet away from the microphones. If you go back and listen to the record, you can hear that Mike and Michael are kinda the same volume on a lot of things, particularly if you listen with headphones. But that Mike is obviously standing behind Michael; he's not as present although he is just as loud. And that's from these binaural recordings of him in the back of a room. And I'll record organs that way, if I know it's going to be a wash instrument, I will pinpoint it, place it in a binaural field so that it's either slightly left or

all the way left, well, "all the way" that you ever get in binaural, or behind you, or whatever, to try to find a place for it in the mix. You have to have a sense of what its job is when you're recording it, which is the great thing about recording live to 2-track, recording as many instruments at once as you can. You get a chance to fine-tune those things. One of the killer things for drum sounds, one of the things that messes up the sound when you're trying to create these multilayer prosceniums, is the phase. You get like 30 mics on a drum set, you get little incremental phase things all over the place. The thing that sounds so good about those Beatles albums, the reason the drums sound the way they do, is because there isn't any phase problem. It's not so much that those EQs are so great, it's that because of the basic technology available, there aren't phase problems.

Well, isn't it also true that those guys knew sound?

I don't really know, that's all relative. You get taught this, you get taught that, but that's only apropos to what you're trying to create at the time.

Yeah, but their practice was as good as their theory. I think more theory would help a lot of the sound of current records.

I think understanding how things work... the training is not particularly good and it never seems to be about the things that really matter.

What are some things that you don't particularly like about current record sounds?

Everything is kind of bright, has this artificial kind of crunch to it, and it's nothing to do with digital-schmigital. The tape recorder, believe me, has less sound than anything else in the chain. It's the least sound of the whole thing. The sound of a guy's drum is much more important than the sound of your tape recorder.

How did you get involved working with REM?

Well, it wasn't that many years later. Mitch and I had become friends because he had moved to Chapel Hill, and was going to school there. We were hanging out, and I was interested in what he was doing. I was selling these little consoles called Quantum, which was a California company started by a guy who had worked for JBL... I'd helped Mitch set up the Drive In studio. I was recording bands there, it was cheap. He had a 2"16-track 3M closed loop, whatever series that is, very good sounding tape recorder, and a 2-track version of that he'd bought someplace. He had that Quantum console, then he outgrew it and got one of those nice Angelas, which was a very good-sounding console made by Amek. Very transparent, sounds a lot like the Sony 3000 series, which is a very clear console. I was using the place a lot without him, and this guy who had gone to Chapel Hill brought REM up to do that stuff that turned into the first EP, *Chronic Town*. They'd already recorded the Hibtone record, "Radio Free Europe" [a 7" single]. They did that down in Athens somewhere. Mitch had made these first recordings, and we were talking about it. He was saying the singer makes these great animal noises and he said, "I don't know what to do with them, they're kind of backwards... the bass player's all over the place." So I listened to the tapes, helped him sort out the sounds. I liked the music, thought they were pretty interesting.

You're not just saying that? [laughter]

No, that's probably my favorite stuff they ever did, that "Box Cars" or whatever it is. In many ways I think that's the most unique, best stuff.

Did you think they were the savior of American rock and roll at that point?

Well, no, I still don't think they are. I think it was very unique, and it has almost nothing to do with America.

Do you think that whole Southern thing is way - overstated? You know, everyone's trying to match that Southern Gothic, William Faulkner, sort of vibe...

There's nothing Faulkner-esque about his lyrics. His lyrics are much more Rimbaud than Faulkner.

Well, you know they put that plant that overgrows everything in Mississippi, kudzu, on the cover [of *Murmur*] and all these critics from the East Coast were like, "this is American Southern Gothic!" But I mean, it wasn't just the lyrics, it was the music, and it was the way you recorded it really! The way you recorded contributed to that.

Here's the atmosphere when this band comes on the scene: their immediate successful influence band was B-52s. And their initial gigs were party gigs, just like B-52s. The way that Stipe got the lyrical content that he did get into these records was that nobody could hear it or gave a shit, not because they had big meetings about what it was going to be. Their lack of knowing what each other was doing was a big part of the success. Mitch and I recognized that that was one of the strengths, and that if we began changing elemental things about them to make them sound more like they were from Memphis, then we would lose the more interesting, but perhaps more commercial, aspects of their party band. The label didn't necessarily understand this, they just said, "Well, here's a band that people seem to like." Despite how cool people perceive IRS as being, they spent a lot of money on the Alarm. And they put a lot of pressure on us to deliver Thompson Twin - like singles for them because that's what was hot. We were looking at an era, where almost especially in hip, college scenes it was almost all British, almost all drum machines, almost all synthesizer. Guitars were dead. As a matter of fact, REM was scared to death of any kind of vague distortion on a guitar at all. We [the producers] had come from the house of the Holy Grail of distorted guitar-land. Guitar sounds to us were boxes turned up loud. It wasn't this clean thing. So we had to work hard to get guitar sounds we could stand, that we felt like did something, that meant anything, that wouldn't also make them [REM] go, "Oh, I heard some distortion, people are going to think that we're a hair band!" or whatever label people were using back then.

Did his playing make your job easier though? Lots of arpeggiation - did you sit there and go, "Roger McGuinn, okay, lemme think of the Byrds records, how they were recorded"?

Maybe, but Byrds records have lots more classic guitar sounds that we were allowed to have, especially on that first album.

A lot more compression too.

Maybe so, but we got the compressors working very hard on those records. But what we tried to do was use them playing almost everything, the basic parts. I played bass on "Perfect Circle" because Mike Mills was playing piano, and it just needed a real plain sort of bass part. So "Perfect Circle" is Mills and Bill Berry, one's playing a tack piano, and the other one's playing the regular Yamaha piano, both at the same time, real close together, I just had one mic on them.

So most of the songs were done live?

No, not necessarily. I always try to make everybody play together, and then I use whatever sounds I can. Typically, if bands already know their songs, they play better all together. If they're hearing the singing, then they know where they are and they don't have to count. That's a big thing, trying to get the guys to sing.

Was REM comfortable in the studio at this point [during the *Murmur* sessions]?

Not really, they didn't know much about it. What happened is that IRS signed them, said, "Okay, now you don't want to make these backwoods records anymore," you know, they're in California. They knew "that Mitch Easter, he's probably in the Klan or something" [laughter]. So they encouraged the band to work with some guy from Boston, relatively well-known guy, Steve "something-or-other". He took them in the studio and made them do the typical thing of beating them to death, made them do 800 takes of a song, told them that Bill sucked, that Bill couldn't possibly play on the record, that they'd have to replace him. He produced these not very good recordings, very modern by 1981 standards, which meant it sounded like the Cars. Which is not horrible, just not exactly what we had in mind. I mean, our records are kind of close, they're not real ambient, and they're kind of simple. The ambiance that is there is live, and then we had one EMT plate that we used a lot. That and slap delay, my favorite, 151 ms with a 440 machine going, [tape] slapping. So anyway, REM had this horrible experience with these guys, and said, "Please let us try some songs with Mitch." At which point, Mitch had never been in a real studio, and they [IRS] said, "Well, okay, but you can't record in his garage, you've got to go to a real studio." So Mitch called me up and asked me if I was interested and willing to help and I said sure. So we went to Charlotte and recorded "Catapult" and "Pilgrimage." The guitar amp on "Pilgrimage" was some sort of solid state amp that just happened to be there, because he didn't bring an amp. It was some little Casino amp, one 12". The guitar sounded great, as good as he ever sounded, before he discovered that yes, you can turn it up. We continually encouraged them to turn it up, and they were pretty open to things, but they would also let you know if they were worried about something, and we'd work around it. They always had a certain kind of fanatical following, even when it was tiny. But nobody thought at the time that this band was going to be the next big thing. There was a lot of pressure at the time, the Police were big, U2 kind of big too. I have always tried to protect what is good about a band, and just kind of softening the things that aren't as good.

So how about the story about Michael singing through a handheld mic out in the stairs. You know, too shy to sing in front of you guys, that sort of thing.

It's not so much that. We did, without asking him, simply set him up in the stairwell. Where nobody could see him. He was definitely using really nice mics, though he might have done one song or something that we gave him a handheld mic for, but I don't remember. Typically we used a FET-47 on him for the whole thing.

Was there a particular reason you set him up in the stairwell?

I personally liked singing in the stairwell a lot. I liked the way it sounded, because it's got a little bit boxy sound, a slight sort of bedroom clank to it, so it wasn't totally dead. And you could turn the lights off, nobody could see you. Now it's got a glass door, so you can peek in there. But at the time, there were two doors between the stairs and the studio.

Did you do that with everybody?

Not everybody, but a lot of singers. To avoid that fishbowl effect. He was pretty secretive and a bit shy. Plus, I'm also the kind of person who is not interested in seeing lyrics. I want to have to hear what's going on, I don't want to be given the opportunity to say, "Oh that's not what he's really saying." It's not a judgmental thing; it's to avoid thinking about whether the singer is articulate enough, because that doesn't matter. And so much of Stipe's writing was sound-oriented anyway. And as a singer myself, I'd been given an earful of, "You're not articulate enough, you fucking shit," my whole life and I would say stuff like, "Well, what is Mick Jagger saying here you asshole?" I was tired of small-minded, idiot producers. I learned most of what not to do from guys [that were] producing me.

It was all over articles for years, though, about how inarticulate he was, as if they'd never heard a guy where you can't understand anything. Which is of course bullshit.

Yeah. And many of our favorite songs became hits because people were obsessed trying to figure out what they were talking about. I wasn't even being that conscious about that. We were mostly like, "Mike, you can sing anything you want to. I'm not going to tell you what to sing. You tell me when you feel like it's good enough, I'll tell you if you're more out of tune than you need to be." It was kind of that simple.

Did you and him have an immediate bond because you were both singers?

Not really. On the whole, they kind of just looked at me as the technical guy anyway. Because they didn't know me as well as they had known Mitch, and they didn't know me musically and they knew Mitch musically. I had records on Warner Brothers with bands that played in coliseums, so I was like the enemy anyway.

Did they ever show any attitude to you? Act standoffish?

No, they were fine, it was no big deal. But I was just sort of Mitch's friend that Mitch wanted to help on this. They didn't know anything about what I had done, really. But they were good. I tried a few things. On one of those records, I did this real sophisticated vocal arrangement for something and we actually recorded it and listened to it, before we all said, "Well, this is too much for you guys." They were relatively patient.

Alright, let's jump ahead to after it comes out. It was starting to make a difference right from the get-go.

Well, the band had huge critical success and a very heavy, diehard serious cult following. The Rolling Stone response to *Murmur* was very strong, but it still didn't sell many records. I mean, it sold maybe 100,000 in the first year. And college radio wasn't very organized, with no real charts for it. And I wish it was still like that, only regional charts.

So did your phone just start ringing at this point? Did your standing in the industry immediately go up, was the industry hip to the critical acclaim coming in, or was it still indifferent to that?

Yes, that stuff helped a lot. The problem was that those people didn't really understand why REM was successful. They thought it was just about being obscure and not playing the guitar very well.

Did you get points on that record?

Not much, I think Mitch and I split 3 points, which is actually pretty decent. We didn't get much of an advance. The budget for the first record was slightly under $15,000 and the second was not much more.

Wow. How long did it take you?

We did our typical kind of 21-day sort of thing on the first one and a few days less on the second.

What kind of days were we talking? Eight hours, twelve?

I never work less than twelve. Probably fourteen, typically.

Okay, here's a big thing, is ear fatigue a myth?

If you don't listen too loud, you don't get ear fatigue. If you're standing in front of loud amps, or mixing at a level that a lot of people mix at, then, yeah it's a real thing. Absolutely.

I've come around to mixing at real low levels. Because you see what jumps out.

You've got to check it out at high volumes every once in a while, to check for squeaks, pops, and noises you don't hear. But your blending should always be done at kind of low levels.

When you mixed those records, were the songs mixed at the same time?

I prefer to record and mix as I go when I'm in a situation where I can do that. I think you stay focused that way.

Was it an intense mixing experience, with tons of mixes on each song?

We would get mixes up, and once everybody was happy with them, we did it. I think it's very important that the band is there for mixing. You have to defend your decisions to them at that point, if one guy says, "turn me up," you have to explain why he's at the right volume already. And also, sometimes they're right. Sometimes you're concentrating on one particular aspect, and yes indeed; the bass is not quite up loud enough. So you say, "Thanks, man," and fix it. Or you get to the third bar, and they say, "Oh, that part is not supposed to be there," and you wouldn't know that, and if they're not there at the time, you have to go back and redo the whole damn thing. So I like having the band around, I almost insist that they are. Unless they completely agree that, when I'm happy with the mixes, they're done.

Well, you know, a lot of bands don't stay for the mixing, obviously. But it's good when a band at least knows the fundamental idea of recording.

Part of what my job is as a producer is to kick the fuckers out of the nest. I'm not interested in doing records for them and perpetuating a career I don't even like. I'm interested in them learning everything they can from me.

That's the most frustrating thing we run into, that so many of these people don't know the basics. And I didn't either, but I tried to listen and learn instead of talk and learn. I don't want to sound like a curmudgeon, but some of these young bands come in, don't know anything, and just start going off and it ends up becoming distracting and taking us away from what we have to do.

Extremely distracting, but it's the real thing. You guys are in a tough position, because until you get a gold record on your wall, they won't shut up.

One more thing on the REM stuff, when you recorded it, is there anything that really stands out, or any secrets or anything? I mean there's a mythology about Murmur, and I think it's funny when you say there's not a lot of ambiance on that record, because most people would think that everything was mic'd twenty-five feet away on that record.

Some things are. Ambiance was the wrong word. It's still kind of a close record. We're not real far away from the drums on that record. We don't have a lot of big, cracking room around them. They're still pretty compact, kind of deep. We were looking for... an alternative way to fill the spectral area where there was no fuzz. Or bass. So what that did was it opened up this darker snare drum area that we could use. A lot of these songs have boxy, sorta Memphis snare drums on them, because they cut up, they filled the spectral area out nicely without covering anything up. Those drum sounds won't make it through big fuzz guitar sounds.

Those records inspired an entire sound. What do you think the essence of that sound was?

I believe you, but it's hard for me to see it that way. Peter was not interested in being a lead guitar player, which is probably the key to his more inventive style. Since he didn't know many chords, he'd make up these arpeggiated things, but he'd listened to lots of records and was real musical, so he had all this stuff swimming around in his head.

Did you use a lot of close mic'ing with 57s?

Hard to remember. I'm not one of those guys who just sets up an amp and does a whole record. We messed around with different things. And Mitch too was hugely involved in these guitar sounds.

Was the Rickenbacker one of the biggest aspects of that sound?

Well, the single-coil sound of the Rickenbacker is a real thing. The pickups are very low output, very smooth. Which can cause an amp with peaks in it to have really peaky notes. [We used] lots of fast limiting to even these things out with under-compression after the fact. Like take [Urei] 1176 [compressor]'s and run the two mixes separate and just push them up under the whole mix. So you're not taking the stuff off the top, you're just bringing everything that is soft up. You've still got more transient than if you were beating it all down here, but you've got an ultra-compressed mix with really fast release times under everything so that the cymbals ring out a little bit more, everything rings out a little bit more. But the top isn't crushed down. [*Get it? It's parallel, compression with the original signal.*]

So what amp were you using at that point? Did you introduce him to the Vox AC30?

We used a lot of different things. Probably we introduced him to the AC30... I brought in one I'd had forever.

But he was conscious not to overdrive it. We've found the Rickenbacker to be thin a lot of times, how do you combat that?

A lot of what you're doing when you're trying to get cleanish guitar sounds and still have some power to them is you've got to have those compressors working overtime. But you've got to be careful with the attack times, because you can't take all the attack away. So one of the things that we would do is under-compression. You take your microphone and you split it into two signals. You have one without any compression coming up on a fader and then you have one

with lots of fast attack and fast release on the fader right beside it. And then you assign both of those faders to one track. What you end up with is a fuller version that still has all the peaks.

The bass on those records is quite good too.

Yeah, the first album was pretty much a direct bass sound. He was playing a Rick then too.

Did you 1176 that as it came through?

Oh, I'm sure. We had lots of compressors. I may have been using something different on that one.

Why go direct?

I go direct almost exclusively just because I'm too lazy to set it up. It depends very specifically on what I want to do. On this other record I did bass entirely through a Twin Reverb. 10s are better for bass than 12s. So with Mike, one of the discussions we had before *Reckoning* was that he wanted a bass sound that was more like his live sound. So I went to see him play in this little pizza place in Greensboro, right before we went in. And we started that record without Mitch. I was in there first about three or four days doing initial setup. So for *Reckoning*, we set up his bass amp in this long tube, a gobo-built tube. It was about twelve feet long, completely isolated with four 12" speakers out at the end, and I mic'd him maybe six or seven feet out into the tube.

Do you remember what mic you used?

It would have been a large diaphragm mic of some sort. Could have been an AKG.

So after the success of those records, what kind of changes have you made [in your production style]?

Well, in some ways those records were successful, but those were not the kind of records that most major labels liked. They would say, "Oh, this band could sound real good if they got a real producer." Because they were different sounding records for the time. And most people I guess just assumed that there wasn't quite as much technique and forethought going into how those records sounded.

Do you think it had anything to do with the South?

Of course it did. There is still a gigantic Southern prejudice. It is unprecedented. It's different now then it was back then. At the time it was more of an LA-New York-Nashville thing. And LA and New York were bowing down to London anyway. We realized that everything grew better in a petri dish of isolation. Out of LA you got Toto, which was extremely successful and extremely technically brilliant, and who fucking cares? Those guys could really play, but I could never even make myself listen to that stuff on the radio.

How quick did IRS let you know that you would do *Reckoning*? Were they happy with *Murmur*?

Well, they came back and said, "Okay, it's time to make another one." Remember, the band had the leverage to get us in the first place. They did what the label asked them to do by trying out the other producer, but the label ultimately let them have their way. The critical success helped, but that didn't really carry over much to us.

Were you aware of how that jangle-pop thing began to formulate? Because in the mid-eighties, it was everything.

We knew those bands were there already. They just didn't have record deals, didn't have hits. Those guitars were still there, they didn't come out of thin air.

Do you feel that *Reckoning* was a continuation of *Murmur* or more of a departure? Did the fact that they were on the road have anything to do with it?

Well, yeah, Mills had a more specific idea of what he wanted to sound like. They hadn't had the same casual atmosphere in which to write their songs, so they were a little more nervous about the material. That record got great reviews, there wasn't a sophomore reaction, and it sold more than *Murmur*.

So the Smithereens were the next big project, right?

Yeah, they were on Enigma, with a ten thousand-dollar budget. They had already got started on some tapes with Jim Ball at the Record Plant. They tricked me into agreeing to make the record by, well, Pat was working at Folk City and Marti and I were playing there and he had a photographer show up to take the picture of me signing the contract that I had not agreed to sign. The whole band was there. No one at Enigma really liked them, except this one guy. And they did really well. That was a great record, a ten-day record. That's all Fender amps, at the Record Plant so it was through a nice API console. And those ATR tape recorders, very good sounding. As if that matters, right?

Was *Green Thoughts* the next one after that?

Green Thoughts we made at Capitol B.

Now how was it to work in there? I mean, oh man...

It was cool, it was good. I don't have a collector's mentality about recording at different studios... what it boils down to is get this thing on tape efficiently and with as little technical interference with the performance as you possibly can. Do all your technical interference as quietly and as unobtrusively as you can so the artist feels like you've done nothing. If the artist can come in and play and thinks they're great and that they sound great, and you just sat there and picked your teeth, then you've done a perfect job, because they're going to be the most relaxed, the most confident, and they're going to have the fire from having that confidence and feeling like they're god. If you get in there and you beat them down, and act like everything is a big deal, then they're just going to get bummed out and feel like they suck.

It's about making the atmosphere and the environment of the session.

And some people respond to different things. Some people like to have their chocolate and their brandy and a little rug, and some people like to feel like they're in a bedroom to make a record.

I think a lot of "small time" studio people get caught up on, "everything has to be done just like this," with the technical aspect.

The technical aspect is so liquid. There are a million different ways to get the thing on tape in a useful fashion. There is no absolutely right way to do anything. It's very specific to the specific singer, guitar amp, or just the atmosphere of that day. The barometric pressure has a huge influence on the way a microphone sounds. And that's not something you can control with air conditioning. There are things that work better than others, or things that you have faith in that you're never going to work without. But this whole thing of, "You've got to stand on this spot in front of this mic to sound like Big Joe Turner," is not apropos to every singer. It's not even apropos to Big Joe Turner, every time he sang. There are incredible sounding Little Richard records that

were made with two mics. The saxophone player stood inside the door to play his background part and turned towards the door to play the solo. And those records sound really good... You had to do that on 4-track when you're trying to make these big records. The Beatles things were a lot of guys playing at the same time. One of the bad things about modern recording is that everything is so isolated that people aren't paying attention to the nature of the interaction. And there is a difference in the way things sound when you're eight feet away and when you're four inches away. If you just record the guy four inches away and turn him up and down, it doesn't sound the same. For example, on old Beatles records, the way the drums sounded when there was singing and when there wasn't singing. Because you would have live vocal tracks and when John would quit singing, the drum leakage would come up because of the compression. So lots of times I'll fake that with ducking or undercompression so the vocal can be loud, the drums actually kind of duck a bit when the singing is happening – you'll have like an ambient mic that ducks a bit and then the singing stops and it fills back in.

Spector records were the same way, when they start singing everything drops down, and then when there's an instrumental passage, everything comes up. You hear the piano start to pound...

Well, a lot of that is just the overall compression. Slow program compression. Another thing that I tried to get everybody to do is do a song live to 2-track. That's some of the most fun I had on REM records; those B-sides were all live to 2-track. Or sometimes we would record binaural, using a binaural head that I'd make just using a box, I don't carry a real binaural head around. I use a tape box and make one. Everybody was positioned around the room to have the right perspective. Lots of times it would be live to 2-track with a live mix. Like Marshall Crenshaw and his "Steel Strings". That's all live, except for Mitch's guitar, up in a big concrete room in a warehouse. And I'm singing my backup part at the console as I mix it...

Did you ever learn drum machine programming, that sort of thing?

I've always owned drum machines, because they're practical. I always used Dr. Rhythm as weird drum machines in their early days. I bought a Drumulator when it first came out, because it had a really good sound. It is still one of the few drum machines that actually sounds kind of like recordings of drums. Recordings are not pumped up at all, they're very kind of plain. So you can fake it pretty well with one of those.

Have you done a lot of your and Marti Jones' solo stuff at home?

Marti's records have been mostly expensive real records. Her last record we did a lot of singing, and we actually did most of that recording at home. The drums were all recorded at this church in Charlotte, using the Reflection mobile unit. But most of the rest of it was done in studios.

What is your home setup like?

It's just ADATs and a Mackie, just like everybody else has. I use a FET-47, an old U-47, but a FET. I have a [Audio Technica] 4050, which is very good for a lot of things. I use a Drawmer, which I like because it's a real fuzzy mic preamp. Compressors...

We don't know much about compression; we're more coloration guys. When we turn on the Joe Meek, we can hear what it does. When we turn on the DBX 160s, we can hear that. So nowadays, do you work out of Reflection mainly?

This year I've made a record in New York, tracked it there and mixed it at Reflection. Also made one at Reflection and my house and mixed it at Reflection. Their basic setup is two rooms and the church. I made one record late last year in the church. They have one big room, A, with a Neve and your choice of 48 analog or 48 digital, but it's the Sony digital systems. The tape recorders can move to either room. And then they have a smaller room, C, that I also like, mostly for jazz stuff.

Good pianos in both rooms, a B-3, vibes, all that stuff. There's a Sony console, a 3000, which is actually the best console ever made, but nobody knows it or gives a shit.

So when you walk into a studio, do you have a rack of stuff that you take?

I take a few things around. Two things that I like to have is a couple 1176s, which studios often have, and then I bought those Distressors, the EL8s, just because not everybody has those. To do some of the drum sound things I like to do you need something that is really fast, on attack and release. They have added benefit of doing the LA2A really well, and doing a respectable Fairchild. But the two things I always take are a Roland 3000 delay line, and I always set it to 151 ms, with the filter in. And I take a PCM60, because its short room, nobody else has that short room and I like that sound.

Do you take any mics with you?

Depends on where I'm going. Usually not, I mean I don't own a big rack of esoteric microphones. Typically I can do pretty much the techniques I need to do as long as they have mics that can do figure-8, and omni. I'm a big fan of omni, I typically keep most mics in omni. And most mics that do omni also will also do figure-8. You need figure-8 for a few plumbline-style techniques, because of your phase. You've got to be very conscious when you're mic'ing of phase planes and making sure that you can see your image through whatever it is you need to see it through. A little added benefit of digital is that you can slow tracks down, like on an ADAT, you can take your close mics and slow them down until they're in a phase plane with your overheads.

One thing that, when you read *MIX* and they interview people who work in the bigger studios like you do, is they kind of become elitist with that equipment, where I can't relate to it. But you, being someone who has worked in huge studios, you still have a positive view towards smaller studios.

Well, the great thing about the technology of starting with these little 4-track cassette decks, or actually with the Teac 3440, it was a real revolution for Chris and Mitch and me, all of us, was that it allowed us to do much better sounding recording at home than we'd ever been able to do. We could afford these tape recorders. We couldn't afford a Scully and keep it working. I bought a Teac and one of those little boxes that had four inputs and two outputs and four switches, left, right, and center. Pan pots should be eliminated anyway, you should just be dealing with left-right-center. You can sit there and obsess about stuff that doesn't matter with panpots. One of the best things about panpots is that you can take something that's fully panned and, just by bringing it slightly in, you can actually make it seem like it's dropping back and out. Panpots are definitely useful, you can take things that are lined up and sometimes expose them, but as soon as you hit the mono switch your blend might not be very good. But if you're

dealing with things where it takes that to expose the part, then there may be another issue with the part that needs to be dealt with. I keep a pair of little Auratones stacked, so you just hit the minis and it's got the mono sound immediately. It's like you have that whole different perspective on the mono blend, so you hear what that TV/boom box thing is going to be. And also, always check the blend from a different room, because that tells you so much more about where your vocals are riding. Leave the room, stand outside, and if something is sticking out too much or not enough, you can easily tell it. But everything sounds a little bit different on every speaker, so you can't mix for every speaker.

Is the [Yamaha] NS-10 the best bet for speakers?

I wouldn't mix a record on NS-10s if somebody paid me an extra million dollars. I just don't like them. Never thought they sounded good. They got famous because [Bob] Clearmountain used them for a year, and he quit using them right away. I love Genelecs, I like the 01s. In general, a two-way is better than a three-way. The fewer crossovers, the less you're trying to guess what is going on with the phase. There is a series of JBLs that I used to mix on that sound very good with certain amps. The best thing about Genelecs is that they sound good and they're powered, which means they sound the same, so your damping factor doesn't change, and the damping factor of the amplifier into the speakers is really the key on what's going on in the low end. The main thing is just getting used to something. If I had gotten used to NS-10s... I have a lot of friends who have made very good sounding records on NS-10s. But the few times I have been listening to things on NS-10s, it has been very hard to tell what is going on in the middle. I think the middle on NS-10s is very colorful, and because of that I don't relate to them. It's all a matter of getting used to something and using it. The rooms all sound a little bit different. Nearfields are more important. If a room has good well-tuned big speakers, that's good to check your deep bass, to make sure you're not overdoing something down low, and to check for noise. But anything that you're used to at low volumes, and especially something that rounds off all the extremes and allows you to hear what is going on in the midrange is really helpful. So, basically, I'm not a snob about any of the equipment. There are certain things that are difficult to do without a very nice piece of equipment. But if somebody put me on a desert island and said I had to make this record with all 635As I think I'd make a pretty good sounding record. It's still more about music than it is about sound.

Do you find the Mackie to be useful?

Mackies are incredible. It's phenomenal that they can make something that costs $1000 and is totally clean, the EQs don't ring, and it's an incredibly useful, workable piece of equipment. The good thing about the particular sound of that 11K shelf that they have in there is that it doesn't ring. You can use a lot of it. The Neve is much ringier in the top end, because of the nature of the feedback loop in the EQ section, and can get kind of obnoxious. Whatever Mackie has done on this shelf, you can use a lot of it and it doesn't ring. It actually sounds very good with those Coles [4038s], which you have to use a lot; you have to turn it all the way up. If you made 11K as your center of a broadband width on the top of the Neve, and made it a shelf and turned it all the way up, it would ring like hell, it would not be as good sounding as the Mackie.

You probably don't use the preamps much on there.

I wouldn't be able to say. I don't cut anything on there at all, so I wouldn't have any judgement of the preamps.

I think they're pretty decent actually. We've cut with them. The thing that brought it home to us was, we were reading an article about Lou Reed recording his last album, and his engineer was talking about preamps. And they had Neves

and Manleys and Mackies. And he said the Mackie came in third place every time, but he couldn't believe how close it was. It was a close third. The gap was a lot smaller than he thought it would be, and those Manleys are like $2000 a channel.

Manleys and Neves are real different, like apples and oranges. The biggest problem with the Manley is that it doesn't load up with every tape recorder and every console well. I use Manleys a lot, and the Manley compressors are really good. But the preamp has a certain load that it works well into. Neves people like it because there is a certain butchness to the way they sound, and that butchness is slightly colored. They're over-engineered with discrete electronics, as are the Manleys.

So talk about the Pat [from Smithereens] record.

We recorded it on 2", and I did all my editing that way. It's a bit quicker than the digital Sony, because that's like video editing in that you do it with copying and SMPTE sync. So 2" editing, state-of-the-art 1970, we go in there and wack it apart and glue it back together. Then we immediately dumped the stuff to digital as we would get tracks that we liked. I made ADAT copies of that and we did all the guitars and the singing at my house. Then went back and laid all the stuff onto the Sony digital.

Now, when you do vocals at your house, how do you do that?

In the basement; I'm in the same room as the singer. I'm recording pretty clean, a little compression.

Was it a conscious decision to jump all around?

Well, we just didn't want to waste a bunch of money at the studio for that stuff. Real expensive musicians, the two guys were really expensive, so a bunch of the money was spent on them. So instead of spending $1500 a day in the studio, we just went back to the house for a week

So who takes care of the editing? The assembly of it?

Well, his record is pretty complicated. We have a lot of cross-fades and a lot of sectional things. But I assembled it all there just to see how things worked, but I reassembled in mastering. The way I master, I master almost everything with Greg Calbi. I've probably done fifty albums with him. He uses Sonic Solutions, so we do pretty much all our analog moves going in to that. And we try different converters. We may use a different converter for every song going in, A to D, depending on what we want it to sound like. Because they all have slightly different characteristics, and you want to bring something out... And here's the thing that bothers me about this anti-digital stuff: people are making all these judgements about what stuff sounds like as if digital can't replicate it. Listening to CDs, which are as about as unsophisticated digital technology as exists, it still sounds pretty good. But if you're making some critical judgements about the top end of digital while listening to a CD, you're an idiot. Because if you're claiming to hear

some difference about your analog recording while listening to a CD, then the subjectivity has become ridiculous. Every digital tape recorder out there sounds better at the fringes, including ADAT, than CDs. But all the converters sound a bit different, as do the players. There are lots of differences out there. As long as you're willing to listen to a CD, then you should not be anti-digital.

But don't you think the fringes are where people prefer analog, because the fringes are rounded slightly?

No. In theory, here's what is happening: Analog goes on forever no matter how far down it gets. Digital, because of memory being so expensive when they developed it, they just picked twenty thousand cycles and cut it off. The truth of the matter is that the stuff that is really going on is gone by 12K anyway. Musically, the residual aspects of these things are so arbitrary, particularly with vinyl recordings. The cartridges all sound so different, and so do the preamps. There are a huge number of variables there that are more consistent with digital. I think a lot of the initial problem with digital is that people were applying analog recording techniques. And especially re-EQ styles to it that brought out a harshness that was not just in digital, it would have been in analog if you actually got back what you put down. And there are a lot of deaf engineers who listen to things too loud, which is why things have gotten brighter and brighter.

How did Connie Francis get that overdriven sound?

Well, listen to Aretha's records. Those mics and tube preamps get into high levels of distortion, bringing out lots of high end. Which is one of the good things about the Drawmers, that it doesn't have very much headroom, so you can get that stuff.

Do you think we can pull the Altecs that far?

Sure, they were probably using those.

You were talking about going to Greg Calbi for mastering. But we have to send stuff away for that, and a lot of times it comes back and people complain it doesn't sound the same. Is there anything that you can recommend for this process? Anything we could tell the mastering engineer?

No, I mean you are at the mercy of whoever is making your copy. You just have to get a relationship with someone you trust. Mastering is very important, because listeners equate volume with quality. If your CD plays back 6 dBs quieter than the new U2 CD, it doesn't matter about the million dollars they spent to record it, it's that it is playing back 6 dBs louder, more than any other single element in the recording chain. So it's worth the extra money. If you're not using esoteric, loud A to D converters, you're going to be about 6 dBs down from where all the other, "real" records are. And 6 dBs is a lot.

Another thing that kills me is the compression aspect. We're very much more about creative compression than we are about limiting. And this one record we did, the mastering engineer just killed everything we did because he went on top and compressed the whole fucker, knocked out everything with too much compression. So the last thing that we did, we sent it to a good guy, and said, "Look, we've compressed it the way we want it. If you need to limit it at one point, fine, but we've done it creatively, so don't do it." And he didn't, said, fine he doesn't have to do that. And it made his job easier too. But you have to say that now, we found out. Just tell them not to do this.

Well, in the old days, where you made vinyl, it was a real technical job above and beyond any sonic changes you might want to make to the record. There's always that last opportunity to change the EQ a bit, add a little compression, even add a little echo. But the big job they had was creating that very technical analog mother, which then turned into stampers, and they made records out of that. Which is, itself, very technical. Greg's training came from that, as did mine. So what we have now is, people think mastering is where you go in and fuck with the record. And while you're at it you make the 1630 with the IDs on it. And you have a lot of horribly underqualified people doing that, who simply have Sonic Sound Tools or something. The only way that you can really protect yourself is make sure that you don't have them press anything up until you've okay'd it. We used to always do that with everything. You'd have test pressings and you'd go back and fix stuff. CDRs don't sound quite the same. The biggest problem you'll have with CDRs is that they'll often be slightly brighter and usually maybe not quite as loud. I usually just listen to DAT's and let somebody else do quality control with the manufacturing. Although CDRs have gotten a lot more consistent.

But the more I think about it, people are judging your studio or your engineering

ability when so much of what we're talking about with mastering and manufacturing can eliminate or contribute to the sound of what you've done. That's a lot of people that can fuck it up, that your reputation is based on. It's scary.

A big big problem in the eighties was judging mixes by cassette. And I've spent a lot of my life trying not to do remixes because the guy was judging by cassette. Especially when you get people who are unfamiliar about what the process really is and they're nervous about it and it's the most money they've ever spent in their life on anything and they're second-guessing everything anyway. It's very difficult when they're judging it all by cassette. At least now most record companies have DATs and you can tell much better how it's mixed. For a while, people were listening to 15 ips, and the only problem with that is they were'nt quite bright enough.

Well, alright, anything else you like to add?

Mitch and I have been drug-free throughout our entire lives. I'm serious.

What did Michael smell like?

He smelled like garlic.

Studio Nightmares

HORROR STORIES FROM ENGINEERS AND MUSICIANS LOCKED IN TINY ROOMS TOGETHER

by Larry Crane

I asked a few pals for horrible recording experiences or stories...

GREG FREEMAN

(Pell Mell, Lowdown, etc)

What about Royal Trux?

That would be one of them. That was probably one of the worst ones. Usually when there are drugs involved that's bad because it just makes for a bad scene.

What about the Dwarves when you thought they slipped you some acid?

That's right! I forgot about that! Yeah, they were doing a different drug every week. "Okay Greg, we want to book 3 hours every Thursday for 7 weeks." One week they'd be really drunk on wine and then the next week they'd come in and they'd be on downers and the 3rd week they'd be tripping, the 4th week they'd be on speed.

Did you notice much difference in the way they played?

No, it all sounded the same. I remember they brought me back that cinnamon roll and I hadn't eaten, so I ate the cinnamon roll and I started to feel really weird and I was like, "Oh fuck, did they put acid in the cinnamon roll?"

That's a new way to take it, I guess.

But actually, the Dwarves, at first they were intense, but we became friends. It was hard, but it was enjoyable; they were kind of funny, they liked me. Greg Semen was my name on the record. They would say a bunch of things and make fun of me all the time.

BARBARA MANNING

(of SF Seals, 28th Day, World of Pooh, solo, etc.)

When I was 19 years old I was pushed around a little easier... now that I'm an older person, I certainly wouldn't allow this kind of thing to happen. I think the most aggravating moment in the studio I've ever had was when I felt stripped of my right to decide how my song was going to be performed, including my own little bass line which I had come up with and was very proud of.

Can we name any names?

I'm not trying to protect Russ Tolman, that's for sure. Russ Tolman, the man who took away our songwriting and kept all the receipts from all the royalties; he was only entitled to half.

What kind of stuff happened while you were in the studio?

Well, it was when we were working on the 28th Day album [1985], on the song "Burnsite" and I had come up with what I felt was a very powerful, strong, muddy bass chord and Russ really didn't like it. He didn't like discordant things in general. He wanted it to sound clean and I recorded it the way I wanted to and he said, no, we had to do it again and told me I had to stick to a 2 note progression, which I was very frustrated with, but I was talked into doing because he told me he kept both tracks and we could decide later. Being open to compromising and open to constructive criticism I thought, "Why not?" and we can decide from then on. However, he didn't keep the other track and he had no intention of ever using it so he just recorded right over it. When I realized that, when it came time to do the vocals, I sorta took it out on him. Noticing he had his headphones on, near the end of "Burnsite" I let out an enormous scream of all my anger and I got a big thrill seeing him throw the headphone set off his ears. I stayed in the studio for a minute before I went in 'cause I was afraid. I was very surprised by the fact that he kept the scream in there, considering that it was certainly directed at him. Not all my recording experiences have been pleasant, but I would say that was the one that was the most aggravating because I felt it had a lot to do with the creative process, not just something going wrong or somebody getting in a fight with somebody else. If you're the writer of the song then you have the ultimate say, in my opinion.

HUGH SWARTS

(Thinking Fellers Union Local 282)

There's getting down to the end of it when you're mixing and having trouble, like with some of the songs that we do, with the density of things... frequency domain, things cancel each other out. Problems like that. Or finishing something and listening back and wondering what we were thinking when we mixed that. A lot of times, this is after going over it very meticulously, phrase by phrase in some cases. I really like Fly Ashtray a lot. They did one record, *Tone Sensations of the Wondermen*, that Kramer did at Noise New York; that's the only one I *don't* like. You know how all that stuff that Kramer does has that lofty sort of sheen to it? It has that on it. I don't know what kind of signal processing he used on it, different kinds of reverb, I'm sure, maybe a very slight delay. We'd played with them and I'd heard all those songs live before I'd heard the record and then I heard that and I was, "Oh my god!" They're great songs and it's passable, but compared to their own production it's not as good. As a matter of fact, they were telling me they were deliberately distracting him and moving knobs behind his back. That's a prime example of somebody making decisions that shouldn't have been his. Everything else I've heard by them, they've done themselves... they had a recording studio for a while. A couple of the guys are engineers, James and Chris, and they pretty much did everything themselves.

MARK ROBINSON

(Teen Beat Recs/re-mix king)

There's definitely times, more than once, where I've showed up at a studio without tape. Some studios have tape and some don't. Usually, it's Sunday or Saturday and you don't have that much money to spend and you're already there in the studio and you're running out to buy tape. A lot of time, I'll go into studios just 'cause they were cheap and not really talking to the producer person much more than 5 minutes on the phone. When we did the Unrest "Skinhead Girl" single, we just went into this guy... I called him up in the classifieds and I was, "Yeah, can we come over and record?" That was at the time when we were working really fast... we were only doing one song. We did the recording part, it couldn't have been more than three hours, and then we were, "So, can we mix now?" and the guy's like, "What? We can't mix today! My ears are getting tired. This is loud stuff, I don't think my ears can take this stuff!" He spent all of his time talking about his "connections" at Columbia Records and stuff like that.

Studio Daze

by Marty Jourard

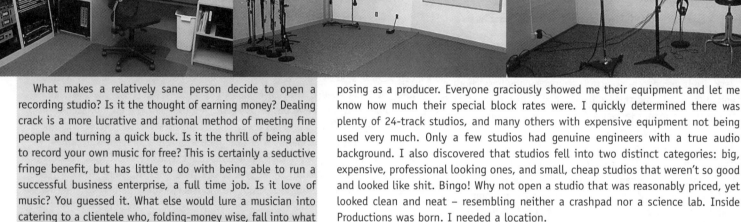

What makes a relatively sane person decide to open a recording studio? Is it the thought of earning money? Dealing crack is a more lucrative and rational method of meeting fine people and turning a quick buck. Is it the thrill of being able to record your own music for free? This is certainly a seductive fringe benefit, but has little to do with being able to run a successful business enterprise, a full time job. Is it love of music? You guessed it. What else would lure a musician into catering to a clientele who, folding-money wise, fall into what can be discretely called the entry-level tax bracket? From 1990 to 1995 I ran and owned a studio in Seattle called Inside Productions, first as an eight – and then a sixteen-track. In those five years I recorded, among the fluff and crud, some truly great music and songs, music I was proud to have put on tape. I also learned an immense amount regarding human nature, taxes, (city, county, state and federal), business licenses, fire marshalls, finding your niche (or not) in a very crowded field, and dealing with the unique mindset of the personality type known as a "musician."

A Little Background

Lest you think I don't understand musicians, not true. I am one. Raised in Gainesville, Florida, I lived in Los Angeles for 13 years, nine of which I spent in a band some of you older readers may remember, The Motels. I played keyboards and saxophone. We made five albums and had a couple top ten singles ("Only the Lonely," "Suddenly last Summer"). I moved to Seattle, not interested in playing professionally, but still wanting to be a part of the music scene. Why not open a studio? I already had some equipment: a Tascam 38 8-track, a 16-channel board (an ergonomic nightmare called the Studiomaster Stellarmix), and a few SM-57s. Did I want to go big-time with the equipment, or stay small and find my niche? I needed to find out what was out there first, so I first called up, then visited most of the studios in the area (12)

posing as a producer. Everyone graciously showed me their equipment and let me know how much their special block rates were. I quickly determined there was plenty of 24-track studios, and many others with expensive equipment not being used very much. Only a few studios had genuine engineers with a true audio background. I also discovered that studios fell into two distinct categories: big, expensive, professional looking ones, and small, cheap studios that weren't so good and looked like shit. Bingo! Why not open a studio that was reasonably priced, yet looked clean and neat – resembling neither a crashpad nor a science lab. Inside Productions was born. I needed a location.

The Early Years

So, in 1991 I signed a lease for a 460 square foot office space in a business park in Bellevue, Washington. Outside, downshifting trucks were heard at all hours. Soundproof this. A capable electronic whiz and serious carpenter friend of mine, Frank Bry, said no problem: we covered the inside of the windows with stiff foam core insulation and sealed them tight, then built studs, added a double layer of sheetrock covered with brown fibreboard and Azonic™ acoustic foam. I stuffed the space above the drop ceiling with many rolls of fiberglass insulation. We covered the 10x15 tracking room walls with more Azonic™ foam – it came in 2x2 foot sheets faced with little foam pyramids, making the room sound deader than Julius Caesar. I ran an eight input snake I bought through Carvin (1-800-854-2235), above the drop ceiling to the other side of the office space.

The tracking room and the recording room were separated by a space occupied by a desk, an upright piano and a sofa. The tracking room, with the door closed, was completely isolated from where I ran the session, so couldn't see what went on inside. In order to have visual contact with the band, I bought a closed-circuit TV system for $300 from Costco, installed a fish-eye lens, mounted the camera in a corner of the tracking room, and voila! – I could see the band, but they couldn't see me. No "band in a fishbowl" vibe. Clients liked being in the tracking room with no-one looking in at them. I was in business at $17 per hour. My first customer was a veterinarian's receptionist who sang along with a karaoke tape. The thrill of operating a studio was finally mine.

How Do You Run this Stuff?

I had no technical background whatsoever. However, having made five albums in L.A. as well as working as a session player on records, I couldn't help but pick up some knowledge of recording. Luckily, the Motels had always worked with great engineers. Of our five albums, two were made with engineer-turned-producer Val Garay, who recorded all those James Taylor and Linda Rondstadt albums that helped usher in punk music in 1976. I watched how he recorded vocals, because he had it figured out. Val told me that mics more or less looked the way they sounded, which makes sense if you think about it, skinny silver mics pick up high end, big fat tube mics are warm, etc.

Suspecting there was even more to be learned about recording I asked recording engineers, used common sense, read my equipment manuals and also a few books available from the Mix Bookshelf catalog, including the pretty good *Modern Recording Techniques* (Huber and Runstein). Learning the mysteries of signal routing practically drove me nuts, though. What the fuck was a "buss send" anyway? I mean, help me. My technically minded friend Frank patiently and repeatedly drew little diagrams for me until I claimed I understood. Certain books explained clearly such concepts as routing, compression, EQ and my personal concept hell, signal flow in patch bays.

I did everything myself - no business partner. In looking back that may have kept me, ultimately, too busy to be effective at everything I was doing. Booking the studio, answering the phone, setting up mics, making coffee, recording, mixing, collecting our modest fee. To run a studio without running yourself ragged, try and find someone you can work with and divide the labor, either business/recording or engineering/dealing with clients. Keeping the client happy is a full time job and so is recording. Be warned.

I ran a small ad in *The Rocket* faithfully for about five years. It acted more as a place marker than an advertisement, a way of acknowledging continuous business presence. After a few years people recognized the name and IP became a known quantity, but that and two dollars will get you a latte. Word of mouth was still the most effective advertising; most bands knew other bands and players and my customers seemed to recommend me to other musicians. Repeat business was good with many bands, especially if a band had tried another studio between their first visit to us and the second. It was my musical knowledge and ability to work with people that made the difference, as well as the overall atmosphere.

Equipment

My equipment was a combination of used and new professional and semipro gear. I found out you could, with careful choices, make a good sounding studio setup without dropping major coin. For instance, I used five Furman PB40 patchbays (20 pairs of i/o jacks) because they were cheap and worked fine. I opened them up and clipped a lead inside selected pairs to "de-normal" them. Building a wiring harness for the deck/board/patchbay took time, solder and hundreds of Switchcraft 1/4" jacks. I bought them through Conquest Sound (1-800-323-7671) for 81 cents apiece. Conquest specializes in ready-made snakes, cables, cords and bulk supplies. I recommend them.

Instead of buying cheap racks or premade cases, I bought two sheets of 3/4" 7-ply birch and built a housing console and rack space for the board, decks, monitors, outboard gear and tape storage for about $120 [see photo]. Not as hard as you think with help from a carpenter-minded friend.

Here are some comments regarding equipment:

Soundcraft Studio Spirit 24x8x2: I know, I know, Mackies are cheaper. Soundcraft boards sound great. This board, chosen over Tascam and Yamaha, had a very good EQ section, many sends, and was solidly built and very quiet.

Carvin EQ2029: 1/3 octave 29 band EQs with very good specs. Carvin still sells these for $229. This unit was clean enough to use for critical EQ effects, especially on drums. Surprisingly few drummers I recorded ever tuned their drums, and this EQ, along with the board EQ, helped "tune" many a kit. For bass drum I would boost around 50-100 Hz, and 2.5kHz for the beater. With toms I would push each individual slider up and back until one of them made a dramatic difference, then twiddle. Just dialing out 60 cycle hum from badly grounded guitars and noisy amps made these worth every penny.

BBE 422 Sonic Maximizer: Bought used for $150. Great for vocals and acoustic guitar, to boost presence in the mix. It was great for bass drum too, you just boosted the bass knob. My approach: any instrument would sound either better or worse through the BBE, so it was always worth a try.

Urei 1176LN limiter: I bought two of these legendary "limiting amplifiers" from Capitol Records engineer Mark Linett in L.A. for $200 each. They were very old, something like serial #157, original silver front. He retrofitted the low noise circuitry for $75 each. These were great for kick drum, acoustic guitar (I tried to duplicate the acoustic guitar production on the second Buffalo Springfield album), and vocals. I had to really tweak the attack and release rate but the 1176 smoothed out stuff beautifully, I used them to really paste vocals onto tape. I made it a point of pride to record vocals so you could always hear, for better or worse, the lyrics.

Effectron II Digital Delay: Bought used for $99. One of the very first non-tape delay units, it had the 1024ms chip, so the longest delay was around one second. This thing was smooth and warm sounding, vastly superior to the Roland SDE-3000 unit most people had. Try to find one.

For weird vocal and guitar sounds I would sometimes insert either a Boss Tremolo/Pan PN2 or Ibanez Tube Screamer into a channel of the patch bay. Stomp boxes are cool to use when mixing; just run it in and out of the chosen insert channel on the patchbay. I found the Alesis Quadraverb to be noisy and basically sucky, good for post-mixing effects on guitars, mostly.

I bought a Sony DPS R7 digital reverb that was very clean. The algorithms were so complex that you only needed a little reverb in the mix to make an effect, so there was little noise added to the overall signal. I tried to use as little reverb as I could in mixes though. Reverb is basically lame. Clients loved it but it made everything sound like a demo. Some clients felt they hadn't gotten their money's worth until there was a lot of reverb on the vocals. You couldn't argue with them.

Monitors

I resisted the temptation to buy big monitors. In fact, salespeople would loan me Tannoy Gold Standards and KRKs and top line Tannoys. The problem was, everything sounded so great on them they didn't put you in a critical state of mind when mixing. The people who were listening to the music I was recording did not have these pricey monitors at home. For years I mixed on a pair of Yamaha NS-10s. Ear fatigue always set in after a few hours of mixing, they had too much high end (tissue over the tweeters helped) and they tended to make vocals louder than they really were on other systems. There had to be life beyond, so I kept the NS-10Ms, but also bought a pair of Tannoy PBM 6.5s. They were nice-sounding, not as harsh as the Yamahas. I also used Auratones. If your mix sounds good on Auratones (esp. the midrange bass guitar frequencies and the vocal/instrumental mix) you have a good mix.

Dream Into Action

After three years in the first location, I decided I needed to move the studio from Bellevue into Seattle itself. Bellevue, to most "alternative" musicians, was a very non-PC place to record, sort of like Fugazi recording in Beverly Hills. I found a basement location in downtown Seattle in the same building that houses *The Rocket* (and for a few months, C/Z Records). As I clapped my hands in the empty concrete basement, on the verge of signing a two-year lease, I realized that the 1100 square feet underground space sounded like a huge racquetball court. Was music even recordable down there? Again, my friend Frank came to my aid, and with his acoustic design knowledge and carpentry chops, we double-walled the tracking room (put a wall in front of each wall), stapled in fiberglass insulation, sheetrocked, and fiberboarded. Carcinogen City. I learned it was worth it to buy ear protection (headphone style) when endlessly assembling 2x4 wall studs. That's a lot of nails being hit at close range. Use the ear protection. If you're not used to operating circular saws and hammers, be extra careful. We musicians need our fingers.

No way was I going to try installing the drop ceiling myself, or do amateur electrical work; I paid for pros. Miraculously, in the middle of downtown Seattle, there were no hum problems when I plugged everything in and turned it on. We cut a rectangular hole in the wall between the tracking room and the control room, built a sturdy wood frame to hold two panes of glass (one perpendicular, one slanted), and took it to an auto glass place. They cut the glass and installed it, we slid the frame in place, filled chinks with expanding foam sealant and silicone seal. Visual contact at last! I replaced the light switches with faders (with LEDs) that allowed you to preset fabulous mood lighting. Of all the money I spent on the interior, this feature got more comments than anything. When a band wasn't grooving too well I would drop the lighting levels

and this often put musicians in Star Mode. Get them faders. I used Lutron Maestros, approx. $40. Try one before buying a bunch to assure non-hum; they worked for me.

From the first day I spent in the new location, I suspected that long daily periods of time in a windowless basement would drive anyone nuts, especially in a space painted a hideous dogshit brown. I wanted the interior to be light, but neutral colored. I painted everything I could off-white and bought many yards of cream-colored sofa fabric cheap from a fabric store that specialized in odd lot industrial fabric overruns. We covered the fiberboard panels on the tracking room walls with sofa fabric, then edged the panels with 1x4" fir trim, painted grey.

To create a usable mixing environment in the control room we insulated the walls surrounding the control room window and on either side of the mixing board. To really deaden this end of the room the walls were covered by 4x8 foot sheets of Owens Corning 703 series fiberglass insulation, covered with sofa fabric. The 703 makes walls highly sound-absorbent. The other end of the rectangular room had a sofa that helped keep reflection to a minimum and was nice to fall asleep on.

I bought some 4x4 square office panel dividers to help isolate the drums from the other instruments by placing them on either side of the drumset, setting up guitar amps up against the panels on the other side, facing away from the drums and close mic'd. Office panels are useful and can be bought from used office furniture stores.

Mixing

As a rule, I found mixing good musicians was much easier then not-so-hot ones. Good musicians played with consistent volume, didn't play stray crud that needed to be edited out while mixing, and produced a sound at their amps or drums (or in their throats) that didn't need heroic EQ measures. Some bands needed open heart surgery on their mixes to make them usable, and their frustration would often build as they wondered why they didn't sound like their favorite records.

I learned to place vocals in the mix by mixing them last, and bringing them up from zero on the fader slowly until they were in the slot. I liked compression and limiting, but found (eventually) that a little goes a long way. Some singers naturally compress their voice when they sing; that's the best sounding kind. After lengthy mixing sessions, I often would leave the mixing console during a playback and listen to the song from the other room, as if I was overhearing a radio or a CD. If it sounded like it might have been the radio or a CD, the mix was probably going in the right direction.

Enter the ADAT

Just as I was preparing to open in my new (Seattle) location, with a brand new Tascam MSR16 1/2" 16-track and a 24-channel Soundcraft Studio Spirit console, industry buzz on the new ADAT abounded. Apparently the Alesis ADAT was going to make my tape format obsolete overnight. Shouldn't I immediately buy one? I soon realized the digital thing was very real in the minds of my potential clients. Everybody had been told that digital was "better" than analog, so some people calling for info and rates wouldn't even look at my studio, merely from the description of my recording deck. 1/2" analog wasn't considered a "pro" format as compared to the ADAT.

What didn't enter the minds of these careful shoppers was this: there were only 8 tracks on an ADAT, and sync was fairly slow and primitive without the $2000 BRC (Big Remote Control) most studio owners neglected to buy. Also, many people bought an ADAT deck, a Mackie board and some monitors and declared themselves a studio, with little or no musical/technical background. The Tascam

MSR16, despite the jeers of the Digital Army, was a great deck; the built in DBX noise reduction worked just fine, and there was no perceptible crosstalk on the record heads. The deck had better specs and transports than the Tascam 38 I used before going 16-track. I also had a Technics 1500 1/4" 2-track; a big, heavy 15 ips reel-to-reel with a huge loop in the tape path. I had it calibrated for Ampex 456. Frankly, mixes sent to the 2-track sounded identical to DAT mixes recorded at the same time.

Although there may have been an audible difference on high end monitors, how many people listened to music on high end systems? Not many of my friends, it was boombox city. So I didn't hop aboard the ADAT bandwagon, for these reasons and also because I had become quite good at razor edits on both the master tape (leadering songs for easy location) and the 1/4", where I could clean up beginnings and endings much quicker than going to a hard disk and editing with a software program.

Equipment vs. Reality: What Really Mattered

Over the years I recorded around 20 projects that in one form or another were released as CDs to the eager public. Of all the ones that sold, none of them were recorded on so called "professional" equipment, i.e. 2" 24-track deck, ADAT etc. Whose product actually did sell? Clients who played live gigs a lot sold their CDs, and so did people with serious musical talent, because they made good music (relatively easy when the music was good), not because the studio had a certain piece of equipment. Ultimately, it's that simple.

Andre Feriante's projects are a good example. This Seattle-based guy is a highly trained classical guitarist as well as a brilliant improviser. His first CD was recorded as he sat on the sofa in my first studio space: He played into a Milab VIP-50 mic plugged into my Sony 75ES DAT deck. He sold 1000 CDs and cassettes and reordered.

His next record was done with more care, but also on the cheap. We used the Milab for the front of the guitar (in a precisely measured location, so we could duplicate the sound in each session), then added an AKG-C414 a few inches from his right ear. He figured if it sounded good to him, a mic placed there would pick up good sound. Both mics were plugged into a Drawmer 1960 stereo tube preamp/limiter, then into two tracks (1 and 2) of the 16-track deck. We didn't use the board. After 30 minutes of takes, I rewound the tape and recorded on tracks 3 and 4. This continued until we used all 16 tracks, recording four hours of stereo music on one $37 reel of tape. Feriante got an indie label deal, and I heard the record one day played over the speakers at a Barnes & Noble store as a featured release in the music section. The music, ultimately, does most of the work.

Artists whose music graced the walls of Inside Productions during the heady Downtown Years included Bananafish, Larry Barrett, Sam Weis, Andre Feriante, Cat Food, the Fire Ants (with the Woods brothers and ex-Nirvana drummer Chad Channing), Sunny Day Real Estate (just before they signed to Sub Pop), Gary Heffern, Monroe's Fur, the Ottoman Bigwigs, and many other Rock and Alt Gods.

Dealing With Those Pesky Musicians

It is a sad fact that some musicians that enter a studio are not fully prepared. There were exceptions, of course. One folksinger cut and mixed a whole record in about four days. A Nashville songwriter cut a demo in one hour with four guitar parts and background vocals, all performed by himself. But unprepared musicians were common. Entire verses would be unwritten as we prepared for vocal overdubs, song arrangements never solidified, and there was almost always my pet peeve, humming Fender guitars. Incredible levels of hum came from countless Teles and Strats plugged into amps supplying their own additional hum. Guitars with Humbuckers, oddly enough, didn't hum. However, there was always one position a guitarist could hold that created the least hum. I would ask the player to slowly make a 360° turn and when the hum was minimal, that was the playing position, I would mark his foot position on the floor in duct tape. Don't move!

No one ever thought to arrive with their own spare 9 volt battery, not once. I had a supply of those. Guitar jacks would buzz, drummers would strip screws on stands, break drumheads or pedals and have no spares, one drummer forgot his drum key and sticks, guitarists would break strings and have no spares, singers (and others) would sometimes lubricate or otherwise alter themselves to nonproductive levels. I was amazed at how many younger musicians didn't fully understand the basic concept of multitrack recording, of combining good parts of several takes into a better whole, of erasing and redoing selected parts of a previously recorded track, and the idea that there was something called a "rough mix," that could be and would be redone. People became genuinely upset with their rough mixes, so making ruffs for clients came with the warning: "These are rough mixes, not the final mix." The next day, they would come in, "Hey man, these mixes aren't right, too much guitar, not enough bass," etc.

Mixing was sometimes challenging for a band with no obvious leader and three or four strongminded instrumentalists. "More bass," the bassist would suggest. "Shouldn't the vocal be a bit higher in the mix?" pondered the singer. "Kick drum, you can't even hear it," the drummer would volunteer. When a first time band began to realize that their premier studio experience was not going to sound like Led Zeppelin II, they would sometimes wonder what went wrong. I explained that the drummer was not in fact John Bonham, I was not producer Jimmy Page, and that the band also had a role in the sound of the final product. I usually recorded drums with a Sennheiser 421 on the kick, SM57 on the snare, two Shure SM81 mics as overheads, individual tom mics as needed. I relied primarily on the overheads for the sound of the drums, with bass drum and snare mics for stereo placement and emphasis. Bass guitar was usually run into a DI and through a DBX 160x compressor, then into the board, although I would mic the bass amp and if the amp sounded good, use it in the mix too. 57s on guitars.

Doubling vocals worked well if the overdub was done as soon as possible after the first vocal. Doubling guitar precisely gave a big fat sound to rhythm and lead parts and was a favorite trick.

I created a Hall of Fame. The corridor that connected the tracking room to the main area I painted white and asked clients to sign the walls with a magic marker. This was a great marketing concept; bands loved signing it, it lent an established air, rappers got way into their tags, and when you walked in to record you passed the names of the previous rock gods that had played music there. It was inspired by my going backstage at the Whisky a Go Go in the '70s and seeing all the rock graffiti. I suggest doing it. You may end up sawing out a panel and selling it if someone gets real famous.

Let's Call The Whole Thing Off

I ran the place for five years, lost money fairly steadily, and realized that running a business in a major city meant not only great musical moments, of which there were many, but: fire inspections, massive paperwork regarding licenses; city, county, state and federal and B&O taxes, employee taxes (don't ever legitimately hire just one person - you or they will spend all their time dealing with the tax and employee paperwork generated by you hiring them), aggressive street people, parking hassles, and more. I decided to sell, and when the lease ran out, the landlord let me stay month-to-month until I sold it, assuring him of a new tenant with no work on his part. I sold all the equipment, the right to negotiate a lease with the owner, and the name to two buyers who had wanted to open a studio for a long time. They wrote me a check, they bought the biz, and within four months, after replacing much of the "not pro enough" gear (board, deck, patchbay, etc.) they folded for lack of business, placing all their equipment on consignment at a local pro audio dealer. The space is now occupied by a highly successful production company that cranks out radio jingles and ads nonstop. They put an additional workstation in the tracking room, and are thriving. Life goes on, and although I learned a lot about recording and music, I found that once a musician, always a musician: I just didn't want to record music for a living. You have to really love working with equipment, people, music, or all three to successfully own and run a recording studio. I hope some of the above info will prove helpful in your efforts.

CHAPTER 4
Knowledge and Techniques

4-Track Basics

RECORDING YOUR BASIC ROCK 'N' ROLL BAND ON 4-TRACK

by Curtis Settino

If you have a cassette 4-track and want to do some recording of your band, or if there's only one of you and you want to sound like a band, here are some suggestions for getting strong, clear recordings. First, remember this: The Beatles recorded *Sgt. Pepper's* on 4-track. Second, forget that. You probably don't have the same high-quality 4-tracks and mics that they had nor the technicians that keep things running in optimum condition nor a George Martin (he helped more than Paul McCartney will ever admit). But, you may have a talent for writing and performing music. If so (and even, if not), you'll want your recording to capture what you do in such a way as to limit the amount of time you spend "disclaimering" your recordings before playing them for people. So, whether the recording is going to be a demo to get gigs or professional attention, something to impress your friends with, or a means to hear your songs more objectively so you can learn from them, the following information and track layouts should work well for you.

Using these track layouts will deliver a nice sense of stereo spacing while retaining a bit of punch. They can all be done by only two people without bouncing tracks or by one person with only one submix.* Although bouncing tracks is wonderfully advantageous at times, it sacrifices sound quality. So try to resist the temptation to layer it on. Also, some people like to record the drums in stereo on a 4-track. I've never been a fan of this approach. I feel it's more important to keep it simple. If, however, the highlight of your piece of music is a drum fill using all fifteen of your rack toms sequentially, you might want to go for the stereo drums. I address the stereo field with subtle track panning (see track layouts). Too much hard left or hard right panning can make your music sound empty and disjointed.

When doing recordings of this kind I always try to think of the song first and the production second. Rarely does snazziness compensate for a lethargic piece of music (but many people try this diversionary tactic). I would suggest that while you prepare to record the first elements (tracks 1 and/or 2) be aware that, very soon, other instruments will be coming into the mix. And all these subsequent elements will want to have their own special spot in the sonic landscape. Often, overplaying can muddy up and confuse a recording. If something you're playing isn't helping, get rid of it. You can always use it in a piece of music where it works. If you finish recording all the tracks and it sounds like a bag of instruments submerged and struggling in molasses, remember the words of non-musician Kurt Vonnegut, "Edit yourself mercilessly!"

Here's a typical track layout for a power trio:

track	instrument	pan position
1	Drums	11 O' Clock
2	Bass and Guitar	1 O' Clock
3	Vocal and Guitar Solo	10 O' Clock
4	Backing Vox and Perc	2 O' Clock

Here's one for a quartet:

track	instrument	pan position
1	Drums and Bass	11 O' Clock
2	Guitar 1 and Back Vox	9 O' Clock
3	Guitar 2 and Perc	3 O' Clock
4	Vocal and Guitar Solo	1 O' Clock

Here's one for a quintet:

track	instrument	pan position
1	Drums	11 O' Clock
2	Bass and Guitar 1	9 O' Clock
3	Keyboard and Guitar 2	3 O' Clock
4	Vocals and Percussion	1 O' Clock

In the spring of 1983, a friend and I purchased a reel-to-reel 4-track. Up to that point, we had been doing multi-track recording by bouncing back and forth between a cassette deck and a boom box. We wanted to upgrade our "studio" (co-opted den), so we started to look around. Shortly thereafter, a classified ad offering a 4-track for $350 caught our eyes.

I don't remember exactly where we went to pick it up, but I do recall that it was out in the glorious razed countryside of southeast Michigan. It was a big, white farmhouse, with no trees and an elaborate alarm system. The owner was an audio engineer. Sound gear filled every room in the house. I got that same uneasy feeling that you get when you see an elderly person living alone with far too many cats (or maybe I was just seeing my future). After a quick look at the 4-track and a couple of questions, we handed over our cash. He even threw in a box of tapes. We were very excited.

The 4-track was an Akai. I have no idea what year the machine was made. It ran at 15 or 7 1/2 ips (If you balanced the tape speed toggle switch between 7 1/2 ips and 15 ips, the machine would run at 3 3/4 ips!) and could handle 4", 7" and 12" reels of 1/4" tape. It was capable of recording on all 4-tracks simultaneously.** It also had a very loud punch-in "ka-click" that seemed to slate directly to tape.

When we got home, we started to record almost immediately. The free tapes he'd given us were used; he'd recorded a religious convention of some sort on them. But instead of erasing all of it and then beginning to record we just left it and started. So our songs all started and ended with little un-erased comments such as, "Folks... folks... if I can have your attention now please..." and, "Love, love... love..." Over the next few months we wrote and recorded almost incessantly.

Listening to those recordings now, a few things come to mind. Mostly, I'm fascinated with the way the music sounds and the structure of the compositions. I believe these recordings are unique because the songs were created on the 4-track. Normally, for us (and many others), songs were written and then learned and played by our band. The songs were always whole before recording started. With the 4-track, we had time (and tracks) to consider things, experiment and make mistakes. Making mistakes was, of course, the best way to learn.

Here are a few things we learned:

1 Coffee cans played with drumsticks sound charming when they distort.

2 Plugging guitar cables into headphone jacks is bad.

3 Having a Hum Buzzer (electronically adept) friend who can fix things such as a fried headphone jack is good.

4 Doubling a distorted guitar tone with a cleaner tone adds clarity and crunch.

5 Doubling a part with the same instrument at a slightly different pitch creates chorusing.

6 Recording very difficult parts at half speed then playing them back at normal speed will trick more people than you think into believing you're a really good player.

7 There is almost no end to the amusement of listening to your music backwards by flipping over the tape.

8 Having a consistent tuning source (a tuner or a keyboard, not a piano because they drift over time) is helpful for doing overdubs at a later date. If you don't have one, record a tuning source (i.e. an open A on a bass) for ten or fifteen seconds before the song starts on the tape. This way, you can tune to it as it plays and then be in position to record your overdub.

9 Recording two instruments with very different timbres (i.e. bass and glockenspiel) on the same track allows you to adjust their relative volumes after they've been recorded with EQ. More bass EQ brings up the bass; more treble EQ brings up the glockenspiel. If you do this kind of combining on all 4-tracks, it's almost like an 8-track... almost.

10 While mixing, putting a short delay on the guitar/bass track and panning the source to the left and the delayed signal to the right creates a richer sound.

11 Not everyone is going to like, understand or care about what you've recorded. Some people are polite listeners, some will stroll away during playback, some will talk, some will tell you who you sound like, and a precious few will ask to hear it again.

12 With repeated listening, the slamming doors, cars, telephones, airplanes, housemates and pets that accidentally infiltrate your recordings will seem more and more musical.

13 Keep your tapes well organized, thoroughly labeled (song titles, dates, recording machine, tape speed, noise reduction, locations, musicians, instruments), in their boxes, tails out (reels) or rewound (cassettes), and away from extreme temperatures, magnets and children. Being organized helps you work faster. Protecting your tapes helps prevent drop-outs.

14 Buy the best tape you can afford. For 4-track reel-to-reel, I recommend Ampex not Radio Shack. For cassette 4-tracks, I recommend TDK metal tape not Three For A Dollar brand. Also, for cassettes, using shorter tapes (15 or 30 minutes a side) will reduce the risk of the tape stretching after a thousand rewinds, fast forwards, plays and records. Again, drop-outs are what you're trying to prevent.

15 Know your equipment really well. That way, you reduce the risk of damaging something if you want to record while drunk, stoned or suffering from a 104-degree fever and hallucinations (my personal favorite!).

16 Non-musicians can be employed to depress then release marked off keys on a keyboard at the right times, while you play something else, thus saving you a submix.

17 Speaking of non-musicians, if you gather all your nearby friends, family and neighbors together to add some group type noise (singing, yelling, clapping...) to a recording, be completely setup and ready to go the second everyone is assembled. The more painless it is for them to record, the greater the odds are that they'll schlep over the next time you need that unfakable "group sound".

18 Still speaking of non-musicians, as people find out that you have a 4-track, you will be asked time and time again if they can come over and record their "really hilarious" rap song. But don't do it. They will make you program the drum machine, teach them where the down beat is, waste your tape, waste your time, and then, they'll scream into the microphone while you're monitoring with headphones on because they think it's funny to surprise you that way.

Another, less tangible, thing that we discovered came about through the sheer repetition of the recording process: our style. Fourteen years later, I still bring to every session many of the methods, tactics and preferences for recording that I developed while locked away for hours at a time 4-trackin'. Of all the songs we recorded, none have ended up being released... yet. Some of them have been played by various bands. Some were re-recorded (only to find that the "essence" of the song was totally lost). Still others sit in the archives and will probably never get heard again. This is all okay. No wasted hours were spent recording these songs. We didn't gain hit singles, riches or fame. We gained experience. The usefulness of these songs was in what we learned while recording them.

So, the main thing I would say is: Go forth and create. You should try to record everything that you can think of. If you're concerned about affording tape, remember: Tape is cheap (for 4-tracks). NEVER re-record over old tapes to save money. For one reason or another, sooner or later, you'll wish you had access to the original multi-track recordings (we recorded over that first free batch of tapes and regretted it immediately). If you feel pressured to create only "finished pieces", you'll never finish anything. If you feel like the cassette 4-track medium is beneath the quality level that you want, you'll never learn what to do when you do get into a professional studio.

A note for the one-person band: If you're going to end up with the bass and drums on one track, try the following. Record the drums on track 1, then the bass on track 2. Before submixing these two together, record a scratch guitar track on track 3. Having the guitar on tape as a reference will help you establish the bass-to-drum ratio on your submix to track 4 more accurately. Sometimes, without the guitar in there eating up space, the bass can easily be undermixed with the drums because there's no sonic battle between percussion and melody (usually).

**This useful feature was not available (due to the cost of adding an additional stereo recording head, I suppose) on most of the cassette 4-tracks that began to hit the market the following year. As a result, using those cassette 4-tracks for recording a band that wanted to record live (all the elements at once) was almost pointless. Even though you could run the machine at an increased pitch (for better sound quality) or add its noise reduction (to lose some hiss), you still ended up with only a cassette two-track recording.*

NERVE GENERATOR
This Is 4-Track! CD (NG)
This Is 4-Track! was recorded in guitarist James Botha's bedroom on a 4-track PortaStudio. To put these songs on tape, Botha first records drums and rhythm guitar on two separate tracks. The drums are recorded with one mic on the kick and two mics overhead, all going to track one. At the same time rhythm guitar goes to track two from a mic'd Fender Twin. On track three goes a second guitar and on track four goes the Moog. These tracks are then mixed down to DAT, which is then recorded to two tracks of a fresh cassette on the 4-track. The remaining two tracks are used for more vocals and miscellaneous solos. By recording this way none of the tracks are bounced within the 4-track, which Botha has found really affects the recording quality. Nerve Generator have made a dynamic, crunchy pop record. The disc's highlight is "The Death Song," an ambitious and beautiful 4-track masterpiece comprised of

several varying sections, including a beautiful flute breakdown. This CD is a great example of what can be done on a 4-track, and a great album regardless of the equipment it was recorded on. –*Rob Christensen*

BILL FOX
Shelter From the Smoke (Cherry Pop)
This solo CD from the ex-leader of the Mice sat on my desk for weeks until tonight when it finally went into the player and shit, by the first song I knew I'd be checking this one out for a long time. Coming on like Roger McGuinn as recorded by Tobin Sprout, it's right up my pop alley. Bill recorded all this on a 4-track cassette and had help from our pals Don Depew at 609 and Mike McDonald of Big Toe Recording [and a *Tape Op* contributor]. It's a great example of 4-track cassette being totally suited to some purposes and I'm sure if it had a "studio sheen" I'd have been a lot less interested on first listen, y'know? –*Larry Crane*

HOOKER O.K. (Sweet Pea)
All I should need to say is that this CD was recorded on a 4-track cassette recorder using only PZM microphones and it sounds great. If that doesn't pique the typical *Tape Op* reader's interest I don't know what will. How about that one member is in the fab Number One Cup combo? Or that it's another Kingsize mastering job. Just buy a copy and quit saying you need new gear. –*Larry Crane*

RICK BAIN
Pet Sounds (Evil Cream Fox)
Rick Bain has released a home recorded 4-track version of *Pet Sounds* all played by himself. This CD rocks. He did it with no bouncing, using a lot of slightly overdriven acoustic guitar, some drum machine, occasionally distorted vocals, and a lot of gusto. It sheds a lot more light on the allure of *Pet Sounds* than the Beach Boys box set does, and it's a hell of a lot more shocking and fun. Rick admitted to me that he was a bit miffed with all the attention paid to everything around *Pet Sounds* at the exclusion of the songs themselves and I had to agree. Plus, the kicker was Janet Weiss (Quasi/Sleater-Kinney) admitting that Rick's version of "Sloop John B" actually made her like the song. Now that's cool. Double bonus: It's available on CDR, which some cool place in Seattle will do runs of for dirt-cheap. Take note... –*Larry Crane*

LUTEFISK
Burn in Hell Fuckers (BongLoad)
This record claims to have been recorded on a Tascam cassette 4-track. At first listen I just didn't believe it, I mean - this is a full band - and I can hear everything really clearly. Repeated listening has led me to believe that they did indeed record this on a 4-track in their practice room. It has that "high-end-missing" quality and mid range squalor that only cassette multitrack can provide, but damn if they didn't do a fine job of it. Plus some of the songs are really good. –*Larry Crane*

Bouncing

IT'S NOT JUST FOR 4-TRACKS ANYMORE

by Brian McTear

My own experience in the recording world goes back about eight years to the summer before my senior year of high school. It was then that I bought a Sansui 6-track cassette recorder, and began recording my songs. In the next few years my band (now The Marinernine) recorded a few demos on that machine, but soon felt it necessary to make the jump to the "real" recording studios, where we had every experience from complete studio euphoria (where the idea of becoming a household name first kicks in) to utter disappointment. In 1995, after years of being away from the DIY life-style, I bought an 8-track and started a studio along with my partner Jason (who also plays in the Marinernine, as well as the recent international ambient/noise craze The Azusa Plane).

Miner Street (our studio and record label) is still 8-tracks and running strong. We just bought a new console, an Allen and Heath Saber 24 X 8, which I must say, should be the envy of all you motherfuckers. But as nice as that is, there are still times when my friends need more than 8-tracks. And if I can't give it to them, they'll probably find some ADAT studio down the street that can for half the price (some friends, huh).

By figuring out the following method for efficiently bouncing tracks, I have actually saved myself from the above scenario on only a few occasions. But I feel like I have learned something of a lost art form. Most people I know think of bouncing tracks only in terms of 4-track recording. But with 1/2" tape, and better yet, the tape compression that comes with it, the results can be beautifully rich and clear as a bell. And although I have never read any of those books on how the greats recorded in the '60s. I am pretty sure that some of the principles laid out here are the very same as they were back then. Give this a shot, and let me know what you think.

1. Record the raw tracks (e.g. rhythm guitar, bass and drums).

From the start, remember these two key guidelines:

1) Always strive for as much separation as possible among instruments. In other words, avoid guitars bleeding into drums and bass mics.

2) At the same time, always strive for as much of an instrument's natural ambience as possible. For this, experiment with mic placement to achieve optimum warmth and minimum bleed.

For the drums, there can be many different approaches. There's the **one-drum-per-track** method in which you can close-mic each drum to its own track with the addition of a room or overhead mic track. For this you can use every available track left over after your initial guitar and bass (or whatever you may be tracking initially) have been accounted for. Another approach would be to **sub out the drums** right off the bat (provided your mixer has sub-outputs). I think I do this out of habit, because I am so used to having to sub out the drums in normal recording scenarios. And if your intention is to send your bounce mix directly to two tracks on the tape, then it is necessary to sub mix the drums (I don't recommend this, though... see sec. 2 "**Make your Bounce Mix**" below).

Drums can be submixed nicely to either two, three or four tracks. On two tracks you could make a **loosely mic'd stereo mix**. By mic'ing loosely, you allow for some of the room ambience to liven your sound a bit. It'll keep things from sounding too dry, and it will actually help the drums to blend with other instruments. On three tracks, there are even more options. There's the **kick + snare + everything else** method, in which the kick and snare are close-mic'd to their own separate tracks and then one ambient mic picks up everything else on a track by itself. Take some time putting that mic in different locations and proximities to the kit to feel out where the best place in your room is. This leans heavily in the direction of the live room sound, which is nice, but you run the risk of losing control over things like cymbal bleed, etc. For me, I find it very hard to maintain balance and separation of drums in my small cutting room using this method. My favorite method, on the other toe, is the **close-mic'd stereo mix + overhead and/or room mic** approach (say that fifty times as fast as you can). I think this gives the best of both worlds: up close definition and separation of each individual piece of the kit on two tracks, brought back to life with some room ambience on a third track. If you have the option of a fourth track, try this with **stereo overheads or room mics on two tracks** instead of just one. This is not, of course, an exhaustive list. There are many more methods, but any of the above are a good place to start.

One thing I should mention briefly before going on, is **phase.** Without going into a deep explanation of this phenomenon, I'll just say that often when two mics are engaged upon the same instrument (e.g. the drums) they can be **out of phase.** You'll know this is happening if the two mic signals, listened to simultaneously, produce a weaker signal than either one by itself. This happens a lot on drums, since, for instance, a rack tom mic may be picking up some snare drum as well, which has its own mic already. Always do a quick test for phase by panning all your drum tracks to center, turning each on, one at a time, then in pairs, all the while listening for volume decreases. To correct phase, either your mics have to be moved into different positions which are in phase with each other, or, if your console has phase reversal buttons (usually marked by a zero with a slash through it), you can fix the problem that way. The only other option would be to alter some XLR cables specifically for phase reversal. To do this, simply switch the wires at one end on pins two and three. Then mark those cables so you only use them in that situation in the future. **When phase is an issue with two mics, only one needs to be altered to correct the situation.**

As for recording your other initial tracks, start off by **close-mic'ing amplifiers** on guitars and the bass. If you want to go the route of **direct boxes** for bass, that's fine (but I usually prefer a mic signal on a bass any day). Keyboards are usually more direct-friendly, though. The benefit to direct signals is that they have no bleed from other instruments. Remember... that's good. The drawbacks, on the other hand, are that the sounds (on a bass in particular) are generally somewhat brittle and cold, unless you spend money on a good box. What work nicely are those ART Tube MPs. Like all ART stuff, they suck for most applications, but as direct boxes, they have a few handy controls you can mess with to get the sound you want. More importantly, they're cheap!

Fig. A. My typical setup for Raw Tracking on my 24x8 console:

Console Channel:	Instrument:	Send to Sub-Channel:	Ends up on Track #:
1	Kick drum	2	2
2	Snare drum	1	1
3	Rack Tom	1	1
4	Floor Tom	2	2
5	Overhead/room	3	3
6	Bass Guitar	4	4
7	Guitar	5	5

Note: There is no rule saying you must use all eight tracks for raw tracks. It's actually much easier to save extra guitars, keyboards, etc., for the overdub stage than it is to decide their final level and EQ in the upcoming bounce-mix stage.

2. Make your Bounce Mix.

Once your raw tracks are recorded, they need to be mixed to stereo, then back onto two tracks of your 8-track. If you have a DAT player or 1/4" 2-track recorder, it's ideal to mix down to these, and then feed the mix back to two tracks of your 8-track.

If not, just bounce to two empty tracks through the submixes on your board. (I prefer the first, though.)

There are two key principles to keep in mind when making this initial mix that are outlined below:

1) For the bounce-mix, maintain the hardest panned separation possible between instruments

Each track/instrument should be panned entirely right or entirely left. This is called a hard-pan bounce mix. Guitar would be on the right, for example, and bass (yes, the bass) would be on the left. The same would go for all the other instruments besides the overhead/room mic track (this needs to be in the middle to liven the drums as a whole and return balance back to the drum mix). Some people object to the idea of a bass guitar, or the kick drum being separated completely off to one side. For the final mix, it doesn't have to be that way. If you pan the tracks with your left and right mixes only to, say, 9 o'clock and 3 o'clock, or 10 and 2, etc., the overall mix should not be too off balance; using this method, however, it will never be right up the middle. But if you listen back to recordings made when 8-track was the best technology out there, by this I mean Beatles, Hendrix, Doors, Stones and the rest of them, you will find highly panned, yet well-balanced recordings. Sometimes the entire drum set was off to one side. When a band allows me to, I pan the mix as drastically as I can. (It's just a phase I'm in.)

2) Since each instrument is being sent to either the left or right channel, mix instruments of like timbre to different sides

By hard panning instruments of like timbre away from one another, you achieve a better-balanced mix in the end. That is why George Martin could get away with having Ringo entirely in the left speaker... because whatever was in the right had complementary tone, fullness, timbre, etc. The overall mix was very carefully balanced. The more important advantage, however, is that by recording two instruments of different timbre to the same track, you increase the flexibility of this mix for later. If bass guitar and snare drum are mixed to the same track intended for the left side, and you need to hear more of the bass in the final mix, then you can turn up the low end on the EQ of that track. This will effectively turn up the bass, but not the snare. But if your bass guitar is on the same track with your kick drum, then altering the bass will have an effect on the kick as well. This is bad. For good measure, make sure you have only one representative from each frequency range (low, mid, and high) on each side of your bounce mix.

3. Over-dubs.

Once you have made your hard-pan mix to two tracks, record the left and right outputs from the DAT player or 2-track to tracks 7 and 8 of your 8-track. Now, call me wasteful, but I don't like to record over the raw track reels, or the DAT/2 track mixes. This way if there is ever the need to go back to any of those stages, you can. Instead, I say at this point suck it up and start a new reel of tape.

Overdubs are simple. At this stage, all you have to do is record whatever else it is that you want. Just make sure, as with all tracks, that the levels are as high as your machine can handle (at which point, I say you punch them a bit higher). At any rate, now you have six more tracks to work with. You could do a three part harmony, another guitar and a keyboard, and still have a track left for something else.

Fig. B. My typical hard-pan bounce mix:

Track #:	List of instruments on that track:	Pan to DAT (Left or Right):
1	Snare drum + Rack tom	L
2	Kick drum + Floor tom	R
3	Overhead/Room	Middle
4	Bass guitar	L
5	Guitar	R

4. Tips for mixing.

Mixing in a bounce mix situation is much easier, I think, than the typical mixing scenario. The reason being that the drums (the most difficult to get sounds for) are already finished. You do have some flexibility for the instruments contained in those bounce mix tracks on 7 and 8.

If you want to hear more kick, turn up the low end on the track it is on. If your board has parametrics, you can get even closer and more specific to the actual frequencies that the kick drum is occupying. If the snare is a bit buried, adjust the mids on its respective track. If the cymbals are sizzling through as a result of the overheads, cut back on some high end. Experiment with the degree to which you pan the bounce-mix tracks. I highly suggest making a mix or two where you hard-pan them. To check how well balanced the overall mix is, listen to one speaker at a time during the play back. To some extent, each side should sound completely different, while the two together should create a much larger picture.

One Last Note: I know of one glitch in this system right off the bat, and that is in the separation of the drums. I have the rack tom in the left drum mix [with the snare] and the floor tom in the Right [with the kick drum]. By this you have the image of snare and hi-hat + rack tom on the left, where they are if you are a right-handed drummer, and the floor tom and ride cymbal on the right. This goes against the principle of keeping instruments of like timbre separated, since the relative timbre of snare and rack tom are somewhat close, but worse-yet, the floor tom and the kick are often very similar. Because of this, any EQ adjustments made to alter the kick drum in either the bounce-mix or the final mix stages are going to result in affecting the floor tom as well. Just be extra careful to get a proper balance between the drums that are sharing tracks. This is a great starting point, though. Please write with comments on this method and any of its pros and cons as you discover them. Good luck.

Two Turntables, A Cheap Sampler and a 4-Track

by Jack Denning

Hip-hop is great, because you can toss all notions of traditional composition and technique out the window and craft the sound to suit your ears. Probably the two key instruments in hip-hop are the turntable and the sampler and these can be obtained on a budget.

For turntables, one model is the king of all kings, and that is the Technics 1200. This baby sports a strong direct drive motor that can stop on a dime, and start back up to speed with the press of a button. Also, it has 8% graduated pitch control (crucial for mixing) and the arm can be fine tuned so that your needle doesn't bounce around while you're hacking away, scratching and cutting that perfect break. These models retail at around $450, which is pretty pricey for entry level experimentation, but is well worth it if your goal is to rock crowds of thousands. Fortunately, these are not necessary for basic 4-tracking. All you really need is a turntable with direct drive (belt-drive will not work!) and pitch control (a must for mixing). It is advisable to get a stylus and cartridge designed for back-cueing (the "proper" term for scratching) and some slipmats, which are felt discs that go on the turntable instead of the rubber mat that usually comes with the turntable. These can be obtained at you local DJ record shop. (STANTON and ORTOFON are the names to look for in cartridges.)

To accompany your turntable, you need a mixer. These control the volume of two turntables with a cross fader. You can plug some headphones in and listen to the record (cueing) while controlling the signal going out with separate volume controls. The retail price of these mixers start at around $100, but you can find them for much less used in pawnshops and electronic surplus shops. Radio Shack also makes an inexpensive model.

Once you have these, just throw on an old record and start hacking. Sounds with a sharp percussive attack are great for scratching. Stuff like a snare or a cowbell. High pitched noises really cut through also. Scratching a bass drum hit is how you get that deep "wooba-wooba-wooba" sound. To see some great technique demonstrated, check out videos from a company called DMC. Every year, they hold the world battle DJ contest, and on these tapes, you will see and hear sound creations that you never dreamed could be possibly made with just some turntables. Truly amazing stuff indeed. Thrift shop record bins are an excellent source for samples. From KTEL disco versions of Broadway hits to children's fairy tales to freaky religious spoken word records you'll find a treasure in every bin.

In the days before the sampler, there were essentially four ways to provide beats:

1. A drummer: Not cost effective, but sounds good.

2. A beat box: Roland 808 & 909 models being the kings here - cost effective, clean and fat-sounding, but also lacking a "human" feel. These are still a prime source for beats today.

3. Cutting breaks off of records: Basically, you get a record with a cool beat on it, get two copies, and do it like this: On turntable #1, let the beat play (we'll say it lasts four bars). As the fourth bar ends, switch to turntable #2, where the same sequence on the same record is set up ready to play. Let turntable #2 play, and while it is playing, spin #1 back to the beginning of the break, and when #2 reaches the end of the fourth bar, switch back to #1 and start rewinding #2. You can repeat this process endlessly, and do some cool shit with it. This method is the classic hip-hop method, and sounds cool as shit. However, it takes a lot of practice, and you pretty much have to have some 1200s (because of their quick-start capabilities). This method is most definitely "old school".

4. Human beat box: made famous by such practitioners as Doug E. Fresh, Biz Markie and the Fat Boys. This method takes some practice, but is fairly easy to do. When I was in grade school, almost every kid rocked this method at every given opportunity (much to the dismay of most teachers). It's super cost effective.

Nowadays, a wonderful invention called the sampler allows us to bypass all of these methods if we so choose. With a sampler, the sky is pretty much the limit. Any noise can be sampled and then looped, creating infinite varieties of rhythms and sonic textures. Just be careful - if you sample another artist's material, and they can prove that you did, then you'll have to pay them if you intend to release the material. Fortunately, a beat can be constructed by simply sampling the first and second beats of a bar, and then looping it. When your sample is this small, the source is nearly impossible to detect. Samplers range from $100 up into the thousands for retail prices, but can be had for much cheaper, if you hunt for bargains. Two things determine the usefulness of a sampler; memory, and the ability to edit. With memory, you can save your samples on disks, and without memory, you have to use the sample while it's in the machine. Obviously, saving a sample is more convenient, but not absolutely necessary. Editing is the ability to trim the starting and stopping pints of a sample to precise points. This is important when sampling beats because you want the timing to be on. Without editing, you have to sample it (your source) dead on. Again, it takes practice, but is not impossible. These features are something you will pay for, but the convenience involved might be worth it.

Now that I've told you about these items, I'll share some of my techniques for getting the sounds to tape. The common practice today for creating hip-hop usually involves programming the beats and music on a sequencer and then multi-tracking the vocals and scratching separately, preferably onto 2" tape. But, if you're like me (broke as a joke), you don't have access to this equipment and must face the challenges of your limitations. That's okay – it fosters creativity. I use a 4-track cassette machine, a sampler and turntables. I supplement these with a bass guitar, an organ and various percussion items. For me, it usually starts with a beat but sometimes something will catch my ear as a great sample, and I'll build a song around that. Usually I just set aside some daily time for recording and go with what my inspirations are at that point. Since my sampler has no memory or editing, I'll sample a good beat and use that as the foundation of the song. In earlier years, I played in bands that had tons of parts in every song, and arranged them in as complicated forms as we possibly could. I gradually learned that audiences really respond to simplistic, flowing grooves. For that reason, I started to drop the number of parts and complexities per song. Lately, I've gotten tired of the notion of a song - verse, chorus, verse, chorus, solo, chorus, end – and have taken to kicking out the ongoing two note jams.

So that's the approach I take to hip-hop – a good beat, a boomin' bass line, a couple of chords here and there, some samples and scratching placed strategically for proper ambience and last but not least, some dope lyrics. Remember that the lyrics are king of what it's all about. The music should compliment them and highlight them. Equal space should exist for both elements. It's important to keep things sparse, because it's so easy to clutter things up with too much instrumentation. Sometimes, it's easy to forget that hip-hop was born of a beat and some lyrics – not from a calculated stylistic choice, but because those were the only resources available. The sound has since developed from that original lack of resources. Again a case of limitations fostering creativity.

I haven't really included that much technical information because there really isn't that much. Hip-hop is the ultimate DIY music, and its applications are limitless. Experimenting with these sounds will add a whole new dimension to other styles you might be interested in. Most of all, it's fun as hell, because there are no rules. The bottom line is, keep it simple, and make it funky.

Recording Recipes

by Curtis Settino

Since I often record alone, I've developed a few techniques to compensate for the lack of extra eyes, ears and hands (until cloning is available to the masses) that I work without. Not all these methods are single-person-dependent, however. So feel free to try them with more than one person around. I'm presenting them in a pseudo-recipe format for easy referencing. The instruments and settings I mention are only for the sake of description. There are countless other instrument combinations and applications. The techniques themselves are also not set in stone, but in some other more transient substance. I think it's sand.

Utilizing Pitch Control for Adding Compression

I only have one compressor (a rms/peak dual channel compressor limiter with gate). Here's a two-step method of compression that I find helpful.

Ingredients: two-channel compressor, kick/snare/hi-hat/cymbal drum set, two microphones.

1) Record the drum set with one microphone in front of the kick and one above the snare. Don't place the mics too close (These positions will help the cymbals come through). Run each mic through a channel on the compressor with these approximate settings: high threshold, fast attack, high ratio.

Essentially this setup uses the compressor as a limiter, more so than as a compressor. My goal is to keep the levels from leaping into the red, which on my ADAT sounds bad.

2) After you've recorded, route the output of each recorded drum track back through the compressor to two new tracks with these approximate settings: medium threshold, fast attack, medium ratio. Bounce the tracks at the slowest speed your deck can go (with my ADAT this is a minor third/three notes lower, -300 pitch, or 75% normal speed if regular speed is zero pitch). You can also record your initial tracks at the fastest speed your deck can go (+100 pitch on the ADAT*). Then you can slow it down that much more while applying the second compression.

Using the slower speed gives the compressor, literally, more time to examine and effect the signal. You can get away with heavier compression because there will be less slur into the part of the signal that doesn't need compression. That slurring, often called "pumping," is like a distracting musical lisp. To help visualize how this slower speed compression works, picture a disco drumbeat: kick, hi-hat, snare, hi-hat, etc. If you were to use a heavier compression on this pattern to rein in the kick and the snare, the hi-hat hits would be unnecessarily effected. At a slower speed, the compressor can detect the space after the kick and before the hi-hat and leave it alone. This adds clarity and punch without boosting up the "Tch" sound of the hi-hat.

The slow-speed track-bouncing technique can also work well with other effects processing. One in particular is pitch shifting. Pitch shifting devices always add a delay to your signal. It may be small, but it's still there. With my pitch-shifting device the inherent delay is .1 ms, that's how long it takes to process the signal. Sometimes that's fine (mostly with slower songs). Sometimes though, after pitch shifting the same signal a few times, such as shifting a high-pitched melody down a few octaves so that it's a bass line, the delay build up is drastic. But, if I do each of my pitch shifting passes at a slower speed, it can save the day.

Creating Harmonic Interest

An adjustable pitch on your recording device helps keep your recordings in tune. If you are overdubbing instruments that aren't easily tunable, such as piano with glockenspiel and didgeridoo, you'll be thankful that you can tune the tape, if not the instruments. But, if you are recording those same instrument sounds using a keyboard, you may want to detune them from each other a little bit. Sometimes the sounds in a keyboard are so in tune that there is not much of the harmonic interest that occurs when live instruments interact with each other. This "interest" is most present when you record multiple instruments live with one microphone or with signal bleed between a few microphones.** The following technique is way to mimic that effect.

Ingredients: one guitar, one keyboard, two microphones and two amps.

1) Record a guitar on one track and then a keyboard on another. Use close mic'ing or a direct signal.

2) Place two amps facing one another about ten feet apart (more or less).

3) Take the playback outputs of the recorded guitar and keyboard tracks and send them to their own amps. Set the amps to the same volumes.

4) Place two microphones between the amps in a stereo pattern. The mic facing the guitar amp will receive the guitar (louder) as well as some slightly delayed keyboard bleed with a changed timbre (quieter) and vice versa.

5) Choose one of the following:

a) Play the guitar and keyboard tracks through their respective amps and record onto two new tracks (four tracks total: two original, two with bleed).

b) While recording the amp signals, mix the original signals into the two new tracks (two tracks total).

6) Experiment with panning and volume [do this before you submix, if you're going the 5b route]:

Try the original guitar at 9-o'clock/100% volume, the bleed guitar at 3-o'clock/60% volume, the original keyboard at 3-o'clock/100% volume, and the bleed keyboard at 9-o'clock/60% volume.

Or, the original guitar hard left/50% volume, the bleed guitar at 10-o'clock/50% volume, the original keyboard hard right/50% volume, and the bleed keyboard at 2-o'clock/50% volume.

How much bleed you get, and the quality of it, will depend on your microphone placements, amp distances, and the room you use. In turn, this will effect your panning and volume choices for submixing.

Making Room for Everybody

Sometimes a song that requires a lot of overdubs will become muddy sounding long before you've finished recording all your intended doubled, tripled, and quintupled parts. What usually happens is that there becomes a build up of room or electrical noise (hum, buzz and hiss) on the tracks. If left unchecked, you'll not only be building up parts, but noise as well with each subsequent overdub. Here are some ways to make room for a bevy of guitars, a bakers' dozen of vocals, and/or too many percussion tracks.

Ingredients: Unlimited tracks and patience (or automation) while mixing... or unlimited patience for bouncing while recording, a microphone with switchable pickup patterns and a lo-cut filter (on the mic or on the mixing board).

1) When layering a guitar part, change your mic placement or tone a little bit with each track to create a richer, thicker sound with fewer tracks.

2) When layering vocals (especially if the same person is singing most or all of them), switch the microphone pickup pattern and/or placement for each track. This, again, will create a richer, thicker sound with fewer tracks.

3) When layering any higher pitched instruments [such as tambourine, recorders, or banjo] use the lo-cut filter. Doing so will eliminate the low-end noise build up on tracks that don't have much low-end information anyway.

4) Whenever possible, use live layering. If there are enough musicians available (two guitarists, three vocalists, fifteen percussionists), ask them to learn and record the part you need. This can take longer sometimes, because everyone thinks they should be featured, but once everyone is humbled and locked-in, it'll sound great. You may still ask them to do two or three tracks of each part.

Catching Cymbal Overtones with Flying Microphones

I overdub cymbals in two main instances. Sometimes I'll play real cymbals with a programmed kick and snare pattern to give it some authenticity. Other times, I use cymbals more as effects and punctuation, rather than as part of a drum set. In both cases, I can take advantage of the fact that there are no drums (or other instruments) competing with the cymbals for the microphone while recording. This gives me the option of using alternate mic'ing techniques. For the first instance (creating the illusion of a live drum set), a standard mic placement is probably best. I usually use two PZMs back-to-back over the drum set. I never put a separate microphone on the hi-hats.*** For the second instance (effects and punctuation), I sometimes use the flying microphone technique to pickup more of the cymbal's overtones.

Ingredients: 1 microphone and cable, 1 cymbal on stand and stick, a piece of rope and a pulley (or screw-eye bolt).

1) Put the pulley (or screw-eye bolt) into the ceiling. Run the rope through it and attach it to the microphone SECURELY and hold the other end. What you want to have here is a situation where the microphone can be smoothly lowered and raised using the rope. A conveniently placed pipe will also work. You may need to experiment with different kinds of rope for maximum smoothness.

2) Raise the mic up with your left hand and place the cymbal below it (a little off center toward you). Lower the mic until it's about six inches from the top of the cymbal. Then, keeping your feet in place (masking tape on the floor helps), reach your right arm up as high as it'll go toward the pulley. Mark the rope with a pen where it meets your right wrist. Tie the rope to your right wrist making sure the marked part ends up in the same spot.

3) Practice lowering and raising the mic while holding a stick in your hand. When the stick meets the cymbal the mic should be about two to three feet above it. When your hand is outstretched the mic should drop to about six inches above again.

4) Start recording. Hold the stick about 1 foot back, ready to strike. At the proper moment hit the cymbal, then quickly and smoothly raise your arm up and lower the mic. The effect is quite interesting. The volume spike of the hit will be softened with the distance (two to three feet) of the mic, then the quieter overtones will be brought into the fore as the mic comes closer.

Other variations include: both arms outfitted with mics and cymbals for stereo recording (be sure to keep them at least three feet apart or there could be some phase problems), and hitting the cymbal quickly picking up the stand and moving it toward the mic or vice verse. Using the rope and pulley is best for situations where you need your other hand free.

Timbral Changes with a Flying Microphone

One thing I like to do is use flying microphones on percussion. Depending on your approach, you can create all sorts of shifts in sound quality during a performance while maintaining volume unity.

Ingredients: A person to hold the microphone, a drummer and a drum set, and someone at the mixer.

1) Position the microphone about three feet away from the drum set. Adjust the input level to your recording device. Mark the fader position "#2".

2) Position the microphone as far from the drum set as possible. Readjust the input level to your recording device. Mark the fader position "#1".

3) Start recording. Very slowly, walk the microphone across the floor toward the drum set. Take the whole song to get there. At the same time and speed, change the fader from position #1 to #2.

When you're done, you'll have a drum performance that plays back at the same volume throughout the song, but with the drum set sound changing from distant to present. You can try different microphones and different settings (omni, cardioid, etc...) as well. Also, the possibility for highly choreographed position switching exists: Maybe the verses are far away and the choruses close. What if you recorded every instrument in a song this way? Or, what if you recorded different combinations... when the guitars switch from far to close sounding, the drum set and bass do just the opposite?

Be careful if you start doing more rapid changing with the microphone position. Make sure your path and cables are clear. Tripping on something and dropping your microphone makes you feel bad. It also helps, for quieter instruments, if the microphone wielder is wearing socks. Boots clomping across a wooden floor arhythmically can be distracting. The main thing I like about this technique is the subliminal effect of subtler applications. A slowly evolving sound picture in a song is felt subconsciously more than heard consciously. It has the ability to change the listeners perception of the song without them realizing it.

Volume Changes With a Flying Microphone

This is the same as the last technique, but without the volume unity. This is a more drastic approach.

Ingredients: A person to hold the microphone, a drummer and a drum set.

1) Position the microphone about three feet away from the drum set. Adjust the input level to your recording device.

2) Reposition the microphone as far from the drum set as possible.

3) Start recording. Very slowly, walk the microphone across the floor toward the drum set. Take the whole song to get there.

Again, and always, countless variations exist for this and other techniques mentioned here. You can use a stereo microphone approaching from the front. You could have two people, each with a microphone, approaching from the opposite sides or walking circles around the drummer. In general, this is "fun in headphones" recording.

*If ADATs could do half speed, double speed, any tempo in between and reverse (possibly achievable using a speed-variable, rotating playback and record head), I would be the happiest recorder of sound ever.

**The fewer mics, the better for room noise reduction as well.

*** To me, the hi-hats are just more cymbals and need not be given any special attention. Putting an additional microphone on the hi-hats usually brings them up in volume unnecessarily. This, in turn, usually brings more snare into the mix. The main thing I don't like about this kind of drum set imaging are the holes that occur whenever the drummer plays a fill, especially short ones. The too-loud hi-hat, which was serving as a sort of metronome or shaker, disappears during fills, and the space is filled with a very different timbre (usually snare or toms), which highlights the absence of the hi-hats even more.

The Secrets of Guitar Amps

AN INTERVIEW WITH GEOFF FARINA

by Larry Crane

Geoff Farina is determined. He won't settle for a crummy guitar sound and this has led him on an amazing quest of knowledge and sound. He is currently a member of Karate (who have albums out on Southern Records) and The Secret Stars (a duo who have some fine albums out on Shrimper Records). But what I find fascinating is what he's learned about tube amps and the ways one can achieve optimum performance and great sounds. Remember though, unplug your amp before trying any of these modifications and don't blame us if you break it.

How did you get into the modifications of tube equipment and building some of the oddball things?

I think mainly because when I was in bands before, and in doing Karate, everything always sounded bad. I always used old amps and everybody's amps sounded bad and the one thing I noticed was that there was a huge amount of myth about tube amps and stuff among people like me and my friends. Not being high-end blues players, the information just isn't there. I just wanted stuff to sound good. When we went into this studio about a year ago to make the Karate record, I wanted to see if I could make things sound better. I read lots of old tube manuals I would find at thrift stores or libraries. Like school libraries with engineering departments and stuff. I started to get a basic knowledge of how a tube works and why it is used. I'm totally a hacker. I know so little math, I'm unable to do a lot of the math work you need to do to be a real engineer. I really have this fragmented knowledge of everything. That's how I got into it. I had this one amp that was a '68 Fender Twin; Fender was sold to CBS in '65 and in '68 they changed to "silver-face" amplifiers which supposedly don't sound as good. What I learned was that the circuitry didn't necessarily change, the things that changed were relatively small for the first couple of years, in '68 and '69. If you know what you're doing, you can go in and rip out some of the parts and go to Radio Shack and get a couple of certain value resistors for a quarter and just make a few little changes and have a really amazing sounding amp. I just happened to have one of these [Fender] amps and since then I've gotten another one from the exact same year that's three serial numbers away from the one that I already owned. I kinda knew what I was doing when we did that record. I wanted a real clean guitar sound and it came out pretty good. So that's basically how I got interested in it… just having everything sounding terrible and everyone having amps that sound mediocre or don't sound good at all.

And they don't really know why.

Yeah, the myth is that you need to get new tubes, but you can buy new tubes and if your amp isn't biased correctly it'll still sound terrible. A lot of Fenders don't even have a bias control. They have what's called a balance control; two of the tubes will be working really hard and two won't be doing anything. You'll spend $50 on new tubes and you're ruining them, basically, and your amp doesn't sound any better. Here in Boston, which is a huge music city, there's a whole lot of mediocre or bad repair people around and a few really good ones. I've taken my stuff out and had it worked on and it doesn't sound any better. There's one guy in particular that's notorious for being just not-good-at-all.

Had you had any experience with electronics before?

Not really. I've always been into trying to fix things myself, but I've never had any real electronics experience. The other guitar player in Karate, my friend Eamomn, is actually this total computer geek and electronics guy, or was at one point in his life. He gave me my first little lesson on it. I was on tour for three months and all I did was read electronics manuals and two or three really good books about tube amps. I just really tried to get a concept of how things worked. The thing that I started to realize about it is that there's no real physical metaphor for how electricity works. Like current is a metaphorical term. That works up until a point, but when you start to think about the difference between voltage and current… current flows in one direction, but what's called holes, this sort of negative space which creates voltage, moves in the other direction simultaneously and it's just kind of weird. The metaphors just kind of break down. You have a certain degree of that and then you have this practical knowledge and you know that if you change these two resistors that it's gonna sound good or it's gonna sound different. It's not something that I've been able to figure out. If anybody has that total grasp on it then that's great for them! It's really difficult!

What are some of the books on tube amps that you mentioned?

There are three books that are really good. The first one I read was by a guy named Gerald Weber and it's called *A Desktop Reference of Hip Vintage Guitar Amps* and it's kinda cheesy, but it's good. He was a weekend-warrior blues guitar player. He was in the meat packing industry and got rich packing meat. He wanted to buy the best tube amp and there wasn't a good tube amp in the '80s to buy. So he learned about them and built one. Now he has this company called Kendrick Amplifiers and if you ever get the chance to hear one, it's a treat. I don't know any punk rockers who would spend $2500 on an amp, but we played in Florida over the summer and the club next door was a blues club - I went over there and there was this really amazing guitar player playing one. It's just a treat - how good they sound. You don't realize what a guitar can sound like 'til you hear one. But anyway, his book is basically a whole bunch of excerpts from his writing for *Vintage Guitar* magazine and it's also got all the Fender schematics. The great thing about the Fender schematics that no other amp company ever did is that Fender printed layouts of amps. A schematic isn't a physical layout. [This book] has a schematic on the top of the page and the layout on the bottom.

Where the parts are on the circuit board.

Which is really valuable when you're not that versed in reading schematics. The thing about this book is that it's really poorly written, actually all three of the books are really poorly written. There's a lot of really great stuff that you have to dig for - little tricks you can do. For example, you can buy a resistor at Radio Shack, solder it to a couple of RCA plugs, plug it into the reverb in and out, use the reverb foot pedal and you have an extra gain stage. It sounds really good. That's what I used in Karate for a couple of years. There's another book by this guy Aspen Pittman, who runs Groove Tubes. It's called *The Tube Amp Book* and it's volume 4.1 by now. That one's cool 'cause its got a lot of pictures of all these old amps and stuff. It's really fun to read and has reproductions of all these old Fender ads and everything. But it's also a huge ad for Groove Tubes, which is kinda annoying. My personal opinion is that they're more of a marketing company. I can't tell the difference between them [Groove Tubes] and Sovteks, which cost half as much. The great thing about that book is that it has this little part of it in the back that has this step-by-step way to troubleshoot an amp. Where to start looking for problems. It's a way to service tube radios; this system you can use to troubleshoot amplifiers, and I've never seen that printed anywhere else. It's really valuable just for that. The other one is a book called *Dave Funk's Tube Amp Workbook*. This guy Dave Funk is really a total goofball. He's a genius, a real electrical engineer, and he's worked designing lab equipment and everything that you can imagine. But he's a terrible writer. The book's terribly written. I have a Master's in English and I edited journals and everything like that, but I don't think I could have read these books without having that knowledge. There's a lot of stuff in there that's really valuable. To really get a sense of what I was doing, just being completely ignorant, I had to read all three of them a lot. The Kendrick book in particular is really great, down-to-earth and the most accessible of all of them.

What other kind of modifications have you done to amps?

This is all stuff that other people have done that I found out about. For example, a lot of Fender amps have two 68K-ohm resistors that come off the two inputs. You can simply remove them. The reason that they're there is so you can use both of the inputs at once, which people used to do so you could put a guitar and a microphone in and you could sing and play guitar, which of course nobody does. So you can remove those and it sounds better without them 'cause they bleed off certain frequencies. There are other things you can do. On a 2-channel Fender amp, pull out the first preamp tube, which runs the first channel. What that does is it makes the second preamp tube run a little hotter. The first channel doesn't work anymore, but nobody uses the first channel. If you don't use the vibrato on a Fender Twin you can disconnect it. The way that a vibrato works on most of the later Fenders is that, even if you have it off, it always bleeds off some of the signal to the ground, so you lose fidelity. There's a brown wire that's connected to the vibrato jack for the footswitch, you can disconnect it and it disconnects the whole vibrato section of the amp. There's something called a negative feedback loop on a lot of amplifiers. That's where the signal goes through the amplifier, then goes through the output transformer and then to the speaker jack. There's a wire that goes from the speaker jack back to another part of the amplifier, like one of the preamp stages. It sends part of the signal back to the preamp stage. The effect that it has - and I don't really understand exactly why - is that it cancels out a lot of the odd-order harmonics and enhances the even-order harmonics. I think it might have something to do with the phase that it's in, but I don't quite understand it. The effect of simply disconnecting that wire is that you get a real sorta' browner, crunchier sound out of the amplifier. Actually, a presence control on an amplifier isn't a tone control. Tone controls are passive circuits. There are different capacitors and resistors that bleed off certain signals depending on how much signal you put through them. A presence control is actually a potentiometer [a variable resistor] on the negative feedback loop. So it's active and that's why that control makes noise. It actually has voltage on it from the negative feedback loop and controls how much of it that goes back into the amplifier so you get that sizzling sound when it's really high. A lot of this is fidelity, making the amp sound clearer and not muddy, but there's also things like changing power filters, which are just these capacitors that are in every amplifier. When electricity comes into an amplifier, it's AC and the rectifier changes it to DC, but it's a pulsating DC and the capacitors even it out. After ten years they [the capacitors] get all brittle and they don't work anymore; that's when you get that 60-cycle hum in the amp and stuff like that. You can change them and build a variac, which is for charging them. I don't know if you have to, and some people don't, but I always do 'cause somebody told me that you did. You can build a variac out of a lightbulb, a 3-prong adapter and a couple other things. The Kendrick book shows you how to do it. So you can charge them yourself and it saves you a hundred dollars. It makes such a dramatic difference. You're talking about getting a ton more volume and a ton more clarity out of the amplifier. Biasing tubes is real important. The way that I bias tubes is there's a certain point on the amp that has to be in this voltage range and you just fuck around with it - you listen to it and see what sounds best within that range. Those are all things that make a ton of difference. A lot of it's about knowing what you want.

I heard you had built these weird reverb units.

I know theoretically how a reverb works. Jodi, the other person in Secret Stars, has this old Danelectro reverb box and we saw one on the back of a Ventures [record] cover so we were kind of excited about it, but it sounds horrible, it's really bad. It says patent pending on it and I have the feeling that it's some kind of prototype or something, I don't know. The theory of how reverb works is that it takes part of the signal and it puts it through a transducer, which is simply like a guitar pickup; it changes mechanical energy to electrical energy or vice versa. It changes the voltage of the signal into mechanical energy that vibrates the spring. On the other end of the spring you have another transducer that takes that mechanical energy and changes it back into a "new" signal and runs it back into the signal path. The spring, of course, vibrates with all these different harmonics and that's how you get the reverb. I tried using guitar pickups as transducers and I built this thing that was in a project box from Radio Shack. Inside, it had two guitar pickups on either end connected to 1/4" jacks and it had the springs that the guitar pickups were supposed to pick up. It kind of worked, but it's more of a feedback machine. It's kind of fun and it's also suspended in this old mail holder from the '50s. I can't even describe it. It's just this weird, hollow, big metal thing that has all these holes in it and I suspended the whole apparatus in this thing. Most reverb boxes, they have the springs, but then the unit is mounted on springs.

For shock resistance.

I think it also facilitates the vibration of the unit. What I learned by doing all this is that in the Fender reverbs, that are in the Twins and stuff, the wires that are the springs have to be magnetized. The transducers in those amps break so easily. If you take it apart you can't fix them 'cause they're so teeny. I don't think that you can build an actual spring reverb, I mean I haven't been able to do it. I'm sure people with "real" knowledge can do it. Fender and all the amp companies don't build them; they buy them from a company that makes them in Canada. The studio that I'm kinda working at wants to build a plate reverb, so I'm interested in getting involved in that.

Those sound really neat.

John Loder, who runs Southern Studios, built a plate reverb and it needs its own separate room.

What kind of studio are you working at?

It's a friend of mine who has a German 16-track, 2" machine and a couple of ADATs. He wants to have an analog 16-studio, but with a pre-production studio where people can go in and do stuff onto these ADATs and figure out what they want before they put anything down on 2". That's his philosophy. He wants me to help on guitar sounds and to bring in bands. I think he wants somebody who knows a little bit of what guitar players want, sort of how to mediate between the engineer and the band. Good engineers might know enough to leave the guitar sound alone, but they might not know the potential of how it could sound. A lot of people who play guitar don't know what their options are.

I'm No Expert: Tubes

by Geoff Farina

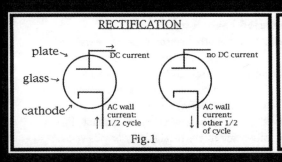

RECTIFICATION

plate, glass, cathode, DC current, no DC current, AC wall current: 1/2 cycle, AC wall current: other 1/2 of cycle

Fig.1

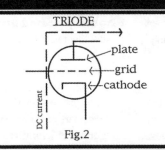

TRIODE

plate, grid, cathode, DC current

Fig.2

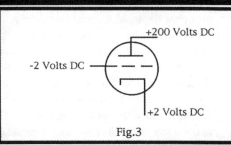

+200 Volts DC, -2 Volts DC, +2 Volts DC

Fig.3

Disclaimer #1: Do not open up your amplifier unless you know what you are doing! Tube amps work with lethal voltages that can remain in the amp even after it is unplugged. If you don't know how to discharge filter caps and how to safely work on your amp, don't try it. If you or your amp die, Larry and I are not responsible.

Disclaimer #2: I'm no expert. I've learned only from blowing shit up, shocking myself, and a little research on the side. Don't trust me. Do research for yourself. Start with a reprint of the *RCA Receiving Tube Manual* from Antique Electronics (602.820.5411).

I thought it might be time for some basic discussion on tubes and how they work, and also some practical knowledge about how we can make our tube equipment sound and work a little better. Now, I'm assuming if your reading *Tape Op* that you have a basic concept of the relationships between current, voltage, and resistance (Ohm's law), as well as AC and DC, parallel and series, etc. If not, spend a few hours with your high school physics books and meet me at the next paragraph.

So how does a tube work? To answer this we need to understand what a tube does. Put simply, tubes in your amp primarily do two very important things: they rectify and amplify.

To understand how, let's start with a little history of the simplest of tubes: the light bulb. As you know, it is a vacuum in which AC current passes back and forth through a filament that heats it up so much that it glows white hot. Now, before the days of multinational, corporate-funded technologies, light bulbs were a bit different. Old bulbs got dirty as the filament burned and produced ash or dust in the bulb. The story goes that some scientist at some point - I forget who and when - tried to add another element to the bulb attract this dust and "clean up" the inside of the bulb. The theory was that if a positive voltage was applied to this second element, the dust would be attracted to it and it would clean up the inside of the tube. What was discovered by this is that

electrons (current) actually flowed from the first element of the tube - the filament or cathode - to the second element of the tube - the anode, more commonly known as the plate because of it's physical appearance.

Stop for a minute and remember your high school physics: current, or electrons, [or burned filament dust particles, for that matter] flow from points of lower voltages to points of higher voltages. When your amp sounds like shit during soundcheck, and you pull the 9-volt out of one of your ten or eleven florescent stomp boxes and lick the contacts, what you feel on your tongue is electrons leaving the negative terminal, traveling through the ol' taste buds [via/saliva which is conductive], and going to the positive terminal, the same way current flows through the tube. This idea is crucial to the operation of a tube, so keep it in mind as we proceed.

Now, the two-element tube created a crucial discovery: this current flowed in only one direction: it was DC, just like a 9-volt battery. As we know, the current that flows through a wall socket to a light bulb is AC, and therefore flows back and forth in both directions. So what was discovered was a way to convert AC to DC, or to rectify: as AC flows back and forth through the filament 120 times per second, the plate produces DC current each time the AC current moves forward. As the AC moves backwards into a negative voltage, the DC stops at zero because a vacuum tube conducts in only one direction. What is left on the plate is 120 pulses of DC per minute. (See Fig. 1)

Your tube amp needs to rectify the wall's AC voltage because most of its guts run on DC. Today this is usually done either with a tube rectifier, or with solid state rectifiers, although there are other methods that have been used. There's a good chance you're amp has a tube rectifier. Look at the tubes: if there is an odd number of big tubes, the farthest tube to the left or right side of the amp is probably the rectifier tube. Common amps with a tube rectifier are Fender Champs, Vibroluxes, Deluxes, 4x10 Bassmans, Ampeg B-15-Ns, Gibson Stereos and lots of older Gibsons and other older amps.

OK, back to work. So far we have a tube with two elements, the cathode with its positive voltage, and the plate with its more positive voltage. The current is flowing in one direction from the cathode to the plate.

At this point, what is needed is a way to control this current to make it useful. Enter the third element: the grid. This is a coil of wire that has space between each wrap of wire to allow electrons to pass through it. Fig. 2 is a schematic representation of this grid in a three-element tube, or triode, and we can see that the grid is inserted between the plate and the cathode, right in the path of the current. This is much like a faucet installed between the water pipe and the spout of the kitchen sink to control the flow of water from the pipe to the drain.

Now, each element of this triode has its own voltage: we already know that the cathode has a positive voltage, and the plate has a more positive voltage, and in between the two is a grid. The grid must have a negative voltage on it in relation to the cathode for it to effectively control the flow of current. Here's why: as the electrons (current) "look" toward the plate - where they would normally go because of the higher voltage, they see the grid instead. In this case, the electrons don't flow toward the plate/grid because they see the grid's negative charge. They stay put and no current flows. This is how the grid electrically "hides" the plate's high positive voltage from the cathode's low positive voltage, and current does not flow

This relatively negative voltage on the grid is called the bias voltage. This is a term most of you have heard, but is often misunderstood: a bias voltage is a [usually negative] DC voltage applied to the grid to make it negative in relation to the cathode. A bias voltage can be positive under certain circumstances, or it can also be zero. As long as it is less positive than the cathode, we're in business.

Let's use a real example: in a Silverface or Blackface Fender Champ, the preamp section of the circuit utilizes one side of a 12AX7 preamp tube [this tube actually has two triodes in it] with around 2 DC volts on the cathode, and about 200 DC volts on the plate. The screen, therefore, needs to be less than 2 volts DC for it to have an effect on current flow. For now, lets assume the grid's bias voltage is -2 volts.

So how does it work? To understand, let's see what happens if we keep the plate and cathode voltages constant, but change the bias voltage from -2 volts to, say -1 or 0 volts DC? The tube turns on and more current flows. (fig. 3) Here's why: as the screen becomes more positive in relation to the cathode, electrons (current) begin to "see" past the grid as it's not so negatively charged, and they start to feel attracted to the much larger positive charge at the plate beyond. As the grid becomes more positive, it puts less pressure on the electrons at the cathode to stay put, and eventually they shoot past the grid toward the plate. Hence, as the grid becomes more positive in relation to the cathode, more current flows from the cathode through the plate. Conversely, as the grid becomes more negative in relation to the cathode, less current flows through the tube.

OK, some of you might be totally bored by now and might be asking yourselves: why is this important? We can control current flow with a change in voltage in any circuit, right? Well, yes, but the important discovery here is that a relatively small change in bias voltage controls a much larger change in plate current. Think of the faucet: when you turn the handle [the bias voltage], you are doing a relatively small amount of work to control the water flow (the current). Only with the faucet can this be done. If you try and control the flow by putting your finger over the end of the spout, water will probably spray out all over the place because the pressure is too much. But with the faucet, a small amount of work is able to control much larger amounts of water than your finger could.

OK. Here's the million-dollar question: where in your arsenal of equipment can you find a small fluctuating AC voltage to "control" this plate current? How about at the other end of your guitar cord? And what happens when we take this plate current and plug it into a speaker? Fucking brilliant. The big current flowing through the plate fluctuates with the same frequency as the small guitar pickup voltage, cacophony ensues, and we all slowly go deaf. Hence, the tube amplifies the guitar signal. It makes the small AC signal coming from your guitar pickups big enough to move a speaker cone.

Addendum for hard-core math geeks: Those of you that already know something about electronics and have been paying attention so far are thinking I fucked up: "You just said that the plate current fluctuates with the much smaller AC grid voltage, but earlier you said that a tube can't conduct AC." Well, perhaps a better way of saying this is that a tube only conducts positive voltages. Keep in mind that the plate always has a high positive voltage on it even when the grid is stagnant. The grid voltage adds and subtracts from the plate voltage. So if the grid goes from, say, -1 to 0 to 1 to 0 and back to -1 to complete the cycle, the plate might go from 200 to 230 to 260 to 230 to 200 to complete the amplified version of the same cycle, but never below 0.

If it does this 220 times per second, we have a very loud A [note]. So that's how your amp works, right? Well, not exactly. A Fender Twin has about 15 of these cathode/grid/plate systems working together, along with about fifty other things going on at once. This is a very simple treatment of a very complex subject, but I hope that I have given you a basic concept of how tubes work.

Now for the practical knowledge I promised. Here's a simple way to bias your Fender amp: First, find a flat head screwdriver, a friend and a guitar, your blackface or silverface Fender Twin Reverb, Deluxe, or Vibrolux that sounds like shit. [this will work on amps with AB763, AB769, AA270 tube charts or the like], a new set of power tubes [four 6L6s on a Twin, two 6v6s on a Deluxe, two 6L6s or 6v6s for the Vibrolux depending on the model], and a new driver tube. The driver tube is the small tube closest to the bigger power tubes. It will be a 12AX7 or 12AT7 depending on the model. [The two are actually interchangeable, and a 12AX7 has about 10% more gain than the 12AT7 and will make the amp a bit louder and raunchier.]

Here's what to do: Turn the amp off and change the tubes. You just replaced your power tubes, but you didn't replace your driver tube, you say? Zealots, this is why your shit is cacophonic! Good tubes can sound like ass without a new driver. Also, if you have matched sets and it's an amp with four power tubes, make sure one set is on the inside and one set is on the outside, not one set on the left and one set on the right.

Next, fire up the amp and have your friend play guitar through it. Turn it up to the loudest you usually play it, and have your friend really lean into it. Now, from behind the amp, look past the power tubes in between the transformers for a small hole. This is the bias adjustment pot. Stick your flat head up in there and turn it a bit in either direction. You will notice that the amp gets slightly louder while you turn in one direction, and slightly quieter while you turn in another direction. While you are turning the screwdriver in the direction that makes the amp louder, watch the plates on the power tubes. These are the big gray parts that seem to surround everything else. When you see the plates start to glow orange, back off just a bit till they are gray again. Don't let the plates glow for more than a second because they will quickly burn up.

Any point before the plates start to glow that the amp sounds best is a good bias point. Although it is subjective, amps generally sound best right before the plates get too hot. Actually, they sound best when the plates are really glowing, but this is highly impractical unless you want to replace the tubes every half-hour. This isn't the most graceful way to bias an amp, but it actually works quite well and it's a good way to do it without killing yourself and without your mom suing me.

All right. Now get to work!

I'm No Expert: Capacitors

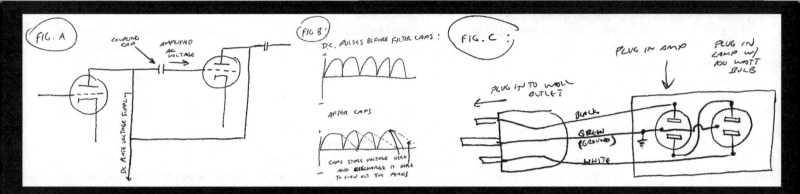

by Geoff Farrina

Disclaimer #1: Do not open up your amplifier unless you know what you are doing! Tube amps work with lethal voltages that can remain in the amp even after it is unplugged. If you don't know how to discharge filter caps and how to safely work on your amp, don't try it. If you or your amp die, Larry and I are not responsible.

Disclaimer #2: I'm no expert. I've learned only from blowing shit up, shocking myself, and a little research on the side. Don't trust me. Do research for yourself. Start with a reprint of the *RCA Receiving Tube Manual* from Antique Electronics (602.820.5411).

Zealots: Capacitors are our friends. I will explain what they are, what they do, and finally how you can change your filter caps and make your amp have something most of us rarely experience: Real BASS!

What do they look like? That's the question that I wish someone answered for me when I first became curious about this stuff. The most identifiable are the ones that look like little brown plain M&Ms, but there are also lots of other kinds as well: some look like little cylinders with obscure codes on them, the old Fender tone caps look like blue Good-N-Plenty's, others don't look like candy at all.

One thing that they all have in common is that they all have two leads, and they are marked with two codes: There is usually voltage number on the cap, which designates the highest voltage the cap can handle. You will also see another code that designates is the amount of capacitance they are capable of, in fractions of *farads*, usually designated by units of 'mfd' or 'uF.' Even smaller fractions of farads, or picofarads, are designated by the unit 'pf', usually referred to as 'puff'. Farads are units of capacitance, but don't worry about what this means now. Just remember that if you see any of these three abbreviations on a part, it's got to be a cap.

To get an idea of what caps do, I'm going to give you a bit of history and this will lead us to a basic understanding of

what capacitance is and how it works. The capacitor story goes something like this: way back in the 1700s two smart guys at the University of Leyden in the Netherlands coated a glass jar with tin foil on the inside and the outside. The inside foil and outside foil were not connected. Then the jar was corked, and a metal rod was stuck through the cork so that it made contact with the foil on the inside. What was discovered was that the jar could be charged on the outside, and then later discharged by way of the metal rod through the cork: the two conductors that were separated by a fraction of an inch of glass were able to store a static charge. It had the *capacity* to store a charge, which is one of the many things that capacitors do.

These days your amplifier [and any other gear you have] has lots of different kinds of capacitors that do lots of different jobs, but basically they all evolved from the Leyden Jar; they all have two plates that are placed very close together, and separated by a nonconductive substance called a *dielectric*, just as the inside and outside tin surfaces on the Leyden Jar were separated from each other by the glass. These days the dielectric is no longer made of glass, but of other materials including some gelatinous material that tends to dry up after a while, as I will get to later.

How do they work? There's some heavy math, but in my opinion, the easiest way to think about capacitors and their characteristics is to think about the specific jobs they do in your amp. First of all, capacitors pass high frequencies and attenuate low frequencies. In essence, they are high pass filters, and the greater the capacitance they have, the lower the frequencies they allow to pass through them. This is how the tone controls work on the amplifier. Your tone controls are a series of resistors that direct parts of your guitar signal through capacitors of certain values to control what frequencies are stopped, and which ones are let through.

Because caps pass high frequencies, they are also used to suppress oscillations in amplifiers. Without getting too involved, this means that when an amplifier starts to freak out and squeal at high frequencies for whatever reason, capacitors can be used to bleed off the higher frequencies to ground, while the more usable part of the signal is allowed to continue through the circuit. This is just what happened in the '70s when Fender was trying to make their amps louder and cleaner. The new designs had a tendency to oscillate due to the new layout of the wiring that evolved after some of the components were changed around, and the transformers were made bigger. Engineers used caps to bleed off some of these annoying oscillations. Although this stopped the problem, most people say they give these amps a sterile sound because they also have a tendency to bleed off the higher harmonics that make tube amps sound good.

(*Note: the high pitched ringing sound your amp usually makes is not parasitic oscillation. It is a microphonic preamp tube, a problem that is far more common. Here's how to tell the difference: pull the guitar cord out of the input jack. Turn it up really loud and smack it. Does it make the amp ring more or stop ringing? Yes? Then reach around back and tap on each preamp tube individually. The one that makes the sound needs to be replaced.*)

Another important characteristic of caps is their ability to store a charge, as I mentioned before. They do this much like the battery in your walkman, but for a much shorter time. What is really cool is that you can use them to store the signal voltage, instead of the power supply voltage that Duracells are usually used for. This can lead to all kinds of great stuff. Vibrato circuits often use caps this way. And have you got an old analog synth with a 'glide' or portamento control? It works by storing up the signal voltage of the key you press and slowly discharging it to the rest of the amplifier circuit.

Another valuable aspect of caps is that they pass AC and do not pass DC, much in the same way transformers block DC. This makes them the likely candidates for many jobs. Caps can get rid of AC by passing it to ground, or get rid of DC by stopping it at the crossroads. This is the case with coupling caps that are used to connect amplifier stages. If you remember in the last issue, I detailed how a tube amplifies. Your amplifier is made up of many such stages, with the plate's output of the first tube going to the grid of the second, and so on. As you'll remember, the plate has a high DC voltage on it, and if this voltage ever got to the grid of the next tube, we'd be scraping you off the ceiling. So how do we keep this DC plate voltage separate from the amplified AC signal that we want to send to the next tube? With a capacitor of course, as shown in Figure A. Here, the capacitor passes the amplified AC voltage on to the grid of the next tube, but keeps the high DC plate voltage where it belongs.

Finally, we need to address a special kind of capacitor: the electrolytic. Basically, electrolytics have all the same characteristics as any other capacitor, except they're polarized. This means that there is a negative lead and a positive lead, and that if you mix up the two, you're screwed. Usually the negative lead is marked, so this is pretty hard to botch up, but I've done it a few times.

One important job that these caps do is 'filter' out the AC component of the power supply voltage. As you probably know, the voltage in your wall outlet is 120 volts AC, and if we put 120 volts AC on *any* part of the tube, we're in deep trouble. So the amplifier needs a way to change this AC to the various DC voltages that the amp needs. The first step is the rectifier tube, or the solid state rectifier, that passes only one side of the wave and leaves us with DC pulses. The filter caps provide another part of this system by smoothing out the DC pulses to create pure DC. As you remember, caps store up voltage and then discharge it, and this is how filter caps work: they store up some of the 'pulse' and then

discharge it as the pulse itself goes back toward ground, as in Figure B. In this way, the cap is providing the voltage in between the pulses of DC, and what comes out the other end is pure DC.

Chances are, if you have an amp that has filter caps that are more than ten years old, they need changed. The dielectric in filter caps, as I mentioned earlier, is a gooey substance that dries up and stops working after ten years or so. When this dries up, your amp will develop a 60-cycle hum, lose volume, have mushy bass, and generally sound like most of the guitars you hear in the punk rock world. The good news is that you can change them and get all the good stuff back: more volume, real bass, and you might even get rid of some of that hum. Here's what to do:

1) Find them *and do not touch them*. Clue: they are way bigger than any of the circuit board components, usually around the size of tubes. They are usually on the outside of the amp chassis with the transformers, not on the inside with the circuit board. In Fenders, they are usually under a pan in front of the tubes. In Marshalls, they are usually all combined into a big brownish-yellow cardboard tube. This tube really contains a few of them all rolled up into one convenient package.

2) *Do Not Touch Them! They Must First be Discharged!* I can not stress this enough. I still have a small blistering burn on my finger from the filter caps in a tiny Fender Champ. A bigger amp can store enough voltage to stop your heart, unplugged. Here's how to discharge them: Unplug the amp, turn it on, and if it has a standby switch, turn that on as well. Touch an insulated screwdriver to pin 1 on any preamp tube, and then touch ground with the screwdriver at the same time, essentially shorting pin 1 to ground. [You are, of course, holding the *insulated* part of the screwdriver, yes?] Hold this connection for a few seconds or so, and you're all set. Any excess voltages are gone.

3) Unsolder the caps and remember how they are connected, find replacements, and solder them in the same way. Use a pencil to remember where the hell they go and what the polarities are! It can be really tricky to try to interpret this from a schematic because the wires are all under the fiberboard on a lot of amps. If you are replacing multi-caps, they might have six or more leads, so be careful.

Replacements are hard to find from electronic warehouses because there is just not that much equipment out there anymore that requires large amounts of filtering. You will have better luck with Mouser, Digi-Key or any of those warehouse-type places if you're looking for smaller values, and of course the price will be right. But for bigger values and voltages you need to find a vintage guitar supplier. The best place to look is in *Vintage Guitar Magazine*. Ignore all the stupid articles about this and that $12,000 Telecaster and go straight to the ads. There are at least five or ten companies like Hoffman and Kendric that sell them. Expect to pay anywhere from $20-$50 to get what you need for bigger amps. Also, if you have a good store in your area that repairs old amps, you can usually get filter caps there.

How do you know what you need? Well, as I mentioned before, you need to get two things right: the voltage and the capacitance. Generally, you can use the same voltage or a higher than the originals, and the capacitance must be in the same ballpark. For example, in a Twin, you might need something like three 20mfd/500v, and then two more 70mfd/350v. [Your caps might say '20uF' instead of '20mfd.' They are the same.] You might find replacement values that are a few mfd in either direction, which is fine as long as the voltages are at least as big as the old ones. Of course, you should always double check with the place you are buying them from. Most amp-parts suppliers that sell them list them as 'filter caps for 50w Marshalls', so it's pretty easy.

4) Charge them. When electrolytics are new, they must be brought up to voltage slowly as to properly form the dielectric and blah blah blah. I haven't decided if filter caps *really* need to be charged or not. Apparently Leo Fender never did, but I always do just in case. First you need a variac, or you need to build a simple current limiter (figure C). A variac is just what it sounds like: it varies the amount of AC you can send from a wall outlet to a device. These are great to have, in general, because if a fuse keeps blowing, you can run your amp at 12 volts and check all the voltages by multiplying what you find by 10, and you won't blow the fuse because you're only drawing 1/10 of the current. Variacs start at around $175, but I got mine at an antique store for $10. So what if it only goes up to 110 volts! Junk stores with old radio parts are the best because hobbyists used to use them. If you have one, use it. Give it a few hours on some small voltage and then increase gradually. Be creative.

If you don't have one, build a simple current limiter out of a three prong extension cord, a lamp, and a 100-watt lightbulb. (see figure C) This project is quite simple, **BUT IT DEALS WITH LETHAL VOLTAGES! DO NOT TOUCH THE BARE WIRES, AND INSULATE EVERYTHING BEFORE YOU PLUG IT IN!** The idea is to put the bulb in series with the amp, so that all the current must first go through the lightbulb before it goes through the amp. This way, the bulb will not glow until the amp is plugged in. When you have both plugged in, the bulb should not glow at its full brightness because some of the current is being used up by the amp. This way, the amp doesn't get the full AC current and the caps are allowed to warm up at a lower voltage before they get the full wall voltage. When I did this before I found a variac, I gave it a couple hours and kept my eye on everything to make sure it didn't blow up.

5) Rock. If you changed and biased your power tubes and your driver tube (see the Tubes article) you should have 100% more volume, less hum, and really firm bass after you change the caps. In fact, you'll be surprised how much you can get out of an amp this way.

Live Recording

RERUN AND THE DOOBIE BROTHERS HAVE RUINED *LIVE RECORDING* FOR AN ENTIRE GENERATION

by Henry H. Owings

Author's Note: Let it be known that the material in this article is intended for recreational use only. Attempting to record a band without their approval is considered in bad taste, and could very well get you into a load of trouble. So you know, you've now been warned.

I'm sure that anybody fortunate enough to suffer through prime time television in the '70s will remember the show *What's Happening!* The most memorable episode for this poor slob is the one where Rerun sneaks a tape recorder into a Doobie Brothers concert. Half way through their lip-synched "performance," the recorder falls out of Rerun's pocket, the Doobs stop playing and then the moral of the story kicks in. I don't really recall what the moral was, but I do remember that it was rather nasty and put recording concerts in a bad light. However, much the same way that photographers take pictures at shows to chronicle an event, people who record shows, for the most part, do it for their own personal recreation.

THE RECORDER

Much like purchasing a 4-track, there's a multitude of options.
Sony WMD3
This model looks almost identical to a real Walkman. And like its lower models, it has only a two-head design, and the factory-supplied microphone doesn't really have a wide range. Like all the other models that will be mentioned, the D3 has a recording level control knob. Some fancier recorders have separate knobs for the left and right channel, but this just always seemed like a bit too much work when you're in a dimly lit club. Regarding the D3, I never had much luck with them, especially when it was so damned easy to accidentally bump the record switch off. However, for many, this suits their needs just fine. It costs around $300, and like the other machines mentioned, can be found at finer electronic stores. However, for my own peace of mind, I've purchased all of my recorders from J&R Music World in Maspeth, New York. [call 1-800-221-8180 to be sent a free catalog] I do this in large part due to the fact

that they've got a very good return policy, a massive selection from inventory, and you can purchase an additional warranty to cover electronic foul-ups.

Sony WMD6

If there is an Econoline van of the portable tape recording world, this would have to be it. It's sturdy, reliable and will last forever. The 3-head design is terrific and, providing that you're not a perfectionist like most, it will suit almost every person's needs. It has select switches for tape type and Dolby, line in/out ports and an attenuation switch. Apart from the Dolby, none of these features are on the wimpier D3. The attenuation switch is of particular importance. If the show is loud (e.g. requires earplugs), the –20dB attenuation helps a lot. For quieter, more acoustic-y shows (sans plugs) the 0dB switch will be the one to go with. The D6 is used more widely than any other recording device on the market. If Whitney, sound man for such bands as the Jesus Lizard, Blues Explosion, and Jawbox, uses it to record their shows; that should give you a good idea of how well these machines travel and perform.

Sony WMD7, WMD8 (aka DAT)

Why get a D7? Because it's one better than a D6! Hoooo! But seriously, I've never been able to figure out the need to record live shows with digital equipment, so my personal knowledge on the subject is rather limited. I do know that with the ever increasing bootleg CD market, DATs are used almost exclusively as master sources. In addition, with regular analog tapes, quality can be lost in two to three generations from the master. With DAT, there's no loss. Big deal.

A D7(or any digital recorder for that matter) will cost almost double of a D6 or similar analog recorder. And if you make copies for fellow traders, you must also remember that you'll need a second DAT machine. Also, you have routine maintenance and additional equipment which could run your total set-up cost well over $1,500! For just a hobby, this seems a bit outrageous, so I've never considered entering the digital realm an option.

Ironically, although, I don't consider myself to have a trained ear by any stretch of the imagination, I'm usually able to pick out which shows are recorded live to DAT just due to the rumbly bass heavy sound. I don't know, it seems to be a big hit, so what do I know? If interested, though, a bevy of information (on DAT, microphones, and other incidental hoo-hah) can be sought out cybernetically at the alt.music.bootlegs.newsgroup.

There has also been the distinct proliferation of MiniDisc (MD) technology to the live audio realm, which seems to be bridging the gap. Again, information can be found on-line (http://www.connact.com/~eaw/minidisc/) and can be answered much more succinctly than I could ever conceive.

MICROPHONES

Although I'm not much of a tech-head like many a Tape Op reader, I do know what works well and what works like crap. Note that there's a countless amount of options when it comes to buying a microphone. With that said, please bear with my lack of big technical words...

PZM (Pressure Zone Mics)

For $120, you can buy two of these rather clumsy looking 3" square mics [at Radio Shack], and get a pretty good sound. But keep in mind that these aren't very portable and must invariably require a special stand and mount for them. When used together, face them towards the band, slightly upwards and apart from each other. There will be a good bit of stereo separation, but I never found the low end to be that remarkable. In fact, that's why I stopped using these mics about 4 years ago. [If you're recording music that's not full bore loud, and you have access to the stage; try throwing a pair on the floor of the stage, out of the way, and it can sound very good. The mics pick up low end the best when they're on a surface and closer to the sound source.]

Core Sound Mics

I picked these capsule mics on the Internet at moskowit@panix.com. And although the microphones themselves are both no bigger than a pencil eraser, they're terribly awkward to use. Also, the version that I purchased cost about $130, which I was told by the manufacturers of the mic, would suit my needs just fine. The other version of the mic cost twice as much and contained a preamp, which is intended for those with digital recorders. I found the version I purchased to be unbelievably bass heavy almost to the point of being distorted. In the mic's own defense, I will say that it works the best in ambient or acoustic settings. These mics are intended for stealth recording at your bigger U2 or Van Halen concerts where there are security pat downs, but for me, I've never had to hide my equipment.

Headphones

I didn't believe it when somebody told me this, but headphones can be used as a stereo microphone. Learn something new every day, huh? Although I have tried these makeshift microphones out of curiosity, they provide unremarkable, tinny sound.

Sony ECM909a

This particular microphone is just slightly larger than a tube of lipstick, has a 2-foot cord, and is as reliable as its D6 counterpart. It requires a AA battery, but allows much fuller sound. There's a toggle switch on the microphone for 90 and 120 degree spreads. Personally, I just stick with the 90-degree setting pointed towards the band slightly upwards. What's more, the 909 is much more convenient to hold or position than anything else I've found.

Ribbon Mics (such as the Coles 4038)

I saw Bob Weston using one once at a show in Chicago, but then again, that's his line of work. Suffice as to say, it is the top of the line and it showed when I was listening to the playback. However, these can cost more than a years tuition at the University of your choice. If you've got the dough though, knock yourself out.

RECORDING

Okay, so you've got the equipment and you're trying to figure out how the hell to use it. Sorry to use this cliche, but the best way to learn is just to practice. But still, here are some pointers that I've found out along the way. And for the record, there's a really great site on the web which goes into great detail over mic placement (http://www.bhm.tis.net/~rob/MICFAQ.html) which I highly recommend visiting.

Huge Clubs (800-2,000+ capacity)

Try to put the microphone as close to the soundman as possible. Usually, the person who is doing sound in such a cavernous place will try to satisfy their ears first and the crowd's second. If you are polite and ask the band for permission (which you should do anyway), you might be able to set everything up at the board. If you're sneaky, you might be ejected from the club and (more importantly) have your equipment confiscated. Like that wouldn't suck. Although I don't intend for this to seem like something exclusive to smaller clubs, sound at larger clubs have always deceived me. Maybe it's due to the noise bouncing off the walls. I dunno.. Find out for yourself, though.

Small Clubs (200-800 capacity)

A lot of the times, the PAs at these size clubs are skimpy at best. They often push the drums and vocals up high in the mix, leaving the guitars pushed to the side. A good rule of thumb is to walk around the club and figure out where it sounds good to you. We'll call this the sweet spot. When you find the sweet spot, that is where you'll get the best recording results.

House Shows (0-200 capacity)

These are always the most fun shows for me personally, but can sometimes become a real challenge when I'm trying to record. If possible, it's always best to get two places to put microphones. The PAs are almost nonexistent, and drums can seem like light years away unless you have a mic directly over them. So it's best to put a mic above the band (to get the drums & vox) and one in front of the PA (for the guitars, bass, etc.), if possible. Otherwise, just use your best judgment.

RECORDING OFF THE BOARD

With rare exception, board tapes have proven to be the albatross of the bootleg field due primarily to the fact that they come out with a mix of nothing but kick drum and vocals. However, in their own defense, I've found a handful of clubs in the States [the Star Bar here in Atlanta comes to mind] where there's a line coming in from the board and another coming from a microphone [or series of mics] in front of the stage going into a mono feed which provides an exquisite mix. Now some of those tapes are remarkable, but they're rare, so I don't bother thinking of them. Another possible suggestion on the board feed is to use a four channel mixer which you can get from Radio Shack and have two lines coming from the board and two from the audience which is basically a rehashing of what I said above, so take from it what you will...

I sincerely believe that this information can be of great use not only to people interested in recording bands of interest, but also for use in their own musical endeavors. And as I've often heard said, "If you're going to do something, do it the best you can." As you can see, there's a number of ways to go about doing the same thing, but depending on your desire for "sonic perfection", recording equipment and methods can vary quite a bit.

My Recording Portfolio

For what it's worth, a few of my recordings have actually been used for various releases that might be of interest.

The Oblivians - *Rock And Roll Holiday* (Pryct)

I recorded this in the very front of the stage at an acoustically horrible sounding club (due in no small part to the coke snorting soundman) called the Midtown Music Hall. This recording was pressed onto LP and was quickly recognized as a definitive work for the band. The release was later mentioned by Byron Coley in the "best of '94" issue of SPIN as one of the most influential underground records of the year. He also said that the record sounded like it was recorded on shoeleather. Whatever, Byron.

The Azusa Plane - *Result Dies With The Worker* (Colorful Clouds)

I think that the biggest reason this release saw the light of day was due to the fact I recorded no fewer than 9 shows by the Azusa Plane and kept hounding J. DiEmilio that their live shows deserved to be documented. He finally gave in. Although the fidelity wavers from time to time, it's a real amazing collection of sounds. The tapes were all dumped onto a computer and then edited using the program called Peak. It was a priceless experience for me.

Providence - *27.4.97* (Little Army/Earworm)

While I was recording this, I was in swept up in a pristine sense of awe. Members of Bardo Pond, Flying Saucer Attack, Azusa Plane and Windy & Carl played in the Rouge Lounge at Terrastock in Providence, RI, and I was front row center, coincidentally. The tape sounds absolutely amazing and remarkably well balanced [as in, you can almost place where each performer was]. A real lu-lu of a recording.

Servotron - *7"*- (Reservation)

I toured with Servotron back in '96 as the first official road slave and I recorded almost every show including an amazing sounding board/live tape at the Moe in Seattle. It's only one song, and it's on the b-side.

Mastering

AN INFORMATIVE DISCUSSION WITH KARL BARLETT OF THE X FACTORY MASTERING AND RECORDING STUDIO

by Larry Crane

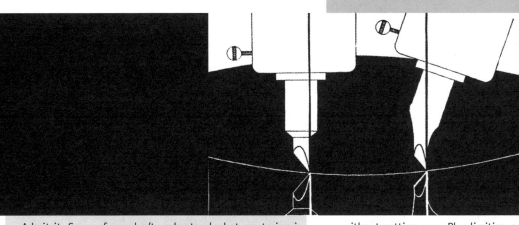

Admit it. Some of you don't understand what mastering is, what it does, and why you need it. I've had a hard time explaining it to clients in the past and thought I'd do good to call my pal Karl Bartlett, who's been mastering records in Nashville for several years now, and ask him to help shed some light on this often misunderstood process.

So why does a release need to be mastered?

It varies. Sequencing and the spacing between songs is definitely part of it. It used to be done on analog tape, but now everyone's mixing to DAT and you can't splice DAT. Any crossfades are much easier to do now than with analog.

You had to get three tape decks.

Oh yeah, and you're adding more noise. Now you just click and drag. You can do 100 second crossfades. So there's the sequencing part of it and there's two sonic parts to it. One is that you want it as loud as possible.

What do you mean when you say "loud"?

I'm talking about VU really. VU versus peak. Meters now, like the meters on DAT machines, are closer to peak, but they're kind of in the middle - they're really neither. If you have a really good set of meters, like a Durrough, it'll show you both. Zero VU is generally about -14 dB from zero these days. That means that if you're sending a zero tone out of your console it should show up at -14 on your DAT machine. What that implies is that you have -14 dB of headroom for your peaks above your average. VU is like your average volume. Let's say you take Oasis or Cracker or somebody that Bob Ludwig (or someone like that) has had his hands on. You'll find average VU on the whole record will be +6 with VU peaks that are insane, at +10 or even a little more. If your VU is +14 you're just pegged. It's zero and the needles won't even move. That does exist in certain cases and it's a little bit overboard. You'll actually start distorting some analog stages of your output devices if you overdo it. Compression is the way that you can bring up your VU

without getting over. Plus limiting on top of that. So the main thing is you want it loud, so it sounds like everything else on the radio and so you get the most out of whatever gear you're playing it out of. The gain is nice and high so you don't have to crank it up and get a lot of extra hiss in there. The other sonic part of mastering, that's probably the biggest thing of all, is that you want consistency from song to song. You want it to sound like one album... you don't want it to sound like 10 different mixes. Even though you probably want some variety, like you didn't just push up the faders and let all 10 songs roll, you want some variety in your songs but you want it all to sound like a consistent album with a consistent amount of bass, treble and volume. So no listener should have to reach for their bass, treble or volume knobs during the whole album. You may want it to breathe more, like a quiet part and a loud part, and that's where it comes into a subjectivity of how squashed (compressed) you want it, from just straight out, in-your-face rock and roll to a jazz project or classical, which is obviously gonna have a lot more dynamic range to it. So those are the three main reasons to master. Make it sound clear, with a proper high end and low end. There's kind of an objectivity about it at that point where I'll use my ear. I've mastered probably 500 albums or more, so I have a pretty good idea now of where the frequency response should be, depending on the kind of music. It's to the point where I'm pretty much objective. Then it'll come back to a subjective point of just how crunchy do you want it, just how bassy do you want it, how bright do you want it - which comes to the producer and other people to tell me what they had in mind beyond the overall objective frequency response and stuff.

But say some band just finished recording, everything came out great, they played the tapes on different systems and it never seems to be lacking. They want to just put it on CD and be done. What are they missing here?

I'd say, "Oh great – go for it." One good thing about it is... even if I produce something – and I'm kinda bad about this 'cause I'll produce something and go ahead and master it myself anyway - but it's good to put an extra pair of ears on it, especially somebody that's a mastering engineer. Hopefully, you'd think if somebody's a mastering engineer that they have good ears and know what they're doing. If people aren't happy with their mastering they should raise all kind of stink about it and take it back and get it right so they are happy. People are paying huge bucks and there's this kind of attitude like, "I'm the mastering guy so I know what's right for your project. This is the way it needs to be and just take it and that's it. Give me my $3000 and we'll talk later." That's not right. People should be happy with their products and I always tell people to let me know if we gotta do a little revision or something, which is harder now 'cause I gotta re-rent the gear. But that's my own problem. It still comes down to the client needs to have it exactly the way they want. I've had people tell me, "No, I don't want any compression on this at all." I'm like, "Yeah, but this is a pop thing and it's a live album and it goes down to -30 for a while and sits there." It's not up to me. I've made my suggestion and they want it a certain way. We did this live "bootleg." It was called *Bootleg Snacks* by the Floating Men, a little alternative/stoner rock band from Nashville. That was the case I'm talking about. The producer, he's a real persnickety kinda guy, didn't want any compression on it, just a little bit of EQ. I was like, "Well, alright." By the end of it, after we'd listened through the thing, I thought it was really refreshing because it's not the way most music is. In fact, I just listened to *Thick as a Brick* [Jethro Tull] today, and I put it on and was looking at my meters and it starts at -30 with that guitar thing at the beginning and it takes a while to build up loud and it's kinda neat. You don't get that anymore. Pearl Jam and all that kind of stuff it just goes right up to zero and just sits there. I think, sometimes, I would prefer less that some of the squashing that's going on. I heard Bob Ludwig is making a call for a little more dynamic range in music. Sometimes it's just so squashed that it just sounds crappy.

In almost all listening environments conditions are less than ideal. If you're keeping it above a certain point it's always gonna be heard.

I think, mainly, a lot of that has to do with radio. You don't want to be quieter than the last thing that was just heard, you wanna be louder.

You definitely hear that on college radio with independently produced stuff next to full on production.

Right there's a good example. You can compare the difference between your pop/rock station versus a college station. They kind of cheat too, cause the big station has 100,000 watts and the little station has 1000 watts.

But even the compressors at the college station aren't as good.

That's true too. A big station squashes it even more. At a little college station you'll get all kinds of different qualities of sounds. We have a station here, that plays Beck and all the "big-name" alternative people, but you'll notice a lot of variety in the EQ. That's partly because people, even though it is mastered, are going different ways. Some bands have a whole bunch of bass and they want it that way. Country music and Christian music and other kinds of music are more consistent. If you listen to a country station, one's gonna sound pretty much the same, EQ wise, as the next. Something you'll notice on

those projects that haven't been mastered is that something is gonna sound really dull. Where's the vocal or where's the bass? There hasn't been one project that I couldn't help. If I couldn't make it sound better, what am I doing? I will always A/B [*compare against the original signal*] it to make sure I'm doing something that's good to it. Hey, if I don't have much to do, that's great. I'll just level them all up, compress it a little, bring it all in the pocket, and just use my EQ to bring in differences between songs. Singles and demos and songs that people are shopping don't matter as much as far as consistency. The consistency from song to song, level and tonally, is the main part of it I think. Everything says, "Digitally Mastered." That's not that cool. Actually, analog mastering is better. What it does is that it's actually adding more coloration, which is actually distortion, the same thing you get off analog tape; that big, fat, warm sound. I love mastering through tubes, especially with all these ADAT studios – these little clean digital studios with clean little mixers and stuff, which are all fine, but we want to get it all big and fat sounding. You can really add a quality. What I'll try to do is maximize the quality of the album that I'm handed. I did this folky, almost like a Nanci Griffith-type, project and worked with this woman a whole lot and it actually got pulled from me after I had already mastered it. These people had some different ideas even though she was the producer – she was pissed. The quality and the character of that whole album that we captured was a really warm, intimate kind of feel. The feel of it you could really get with mastering a lot.

I assume when you're talking about tubes you're not talking about a single 12AX7 device. You were talking before about the Fairchild and the Manley compressors.

I'm just about to get into the Manley. We had a Fairchild 670 at Final Stage [Karl's old employer] and the album I just did here I did rent a Fairchild. It has 23 or 24 tubes and it's real finicky. The Fairchild 670 is the grandaddy of all compressors and it's a beautiful thing. It's a $20,000 piece of gear if you can even find one anymore.

How old are they?

They're 20 or 30 years old. Beautiful things. There are only a couple of knobs - you can't adjust many parameters. You actually can, once you know the device, learn how to get out of it what you want - more kick or more bass. I can do a lot of that kind of work before I even touch the EQ.

So what's the signal path you use when mastering a CD?

This kind of comes back to how people should prepare their masters. The masters I get from Greg Freeman are on 1/4" tape but almost everything I do is off DAT. A couple of things are off 1/2" tape. The biggest, most finicky people used to always mix to 1/2". There's really good analog-to-digital converters now and there's also some 24 bit storage mediums and things people are going to cause it's really bordering on being better than 1/2". 1/2" can be better than DAT if it's all calibrated and aligned right and the engineer really knows what they're doing, you can get a real nice mix going to a 1/2". My personal belief, and this may stir a little controversy with Greg, is that I personally think that DAT has a better sound than 1/4". That's not necessarily always the case, but at some place like Greg Freeman's (Lowdown, S.F.), where they're cutting on 2" 16-track anyway, you've already got the big, fat analog sound – go ahead and capture it as nicely as you can onto a nice clear medium cause the sound that you're after is already there. Maybe, if you had a really nice 1/4" machine and a really clean studio with ADATs or a DA88 maybe you'd go to that. That's just my personal thing. I think Greg likes to cut the tape up and edit that way. One thing that I get from him is A and B side reels that are exactly spaced how they want them. That can be good, for them, mastering across the country. Generally I'll go from DAT and through some nice converter, like an Apogee, from the DAT.

Do you have a converter there?

No, I don't have any here. This last project I did I was able to use some converters from the studio where I used to work. I don't know how long that's gonna happen! Good converters, especially on the way back in, are a good call. Especially when you're trying to recapture the analog mastering. So we go analog out of a DAT and into a real nice, stereo, parametric EQ. There's some mastering ones that are clickable, with detents, so you can exactly recall what you did even though it's analog. The one I've been using here is not a mastering EQ, but it's a regular GML 5 band parametric. It's a real nice sounding thing. I was using the GML mastering EQ at Final Stage and it's almost exactly the same. I EQ before compression and I think that's what most people do. Some people EQ before and after. I like to EQ on the way into the tube compressor and after that it'll go into an analog-to-digital converter, hopefully a nice Apogee or something like that, and then a digital limiter.

Can you explain the difference between a limiter and a compressor?

I can explain how we do it. Those compressors I was talking about don't have things on it like "ratio," 2 to 1, 3 to 1. It's more of a threshold, input gain, and time. The end result is that the compressor gives you the VU and the limiter just keeps you from having any "overs." You set your limiter to a third or half a dB under zero. I've found it to be one of the weakest links in the chain, depending on what you're using. The limiter just cuts off the zeros, it's like a real hard knee, right at the very top. You don't have overs. Hopefully it doesn't do anything sonically. When you push a digital limiter too hard it gets crackly. Compressors do that too, and it's sort of an effect where it's all crunchy and compressed. The guy who masters Reba (McEntire) and some of those big country acts does it all digitally with Pro Tools and an L1 limiter and he squashes the shit out of stuff. It'll be like a Reba ballad and it sounds great for the first verse but when it gets to the chorus it just goes to zero and doesn't move. It's out of hand. It gets crunchy and crackly and it also thins out. The more you compress stuff the more bass gets added. That's one tip; people should leave a little less bass on their mix than they're gonna want in the long run. When you squash it, the bass will come up, get sustained more and be more in your face and generally louder. If you go past that, to the point where you're just squashing this thing, it'll start thinning back out. When things are too bassy, I'll do that. Generally, a good, decent amount of compression will add more bass. I find that the trend is that people are getting more and more bass than they did 5 or 10 years ago. That was the digital craze, where everyone wanted it really bright, real clear sounding. That's a hard call 'cause some people want normal sounding bass and some people want a lot more. Bass, to me, is the most variable thing. As you get to the top end it's more objective and the mid-range is

pretty objective too. You can tell if the vocal's clear sounding or if there's a wet blanket over it. It's easier to tell in the high end and a little bit of EQ goes a lot farther in the upper register. I usually don't get past a dB or a couple of dBs in extreme cases whereas sometimes with low end I'll go 5, 6, 7 or 8 dBs that I'm having to cut or boost if the mix is way off. Generally it's not that bad.

And people don't perceive bass the same.

Yeah, that's a bonafide physiological fact that people should take into account when they're mixing. I definitely take it into account when I'm mastering. I master at a pretty nominal volume, about 90 dB. I'll turn it down and up a little bit so that I don't get burned out or ear fatigue. That does occur too. You can't hear, even if you want to and you're still attentive, your ears just burn out, they really do, and they just need a rest. I tried mastering three albums in a day. By the third one I was still up for it, but I couldn't literally hear what I was doing. I can still hear changes that I'm making but I'm having a harder time telling which direction it needs to go. I lose the perspective on it and it's just sheer ear fatigue. That's a bonafide thing too. There's people in Nashville that mix at all different volumes, some people that mix really loud. They must know what they're doing cause the people I'm talking about are big-name people. In general, unless you're those people, I would recommend mixing at a pretty nominal volume. Not too loud. Do your mix and then go ahead and listen to it cranked up if you want. Take it out to your car on a cassette. Check it out and get a good idea, before it's mastered, that you're in the right ballpark. When people mix and it's way too loud, and you play it back at a listening volume on a home stereo, it'll sound flat, like it's just laying there. That's something to watch out for. You can shoot yourself in the foot like that. So anyway, what I'm doing here now is I'll put the signal back on another DAT, because I don't have a computer here. I do all my digital editing and PM CDs and stuff at another studio that has Sonic Solutions. I'll go song by song. I'll dump a song to DAT, write down all my settings, and go onto the next song. If no one's talking, and I'm on a roll, I can pretty much go right on through. If we've taken a break, or we had to chat about something, sometimes all go back and skip through and listen to a little bit of all the songs before and get back on track tonally. Tonally, now, it's real easy for me to make sure that they're real consistent. It's a real easy thing for my ear now. When we get it in the computer, we can do some final touches on the leveling. One thing I've used here, instead of a limiter, is the soft-limit feature on the Apogee. It's a pretty nice sounding limiter actually. One thing it does is it puts the peak at -2 dB, so it leaves you 2 dB of headroom. What I'll generally do is go ahead and boost it all up 1 dB in the computer, which leaves me 1 dB to come up with the quietest things again. We'll bring it right up to zero. Even the occasional over is okay. Different DAT machines show overs at different numbers of consecutive words of over. (Panasonic) 3700s will show overs at 8 consecutive words of full value. The 7010s and real nice, pro Sony's will show up at 3 words of over. Sonic Solutions will show you on your Mac screen at one word. The number where it shows an over on the CD, if you were gonna go to a CD production, is 8 words. At the CD plant, I don't even know if there is an official number where they'll send it back to you because of overs. There are production CDs that have overs on them and that's okay.

When you're mastering do you ever put in other CDs to A/B against what you're working on or do you find that that's just useless?

It's not useless. I don't usually do that, unless, for example: The very first album that I just did here, which it's new... there's so many new variables. I know my speakers, but I don't know how they're sounding in this room. We took an old bluegrass album – I've mastered about a dozen albums for this guy - so we took one that we'd already done that we liked the sound of, and A/B'd to that for sure when we were starting.

Just to see how it was coming out and how the room sounds?

We figured that we know the sound of the CD and we'll take that as a constant and get familiar with the room. I had it so I could switch back and forth while they were both playing and make sure that our bass and treble were comparable. That's a good way to do it. Sometimes people will give me a suggestion... there was this Christian hard rock thing I did, I think they were called Prophecy, and they said they wanted to sound like 311. I really liked 311 a lot and had listened to it a lot so I didn't need to stick it in and A/B it. Those kind of tips can help me with which direction to take it. 311's really compressed and has a little bit of really overpowering bass. It's almost like rap a little bit. Usually I'll end up mastering alone, but sometimes there's clients and if they want to get used to the room they'll bring in CDs. That's a good idea for them. Especially if they're gonna be leaning over my shoulder and telling me they want another 1/2 dB at 420 Hz. I hate that! I hate it when people lean over my shoulder and tell me what to do. "Sit back, be quiet, and let me do my tweaks. I'll give you the nod when I want your opinion."

What kind of things can people do to prepare for mastering as they work on an album?

One thing that just came to mind... the first rule of all is: There are no rules. You should use your ear. Look at somebody like Beck or even Jimi Hendrix in his day. "What's this crunchy guitar panned left and right?" There are no rules and you should never sell yourself short. Go ahead with an idea. If you want a vocal to sound a certain way make it really that way. I don't mean overdo effects. What I mean is don't be hesitant with your work. When I first started doing mixes what I found is they were very well balanced, everything was in its place, you could hear everything very clearly and there it was... it just kind of sat there. It didn't have a lot of life and I didn't take any chances. There's no rule, other than your own ear and your own feeling to it. If you're gonna be the original one to set out to start a whole new trend and a whole new sound it better not sound just like that album that you really like. It's just gonna be another Weezer copy or whatever. It keeps you enthusiastic and always looking for new sounds. As far as more specific tips: It used to be that places would say to leave a few dB at the top for the mastering engineer. It doesn't really matter now cause we can adjust the gain up or down. If you're mixing to DAT you get higher resolution the higher you record. It is actually better to get it right up to zero. I can add or subtract just about anything. It's easier to add bass than to take it away. Compression you can't take away. When I get something in that's just squashed, usually it's with a DBX or something, nothing like what I have to work with. Plus it wasn't EQ'd first on the way in. Basically I just throw my hands up. "What am I supposed to do with this? I can EQ it but I can't compress it now that it's already squashed. I can't expand it!" When it's overcompressed you can't go back. That's the worst thing. Even if you want a lot of compression, I would leave some room, so it can be EQ'd

first, and tell the mastering guy to squash the hell out of this. If you know your recordings gonna be mastered, you should ask if it's gonna be digitally mastered or analog. If it's gonna be analog mastered, you might as well go ahead and record [your mixes] at 48 kHz. It's just about 10% better, more samples, there's certainly a little bit more resolution in the higher frequencies. When we bring it to analog we bring it to 44.1 kHz on the way back in to digital. If you're gonna master digital, there's lots of digital sample rate conversion you can do to get it to 44.1 kHz anyway, but you might as well go ahead and mix at 44.1 kHz.

I've heard the sample rate conversions can be a little bit sketchy at times.

It can. Even in a digital-to-digital transfer, where it's supposed to be exact, there have been people noticing differences in that, which is unsettling. That's scary stuff. Usually the differences you notice there are in imaging. The image will seem to close down a bit and not be quite as big. So 48 kHz is good if you're mastering in analog. It doesn't matter if you mix in order, of course.

How much should people budget for if they're planning to have someone like you master their CD?

About $500 to $600. I'm pretty cheap. This whole niche of people, exactly the kind of people who are going to be reading this, that's the market I wanna be in. I don't give a shit about mastering some big-name country guy. I don't even want to do it! I used to master a whole lot of Christian music. We would do a fine job, but I want to be able to get the bands in here that I want to do. We're looking at over $500 but certainly under $1000, and I know mastering can go well over that. It's $100 an hour plus some editing and other parts and I cover the cost of rentals and the other studio to cut the CD.

Are there extra costs for revisions?

No, if it's not major. If someone told me the wrong ID and I got the wrong song on there, something's that really not my fault, I'll have to charge. If there's a glitch on the PMCD, that's me. I do recommend that people listen to their masters. I usually don't have revisions.

They just go out and bad-mouth you!

I hope not. That would be pointless. If people really need to have it changed they should tell me and get it done right.

So you do mastering out of your own studio there?

Yeah. I just started doing it since I got laid off at the mastering place where I used to work. I was due for a raise and they said, "Work's light right now" and laid me off. I said, "Fine." I'm kind of in with some boys that do a rental company here and they've got all kinds of nice analog gear. The same stuff I was using before and some other choices too. They give me a good deal.

Do you rent stuff for projects or by the month?

Yeah, I rent it by the project. I kind of have to eat it if I have to go back and do revisions and stuff... or I'll just try to time it when there are other projects going on.

So what else goes on at your studio?

I have a 1/2" 8-track, a Mackie 1604, a (Panasonic) 3700 DAT and a little bit of outboard gear.

Do you record bands there?

I'm going to. Right now I'm still trying to get it finished up. The mastering is an easier thing to come by. I already had the business and the control room is good enough that I can do mastering in it but the rest of the place isn't really finished yet. A lot of people are waiting to come in and work in here so I gotta hurry up. I might do a little bit of low-key, indie band projects. Get some big huge tie-dyes on the walls – some big candleholders and oil lamps and colored lights...

To make a different kind of place?

Yeah, a real vibe. An anti-professional, anti-music row kind of thing `cause that already exists here.

A LETTER FROM GREG FREEMAN

I enjoyed the interview with Karl about mastering but feel compelled to throw in a couple of comments. This is so obvious that I'm sure Karl simply forgot to mention it, but the primary reason for mastering is to convert a final mix tape [analog or digital] to a format from which it can be reproduced in mass quantities. In the old days you would cut a lacquer master, which would then go through a few intermediate steps and be turned into stampers for pressing records. These days you transfer your mix to one of three formats for CD duplication, either a Sony 1630 [a 3/4" videocassette storage format], a CD-R or an Exabyte digital data tape. Along with your audio goes the control track information, the "pq subcode", which tells your CD player times and tracks. This is really a "pre-master", since the plant then cuts a "glass master" from which CDs are stamped [like records!] The aesthetic stuff is really the gravy [and the fun part] of mastering,

and gets all the glory, but the nuts and bolts stuff is the reason you have to go through the process.

And, uh er um, not everyone is mixing to DAT these days! [In fact I'll bet at most mastering houses, it's either 1/2"or 1/4" analog or some higher-bit digital storage medium.] For my money you are served better by holding off converting to digital [A-D conversion being the weakest link, in my opinion] until you can go in at a higher bit-rate than CD, which these days is 20-bit or 24-bit. [And - very important! - any pro mastering studio will have FAR better A-D convertors than those that live in any DAT deck.] This is better because the higher bit rate is better able to accommodate the extra information you create whenever you do any sort of calculation on your digital audio. [Example: divide 10 by 3. You get 3.33333333... to infinity. The higher your bit-rate, the more of those infinite threes you can squeeze into your word in your digital data. Usually when I've had a beer or two I'm able to start in on my theory of why analog is better at capturing those infinite threes!] Once you're ready, you can then dither down to 16-bit and squeeze some extra resolution to your final product.

You should check out Bob Katz' Digital Domain website for some very good information about mastering, how to prep your analog or digital tape for mastering, and lots more. Here's the URL: <www.digido.com>

Oh yeah, avoid sample rate conversion like the plague!

–Greg Freeman, San Francisco

How to Overproduce a Rock Record

by Jack Endino

A correspondent finally got me started writing it. I've been stewing over it for a long time, and felt I should share. I hope you are amused. However, this is not entirely funny. Everything described actually has happened to bands I know. All of it is happening somewhere, right now. What's worse is that, taken one at a time, I have done many of these things to some extent, at one point or another in my career! No one is innocent! What a biz.

First, spend about a month on "pre-production", making sure that everything is completely planned out so that no spontaneity is necessary or possible in the studio. If there are no "hits" there, make the band collaborate with outside songwriters. Line up extra studio musicians who are better players than the band themselves, just in case.

Next, book the most expensive studio you can find so that everyone but the band gets paid lots of money. The more expensive, the more the record label will take the project seriously, which is important. Book lots and lots of time. You'll need at least 48 tracks to accommodate all the room mics you'll set up for the drums, all of which will be

buried by other instruments later anyway, and for the added keyboard tracks, even if the band has never had a keyboard player. And for all the backing vocal tracks, even if the band only has one singer.

Then, record all the instruments one at a time, but make the drummer play to a click track for every song so the music has no chance to breathe whatsoever. That way you can use lots of MIDI gear. Do multiple takes of each song. Use up at least 30 reels of 2" tape. Take the best parts of each take and splice them all together. You might even use a hard-disk recording system like Pro Tools, then transfer it all back to analog 2". Spend at least two weeks just compiling drum tracks like this. You'll need to rent at least a half a dozen snare drums, and you'll have to change drumheads every couple hours. If you really do it right, the entire band will never have to actually play a song together.

Now, start overdubbing each instrument, one at a time. Make sure everything is perfect. If necessary, do things over and over until absolute perfection is achieved. Do a hundred takes if you must. If this doesn't work, get "guest musicians" in to "help out".

Don't forget to hire someone who's good with samples and loops so the kids will think its hip! Better get some turntable scratching on there too.

Be sure to spend days and days just experimenting with sounds, different amplifiers, guitars, mics, speakers, basically trying every possible option you can think of to use up all that studio time you've booked. No matter how much time you book, you can use it up this way easily. Everyone involved will think they're working very hard.

Make sure you rent lots of expensive mics and expensive compressors and expensive preamps so you can convince yourself and everyone else how good it's sounding. Charge it to the band's recording budget of course. Make sure you have at least two or three compressors IN SERIES on everything you're recording. Any equipment with tubes in it is a sure bet, the older the better. The best is early - 1970s - era Neve equipment, old Ampex analog recorders, and WWII-vintage tube microphones, since everyone knows that the technology of recording has continuously declined for the past 30+ years. Don't forget to get some old "ribbon" mics too.

Make sure that by the time it's finished everyone is absolutely, totally sick of all the songs and never wants to hear any of them again. Oops! Now it's time to mix it!

Better get someone with "fresh ears" [who's never heard any of it before] to mix it in a $2000/day SSL room with full automation. Make sure they're pretty famous, and of course you have to fly to LA, NYC or Nashville to do this, because there simply are no decent studios anywhere else. Make sure they compress the hell out of everything as they mix it. Compress each drum individually and then compress an overall stereo submix of 'em. Make sure to compress all the electric guitars even though a distorting guitar amp is the most extreme "compressor" in existence. Compress everything else, and then compress the overall mix. Add tons and tons of reverb to the drums on top of all those room mics, and add stereo chorus on everything else. Spare no expense. Spend at least two weeks on it. Then take it home and decide to pay for someone else to remix the whole thing.

Then get some New York coke-head mastering engineer to master it, and make sure he compresses the hell out of everything again and takes away all the low end and makes it super bright and crispy and harsh so it'll sound really LOUD on the radio. [Too bad about all those people with nice home stereos.]

Oh-oh! Your A and R guy just got fired! Looks like the record will never be released!

CHAPTER 5
Recording Equipment

Microphones

by Larry Crane, Andy Brown, Rex Ritter and Michael McDonald

Normally, in the recording magazine world, you'll pick up a current issue and find reviews of products that have just come on to the market and may cost *LOTS* of money. Here at *Tape Op* we're not only behind the times, but we're also quite broke. What follows is a list of mics that we've been using with some general thoughts about the mics and their sounds. This isn't a comprehensive list of every mic you can find out there or a [very] knowledgeable scientific treatise on how diaphragms work – it's just some tips for y'all.

SHURE SM 57

If you're recording music and you don't have one of these what's wrong with you? Probably every professional studio and every 4-trackin' geek has some of these mics lying around. 57s, the rugged workhorses of the mic world, have dictated to our ears the way we think guitar amps should sound on so many recordings it's almost scary. I use them a lot, and the following techniques can be applied to just about any type of mic. On guitar amps, try using two, side-by-side, pointing at the sweet spots just to the sides of the speaker dome in the center, and mixing the signals together onto one channel. If you're mic'ing a two speaker amp, like a Fender Twin, put one on each speaker for a fuller tone range. For drums, 57s are the standard snare mics. I try to angle down 1/2" above the rim in a way that picks up the side and bottom of the snare so you can hear its crispness. I tried mic'ing from the side of the snare but the high-hat leakage and wimpiness of the attack made me stop. On toms, get them where they are pointing in halfway to the center for a good slapping sound. I usually EQ the rack tom up a bit at 3K and the floor tom around 4-5K, with a low-end boost on both. I like loud toms, and this works well. If you want a sharp, tapping kick drum sound throw a 57 in there too. Don't point right at the spot where the beater hits or you'll probably get a blown-out mic sound. A little off-center and a lot of EQ boost on the low end can garner a fine kick tone.

For vocals, you can try a 57. They seem kinda dead and dry to my ears, but I've had some takes that came out just fine. Fancier preamps can bring out a lot of character in the mic at this point but that's a whole other subject.

PZM

I usually use them for stereo overhead mics for the drum kit. They have a nice, clear high frequency sound that picks up cymbals really well and the fact that they are immune to phase cancellation allows the other mics on the kit to come up as loud as needed without causing trouble. Right now, they're mounted on small sheets of particleboard and suspended on old cymbal stands so I can move them around the room and balance out the levels of the cymbals that they are picking up. I roll off the low end and pull back the highest high end a bit too. This seems to give a good picture of the cymbal action, while also building a stereo image of the drum kit (which I think adds a lot to the drum sound in general). Sometimes, I try to use them as ambient mics for acoustic guitar or ethnic percussion tracks but most of the time they've generated too much internal hum to be really useful.

CROWN CM 700

This mic, looks a lot like a Mag Light. Someone traded me this for recording time, but I think they list at $300, so you should be able to find one for a little over $200. It's worth every penny. This mic is a cardioid condenser, and it somehow has all the clarity of a condenser mic with the ability to handle high sound pressure levels (SPL). It also has a built in bass-tilt switch, which can be set for flat, roll-off, or low-cut and rolls off around 200 Hz. These can be helpful for reducing rumble or unwanted proximity effect. I've been using this mic for recording the snare during basic tracks and later lead vocal tracks during final overdubs. It's amazing that one mic could be great at both. It has many other uses too, like for capturing the ugly glory of a death-metal Marshall guitar cabinet, violin overdubs, and Indian hand drums. I find it to be one of the most versatile mics I've ever used and sometimes wonder how I recorded without one. I guess that says it all.

AUDIO TECHNICA AT 37R

I've been seeing more of these around lately. It's a little condenser mic, about the size of a half-smoked cigar, with a very crisp, bright sound. It works well as a drum overhead mic, especially in pairs for picking up the cymbals, but I'll tell you what I think this mic is best at... acoustic guitars. You can just point this mic at an acoustic and it sounds fine. I've pointed it at the soundhole, hung it over the musician's shoulder and aimed it at the fretboard. It always sounds great, even without much EQ. It's also really great on percussion overdubs, especially if you're trying to pick up some of the room acoustics as well. I've used it on vocalists, and sometimes it works, but usually the crispness brings out too much of their sibilance (sssssssssssss sounds) and is a bit obnoxious. It's definitely a handy mic to have around and at $130 or so is a good buy.

AKG D112

This mic is *THE* kick drum mic. Plus it looks like a rocket. It has a well-defined low end, due to the large diaphragm, and makes a good-sounding kick drum sound great. Just put it in there and roll tape. It's also great for mic'ing up bass guitar cabinets, giving them a much needed clarity. One other thing it can do is provide real breathy vocal overdubs. You see, since the diaphragm is so much larger than a "standard" mic, the amount of pressure it takes to move it is greater, thus a singer's voice won't be creating a lot of voltage variation. This gives you a dynamically flat vocal sound with a very "breathy" feel to it. There are many times where this effect will work wonders. Another good thing is that this mic can be found, new, for around $210. That's a great deal, considering the jump in low-end definition your recordings will get.

There's this cool band, Jessamine, who have several albums out that they've recorded themselves [on Kranky and their own Histrionic label]. The music is great, dreamy weird stuff [trust me]. I got together with Andy (keyboards) and Rex (guitar/vox) to talk about a bunch of their new microphone acquisitions and some of their old standbys. "The thing that we should say is that all of these things came recommended to us..."

Altec "Lipstick" microphones

Too bad we don't have a picture. They're about the size of a lipstick canister-thing and sort of grayish and permanently attached to this cable that goes to the tube preamp 1/2 rack sized thing. *So they're little tube powered condensers?* Yeah, they have different capsules for them and we have the omni ones, we determined, but we don't really know. Maybe a wide pattern cardioid. *What do you use them for?* Mainly just on overheads but they sound great on just about anything. We used them, stereo, on guitar amps, with an AKG 414, which sounds incredible. They're really good and crisp. Great room sound, a really good ambient mic. The most incredible sounds we'd get were when we used these as a stereo pair with another mic to fill in the bass range. We haven't really experimented too much with vocals. We just got all these things recently. [Pair for $1000, used]

Audio Technica 4033

It's really amazing for the price. That's the thing that we've been into... the best things we could get for the little amount of money we had to spend. We use it for the bass right now.

It sounded good any time we used it on anything. We tried it on drums. It just gets the full frequency spectrum. We're trying to find specific microphones for specific jobs. We got 4 or 5 new mics in 2 weeks so we'd just track all the mics on each thing, with combinations too. We'd have 5 or 6 mics on one tom, record 6 tracks of that and then listen back and see how they sound. We just had to know what they were gonna do. ($420 used/$500 new)

Sennheiser 421

We picked one up and I've been incredibly disappointed with it. I think we might have gotten ripped off. This one, in particular, sounds super high-endy, with no upper mids, and then a low end. It's supposed to be famous for its good low end. Whatever we were trying to do with it wasn't working out for toms or bass or anything. *Did you get it used from someone?* Yeah. *Should we get it serviced?* We'll send them a note, "Is this mic supposed to sound like this?" *"Please send me a 57!""* ($380 new)

Beyer 260

We should just let you borrow it sometime! I cannot believe how smooth it sounds. You hear that about ribbon mics, "Oh, they're smooth," but actually hearing it... it just smooths it out. I don't know how to explain it. It still sounds really good and clear. We haven't really tried it on drums. It's recommended for female vocals and strings. We tried it out on vocals but that was live. ($250 new)

Beyer 201

We use it, right now, on our upper tom. We heard that, in combination with a SM 98 (which we don't have) this makes a great snare mic. It's got the punch. The initial attack is so present, but it doesn't fill out the high range of the snare sound. On a tom it sounds great and it's a good step up, especially on drums, from an SM 57. ($200 new)

AKG 414

On our record [*The Long Arm of Coincidence*] that was our only "good" mic. Everything was 57s until we got the vocals. *Even your drum overheads?* Yeah. We had a snare mic and two 57s that picked the overheads. For a while, a 57 on the kick until we got the D 112. You can definitely tell which songs it's on. Anyway, we used the 414 on vocals and since on guitar quite a bit. It's got a really nice bass range. Initially we borrowed a 414 and we heard the difference. The person [singing] was right here! And weird things like switchable mic patterns... we never had any of them! We were using it for a room mic and we've used it for a drum overhead. It's really nice and versatile. ($1000 new)

Mike McDonald has been recording bands in the Cleveland area with his mobile Big Toe Recording setup, at Don Depew's 609 studio and others. Here's some of his "more pricey" picks for cool mics to have:

Beyer MC834

This large-diaphragm condenser mic has excelled in almost every application. It's got a wide, flat frequency response and is able to handle extremely high SPLs. The tone is natural without being dull and crisp with being shrill. It's a nifty choice for bass guitar amplifiers. If at first listen, the bass doesn't poke through in the upper-middle frequencies, realize that most ears are used to hearing the usual dynamic mics (Sennheiser MD421, AKG D112, Shure SM57) with presence peaks in that range. A boost in that area at the amp helps considerable. I've also had great luck with this mic on drum sets, guitar amps, vocal, piano... This is a great "main mic" for those on a budget. I got mine new for only $625 through Full Compass. It's a great alternative to the similarly-priced and now all-too-common AT 4033.

Coles 4038

Speaking of all-too-common, this ribbon mic has soared in popularity in the last few years. Its success is not unwarranted, however. I have been attracted to ribbon mics since hearing an RCA DX 77 many months ago, and when I found out that the Coles was used as the drum overhead at Abbey Road, it became a must have. This mic imparts a thickness to anything it touches: drums, acoustic guitars, guitar amps, vocals... My favorite use is as a drum overhead. The high-end in the cymbals is smoothed out [or chopped off, as some drummers I've recorded have complained], and the drums themselves have an incredible amount of punch. Steve Albini is a massive advocate of this mic on guitar amps, where it does shine brightly. The cool thing about this, or any ribbon mic, is the contrasting tone as opposed to the brighter condenser or the more mid-rangy dynamic. They give the recordist greater flexibility to mix with microphones, rather than with processing.

Shure SM81

I've never been too fond of these mics, probably because I used a pair for a year while recording classical ensembles direct to DAT with a pair of headphones as my only monitors. Man, after an hour of recording, I would suffer from a major case of ice-pick-in-ear syndrome. [Switching to another mic preamp helped considerable, so maybe it wasn't entirely the mics fault.] However, I recently experienced Don Depew (609, Cleveland) using these on guitar amps and was blown away. Aimed with the diaphragm parallel to the speaker cone, this mic yielded an absolutely huge guitar sound. The bottom-end was intact and the mids and top were detailed, though still a little harsh at times. Really great sound from an unassuming mic in an unexpected application.

Microtech Gefell UM 70k

This is a dandy of a mic with a cool background. It's made by the East German half of Neumann and marketed as a piece of history to American boobs like myself. It uses the M7 capsule, which was used in the U47 and other Neumanns. This is a large-diaphragm, multi-patterned mic, which seems to emphasize the upper-mids highs. It's my first choice for a vocal mic, because it allows the vocal to cut through without EQ. I find it a little much top-end wise for use as a drum overhead mic, but it works great for percussion. I basically use it for anything I want to emphasize or poke through better in a mix. This particular model, the "k" version, seems to be only available through Full Compass. It's got a difference in noise specs and is a few hundred bucks cheaper than the non-"k" version. I should also add that in trying to discover what the "k" version was all about, I spoke with the guy who imports and helps develop these mics, and he was very cool and treated me like a person when most would have talked down to me. More people like this should be in the recording game.

AKG C-414 B/ULS

I must have waited on a thousand tables to get my pair of 414s. I thought that owning these would make me "professional." A few years later, I'm more of a professional waiter than anything else. These just don't floor me. They are on the dull side with no sparkle on top. They're my standard for overheads when I record drums in stereo. They sound fine, but they've got a reputation for sounding great in that application. I've heard the C-414 EB version, and it sounds much more like what I had expected, so maybe it's just the B/ULS model that I've got this beef with. I do like these as blending or room mics for guitar amps and drums. Their natural sound can provide a nice compliment to mics with more "personality" without getting in the way.

Building the PAIA Mic Preamp Kit

by Larry Crane

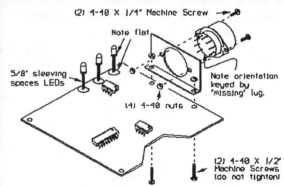

A while back I received a mail order catalog from PAIA, a company in Oklahoma that manufactures electronic project kits to build music-orientated devices. I remember seeing this catalog in high school when I was an electronics class geek, but back then, most of the things they offered were of little use to me. Now, with my cozy little recording studio in full swing, things like headphone amps, signal processors, and the cheapest Theremin ($166!) I've ever heard of, sound like fun. But the one thing that really caught my eye was a $68.85 tube mic preamp, so I ordered one.

Now, keep in mind that these are *kits*. You get a bag of parts and a little booklet and you're expected to know how to solder, identify components and be able to follow instructions. Luckily for me, I had years of tech-goon experience having built electronic stuff from scratch, and I worked in a factory for a bit, soldering computer circuit boards under a microscope. Maybe overqualified, but assembling this kit still took me a ten-hour day, three aspirin and four beers.

The way they sell their mic preamp kits, they'd like you to purchase two kits and the custom rack-mount case to install them in, still not a bad deal at $160, but leave it to me to buck the trend. I figured I'd order one and see if I liked it. That way I'd only spend $69, less than half the price of the new ART Tube MP mic pre that I'd been eyeing. I also figured I'd mount in a cheap Radio Shack case, which would especially terrify clients in the studio ["Don't run my vocals through *that* thing!"].

That's where the problems began. Soldering all the components to the circuit board was no problem. I actually enjoy this kind of work, sick person that I am. Once I had all the pieces soldered on with wires hanging off and switches and potentiometers dangling away, I drove over to weird ol' Radio Shack to pick out a suitably ugly case to mount this project in. I found a dorky looking box, brought it home, and found out it was too small. I made do by flipping the tube over so it's above the circuit board, which is probably not a good idea, due to heat and RF-type leakage. Oh well.

Then I discovered that the instructions are geared solely towards mounting the preamp in the rack mount case that they wanted me to buy. This meant that parts were identified by numbers, i.e. J1 for the phono jack, S3 for a switch, etc. and that meant that even if I mounted these in my dumb box, I didn't know what they did. Is this the power switch or the polarity switch? Some, I could identify by how they were connected, but the rest? I ended up mounting them in my case in the same order as shown for the *real* case, except I put the input jack (J3) in the rear of the cabinet instead of the front. Anyway, I then grabbed the PAIA catalog and looked really close at the fuzzy picture of the preamp case and was barely able to read which knob and switch was what.

The controls give you knobs for tube overdrive, blend, and output with switches for phantom power, phase inversion, and power. The tube overdrive does what it says; pushing the tube harder as it's turned to the right. Distortion starts occurring on most sounds about 1/3 or 3/4 of the way to full and it's a sweet overdrive, not a scratchy or ugly sound. You can also change the setting on the internal trimmer (R22) pot to provide more gain and different distortion harmonics generated if you're looking for brighter distortion sounds. The blend control mixes straight input signal with tube-derived signal. I've been running it fully on the tube side and it sounds best. The output knob controls the output level, obviously. Like most gear, it seems to work best around 3/4 of the way up. The phantom power switch is for powered condenser mics, a nice bonus feature you might not expect on an inexpensive preamp. The phase inversion switch is for eliminating mic cancellation, a whole other topic in itself, but a convenient little feature, and the power switch's function should be obvious.

Anyway, it all worked out. This is what I've been using for all the vocal tracks lately, and it sounds quite fine, not as bright and raspy as my board's preamp, but instead a warm, natural sound. It also made a cheap little condenser mic sound better when mic'ing an acoustic guitar [from about three feet away] and I gave some drum tracks a bit of edge by running an extra mic across the room from the drums, maxing out the controls and blending a little into the mix.

For sonic clarity, you can take the output of the preamp right into your tape deck, eliminating any extra noise and tonal shaping your mixer may introduce. A friend of mine built some of these preamps and he, being way more knowledgeable than I about electronics, called PAIA and got information over the phone for some interesting modifications. One involves eliminating the "blend" control stage, thus cleaning up the signal a bit by running it through fewer circuits and giving the user a tube-processed-only signal. Another modification has to do with building a separate power supply for the tube, and running it hotter for more "tube" effect. He says this is easy to construct, but I have no idea how. Feel free to call PAIA, if you buy any of their kits, since they seem to be real supportive of modifications and know what they're talking about.

In conclusion, I feel the PAIA Tube Mic Preamp is well worth the money spent on it, providing one knows the basics of electronic construction. It's helped me obtain higher quality sounds out of my microphones for less that the cost of a new, cheap mic. It can also help create some interesting mic overdrive sounds with a much clearer distortion than an old stomp box effect. All of these uses and the low price definitely make it a product worth checking out for any small studio or 4-tracker.

PAIA Electronics, Inc., 3200 Teakwood Lane, Edmond OK 73013. (405) 340-6300

An Interview with Warren Defever (of His Name is Alive)

SOMEWHERE BETWEEN INNOVATION AND ANTIQUITY

by Michael Walsh

On a recent visit to Detroit, my friend Chad Gilchrist [a member of His Name is Alive, Outrageous Cherry, and his own Symphony of Science & Sound] played me a cassette under the name E.S.P. Family. It was a recording of communist miners' folk songs played and recorded by Warren Defever on an old wire recording system - sounding faint from time, but recorded recently. It was as if he turned on the old AM transistor radio to a distant station. It was a great medium for the simple folk songs that could be picked out of the tin. I wanted to find out more.

Long before this project, I was aware of Warren's innovative production through recordings of H.N.I.A, only recently becoming aware of the many other projects he has been involved in. I called Warren at his home/studio in Michigan and we had this discussion which started with the wire recorder then wound through the decades back to somewhere near where it started.

What was the device used to the tape of old communist miners' songs (E.S.P. Family)?

A Webster Wire Recorder, and as far as I can tell, it goes back to the late '30s.

What was the "tape"?

Early on, when they were experimenting with basically magnetic tape, they tried other substances as well. They used magnetic ribbons, magnetic wire, and magnetic tape. This uses spools of wire.

Is the wire round or is it flattened?

Basically round, but it's really, really thin. Extremely thin and very breakable. In the owners manual it recommends using shorter reels until you've gotten used to it, before you use the longer reels. Early on, I lost some really good performances that were on a one-hour spool of wire. It was incredibly difficult to work with. The good part is, when it breaks, you can just tie it back in a knot.

Any loss of time?

It moves very, very quickly. I imagine it's 30 ips. When it's going that fast, chances are there are potentials for danger. But at the same time, if you just wind on it then you can get it to go pretty smooth, once you know what you're doing.

Is the recording mechanism based in magnetic tape technology similar to what we have now?

Yep.

Do you use whatever microphone you needed?

Actually, the way it's designed, it's got a built-in mic and a built-in speaker. For me, with that kind of thing, it's important not to mess with it, not to "fix it up", not to modernize it. So, we used that microphone. We used that speaker. And if we're going to record something with it, we use that microphone and we'll transfer that to something else. We'll actually mic the wire recorder and transfer [the original recording] onto DAT or reel-to-reel or whatever.

You just do a play back and mic the output [of the built-in Webster speaker]?

Yep. And it was before they had the word "play". They used the word "run." [Laughs] I really like that one.

Can you play it over and over again, or is it a pretty temporary recording, like earlier home-recordable 78s?

As far as I can tell, it's actually pretty sturdy. It's up to the actual tape itself. And I've had really good luck with it. As long as you don't break the wire, you can continue to play it back. I've got a couple boxes of wire now but I don't know what I will do if I run out. I don't know that you can go to the hardware store and get spools of wire... I don't think you can do it, plus I don't think there are sources to get it.

So the wire came magnetized already?

Right.

So it has a little 3 or 4-inch speaker you play it back through?

Yeah, it sounds really good. It's all tubes and it gets super hot and it's really great. You can kind of smell it kind of burning all kinds of dust.

Like an early 78 player - all self-contained?

Yeah, and it takes a while to warm-up.

Do you know when these recorders were first developed?

The earliest known reference I've seen to wire recorders, was the early '30s... '32.

Where was yours manufactured?

It was manufactured in Chicago. Compared to tape, they aren't quite as easy to deal with. A couple of times I've had it fly off the reel and when you get hit in the eye with this... it's a little different than getting hit in the eye with tape.

Were wire recorders developed for any particular use?

I have heard that originally they were used in the home but I don't think it really caught on very well in the general public. At the same time you could get one of these, it was just as easy to get a disc cutter, you know, cut your own 78s on a recordable disc.

The all in one kind that came with built-in speakers, a radio, a record player, as well as a separate platter for recording? I had a chance to buy one at an estate sale with a big old mic included, and a guy that saw me looking at it snatched it from under me for about $90.

That's too bad. I have one that's a little different. It's from the '50s and it's probably meant for people doing speeches and stuff, that someone is going to type it up, but it records on little flexi-disks. It's really cool. It sounds great, plus it has very old time, lo-fi microphone.

So, do I dare ask - do you lean towards analog or digital?

I like both. I record a lot of stuff to tape. I've got a really good 4-track 1/4" recorder. At the same time I record a lot of stuff on 24-track ADAT. Early on when I was in high school I recorded at a studio (Garageland Studios in New Boston, MI). I had a job there. It was the home of Len Puch, with records by The Gories, and Snake-Out and Elvis Hitler. When I was there, everything was tape, and I learned things like editing, mastering, stuff like that, and I'm still pretty good at that, but lately I've been using Pro Tools, so I do a lot of editing on that, as well.

Do you generally go direct to digital when you do that?

No, usually not.

You blend the two?

Yeah, I like just constantly moving stuff around.

No worry about signal loss or anything like that?

I would rather you get a little extra loss in there. I would rather it sound a little bit worse.

And have the flexibility?

Yeah. Ninety percent of records I hear, it's not what I want to hear. A lot of time I find a lot of really bad records... like records from smaller countries, third world countries – recordings in places where they just didn't "have it together", where it wasn't a giant industry... they can really have got a good vibe. There are so many bad Jamaican records, where the kick hiss is so loud or whatever, but they've really got such a vibe, and that's maybe more what's happening.

That's what's important. The music, essentially, is always the bottom line.

Right.

Were you into digital pretty early on, with keyboards, or anything like that?

No, that kind of came later when I got various samplers and drum machines and stuff like that. I've got a number of different synthesizers and samplers now, sort of on the side. I call that my hobby.

Do you like Pro Tools as an editing unit?

Yeah.

Do you do mastering for your group, His Name Is Alive, as well?

I do pre-mastering, essentially.

Have you ever worked with mastering?

Yeah... It's really great. When we mastered the Stars on E.S.P. album I went to Los Angeles and we did it at the super-most expensive mastering place in Hollywood. They have a chef that works there so at noon all the engineers and clients take a break and this guy cooks a magnificent lunch. The place itself was really cool. It'd been around for a long time and it really had the vibe of... not so much this is, you know, the future of mastering. It's more like we know how records are made, this is how the good ones have been made and that's how we're going to make ours.

Good work ethic over the latest dials and whistles?

Yeah, they had a good blend of this is the way we used to do it, this is the way we're doing it now, mixed with here's some new stuff that we've tested out and it's working good. It fits in with, at least, the moral outlook of previous masterings. I think there are so many good sounding records that are old, and there are so many bands, or even producers, that think they're just improving on what went on before. Really it's just a new bad idea, and there is such a lack of research [or the knowledge of the history of records] in music within the record industry.

People don't listen enough to the greats, or the variety even.

They don't even realize that everything they're doing, someone else has gone through that before. They're not learning from those mistakes or from what was done right.

So you don't see any advantage to starting and/or ending in analog or digital?

Right, it makes no difference. There are really good all digital recordings, and it depends on what your mood is that day. I can see the advantage in the simplicity that you can probably get to, once you know what you're working with, in digital editing.

Pro Tools I've heard of. Do you know of any affordable entry-level digital editors to start with?

I started with what was called Session 8, which was still high end but not very expensive digital editing system, by DigiDesign. I've gradually upgraded to what they call Pro Tools Project, and now I've got the full Pro Tools, but it was a real gradual process.

Have you done much with vinyl?

Yeah, all our records thus far have come out on vinyl as well. The last record we did a whole separate mix for the vinyl. So... we did it all in mono. We added a whole extra layer of tape echo and spring reverb. We had a good spring reverb lying around, pretty old, it also had a tremolo, and it was all tube.

Nice. Have you ever made any interesting gadgets of sorts, recording tricks?

Occasionally, I'll make something. I have this thing called the "electric gourd," but I usually am not that involved in that sort of business. The guy I live with, who plays in a band called Princess Dragon Mom, built this thing called the "electric bear."

The Electric Bear? What miraculous wonders can the Electric Bear produce?

It sounds just like you're being attacked by a bear.

Do you have to get near it?

Yeah, and he plays it. I think making stuff is cool, but I guess I'm in too much of a hurry to make stuff. You know, sometimes you'll make something by accident, or you'll be working on something and you cross the wires the wrong way and you'll get something new.

If you don't break it.

But to specifically make something new, no.

Any studio tricks that you've accidentally fallen into that you recommend?

There was one studio that I'd been working with a band in, around Detroit, and it was a really good studio. It had all super expensive vintage gear and the engineers and owner were really well versed in that sort of equipment, and had been around a while. I figured out the way I leaned on the board, leaning my arms on the board, one of the tracks which was the track the guitar was on, it actually got brighter – there was more high end – depending on how hard I leaned on the board. So, pretty much you just gotta fool around a little bit. I got this one drum machine, this old drum machine, that's meant for, you know, you connect it to an organ; there is one knob for drum fills, but if you have the drum fill turned off, and if you turn that knob while there's a beat playing, it turns into kind of a wah-wah. So really you just kind of gotta kind of stick your fingers in there and turn stuff that isn't supposed to do anything.

I take it you record other people as well as yourself. Do you work differently with your own material?

Occasionally, I'll do that. But the main thing really, if something sounds bad, then I'm more likely to work hard on it.

But if it sounds good just let it go?

Yeah. Why wreck it? But as far as wrecking stuff, yeah, I could wreck anything. I can make anything sound bad.

How do you best avoid that, get opinions?

No, no. That's fine. That's what I'm trying to do.

Oh? O.K. Well, any more about the wire recorder? Can you still get one?

It's really the only one I've seen, but once I got it, once I saw what it was, then I noticed – just going to different resale shops, church rummage sales – that I would find the spools of wire, whereas before I may have seen them, but never even recognized what they were. Now, I've been finding more and more spools of wire, which is good, because I think there is a finite amount of pre-recorded wire in the world. I need to collect as much as I can.

So you've been collecting stuff that's already been recorded?

Yeah. I got a whole box of spools by a man, an older man, whose son had been a Baptist preacher, who recorded many of his sermons, many songs of himself, at church, and there is a compilation of that stuff that isn't finished, before I tape over those. That's real good.

Nice. So you can even do re-recording over those. Any groups that you've really enjoyed working with?

Pretty much, I've tried only to record those I've been friends with, or really, really liked. We're not really, like, "open for business" here since it's all in my house. Lately I've been turning down more things than ever just cause, you know, "Who are these people, what do they want," how do I know?

Yeah, it's wonderful to work with people you already know you want to work with.

Right. And it's good that they understand that, you know, I'm gonna sit here and try to mess 'em up and that's my job and that's why they're here.

Jenny Toomey, of Simple Machines, said good things about your easy, laid back ways of recording people.

We have a real friendly recording studio here. She's really good, has got a good ear and she's very open, so it always goes good working with her. You know, I'll go, "Here's your song back. I took out all the music. I just added noise and I ruined your vocals so they sound really bad." and she'll just go, "That's great." She'll like that.

Great. Where could one get a recording of these wire recording's of communist mining songs [known as E.S.P. Family]?

You should be able to get it on a tape on a local label that I try to help out with. It's called timeSTEREO.

timeSTEREO, P. O. Box 531671, Livonia, MI, 48153
[They have a catalog with cool stuff from the Detroit area like: Godzuki, Princess Dragon Mom, Noise Camp - "read kids, noise, camp", Noise Camp Remix, Little Princess, Control Panel 2, and even the chance to buy a small table "Made of sturdy wood. Choose whale or gorilla".]

CHRIS BUTLER

The Wilderness Years, vol. 1 and *The Wilderness Years, vol. 3* 7" singles (Future Fossil)

If the name Chris Butler sounds familiar, it's likely because you still listen to your Waitresses' records. As guitarist/songwriter for that band, Butler claimed a place in the annals of New Wave as a creative, offbeat artist responsible for tunes such as "I Know What Boys Like" and "Christmas Wrapping". Butler has continued his career producing other artists ranging from Joan Osborne to Charlie Chesterman, as well as recording his own projects. Recently, Chris finished "The Devil Glitch", a 68 minute-long song which holds the current Guinness World Record for "Longest Pop Song". Consequently, it's not surprising that Butler has released *The Wilderness Years* 7-inch series, a project that reveals his passion for antiques. In the notes to *Volume 1*, we discover that "A Hole In the Sky" and "Davey's Sister's Home From College" were "recorded without electricity or microphones on 100-year-old wax cylinders using a hand-cranked Edison 'Spring Motor' phonograph circa 1898." While listening to the record you can study the sleeve photo of the machine and consider that the scratchy, old-time sound is genuine rather than affected. It's interesting to note that playback had to be hand-cranked as well. The format for *Volume 3* was "a Webster-Chicago 180-1 wire recorder (c.1946-49) using World War II Navy surplus stainless steel wire, Type W-174 consumer wire and period crystal microphones." Behind Butler's vocal and slide guitar of "The Bottom of a Workingman's Beer", he leaves in "half-erased shadow talk... [That] dates from the Korean War, when a Northeastern Ohio family sat down at a kitchen table to play cards on a Saturday night... and someone pushed 'record.'" These records are incredible documents created lovingly by a master tinker. The songs themselves can be described as acoustic, minimalist, and avant-blues rock. Chris's obvious songwriting skills have matured and continue to tickle the ear. *The Wilderness Years* series is a case in which you'd expect the method to overshadow the content, but thankfully this doesn't occur. Consider lyrics like "and there's a jar of purple eggs on the bar/oh, I begs to be so embalmed" and I think you'll agree. Chris Butler's next project is an entire album of songs performed only by musicians named "Chris Butler". This guy knows how to entertain himself as well as others. –Bob Toevs

A Beginners Guide to Digital Recording with your PC *(MAYBE IT'S TIME TO SAY GOODBYE TO YOUR TRUSTY 4-TRACK CASETTE DECK!)*

by Rich Hardesty

In 1984 I purchased a Yamaha MT44 4-track cassette recorder. For almost 15 years it's served as my main "sketch-pad" for musical ideas, but over the last year it has begun to show its age. I had been deliberating over whether or not to replace it, when I began to see a not so terrifying alternative: abandon cassettes and go digital.

Although I've used PCs for over five years, I stayed away from the whole midi and digital recording scene; either due to blithe ignorance or perhaps a lingering sense that I was contributing to the overall decline of the 'natural' process of artistic creativity. Maybe I've been subconsciously resentful of the proliferation of canned music beds and sample-based plagiarism perpetrated by a new generation of 'plug-and-play' clueless nimrods seeking talent-in-box. Okay, I know that sounds a bit harsh, but now I've seen the light -these are just new tools and all kinds of people can use them for the pursuit of good or evil. Now on to what this primer is all about.

This article is primarily aimed at those of you out there like me, who have come from the world of traditional recording techniques. If you're already a long-time PC 'midi-head' you won't find anything here particularly enlightening. This is for technical neophytes and curmudgeons like me who have resisted the migration to digital for various reasons. I'm here to tell you that the time is right to jump in and test the water, for it may well open up a whole new set of possibilities for you; letting you do things your analog tape decks would never be able handle and do it *faster* and *cheaper* to boot.

WHAT DO YOU WANT TO DO?

Let's assume you primarily play and record analog instruments like guitars, bass, percussion or wind instruments. If I say "keyboards" and you think old Wurlitzer electric piano instead of Korg M-1, then you're among friends. This won't be about digital composing or notation. This is for the songwriter who sits down alone with a guitar or at the piano, sketches out a new tune and then sets up a microphone and puts it on tape.

If you have a fairly new home PC, you can still stick with your favorite instruments and song building processes and make great digital recordings. In fact, you still may want to hang on to the worn out cassette multi-track unit because later on I'll tell you how it may still play an important role in your PC-based recording process.

The Hardware
The basic things you'll need for PC-based recording are these:
A newer PC running Windows '95 or later [sorry Mac folks, I don't speak your language]
A decent (full-duplex, 16-bit) soundcard
Recording software

1. General guidelines for your PC hardware platform.

To get the most out of digital multi-track recording, you just won't be happy with anything less than a later model Pentium-class machine. Recording and synchronizing lots of audio files is processor-intensive. Add to that the capability of using real-time effects via Active-X plug-ins [more about that later] and you'll find that a realistic beginning point is a 200Mhz machine. I know there are folks out there managing 4-track recording on a 486 machine, but believe me, they're miserable and just barely squeaking by.

The other thing your PC will need is a fast and very big hard drive. Here's why: Each track you create will be saved as a Wave file. If you record at the preferred sample rate of 44.1kHz [anything lower will sound pretty awful], each Wave file recorded in mono will run about 5.2 Megabytes per minute. If you create a song made up of eight different recorded tracks, that's over 42 MB per minute. Including the final mixed-down versions, I find that a typical song will eat up 300-400 MB.

Your hard drive will also need to be pretty fast. Speedy access to your Wave files is important or synchronization problems in the form of extreme lag times during playback will occur. While a SCSI-based drive would be nice, you'll do just fine with an Ultra DMA 33-drive interface. You'll also want a decent amount of RAM for this job. I would recommend 64 MB as satisfactory. Again, with lots of tracks and program events to manage, you'll want to minimize how often Windows has to access the 'swap-file' on your hard drive. Besides, like hard drives, RAM has become faster and cheaper.

2. The Soundcard

I don't profess to be any sort of authority on the virtues of all kinds of hardware products. There are many good soundcard choices out there and like everything related to computer products, they just keep getting better and cheaper. Also bear in mind that I'm focusing only on soundcards geared for the general consumer market, which fall into the $50-200 price range. There are some amazing, high-end products out there for professional applications, but they're expensive, often not easy to configure and assume that you have a workstation dedicated to music production and not much of anything else.

Before you dive in and go shopping, there are some basic requirements that you should be aware of before you make your purchase. At the top of that list, you must make sure it is a full-duplex card. This means it can handle simultaneous input and output. For many people, this capability is used for telephone and video-conferencing applications. For the home recorder, this basic requirement allows you to record and monitor what you're playing at the same time. Another tip: some cards only provide 16-bit recording and 8-bit simultaneous monitoring. Make sure yours supports full-bandwidth duplex, which is 16-bit input and output in both directions.

The other requirement is just one for your own convenience: Buy only from a well known, established company with a solid record of reliable customer support.

These dang things are complicated and if something runs afoul during the installation process or your Windows settings are not just right, you'll get nothing but heartache and frustration. You'll want to have access to regularly updated software drivers and tech support available when you need it. So don't be tempted by the 'NoNamo Rocket-Science Ultra-16' soundcard for only $18.99 from Fry's electronics or a web-based computer liquidator.

Some other things to consider when making a soundcard choice involve compatibility for features that are just now starting to hit the mainstream market. The current generation of decent cards all support the recording of 16-bit audio at a sampling rate of 44.1kHz. Just now coming onto the mainstream market are new cards that offer 24-bit recording at up to 96kHz. This is good news for those wanting the absolute best resolution for recording, but many of the ears out there will probably be satisfied with today's standard for some time.

The other advanced feature available on some cards involves better input and output options. The 'standard' soundcard today offers one microphone input, one stereo 1/8" line input and a 15-pin midi in/out/through port and a stereo 1/8" output. Higher-end cards are offering stereo RCA-type jacks and SP/DIF coaxial digital in/out connections so your signal path stays completely digital; allowing you to interconnect to other digital gear like DAT's. Again, most of you probably won't care too much about this right now, but it's something to consider.

In addition, you may want to tilt in favor of a card that uses the PCI bus interface instead of the old ISA bus architecture. The big benefit is that it will reduce the load on your CPU and directly process wavetable synth sounds.

My suggestion is to do some intelligent shopping; read the hardware reviews on some of the computer magazine web sites or sites that specialize in PC-based recording and sampling. This list is by no means all-inclusive, but to get you started, here are a few of the larger, established soundcard vendors that have produced some fine products over the years and still do to this day:

Creative Sound Labs: (www.soundblaster.com)

Makers of the Soundblaster product line that has dominated the industry standard; particularly for gaming applications. Their Soundblaster PCI 128 card is one to look at. They've also taken over the U.S. Marketing of a real nice [and amazingly inexpensive] card from Ensoniq, and now call it the Creative Labs Audioblaster PCI from Ensoniq. This is the one I'm using right now.

Voyetra/Turtle Beach: (www.voyetra.com)

Turtle Beach has been making some of the nicer, but not real expensive higher-end cards for the past five years. Their on-board wavetable sounds rank among the best and they often earn some of the industry's better signal-to-noise measurements. Recently they've teamed with Kurzweil and incorporated their wavetable synth onboard sound chips into their cards. They have at least several models worth considering. Their modestly priced Daytona II uses the newer PCI-bus interface and has loads of nice features. To get a glimpse of the higher-end, you should check out their Pinnacle series. It features many top-of-the-line characteristics and is priced accordingly.

Diamond Multimedia: (www.diamondmm.com)

Diamonds' soundcard product line tilts more towards the hardcore gaming crowd; especially with their highly rated Monster 3-D soundcard leading the trend towards supporting 'immersive' positional audio technology. Worth examining in the category of "low-cost music applications" is their inexpensive Sonic Impact S-90. Comparable to the Ensoniq PCI mentioned earlier, it has a pretty decent s/n ratio of +90dB and has speaker and stereo line outputs – something not found on most other low-cost cards. This is a nice extra, because it is far preferable to bypass the soundcard's onboard output section [it just adds unwanted noise into the signal path] and run it to a better external amp.

3. Recording Software

This is the heart of it all and probably the main reason why things are really getting interesting for those who want to record with their PC. In the past two years, PC-based music has moved beyond the midi-workstation phase and into a production environment suitable for recording real instruments with good fidelity.

The larger, established music software companies are of course meeting the demands for greater recording options in addition to midi composition and sequencing. However, of greatest benefit to musicians is the growing number of very small companies or solo software developers who have created vast libraries of literally hundreds of music software programs. That's great news for your pocketbook, but like any category of software programs you may want to buy, you need to know what your primary needs are and which programs will best meet them.

Music Software: Finding The Right Tool For the Job

The general categories of products include:
Midi sequencing/composition/editing and notation
Software sound synthesis and sampling
Wave editing/recording
Multi-track recording/editing
Utilities - players, format encoders/converters, diagnostic tools, midi patch librarians and CD-rippers.

Rather than delve into the specifics of each of these categories, let's return to the original question at hand: What do you want to do? If you're like me and your primary interest is in wanting to create a digital multitrack production environment to replace that worn-out cassette recorder, your choices are initially rather narrow: multi-track recording/editing. However, as you get more involved in making recordings, you'll find your needs may eventually encompass nearly all of the aforementioned product category.

To illustrate this point, I've created this diagram depicting each stage of the PC-based recording process and the tasks and tools that are commonly used:

2. Multi-track Recording Software

To me, this is the part that is really exciting and the reason for my sudden interest in moving to the PC. Massive improvements in processor speed and related hardware over the past two years have made multi-track recording practical for the average home user. All that remains is for you to choose the software package that meets your needs. While there are comparatively few choices available [unlike pure midi composition, score and notation, for instance],

multi-track recording software today falls into two distinct categories: fairly expensive and downright cheap. The prices I mention reflect the manufacturer's list but are often deeply discounted at retail stores. This brief overview reflects the products for which I was able to acquire demo versions. Here goes:

The Fairly Expensive Choices
Cakewalk (www.cakewalk.com)

Cakewalk is the industry leader in this category. Their multi-track software comes in three flavors: Home Studio, Studio and Professional and their prices range from under $100 to $319. From the standpoint of multi-track recording, the price difference is mainly tied to the number of tracks the program will allow you to record: only four for Home Studio to virtually unlimited with the Pro version The key to the Cakewalk line is that these are full-featured programs that integrate well, the twin aspects of midi and wave recording.

The slick and highly detailed user interface is attractively laid out and yet kind of daunting at the same time – especially for someone who's new to these kinds of programs. There is so much it is capable of that it's not obvious where to begin in the song creation process. Set up can be a somewhat complex arrangement as well. Cakewalk also provides direct support for specific hard-disk recording interfaces from Roland, Aardvark, Yamaha and others as well as instrument support for quite a laundry list of synth and keyboard manufacturers. You can also expect full midi composition, editing and notation capabilities with this program. This after all, is what the earliest Cakewalk programs were all about, but if your focus is not on midi-based production such features will probably hold little interest for you.

You get extensive waveform editing features, including the ability to draw panning and envelope events on each track; giving you a high degree of control during mixdown. You can sync to AVI and Quicktime movie files with midi and audio tracks. Cakewalk also includes 256 realtime effects that conform to the new Direct-X plug-in standard. These can be applied non-destructively [the only way to go]. One of the things I liked the best about the newest version is the mixing control panel. It's very nicely rendered and has all the controls and buttons laid out logically; just like a real mixer: faders, mutes, solo and record enable buttons. One nice automation feature is that you can select and group mutes and set a predefined point at which they're enabled.

For multi-track Wave recording, I think the only two reasonable choices are Studio and perhaps Professional versions. The Home Studio version, while set at a decent price point, is unfortunately limited to 4 tracks of recording. Studio, which lets you record up to 24 wave tracks is more like it; but then again, it retails for $249.00. The $319.00 Pro version ups the ante even further by offering 128 tracks and support for 24-bit recording at 96kHz. If you make your living sitting at a digital audio workstation, I can see why Cakewalk Pro would be one of your top choices. If on the other hand, you don't require the depth and complexity of its offerings, you may find it a bit overwhelming and pricey.

Voyetra Digital Orchestrator Pro (www.voyetra.com)

Voyetra's pro package covers many of the same features and functionality of Cakewalk, but does so at a lower price. At $249, DOP is a reasonable bargain. It offers support for up to 1,000 tracks [that's what I call virtually unlimited], a nice selection of on-board effects and a clean, though very Win 3.1 in it's appearance user interface. It features comprehensive midi support and editing functions. I particularly like the hardware settings dialogue box and the many routing and control options it affords. Setting up a recording is a breeze and I was able to lay down a mix of midi drums and two guitar parts within 20 minutes. After that, however I didn't particularly like how DOP handles the next stage: mixing and rendering. Nestled within the very compact and detailed track window is a tiny group of volume sliders for setting individual levels. No pan, no mutes, no individual effects settings buttons or master volume control like I'd hoped for. Instead, you must initiate such steps by opening individual dialogue boxes and it ain't pretty. They should have created a new multi-channel mixer window that looks something like an actual mixer - laid out vertically. Curiously, this is precisely what they did for handling settings for the midi tracks, but why this was not integrated for the task of mixing wave files I have no idea.

The rendering dialogue box was also a letdown. It just launched into the rendering process without asking for render-to options like creating an MP3 version for your convenience; though the product literature claims it offers such support. If you download their demo version, be aware that their trimmed-down help file won't tell you much about the program's inner-workings. You'll just have to muddle through it. Electronic Musician magazine chose Voyetra's earlier product; Midi Orchestrator Deluxe as sequencing product of the year for 1997. They may well have earned it for their midi functionality and exceptional price ($129.00), but their attempt at incorporating digital audio tracking falls short in my view. Maybe they'll get it right in the new version.

CoolEdit-Pro (www.syntrillium.com)

This beautiful program is the pro-level, multi-track version of Syntrillium Software's highly acclaimed Windows-based shareware Wave editor - CoolEdit 96. People who used CoolEdit marveled at its elegant simplicity, power and versatility for manipulating wave files. Once you start up their Pro version, it's plain from the get-go that wave file recording and feature-rich editing is indeed its core strength.

CEP lets you record and manage up to 64 tracks at 20-bit resolution you can easily switch views from multiple to single track waveforms. One nice touch is that you can double click on any single track in multiple wave view and it will bring the selected track into single waveform view for precise editing procedures. It also has a marvelously detailed range of set up options and supports multiple soundcard configurations as well as direct support for very high-end hardware.

In order to meet the demands of the professional market it offers a wealth of conveniences. This includes SMPTE timecode sync functions, CD player controls, and multiple file type support and conversions in single and batch mode. Although it was disabled in the demo version, CEP handles RealAudio and MP3 files.

In testing the program, I started by inserting a group of wave files from a different project and recorded one new track for a vocal. It was fast and efficient and apparently my set up choices worked the first time, as I experienced no difficulties at all. The only thing that raised an eyebrow was the furious level of disk activity that ensued during the playback process. I hadn't experienced that with other programs that I tested, as I have a 400Mhz Pentium II with a reasonably fast hard drive and more than enough memory. With so much reading and writing to disk going on, I had a feeling that the level of real-time interactivity possible with individual track settings (volume, pan, etc.) while in play mode would be a problem. It was.

Every time I tried to alter the volume settings, the play function would stop. I messed around with some of the playback buffer settings to fix the response time, but that produced no improvement. However, when I switched to single track view, any changes I made in the volume took effect almost immediately. This is not a very facile arrangement for testing levels and other settings prior to rendering.

I admired the design the individual track controls while in multi-track view mode. Small, but nicely rendered mute, solo and record enable buttons resided next to the record source and track name labels. However, everything is laid out horizontally and I still find it somewhat hard to get used to. I can understand this choice, as computer monitors provide more screen real estate in the horizontal aspect. Go ahead and say I'm hopelessly stuck in the tired conventions of the analog world, but I just wish the developers had tried to make it look a bit more like a typical recording console.

When I was getting ready to mix and render my little demo project I came across another annoying hurdle in the process. In order to add any effects in a non-destructive fashion, you must make an additional copy of each and every track to which you want effects applied. Then you select how you want the settings applied to that new track with respect to the original. It's a bit cumbersome and it just eats up gobs of disk space [make sure you have at least a gigabyte or two available to you for each multi-track session!]. Once you make your track copies you can apply the approximately 50 DSP effects that are included.

Once a song is rendered, the view automatically switches into single waveform mode [actually two stereo tracks] so you can quickly dive into fine tuning the file. I should also mention that in any of the wave form views you can include an envelope and pan control line that you can grab and redraw. Again, these are niceties, which are a distinct legacy from CEP's junior predecessor; recast for the more demanding professional user.

In some respects, this program resembles SoundForge in that it too offers powerful, comprehensive tools and capabilities for working wonders on sound files and prepping them for professional multimedia productions. It's also in the same price league: $399.00 As much as I admired the depth and attention to details evident in so many parts of the program, I just couldn't see myself using it as a replacement for my cassette multi-track unit. In a nutshell, it has too many advanced features I probably won't ever use and not enough of the ones I care about most.

Steinberg Cubase VST (www.steinberg-na.com)

Cubase is a long time player in the midi software scene; at least going back to the mid-1980s. They made the early migration from Atari to Mac to Windows and are still going strong with their latest version of the venerable Cubase product: VST (virtual studio technology). Cubase VST comes in three flavors; depending on what you require and how much you're willing to spend on this obviously feature-crammed, complex suite that's pretty much aimed at serious users. In any case, all the versions rank up at the top of the pricing tree: $549 for VST/Audio, $649 for VST/Score, and $749 for VST/24.

From my vantagepoint, the biggest difference that separates the packages is that VST/24 supports 24-bit hardware, audio-sampling rates to 96kHz and up to 96 tracks of recording. The others support 16-bit hardware at up to 48kHz and 64 tracks of recording. VST also handles support for a wide array of recording hardware from the most of the ones you'd expect. I just have a 16-bit card, so I tried out VST/audio.

Right out of the box you know right away this product is not aimed at casual users who just want to lay down a few tracks from time to time. There is a pretty steep learning curve involved. But it's not that the program itself is overly complicated and hard to understand – there's just so many very detailed parts to it. The printed and online documentation exceeds 700 pages and believe me that can be intimidating if you're a relative beginner. I'm happy to report though, t that it installed quickly and ran flawlessly the first time I fired it up; something that I cannot say about some of the other packages I tested. The setup program correctly identified my hardware and system settings and within 30 minutes after launching VST I was laying down a guitar track.

The Cubase interface has some interesting distinguishing characteristics that run somewhat counter to the user interface design most others have adopted: Except for the transport control panel, the main 'arrange' window is almost completely devoid of buttons and modern toolbar design elements you might expect. Everything pretty much revolves around drop-down menu lists and keyboard macro commands for basic functions. As with the other upper-end products, the midi composition and editing functions were many and quite deep. Frankly, I didn't spend much time getting familiar with them other than just quickly composing a simple drum track to accompany my guitar parts. I'll probably go back to those functions later on at some point, but my focus was on recording audio and I wanted to get on with it as quickly as possible.

After recording six parts along with the midi track I was ready to start mixing and Cubase did not disappoint. I really liked the attention to detail and familiarity evident in the mixing panel. Just like one of the real big consoles, you'll have at your disposal four channels of parametric EQ for each track. It also has 16 channels of group master outputs and EQ/effects. In staying consistent with a pro studio design approach, it provides four effects inserts and eight auxillary sends for each channel. As I mentioned before, software effects plug-ins are the rage right now and Cubase puts an interesting spin on that feature. While it supports Active-X plug-ins, VST also utilizes it's own plug-in architecture that gives it a bit of an edge in the mixdown process: effects can be programmed for each channel giving you quite a bit of automation control over the final mix. VST comes with eight different effects plug-ins -the best of the bunch being the Wonderverb. It was quite clean and impressive sounding. Just to test compatibility I also ran a couple of the Active-X effects I already had through VST and they performed just fine.

It took about five hours to record my demo song and another hour to mix. It was actually less difficult than I thought it would be and the results were quite satisfying for a number of reasons. First, the recorded result sounded cleaner than what I had experienced with some of the other products. With some other programs I ended up with a few ticks, pops and periodic hiccups, but recording in Cubase produced nary a one. Since the underlying basic digital recording technology is virtually identical among all these kinds of software programs, the difference could have been a superior hardware detection and setup program; which given what I now know, is no small accomplishment with programs of this type.

This possibility was also borne out by the fact that it appeared that my system load (CPU and hard disk activity) wasn't as heavy while using Cubase. On some programs, I got playback lag using only 6 tracks and my hard drive would be blinking and chattering non-stop. VST includes a nifty little system monitoring panel that lets you see how you're coping as you pile on the tracks and effects. If things do bog down it's easy to alter the system settings while Cubase is running so you can quickly resume your tasks.

Of all the upper-end packages I tested, I felt most comfortable with Cubase VST. Make no mistake about it; it's big, stuffed with features I may never fully utilize [or adequately understand] and the price is real pricey. I can imagine professionals who make a living composing music in a desktop environment gravitating towards Cubase VST. However, for newbies looking to get their feet wet in digital audio, I suspect the program's girth and price tag will represent too much of stretch.

The 'Cheap' seats

I scoured the software libraries all over the world and only came up with one product designed for multi-track recording that fit the category of cheap. I'm sure however, that more products will soon appear that meet this criteria. Surprisingly, the one available choice turned out to be perhaps the best match so far for my somewhat narrow vision and limited technical skills.

NTrack (www.fasoft.com)

NTrack is the shareware sole creation of an Italian named Flavio Antonioli. He's a real earnest and thoughtful fellow and seems to have correctly anticipated [mostly] what many people would want as a PC-based replacement for a multi-track cassette unit. At the miraculous price of $30, one should probably characterize every purchase of his product as Flavio's way of making an in-kind charitable donation to cash-strapped musicians around the world who are also technically challenged.

NTrack is very simple to use. It even looks that way the moment you start the program. It follows many of the Windows 95 GUI conventions, though it still has a bit of a homemade quality to it and a few quirks. For instance, the activity window below the main toolbar flashes "ECORDING" while you're, uh recording. The re-sizable VU-meter panels have a bad habit of not staying anchored to where you last positioned them. I also experienced a few crashes when saving or exiting the program. Some of the English translation in the online help file and dialogue boxes is reminiscent of an early '60's Alfa Romeo U.S. owner's manual, [of course no one's criticized my inability to read or write in Italian lately]. All in all, these are comparatively petty annoyances in what is fundamentally a nice, versatile little program. This is the core issue: Can Ntrack record and mix an almost unlimited number of tracks with relative ease? The answer from my perspective is a resounding YES.

I should qualify my previous statement. Although NTrack is supposedly able to record a virtually unlimited number of tracks, I have no idea if anyone has tested that assertion in the real world. The truth is, anything beyond 16 tracks of Wave files seems pretty unlimited to me. I think the average non-professional users' system hardware and CPU speed today will put a more practical limit on Wave tracks to anywhere from 6 to 20. Flavio might take issue with me on that point, but my own experience, as well as surveying comments from other users of this and similar programs tends to support to that.

To get started, you just go through a fairly concise set-up of your preferences and select the input and output sources. While the current version supports 16-bit recording and playback at up to 44.1kHz, I just downloaded the beta version 1.1 which now handles 24-bit resolution. There are accommodations to midi input but midi is not one of the central strengths of the program. Don't expect all the comprehensive composition, editing and notation functionality touted by the other big league competitors of NTrack. NTrack can record from midi input and import midi files and synchronize them; allow you to initiate program changes and otherwise get by at a very basic level. For recording control, you have options like overdub, overdub onto selected file, multiple punch-in takes and precise punch-in intervals set by markers placed along the timeline.

Once you've recorded all your wave and midi files you'll find that rendering to a single wave file is a pretty straightforward affair. [Note: to include any midi program tracks into your rendered wave file, you'll have to 'bounce' them onto a new wave file, and to make that more practical, you'll want a soundcard that allows you to select simultaneous, multiple recording inputs]. I really appreciated having two render-to-file options. With one, you simply select render from the 'file' menu and then a dialogue box pops up and you're presented with several options including the ability to simultaneously create an MP3 version. Unfortunately, my version had a bug that prevented it from working as a frontend with the included MP3 encoder(BladeEnc -a freeware encoder), but no matter; I just went outside of Ntrack and handled the conversion separately.

The other render option I like is to render while playing. This is where NTrack really starts to act 'familiar.' This is the kind of behavior that connects me to things I already understand: the real-time mixdown process. Activate the Big Mixer toolbar button and a re-sizable mixer control panel appears. Each of your tracks has a vertical volume slider, pan control, mute and solo enable buttons. At the top-left is a master volume control. While it's not as detailed and refined in appearance as other on-screen representations of mixer panels I've seen, it is nonetheless clear as to its functions.

Below each channel strip is an inset window that also lists any of the effects assigned to each track. Just click in that window and a dialogue box pops up to let you add, configure and delete any DSP effects. I should also mention that all effects you assign each channel are applied non-destructively. They won't become permanently applied until you decide to render them to your master track. This is the way to go, for just as in the traditional studio environment, you can set outboard effects and fuss with individual track and master channel settings to your heart's content. Nothing goes onto the master tracks [or in this case the rendered file],until you think you have precisely what you want. NTrack is not designed as an all-inclusive digital audio production suite and it knows it. In the preferences set up box, you can provide the path to an external Wave editor and you can then launch it with just a click from the main toolbar. This is a wise decision. While you can copy/paste any selection to create loops from Wave files and edit/redraw within the waveform it does not compare to the kind of depth you get with SoundForge or CoolEdit Pro. My suggestion is to acquire another program that shines in that area. But who's quibbling -at NTrack's price you'll be happy to do it.

Also, if you must have total mastery over the midi domain or you're thinking about a career in audio post-production, you may want to carefully examine the products in the upscale end of the market. [I understand there's still lots of radio jingles and TV commercial music beds that need to be written for local auto dealers and personal injury law firms -sorry, but I had to toss that in.]

If however, you're more like me and think of midi as just an easy way to lay down a steady beat to which you then record electric guitars and vocals over, NTrack might be just right for you. I personally think it's a terrific find. It's simple, fun, easy to learn and master and a fantastic value. Download the demo version and give it a whirl.

A Final Note On Digital Multi-track Recording

Towards the beginning of this piece I made reference to the fact that you might find a use for your tired cassette multi-track recorder in your new, all-digital environment. Invariably, these units eventually fall prey to worn out parts in the transport or excessive head wear; rendering them no fun to play with anymore. Some people don't bother to get them fixed; either it's too costly or they've become enamored with their new PC-based set up so they just cast their decks off to the land of misfit toys. It doesn't always have to end that way. Let me tell you why.

Most consumer grade soundcards only accept one stereo 1/8" line input. This is pretty limiting on its face. How did you think you were going to connect up one or more decent microphone inputs to the soundcard, smartguy? It's real fundamental to be able to control the mic input signal and even pre-mix and send multiple mic signals to the single input source on the soundcard.

Face it, you need some sort of rudimentary preamp or mixer. One solution may be in acquiring a decent microphone preamp that you can build from a kit or purchase ready to go. The other solution may already be at hand: use your old multi-track recorder. If the mixer section of your recorder has either individual channel line-out jacks or a stereo or line-level output connections, you may have a reasonable alternative that costs you nothing. My first choice would be to use an output that comes before the units' internal amplification circuitry: the channel-outs or line-level outputs. That way you'll introduce less noise into the signal path.

Think of the possibilities: using two mics on a guitar track - one in front of the amp; the other 20 feet away catching some room reflections. Being able to record a real drum set with multiple mics and then pre-mix it as a stereo line input to the soundcard. Record a barbershop quartet in one pass. Uh scratch that last one. Anyway, you get the idea.

The other tip has to do with monitoring. For God's sake, make sure you have a decent set of speakers. If you don't have a separate power amp and nice near-field monitors available to connect to your line-out jack on the soundcard, then at the very least, be picky about the speakers designed for use with your computer. Most of the ones that come bundled with computers are little more than twin AM- band transistor radios. Some of the upgraded packages toss in a mini sub-woofer but then you get a mix of shrill highs and shoe-box thuds and almost no midrange - it's OK for the gaming crowd but not for your recordings.

Shop around for the nicer three [or even five] piece multimedia speaker packages. I know that some pretty decent ones have come out of companies like Cambridge Soundworks and Bose Audio to name just two.

The 'Other' Software Pieces in Your Digital Recording Set-up
1. Effects Plug-ins

This latest generation of multi-track recording software all support what has become a standardized means of applying digital effects in PC-based recording: open extensions to Microsoft's Direct-X Media library. I won't bother getting into detail about the how's and why's of the approach; it's too boring and I'd probably get it wrong anyway. What's important is that this marks the clear departure from using relatively expensive, rack-mounted gadgets with lots of knobs and lights to cheap, software-only solutions.

Again, if your PC has enough horsepower you can apply these real-time effects and be amazed at the flexibility and sonic quality available to you at such a miniscule price. How inexpensive are they? That depends on the company and the product, of course. Everyone has their own pricing/packaging strategy to maximize profitability. Some like to sell single effects plug-ins for about $18-25. Others prefer to bundle their choicest products into a plug-ins suite for upwards of $150. You'll be fascinated with what's currently available: 24-bit [even some 32-bit] dynamic effects processing allowing you to chain multiple plug-ins together, regardless of which company it came from.

I played around with demo products from several different vendors. Some the reverbs I tried were quite nice – clean with no nasty artifacts or undue coloration. Parametric EQ's that nicely mimicked the kind of control you'd expect from a nice mixing console. Compressor/limiters that perform as well as a hardware-only version costing hundreds of dollars. So far, I've found almost a dozen creators of Active-X compatible effects plug-ins – and I was just casually looking. As each month goes by their ranks will surely grow. We end users will reap the benefits of expanding choices, improved performance and very healthy price/feature competition among the players.

2. Wave Editors

If you don't want to spring for one of the big digital recording suites that include extensive editing capabilities, there are quite a few standalone programs out there, ranging from utilitarian shareware creations to tightly integrated professional products aimed at the upper brackets.

In any case, if you want to record Wave files, you'll need some kind of application that takes care of fine-tuning your tracks. Basic functions include cut, copy and paste, looping, waveform re-drawing, volume fades, cross-fades, normalization, equalization, sample-rate conversions and some other things that don't readily come to mind.

Like everything else, your program choices will become clearer to you once you decide what your primary needs are and what you can afford. Some examples that merit your consideration include the aforementioned CoolEdit 96, GoldWave Editor for Windows, and of course Sonic Foundry's Sound Forge. That should get you started.

3. The Utility Grab Bag

In varying degrees, all the multi-track programs discussed here offer all kinds of little 'helper' applications needed to complete your project, from first track to CD-master. Over the course of your digital recording project you're likely to find the need to do one or even all of the following:

-Convert a file format from one type to another; e.g. a Wave to an MP3.
-Pull tracks or sample sounds from another CD (CD-rippers)
-Modify or create a new synth sound,
-Organize your midi patch library.
-Run diagnostics on your midi system, soundcard or even Windows' multimedia settings.
-Obtain a player for a special type of audio file.
-Add in a new library of sounds if your soundcard supports Soundfont technology.

I won't even attempt to list the choices available for each of these special utility categories because there are far too many and I haven't had enough direct experience in comparing their features. You'll find that utilities like these come in all varieties. Some are fairly crude, no-frills 'freeware'; others are nicely executed and modestly priced shareware products.

Part of the fun in assembling your digital studio is in mixing and matching the pieces and experimenting with newfound toys. Naturally, the Web offers a wonderful, virtual swap meet for buyers, sellers and casual developers of such programs. While the big, general purpose software demo download spots like Download.Com and Shareware.Com are good places to poke around, you will probably find it more rewarding to seek out the sites devoted to music creation. There's quite a few out there. Some are devoted to software distribution and reviews; some cover nearly all aspects of digital recording. To jumpstart your search, here's just a few links that should prove useful to you:

The Digital Sound Pages: (www.xs4all.nl/~rexbo/main.htm) Has an excellent intro primer on all aspects of digital music production and some other good links.

SampleNet: (www.futurenet.com/samplenet) U.K.-based web-zine that does a fine job of covering the world of sampling from the multiple vantage points of hardware, software, philosophy, tips, techniques; offers downloadable samples too.

Shareware Music Machine: (www.hitsquad.com/smm) An exhaustive collection of music software of almost every of kind. It includes sw for Mac, beOS, and even Atari!

ZicWeb: (www.zicweb.com/mainframe.html) Tips, techniques, product reviews, software downloads and even more links.

Tails Out...

Congratulations, you've made it to the end of *Tape Op: The Book About Creative Music Recording*. You didn't fast-forward did you? Good. So what have you learned? What are we trying to say?

If there's one point I hope is made here it is that creativity, sweat and talent is far more important in the recording process than gear. Many great records are made in home studios as well as in top-of-the-line studios. What makes them great are memorable songs, arresting performances and the sounds that reinforce the first two qualities. You can't buy any of this in a box - it has to come from the hearts and minds of the people involved.

It's fascinating to learn of the process and gear used in creating a great album, but in the end it doesn't really matter. It's the music that matters, and the connection that the music makes with the listener that really counts. Through all the talk about gear and techniques and such we can learn ways to help capture performances and sounds that might be part of a great new album that will excite a listener who, with no care of how records are made, just thrills in the power that a great piece of music can unleash. Being part of that creation can be the most rewarding feeling in the world.

– Larry Crane

TAPE OP

The Creative Music Recording Magazine

Subscribe Free

*3rd class subscription

Get a free subscription to Tape Op. All you have to do is fill out one of the cards below and mail it to the address at the bottom of this page. The next issue will be delivered to you by a smiling US postal worker

Subscribe online at www.tapeop.com and give those hard working postal employees a break

*3rd class subscriptions are not guaranteed to arrive, or may arrive torn.
*First class subscription $12 for 6 issues guranteed to arrive in a manila envelope in good condition.

Mail completed form in a regulation sized envelope to: Tape Op PO Box 507 Sacramento, CA 95812

Please send me a Free Subscription to TAPE OP

Canadian & foreign Subscription are $37.50 for six issues. Don't blame us, it's the postal system

TAPE OP
The Creative Music Recording Magazine

Because I am a very important person:
(check one)
☐ I have the first Black Sabbath LP on vinyl
☐ I know the difference between a ribbon mic and a bowtie
☐ I saw Nirvana play in a little club with 17 people
☐ I can name every member of every line-up of Yes
☐ I like to record good music
And in addition, (check one)
☐ I have a 4-track
☐ I have an 8-track
☐ I have a 16-track
☐ I have a pretty nice studio
☐ I work at a really nice studio
☐ I make/record music on my PC
☐ I'm in a band
☐ I'm a student of the recording arts
☐ I'm not shit, have pity on me

Name _____

Address _____

City _____ State ____ Zip _____

(You can attach your business card instead of filling this out, but you still have to check the boxes)